THE SELF-CONSCIOUS EMOTIONS

THE SELF-CONSCIOUS EMOTIONS

Theory and Research

Edited by
JESSICA L. TRACY
RICHARD W. ROBINS
JUNE PRICE TANGNEY

Foreword by Joseph J. Campos

THE GUILFORD PRESS
New York   London

© 2007 The Guilford Press
A Division of Guilford Publications, Inc.
72 Spring Street, New York, NY 10012
www.guilford.com

Printed in the United States of America

This book is printed on acid-free paper.

Last digit is print number: 9 8 7 6 5 4 3 2 1

Library of Congress Cataloging-in-Publication Data

The self-conscious emotions : theory and research / edited by Jessica L.
Tracy, Richard W. Robins, June Price Tangney ; foreword by Joseph J.
Campos.
     p. cm.
  Includes bibliographical references and index.
  ISBN-13: 978-1-59385-486-7 (hardcover : alk. paper)
  ISBN-10: 1-59385-486-2 (hardcover : alk. paper)
1. Emotions. 2. Affect (Psychology) I. Tracy, Jessica L. II. Robins,
Richard W. III. Tangney, June Price.
  BF511.S3453 2007
  152.4—dc22
                                                    2007015304

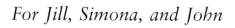

For Jill, Simona, and John

About the Editors

Jessica L. Tracy, PhD, is Assistant Professor of Psychology at the University of British Columbia. Her research focuses on the expression, psychological structure, and cognitive elicitors of self-conscious emotions, as well as their links to personality and self-esteem regulation. She has published articles in the *Annals of the New York Academy of Sciences, Psychological Science,* and *Psychological Inquiry,* as well as in specialized journals in personality, social, and developmental psychology, and the psychology of emotion. Her research has been funded by the National Institute of Mental Health and the Social Sciences and Humanities Research Council of Canada. Dr. Tracy founded the annual Society for Personality and Social Psychology Pre-Conference on Emotion, and her work has been honored by the Wellcome Trust–*New Scientist* Essay Competition, as well as by dissertation awards from the New York Academy of Sciences and the American Psychological Association.

Richard W. Robins, PhD, is Professor of Psychology at the University of California, Davis. His research and publications focus on personality, emotions, and the self. Dr. Robins is coeditor of the *Handbook of Research Methods in Personality Psychology* and the forthcoming *Handbook of Personality, Third Edition,* and he has served as associate editor of the *Journal of Personality and Social Psychology.* His research has been funded by the National Institute of Mental Health and the National Institute on Aging. Dr. Robins was awarded the American Psychological Association's Distinguished Scientific Award for Early Career Contribution to Psychology and the Society for Personality and Social Psychology's Theoretical Innovation Prize.

June Price Tangney, PhD, is Professor in the Department of Psychology at George Mason University. She is coauthor of *Shame and Guilt* (with Ronda L. Dearing), and coeditor of *Self-Conscious Emotions: The Psychology of Shame, Guilt, Embarrassment, and Pride* (with Kurt W. Fischer) and the *Handbook of Self and Identity* (with Mark R. Leary). She has served as associate editor for *Self and Identity,* consulting editor for the *Journal of Personality and Social Psychology, Personality and Social Psychology Bulletin, Psychological Assessment,* the *Journal of Social and Clinical Psychology,* and the *Journal of Personality,* and is currently associate editor of *American Psychologist.* Dr. Tangney's research on the development and implications of moral emotions has been funded by the National Institute on Drug Abuse, the National Institute of Child Health and Human Development, the National Science Foundation, and the John Templeton Foundation. Currently, her work focuses on moral emotions among incarcerated offenders.

Contributors

Jennifer S. Beer, PhD, Department of Psychology, University of California, Davis, Davis, California

Jennifer K. Bosson, PhD, Department of Psychology, University of South Florida, Tampa, Florida

Daniel Brugman, PhD, Department of Developmental Psychology, Utrecht University, Utrecht, The Netherlands

Sally S. Dickerson, PhD, Department of Psychology and Social Behavior, University of California, Irvine, Irvine, California

Robin S. Edelstein, PhD, Department of Psychology and Social Behavior, University of California, Irvine, Irvine, California

Jeff Elison, PhD, Department of Psychology, Southern Utah University, Cedar City, Utah

Heidi L. Eyre, PhD, Department of Psychology, Jacksonville State University, Jacksonville, Alabama

Tamara J. Ferguson, PhD, Department of Psychology, Utah State University, Logan, Utah

Daniel M. T. Fessler, PhD, Department of Anthropology, University of California, Los Angeles, Los Angeles, California

Kurt W. Fischer, PhD, Graduate School of Education, Harvard University, Cambridge, Massachusetts

Paul Gilbert, PhD, DClinPsych, Mental Health Research Unit, Kingsway Hospital, Derby, United Kingdom

Jennifer L. Goetz, BS, Department of Psychology, University of California, Berkeley, Berkeley, California

Jamie L. Goldenberg, PhD, Department of Psychology, University of South Florida, Tampa, Florida

Tara L. Gruenewald, PhD, Department of Medicine—Division of Geriatrics, University of California, Los Angeles, Los Angeles, California

Daniel Hart, EdD, Camden College of Arts and Sciences, Rutgers University, Camden, New Jersey

Susan Harter, PhD, Department of Psychology, University of Denver, Denver, Colorado

Dacher Keltner, PhD, Department of Psychology, University of California, Berkeley, Berkeley, California

Margaret E. Kemeny, PhD, Department of Psychiatry, University of California, San Francisco, San Francisco, California

Kristin Hansen Lagattuta, PhD, Department of Psychology, University of California, Davis, Davis, California

Mark R. Leary, PhD, Department of Psychology and Neuroscience, Duke University, Durham, North Carolina

Michael Lewis, PhD, Institute for the Study of Child Development, Robert Wood Johnson Medical School, New Brunswick, New Jersey

Jin Li, EdD, Department of Education, Brown University, Providence, Rhode Island

Brian Lickel, PhD, Department of Psychology, University of Southern California, Los Angeles, California

Debra J. Mashek, PhD, Department of Humanities and Social Sciences, Harvey Mudd College, Claremont, California

M. Kyle Matsuba, PhD, Department of Psychology, University of Northern British Columbia, Prince George, British Columbia, Canada

Rowland S. Miller, PhD, Department of Psychology and Philosophy, Sam Houston State University, Huntsville, Texas

Erik E. Noftle, PhD, Department of Psychology, University of California, Davis, Davis, California

Jennifer L. Prewitt-Freilino, MS, Department of Psychology, University of Oklahoma, Norman, Oklahoma

Tomi-Ann Roberts, PhD, Department of Psychology, Colorado College, Colorado Springs, Colorado

Richard W. Robins, PhD, Department of Psychology, University of California, Davis, Davis, California

Thomas J. Scheff, PhD, Department of Sociology, University of California, Santa Barbara, Santa Barbara, California

Toni Schmader, PhD, Department of Psychology, University of Arizona, Tucson, Arizona

Phillip R. Shaver, PhD, Department of Psychology, University of California, Davis, Davis, California

Marija Spanovic, BA, Department of Psychology, University of Southern California, Los Angeles, California

Jeffrey Stuewig, PhD, Department of Psychology, George Mason University, Fairfax, Virginia

June Price Tangney, PhD, Department of Psychology, George Mason University, Fairfax, Virginia

Ross A. Thompson, PhD, Department of Psychology, University of California, Davis, Davis, California

Jessica L. Tracy, PhD, Department of Psychology, University of British Columbia, Vancouver, British Columbia, Canada

Jeanne Tsai, PhD, Department of Psychology, Stanford University, Stanford, California

Jennifer White, BS, Department of Psychology, Utah State University, Logan, Utah

Ying Wong, MA, Department of Psychology, Stanford University, Stanford, California

Foreword

This book makes an important contribution to our ever-changing thoughts about the nature of emotions. Like its predecessor, *Self-Conscious Emotions: The Psychology of Shame, Guilt, Embarrassment, and Pride* (Tangney & Fischer, 1995), this book reflects a major change in the way that emotions are conceptualized. In my foreword to the previous book, I noted the *zeitgeist* about emotion that it captured, and pointed out that research on the so-called "basic emotions" of joy, fear, sadness, surprise, anger, and disgust/contempt (the "basic six") appeared to be diminishing. In addition, both theory and research in the study of emotion had begun to emphasize the many ways in which the same expressive response could be made in the service of several different emotions, and morphologically different responses could reflect the same emotion (i.e., emotional responses showed equipotentiality). Furthermore, at that time, four major developments were changing how we viewed emotions. The first two concerned theoretical innovations: Karen Barrett's functionalist theory of emotion, and Fischer and Mascolo's cognitive sequential explanation of emotional development. New methodological advances in the measurement of the elusive concept of "self-recognition" were also making links between self-understanding and emotional development possible. Finally, an important contribution came from new observational, self-report, and narrative assessments of emotions more complex than the "basic six," which were being developed by June Price Tangney, Karen Barrett, and Nico Frijda, among others. The previous book thus not only captured a *zeitgeist* in the making; it laid the foundation for the theoretical and empirical developments that are captured in this new volume.

The editors of the present volume are to be congratulated for a rarity in our time—compiling chapters that are both broad in content and important in their likely impact. The chapters as a whole nicely represent the field of emotion study, presenting to the reader much of the rich diversity that now characterizes research on the so-called "self-conscious emotions." They include contributions on theoretical, methodological, and empirical work that cannot readily be found elsewhere, as well as literature reviews that are priceless for the scholar.

In particular, the book contains a brilliant and provocative theoretical chapter on the appraisal criteria that enter into the generation of self-conscious emotions. There is also a chapter specifying the measurement of these emotions, which not only serves as an invaluable repository of the advances made by pioneers in the study of self-conscious emotions, but also makes it possible to develop new and improved assessments of pride, shame, guilt, and other complex emotions. This chapter and others also present the limitations of current approaches to quantifying the more complex emotions, which should motivate a new generation of researchers to build on contemporary contributions. Thus, on both conceptual and methodological grounds, the book simultaneously synthesizes the field and points to its future. No editors can set a higher goal for themselves than bringing together a set of chapters and making them an exciting and coherent contribution to the field of study.

This book also captures five major research themes that have been building in the field of emotions for the past decade. The first theme is evolutionary psychology. In 1995, little systematic thought was devoted to the evolutionary basis of self-conscious emotions. Moreover, evolutionary arguments too often rested on prehistoric scenarios that were plausible but untestable, because they had no fossil record in their support. This volume takes a refreshingly different approach, rooted in anthropological, psychological, and sociological findings on shame, pride, and guilt. The chapters on evolutionary thought are clearly written, thought-provoking, and sophisticated.

A second theme, a powerful force in the contemporary study of emotion, is neuroscience. It is unclear exactly when affective neuroscience had its beginnings. Like the Nile River, it probably had many sources. However, there is no doubt that at present the role of the brain in emotion has thoroughly captured the imagination of emotion researchers. Views of the link between the brain and emotion are no longer gross (e.g., the dichotomy in hemispheric specialization between emotion and language); nor are they extremely specific (e.g., the quest for localization of discrete emotions in "affect programs"). Rather, the brain and emotion are seen as standing in relation to each other through the orchestration of multiple cerebral areas, working together to generate complex and flexibly manifested (not reflexive) responses. This volume reflects this new and complex approach in affective neuroscience, through its inclusion of a well-written and cogent treatment of the brain's role in processing social information and integrating it into adaptive emotional behavior.

A third theme is the recent sharp increase in the study of culture and emotion. Initially motivated by attempts to demonstrate, following Ekman's classic studies, that a given pattern of expressing an emotion was recognizable across a wide array of cultures, studies of culture and emotion have dealt more recently with matters of cultural specificity. The searches for both universality and cultural specificities are reflected in this volume. Important themes emerge as cultural-specific processes, including individualism and collectivism. In addition, several chapters address the specific ways in which cultures (e.g., Japan and the United States) use complex emotions, such as shame, for culturally desired outcomes. Although the book does not provide an extensive treatment of culture and emotion vis-à-vis self-conscious emotions, it does provide a useful sample of research in this enormous area of study.

A fourth theme is the question of whether self-conscious emotions are "good" or "bad." We often lose sight of the fact that some philosophical approaches to moral development place emotions, such as shame and guilt, at the center of their explanations of morality. On those occasions when we see a link between emotion and morality, more often than not we see emotion as disruptive to normal moral development. Consider that in Freudian theory, guilt and the superego are clearly and necessarily destructive and maladaptive. The "morality" that develops from guilt, in the classic Freudian tradition, is rigid and neurotic. In that sense, guilt is "bad." However, not all emotion researchers agree that guilt is "bad." Some investigators, such as Martin Hoffman and Nancy Eisenberg, view the proper experience of guilt as central for the prosocial aspects of human behavior. In their view, guilt can be "good." In this volume, several contributors struggle with whether shame and embarrassment, as well as guilt, are good or bad; others consider what makes guilt damaging and what makes it helpful; still others investigate when emotional communication becomes so extreme as to cause a bitter state of humiliation. These chapters pose extraordinarily thoughtful and valuable questions—questions not often considered in other sources.

This volume helps clarify certain aspects of the current controversy about positive versus negative emotions in some areas of emotion research. The consensus of the work presented in this volume is that any emotion can be positive or negative, depending on context. But context is not used as an explanatory panacea; various exemplars of context are specified concretely and convincingly within this book. In sum, the chapters struggling with how emotions can be good or bad bring to light important and relatively neglected issues, and bring to our attention much prior literature that is little cited. These chapters leave the reader to extrapolate from a subset of emotions how any emotion can be good or bad.

The fifth theme is that of early development. One cannot study "self-conscious emotions" without struggling with issues of conceptualizing the self, its many levels, and its precise role in generating the emotions that are the primary focus of this book. The seminal work of Michael Lewis, who generated the seeds of research on self-conscious emotions in the book *Social Cognition and the Acquisition of Self* (Lewis & Brooks-Gunn, 1979), is represented in his chapter in this book. Moreover, many other contributors either allude to the importance of a developmental perspective in understanding self-conscious emotions, or devote considerable thought to propositions about the origins of and the cognitive skills required for guilt, shame, embarrassment, and pride. No treatment of self-conscious emotions can be complete without a developmental perspective, since these emotions can be shown in rudimentary forms at a much earlier age than is typically believed possible. Just as the basic emotion of fear can initially be shown in response to physical events (e.g., looming), then to more cognitively complex phenomena (e.g., maternal loss), and then to very abstract sources of fear (e.g., threat to one's retirement), so shame, guilt, and pride can be shown in rudimentary ways in late infancy and then become more cognitively sophisticated as the child becomes an adult. It is the task of the researcher to describe these developmental levels, and to explain the transitions from one to the other.

I further maintain that this book is significant not only for the wealth of information it covers, but also for what it does not cover—what it leaves open as future directions for research in the field. I note two such directions. First is the question of whether we should continue to label pride, shame, guilt, and embarrassment as "self-conscious emotions," or whether a new designation would now be more heuristic. The ability of a person to stand back and reflect on his or her emotions is undoubtedly important; indeed it is probably uniquely human. However, do all instances of shame, pride, and guilt require standing back and treating oneself as both the subject and the object of an emotion? There is good reason to argue that self-reflection may not be required for complex emotions. Daniel Fessler has stated this point well in his chapter: "Shame, and its opposite, pride, are quintessentially *other-oriented* emotions" (p. 187, emphasis added). In short, a person who feels a "self-conscious emotion" is actually perceiving that another person is expressing an emotion about him or her. That is, self-conscious emotions involve appraising others, not primarily standing back and reflecting on one's own emotions. I predict that as more empirical research is conducted, the designation "self-conscious emotions" will begin to be offset by the term "other-conscious emotions," until we learn that neither term is entirely apt and a new, more accurate term is created.

A second direction concerns the expansion of the components of appraisal, including elaboration on the appraisals of others. Such appraisals are communicated by specific social signals, such as those classically described for basic emotions. More specifically, different patterns of emotional communication are linked to different complex emotions, and these must be considered in future treatments of this topic. For example, the emotional signals from others that help generate shame are not the same as those that generate guilt. Rather, shame is typically produced when the action of a protagonist is followed by a significant person's sadness, anger, contempt, or ridicule (laughter in the service of contempt), but not by another person's fear or suffering. The generation of shame by another may be discrete-emotion-specific. Similarly, guilt may arise when a protagonist's actions are followed by another person's conveying authentic and strong pain, suffering, fear, disappointment, sadness, and possibly a subset of other emotions. However, the expression of emotions other than those just listed will not generate guilt, even when other circumstances are kept constant. For instance, anger communicated by another may not bring about guilt. Indeed, anger may short-circuit the generation of guilt. If these speculations are correct, then not only will the complex emotions (e.g., shame, guilt, and pride) that are the subjects of this book be seen as involving other persons, but they will also open up the experimental investigation of the role of emotional communication in the generation of complex emotions.

I foresee that this book will lead to a new and more accurate depiction of the nature of complex emotions. In addition, it will help to bridge two currently separate literatures: that on social referencing (noticing the emotional reactions of others in relation to how one behaves) and that on the generation of new and more complex emotions in oneself. Few current books both crystallize the present state of knowledge and blend different research traditions in novel ways. This volume is extraordinary in accomplishing both of these aims.

JOSEPH J. CAMPOS, PhD
University of California, Berkeley

REFERENCES

Lewis, M., & Brooks-Gunn, J. (1979). *Social cognition and the acquisition of self.* New York: Plenum Press.

Tangney, J. P., & Fischer, K. W. (Eds.). (1995). *Self-conscious emotions: The psychology of shame, guilt, embarrassment, and pride.* New York: Guilford Press.

Preface

In Arthur Miller's *Death of a Salesman*, Miller's protagonist Willy Loman experiences such profound shame from failing to achieve the American dream that he commits suicide by the play's final act. In Ovid's *Metamorphoses*, the infamous Narcissus is so consumed by pride that he chooses eternal self-reflection over the possibility of a meaningful romantic relationship. Indeed, self-conscious emotions such as shame and pride play a central role in motivating and regulating people's thoughts, feelings, and behaviors. These emotions drive people to work hard and to behave in moral, socially appropriate ways. As Goffman (1955) noted, our every social act is influenced by even the chance of public shame or loss of "face." At the same time, most people spend a great deal of time pursuing achievements and relationships that have the potential for a boost of pride.

Despite their centrality to psychological functioning, self-conscious emotions have received considerably less research attention than the so-called "basic" emotions such as joy, fear, and anger. Over the past several decades, the field of emotion research has expanded dramatically, but only recently has there been a corresponding increase in research on self-conscious emotions. Theoretical and methodological advances of late have led to important insights into the cognitive, behavioral, and physiological causes and consequences of self-conscious emotions, as well as the cultural and developmental contexts in which these emotions are experienced and expressed. Early advances in the area were documented in Tangney and Fischer's highly influential 1995 volume, *Self-Conscious Emotions: The Psychology of Shame, Guilt, Embarrassment, and Pride*—the first comprehensive source for psychological research on the topic. That book paved the way for affective scientists and self researchers who, for the first time, found a community of like-minded scholars, individuals who agreed that pride, shame, guilt, and embarrassment are worthy topics of scientific investigation.

The field has expanded exponentially in the years since the publication of Tangney and Fischer's volume. New theories have emerged that provide compelling accounts of the social, cognitive, and biological underpinnings of self-conscious emotions. These theories tackle broad-level issues, explaining how self-conscious emotions differ from other emotions, why they might have evolved, and how they help (and hurt) the self. These theories also tackle more specific questions, making fine-grained distinctions among related emotions and their subtypes, and pinpointing the particular mechanisms that influence each emotional process. At the same time, new empirical findings demonstrate the importance of self-conscious emotions to a wide array of psychological phenomena, ranging from altruism, achievement, and aggression to narcissism, nationalism, and terror management. Many contemporary self-conscious emotion researchers adopt a functionalist perspective, assuming that self-conscious emotions are an adaptive part of human nature—especially of humans' uniquely social nature.

The goal behind *The Self-Conscious Emotions: Theory and Research* was to develop an up-to-date, "one-stop" resource covering the current state of self-conscious emotion research. However, as researchers who tend to think that self-conscious emotions are, perhaps, the most psychologically interesting and socially essential of all affective states, we had another motive as well: to demonstrate the importance and wide-ranging implications of emotions like pride, shame, guilt, and embarrassment. What better way to demonstrate that self-conscious emotions are every bit as fundamental as the "basic" emotions than to ask the field's leading experts to provide thoughtful and comprehensive reviews of their work?

The book is divided into six sections. The first is devoted to broad, overarching theories of the nature and function of self-conscious emotions. Given the interdisciplinary nature of affective science, it is no surprise that these theories conceptualize self-conscious emotions from multiple levels of analysis, ranging from basic brain mechanisms to complex social processes. The second section includes chapters that address the developmental pathways that underlie self-conscious emotions. In the book's third section, authors tackle the thorny question of what role culture plays in the experience, expression, and recognition of self-conscious emotions. Moving beyond simplistic debates about the universality versus cultural specificity of emotions, these chapters highlight both similarities and differences across cultures, and provide insights into the ways in which cultural similarities address questions about phylogeny. The fourth section covers research on each specific self-conscious emotion. The fifth section has the broadest scope, focusing on the applications and implications of self-conscious emotions in a wide range of areas. In this section, we learn about the role of shame, guilt, and pride in group behavior, criminality, terror management, body image, narcissism, and international aggression. Finally, the sixth section includes a single chapter that provides a comprehensive overview of both self-report and nonverbal approaches to assessing self-conscious emotions. We hope that this chapter will become an invaluable tool for researchers who seek guidance on how best to measure their self-conscious construct of interest.

The contributors to this volume are an elite group of researchers, some of whom are well known for their important contributions to the field since its inception and others who are relatively new to the field but have already made significant advances and are likely to play a key role in the field's future. Collectively, the chapters in this volume reflect the breadth and diversity of this exciting area of research, while at the same time revealing a field that is united by a common set of concerns: the importance of self processes, of focusing on specific emotions rather than broad underlying affective dimensions, and of adopting an explanatory, process-oriented approach.

We wish to thank Seymour Weingarten, editor-in-chief of The Guilford Press, for his encouragement and guidance throughout the project, and for his long-standing support of emotion research. We would also like to thank Carolyn Graham and the other members of the Guilford staff for their help in facilitating the creation of a final product that we feel quite proud of. We also offer our heartfelt gratitude to each of the volume's contributors, from whom we learned a tremendous amount. We took great pleasure in reading and rereading these chapters, and we trust that others will as well.

We developed this volume with the goal of representing what the field has learned about self-conscious emotions in the past 12 years, what the future holds for self-conscious emotion research, and how the insights gained have enhanced our understanding of important areas of human behavior. We leave this project with a strong sense of the import, relevance, and unique humanity of the self-conscious emotions. There may be no clearer affective window through which to study human nature.

REFERENCES

Goffman, E. (1955). On face-work: An analysis of ritual elements in social interaction. *Psychiatry: Journal for the Study of Interpersonal Processes, 18,* 213–231.

Tangney, J. P., & Fischer, K. W. (Eds.). (1995). *Self-conscious emotions: The psychology of shame, guilt, embarrassment, and pride.* New York: Guilford Press.

Contents

PART IV. SPECIFIC EMOTIONS: FUNCTION AND CONCEPTUALIZATION

PART V. SPECIAL TOPICS AND APPLICATIONS

PART VI. ASSESSMENT

PART I

THEORETICAL PERSPECTIVES

Social, Cognitive, and Neural Mechanisms
Underlying Self-Conscious Emotions

The Self in Self-Conscious Emotions

A Cognitive Appraisal Approach

JESSICA L. TRACY
RICHARD W. ROBINS

When Jeff Skilling, former CEO of Enron, applied to Harvard Business School at the age of 26, he had trouble coming across positively to the admissions officer. He had spent most of his college years gambling (and losing) thousands of dollars in the stock market rather than focusing on schoolwork, and this was evident from his transcript. At some point during the interview the admissions officer finally lost his patience with the young man, and asked Skilling, point blank, "Jeff, are you smart?" To which Skilling replied, without missing a beat, "I'm f*cking smart" (Clark, 2006).

Although this kind of unabashed hubristic pride may have won Skilling a place in the Harvard Business School's class of 1979, it also may have been a cause of Skilling's impulsive risk taking, his willingness to exaggerate his successes, and his development of reckless policies that eventually led to the downfall of Enron and Skilling's criminal indictment for fraud. As psychologists who seek to understand the affective roots of Skilling's behavior, we cannot be satisfied by simply blaming it on a pattern of high positive or negative affect, or high or low activation. Skilling's actions and personality can only be fully understood by invoking the discrete self-conscious emotions of pride and shame, which likely motivated much of his behavior throughout his life.

In fact, self-conscious emotions play a central role in motivating and regulating almost all of people's thoughts, feelings, and behaviors (Campos, 1995; Fischer & Tangney, 1995). Most people spend a great deal of time avoiding social approbation, a strong elicitor of shame and embarrassment. We worry about losing social status in the eyes of others and, as Goffman (1955) noted, our every social act is influenced by even the slight chance of public shame or loss of "face." In fact, according to the "Cooley–Scheff conjecture," we are "virtually always in a state of either pride or shame" (Scheff, 1988, p. 399).

Researchers have linked self-conscious emotions to a wide array of empirical outcomes, many of which are reviewed in this volume. Embarrassment, guilt, pride, and shame drive people to work hard in achievement and task domains (Stipek, 1995; Weiner, 1985), and to behave in moral, socially appropriate ways in their social interactions and intimate relationships (Baumeister, Stillwell, & Heatherton, 1994; Leith & Baumeister, 1998; Retzinger, 1987). To take just a few specific examples, guilt is a central part of reparative and prosocial behaviors such as empathy, altruism, and caregiving (e.g., Batson, 1987; Baumeister et al., 1994; Tangney & Dearing, 2002; Tangney, Stuewig, & Mashek, Chapter 2, this volume). Shame mediates the negative emotional and physical health consequences of social stigma. Victims of physical abuse (Feiring, Taska, & Lewis, 2002) and HIV-positive males (Gruenwald, Dickerson, & Kemeny, Chapter 5, this volume) suffer poorer emotional and physical health if they feel ashamed of their stigma. Shame is also associated with depression and chronic anger (Harder, 1995; H. B. Lewis, 1971), and is a core component of the narcissistic, antisocial, and borderline personality disorders (Harder, 1995).

Yet, despite their centrality to psychological functioning, the self-conscious emotions have received considerably less attention from emotion researchers than the so-called basic emotions such as joy, fear, and sadness (Campos, 1995; Fischer & Tangney, 1995). Overall, the field of emotion research has expanded dramatically in recent years, yet this increase is only beginning to be matched by a corresponding increase in research on self-conscious emotions. Instead, emotion researchers have focused on emotions that are biologically based, shared with other animals, panculturally experienced, and identifiable via discrete, universally recognized facial expressions—in other words, emotions that can be studied without reliance on verbal reports of internal experience. From this perspective, only a small subset of emotions represented in the natural language—anger, fear, disgust, sadness, happiness, and surprise—are considered important (Ekman, 1992; Izard, 1971). These six have been labeled "basic" emotions because of their biological basis, evolved origins, universality, and location (in most cases) at the basic level in hierarchical classifications of emotion terms (Johnson-Laird & Oatley, 1989; Shaver, Schwartz, Kirson, & O'Connor, 1987). Self-conscious emotions, in contrast, show weaker evidence of universality: their antecedents, subjective experience, and consequences may differ across cultures (Eid & Diener, 2001; Kitayama, Markus, & Matsumoto, 1995; Menon & Shweder, 1994; Wong & Tsai, Chapter 12, this volume; Li & Fischer, Chapter 13, this volume; but see Breugelmans & Poortinga, 2006), and researchers have only recently identified cross-culturally recognized nonverbal expressions (Haidt & Keltner, 1999; Tracy & Robins, 2006a). Moreover, self-conscious emotions are subsumed by basic emotions in linguistic hierarchical classifications (e.g., sadness subsumes shame, joy subsumes pride; Shaver et al., 1987; Edelstein & Shaver, Chapter 11, this volume).

Methodological roadblocks have also hindered research on the self-conscious emotions, which in some cases may be more difficult to elicit in the laboratory than basic emotions such as fear, disgust, and joy. Experimental procedures used to elicit basic emotions (e.g., photographs, film clips) seem less effective in eliciting self-conscious emotions. Indeed, it is difficult to imagine an ethical manipulation that would generate shame in all individuals, partly because self-conscious emotions require more psychologically complex and individualized elicitors. Furthermore, even if self-conscious emotions could be effectively elicited, it may be more difficult to reliably assess the resultant experiences. There are several reliable self-report measures of self-conscious emotional dispositions, but standardized procedures for assessing online self-conscious emotions from nonverbal behaviors are only beginning to be developed (Robins, Noftle, & Tracy, Chapter 24, this volume). In contrast, there are a variety of coding schemes for assessing basic emotions through both verbal and nonverbal behaviors, such as the Emotion–Facial Action Coding System (EM-FACS) for coding facial expressions (Ekman & Rosenberg, 1997).

Although the historical emphasis on basic emotions is understandable, we believe the time is ripe to devote greater attention to self-conscious emotions. The theoretical and methodological lessons learned from the study of basic emotions can be applied to research on the more psychologically complex self-conscious emotions. Regardless of whether self-conscious emotions are universal and have clear-cut neurobiological bases, if an individual subjectively feels ashamed, guilty, embarrassed, or proud, then that, in itself, is an important psychological event with implications for the individual's future behavior, decisions, and mental and physical health. Moreover, the methodological impediments to the study of self-conscious emotions are not intractable. Similar issues were raised several decades ago when many psychologists argued that emotions in general could not be studied scientifically. A handful of emotion researchers questioned this claim and struggled against the zeitgeist to develop the field of affective science. We believe it is time to approach the study of self-conscious emotions in the same systematic and comprehensive manner.

In our view, self-conscious emotions should be treated as a special class of emotions. As "cognition-dependent" emotions (Izard, Ackerman, & Schultz, 1999), self-conscious emotions require a distinct theoretical model specifying their antecedent cognitions. In fact, the absence of such a model may have impeded self-conscious emotion research and contributed to their relative neglect.

In this chapter, we briefly describe the unique features that distinguish self-conscious from basic emotions, and explain why these features prevent generally accepted models of emotions from adequately capturing the self-conscious emotion process. We next present an appraisal-based process model of self-conscious emotions. This model was first formulated in Tracy and Robins (2004a), but has since been amended in response to thoughtful commentaries (*Psychological Inquiry*, 2004, vol. 15, pp. 126–170) and recent empirical research (Tracy & Robins, 2006b; Tracy & Robins, 2007a). We conclude by discussing the model's broader implications for research on self and emotion.

THE NEED FOR A THEORETICAL MODEL

Distinct Features of Self-Conscious Emotions

Below, we briefly describe five major features of self-conscious emotions that distinguish them from non-self-conscious emotions (for greater detail, see Tracy & Robins, 2004a). In our view, a comprehensive model of self-conscious emotions must account for each of these features.

1. *Self-conscious emotions require self-awareness and self-representations.* First and foremost, self-conscious emotions differ from basic emotions because they require self-awareness and self-representations. Although basic emotions like fear and sadness *can* and often do involve self-evaluative processes, only self-conscious emotions *must* involve these processes (Buss, 2001; Lewis, Sullivan, Stangor, & Weiss, 1989; Tangney & Dearing, 2002). A sense of self as conceived by theorists since William James (1890) includes both an ongoing sense of self-awareness (the "I" self) and the capacity for complex self-representations (the "me" self, or the mental representations that constitute one's

identity). Together, these self processes make it possible for self-evaluations, and therefore self-conscious emotions, to occur.

Importantly, by self-representations, we do not mean simply the cognitive contents of the personal self, but also relational, social, and collective self-representations. We are social creatures, so our self-representations reflect how we see ourselves vis-à-vis close others (e.g., as a romantic partner), social groups (e.g., as a professor), and broader cultural collectives (e.g., as a woman, as an American).

2. *Self-conscious emotions emerge later in childhood than basic emotions.* A second distinctive feature of self-conscious emotions is that they develop later than basic emotions (Izard, 1971). Most basic emotions emerge within the first 9 months of life (e.g., Campos, Barrett, Lamb, Goldsmith, & Stenberg, 1983); in fact, the primacy of these emotions in ontogeny is one reason for their classification as "basic" (Izard, 1992). In contrast, even generalized feelings of self-consciousness (sometimes considered an early form of embarrassment) do not develop until around 18–24 months (M. Lewis, 2000). More complex self-conscious emotions, such as shame, guilt, and pride, emerge even later, possibly by the end of the child's third year of life (Izard et al., 1999; Lagattuta & Thompson, Chapter 6, this volume; Lewis, Alessandri, & Sullivan, 1992; Stipek, 1995).

3. *Self-conscious emotions facilitate the attainment of complex social goals.* Emotions are assumed to have evolved through natural selection to facilitate survival and reproductive goals (which we will refer to as "survival goals"). It is easy to understand how a basic emotion might promote survival goals—for example, fear may cause an individual to run away from a predator, thereby enhancing his or her chances for survival in the face of threat. In contrast, we believe that self-conscious emotions evolved primarily to promote the attainment of specifically *social* goals, such as the maintenance or enhancement of status, or the prevention of group rejection (Keltner & Buswell, 1997; Tracy & Robins, 2004b). Humans evolved to navigate within a social structure that has complex layers of multiple, overlapping, and sometimes nontransitive social hierarchies (e.g., the highest status hunters were not always the highest status warriors). Survival, in our evolutionary history, depended on our capacity to overcome numerous complicated social problems, including "dyadic, triadic, or group-level cooperation; smooth group functioning; cheating; detection of cheaters; intragroup (and, particularly, intrasexual) competition, and intergroup competition" (Sedikides & Skowronski, 1997, p. 92). These dynamics may have promoted the evolution of a special set of emotions geared toward facilitating the achievement of social goals alone. Consistent with this account, self-conscious emotions seem to be present only in humans and other species (e.g., great apes) with highly complex and frequently shifting social hierarchies (de Waal, 1989; Keltner & Buswell, 1997; Leary, Chapter 3, this volume).

Collectively, the self-conscious emotions are assumed to promote behaviors that increase the stability of social hierarchies and affirm status roles (Tracy & Robins, 2007b). More specifically, shame and embarrassment may promote appeasement and avoidance behaviors after a social transgression, guilt may promote apology and confession after a social trespass, and pride may promote boastfulness and other approach-oriented behaviors after a socially valued success (Keltner & Buswell, 1997; Noftle & Robins, 2006; Tangney & Dearing, 2002; Tracy & Robins, in press). These social goals, in turn, facilitate survival and reproduction—for example, the social goal of befriending an ally can be seen as an intermediary step toward the survival goal of finding food.

4. *Self-conscious emotions do not have discrete, universally recognized facial expressions.* Each of the six basic emotions has a discrete, universally recognized facial

expression (Ekman, 2003). In contrast, researchers have failed to identify distinct facial expressions for any self-conscious emotion. They have, however, found distinct expressions that include bodily posture or head movement combined with facial expression for embarrassment, pride, and shame (Izard, 1971; Keltner, 1995; Tracy & Robins, 2004b). Furthermore, recent research conducted among isolated tribal villagers in Burkina Faso suggests that at least two of these expressions—pride and shame—may be universally recognized (Tracy & Robins, 2006a).

There are several possible explanations for the absence of discrete face-only expressions in self-conscious emotions. First, the more complex postural or bodily signals associated with embarrassment, pride, and shame may better fit the more complex messages likely sent by these emotions. A quick facial expression may be adequate for telling conspecifics "Run!," but a more complex bodily expression may better convey the more complicated message "I just did something that makes me deserve high status." Second, self-conscious emotions may be expressed more frequently through language than through nonverbal expressions. Although facial expressions have the advantage of being automatic and immediate, self-conscious emotions communicate messages that are typically less urgent, perhaps allowing for more deliberate processing and the production of verbal language. For example, conveying one's guilt over a social transgression is important, but it is important over a longer time frame than conveying one's fear about the presence of a predator.

Third, the expression of self-conscious emotions may, at times, be maladaptive, making it more important that these expressions be regulated. Facial expressions are more difficult to regulate than body movements and posture because many of the facial muscle contractions involved are involuntary (Eibl-Eisenfeldt, 1989). Although in contemporary society we may wish we could control the expression of all of our emotions, in our evolutionary history it was clearly more adaptive that our (basic) emotions be automatically expressed. The expression of self-conscious emotions, in contrast, may be detrimental to fitness. For example, in many cultures it is not acceptable to openly display pride, and such displays may lower likeability (Eid & Diener, 2001; Mosquera, Manstead, & Fischer, 2000; Paulhus, 1998; Zammuner, 1996).

5. *Self-conscious emotions are cognitively complex.* A fifth distinctive feature of self-conscious emotions is that they are more cognitively complex than basic emotions (Izard et al., 1999; M. Lewis, 2000). In order to experience fear, individuals need very few cognitive capacities; they must simply appraise an event as threatening their survival goals (e.g., Lazarus, 1991). To experience shame, however, an individual must have the capacity to form stable self-representations and to consciously self-reflect (i.e., direct attentional focus toward those representations). These two capacities allow the individual to engage in a host of complex self-evaluative processes that elicit self-conscious emotions, as we explain below. Basic emotions can involve these complex processes, but, unlike self-conscious emotions, they also can (and often do) occur with much simpler appraisals (e.g., LeDoux, 1996).

Importance of the Distinction

As these five distinctive features make clear, the self-conscious emotions are a unique class of emotions that cannot be simplistically grouped with other emotions that do not critically involve the self. This does not mean, however, that the self-conscious emotions have nothing in common with the basic emotions. Kemeny, Gruenewald, and Dickerson

(2004) have argued that emotions can be viewed as varying on a continuum from basic to self-conscious rather than as existing in one of two discrete classes. In our view, basic and self-conscious emotions are best conceptualized as "fuzzy" categories, with each emotion varying in the extent to which it is a good or bad exemplar of each category. From this perspective, shame and pride are particularly good exemplars of the self-conscious emotion category because they require self-representations and self-awareness, emerge later in development, do not have nonverbal expressions that can be recognized from the face alone, and are cognitively complex. Yet, if these two emotions are also universal, adaptive, and accompanied by functional physiological or endocrine responses, as accumulating evidence seems to suggest (Gruenwald et al., Chapter 5, this volume; Tracy & Robins, 2006a), then they may also meet the criteria for good exemplars of the basic emotion category.

In contrast, guilt seems to lack any kind of recognizable nonverbal expression, shows little evidence of universality (Haidt & Keltner, 1999), and is unlikely to have discrete physiological correlates. Thus, guilt may be a worse exemplar of the basic emotion category. However, guilt is cognitively complex, requires the capacity to self-reflect and make causal attributions (a prerequisite for self-conscious emotions, explained below), and serves important social functions. For these reasons, guilt is a very good exemplar of the self-conscious emotion category.

The important point, for the purposes of this chapter (and this book as a whole), is that distinguishing between these two categories is important and meaningful, and will provide a valuable framework for research on the similarities and differences between emotions within and across categories. For example, despite recent evidence that at least one self-conscious emotion expression (pride) shows the basic emotion characteristics of brief duration, high recognizability, and recognition even among children (Tracy, 2005; Tracy & Robins, 2004b; Tracy, Robins, & Lagatutta, 2005), the question remains: Why are basic emotions expressed in the face, whereas self-conscious emotions clearly require nonfacial elements? This is a noteworthy distinction, and examining it further may help clarify how and why the self-conscious emotions evolved. By conceptualizing the two classes as fuzzy rather than as discrete categories, we can avoid debates about whether a particular emotion is basic or self-conscious, and begin to explore the phylogenetic reasons these categories exist. Perhaps the degree to which an emotion is a good exemplar of each category reveals something important about when and why it came to be a part of the human behavioral repertoire.

Furthermore, this distinction provides the basis for the development of a process model delineating the cognitive antecedents of self-conscious emotions. Such a model can help move the field beyond intuitive definitions of self-conscious emotions—which are ubiquitous in the literature—by defining them in terms of underlying (and presumably universal) processes. If emotions are defined in terms of processes, questions about individual and cultural differences need not be about whether the emotion is the same or different, experienced or not experienced, or important or not important in different individuals or cultures, but rather whether (and how) the underlying process varies. This framework would promote a more explanatory and less descriptive approach.

Limitations of Extant Models of Emotion

According to most emotion theorists, emotions are initiated by the perception of a stimulus, which is evaluated (appraised) either consciously or unconsciously, setting off an "affect program" (e.g., Ekman, 1992). This program is assumed to be a discrete neural pattern that produces a coordinated set of responses, including action readiness and associated behaviors, physiological changes, a discrete facial expression, and a subjective feeling state. This model assumes a very simple appraisal process, which may not be accurate for the self-conscious emotions. Although appraisal theories of emotion have revised and extended the generic model by suggesting potentially relevant appraisal dimensions (e.g., Lazarus, 1991; Roseman, 2001; Scherer, 2001; Smith & Ellsworth, 1985), they do not provide a clear, consensual picture of the precise set of appraisals that generate self-conscious emotions.

Another limitation of extant models, as applied to the self-conscious emotions, is that they do not fully incorporate self-evaluative processes. There is typically little discussion of complex self processes such as self-focused attention, the activation of stable self-representations, and reflection upon discrepancies between a current self-state and some evaluative standard relevant to one's identity (e.g., an ideal self-representation). A complete process model of self-conscious emotions requires the inclusion of these elements, which constitute a large part of what differentiates self-conscious from non-self-conscious emotions.

A THEORETICAL PROCESS MODEL OF SELF-CONSCIOUS EMOTIONS

Figure 1.1 shows our model of the self-conscious emotion process (Tracy & Robins, 2004a). The model builds on previous theory and research on causal attributions and emotions (e.g., Covington & Omelich, 1981; Jagacinski & Nicholls, 1984; Weiner, 1985); cognitive appraisals and emotions (e.g., Lazarus, 1991; Scherer, 2001; Roseman, 2001; Ellsworth & Smith, 1988); the cognitive antecedents of shame, guilt, and pride (e.g., M. Lewis, 2000; H. B. Lewis, 1971; Tangney, 1991); and self-evaluative processes (e.g., Carver & Scheier, 1998; Cooley, 1902; Duval & Wicklund, 1972; Higgins, 1987).

Survival-Goal Relevance: Is the Event Relevant to Survival and Reproduction?

As shown in Figure 1.1, the first appraisal in the model is an evaluation of whether the eliciting event is relevant to survival and reproduction (e.g., Lazarus, 1991).[1] Events appraised as relevant to an individual's survival goals will lead to one of the basic emotions, according to appraisal and functionalist theories of the basic emotion process (e.g., Lazarus, 1991; Nesse, 1990; Roseman, 2001; Scherer, 2001). If an event is appraised as irrelevant to survival goals, it will elicit no emotion—unless it is appraised as relevant to identity goals (see below).[2]

Attentional Focus on the Self: Activation of Self-Representations

The next cognitive process in the model involves attentional focus (the "I" self) directed toward one's self-representations (the "me" self), resulting in a state that has been labeled "objective self-awareness" (Duval & Wicklund, 1972) or "self-focused attention" (Carver & Scheier, 1998). This state and its corresponding activated self-representations allow individuals to make reflexive self-evaluations.

The self-representations activated in this process include actual or current self-representations ("I am independent"), ideal or hoped-for self-representations ("I want to

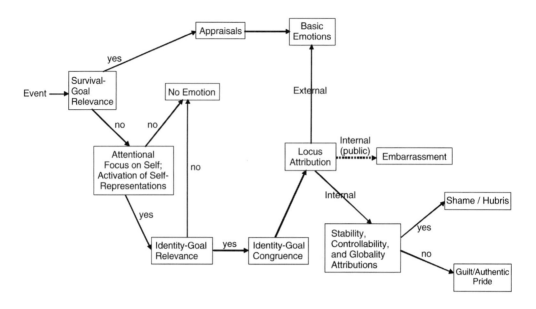

FIGURE 1.1. Process model of self-conscious emotions. The dotted arrow connecting "Locus Attribution" and "Embarrassment" indicates that a public self-representation must be activated in order for embarrassment to occur. From Tracy and Robins (2004a). Copyright 2004 by Jessica L. Tracy. Reprinted by permission.

become more independent"), and ought self-representations about fulfilling important obligations and duties ("My parents think I should become more independent"; Higgins, 1987). These self-representations may concern past, present, and future selves (Markus & Nurius, 1986; Wilson & Ross, 2001), and may refer to private (personal) and public (relational, social, and collective) aspects of the self (Robins, Norem, & Cheek, 1999). Collectively, these various representations constitute a person's identity.

According to our theoretical model, self-representations must be activated (either explicitly or implicitly) in order for self-conscious emotions to occur; only through self-focused attention can the individual make comparisons between self-representations and the external emotion-eliciting event. In fact, recent research suggests that self-focused attention is a necessary precursor for the occurrence of several distinct emotions in response to self-discrepancies (Phillips & Silvia, 2005).

Identity-Goal Relevance: Does It Matter for Who I Am?

Once attentional focus is directed toward self-representations, events can be appraised for their relevance to identity goals (e.g., "Does it matter for who I am or would like to be?"). According to our model, any event that relates to an important self-representation is likely to be appraised as relevant to an identity goal and, assuming that additional appraisals (described below) occur, will generate a self-conscious emotion. In contrast, an event that is relevant only to an individual's proximal adaptive fitness (and thus to the more simplistic, biological self that is shared with even single-cell organisms) will be appraised as survival-goal relevant. Importantly, events appraised as relevant to identity goals can also generate basic emotions (see below).

Several researchers have argued that the key goals at stake for self-conscious emotion elicitation are not about identity concerns, broadly defined, but rather about a more specific range of identity concerns involving interpersonal, social, or public evaluation (Baldwin & Baccus, 2004; Kemeny et al., 2004; Leary, Chapter 3, this volume). From our perspective, self-conscious emotions are experienced when a person's identity is threatened or elevated—which can occur in public or private, and in interpersonal or task contexts, as long as the eliciting event is relevant to the aspirations and ideals (as well as the fears) of the self. In fact, social evaluations will not elicit self-conscious emotions if the evaluated individual does not make the corresponding self-evaluative appraisals. For example, the public praise of others will not produce pride in individuals who discount the evaluations (e.g., if they have low self-esteem; Brown, 1998), and negative evaluations will not produce shame if they pertain to non-self-relevant domains, as James (1890) noted: "I, who for the time have staked my all on being a psychologist, am mortified if others know much more psychology than I. But I am contented to wallow in the grossest ignorance of Greek" (p. 310).

Thus, based on decades of research on the self, we argue that negative social evaluations elicit shame *because* they activate a host of self-evaluative processes, which are described by our model. These self-evaluative processes necessarily mediate the relation between social evaluation and self-conscious emotions. By emphasizing a broader range of identity processes than social evaluation, our model allows for the potentially private nature of these emotions—the fact that they can occur in response to events of which only the self is aware—and places social evaluation at the origins of the self-concept (i.e., our identities are created through early socialization), and not of the emotions that are triggered by it.

Identity–Goal Congruence: Is This Event Congruent with My Goals for Who I Am and Who I Want to Be?

Once an event has been appraised as relevant to identity goals, the next step is for it to be appraised as congruent or incongruent with these goals (see Figure 1.1). This appraisal determines the valence of the outcome emotion: positive or pleasurable emotions are elicited by goal-congruent events, and negative or displeasureable emotions are elicited by goal-incongruent events (Lazarus, 1991).[3]

How do individuals decide whether an event is congruent or incongruent with identity goals? Current self-representations, activated by the emotion-eliciting event (e.g., failure on an exam), are compared with stable, long-term self-representations, including actual ("I am a successful student") and ideal self-representations ("I want to be a successful student"; Higgins, 1987). Individuals may notice a discrepancy between current, actual, and ideal self-representations, and appraise the event as identity-goal incongruent. As shown in Figure 1.1, this appraisal would eventually elicit a negative self-conscious emotion such as shame or guilt.

Our emphasis on the role of discrepancies between current self-representations and more stable self-representations is based on conceptualizations of self and emotions first articulated by Cooley (1902) and James (1890). More recently, Carver and Scheier (1998) proposed that positive and negative affect are the output of a cybernetic self-regulation process, such that awareness of a discrepancy between a current self-state and some evaluative standard (e.g., an ideal self-representation) generates negative affect, whereas reduction of such a discrepancy generates positive affect. Our model builds on this view by specifying the distinct types of negative and positive emotions that are generated by these discrepancies.

Internality Attributions: Did the Event Occur Because of Something about Me?

Once an event has been appraised as either congruent or incongruent with identity goals, the next step is to determine its cause. This decision involves a set of appraisals, the most important of which concerns causal locus: Is the event due to an internal (within the individual) or an external (outside the individual) cause? The attribution of causal locus (Heider, 1958) has been studied by previous appraisal theorists, who refer to it as "credit or blame to oneself" (Lazarus, 1991), "accountability" (Smith & Lazarus, 1993), "agency" (Ellsworth & Smith, 1988; Roseman, 1991), "responsibility" (Frijda, 1987), or "causal attribution check" (Scherer, 2001).

Of note, we do not conceptualize this appraisal in the narrow sense of attribution theory (e.g., "Did I cause the event?"), but rather in the more general sense of "Is something about me or related to me the cause of the event?," where "me" is broadly defined to include all aspects of one's identity. This distinction is particularly important in the case of embarrassment, where internal appraisals are often made about events for which one had no responsibility or intentionality (e.g., being the recipient of spilled soup). This broader sense of internalization is also relevant for situations where individuals feel shame or pride about the actions of someone else—such as a family member, close friend, or even a stranger who represents a shared collective identity (e.g., an Olympic athlete from one's country). In such cases, the self-conscious emotion may be experienced "vicariously" (Lickel, Schmader, & Spanovic, Chapter 19, this volume) or more directly, if the individual responsible for the emotion's elicitation represents a shared identity with the individual experiencing the emotion. In other words, we may be aware of and empathic toward someone else's embarrassment without feeling it ourselves (e.g., the vicarious embarrassment that occurs when we watch an actor in a play forget his lines), but if we identify with the individual such that his or her mishap feels like our own, where "our own" is defined in the broader, collective sense, then the embarrassment we feel is likely to be direct, and not vicarious (e.g., if our romantic partner commits a social faux pas). Self-conscious emotions may be unique in this regard, due to the particular importance of self-evaluations in their elicitation, and the fact that the self can, and often does, include collective self-representations.

As shown in Figure 1.1, self-conscious emotions occur when individuals attribute the eliciting event to internal causes (M. Lewis, 2000; Tangney & Dearing, 2002; Weiner, 1985). Supporting this claim, studies have shown that internal attributions for failure tend to produce guilt and shame, and internal attributions for success tend to produce pride (Tracy & Robins, 2007a; Weiner, 1985; Weiner, Graham, & Chandler, 1982). Similarly, the appraisal dimensions of "agency" and "self-accountability" have been found to predict self-conscious emotions (Ellsworth & Smith, 1988; Roseman, 1991; Smith & Lazarus, 1993). In contrast, attributing events to external causes typically leads to basic emotions (Russell & McAuley, 1986), even when the event is identity-goal relevant. In fact, in contemporary society, this causal pathway may be the most typical route for the elicitation of basic emotions, given that threats to survival are less frequent than threats to identity. When people feel angry or afraid, their feelings were more likely to have been triggered by an external attribution for an identity (or "ego") threat, such as an insult from a coworker, than by a direct threat to their survival.

Stability, Globality, and Controllability Attributions: Is It Something I Always Do and Can't Control? Is It Something about Who I Am?

Besides locus, three other causal attributions are important for the elicitation of self-conscious emotions, and especially for differentiating among self-conscious emotions. These attributions concern the *stability, controllability,* and *globality* of causes. Central to the attribution process, these causal factors have been empirically linked to various emotional states (e.g., Brown & Weiner, 1984; Covington & Omelich, 1981; Niedenthal, Tangney, & Gavanski, 1994; Tangney, Wagner, & Gramzow, 1992; Tracy & Robins, 2006b, 2007a; Weiner et al., 1982; Weiner & Kukla, 1970). Although theoretically independent, controllability and stability are highly correlated; stable causes are more likely to be global and uncontrollable, and unstable causes are more likely to be specific and controllable (Peterson, 1991). Nonetheless, others have argued that controllability contributes additional variance to emotion outcomes beyond other dimensions (Weiner, 1991). As described below, we believe that globality, stability, and controllability attributions influence which particular self-conscious emotion is elicited after events are internalized.

Shame and Guilt

Several emotion theorists have argued that shame involves negative feelings about the stable, global self, whereas guilt involves negative feelings about a specific behavior or action taken by the self (H. B. Lewis, 1971; M. Lewis, 2000; Tangney & Dearing, 2002). Following this theoretical conception, our model specifies that internal, stable, uncontrollable, and global attributions ("I'm a dumb person") lead to shame, whereas internal, unstable, controllable, and specific attributions ("I didn't try hard enough") lead to guilt. Supporting this distinction, studies have shown that individuals who blame poor performances on ability (an internal, stable, uncontrollable factor) are more likely to feel shame, whereas those who blame poor performance on effort (an internal, unstable, controllable factor) are more likely to feel guilt (Brown & Weiner, 1984; Covington & Omelich, 1981; Jagacinski & Nicholls, 1984; Tracy & Robins, 2006b). Furthermore, individuals who tend to make internal, unstable, controllable attributions tend to be prone to guilt, whereas those who tend to make internal, stable, uncontrollable attributions tend to be prone to shame (Tangney et al., 1992; Tracy & Robins, 2006b). In addition, Niedenthal et al. (1994) found that counterfactual statements about changing a stable, global aspect of the self-concept (e.g., "if only I were a better friend") lead to greater shame and less guilt than do counterfactuals changing a specific behavior (e.g., "if only I had not flirted with his date").

Embarrassment

Like shame and guilt, embarrassment requires an appraisal of identity-goal relevance and identity-goal incongruence, and attributions to internal causes. However, unlike shame and guilt, embarrassment does not seem to require any further attributions, and, as conceptualized in our model, can occur only when attentional focus is directed toward the *public self,* activating corresponding public self-representations (Miller, Chapter 14, this volume). That is, an individual can become embarrassed by events caused by internal, stable, uncontrollable, and global aspects of the public self, such as repeatedly being publicly exposed as incompetent; or by events caused by internal, unstable, controllable, and specific aspects of the public self, such as spilling soup on one's boss. Importantly, activation of the public self does not require a public context. Rather, the public self is always present because it reflects the way we see ourselves through the (real or imagined) eyes of others. Thus, with regard to whether embarrassment is likely to occur, the crucial question is whether the public self has been activated, not whether the action occurred in a public context.

This account implies that embarrassment is less cognition-dependent than shame or guilt, both of which seem to depend on additional appraisal dimensions (i.e., stability, controllability, and globality). Supporting this claim, embarrassment emerges earlier in childhood than shame or guilt (Lewis et al., 1989), and, as a result, several researchers have placed it within a "first class" of self-conscious emotions, in contrast to the "second class" of guilt, shame, and pride, which require greater cognitive capacity (Izard et al., 1999; Lewis et al., 1989).[4]

Authentic and Hubristic Pride

According to our model, there are two facets of pride that parallel shame and guilt. Global pride in the self ("I'm proud of who I am"), referred to as "hubris" by M. Lewis (2000) and as "alpha pride" by Tangney et al. (1992), may result from attributions to internal, stable, uncontrollable, and global causes. Conversely, a feeling of pride that we refer to as "authentic" based on specific achievements ("I'm proud of what I did") may result from attributions to internal, unstable, controllable, and specific causes.

Recent research provides empirical support for this distinction (Tracy & Robins, 2007a, and Chapter 15, this volume). Two distinct facets of pride emerge from analyses of the semantic meaning of pride-related words, the dispositional tendency to experience pride, and the feelings associated with an actual pride experience. The content of these facets fits with the theoretical distinction between "authentic" and "hubristic" pride; specifically, authentic pride is associated with concepts and feelings like "accomplished," "confident," and "self-worth," whereas hubristic pride is more associated with such concepts as "arrogant," "egotistical," and "pompous." Moreover, the findings from several studies support our claim that authentic pride is more likely to result from internal, unstable, and controllable attributions for a positive event, whereas hubristic pride is more likely to result from internal, stable, and uncontrollable attributions for the same event (Tracy & Robins, 2007a, and Chapter 15, this volume).

IMPLICATIONS AND CONCLUSIONS

The theoretical model presented in this chapter uses an appraisal-based approach to integrate two prominent areas of research in social-personality psychology: the self and emotions. The resulting synthesis has the potential to provide insights into extant findings in both literatures and to suggest important directions for future research.

Specifically, to better understand the functions and outcomes of the emotions that mediate self processes (e.g., self-esteem, self-enhancement), self researchers can utilize our theoretical model to specify the exact emotions that may be involved. If, for example, self-enhancement increases positive affect, researchers can test whether it causes people to feel joy, authentic pride, hubristic pride, or some combination of these. From a discrete emotions perspective, each of these will produce divergent behaviors, thoughts, and feelings, so differentiating among them will facilitate our understanding of the larger process and our ability to make predictions. If we can focus on the particular emotion that accounts for the relation between two variables, the resultant correlation will be stronger than one found using a composite of different emotions, some relevant and some not.

To take a more specific example, our model has implications for the large body of experimental research on reactions to feedback. Numerous studies have shown that, following an ego threat, low self-esteem individuals tend to experience negative affect and withdraw from the task (Baumeister, Tice, & Hutton, 1989; Brown & Dutton, 1995). From a discrete emotions perspective, this withdrawal can be interpreted as a behavioral outcome of shame (H. B. Lewis, 1971; Lindsay-Hartz, 1984). Thus, the negative affect reported may more specifically reflect feelings of shame, and the outcome behaviors may be part of a coordinated functional response associated with the emotion. If failure represents a stable, global shortcoming of the self, the adaptive solution *is* to withdraw and avoid repeated attempts at success or social contact, which could further reveal the self's inadequacies.

In contrast, individuals high in narcissism do not respond to ego threats with withdrawal; instead, they typically become angry and aggressive (Bushman & Baumeister, 1998). This pattern may characterize Jeff Skilling's response to having his intelligence questioned by a Harvard admissions officer or to being indicted for fraud. One explanation for this alternate response to failure is that narcissists invoke a defensive process, using anger and aggression to avoid feeling shame (Scheff, 1998; Tracy & Robins, 2007b). Our model points to the specific cognitive pathways that may make this process possible. Narcissists may make external attributions for ego threats, blaming others for their failures. This regulatory strategy would promote a basic emotion, like anger, and would allow for the circumvention of conscious shame. This account suggests testable hypotheses—for example, individuals with genuine, nonnarcissistic, high self-esteem should respond to ego threats by taking responsibility and making internal, unstable, specific attributions; they thus should feel guilt rather than shame or anger.

To take another prominent example from the self literature, our model has implications for affective self-regulation. As was mentioned above, Carver and Scheier (1998) have argued that awareness of a discrepancy between a current self-state and a goal state results in negative affect. We have built on their model to argue that discrepancies between current and ideal states more specifically generate shame or guilt; this reinterpretation may improve our understanding of the behavioral outcomes associated with these discrepancies. In the Carver–Scheier (1998) model, discrepancies motivate behaviors that produce faster progress toward a goal state (i.e., increased effort to achieve goals). When we view the negative affect that is generated by the discrepancy as guilt, we can integrate functionalist theories of emotions into our interpretation and explain the progress-oriented behaviors: guilt functions to promote reparative action and increased future efforts (Barrett, 1995; Lindsay-Hartz, 1984; Tangney & Dearing, 2002). Furthermore, when discrepancies motivate withdrawal and avoidance rather than increased effort toward reducing the discrepancy, we can make predictions about why this might be the case. From a functionalist perspective, we need not assume that the overarching Carver–Scheier model is wrong; instead, we can hypothesize that shame, rather than guilt (and rather than overly broad negative affect), is the mediating emotion in such cases.

In conclusion, the literature on self-conscious emotions is still in its infancy, and needs an overarching, integrative model to provide structure and direction to the field. The model presented here may serve as one potential starting point, and we hope that, with reformulations and extensions from the growing body of empirical research on the topic (much of which is described in subsequent chapters in this volume), the field will progress toward a consensual model that can provide the foundation for a cumulative science of self-conscious emotions.

NOTES

1. Figure 1.1 implies a clear order and a serial, step-by-step sequence of conscious appraisals. However, the actual process presumably includes numerous feedback loops and may work bidirectionally and in parallel. Moreover, many of the appraisal processes are likely to occur implicitly. Nonetheless, to simplify explanation of the model, we discuss the emotion process described in Figure 1.1 as if it occurred in a simple serial order. Appraisal theorists have argued that representational models such as this usefully elucidate appraisal theories of emotions (Kappas, 2001), and several theorists have proposed models that seem to work in a clear sequential order (e.g., Scherer, 2001). Furthermore, even if the processes described in Figure 1.1 actually occur simultaneously or in parallel, our model can elucidate the mental algorithms through which these processes determine which particular self-conscious emotion is produced.
2. It is possible, however, that there exists a small class of eliciting events that can produce emotions without appraisals of goal relevance. For example, viewing a work of art or a beautiful landscape might elicit joy or awe with no cognitive mediation.
3. Although not shown in Figure 1.1, the appraisal of goal congruence would lead to two separate paths, depending on congruency or incongruency. The subsequent series of appraisals are identical, but the outcome emotions are either positive or negative. To simplify the figure, we combine the two paths and show the specific positive and negative emotions at the end of the model.
4. However, it is possible that a low-level, pre-"first-class" self-conscious emotion—"generalized self-consciousness"—can occur in response to the activation of self-representations but prior to any further appraisals. Lewis (2000) labeled this state "embarrassment as exposure," and noted that it occurs in response to praise or public attention and does not require any negative evaluation of self. Most researchers distinguish this state from the later developing, more cognitively complex form of embarrassment, which results from additional appraisals in our model (M. Lewis, 2000; Miller, 1995).

REFERENCES

Baldwin, M. W., & Baccus, J. R. (2004). Maintaining a focus on the social goals underlying self-conscious emotions. *Psychological Inquiry, 15,* 139–144.

Barrett, K. C. (1995). A functionalist approach to shame and guilt. In J. P. Tangney & K. W. Fischer (Eds.), *Self-conscious emotions: The psychology of shame, guilt, embarrassment, and pride* (pp. 25–63). New York: Guilford Press.

Batson, C. D. (1987). Prosocial motivation: Is it ever truly altruistic? In L. Berkowitz (Ed.), *Advances in experimental social psychology* (Vol. 20, pp. 65–122). New York: Academic Press.

Baumeister, R. F., Stillwell, A. M., & Heatherton, T. F. (1994). Guilt: An interpersonal approach. *Psychological Bulletin, 115,* 243–267.

Baumeister, R. F., Tice, D. M., & Hutton, D. G. (1989). Self-presentational motivations and personality differences in self-esteem. *Journal of Personality, 57,* 547–579.

Breugelmans, S. M., & Poortinga, Y. H. (2006). Emotion without a word: Shame and guilt among Rarámuri Indians and rural Javanese. *Journal of Personality and Social Psychology, 91,* 1111–1122.

Brown, J. D. (1998). *The self.* New York: McGraw-Hill.

Brown, J. D., & Dutton, K. A. (1995). The thrill of victory, the complexity of defeat: Self-esteem and people's emotional reactions to success and failure. *Journal of Personality and Social Psychology, 68,* 712–722.

Brown, J. D., & Marshall, M. A. (2001). Self-esteem and emotion: Some thoughts about feelings. *Personality and Social Psychology Bulletin, 27,* 575–584.

Brown, J. D., & Weiner, B. (1984). Affective consequences of ability versus effort ascriptions: Controversies, resolutions, and quandaries. *Journal of Educational Psychology, 76,* 146–158.

Bushman, B. J., & Baumeister, R. F. (1998). Threatened egotism, narcissism, self-esteem, and direct and displaced aggression: Does self-love or self-hate lead to violence? *Journal of Personality and Social Psychology, 75,* 219–229.

Buss, A. H. (2001). *Psychological dimensions of the self.* Thousand Oaks, CA: Sage.

Campos, J. J. (1995). Foreword. In J. P. Tangney & K. W. Fischer (Eds.), *Self-conscious emotions: The psychology of shame, guilt, embarrassment, and pride* (pp. ix–xi). New York: Guilford Press.

Campos, J. J., Barrett, K. C., Lamb, M. E., Goldsmith, H. H., & Stenberg, C. (1983). Socioemotional development. In M. M. Haith & J. J. Campos (Eds.), *Handbook of child psychology: Vol. 2. Infancy and developmental psychobiology* (4th ed., pp. 783–915). New York: Wiley.

Carver, C. S., & Scheier, M. F. (1998). *On the self-regulation of behavior.* New York: Cambridge University Press.

Clark, A. (2006, October 24). White-collar criminals find quality of mercy increasingly strained. *The Guardian.*

Cooley, C. H. (1902). *Human nature and the social order.* New York: Scribner's.

Covington, M. V., & Omelich, C. L. (1981). As failures mount: Affective and cognitive consequences of ability demotion in the classroom. *Journal of Educational Psychology, 73,* 796–808.

de Waal, F. B. M. (1989). *Chimpanzee politics: Power and sex among apes.* Baltimore: Johns Hopkins University Press.

Duval, S., & Wicklund, R. A. (1972). *A theory of objective self-awareness.* New York: Academic Press.

Eibl-Eibesfeldt, I. (1989). *Human ethology.* New York: Aldine de Gruyter.

Eid, M., & Diener, E. (2001). Norms for experiencing emotions in different cultures: Inter- and intranational differences. *Journal of Personality and Social Psychology, 81,* 869–885.

Ekman, P. (1992). An argument for basic emotions. *Cognition and Emotion, 6,* 169–200.

Ekman, P. (2003). *Emotions revealed.* New York: Times Books.

Ekman, P., & Rosenberg, E. L. (1997). *What the face reveals: Basic and applied studies of spontaneous expression using the Facial Action Coding System (FACS).* New York: Oxford University Press.

Ellsworth, P. C., & Smith, C. A. (1988). Shades of joy: Patterns of appraisal differentiating pleasant emotions. *Cognition and Emotion, 2,* 301–331.

Feiring, C., Taska, L., & Lewis, M. (2002). Adjustment following sexual abuse discovery: The role of shame and attributional style. *Developmental Psychology, 38,* 79–92.

Fischer, K. W., & Tangney, J. P. (1995). Self-conscious emotions and the affect revolution: Framework and overview. In J. P. Tangney & K. W. Fischer (Eds.), *Self-conscious emotions: The psychology of shame, guilt, embarrassment, and pride* (pp. 3–24). New York: Guilford Press.

Frijda, N. H. (1987). Emotion, cognitive structure, and action tendency. *Cognition and Emotion, 1,* 115–143.

Goffman, E. (1955). On face-work: An analysis of ritual elements in social interaction. *Psychiatry: Journal for the Study of Interpersonal Processes, 18,* 213–231.

Haidt, J., & Keltner, D. (1999). Culture and facial expression: Open-ended methods find more expressions and a gradient of recognition. *Cognition and Emotion, 13,* 225–266.

Harder, D. W. (1995). Shame and guilt assessment, and relationships of shame- and guilt-proneness to psychopathology. In J. P. Tangney & K. W. Fischer (Eds.), *Self-conscious emotions: The psychology of shame, guilt, embarrassment, and pride* (pp. 368–392). New York: Guilford Press.

Heider, F. (1958). *The psychology of interpersonal relations.* New York: Wiley.

Higgins, E. T. (1987). Self-discrepancy: A theory relating self and affect. *Psychological Review, 94,* 319–340.

Izard, C. E. (1971). *The face of emotion*. East Norwalk, CT: Appleton-Century-Crofts.

Izard, C. E. (1992). Basic emotions, relations among emotions, and emotion–cognition relations. *Psychological Review, 99,* 561–565.

Izard, C. E., Ackerman, B. P., & Schultz, D. (1999). Independent emotions and consciousness: Self-consciousness and dependent emotions. In J. A. Singer & P. Singer (Eds.), *At play in the fields of consciousness: Essays in honor of Jerome L. Singer* (pp. 83–102). Mahwah, NJ: Erlbaum.

Jagacinski, C. M., & Nicholls, J. G. (1984). Conceptions of ability and related affects in task involvement and ego involvement. *Journal of Educational Psychology, 76,* 909–919.

James, W. (1890). *The principles of psychology*. Cambridge, MA: Harvard University Press.

Johnson-Laird, P. N., & Oatley, K. (1989). The language of emotions: An analysis of a semantic field. *Cognition and Emotion, 3,* 81–123.

Kappas, A. (2001). A metaphor is a metaphor is a metaphor: Exorcising the homunculus from appraisal theory. In K. R. Scherer, A. Schorr, & T. Johnstone (Eds.), *Appraisal processes in emotion: Theory, methods, research* (pp. 157–172). New York: Oxford University Press.

Keltner, D. (1995). Signs of appeasement: Evidence for the distinct displays of embarrassment, amusement, and shame. *Journal of Personality and Social Psychology, 68,* 441–454.

Keltner, D., & Buswell, B. N. (1997). Embarrassment: Its distinct form and appeasement functions. *Psychological Bulletin, 122,* 250–270.

Kemeny, M. E., Gruenewald, T. L., & Dickerson, S. (2004). Shame as the emotional response to threat to the social self: Implications for behavior, physiology, and health. *Psychological Inquiry, 15,* 153–160.

Kitayama, S., Markus, H. R., & Matsumoto, H. (1995). Culture, self, and emotion: A cultural perspective on "self-conscious" emotions. In J. P. Tangney & K. W. Fischer (Eds.), *Self-conscious emotions: The psychology of shame, guilt, embarrassment, and pride* (pp. 439–464). New York: Guilford Press.

Lazarus, R. S. (1991). *Emotion and adaptation*. New York: Oxford University Press.

LeDoux, J. E. (1996). *The emotional brain: The mysterious underpinnings of emotional life*. New York: Simon & Schuster.

Leith, K. P., & Baumeister, R. F. (1998). Empathy, shame, guilt, and narratives of interpersonal conflicts: Guilt-prone people are better at perspective taking. *Journal of Personality, 66,* 1–37.

Lewis, H. B. (1971). *Shame and guilt in neurosis*. New York: International Universities Press.

Lewis, M. (2000). Self-conscious emotions: Embarrassment, pride, shame, and guilt. In M. Lewis & J. M. Haviland-Jones (Eds.), *Handbook of emotions* (2nd ed., pp. 623–636). New York: Guilford Press.

Lewis, M., Alessandri, S. M., & Sullivan, M. W. (1992). Differences in shame and pride as a function of children's gender and task difficulty. *Child Development, 63,* 630–638.

Lewis, M., Sullivan, M. W., Stanger, C., & Weiss, M. (1989). Self development and self-conscious emotions. *Child Development, 60,* 146–156.

Lindsay-Hartz, J. (1984). Contrasting experiences of shame and guilt. *American Behavioral Scientist, 27,* 689–704.

Markus, H., & Nurius, P. (1986). Possible selves. *American Psychologist, 41,* 954–969.

Menon, U., & Shweder, R. A. (1994). Kali's tongue: Cultural psychology and the power of shame in Orissa, India. In S. Kitayama & H. R. Markus (Eds.), *Emotion and culture: Empirical studies of mutual influence* (pp. 241–282). Washington, DC: American Psychological Association.

Miller, R. S. (1995). Embarrassment and social behavior. In J. P. Tangney & K. W. Fischer (Eds.), *Self-conscious emotions: The psychology of shame, guilt, embarrassment, and pride* (pp. 322–339). New York: Guilford Press.

Mosquera, P. M., Manstead, A. S. R., & Fischer, A. H. (2000). The role of honor-related values in the elicitation, experience, and communication of pride, shame, and anger: Spain and the Netherlands compared. *Personality and Social Psychology Bulletin, 26,* 833–844.

Nesse, R. M. (1990). Evolutionary explanations of emotions. *Human Nature, 1,* 261–289.

Niedenthal, P. M., Tangney, J. P., & Gavanski, I. (1994). "If only I weren't" versus "If only I hadn't":

Distinguishing shame and guilt in counterfactual thinking. *Journal of Personality and Social Psychology, 67,* 585–595.

Noftle, E. E., & Robins, R. W. (2006). *How are actions and inhibited actions related to discrete emotions?: A functionalist perspective.* Manuscript submitted for publication.

Paulhus, D. L. (1998). Interpersonal and intrapsychic adaptiveness of trait self-enhancement: A mixed blessing? *Journal of Personality and Social Psychology, 74,* 1197–1208.

Peterson, C. (1991). The meaning and measurement of explanatory style. *Psychological Inquiry, 2,* 1–10.

Phillips, A. G., & Silvia, P. J. (2005). Self-awareness and the emotional consequences of self-discrepancies. *Personality and Social Psychology Bulletin, 31,* 703–713.

Retzinger, S. M. (1987). Resentment and laughter: Video studies of the shame–rage spiral. In H. B. Lewis (Ed.), *The role of shame in symptom formation* (pp. 151–181). Hillsdale, NJ: Erlbaum.

Robins, R. W., Norem, J. K., & Cheek, J. M. (1999). Naturalizing the self. In L. A. Pervin & O. P. John (Eds.), *Handbook of personality: Theory and research* (2nd ed., pp. 443–477). New York: Guilford Press.

Roseman, I. J. (1991). Appraisal determinants of discrete emotions. *Cognition and Emotion, 5,* 161–200.

Roseman, I. J. (2001). A model of appraisal in the emotion system: Integrating theory, research, and applications. In K. R. Scherer & A. Schorr (Eds.), *Appraisal processes in emotion: Theory, methods, research* (pp. 68–91). New York: Oxford University Press.

Russell, D., & McAuley, E. (1986). Causal attributions, causal dimensions, and affective reactions to success and failure. *Journal of Personality and Social Psychology, 50,* 1174–1185.

Scheff, T. J. (1988). Shame and conformity: The deference-emotion system. *American Sociological Review, 53,* 395–406.

Scheff, T. J. (1998). Shame in the labeling of mental illness. In P. Gilbert & B. Andrews (Eds.), *Shame: Interpersonal behavior, psychopathology, and culture* (pp. 191–205). Oxford, UK: Oxford University Press.

Scherer, K. R. (2001). Appraisal considered as a process of multilevel sequential checking. In K. R. Scherer, A. Schorr, & T. Johnstone (Eds.), *Appraisal processes in emotion: Theory, methods, research* (pp. 92–120). New York: Oxford University Press.

Sedikides, C., & Skowronski, J. J. (1997). The symbolic self in evolutionary context. *Personality and Social Psychology Review, 1,* 80–102.

Shaver, P., Schwartz, J., Kirson, D., & O'Connor, C. (1987). Emotion knowledge: Further exploration of a prototype approach. *Journal of Personality and Social Psychology, 52,* 1061–1086.

Smith, C. A., & Ellsworth, P. C. (1985). Patterns of cognitive appraisal in emotion. *Journal of Personality and Social Psychology, 48,* 813–838.

Smith, C. A., & Lazarus, R. S. (1993). Appraisal components, core relational themes, and the emotions. *Cognition and Emotion, 7,* 233–269.

Stipek, D. (1995). The development of pride and shame in toddlers. In J. P. Tangney & K. W. Fischer (Eds.), *Self-conscious emotions: The psychology of shame, guilt, embarrassment, and pride* (pp. 237–252). New York: Guilford Press.

Tangney, J. P. (1991). Moral affect: The good, the bad, and the ugly. *Journal of Personality and Social Psychology, 61,* 598–607.

Tangney, J. P., & Dearing, R. L. (2002). *Shame and guilt.* New York: Guilford Press.

Tangney, J. P., & Fischer, K. W. (Eds.). (1995). *Self-conscious emotions: The psychology of shame, guilt, embarrassment, and pride.* New York: Guilford Press.

Tangney, J. P., Wagner, P., & Gramzow, R. (1992). Proneness to shame, proneness to guilt, and psychopathology. *Journal of Abnormal Psychology, 101,* 469–478.

Tracy, J. L. (2005, May). *The automaticity of emotion recognition.* Paper presented at the American Psychological Society's 17th Annual Convention, Los Angeles, CA.

Tracy, J. L., & Robins, R. W. (2004a). Putting the self into self-conscious emotions: A theoretical model. *Psychological Inquiry, 15,* 103–125.

this self-imposed affective consequence is based both on an evaluation of the ethics of the behavior (e.g., its propriety, its effect on others) and on an assessment of what that behavior reveals about the self (e.g., our character, our talent, our worth). In effect, shame, guilt, embarrassment, and pride function as an emotional moral barometer, providing immediate and salient feedback on our social and moral acceptability. Moreover, these emotions provide a countervailing force to the reward structure based on more immediate, selfish, id-like desires.

Importantly, actual behavior is not necessary for the press of moral emotions to have effect. People can *anticipate* their likely emotional reactions (e.g., guilt vs. pride/self-approval) as they consider behavioral alternatives. Thus, the "self-conscious" moral emotions can exert a strong influence on moral choice and behavior by providing critical feedback regarding both anticipated behavior (feedback in the form of *anticipatory* shame, guilt, or pride) and actual behavior (feedback in the form of *consequential* shame, guilt, or pride). Moreover, there is a functional relationship between anticipatory and consequential emotional reactions. Anticipated, or "forecasted," affective responses to behavior not yet enacted are inferred from past consequential emotions to similar behaviors and events.

Thus far, we have focused on *emotion states*, situation-specific experiences of consequential and anticipatory feelings of shame, guilt, embarrassment, and pride. In the realm of moral emotions, researchers are also interested in *dispositional* tendencies to experience these self-conscious emotions (e.g., shame-proneness, guilt-proneness). A "moral emotion disposition" is defined as the propensity to experience that emotion across a range of relevant situations (Tangney, 1990). From this perspective, shame-prone individuals would be more susceptible to both anticipatory and consequential experiences of shame, relative to their less shame-prone peers. Theoretically, shame-prone people are inclined to anticipate shame in response to a range of *potential* behaviors and outcomes. In turn, shame-prone individuals also are inclined to experience shame as a consequence of a range of *actual* failures and transgressions.

A CONCEPTUAL MODEL OF MORAL BEHAVIOR: WHERE DO SELF-CONSCIOUS EMOTIONS FIT IN?

What roles do shame, guilt, embarrassment, and pride play in the larger human moral apparatus? Figure 2.1 presents a framework for thinking about how intrapersonal factors from three domains might jointly influence moral behavior—moral behavior enacted in particular situations and moral behavior across time, as in "a life lived morally." Not included in this model are the myriad situational factors that bear importantly on individuals' behavior in morally relevant contexts, factors studied in considerable detail in the social psychological literature. According to the model in Figure 2.1, moral intentions and behaviors are influenced by moral standards, moral cognitions, and moral emotions.

Moral Standards

Moral standards represent an individual's knowledge and internalization of moral norms and conventions. People's moral standards are dictated in part by universal moral laws and in part by culturally specific proscriptions. In his comprehensive review of moral reasoning and moral behavior, Blasi (1980) largely dismissed moral standards, arguing that

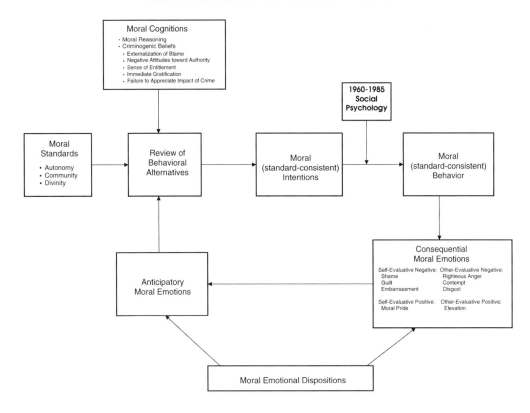

FIGURE 2.1. A conceptual model of moral emotions, moral cognitions, and moral behavior.

there are very small individual differences in knowledge of accepted rules and norms beyond the early age of 7 or 8. Most people recognize that, barring extenuating circumstances, it is wrong to murder, cheat, steal from, or otherwise do harm to others. The U.S.
judicial system rests heavily on this assumption of minimal variance. Television drama
notwithstanding, the not-guilty-by-reason-of-insanity defense rarely prevails in real
courtrooms (Jones, 1996)—reflecting the belief that the vast majority of people (of highly
deviant people, even) understand the difference between "right and wrong."

More recently, psychologists have recognized that moral standards are multifaceted,
diverse, and to a considerable extent culturally relative. The definition of "right" and "wrong"
is not universally consistent across groups varying by culture, age, status, and so on.

Shweder, Much, Mahapatra, and Park (1997) offer a framework for reconciling
these divergent views of moral standards, identifying three "ethics" that inform our standards for moral behavior: autonomy, community, and divinity. The ethic of autonomy
focuses on individual rights, justice, and especially prohibitions against *harming others*—
physically, psychologically, or spiritually. The ethic of community focuses on duty,
loyalty, and *shared social conventions*—standards and rules that support community and
hierarchy. The ethic of divinity encompasses interrelated concepts of divinity and physical
purity. Importantly, standards emanating from the ethic of autonomy are relatively universal. Standards emanating from the ethics of community and divinity are more likely to
show variability across cultures.

Moral Cognitions

Of the three components that come to bear on moral behavior (moral standards, moral cognitions, and moral emotions), most research has focused on moral cognitions. Moreover, the preponderance of the moral cognitions research focuses on a particular kind of moral cognition: moral reasoning.

In his theory of moral development, Kohlberg (1969) proposed that people's thinking about moral issues progresses in stages, paralleling Piaget's (1952) more general theory of cognitive development. At the lowest levels of moral reasoning, people focus on concrete ideas of right and wrong (e.g., "that's the rule") and consequences for oneself (e.g., "getting in trouble"). At successively higher levels of moral reasoning, the arguments become more complex and less egocentric, incorporating notions of community, justice, and reciprocity (e.g., "fairness for the common good").

How does level of moral reasoning relate to moral behavior? The very strong assumption among moral developmentalists is that people who reason at more sophisticated levels behave better. In the vast literature on moral reasoning, remarkably few studies have actually examined people's *behavior*, but the available evidence suggests that the link between level of moral reasoning and moral behavior is positive but at best modest (Blasi, 1980; Arnold, 1989; Kurtines & Greif, 1974; Mischel & Mischel, 1976; Tangney, Stuewig, Mashek, Feshbach, & Feshbach, 2006). Level of moral reasoning does not account for the lion's share of variance in people's choices to engage in moral versus immoral behavior, suggesting that additional cognitive factors are important in influencing moral behavior.

Theory and research from social psychology (Bandura, 1990) and criminology (Andrews & Bonta, 1994; Maruna & Copes, 2005; Sykes & Matza, 1957; Yochelson & Samenow, 1976) converge to underscore the importance of certain cognitive processes in fostering and maintaining behavior at odds with one's moral standards. Although the field of psychology has long focused on moral reasoning, other aspects of moral cognition—such as the propensity to engage in cognitive distortions, rationalizations, and techniques of "neutralization"—may be more powerful predictors of moral versus immoral behavior.

Clinicians working with serious criminal offenders, too, note that criminals who persist in a life of crime often hold a distinct set of beliefs—(im)moral cognitions—that serve to rationalize and perpetuate criminal activity (Tangney, Mashek, & Stuewig, 2007). For example, it is not unusual for inmates to make external attributions for the cause of their conviction (externalization of blame). More than a few offenders genuinely perceive that the primary reason they are in jail—the heart of responsibility—is an overzealous cop, an associate's betrayal, or society's failure to provide adequate employment opportunities. Another common cognitive distortion among offenders centers on the experiences of a victim. Many offenders view a broad range of crimes as "victimless." They may believe that a victim (e.g., of burglary, fraud, or even rape) is not really harmed unless there is concrete physical injury, in effect downplaying the validity of psychological pain.

Distinct from moral standards (judgments of "right" and "wrong"), criminogenic cognitions represent patterns of thought apt to attenuate the relationship between one's standards and one's behavioral decisions and associated actions (see Figure 2.1). For example, criminologists Sykes and Matza (1957) described "techniques of neutralization"—

for example, minimizing harmful consequences, dehumanizing the victim—the function of which is to reduce dissonance between moral standards and moral behavior.

Moral Emotions

After decades of neglect, the scientific study of moral emotions has come into its own. Recently, Haidt (2000, 2003) added importantly to our thinking about the nature of moral emotions. He defines "moral emotions" as those "that are linked to the interests or welfare either of society as a whole or at least of persons other than the judge or agent" (2003, p. 276). Moral emotions provide the motivational force—the power and the energy—to do good and to avoid doing bad (Kroll & Egan, 2004).

In addition to the negative self-conscious emotions shame, guilt, and embarrassment, Haidt has identified a number of other-evaluative emotions that serve moral functions. For example, elevation and gratitude are emotions experienced upon observing the admirable deeds of *others*; both motivate observers to engage in admirable deeds themselves, contributing to the common good. By crossing the two dimensions of focus/evaluation (on the self vs. on the other) and valence (positive vs. negative) (see "Consequential Moral Emotions" in Figure 2.1), one can conceptualize a two-dimensional space of moral emotion (Haidt, 2003, following Ortony, Clore, & Collins, 1988).

THE NEGATIVE SELF-EVALUATIVE EMOTION QUADRANT

A triad of negatively valenced "self-conscious" emotions—shame, guilt, and embarrassment—are widely recognized as playing an important moral self-regulatory role. Here we summarize theory and research on the distinction between shame and guilt.

What Is the Difference between Shame and Guilt?

Attempts to differentiate between shame and guilt fall into three categories: (1) a distinction based on types of eliciting events, (2) a distinction based on the public versus private nature of the transgression, and (3) a distinction based on the degree to which the person construes the emotion-eliciting event as a failure of self or behavior (for a review, see Tangney, Stuewig, & Mashek, 2007).

Research indicates that type of event has surprisingly little to do with the distinction between shame and guilt (Keltner & Buswell, 1996; Tangney, 1992; Tangney, Marschall, Rosenberg, Barlow, & Wagner, 1994; Tracy & Robins, 2006). Most types of events (e.g., lying, cheating, stealing, failing to help another, disobeying parents) are cited by some people in connection with feelings of shame and by other people in connection with feelings of guilt. Neither is shame necessarily the more "public" emotion arising from public exposure and disapproval, as often claimed (Benedict, 1946). When experiencing shame, people may *feel* more exposed—more aware of others' disapproval—but the reality is that situations causing both shame and guilt are typically social in nature (Tangney, Stuewig, & Mashek, 2007).

Currently, the most dominant basis for distinguishing between shame and guilt centers on the object of negative evaluation and disapproval. Shame involves a negative evaluation of the global self; guilt involves a negative evaluation of a specific behavior (H.

B. Lewis, 1971; Tangney, 1990; Tangney & Dearing, 2002; Tracy & Robins, 2004). This differential emphasis on self ("*I* did that horrible thing") versus behavior ("I *did* that horrible *thing*") gives rise to distinct emotional experiences associated with distinct patterns of motivation and subsequent behavior.

On balance, shame is the more painful emotion because one's core self—not simply one's behavior—is at stake. Feelings of shame are typically accompanied by a sense of shrinking or of "being small," and by a sense of worthlessness and powerlessness. Guilt, on the other hand, is typically a less devastating, less painful experience because the object of condemnation is a specific behavior, not the entire self. Rather than needing to defend the exposed core of their identity, people in the throes of guilt are drawn to consider their *behavior* and its consequences. This focus leads to tension, remorse, and regret over the "bad thing done."

There is impressive empirical support for H. B. Lewis's (1971) distinction between shame and guilt, including experimental and correlational studies employing a range of methods, qualitative case study analyses, content analyses of shame and guilt narratives, participants' quantitative ratings of personal shame and guilt experiences, analyses of attributions associated with shame and guilt, and analyses of participants' counterfactual thinking (for reviews, see Tangney & Dearing, 2002, and Tangney, Stuewig, & Mashek, 2007). Most recently, for example, Tracy and Robins (2006) employed both experimental and correlational methods to show that internal, stable, uncontrollable attributions for failure were positively related to shame, whereas internal, unstable, controllable attributions for failure were positively related to guilt.

Shame and Guilt Are Not Equally "Moral" Emotions

Empirical research suggests that shame and guilt are not equally "moral" emotions. On balance, guilt appears to be the more adaptive emotion, benefiting individuals and their relationships in a variety of ways (Baumeister, Stillwell, & Heatherton, 1994; Tangney, 1991; Tangney & Dearing, 2002). Five lines of research illustrate the adaptive functions of guilt, in contrast to the hidden costs of shame (see Tangney, Stuewig, & Mashek, 2007).

Hiding versus Amending

Research consistently shows that shame and guilt lead to contrasting motivations, or "action tendencies" (Ketelaar & Au, 2003; H. B. Lewis, 1971; Lindsay-Hartz, 1984; Tangney, 1993; Tangney, Miller, Flicker, & Barlow, 1996; Wallbott & Scherer, 1995; Wicker, Payne, & Morgan, 1983). Shame often motivates efforts to deny, hide from, or escape the shame-inducing situation. Guilt often motivates reparative action (e.g., confession, apology, efforts to undo the harm done).

Other-Oriented Empathy versus Self-Oriented Distress

Shame and guilt are differentially related to empathy. Specifically, guilt goes hand in hand with other-oriented empathy. Feelings of shame apparently disrupt individuals' ability to form empathic connections with others. This differential relationship of shame and guilt to empathy is apparent both at the level of emotion disposition and at the level of emotional state (Joireman, 2004; Leith & Baumeister, 1998; Tangney, 1991, 1995; Tangney & Dearing, 2002; Tangney et al., 1994).

Constructive versus Destructive Reactions to Anger

Research indicates a robust link between shame and anger, again observed at both the dispositional and the state levels. For example, across individuals of all ages, proneness to shame is positively correlated with anger, hostility, and the propensity to blame others (Andrews, Brewin, Rose, & Kirk, 2000; Bennett, Sullivan, & Lewis, 2005; Harper, Austin, Cercone, & Arias, 2005; Harper & Arias, 2004; Paulhus, Robins, Trzesniewski, & Tracy, 2004; Tangney & Dearing, 2002). In an effort to escape painful feelings of shame, shamed individuals are apt to defensively "turn the tables," externalizing blame and anger outward onto a convenient scapegoat. In this way, shamed individuals may regain some sense of control and superiority in their life, but the long-term costs are often steep. Friends, coworkers, and loved ones are apt to feel confused and alienated by seemingly irrational bursts of anger. Guilt-proneness, in contrast, is consistently associated with more constructive responses to anger (e.g., nonhostile discussion, direct corrective action) and a disinclination toward aggression (Tangney, Wagner, Hill-Barlow, Marschall, & Gramzow, 1996).

Psychological Symptoms

Research over the past two decades consistently indicates that proneness to shame is related to a wide variety of psychological symptoms, including low self-esteem, depression, anxiety, eating disorder symptoms, posttraumatic stress disorder (PTSD), and suicidal ideation (for a review, see Tangney, Stuewig & Mashek, 2007). The negative psychological implications of shame are evident across measurement methods, diverse age groups, and populations.

While the traditional view is that guilt plays a significant role in psychological symptoms, the empirical findings have been more equivocal. Tangney (1996) argued that once one conceptualizes guilt as a negative emotion in response to a specific failure or transgression, there's no compelling reason to expect guilt to be associated with poor psychological adjustment. Instead, guilt is most likely to be maladaptive when it becomes fused with shame. Consistent with this conceptual analysis, empirical studies that employ measures that are ill-suited to distinguish between shame and guilt report that guilt-proneness is associated with psychological symptoms. On the other hand, measures sensitive to H. B. Lewis's (1971) distinction between shame about the self versus guilt about a specific behavior show that the propensity to experience "shame-free" guilt is essentially unrelated to psychological symptoms. Problems with guilt are likely to arise when people have an exaggerated or distorted sense of responsibility for events (Tangney & Dearing, 2002; Zahn-Waxler & Robinson, 1995), but the propensity to experience "shame-free" guilt in response to clear transgressions is generally unrelated to psychological problems.

Risky, Illegal, and/or Immoral Behavior

Because shame and guilt are painful emotions, it is often assumed that they motivate individuals to avoid "doing wrong." But as discussed in greater detail by Stuewig and

Tangney (Chapter 20, this volume), when considering actual moral behavior, empirical support for the moral functions of guilt is much stronger than for shame. Among children, adolescents, college students, parents, grandparents, and incarcerated felons, guilt-proneness is associated with low levels of consensually immoral behavior. There is virtually no evidence for the presumed moral functions of shame.

Vicarious or "Collective" Shame and Guilt: Group-Based Self-Conscious Emotion

Thus far, we have discussed shame and guilt experienced in reaction to one's *own* misdeeds. In recent years, a number of investigators have substantially expanded the literature on self-conscious emotions by considering "vicarious" or "group-based" shame and guilt—feelings experienced in response to the transgressions and failures of *other* individuals (see Lickel, Schmader, & Spanovic, Chapter 19, this volume). This research represents an exciting integration of self-conscious emotions theory with the social psychological literature on social identity, group processes, and intergroup processes. In many ways, the phenomena of vicarious shame and guilt parallel personal shame and guilt experiences. Of particular applied relevance to current international conflicts, when people are provided with ambiguous information about group members' transgressions, those who are highly identified with the group appear to capitalize on the ambiguity, reporting less vicarious shame (Johns, Schmader, & Lickel, 2005) and group-based guilt (Doojse, Branscombe, Spears, & Manstead, 1998), relative to those who are less identified, and whose self is presumably less threatened.

As with personal guilt experiences, group-based guilt has been associated with empathy (Zebel, Doojse, & Spears, 2004) and a motivation to repair or make amends (Zebel et al., 2004; Iyer, Leach, & Crosby, 2003; Swim & Miller, 1999; Lickel, Schmader, Curtis, Scarnier, & Ames, 2005). And, as with personal shame experiences, vicarious group-based shame (but not guilt) has been linked to a desire to distance oneself from the shame-eliciting event (Lickel et al., 2005; Johns et al., 2005). Furthermore, the link between anger and shame is evident when considering vicarious shame (Schmader & Lickel, 2006; Johns et al., 2005; Iyer, Schmader, & Lickel, 2007). There are, however, some indications that group-based shame may have a "kinder, gentler" side than personal shame. For example, under some circumstances, group-based shame appears to motivate a desire to change the image of the group in a proactive fashion (Lickel, Rutchick, Hamilton, & Sherman, 2006).

Although research on shame and guilt—at the individual or group level—has dominated the literature on moral emotions thus far, they are just part of the story. Haidt (2003) has delved into morally relevant affective responses to the behavior of *others.*

NEGATIVE OTHER-EVALUATIVE EMOTIONS

Righteous anger, contempt, and disgust lie in the negatively valenced/other-evaluative quadrant of moral emotions in Figure 2.1. Righteous anger arises in response to a special class of anger-eliciting events, those in which the perpetrator's behavior represents a violation of *moral* standards. Rozin, Lowery, Imada, and Haidt (1999) presented evidence that righteous anger tends to occur more specifically in response to violations of the ethic of autonomy—the ethic most familiar in Western culture. Righteous anger can serve moral functions in that it can motivate "third party" bystanders to take action in order to remedy observed injustices.

The emotions of contempt and disgust also stem from negative evaluations of others. Rozin et al. (1999) present evidence that feelings of contempt are differentially linked to violations of the ethic of community (e.g., violations of social hierarchy), whereas feelings of disgust are linked to violations of the ethic of divinity (e.g., actions that remind us of our animal nature, assaults on human dignity).

POSITIVE OTHER-EVALUATIVE EMOTIONS

Just as disgust is the moral emotion people experience when observing violations of the ethic of divinity, elevation is the positive emotion people experience when observing others behaving in a particularly virtuous, commendable, or superhuman way (Haidt, 2000). Gratitude is another example of an other-oriented, positively valenced moral affect. People are inclined to feel gratitude specifically in response to another person's benevolence—that is, when they are the *recipient* of benefits provided by another, especially when those benefits are unexpected and/or costly to the benefactor. Underscoring the moral relevance of gratitude, McCullough, Kilpatrick, Emmons, and Larson (2001) observed that grateful people are often motivated to respond prosocially—both to their benefactor and toward others not involved in the gratitude-eliciting act.

POSITIVE SELF-EVALUATIVE EMOTIONS

Moving back to the self-conscious (vs. other-evaluative) emotions, but now on the positive end of the valence dimension, we have pride. Although infrequently discussed in the literature, pride can play a role in fostering (or undermining) moral motivation and behavior as well. Most theoretical and empirical research on pride emphasizes achievement-oriented pride (Tracy & Robins, 2004). Although pride may most often arise in response to scholastic, occupational, or athletic achievement, self-conscious experiences of pride in moral contexts may be an important component of our moral emotional apparatus. Feelings of pride for meeting or exceeding morally relevant standards (and for inhibiting impulses to behave immorally) may serve important motivational functions, rewarding and reinforcing one's commitment to the ethics of autonomy, community, and divinity.

A THIRD DIMENSION FOR DELINEATING MORAL EMOTION: EVALUATION OF PERSON VERSUS BEHAVIOR

The two-dimensional space of moral emotions defined by focus/evaluation (on the self vs. on the other) and valence (positive vs. negative) can be further differentiated along a third dimension, the degree to which the object of evaluation is a behavior versus a person. In effect, this dimension reflects the degree to which a characteristic is conceived as time-bound and potentially unstable versus something more trait-like, pertaining to the person him- or herself. Most familiar is the distinction between shame and guilt. Negative evaluations of the self versus behavior are a key factor in distinguishing between shame and guilt (H. B. Lewis, 1971; Tangney, 1990; Tangney & Dearing, 2002).

Recent advances in emotions research confirm that this person versus behavior distinction is relevant not only to the *negative* self-conscious emotions, but also to the positively valenced self-conscious emotions. Drawing on multiple methods, Tracy and Robins (2006) present compelling empirical evidence for two types of pride: event-specific "authentic" pride and trait-like "hubristic" pride. (Similar distinctions have been made using somewhat less optimal terms by Tangney [1990]—"beta" pride [pride in behavior] versus "alpha" pride [pride in self], and M. Lewis [1992]—pride vs. hubris.) Tracy and Robins's (2006) research suggests that, paralleling the distinction between shame and guilt, hubris may be the dark side of pride owing to a range of co-occuring social and personality features. If anything, hubris is associated with more selfish motives than moral ones. For example, individual differences in hubris are related to narcissism and Big Five disagreeableness (Tracy & Robins, 2006). To reiterate, although the prototypical pride episode is prompted by nonmoral contexts (e.g., achievement), a potentially important subset of pride experiences arise in moral contexts, such as engaging in philanthropy or altruism, success in desisting from a tempting morally inconsistent behavior, or reflecting on a good life lived. Our guess is that morally relevant pride is most often experienced as the "authentic" behavior-specific variety.

One question yet to be discussed is the possibility that the person versus behavior dimension may be important in understanding *other*-evaluative moral emotions—the two remaining quadrants in Figure 2.1. Is there a useful distinction to be made between feelings of contempt or disgust for a person's behavior versus a person's presumed character? Is there a useful distinction to be made between feelings of elevation or awe at witnessing a morally inspirational behavior versus perceiving that one is in the presence of a saint? So much new territory remains to be explored in the domain of moral emotions!

MORAL EMOTIONAL PROCESSES: EMPATHY, FORGIVENESS, SELF-COMPASSION

In addition to the moral emotions described thus far, there are a number of morally relevant emotional *processes* (not shown in Figure 2.1). Although beyond the scope of the current chapter, other-oriented empathy (for more complete reviews, see Eisenberg, Spinrad, & Sadovsky, 2006, and Eisenberg, Valiente, & Champion, 2004), forgiveness (McCullough, Pargament, & Thoresen, 2000; Worthington, 1998, 2005), and self-compassion (Leary, Tate, Adams, Allen, & Hancock, 2007) figure importantly in the cognitive, affective, and motivational dynamics of moral behavior. These affective processes, too, may moderate the link between moral standards and moral behavior.

Moral Intentions versus Moral Behaviors

On the dependent-variable side of the model, it is useful to make a distinction between moral intentions and moral behaviors. "Moral behavior" is defined by what people actually do (or desist from doing). "Moral intentions" include behavioral intentions, plans, and decisions in morally relevant contexts. Owing to ethical and practical constraints, researchers often operationalize moral behavior in terms of people's intentions to behave. At the same time, one of the maxims of social psychology is that intentions do not always translate into actual behavior. Rather than conceptualizing methods relying on the assessment of behavioral intentions (or responses to hypothetical scenarios) as "second best," researchers might be better served by explicitly considering the distinction in their conceptual models. There is an extensive social psychological literature devoted to understanding the imperfect link between intentions and behavior (Ajzen, 1991; DeVisser &

Smith, 2004; Latane & Darley, 1968; Lewin, 1943)—in the moral realm and more generally. In cases where both intentions and behavior cannot be measured, researchers can draw on this social psychological literature to estimate the degree to which other factors, further "downstream," would be likely to moderate (or attenuate) the link between intentions and behavior—that is, the degree to which intentions are likely to be valid markers for actual behavior—typically the ultimate interest.

SUMMARY OF THE CONCEPTUAL MODEL

In sum, moral emotions influence moral behavior in two distinct contexts: as anticipatory emotions that come into play as we review and contemplate behavioral alternatives, and as consequential emotions in the wake of actual behavior, motivating subsequent behaviors such as altruism, reparation, or defensiveness. Moral emotional styles (e.g., shame-proneness, guilt-proneness) are relevant to both emotion functions, representing people's propensity to both anticipate and experience these emotions in relevant contexts.

Of central interest is the degree to which people's behaviors match their moral standards. According to the conceptual model in Figure 2.1, anticipatory moral emotions and moral cognitions serve to moderate the link between people's moral standards, on one hand, and their moral intentions and behaviors, on the other. Guilt, higher levels of moral reasoning, and low levels of criminogenic thought should be associated with a relatively close match between standards and behavior. Shame, less sophisticated levels of moral reasoning, and criminogenic cognitions are apt to attenuate the match between moral standards and moral behavior.

One might be tempted to include moral standards under the umbrella of moral cognitions. (Moral standards are indeed cognitions with obvious moral relevance, and the line between moral standards and moral cognitions can be grey.) For the purposes of this model, however, we find it helpful to distinguish between (1) moral standards—which play one role in the model: as values/standards against which we evaluate behavior—and (2) moral cognitions—which play a different role: as moderators that strengthen or weaken the match between values/standards and actions, and perhaps as a direct influence on moral intentions and moral behavior as well.

Although moral behavior is typically of greatest interest, researchers do not always have the option of measuring actual behavior. Researchers often elect instead to assess behavioral intentions. In evaluating the validity of inferences about behavior drawn from intentions, researchers can draw on the extensive social psychological literature delineating factors that moderate consistency between intentions and behavior.

DIRECTIONS FOR FUTURE RESEARCH

We close this chapter by offering a sampling of research questions suggested by the conceptual model presented here.

Cross-Emotion Variability in the Structure of Emotion States and Traits

According to Figure 2.1, emotion dispositions (e.g., shame-proneness) are related to two types of "state" or situation-specific emotional experiences: *anticipatory* and *consequen-*

tial emotions. For example, relative to their less guilt-prone peers, people with guilt-prone dispositions should be more likely to experience guilt in guilt-relevant situations (e.g., hurting another person), and they should be more likely to anticipate feeling guilt when contemplating guilt-relevant behaviors (e.g., those that violate standards based on an ethic of autonomy). An analogous pattern would be expected for pride. Owing to the defensiveness often prompted by shame, however, one might expect a somewhat attenuated link between shame-proneness and anticipatory shame. People, especially shame-prone individuals, may have relatively less insight into the causes and consequences of shameful feelings. (Indeed, relative to other emotions, when shamed, people may have less insight—less explicit, readily retrievable knowledge—to identify the nature of the emotional experience itself. Shame may be a difficult emotion to identify, as suggested by H. B. Lewis [1971] 35 years ago.) Empirical research has yet to directly evaluate this possibility.

Researchers might also expect, in general, a robust link between consequential emotional reactions to actual behaviors and anticipatory emotions when contemplating similar future behavior. People who have felt guilty for lying to a friend in the past are likely to *anticipate* feeling guilt when contemplating a future lie. Likewise for pride. But the picture may differ for shame. A range of empirical studies indicate that consequential shame reactions are likely to be defended against (e.g., denied, blamed on others) rather than owned. As a result, the link between consequential shame and anticipated shame may be attenuated. It would be useful to examine this possibility in future research.

Toward Predicting and Enhancing Standard-Consistent Intentions and Behavior

As discussed at the beginning of this chapter, moral standards vary across the dimensions of universality and social consensus. Figure 2.1 suggests that where there are individual differences in moral standards for a particular class of behaviors—for example, in domains with less social consensus—moral emotions and moral cognitions will serve as moderators of the link between standards and intentions/behaviors.

Although not tested explicitly, extant empirical research is consistent with the notion that guilt strengthens the link between one's moral standards and one's behavior, whereas shame may in fact disrupt (attenuate) this link. Research on the moral implications of shame and guilt has thus far focused largely on unambiguous moral and immoral behavior. That is, studies are typically conducted in such a way that there is effectively little variance in moral standards. For example, researchers may ask participants about their history of behaviors for which consensual moral standards exist—for example, lying, cheating, stealing in the absence of extenuating morally relevant circumstances. In effect, "moral standards" become a constant, and the construct drops out of Figure 2.1.

It is worth embellishing Figure 2.1, nonetheless. The implication is that where individual differences in moral standards exist (e.g., across culturally relative standards, such as many based on ethics of community and divinity), shame and guilt are likely to moderate—importantly and in opposite directions—the match between values and deeds. This may be expected at both state and dispositional measures. For example, people vary in the degree to which they construe drinking alcohol as immoral. Among those who view alcohol consumption as a moral offense, those who anticipate feeling guilt if they drank should be more likely to desist relative to those who fail to anticipate guilt (and relative to those who anticipate shame). Among those who construe drinking alcohol as a matter of personal choice, anticipatory shame and guilt are irrelevant to predicting whether a person will drink or not. Similarly, at the dispositional level, across a range of behaviors, guilt-prone individuals should demonstrate a closer match between their personal moral code and their actual behavior, compared to less guilt-prone and more shame-prone peers.

Moral cognitions play a similar moderating role, according to Figure 2.1. Criminogenic patterns of thought, such as minimizing victim impact and perceived entitlement, are apt to weaken the link between moral standards and moral behavior. Such perceptions and beliefs cloud the issue, as justifications for behaviors that one would ordinarily find unacceptable.

Of special interest, although not easily conveyed in Figure 2.1, are the ways in which moral cognitions and emotions may interact/conspire/work together in determining one's moral behavioral path. One might hypothesize, for example, that to the extent that a person anticipates (or fears) shame for a contemplated prohibited behavior, he or she may be more inclined to engage in criminogenic thinking likely to weaken (moderate) the link between moral standards and moral intentions. In the coming decade, a new generation of researchers is likely to model and evaluate sophisticated hypotheses concerning the mediating and moderating roles of shame, guilt, and other self-conscious emotions.

Also of theoretical and applied importance is the degree to which key findings are specific to particular populations of interest. Is shame an equally problematic emotion among criminal offenders as among state college freshmen? Or might shame serve more constructive "moral" functions in populations extreme on moral behavior itself? Exciting research is yet to be conducted to define the parameters of generalizability and to identify population moderators of the links pictured in Figure 2.1. It is easy to imagine ways in which particular moral cognitive and moral emotional factors might be differentially relevant as a function of population characteristics (e.g., college freshmen vs. corporate managers vs. criminal offenders) and developmental level (e.g., preoperational children, adolescents, midlife adults).

Reevaluating Assumptions and Conclusions

We have found the joint consideration of moral standards, cognitions, and emotions to be illuminating and challenging. One outcome is that we have been drawn to reexamine assumptions and earlier, empirically based conclusions. One such area concerns the types of situations that elicit shame and guilt. In earlier work, Tangney (1992) emphasized the similarity of shame- and guilt-inducing situations, noting that most types of behaviors (e.g., lying, cheating, stealing) are mentioned by some people in describing shame-inducing situations and by others in describing guilt-inducing situations. Following H. B. Lewis (1971) and much supporting empirical data, we have emphasized that the crux of the difference between shame and guilt lies in the focus of negative evaluation: whether people focus on their bad behavior or on themselves as a bad or defective person. However, Shweder's (Schweder et al., 1997) elegant work on the three ethics of morality (autonomy, community, and divinity) have led us to question whether there *are* situational differences in the elicitors of shame and guilt along ethical lines. It is plausible that whereas violations of the ethic of autonomy are apt to prompt feelings of shame, guilt, or both, violations of the ethics of community and divinity may be more highly skewed toward the elicitation of shame. We look forward to future research examining the moral emotions within Shweder's framework of moral ethics.

CONCLUSION

Little research has examined the relation between moral cognitions and moral emotions, much less their interactive influence in moderating the link between moral standards and people's moral behavior. We have found this conceptual model—the result of a good amount of conceptual stumbling and consequent revision—helpful for articulating, in testable terms, some of the dynamics surrounding shame observed by clinicians working with diverse populations. We hope that others will also find it a useful tool. Equally important, this conceptual model may help identify potential points of prevention and intervention—also testable endeavors.

It is exciting to see the enormous advances in the scientific understanding of self-conscious emotion over a mere 10 years. No doubt, the next 10 years of research will bring even greater returns, importantly informing not only treatment, but also educational, judicial, and social policies that foster adaptive moral processes and ultimately moral behavior to the benefit of all.

ACKNOWLEDGMENTS

This research was supported by Grant No. RO1 DA14694 to June Price Tangney from the National Institute on Drug Abuse.

REFERENCES

Ajzen, I. (1991). The theory of planned behavior. *Organizational Behavior and Human Decision Processes, 50*, 179–211.

Andrews, B., Brewin, C. R., Rose, S., & Kirk, M. (2000). Predicting PTSD symptoms in victims of violent crime: The role of shame, anger, and childhood abuse. *Journal of Abnormal Psychology, 109*, 69–73.

Andrews, D. A., & Bonta, J. (1994). *The psychology of criminal conduct.* Cincinnati: Anderson.

Arnold, M. L. (1989, April). *Moral cognition and conduct: A qualitative review of the literature.* Poster presented at the meeting of the Society for Research in Child Development, Kansas City.

Bandura, A. (1990). Selective activation and disengagement of moral control. *Journal of Social Issues, 46*(1), 27–46.

Baumeister, R. F., Stillwell, A. M., & Heatherton, T. F. (1994). Guilt: An interpersonal approach. *Psychological Bulletin, 115*, 243–267.

Benedict, R. (1946). *The chrysanthemum and the sword.* Boston: Houghton Mifflin.

Bennett, D. S., Sullivan, M. W., & Lewis, M. (2005). Young children's adjustment as a function of maltreatment, shame, and anger. *Child Maltreatment: Journal of the American Professional Society on the Abuse of Children, 10*(4), 311–323.

Blasi, A. (1980). Bridging moral cognition and moral action: A critical review of the literature. *Psychological Bulletin, 88*, 1–45.

DeVisser, R. O., & Smith, A. M. A. (2004). Which intention? Whose intention?: Condom use and theories of individual decision making. *Psychology, Health and Medicine, 9*, 193–204.

Doojse, B., Branscombe, N. R., Spears, R., & Manstead, A. S. R. (1998). Guilty by association: When one's group has a negative history. *Journal of Personality and Social Psychology, 75*, 872–886.

Eisenberg, N., Spinrad, T. L., & Sadovsky, A. (2006). Empathy-related responding in children. In M. Killen & J. G. Smetana (Eds.), *Handbook of moral development* (pp. 517–549). Mahwah, NJ: Erlbaum.

Eisenberg, N., Valiente, C., & Champion, C. (2004). Empathy-related responding: Moral, social, and socialization correlates. In A. G. Miller (Ed.), *The social psychology of good and evil* (pp. 386–415). New York: Guilford Press.

Haidt, J. (2000). The positive emotion of elevation. *Prevention and Treatment, 3*, n.p.

Haidt, J. (2003). Elevation and the positive psychology of morality. In C. L. Keyes & J. Haidt (Eds.), *Flourishing: Positive psychology and the life well-lived* (pp. 275–289). Washington, DC: American Psychological Association.

Harper, F. W. K., & Arias, I. (2004). The role of shame in predicting adult anger and depressive symptoms among victims of child psychological maltreatment. *Journal of Family Violence, 19*(6), 367–375.

Harper, F. W. K., Austin, A. G., Cercone, J. J., & Arias, I. (2005). The role of shame, anger, and affect regulation in men's perpetration of psychological abuse in dating relationships. *Journal of Interpersonal Violence, 20*, 1648–1662.

Iyer, A., Leach, C. W., & Crosby, F. J. (2003). White guilt and racial compensation: The benefits and limits of self-focus. *Personality and Social Psychology Bulletin, 29*, 117–129.

Iyer, A., Schmader, T., & Lickel, B. (2007). Why individuals protest the perceived transgressions of their country: The role of anger, shame, and guilt. *Personality and Social Psychology Bulletin, 33*, 572–587.

Johns, M., Schmader, T., & Lickel, B. (2005). Ashamed to be an American?: The role of identification in predicting vicarious shame for anti-Arab prejudice after 9-11. *Self and Identity, 4*, 331–348.

Joireman, J. (2004). Empathy and the self-absorption paradox II: Self-rumination and self-reflection as mediators between shame, guilt, and empathy. *Self and Identity, 3*, 225–238.

Jones, P. R. (1996). Risk prediction in criminal justice. In A. Harland (Ed.), *Choosing correctional options that work: Defining the demand and evaluating the supply* (pp. 33–68). Thousand Oaks, CA: Sage.

Keltner, D., & Buswell, B. N. (1996). Evidence for the distinctness of embarrassment, shame, and guilt: A study of recalled antecedents and facial expressions of emotion. *Cognition and Emotion, 10*, 155–171.

Ketelaar, T., & Au, W. T. (2003). The effects of feelings of guilt on the behavior of uncooperative individuals in repeated social bargaining games: An affect-as-information interpretation of the role of emotion in social interaction. *Cognition and Emotion, 17*, 429–453.

Kohlberg, L. (1969). Stage and sequence: The cognitive developmental approach to socialization. In D. A. Goslin (Ed.), *Handbook of socialization theory and research* (pp. 347–480). Chicago: Rand McNally.

Kroll, J., & Egan, E. (2004). Psychiatry, moral worry, and moral emotions. *Journal of Psychiatric Practice, 10*, 352–360.

Kurtines, W., & Greif, E. B. (1974). The development of moral thought: Review and evaluation of Kohlberg's approach. *Psychological Bulletin, 81*, 453–470.

Latane, B., & Darley, J. M. (1968). Group inhibition of bystander intervention. *Journal of Personality and Social Psychology, 10*, 215–221.

Leary, M. R., Tate, E. B., Adams, C. E., Allen, A. B., & Hancock, J. (2007). Self-compassion and reactions to unpleasant self-relevant events: The implications of treating oneself kindly. *Journal of Personality and Social Psychology, 92*, 887–904.

Leith, K. P., & Baumeister, R. F. (1998). Empathy, shame, guilt, and narratives of interpersonal conflicts: Guilt-prone people are better at perspective taking. *Journal of Personality, 66*, 1–37.

Lewin, K. (1943). Defining the "filed at a given time." *Psychological Review, 50*, 292–310.

Lewis, H. B. (1971). *Shame and guilt in neurosis.* New York: International Universities Press.

Lewis, M. (1992). *Shame: The exposed self.* New York: Free Press.

Lickel, B., Rutchick, A., Hamilton, D. L., & Sherman, S. J. (2006). Intuitive theories of group types and relational principles. *Journal of Experimental Social Psychology, 42*, 28–39.

Lickel, B., Schmader, T., Curtis, M., Scarnier, M., & Ames, D. R. (2005). Vicarious shame and guilt. *Group Processes and Intergroup Relations, 8*, 145–147.

Lindsay-Hartz, J. (1984). Contrasting experiences of shame and guilt. *American Behavioral Scientist, 27,* 689–704.

Maruna, S., & Copes, H. (2005). What have we learned from five decades of neutralization research? In M. Tonry (Ed.), *Crime and justice: Vol. 32. A review of research* (pp. 221–320). Chicago: University of Chicago Press.

McCullough, M. E., Kilpatrick, S., Emmons, R. A., & Larson, D. (2001). Is gratitude a moral effect? *Psychological Bulletin, 127,* 249–266.

McCullough, M. E., Pargament, K. I., & Thoresen, C. E. (Eds.). (2000). *Forgiveness: Theory, research, and practice.* New York: Guilford Press.

Mischel, W., & Mischel, H. N. (1976). A cognitive social learning approach to morality and self-regulation. In T. Lickona (Ed.), *Moral development and behavior: Theory, research and social issues* (pp. 84–107). New York: Holt.

Ortony, A., Clore, G. L., & Collins, A. (1988). *The cognitive structure of emotions.* Cambridge, UK: Cambridge University Press.

Paulhus, D. L., Robins, R. W., Trzesniewski, K. H., & Tracy, J. L. (2004). Two replicable suppressor situations in personality research. *Multivariate Behavioral Research, 39,* 301–326.

Piaget, J. (1952). *The origins of intelligence in children.* New York: International Universities Press.

Rozin, P., Lowery, L., Imada, S., & Haidt, J. (1999). The CAD triad hypothesis: A mapping between three moral emotions (contempt, anger, disgust) and three moral codes (community, autonomy, divinity). *Journal of Personality and Social Psychology, 76,* 574–586.

Schmader, T., & Lickel, B. (2006). Stigma and shame: Emotional responses to the stereotypic actions of one's ethnic ingroup. In S. Levin & C. van Laar (Eds.), *Stigma and group inequality: Social psychological approaches* (pp. 261–285). Mahwah, NJ: Erlbaum.

Shweder, R. A., Much, N. C., Mahapatra, M., & Park, L. (1997). The "Big Three" of morality (autonomy, community, divinity) and the "Big Three" explanation of suffering. In A. Brandt & P. Rozin (Eds.), *Morality and health* (pp. 119–169). New York: Routledge.

Swim, J. K., & Miller, D. L. (1999). White guilt: Its antecedents and consequences for attitudes toward affirmative action. *Personality and Social Psychology Bulletin, 25,* 500–514.

Sykes, G. M., & Matza, D. (1957). Techniques of neutralization: A theory of delinquency. *American Sociological Review, 22,* 664–670.

Tangney, J. P. (1990). Assessing individual differences in proneness to shame and guilt: Development of the Self-Conscious Affect and Attribution Inventory. *Journal of Personality and Social Psychology, 59,* 102–111.

Tangney, J. P. (1991). Moral affect: The good, the bad, and the ugly. *Journal of Personality and Social Psychology, 61,* 598–607.

Tangney, J. P. (1992). Situational determinants of shame and guilt in young adulthood. *Personality and Social Psychology Bulletin, 18,* 199–206.

Tangney, J. P. (1993). Shame and guilt. In C. G. Costello (Ed.), *Symptoms of depression* (pp. 161–180). New York: Wiley.

Tangney, J. P. (1995). Shame and guilt in interpersonal relationships. In J. P. Tangney & K. W. Fischer (Eds.), *Self-conscious emotions: The psychology of shame, guilt, embarrassment, and pride* (pp. 114–139). New York: Guilford Press.

Tangney, J. P. (1996). Conceptual and methodological issues in the assessment of shame and guilt. *Behaviour Research and Therapy, 34,* 741–754.

Tangney, J. P., & Dearing, R. (2002). *Shame and guilt.* New York: Guilford Press.

Tangney, J. P., Marschall, D. E., Rosenberg, K., Barlow, D. H., & Wagner, P. E. (1994). *Children's and adults' autobiographical accounts of shame, guilt and pride experiences: An analysis of situational determinants and interpersonal concerns.* Unpublished manuscript, George Mason University, Fairfax, VA.

Tangney, J. P., Mashek, D. J., & Stuewig, J. (2007). Working at the social-clinical-community-criminology interface: The GMU Inmate Study. *Journal of Social and Clinical Psychology, 26,* 1–21.

Tangney, J. P., Miller, R. S., Flicker, L., & Barlow, D. H. (1996). Are shame, guilt and embarrassment distinct emotions? *Journal of Personality and Social Psychology, 70,* 1256–1269.

Tangney, J. P., Stuewig, J., & Mashek, D. J. (2007). Moral emotions and moral behavior. *Annual Review of Psychology, 58,* 345–372.

Tangney, J. P., Stuewig, J., Mashek, D. J., Feshbach, N. D., & Feshbach, S. (2007). *Moral emotion, moral cognition, and moral behavior.* Manuscript in preparation

Tangney, J. P., Wagner, P. E., Hill-Barlow, D., Marschall, D. E., & Gramzow, R. (1996). Relation of shame and guilt to constructive versus destructive responses to anger across the lifespan. *Journal of Personality and Social Psychology, 70,* 797–809.

Tracy, J. L., & Robins, R. W. (2004). Show your pride: Evidence for a discrete emotion expression. *Psychological Science, 15*(3), 194–197.

Tracy, J. L., & Robins, R. W. (2006). Appraisal antecedents of shame, guilt, and pride: Support for a theoretical model. *Personality and Social Psychology Bulletin, 32,* 1339–1351.

Wallbott, H. G., & Scherer, K. R. (1995). Cultural determinants in experiencing shame and guilt. In J. P. Tangney & K. W. Fischer (Eds.), *Self-conscious emotions: The psychology of shame, guilt, embarrassment, and pride* (pp. 465–487). New York: Guilford Press.

Wicker, F. W., Payne, G. C., & Morgan, R. D. (1983). Participant descriptions of guilt and shame. *Motivation and Emotion, 7,* 25–39.

Worthington, E. L. Jr. (1998). *Dimensions of forgiveness: Psychological research and theological perspectives.* Philadelphia: Templeton Foundation Press.

Worthington, E. L. Jr. (Ed.). (2005). *Handbook of forgiveness.* New York: Brunner-Routledge.

Yochelson, S., & Samenow, S. E. (1976). *The criminal personality: A profile for change* (Vol. 1). New York: Aronson.

Zahn-Waxler, C., & Robinson, J. (1995). Empathy and guilt: Early origins of feelings of responsibility. In J. P. Tangney & K. W. Fischer (Eds.), *Self-conscious emotions: The psychology of shame, guilt, embarrassment, and pride* (pp. 143–173). New York: Guilford Press.

Zebel, S., Doosje, B., & Spears, R. (2004). It depends on your point of view: Implications of perspective-taking and national identification for Dutch collective guilt. In N. R. Branscombe & B. Doosje (Eds.), *Collective guilt: International perspectives* (pp. 148–168). New York: Cambridge University Press.

3

How the Self Became Involved in Affective Experience

Three Sources of Self-Reflective Emotions

MARK R. LEARY

During much of the 20th century, behaviorists doggedly asserted that human behavior may be explained by precisely the same processes that account for the behavior of nonhuman animals. Human beings were regarded as more "intelligent" in the sense of being able to learn more complex associations than other species, but the underlying psychological processes were assumed to be the same. The radical behaviorist agenda was ultimately abandoned for many reasons, but one was that it failed to take into account the fact that a good deal of human behavior arises from the ways in which people think about themselves in their own minds. Although certain other animals appear to have a rudimentary capacity for self-awareness (Gallup, 1977), no other animal seems able to think consciously about itself in the abstract and complex ways that are characteristic of human beings.

The fact that people have an advanced capacity for self-awareness has important implications for understanding human emotion. A number of theorists have examined the links between self-relevant thought and emotional experience (see Dickerson, Gruenewald, & Kemeny, 2004; Keltner & Beer, 2005; Leary, 2003; Tangney & Fischer, 1995; Tracy & Robins, 2004a). However, previous discussions of the role of the self in emotion have failed to address three central issues. First, what psychologists call the "self" actually consists of a number of distinct cognitive processes that may bear different relationships to emotional experience. A full understanding of the relationship between self-reflection and affect requires that we distinguish among these various self processes. Second, as we will see, many theorists have drawn a distinction between "self-conscious" emotions (such as guilt, shame, pride, and embarrassment) and other "non-self-conscious" emotions (such as sadness, fear, and anger) despite the fact that these other emotional states often involve self-awareness as well. If most, if not all, emotions may sometimes be generated by self-reflection, in what sense may some affective states be classified as "self-conscious" whereas other, similar states are not? Third—and perhaps most central to understanding the relationship between self and emotion—little attention has been paid to the question of why self processes became involved in emotional experience. After all, animals with no capacity for self-awareness appear to experience an array of emotions. Why, then, is the self intimately involved in emotional experience among human beings?

The goal of this chapter is to examine the fundamental ways in which self-reflection influences emotional experience. After considering the nature of emotion in the absence of self-awareness, we examine three distinct ways in which self-reflective emotions arise. Along the way, we explore the difference between the so-called self-conscious emotions—such as shame, pride, and embarrassment—and other emotions that also involve self-awareness. We conclude with speculations regarding why the self became involved in human emotional experience.

EMOTIONS WITHOUT A SELF

To discuss self-reflective emotions, it is first necessary to define precisely what we mean by the term "self." Writers have used the word *self* in several distinct ways—to refer to the individual person, to all or some of the human personality, to cognitive processes that mediate self-awareness and reflexive thinking, to thoughts and feelings about oneself, and to the executive processes underlying agency and self-control (see Katzko, 2003; Leary & Tangney, 2003; Olson, 1999). If we set aside uses of "self" that refer to the person or the personality, neither of which refer to the construct of interest to behavioral scientists who study self and identity, we can roughly define "self" as the mental apparatus that allows an organism to think consciously about itself. To avoid confusion, I will use terms other than "self"—such as "self-concept" or "self-representation"—to refer to the *content* of people's thoughts about themselves.

Animals do not need a self—a capacity for conscious self-awareness—in order to experience emotion. Of course, we cannot know for sure what other animals feel, but their behavior suggests that they experience a wide array of emotions including fear, sadness, joy, and rage (Darwin, 1872/1998; Masson & McCarthy, 1994). Animals' emotional reactions appear to result primarily from one of two processes.

First, some emotional reactions are innate, hardwired responses to particular stimuli. For example, most species react naturally with fear to certain releasing stimuli, such as signs of predators, loud noises, staring eyes, or the threat gestures of conspecifics. Human beings also appear to be innately prepared to experience fear in response to certain stimuli, such as looming objects, snakes, bared fangs, and being alone in the dark (Marks, 1987). Presumably, natural selection favored animals, including human beings, that were wary around stimuli that posed a consistent threat to survival or reproduction, resulting in evolved reactions to certain threatening stimuli. In the same way, other emotions (such as anger, sadness, and perhaps joy) appear to be hardwired in many species.

Second, animals may also learn to experience emotions in response to previously neutral stimuli through the process of classical conditioning. Classically conditioned emotional responses have been demonstrated in a large number of species, including human beings (starting with John Watson's study of Little Albert). In addition, conditioning has been used to change maladaptive emotions, such as phobias, through systematic desensi-titization and counterconditiong. Clearly, neutral stimuli that become associated with emotion-producing events can come to elicit emotions on their own.

Both of these processes—one involving innate, species-specific reactions and the other involving conditioning—can occur without conscious self-thought. Self-awareness is not needed to respond to natural emotion-evoking stimuli or classically conditioned events, and both human and nonhuman animals respond automatically, without conscious mediation, to a wide array of emotion-producing situations.

SELF-AWARENESS AND EMOTION

The evolution of self-awareness among human beings and their prehistoric ancestors rendered people's emotional lives far more extensive and complex than those of self-less animals because, as we explore below, human emotion often arises from the ways in which people think about themselves and the events that happen to them. In an article that traced the evolution of the self, Leary and Buttermore (2003) proposed that self-awareness involves several distinct mental abilities that evolved independently. Three of these abilities—those involving the extended, the private, and the conceptual selves (see Neisser, 1988)—have important implications for understanding human emotion.

The first self-relevant ability to evolve may have been the *extended self*, which allowed prehuman hominids to reflect on themselves over time. The extended-self ability permits people to transcend the present moment to remember themselves in the past or to imagine themselves in the future. Most nonhuman animals show no signs of consciously reflecting on their pasts or contemplating their futures, and thus appear to live perpetually in the present moment. Even chimpanzees, one species known to possess a rudimentary form of self-awareness (Gallup, 1977), seem to be able to project themselves only a short time into the future (Kohler, 1925), and thus do not show the long-range planning that we see in human beings.

The earliest concrete evidence that prehistoric hominids could think consciously about themselves in the future appears in the archeological record around 2 million years ago. About that time, *Homo habilis* carried stones long distances to make tools (Potts, 1984), suggesting that this prehuman species was able to look ahead to plan its tool making and tool use (Leary & Buttermore, 2003). As we explore momentarily, the ability to think about oneself in a temporal fashion enables human beings to experience emotions in response to imagined past and future events.

The *private self* is involved in thinking about private, subjective information such as one's thoughts, feelings, intentions, memories, and other internal states. Presumably, other animals experience subjective states, but only those with a private self can consciously think about them. The private-self ability is relevant to understanding human emotion for two reasons. First, an organism that can think consciously about its internal states is privy to subjective knowledge that may facilitate adaptive behavior. For example, by thinking consciously about one's experiences and why one has them, people can sometimes modify their reactions to events. By understanding the events that "push their buttons," people can prepare in advance to execute or inhibit particular reactions when certain circumstances arise. Furthermore, when paired with the extended self, the ability to reflect on inner experience permits people to imagine how they will feel at a later time. Doing so allows people to regulate their present behavior in terms of how they will feel about it later (e.g., "I would regret doing this"), which provides the basis for a great deal of self-control.

Second, the private self is important in emotional experience because thinking about one's private states may be necessary in order to infer others' internal states. In fact, some theorists have proposed that the ability to reflect on one's private thoughts and feelings evolved specifically to help people read others' minds (Gallup, 1997; Humphrey, 1980). Essentially, people can infer others' emotions, thoughts, and motives only by extrapolating from their own experiences. In order to imagine what another person is thinking or feeling, an individual must imagine what he or she might think or feel if in the other person's position, with appropriate adjustments made for the other's idiosyncratic characteristics. Furthermore, intentional communication may rely on this ability to imagine others' reactions to what one communicates (Donald, 1991). For our purposes, the private self is relevant both because thinking about one's inner states can create additional emotions (a man might become upset at himself for how jealous he feels) and because many emotions arise from people's inferences about what other people might be thinking (a woman on a job interview may worry that the interviewer is forming a negative impression of her).

The last self ability to evolve was probably the *conceptual* (or *symbolic*) *self,* which involves the capacity for abstract, symbolic self-thought. The archeological record reveals no evidence that people could think about themselves in an abstract or conceptual manner until the time of the Middle–Upper Paleolithic Transition (sometimes called the "cultural big bang"), around 60,000 years ago (Leary & Buttermore, 2003; for an alternative perspective, see Sedikides & Skowronski, 1997). After millions of years of living essentially as intelligent apes, members of the hominid line began to show the first evidence of art, body adornment, identity, culture, and ritualistic burial during this period. The emergence of the conceptual self not only allowed people to characterize themselves in abstract ways but also to evaluate those self-characterizations according to arbitrary cultural criteria. Of course, self-evaluations—both positive and negative—can evoke emotional responses, so the conceptual-self ability also contributes to human emotion.

Although these three self abilities each involve conscious self-reflection, they appear to rely on somewhat different cognitive abilities. It seems to be a quite different cognitive task to imagine oneself in the past or the future (extended self) than to think about one's private feelings or other people's subjective reactions (private self) or to conceptualize or evaluate oneself symbolically (conceptual self). Most behavioral researchers have clumped these three processes under the single heading of "self," but there may be good reasons to distinguish among them. Perhaps future neuroimaging studies will identify distinct parts of the brain associated with these three activities, although we should expect there would be some overlap given that they all involve conscious self-awareness. In the meantime, I will simply assume that distinguishing among these three self abilities provides heuristic value in understanding the effects of self-awareness on human emotion.

Importantly, these three self abilities may be applied in tandem. For example, when people think about how they will feel in the future, they are employing both the private- and the extended-self abilities. Likewise, a person who positively judges his past performance on arbitrary, symbolic criteria (such as grades) is employing the extended and the conceptual selves, and one who negatively evaluates herself today for thoughts that she had in the past is using the conceptual, private, and extended selves.

These capacities for self-relevant thought provide innumerable benefits. The extended self allows planning and the ability to maintain motivation over long periods of time even when behavior is not being immediately rewarded, the private self allows private self-examination and the capacity to infer others' thoughts and feelings, and the conceptual self underlies abstract self-evaluation and thus volitional self-change. Most of the foundations of modern human life—culture, government, religion, science, and philosophy, for example—would be impossible without these self abilities.

The extended, private, and conceptual self abilities—singly and in combination—contribute to human emotional experience. I will call emotions that are elicited by self-relevant thought—as opposed to emotions that do not require self-awareness—"self-reflective emotions." Importantly, self-reflective emotions are not the same as what many writers have called "self-conscious emotions." In point of fact, every emotion can, under some circumstances, be elicited by self-relevant thoughts, and this is true both of emotions that are typically regarded as "self-conscious" emotions (such as shame, pride, guilt, and embarrassment) and those that are not typically viewed as self-conscious (such as fear, anger, or happiness). For example, a person may experience fear simply from imagining a painful medical test that he or she must undergo next month or experience happiness from reflecting on what a wonderful person he or she is. As I am using the term, self-reflective emotions are not distinguished by the emotions themselves but rather by whether the emotion is elicited by conscious self-thought as opposed to an automatic or classically conditioned process that does not involve conscious self-reflection.

The so-called self-conscious emotions are only one category of self-reflective emotion. Self-conscious emotions undoubtedly require self-reflection (and thus are self-reflective emotions), but they also share the property of involving inferences about other people's evaluations of the individual. When people feel ashamed, guilty, embarrassed, socially anxious, or proud, they are assessing themselves from the perspectives of other people. In some cases the reaction is in response to the real or imagined judgments of specific other individuals, whereas in other cases it is in response to an internalized standard of some "generalized other" (Mead, 1934). In either case, self-conscious emotions, and the appraisals that underlie them, are inherently social in nature. I return to this point later in the chapter.

THE EXTENDED SELF

The extended-self ability allows people to think about themselves in other places and at times outside of their current situation. When people ruminate on past events or anticipate future ones, they are relying on the cognitive ability to imagine themselves in their own "mind's eye." Jaynes (1976) suggested that people are able to create an "analogue-I" in their mind, which they can then manipulate cognitively to remember or imagine themselves in other contexts.

The extended self is responsible for all behaviors that require people to think of themselves over time. All planning, for example, requires people to project an image or thought of themselves into an imagined future in order to anticipate what needs to be done now to bring about certain outcomes later on. The extended self also allows people to deliberately recall situations that they have experienced in the past in order to bask in delightful memories, try to understand why certain situations turned out as they did, or learn from their mistakes.

A great deal of human emotion arises from imagining past and future events. The machinations of the analogue-I evoke an array of emotions. For example, ruminating on one's past mistakes or misdeeds can create regret, guilt, or shame, and thinking about previous losses (such as the death of a loved one or a romantic breakup) can evoke sadness, even after a great deal of time has passed. Similarly, people may nurse grudges by recalling past instances in which they were mistreated or bask in happiness by remembering the "good old days." Such emotional reactions to the past are possible only because people are able to think consciously about themselves in a temporal fashion. Although thinking about oneself in the past sometimes generates positive feelings, the extended self may inflict a great deal of unnecessary suffering as well. When people ruminate on past failures, rejections, losses, and other negative events, their self-thoughts may do nothing more than to make them quite miserable without providing any pragmatic benefits (Leary, 2004).

Similarly, a great deal of emotion results from thinking about the future. Most notably, all worry involves mentally projecting oneself into an imagined future. Whereas other animals experience fear when they perceive threatening stimuli in their current environment, human beings appear to be the only animal that experiences anxiety from imagining negative events in their own minds. Simply imagining that one's "future self" may not live up to one's hopes or expectations can cause people to become quite upset (Markus & Nurius, 1986). Of course, people may also experience positive feelings from imagining themselves in the future, feelings that may provide an incentive to work toward future goals or serve as a balm for present unhappiness.

Past- and future-based emotions are sometimes quite useful for self-regulation. For example, thinking about how one felt in a past situation may steer one's present behavior in a hedonically satisfying direction. Remembering how badly he felt when he previously cheated on a test may help a student resist cheating again, and recalling the positive feelings of behaving altruistically in the past may lead a person to be helpful in the present situation. Likewise, imagining how one will feel in the future helps people to behave in ways that will lead to desired emotional outcomes. By forecasting how they might feel if they behave in certain ways, people can make more judicious behavioral choices. To the extent that current behavior has future affective consequences, a person who is unable to imagine how he or she may feel later would have great difficulty regulating his or her behavior now.

Similarly, anticipating future threats is often beneficial because it permits people to take precautions or, if the threat is inevitable, to prepare to cope with it. Unfortunately, people typically imagine far more frequent and serious threats than actually occur, and so experience anxiety more often than is necessary. And, even when dreaded events do arrive, the anticipatory anxiety typically does little to help the person avoid or minimize the unpleasant event but rather only makes the individual suffer well in advance. Many people's lives are filled with chronic anxiety because they dwell on unpleasant events that might occur in the future (Segerstrom, Tsao, Alden, & Craske, 2000). In the ancestral environment in which human evolution occurred, life was lived mostly day to day, and self-reflection would have helped people avoid or prepare for potential threats in the very near future. Today, however, people's present behavior is often focused on long-term goals, leading to an extended time horizon that prompts people to worry about things that may occur far in the future (Leary, 2004; Martin, 1999).

The role of the extended self in emotion was recognized at least 3,000 years ago by Eastern wisdom traditions such as Taoism, Buddhism, and Zen. Seeing that a great deal of human suffering arises from imagining oneself in the past or the future, sages espoused practices that help to quiet one's self-chatter about past and future and to root one's attention in the present moment (Claxton, 1990). Today, clinicians are employing similar mindfulness-based strategies to help clients control excessive self-thought by focusing nonjudgmentally on the present moment (Hayes & Linehan, 2004).

THE PRIVATE SELF

Traditionally, when psychologists have discussed self-awareness, they have typically referred to processes that involve the private-self ability, which, as noted, involves the capacity to think consciously about one's internal states. People think a great deal about their inner psychological lives, such as thoughts, emotions, motives, reactions, values, memories, physical sensations, and so on.

Self-Awareness

Research on self-awareness has demonstrated that being aware of aspects of one's private experience can have at least three effects on emotion. First, in their initial exposition of self-awareness theory, Duval and Wicklund (1972) suggested that self-awareness induces an evaluative state in which people compare their current situation or behavior with relevant private standards. Because people rarely meet their standards completely, self-awareness often evokes negative feelings—a natural consequence of failure to meet one's standards. Early research confirmed the notion that private self-awareness induces negative affect, but later studies showed that this effect occurs primarily when people detect a discrepancy between their standards and their behavior that they are unable to reduce (Steenbarger & Aderman, 1979). Even so, by making discrepancies between one's behavior and one's standards salient, self-awareness often induces negative emotions.

Second, self-awareness may change the nature of people's emotional experiences. Early research on this topic suggested that being self-aware leads people to be more aware of their affective reactions, and thus to experience their emotions more strongly (Scheier, 1976; Scheier & Carver, 1977). However, other work showed that self-awareness can also dampen subjective emotions, presumably by distracting people from their feelings (Silvia, 2002). Whether self-awareness intensifies or dampens emotional experience may depend on precisely what aspect of one's inner experience is most salient. Focusing on one's feelings may make people more aware of their emotions, whereas focusing on other aspects of one's inner experience (such as plans or daydreams) may distract people's attention from their feelings.

Third, thinking about oneself contributes directly to a great deal of emotional experience. Even in the absence of any emotion-producing stimuli whatsoever, people may experience emotions from analyzing their motives, evaluating themselves, ruminating over their shortcomings, replaying unpleasant experiences, and talking to themselves in particular ways. For example, it is widely recognized that certain kinds of ruminative self-thoughts can precipitate and maintain depressive episodes (Siegle, Moore, & Thase, 2004). Furthermore, thinking about the reasons for their feelings can change how people feel (Wilson & Schooler, 1991).

Social Self-Reflection

As noted previously, the ability to think about private, subjective aspects of one's experience may underlie the ability to infer the perspectives, thoughts, and reactions of other people (Gallup, 1997; Humphrey, 1986). Imagining how one is (or is likely to be) perceived and evaluated by other people can induce an array of emotions, such as social anxiety, embarrassment, pride, guilt, and shame. Importantly, these emotions are precisely those that previous researchers have sometimes called "self-conscious" emotions (or, sometimes, "social emotions" or "self-affects"). Viewed from this perspective, this group of emotions arises not from self-reflection per se (as we have seen, other emotions also involve self-awareness) but rather from imagining oneself through the eyes of other people. Self-conscious emotions are fundamentally social emotions that are elicited by real and imagined events that have potential implications for how the individual is perceived and evaluated by other people. Ascertaining other people's perceptions and evaluations of us necessarily involves imagining ourselves through their eyes, and this process involves self-awareness. As other theorists have noted, the self-conscious emotions inherently involve reactions to social-evaluative events or perceived transgressions of social standards (see Dickerson et al., 2004; Keltner & Beer, 2004).

So, for example, people feel socially anxious when they are afraid that others may form undesired impressions of them (Leary & Kowalski, 1995) and embarrassed when they think that others have already formed an undesired impression (Miller, 1996). Likewise, guilt occurs when people believe that others might think they have performed a harmful or ethically undesirable behavior and shame occurs when they believe that others might think that they are an inherently bad person (Schott, 1979). And, although little direct evidence exists, it seems that pride involves the belief that one has done something (or perhaps possesses characteristics or resources) that could potentially increase one's relational value and acceptance by other people.

Although the emotion that people colloquially call "hurt feelings" has not been included among the self-conscious emotions, it may qualify because it involves imagining oneself through the eyes of other people. Evidence suggests that hurt feelings is a distinct emotion that arises when people infer that others do not regard their relationship with them as sufficiently valuable or important (Leary & Springer, 2000; Leary, Springer, Negel, Ansell, & Evans, 1998). Thus, hurt feelings involve conscious reflection on how one is being perceived by others, specifically the degree to which others value their relationship with the individual. Believing that one is shunned, avoided, criticized, or rejected hurts people's feelings and leads them to dwell self-consciously on other people's perceptions of them (see Leary & Leder, in press, for evidence regarding the status of hurt feelings as a distinct emotion).

As a group, the so-called self-conscious emotions differ in an important way from emotions—such as anger, sadness, and fear—that have not been regarded as self-conscious in nature. The self-conscious emotions require self-awareness, and thus are not seen in animals without the capacity for self-reflection or in human infants who have not yet acquired the ability to think consciously about themselves (Barrett, 1995; Lewis, 1991; Lewis & Brooks-Gunn, 1979; Mitchell, 2003). These emotions must have emerged relatively late in evolutionary history, after self-awareness appeared (see Leary & Buttermore, 2003), although their evolutionary precursors may be seen in reactions relevant to dominance, appeasement, and acceptance in nonhuman animals (Gilbert, 2000; MacLean, 1990; Parker, 1998).

Understanding that self-conscious emotions are fundamentally reactions to other people's real, implied, or imagined judgments also explains why guilt, shame, embarrassment, social anxiety, and, to a lesser extent, pride involve the subjective experience of feeling "self-conscious" in the everyday use of the term. These emotions involve the sense of being conspicuous, accompanied by ruminative thoughts about what other people might be thinking about the individual (Leary & Kowalski, 1995; Miller, 1996; Tangney & Fischer, 1995). These reactions are not a property of other self-reflective emotions that do not involve concerns about other people's evaluations. Becoming enraged as one reflects on how badly one was mistreated or feeling happy thinking about one's recent vacation do not make people feel "self-conscious" (in the ordinary use of the term), even though the individual is clearly in a state of self-awareness.

This conceptualization of self-conscious emotions differs from models that conceptualize these emotions as emerging directly from people's own private self-evaluations. For example, Mascolo and Fischer (1995) traced emotions such as pride, shame, and guilt to people's evaluations of their own value, worth, or wrongdoing, and Tracy and Robins (2004a) proposed that people experience self-conscious emotions "only when they become aware that they have lived up to, or failed to live up to, some actual or ideal self-representation" (p. 105). According to their perspective, self-conscious emotions promote adherence to people's actual or ideal self-representations and promote the attainment of social goals, but for Tracy and Robins (2004b), "the key question is not whether social goals are at stake, but whether identity goals are at stake. These identity goals can be interpersonal or task focused, public or private, but most important, must be about the aspirations and ideals (as well as the fears) of the self" (p. 174).

The Tracy–Robins analysis suggests that the self is involved in self-conscious emotions because these emotions require stable self-representations and the ability to assess whether one is living up to those self-representations. In contrast, I suggest that self-relevant thought underlies self-conscious emotions not because people are comparing their behavior to their self-representations but rather because thinking about other people's perceptions and evaluations of oneself requires self-awareness. The self-conscious emotions are much more strongly tied to what we think other people might think of us than to what we think of ourselves. We may become embarrassed when other people perceive us in an undesired fashion even when we know that those people's perceptions of us are inaccurate (Miller, 1996), and other people can make us feel guilty or ashamed even though we know that we did nothing wrong. Similarly, people experience social anxiety when they think others will not form desired impressions of them even though they know that they possess attributes that, if observed by others, would lead them to be impressed (Leary & Kowalski, 1995). Likewise, people may feel proud while knowing that they did nothing exemplary, as when people bask in the reflected glory of those who have excelled (Cialdini et al., 1976) or feel ashamed when those with whom they are associated misbehave (Lickel, Schmader, & Barquissau, 2004). Fundamentally, self-conscious emotions evolved not to respond to people's private evaluations of themselves but rather to regulate their interactions and relationships with other people (Baumeister, Stillwell, & Heatherton, 1994; Keltner & Beer, 2004; Keltner & Buswell, 1997; Miller & Leary, 1992).

Internalized Standards

This does not mean, of course, that people do not experience emotions, including self-conscious emotions, as a result of thinking about or evaluating themselves in their own minds. People internalize other people's values, then use those internalized values to judge themselves. Even so, the fundamental cause of self-conscious emotions involves the real or imagined appraisals of other people, even if those appraisals are internalized and the individual is no longer consciously aware of their source (see Baldwin & Baccus, 2004).

In fact, developmental theorists largely agree that children do not experience self-conscious emotions until they have internalized knowledge of others' standards and judgments (Barrett, 1995; Harter, 1999; Lewis, 1994; Stipek, 1995; Stipek, Recchia, & McClintic, 1992). Occasionally, people may develop idiosyncratic standards for self-evaluation that do not appear to be related to other people's judgments of them, but I suggest that these rare occasions arise when people erroneously misapply a psychological system that was designed to regulate social behavior.

Indeed, from an evolutionary standpoint, it is difficult to imagine what sort of selection pressures would have led human beings to be concerned about their own self-evaluations unless those evaluations were linked to important, reproductively meaningful outcomes. If we accept the assumption that emotions evolved because they helped animals deal with challenges and opportunities in their physical and social environments (a relatively non-controversial assertion in emotion science; see Frijda, 1986), then we must locate the function of emotion in its ability to help animals respond adaptively to their environments. Given that self-conscious emotions do not seem to be reactions to the physical, nonsocial environment, we can safely assume that they evolved to facilitate interpersonal encounters. With their high powers of conceptualization and representation, people may experience self-conscious emotions even when they are by themselves, but this internalized effect is not different in principle than people worrying about going to the dentist while sitting alone at home with no sharp dental instruments in sight. Thus, self-conscious emotions are involved in the maintenance of social relationships. Not only do self-conscious emotions steer people's behavior in adaptive interpersonal directions (see Keltner & Beer, 2005; Leary, Koch, & Hechenbleikner, 2000; Miller & Leary, 1992; Tracy & Robins, 2004a, 2004b), but they may also cue people regarding which thoughts and actions they should try to conceal versus reveal to other people. However, I do not think that self-conscious emotions are fundamentally about living up to one's actual or ideal self-representations.

THE CONCEPTUAL (OR SYMBOLIC) SELF

Nonhuman animals' emotions are largely in response to concrete events. Even a classically conditioned stimulus which, in a sense, is a "sign" of the actual emotion-producing stimulus, is concrete rather than abstract or conceptual, and it is not fundamentally about the animal itself.

In contrast, self-reflective emotions may arise when people conceptualize themselves in abstract, symbolic, and largely arbitrary ways. After the hominid ability to conceptualize oneself evolved, perhaps as late as 60,000 years ago (Leary & Buttermore, 2003), people could experience emotions in response to their abstract thoughts about themselves. Furthermore, the conceptual self allowed people to develop symbolic culture rooted in shared but relatively arbitrary meanings, and thus to evaluate themselves according to cultural standards. Before acquiring the conceptual-self ability, people could presumably not form abstract cognitive representations about themselves or evaluate themselves along symbolic, much less cultural, dimensions.

The ability for abstract self-thought allows people to experience emotions simply from thinking about their own characteristics or behavior. Thinking about evidence of one's incompetence, lack of social skill, or immoral actions can make the person experience a range of aversive emotions even when the standards he or she is applying are abstract and symbolic. Similarly, ruminating about one's symbolically positive characteristics can induce happiness, security, and contentment. Furthermore, when people conceptualize themselves, they sometimes ponder the causes of their actions or outcomes, and people's beliefs about the causes of the events that happen to them greatly affect their emotional reactions to those events. For example, attributing one's failures to lack of ability fosters different emotions than attributing one's failures to lack of effort or bad luck (Weiner, Russell, & Lerman, 1978). Likewise, attributing negative events to momentary mistakes (i.e., behavioral self-blame) results in different feelings than believing that negative events were due to long-standing personal shortcomings (i.e., characterological self-blame) (Janoff-Bulman, 1979; Winkel & Vrij, 1993). Presumably, most other animals lack the symbolic and linguistic capability to contemplate their personal characteristics or to make attributions for their actions, and thus do not experience emotions as a result of abstract and conceptual self-thought (Mitchell, 2003).

People's self-representations also set them up to be affected by the fortunes of the people and groups with whom they symbolically identify. Once people conceptualize themselves as a member of a particular group—a religion, a nation, a racial or ethnic group, a university, or a civic club, for example—the ups-and-downs of that group can greatly affect their emotions even when nothing personal is at stake (Cialdini et al., 1976). Furthermore, people experience vicarious shame and guilt when those who are associated with them behave in ways that reflect negatively on the group even though they personally did nothing wrong (Branscombe & Doosje, 2004; Lickel et al., 2004; Lickel, Schmader, Curtis, & Ames, 2005), and the more strongly people identify with their groups, the worse they feel about other group members' misbehaviors (Johns, Schmader, & Lickel, 2005). These emotional reactions arise solely from how people conceptually identify themselves in their own minds.

CONCLUSION

I recently saw a television interview with Noble Doss who, as a college football player in 1941, dropped an easy pass that would have likely led the University of Texas to the Rose Bowl and a national football championship. We would not be surprised that Doss felt horribly about this event at the time. One can only imagine the embarrassment, guilt, sadness, regret, and self-doubt that a college student would have felt after letting his team and his university down in such a public manner. What surprised me was how distressed Doss, now 85 years old, still is. "I've thought about it every day of my life," he said quietly, his eyes glistening with tears. "It cost us the national championship and the trip to the Rose Bowl."

Self-reflection has kept the event, and its self-relevant implications, alive in Noble Doss's mind for over 60 years. The extended self still conjures up memories of the dropped pass; the private self allows him to ruminate over his thoughts and feelings, as well as to imagine other people's reactions to his lapse; and the conceptual self leads Doss to construe what at one level was a simple momentary failure to hold on to a pigskin ball as a symbolic loss of a national championship. And, together, these self-reflective abilities generate a kaleidoscope of unpleasant emotions many years after the event.

Since Darwin's (1872/1998) evolutionary analysis of emotion, virtually all theorists have assumed that emotions evolved to help organisms deal with recurrent challenges, threats, opportunities, and benefits in their physical and social environments (Frijda, 1986). With the emergence of self-awareness among our hominid ancestors, however, human beings became capable of generating emotional responses with their own thoughts.

By and large, this was a functional adaptation because it meant that people no longer had to wait to respond to actual events but could imagine events that might occur (the extended self), infer others' reactions to them (the private self), and assess their actions from the perspective of internalized abstract standards (the conceptual self). Thus, self-reflective emotions allowed people to regulate their behavior preemptively on the basis of consciously remembered and anticipated consequences rather than reactively on the basis of immediate physical and social cues. Furthermore, self-reflection allowed people to override their natural emotional reactions to events when conscious analysis revealed that their immediate reaction was inappropriate, maladaptive, or unwise.

This self-reflective component of the emotional system would have been an improvement over the purely automatic system that presumably preceded it evolutionarily. Even so, it seems likely that self-reflective emotions are often a burden to modern people in a way that they were not in the evolutionary past. As noted, when prehuman hominids lived day to day as nomadic hunters and gatherers, their time horizon spanned only a few hours to a few days ahead. Thus, when the extended self conjured up thoughts about the individual's future, the person could anticipate only a fairly small range of outcomes within a very constricted time frame. In contrast, after the agricultural revolution led people to settle down into communities, accumulate possessions, and plan for planting and harvesting crops, people began to imagine a much longer expanse of self-relevant time (Martin, 1999). Because this protracted future was typically quite uncertain (Will the crops I plant this spring grow to provide food for next winter?), people began to plan for and worry about a future that extended months or years ahead of them. Today, of course, modern people are exceptionally future-oriented, devoting considerable effort now for uncertain outcomes in the future. As a result, people today are plagued by much self-generated doubt and anxiety about the future (Leary, 2004).

A second historical change that probably increased the frequency and potency of self-reflective emotions involves the fact that most people today live in a much larger number of changing social groups than did our prehistoric ancestors, and thus must pay greater attention to how they are regarded by a larger number of people. A hunter-gatherer who spent his or her entire life in a single clan would undoubtedly have needed to behave in ways that maintained acceptance by other members of the group (Baumeister & Leary, 1995), but the criteria for acceptance would have been both unambiguous and consensual. Today, however, many people's lives are characterized by a constantly shifting panorama of new faces, and, with each new person or group, the individual must reestablish his or her social identity and relational value among people whose values and standards are often unknown or discrepant from his or her own. As a result, many people today are probably more acutely aware of others' perceptions and evaluations of them and more consciously worried about establishing and maintaining interpersonal connections. As a result, I suspect that the self-conscious emotions—social anxiety, embarrassment, pride, guilt, and shame—are more common today than they were in the prehistoric past.

Third, prior to the emergence of the conceptual self, people would have not concerned themselves with abstract and symbolic aspects of their identity. One might have been concerned about relatively concrete self-images—of being physically strong or helpful, for example—but people would not have concerned themselves with the kinds of abstract identity issues that affect people today. We not only have a larger number of arbitrary criteria on which to evaluate ourselves but also a much larger number of other people to use for social comparison. As a result, people today are probably more self-evaluative and more likely to experience negative emotions stemming from unflattering comparisons with other people.

Self-awareness was a remarkable evolutionary innovation that changed many things about hominid psychology. Among these changes was the fact that we developed the ability to influence our emotions by our own self-reflection. This adaptation was a double-edged sword, however, allowing for improved self-regulation (and, perhaps, the existence of human culture itself), but also creating a great deal of emotional distress generated purely by our self-thoughts.

REFERENCES

Baldwin, M. W., & Baccus, J. R. (2004). Maintaining a focus on the social goals underlying self-conscious emotions. *Psychological Inquiry, 15,* 139–144.

Barrett, K. C. (1995). A functionalist approach to guilt and shame. In J. P. Tangney & K. W. Fischer (Eds.), *Self-conscious emotions: The psychology of shame, guilt, embarrassment, and pride* (pp. 25–63). New York: Guilford Press.

Baumeister, R. F., & Leary, M. R. (1995). The need to belong: Desire for interpersonal attachments as a fundamental human motivation. *Psychological Bulletin, 117,* 497–529.

Baumeister, R. F., Stillwell, A. M., & Heatherton, T. F. (1994). Guilt: An interpersonal approach. *Psychological Bulletin, 115,* 243–267.

Branscombe, N. R., & Doojse, B. (Eds.). (2004). *Collective guilt: International perspectives.* Cambridge, UK: Cambridge University Press.

Cialdini, R. B., Borden, R. J., Thorne, A., Walker, M. R., Freeman, S., & Sloan, L. R. (1976). Basking in reflected glory: Three (football) field studies. *Journal of Personality and Social Psychology, 34,* 366–375.

Claxton, G. (1990). *The heart of Buddhism.* London: Thorsons.

Darwin, C. (1998). *The expression of the emotions in man and animals.* New York: Oxford University Press. (Original work published 1872)

Dickerson, S. S., Gruenewald, T. L., & Kemeny, M. E. (2004). When the social self is threatened: Shame, physiology, and health. *Journal of Personality, 72,* 1189–1216.

Donald, M. (1991). *Origins of the modern mind.* Cambridge, MA: Harvard University Press.

Duval, S., & Wicklund, R. A. (1972). *A theory of objective self-awareness.* New York: Academic Press.

Frijda, N. (1986). *The emotions.* New York: Cambridge University Press.

Gallup, G. G. Jr. (1977). Self-recognition in primates. *American Psychologist, 32,* 329–338.

Gallup, G. G. Jr. (1997). On the rise and fall of self-conception in primates. In J. G. Snodgrass & R. L. Thompson (Eds.), *The self across psychology* (pp. 73–82). New York: New York Academy of Sciences.

Gilbert, P. (2000). Varieties of submissive behavior as forms of social defense: Their evolution and role in depression. In L. Sloman & P. Gilbert (Eds.), *Subordination and defeat: An evolutionary approach to mood disorders and their therapy.* (pp. 3–46). Mahwah, NJ: Erlbaum.

Harter, S. (1999). *The construction of the self.* New York: Guilford Press.

Hayes, S. C., & Linehan, M. M. (2004). *Mindfulness and acceptance: Expanding the cognitive-behavioral tradition.* New York: Guilford Press.

Humphrey, N. (1980). Nature's psychologists. In B. D. Jospehson & V. S. Ramachandran (Eds.), *Consciousness and the physical world* (pp. 276–298). Cambridge, UK: Cambridge University Press.

Humphrey, N. (1986). *The inner eye.* London: Faber & Faber.

Janoff-Bulman, R. (1979). Characterological vs. behavioral self-blame: Inquires into depression and rape. *Journal of Personality and Social Psychology, 31,* 1798–1809.

Jaynes, J. (1976). *The origin of consciousness in the breakdown of the bicameral mind.* Boston: Houghton Mifflin.

Johns, M., Schmader, T., & Lickel, B. (2005). Ashamed to be an American?: The role of identification in predicting vicarious shame for anti-Arab prejudice after 9–11. *Self and Identity, 4,* 331–348.

Katzko, M. W. (2003). Unity versus multiplicity: A conceptual analysis of the term "self" and its use in personality theories. *Journal of Personality, 71,* 83–114.

Keltner, D., & Beer, J. S. (2005). Self-conscious emotion and self-regulation. In A. Tesser, J. V. Wood, & D. A. Stapel (Eds.), *On building, defending, and regulating the self* (pp. 197–215). New York: Psychology Press.

Keltner, D., & Buswell, B. N. (1997). Embarrassment: Its distinct form and appeasement functions. *Psychological Bulletin, 122,* 250–270.

Kohler, W. (1925). *The mentality of apes.* New York: Harcourt, Brace.

Leary, M. R. (2003). The self and emotion: The role of self-reflection in the generation and regulation of affective experience. In R. J. Davidson, K. R. Scherer, & H. H. Goldsmith (Eds.), *The handbook of affective sciences* (pp. 773–786). New York: Oxford University Press.

Leary, M. R. (2004). *The curse of the self: Self-awareness, egotism, and the quality of human life.* New York: Oxford University Press.

Leary, M. R., & Buttermore, N. E. (2003). Evolution of the human self: Tracing the natural history of self-awareness. *Journal for the Theory of Social Behaviour, 33,* 365–404.

Leary, M. R., Koch, E., & Hechenbleikner, N. (2001). Emotional responses to interpersonal rejection. In M. R. Leary (Ed.), *Interpersonal rejection* (pp. 145–166). New York: Oxford University Press.

Leary, M. R., & Kowalski, R. M. (1995). *Social anxiety.* New York: Guilford Press.

Leary, M. R., & Leder, S. (in press). The nature of hurt feelings: Emotional experience and cognitive appraisals. In A. Vangelisti (Ed.), *Hurt feelings in close relationships.* Cambridge, UK: Cambridge University Press.

Leary, M. R., & Springer, C. (2000). Hurt feelings: The neglected emotion. In R. M. Kowalski (Ed.), *Behaving badly: Aversive behaviors in interpersonal relationships* (pp. 151–175). Washington, DC: American Psychological Association.

Leary, M. R., Springer, C., Negel, L., Ansell, E., & Evans, K. (1998). The causes, phenomenology, and consequences of hurt feelings. *Journal of Personality and Social Psychology, 74,* 1225–1237.

Leary, M. R., & Tangney, J. P. (2003). The self as an organizing construct in the behavioral and social sciences. In M. R. Leary & J. P. Tangney (Eds.), *Handbook of self and identity* (pp. 3–14). New York: Guilford Press.

Lewis, M. (1991). Ways of knowing: Objective self-awareness or consciousness. *Developmental Review, 11,* 231–243.

Lewis, M. (1994). Myself and me. In S. T. Parker, R. W. Mitchell, & M. L. Boccia (Eds.), *Self-awareness in animals and humans: Developmental perspectives* (pp. 20–34). New York: Cambridge University Press.

Lewis, M., & Brooks-Gunn, J. (1979). *Social cognition and the acquisition of self.* New York: Plenum Press.

Lickel, B., Schmader, T., & Barquissau, M. (2004). The evocation of moral emotions in intergroup contexts: The distinction between collective guilt and collective shame. In N. Branscombe & B. Doojse (Eds.), *Collective guilt: International perspectives* (pp. 35–55). Cambridge, UK: Cambridge University Press.

Lickel, B., Schmader, T., Curtis, M., & Ames, D. R. (2005). Vicarious shame and guilt. *Group Processes and Intergroup Relations, 8,* 145–147.

MacLean, P. D. (1990). *The triune brain in evolution.* New York: Plenum Press.

Marks, I. M. (1987). *Fears, phobias, and rituals.* New York: Oxford University Press.

Markus, H., & Nurius, P. S. (1986). Possible selves. *American Psychologist, 41,* 954–969.

Martin, L. (1999). I-D compensation theory: Some implications of trying to satisfy immediate-return needs in a delayed-return culture. *Psychological Inquiry, 10,* 195–208.

Mascolo, M. F., & Fischer, K. W. (1995). Developmental transformations in appraisals for pride, guilt, and shame. In J. P. Tangney & K. W. Fischer (Eds.), *Self-conscious emotions: The psychology of shame, guilt, embarrassment, and pride* (pp. 64–113). New York: Guilford Press.

Masson, J. M., & McCarthy, S. (1994). *When elephants weep: The emotional lives of animals.* London: Cape.

Mead, G. H. (1934). *Mind, self, and society*. Chicago: University of Chicago Press.

Miller, R. S. (1996). *Embarrassment: Poise and peril in everyday life*. New York: Guilford Press.

Miller, R. S., & Leary, M. R. (1992). Social sources and interactive functions of emotion: The case of embarrassment. In M. S. Clark (Ed.), *Emotion and social behavior* (pp. 202–221). Beverly Hills, CA: Sage.

Mitchell, R. W. (2002). Subjectivity and self-recognition in animals. In M. R. Leary & J. P. Tangney (Eds.), *Handbook of self and identity* (pp. 567–593). New York: Guilford Press.

Neisser, U. (1988). Five kinds of self-knowledge. *Philosophical Psychology, 1*, 35–59.

Olson, E. T. (1999). There is no problem of the self. In S. Gallagher & J. Shear (Eds.), *Models of the self* (pp. 49–61). Thorverton, UK: Imprint Academic.

Parker, S. T. (1998). A social selection model for the evolution and adaptive significance of self-conscious emotions. In R. J. Sternberg & M. D. Ferrari (Eds.), *Self-awareness: Its nature and development* (pp. 108–134). New York: Guilford Press.

Potts, R. B. (1984). Home bases and early hominids. *American Scientist, 72*, 338–347.

Scheier, M. F. (1976). Self-awareness, self-consciousness, and angry aggression. *Journal of Personality, 44*, 627–644.

Scheier, M. F., & Carver, C. S. (1977). Self-focused attention and the experience of emotion. *Journal of Personality and Social Psychology, 35*, 625–636.

Schott, S. (1979). Emotion and social life: A symbolic interactionist analysis. *American Journal of Sociology, 84*, 1317–1334.

Sedikides, C., & Skowronski, J. J. (1997). The symbolic self in evolutionary context. *Personality and Social Psychology Review, 1*, 80–102.

Segerstrom, S. C., Tsao, J. C., Alden, L. E., & Craske, M. G. (2000). Worry and rumination: Repetitive thought as a concomitant and predictor of negative mood. *Cognitive Therapy and Research, 24*, 671–688.

Siegle, G. J., Moore, P. M., & Thase, M. E. (2004). Rumination: One construct, many features in healthy individuals, depressed individuals, and individuals with lupus. *Cognitive Therapy and Research, 28*, 645–668.

Silvia, P. J. (2002). Self-awareness and emotional intensity. *Cognition and Emotion, 16*, 195–216.

Steenbarger, B. N., & Aderman, D. (1979). Objective self-awareness as a nonaversive state: Effect of anticipating discrepancy reduction. *Journal of Personality, 47*, 330–339.

Stipek, D. (1995). The development of pride and shame in toddlers. In J. P. Tangney & K. W. Fischer (Eds.), *Self-conscious emotions: The psychology of shame, guilt, embarrassment, and pride* (pp. 237–252). New York: Guilford Press.

Stipek, D., Recchia, S., & McClintic, S. (1992). Self-evaluation in young children. *Monographs of the Society for Research in Child Development, 57*(Serial No. 116), 1–84.

Tangney, J. P., & Fischer, K. W. (Eds.). (1995). *Self-conscious emotions: The psychology of shame, guilt, embarrassment, and pride*. New York: Guilford Press.

Tracy, J. L., & Robins, R. W. (2004a). Putting the self into self-conscious emotions: A theoretical model. *Psychological Inquiry, 15*, 103–125.

Tracy, J. L., & Robins, R. W. (2004b). Keeping the self in self-conscious emotions: Further arguments for a theoretical model. *Psychological Inquiry, 15*, 171–177.

Weiner, B., Russell, D., & Lerman, D. (1978). Affective consequences of causal attributions. In J. H. Harvey, W. Ickes, & R. F. Kidd (Eds.), *New directions in attribution research* (Vol. 2, pp. 59–89). Hillsdale, NJ: Erlbaum.

Wilson, R. D., & Schooler, J. W. (1991). Thinking too much: Introspection can reduce the quality of preferences and decisions. *Journal of Personality and Social Psychology, 60*, 181–192.

Winkel, F. W., & Vrij, A. (1993). Crime victims' attributional activities and differential psychological responding to victimization: The influence of behavior, character, and external explanations. *Issues in Criminology and Legal Psychology, 20*, 58–69.

4

Neural Systems for Self-Conscious Emotions and Their Underlying Appraisals

JENNIFER S. BEER

"Limbic system! Limbic system!" For many, this might be their first guess when asked about the neural underpinnings of self-conscious emotions. However, the limbic system is no longer a useful way to collar[1] the emotional networks in the brain (LeDoux, 1993). Many structures in the limbic system are not involved in emotional functions and many more are not specific to emotional function. Instead of considering which brain areas are "emotional," an answer to the question of the brain structures involved in self-conscious emotions should be derived from a consideration of the discrete self-conscious emotions and their component processes.

Entire books have been written on self-conscious emotions (e.g., Tangney & Fischer, 1995; this volume). Most theorists include embarrassment, shame, guilt, and pride in this emotion category. What is special about these emotions and why have they been rounded up and herded together into their own category of emotion? Perhaps one of their most unique characteristics is that they function to keep behavior within the constraints of social norms (Beer, Heerey, Keltner, Scabini, & Knight, 2003; Beer & Keltner, 2004; Lewis, 1993; Tangney & Fischer, 1995). In other words, self-conscious emotions keep us handcuffed to the social contract. The negative flavors of self-conscious emotions such as embarrassment, shame, and guilt that arise from social misdeeds are sufficiently unpleasant that, once given a taste, people are highly motivated to regulate their behavior so as to avoid experiencing them (e.g., Brown, 1970). Similarly, pride is a pleasant feeling that individuals may be drawn toward again and again. These diverse emotional experiences share several psychological computations. In order to experience a self-conscious emotion, one must have an awareness of self (self-perception), an awareness that others are judging that self (person inference), and an awareness that there are a set of rules or social norms that determine whether the actions of the self are "right" or "wrong" (social norms).

This chapter addresses the question of the neural underpinnings of self-conscious emotions by first considering the neural systems recruited for self-perception, person inference, and knowledge of social norms. Second, the small amount of work directly addressing neural systems recruited for self-conscious emotions is reviewed. The chapter concludes with comments on future directions for work in this area.

SELF-PERCEPTION PROCESSES

A host of psychological processes have been examined by neuroscientists in search of the self. These processes include self-referent encoding (i.e., using one's self vs. another construct as a point of encoding; see Symons & Johnson, 1997), self-reflection (i.e., evaluating one's identity), and self-monitoring (assessing one's behavior). Together these studies suggest that the brain areas most commonly associated with self-processing are the frontal lobes including the cingulate (see Table 4.1).

Neuroimaging work has focused on activity related to self-reference encoding and found that medial prefrontal cortex is involved in the effective encoding of information in reference to the self. Studies using positron emission tomography (PET) (Craik et al., 1999) and functional magnetic resonance imaging (fMRI) (Fossati et al., 2003; Kelly et al., 2002; Kircher et al., 2002; see Gillihan & Farah, 2005) techniques have found

TABLE 4.1. Brain Areas Most Commonly Associated with Self-Perception

Task	Brain structure/area of damage	Citation
	Anterior cingulate	
Self-reference	Anterior cingulate (BA 24)	Craik et al. (1999)
Positive versus negative self-judgments	Anterior cingulate (BA 32)	Fossati et al. (2003)
Self- versus other-person judgments	Anterior cingulate (BA 32)	Gusnard et al. (2001)
	Posterior cingulate	
Self-reference	Posterior cingulate (BA 31)	Fossati et al. (2003); Kelley et al. (2002); Kircher et al. (2000); Kircher et al. (2002)
	Frontal lobes	
Self-reference	Medial frontal lobe (BA 9/10)	Craik et al. (1999); Fossati et al. (2003); Kelley et al. (2002)
Self-reference	Inferior frontal gyrus (BA 47)	Craik et al. (1999)
	Inferior frontal cortex	Kelley et al. (2002)
	Inferior frontal gyrus (BA 44)	Kircher et al. (2002)
Own face versus unknown face	Inferior frontal gyrus (BA 45/46)	Kircher et al. (2000)
Own face versus partner's face	Middle frontal gyrus (BA 8/9)	Keenan et al. (2000)
Own face versus self-descriptions		
Impaired self-perception	Orbitofrontal cortex damage	Beer et al. (2005)
	Right frontal lobe damage	Keenan et al. (2000)

Note. BA, Brodmann's area.

increased activity in the medial prefrontal cortex (Bradmann's areas [BA] 9 and 10) and inferior frontal gyrus (BA 44, 47) when encoding information in relation to the self when compared with a famous political figure, general social desirability, and syllabic structure. Similar findings are associated with comparisons between reflecting on one's characteristics as opposed to non-self-relevant characteristics (Kircher et al., 2002) and one's feelings of pleasantness versus perception of external scenery (Gusnard, Akbudak, Shulman, & Raichle, 2001). Similarly, fMRI research has consistently shown that the right frontal lobe (e.g., BA 9/10) has increased activity when observing one's own face versus that of a close other or another person (e.g., Keenan, Wheeler, Gallup, & Pasucal-Leone, 2000; Kircher et al., 2000). However, some studies have found medial prefrontal activation for self- and other-referential tasks but failed to find a difference in the intensity of activation in these areas between those two conditions (e.g., Ochsner et al., 2005).

A related self process, self-monitoring, has been a greater focus in clinical case studies and lesion patient research. Together these studies suggest that the frontal lobes support monitoring abilities, that is, the ability to accurately compare actual behavior to abstract behavioral standards (e.g., Beer, Shimamura, & Knight, 2004; Beer, John, Scabini, & Knight, 2006; Lhermitte, 1986; Luria & Homskaya, 1970; Stuss & Benson, 1984). For example, the stimulus-bound behavior classically associated with frontal lobe damage epitomizes a failure to monitor the appropriateness of behavior (Luria & Homskaya, 1970; Lhermitte, 1986; Lhermitte, Pillon, & Serdaru, 1986). Behavior is considered stimulus-bound when it is driven by the context and not under the individual's control. For example, a frontal lobe patient is likely to use any object he or she encounters or to imitate someone else's actions without taking into account whether that activity is appropriate for the context (utilization behavior; Lhermitte, 1986). These case histories suggest that prefrontal damage impairs the ability to choose behaviors as a function of whether they are appropriate for a given context.

In addition to the classic case studies, one empirical study has shown that orbitofrontal patients, in comparison to lateral prefrontal patients and healthy controls, tend to lack insight into the inappropriateness of their social behavior (Beer et al., 2006). Participants performed a task in which they had to control the amount of personal information they disclosed. Transcripts of the task were coded by trained judges for appropriateness of self-disclosure. Self-monitoring accuracy was assessed by comparing self-reports of self-disclosure to the trained judges' codes. Orbitofrontal patients tended to overestimate the appropriateness of the intimacy of their self-disclosure. No differences were found for dorsolateral prefrontal patients or healthy controls. Furthermore, the importance of self-monitoring for self-conscious emotions is most clearly seen in this study. Orbitofrontal patients only became embarrassed by their inappropriate self-disclosure after their ability to monitor their performance was facilitated. Specifically, watching a videotape playback drew orbitofrontal patients' attention to themselves and their behavior and increased their feelings of embarrassment (Beer et al., 2006).

Together the neural studies of self-perception processes suggest that the frontal lobes, extending from the orbital portion to the cingulate to the dorsolateral regions, are involved in a variety of self processes such as using one's self as reference for new information or evaluating how one is impacting the environment. Aptly named, self-conscious emotions require that an individual have a sense of "self." As such, it is likely that the frontal lobes are an important part of the neural network that gives rise to self-conscious emotions by virtue of their involvement in self-processing.

PERSON-INFERENCE PROCESSES

Self-conscious emotions are also sometimes referred to as "social emotions." This is the first clue that the "self" moniker means that not only one's own self but the selves of others need to be considered in discussions of the self-conscious emotions. These feelings arise from the awareness that other people have selves and that these selves have the potential to be judging your self. Therefore, neural systems involved in making inferences about other people's minds and emotions are likely to be involved in self-conscious emotions.

Both lesion and imaging research suggest that prefrontal cortex, the temporal lobes, and the amygdala are involved in making inferences about others such as understanding other people's mental and emotional states (see Table 4.2).

Making inferences about others' mental states is most commonly associated with the frontal lobes and, to a lesser extent, the superior temporal sulcus. Two imaging studies found that left medial prefrontal areas (i.e., BA 8 and 9) showed increased activation when participants were asked to make a mental inference versus a physical inference. In one study, participants had to decide whether a person living in the 15th century would know the function of an object or decide what function an object had. When these two conditions were compared, increased activity in left BA 9 was found (Goel, Grafman, Tajik, Gana, & Danto, 1997). Another study examined activation in relation to story comprehension that required the participants either to make mental inferences or physical inferences about a character's actions. When these two conditions were compared, increased activity in left BA 8 and the superior temporal sulcus was found (Fletcher et al., 1995; see also Rilling, Sanfey, Aronson, Nystrom, & Cohen, 2004, and Saxe, Carey, & Kanwisher, 2003, for studies associating superior temporal sulcus with theory of mind tasks). In contrast, another imaging study showed increased activation in right orbitofrontal regions in comparison to left polar frontal regions during a mental state recognition task that required participants to decide whether a word described a mind state or a body state (Baron-Cohen, Ring, Moriarty, Schmitz, Costa, & Ell, 1994). Finally, one study compared inferences about people to inferences about dogs and found middle frontal gyrus (BA 9) activation (Mason, Banfield, & Macrae, 2004).

Lesion research also suggests that prefrontal areas and, to a lesser extent, the temporal lobes are involved in making mental inferences. Price, Daffner, Stowe, and Marsel-Mesulum (1990) found that dorsolateral prefrontal patients were impaired at giving directions to another person when compared to normals. Although some studies suggest that orbitofrontal cortex, particularly the right side, is critically involved in theory of mind on a visual perspective task (Stuss, Gallup, & Alexander, 2001), another study found that orbitofrontal and dorsolateral prefrontal patients did not have trouble with basic-level theory of mind tasks (Stone, Baron-Cohen, & Knight, 1998). However, in this study, orbitofrontal patients were impaired in their ability to make inferences about the intentions of characters in vignettes about social faux pas when compared to normals and dorsolateral prefrontal patients.

The lack of insight into others' minds is also reflected in the conversational style of orbitofrontal patients. Kaczmarek (1984) found that damage to the left orbitofrontal cortex was associated with confabulation, misnamings, and digressions from the topic. These findings were interpreted to reflect a decreased appreciation for the necessity of a coherent description to ensure that the audience understood the speaker. These data might also be interpreted as support for impaired self-monitoring. The orbitofrontal patients may have been tangential and incoherent in their responses because

TABLE 4.2. Brain Areas Most Commonly Associated with Person Inference

Task	Brain structure/area of damage	Citation
	Amygdala	
Recognizing sadness versus anger	Amygdala	Blair et al. (1999)
Recognizing emotion versus neutral (or age judgment)	Amygdala	Gur et al. (2002)
Recognizing fear versus happy	Amygdala	Morris et al. (1998)
Recognizing fear versus neutral	Amygdala	Breiter et al. (1996); Phillips et al. (1997); Sato et al. (2004)
Recognizing happy versus fear	Amygdala	Breiter et al. (1996)
Impaired perception of emotion in others	Amygdala damage	Adolphs et al. (1994); Adolphs et al. (1995); Adolphs et al. (1998); Adolphs et al. (1999); Adolphs, Baron-Cohen, & Tranel (2002a); Adolphs & Tranel (2003); Adolphs & Tranel (2004); Anderson & Phelps (2000); Broks et al. (1998); Glascher & Adolphs (2003); Scott et al. (1997); Sprengelmeyer et al. (1999); Young et al. (1995); Young et al. (1996)
Impaired theory of mind	Amygdala damage	Shaw et al. (2004); Stone et al. (2003)
	Frontal lobes	
Inferences about people versus dogs	Middle frontal gyrus (BA 9)	Mason, Banfield, & Macrae (2004)
Empathic judgments	Orbitofrontal gyrus Superior frontal gyrus Inferior frontal gyrus	Farrow et al. (2001)
Impaired empathy	Frontal lobe damage	Eslinger (1998); Grattan & Eslinger (1992); Grattan et al. (1994); Price et al. (1990); Shamay-Tsoory et al. (2003)
Theory of mind	Medial frontal gyrus (BA 8/9)	Baron-Cohen et al. (1999); Fletcher et al. (1995); Goel et al. (1995)
Impaired theory of mind	Orbitofrontal cortex damage	Stone, Baron-Cohen, & Knight (1998)
	Frontal lobe damage	Happe, Malhi, & Checkley (2001)
Impaired perception of emotion in others	Orbitofrontal cortex damage	Adolphs, Damasio, & Tranel (2002b); Beer et al. (2003); Hornak, Rolls, & Wade (1996)
	Superior temporal sulcus/gyrus	
Theory of mind	Superior temporal gyrus (BA 22/39)	Fletcher et al. (1995); Rilling et al. (2004)
	Anterior superior temporal sulcus	Saxe, Carey, & Kanwisher (2003)
Impaired perception of emotion in others	Anteriomedial temporal lobe	Adolphs et al. (2001)

Note. BA, Brodmann's area.

they failed to monitor the appropriateness of their responses in reference to the questions posed.

It is worth noting that two studies have also found a relation between amygdala damage and theory of mind impairment. In one study, patients with childhood amygdala damage (as opposed to damage incurred in adulthood) failed a series of theory of mind tasks requiring ironic or nonliteral inferences (Shaw et al., 2004). In another study, two patients with amygdala damage acquired in adulthood showed deficits on interpreting social faux pas vignettes and pictures of eye gaze (Stone, Baron-Cohen, Calder, Keane, & Young, 2003).

Inferences about the emotional states of others have been most commonly associated with the amygdala, with mixed evidence for the involvement of the frontal lobes. Perception of emotional faces is associated with amygdala activation (e.g., Breiter et al., 1996; Blair, Morris, Frith, Perrett, & Dolan, 1999; Gur et al., 2002; Morris et al., 1998; Phillips et al., 1997; Sato, Kochiyama, Yoshikawa, Naito, & Matsumura, 2004) and impaired in cases of amygdala damage (e.g., Adolphs, Tranel, Damasio, & Damasio, 1994, 1995; Adolphs, Tranel, & Damasio, 1998; Adolphs et al., 1999; Adolphs, Baron-Cohen, & Tranel, 2002a; Adolphs, Damasio, & Tranel, 2002b; Adolphs & Tranel, 2003, 2004; Adolphs, Tranel, & Damasio, 2003; Anderson & Phelps, 2000; Broks et al., 1998; Glascher & Adolphs, 2003; Scott et al., 1997; Sprengelmeyer et al., 1999; Young, Hellawell, Van De Wal, & Johnson, 1996). These studies typically require participants to make judgments about standardized sets of emotional facial expressions of various emotions in comparison to neutral expressions.

Some evidence suggests that the frontal lobes may also be involved in perceiving the emotional states of others. For example, orbitofrontal patients show impairments on empathy trait measures of empathy (Grattan, Bloomer, Archambault, & Eslinger, 1994; Shamay-Tsoory, Tomer, Berger, & Aharon-Peretz, 2003). Similarly, two studies found that orbitofrontal patients were impaired at inferring emotional states from pictures of various emotional facial expressions (Hornak, Rolls, & Wade, 1996), although in one study this impairment only held for expressions of embarrassment and shame (Beer et al., 2003). However, Stone et al. (1998) did not find that orbitofrontal patients had trouble inferring the feelings of story characters that had been on the receiving end of a social faux pas. Unfortunately, this study did not require participants to identify the emotion of the character who committed the faux pas.

Together the neural studies of person-inference processes suggest that the frontal lobes are important for making inferences about the mental states of others whereas the amygdala is most commonly associated with making inferences about the emotional states of others. Self-conscious emotions require that an individual is aware that others may be evaluating one's behavior and that these evaluations may evoke positive or negative emotional reactions that will shape future social interactions. Therefore, it is likely that the frontal lobes and the amygdala (and to a lesser extent the superior temporal sulcus) are an important part of the neural network that gives rise to self-conscious emotions by supporting person-inferences processing.

KNOWLEDGE OF SOCIAL NORMS

A final piece of the self-conscious emotion puzzle is the knowledge of the "rules" that you and others are using to judge behavior. Therefore, neural systems involved in learning and applying social norms are likely to support self-conscious emotions. An abundance of theories on the social brain await harvest (e.g., Adolphs, 1999; Beer et al., 2004; Brothers, 1996; Blakemore & Frith, 2004; Chayer & Freedman, 2001; Grafman, 1995; Stuss & Benson, 1984; Tooby & Cosmides, 1990; Tucker, Luu, & Pribram, 1995; Wood, 2003). Whereas theorists disagree on whether the social brain is a unique neural network equipped only to handle interpersonal negotiations or whether it is a network that has been adapted for those situations, almost all agree that this network includes the frontal lobes (including anterior cingulate), the amygdala, the temporal lobes, and the insula/somatosensory cortices. Although the actual empirical work in this area has not been systematic, several studies support the involvement of many of the hypothesized brain structures (see Table 4.3).

The involvement of the frontal lobes in social knowledge has been demonstrated in both lesion patients and neuroimaging research. The bulk of the research in this area has

TABLE 4.3. Brain Areas Most Commonly Associated with Social Knowledge

Task	Brain structure/area of damage	Citation
	Amygdala	
Nonmoral versus neutral	Left amygdala	Moll et al. (2002)
Untrustworthy versus trustworthy	Right amygdala	Winston et al. (2002)
Impaired social knowledge	Amygdala damage	Adolphs et al. (1998); Adolphs et al. (2002a); Bar-On et al. (2003)
	Frontal lobes	
Moral versus nonmoral judgments	Medial frontal (BA 9/10)	Greene et al. (2001)
Person versus object	Inferior frontal gyrus	Mitchell, Heatherton, & Macrae (2002)
	Superior frontal gyrus	
Impression formation versus sequencing	Dorsomedial prefrontal cortex	Mitchell, Macrae, & Banaji (2004)
Moral versus neutral	Medial frontal (BA 10/11)	Moll et al. (2002)
Explicit versus implicit trustworthiness	Superior frontal sulcus	Winston et al. (2002)
Impaired social knowledge	Orbitofrontal/ventromedial cortex damage	Bar-On et al. (2003); Cicerone & Tannenbaum (1997); Saver & Damasio (1991)
	Prefrontal cortex damage	Anderson et al. (1999); Blair & Cipolotti (2000); Goel et al. (1997); Gomez-Beldarrain et al. (2004); Grattan & Eslinger (1992); Mah et al. (2004); Price et al. (1990)
	Superior temporal sulcus/gyrus	
Person versus object	Superior temporal lobe	Mitchell et al. (2002)
Untrustworthy versus trustworthy judgment	Superior temporal sulcus/gyrus	Winston et al. (2002)

Note. BA, Brodmann's area.

examined the performance of frontal lobe patients on various gambling tasks and found that frontal lobe damage may increase or decrease risk taking (e.g., Bechara, Damasio, & Damasio, 2000; Rahman, Sahakian, Cardinal, Rogers, & Robbins, 2001; Shiv, Loewenstein, & Bechara, 2005; Sanfey, Hastie, Calvin, & Grafman, 2003). Gambling tasks are purported to be good models of social decision making as they inherently involve risk. However, gambling seems a poor proxy for the kind of social assessments that underlie self-conscious emotion. Studies of lesions patients more relevant for the purpose of this chapter have found that damage to the frontal lobes impairs the ability to prioritize solutions to interpersonal problems (Bar-On, Tranel, Denburg, & Bechora, 2003; Cicerone & Tanenbaum, 1997; Dimitrov, Grafman, & Hollnagel, 1996; Price et al., 1990; Saver & Damasio, 1991), impairs understanding of social relationships (Mah, Arnold, & Grafman, 2004); and eliminates gender stereotyping (Milne & Grafman, 2001). Similarly, imaging studies have found frontal lobe activation in relation to moral evaluation (Greene, Sommerville, Nystrom, Darley, & Cohen, 2001; Moll et al., 2002; Winston, Strange, O'Doherty, & Dolan, 2002), social words and phrases (Wood, Romero, Makale, & Grafman, 2003), knowledge about people in comparison to objects (Mitchell, Heatherton, & Macrae, 2002), and forming impressions of people in comparison to temporal sequencing (Mitchell, Macrae, & Banaji, 2004). However, evidence for the involvement of frontal lobes in explicit knowledge of social norms is mixed. A study of two orbitofrontal patients has found that childhood damage may impair acquisition of social norms (Anderson, Bechara, Damasio, Tranel, & Damasio, 1999), whereas a study of eight patients with adult damage did not find a deficit in social norms (Beer et al., 2006).

Lesion studies have also supported the involvement of amygdala in social knowledge. Damage to this area impairs social intelligence (Bar-On et al., 2003) and impairs judgments of trustworthiness (Adolphs, Tranel, & Damasio, 1998). Similarly, neuroimaging studies have found activations in amygdala for judgments of trustworthiness (Winston et al., 2002). It is important to note that the studies of trustworthiness do not norm faces to correlate with varying degrees of actual trustworthiness in the individual pictured. Therefore, these studies are best interpreted as investigations of shared stereotypes regarding trustworthiness.

Together the studies on neural networks of social knowledge suggest that the frontal lobes and amygdala are important for understanding and applying social norms to behavior. Self-conscious emotions arise when social norms have been transgressed. In addition to their role in self-perception and person inference, the frontal lobes and amygdala are likely involved in self-conscious emotional experiences by virtue of their involvement in declarative and procedural social knowledge.

SELF-CONSCIOUS EMOTIONS

An explosion of work addressing the neural underpinnings of self-conscious emotions has yet to occur. A few studies have been conducted on self-conscious emotion favorites such as embarrassment (Beer et al., 2003, 2006; Berthoz, Armony, Blair, & Dolan, 2002; Blair & Cipolotti, 2000; Devinsky, Hafler, & Victor, 1982; Ruby & Decety, 2004; Takahashi et al., 2004), guilt (Shin et al., 2000; Takahashi et al., 2004), and pride (Beer et al., 2003). Research on the related field of moral emotion and judgment has enjoyed much more popularity than self-conscious emotions per se (e.g., Anderson et al., 1999; Greene et al.,

2001; Moll, de Oliveira-Souza, Bramati, & Grafman, 2002; Moll et al., 2005). Although still in its infancy, the research on the neural bases of self-conscious emotions has already generated some convergent findings.

Embarrassment has been mainly associated with the frontal and temporal lobes (Beer et al., 2003, 2006; Berthoz et al., 2002; Blair & Cipolotti, 2000; Devinsky et al., 1982; Ruby & Decety, 2004; Takahashi et al., 2004). Three studies with lesion patients have found evidence of disrupted embarrassment associated with frontal damage. For example, orbitofrontal patients fail to experience embarrassment even after behaving inappropriately (Beer et al., 2003, 2006) unless they are shown a videotape of their social mistakes (Beer et al., 2006). Case studies have found that right-sided frontal lobe damage impairs understanding of embarrassing scenarios (Blair & Cipolotti, 2000) and that seizures from the medial prefrontal cortex may be preceded by an aura of embarrassment (Devinsky et al., 1982). In addition to the lesion work, three imaging studies have found brain activity in the frontal and temporal lobes in relation to embarrassment. One study had individuals read sentences that evoked embarrassment or an emotionally neutral state (Takahashi et al., 2004). The embarrassment condition was associated with activation in the frontal lobes (BA 6/8/9/10/47), the temporal lobes (BA 21/20/39), the visual cortex (BA 17/18/19), and the left hippocampus. Similarly, another study asked participants to imagine themselves in scenarios in which they mistakenly violated social norms (embarrassment condition) or scenarios in which no social norms were violated (Berthoz et al., 2002). The embarrassment condition was associated with increased activity in various subregions of the frontal lobes (BA 6/8/9/10/44/45/47), the temporal lobes (BA 21/37/38), and visual areas (BA 17/18). Finally, another study found increased amygdala activity in relation to judgments of embarrassment for the self and for one's mother (Ruby & Decety, 2004).

Guilt has been associated with diffuse activation in the frontal and temporal lobes (Shin et al., 2000; Takahashi et al., 2004). In one study, participants' brain activity was measured while they read sentences that evoked guilt or an emotionally neutral state. In comparison to the neutral condition, the guilt condition was associated with activation in the medial prefrontal cortex (BA 6/8/9/10) and posterior superior temporal sulcus (BA 39) (Takahashi et al., 2004). Another study compared participants' brain activity while they recalled a guilty or an emotional neutral event (Shin et al., 2000). The guilt condition was associated with increased activity in bilateral temporal poles, anterior cingulate (BA 32), and left inferior frontal gyrus/anterior insula (BA 47/48). However, it is difficult to conclude that this activation is specific to guilt as participants self-reported significantly higher levels of guilt as well as shame, disgust, anger, and sadness after the guilt condition in comparison to the neutral condition.

CONCLUSIONS

This chapter suggests that the neural networks involved in self-conscious emotion spans the frontal and temporal lobes (including cingulate and amygdala). Although very little work has directly addressed this question, research on the neural bases of the psychological processes underlying self-conscious emotions has begun to provide some answers. The frontal lobes have been associated with self- and other processing, acquisition and application of social norms, and the generation of embarrassment, pride, and guilt. The temporal lobes have been associated with making inferences about the minds of others and knowledge about the social world in addition to the experience of embarrassment and guilt. Finally, the amygdala has been associated with interpreting the emotions of others and knowledge about the social world as well as embarrassment. In other words, each area is involved in one or more of the appraisal processes underlying self-conscious emotion as well as the experience of one or more self-conscious emotions.

Many more questions are raised than answered by a review of work on the neural bases of self-conscious emotions. What should be the goal of this area? Work in this area is sometimes motivated by a desire to map function onto neuroanatomy while other studies aim to learn something about the psychological processes underlying self-conscious emotions. Scientists with either of these goals will want to consider a number of issues when designing future research.

First, better and more comprehensive methodology is needed to draw stronger conclusions about the involvement of these brain areas in self-conscious emotions. Most current research has focused on embarrassment, with a few studies examining guilt; almost nothing is known about shame or pride. For example, the mixed lesion evidence regarding the role of orbitofrontal cortex in emotional perception might be resolved if more studies included stimuli of basic emotional expressions as well as more complex emotional expressions (e.g., contempt, shame, embarrassment). Additionally, eliciting discrete emotions may be particularly difficult for neuroimaging techniques that require a large number of repeated, fast trials. If the emotion system is designed to activate in relation to meaningful environmental changes, it is possible that self-conscious emotion neural responses will habituate before they can be assessed using fMRI. In this case, lesion studies may be more promising. Second, studies should be designed to compare brain activity between discrete self-conscious emotion states, other emotion states, and emotionally neutral states. It is certainly the case that the brain regions mentioned in this review have been associated with non-self-conscious emotions. In order to understand whether there are neural distinctions that parallel the basic and self-conscious distinction made by many emotion researchers, future research must include conditions from both categories. For example, a study might compare the experience of anger and shame. Anger and shame are similar because both may arise in reaction to offensive behavior. However, these two emotions differ because anger arises when someone else commits the offensive acts and shame arises when the acts are committed by the self. Third, if future research continues to consider the appraisals that underlie self-conscious emotions, studies comparing declarative and procedural social knowledge will be valuable as they are often confounded in the current research. How much do self-conscious emotions arise from knowing norms in comparison to knowing specific behaviors to satisfy those norms? Finally, research on patients with brain damage acquired in childhood has sometimes yielded extremely different results than research with patients whose brain damage was acquired in adulthood. Future developmental research will be beneficial for understanding how children's development of self-conscious emotions parallels their neural development.

NOTE

1. The term "limbic" was derived from *limbus,* the Latin word for collar, because of its circular shape.

REFERENCES

Adolphs, R. (1999). Social cognition and the human brain. *Trends in Cognitive Sciences, 3,* 469–479.

Adolphs, R., Baron-Cohen, S., & Tranel, D. (2002a). Impaired recognition of social emotions following amygdala damage. *Journal of Cognitive Neuroscience, 14,* 1264–1274.

Adolphs, R., Damasio, H., & Tranel, D. (2002b). Neural systems for recognition of emotional prosody: A 3-D lesion study. *Emotion, 2,* 23–51.

Adolphs, R., & Tranel, D. (2003). Amygdala damage impairs emotion recognition from scenes only when they contain facial expressions. *Neuropsychologia, 41,* 1281–1289.

Adolphs, R., & Tranel, D. (2004). Impaired judgments of sadness but not happiness following bilateral amygdala damage. *Journal of Cognitive Neuroscience, 16,* 453–462.

Adolphs, R., Tranel, D., & Damasio, A. R. (1998). The human amygdala in social judgment. *Nature, 393,* 470–474.

Adolphs, R., Tranel, D., & Damasio, H. (2001). Emotion recognition from faces and prosody following temporal lobectomy. *Neuropsychology, 15,* 396–404.

Adolphs, R., Tranel, D., & Damasio, A. R. (2003). Dissociable neural systems for recognizing emotions. *Brain and Cognition, 52,* 61–69.

Adolphs, R., Tranel, D., Damasio, H., & Damasio, A. (1994). Impaired recognition of emotion in facial expressions following bilateral damage to the human amygdala. *Nature, 372,* 669–672.

Adolphs, R., Tranel, D., Damasio, H., & Damasio, A. R. (1995). Fear and the human amygdala. *Journal of Neuroscience, 15,* 5879–5891.

Adolphs, R., Tranel, D., Hamann, S., Young, A. W., Calder, A. J., Phelps, E. A., et al. (1999). Recognition of facial emotion in nine individuals with bilateral amygdala damage. *Neuropsychologia, 37*(10), 1111–1117.

Anderson, A. K., & Phelps, E. A. (2000). Expression without recognition: Contributions of the human amgydala to emotional communication. *Psychological Science, 11,* 106–111.

Anderson, S. W., Bechara, A., Damasio, H., Tranel, D., & Damasio, A. R. (1999). Impairment of social and moral behavior related to early damage in human prefrontal cortex. *Nature Neuroscience, 2,* 1032–1037.

Bar-On, R., Tranel, D., Denburg, N. L., & Bechara, A. (2003). Exploring the neurological substrate of emotional and social intelligence. *Brain, 126,* 1790–1800.

Baron-Cohen, S., Ring, H., Moriarty, J., Schmitz, B., Costa, D., & Ell, P. (1994). Recognition of mental state terms. *British Journal of Psychiatry, 165,* 640–649.

Baron-Cohen, S., Ring, H. A., Wheelwright, S., Bullmore, E. T., Brammer, M. J., Simmons, A., et al. (1999). Social intelligence in the normal and autistic brain: An fMRI study. *European Journal of Neuroscience, 11,* 1891–1898.

Bechara, A., Damasio, H., & Damasio, A. R. (2000). Emotion, decision making, and the orbitofrontal cortex. *Cerebral Cortex, 10,* 295–307.

Beer, J. S., Heerey, E. A., Keltner, D., Scabini, D., & Knight, R. T. (2003). The regulatory function of self-conscious emotion: Insights from patients with orbitofrontal damage. *Journal of Personality and Social Psychology, 85,* 594–604.

Beer, J. S., John, O. P., Scabini, D., & Knight, R. T. (2006). Orbitofrontal cortex and social behavior: Integrating self-monitoring and emotion–cognition interactions. *Journal of Cognitive Neuroscience, 18,* 871–880.

Beer, J. S., & Keltner, D. (2004). What is unique about self-conscious emotions?: Comment on Tracy & Robins' "Putting the self into self-conscious emotions: A theoretical model." *Psychological Inquiry, 15,* 126–129.

Beer, J. S., Shimamura, A. P., & Knight, R. T. (2004). Frontal lobe contributions to executive control of cognitive and social behavior. In M. S. Gazzaniga (Ed.), *The newest cognitive neurosciences* (3rd ed., pp. 1091–1104). Cambridge, MA: MIT Press.

Berthoz, S., Armony, J. L., Blair, R. J., & Dolan, R. J. (2002). An fMRI study of intentional and unintentional (embarrassing) violations of social norms. *Brain, 125,* 1696–1708.

Blair, R. J. R., & Cipolotti, L. (2000). Impaired social response reversal: A case of "acquired sociopathy." *Brain, 123,* 1122–1141.

Blair, R. J., Morris, J. S., Frith, C. D., Perrett, D. I., & Dolan, R. J. (1999). Dissociable neural responses to facial expressions of sadness and anger. *Brain, 122,* 883–893.

Blakemore, S. J., & Frith, U. (2004). How does the brain deal with the social world? *Neuroreport, 15,* 119–128.

Breiter, H. C., Etcoff, N. L., Whalen, P. J., Kennedy, W. A., Rauch, S. L., Buckner, R. L., et al. (1996). Response and habituation of the human amygdala during visual processing of facial expression. *Neuron, 17,* 875–887.

Broks, P., Young, A. W., Maratos, E. J., Coffey, P. J., Calder, A. J., Isaac, C. L., et al. (1998). Face processing impairments after encephalitis: Amygdala damage and recognition of fear. *Neuropsychologia, 36,* 59–70.

Brothers, L. (1996). Brain mechanisms of social cognition. *Journal of Psychopharmacology, 10,* 2–8.

Brown, B. R. (1970). Face-saving following experimentally induced embarrassment. *Journal of Experimental Social Psychology, 6,* 255–271.

Chayer, C., & Freedman, M. (2001). Frontal lobe functions. *Current Neurology and Neuroscience Reports, 1,* 547–552.

Cicerone, K. D., & Tanenbaum, L. N. (1997). Disturbance of social cognition after traumatic orbitofrontal brain injury. *Archives of Clinical Neuropsychology, 12,* 173–188.

Craik, F. I. M., Moroz, T. M., Moscovitch, M., Stuss, D. T., Wincour, G., Tulving, E., et al. (1999). In search of the self: A positron emission tomography study. *Psychological Science, 10,* 26–34.

Devinksy, O., Hafler, D. A., & Victor, J. D. (1982). Embarrassment as the aura of a complex partial seizure. *Neurology, 32,* 1284–1285.

Dimitrov, M., Grafman, J., & Hollnagel, C. (1996). The effects of frontal lobe damage on everyday problem solving. *Cortex, 32,* 357–366.

Eslinger, P. J. (1998). Neurological and neuropsychological bases of empathy. *European Neurology, 39,* 193–199.

Farrow, T. F., Zheng, Y., Wilkinson, I. D., Spence, S. A., Deakin, J. F., Tarrier, N., et al. (2001). Investigating the functional anatomy of empathy and forgiveness. *Neuroreport, 12,* 2433–2438.

Fletcher, P. C., Happe, F., Frith, U., Baker, S. C., Dolan, R. J., Frackowiak, R. S. J., et al. (1995). Other minds in the brain: A functional imaging study of "theory of mind" in story comprehension. *Cognition, 57,* 109–128.

Fossati, P., Hevenor, S. J., Graham, S. J., Grady, C., Keightley, M. L., Craik, F., et al. (2003). In search of the emotional self: An fMRI study using positive and negative emotional words. *American Journal of Psychiatry, 160,* 1938–1945.

Gillihan, S. J., & Farah, M. J. (2005). Is self special?: A critical review of evidence from experimental psychology and cognitive neuroscience. *Psychological Bulletin, 131,* 76–97.

Glascher, J., & Adolphs, R. (2003). Processing of the arousal of subliminal and supraliminal emotional stimuli by the human amygdala. *Journal of Neuroscience, 23,* 10274–10282.

Goel, V., Grafman, J., Sadato, N., & Hallet, M. (1995). Modeling other minds. *Neuroreport, 6,* 1741–1746.

Goel, V., Grafman, J., Tajik, J., Gana, S., & Danto, D. (1997). A study of the performance of patients with frontal lobe lesions in a financial planning task. *Brain, 120,* 1805–1822.

Gomez-Beldarrain, M., Harries, C., Garcia-Monco, J. C., Ballus, E., & Grafman, J. (2004). Patients with right frontal lesions are unable to assess and use advice to make predictive judgments. *Journal of Cognitive Neuroscience, 16,* 74–89.

Grafman, J. (1995). Similarities and distinction among current models of prefrontal cortical functions. In J. Grafman, K. J. Holyoak, & F. Boller (Eds.), *Structures and functions of the human prefrontal cortex* (pp. 337–368). New York: New York Academy of Sciences.

Grattan, L. M., Bloomer, R. H., Archambault, F. X., & Eslinger, P. J. (1994). Cognitive flexibility and empathy after frontal lobe lesion. *Neuropsychiatry, Neuropsychology, and Behavioral Neurology, 7,* 251–259.

Grattan, L. M., & Eslinger, P. J. (1992). Long-term psychological consequences of childhood frontal lobe lesion in patient DT. *Brain and Cognition, 20,* 185–195.

Greene, J. D., Sommerville, R. B., Nystrom, L. E., Darley, J. M., & Cohen, J. D. (2001). An fMRI investigation of emotional engagement in moral judgment. *Science, 293,* 2105–2108.

Gur, R. C., Schroeder, L., Turner, T., McGrath, C., Chan, R. M., Turetsky, B. I., et al. (2002). Brain activation during facial emotion processing. *Neuroimage, 16,* 651–662.

Gusnard, D. A., Akbudak, E., Shulman, G. L., & Raichle, M. E. (2001). Medial prefrontal cortex and self-referential mental activity: Relation to a default mode of brain function. *Proceedings of the National Academy of Sciences of the United States of America, 98,* 4259–4264.

Happe, F., Malhi, G. S., & Checkley, S. (2001). Acquired mind-blindness following frontal lobe surgery?: A single case study of impaired "theory of mind" in a patient treated with stereotactic anterior capsulotomy. *Neuropsychologia, 39,* 83–90.

Hornak, J., Rolls, E. T., & Wade, D. (1996). Face and voice expression identification in patients with emotional and behavioural changes following ventral frontal lobe damage. *Neuropsychologia, 34,* 247–261.

Kaczmarek, B. L. J. (1984). Neurolinguistic analysis of verbal utterances in patients with focal lesions of frontal lobes. *Brain and Language, 21,* 52–58.

Keenan, J. P., Wheeler, M. A., Gallup, G. G., & Pasucal-Leone, A. (2000). Self-recognition and the right prefrontal cortex. *Trends in Cognitive Sciences, 4,* 338–344.

Kelley, W. M., Macrae, C. N., Wyland, C. L., Caglar, S., Inati, S., & Heatherton, T. F. (2002). Finding the self?: An event-related fMRI study. *Journal of Cognitive Neuroscience, 14,* 785–794.

Kircher, T. T., Brammer, M., Bullmore, E., Simmons, A., Bartels, M., & David, A. S. (2002). The neural correlates of intentional and incidental self processing. *Neuropsychologia, 40,* 683–692.

Kircher, T. T., Senior, C., Phillips, M. L., Benson, P. J., Bullmore, E. T., Brammer, M., et al. (2000). Towards a functional neuroanatomy of self processing: Effects of faces and words. *Cognitive Brain Research, 10,* 133–144.

LeDoux, J. E. (1993). Emotional networks in the brain. In M. Lewis & J. M. Haviland (Eds.), *Handbook of emotion* (pp. 109–118). New York: Guilford Press.

Lewis, M. (1993). Self-conscious emotions: Embarrassment, pride, shame, and guilt. In M. Lewis & J. M. Haviland (Eds.), *Handbook of emotions* (pp. 353–364). New York: Guilford Press.

Lhermitte, F. (1986). Human autonomy and the frontal lobes: Part II. Patient behavior in complex and social situations: The "environmental dependency syndrome." *Annuals of Neurology, 19,* 335–343.

Lhermitte, F., Pillon, B., & Serdaru, M. (1986). Human anatomy and the frontal lobes: Part I. Imitation and utilization behavior: A neuropsychological study of 75 patients. *Annuals of Neurology, 19,* 326–334.

Luria, A. R., & Homskaya, E. D. (1970). Frontal lobes and the regulation of arousal process. In D. I. Mostofsky (Ed.), *Attention: Contemporary theory and analysis* (pp. 303–330). New York: Appleton-Century-Crofts.

Mah, L., Arnold, M. C., & Grafman, J. (2004). Impairment of social perception associated with lesions of the prefrontal cortex. *American Journal of Psychiatry, 161,* 1247–1255.

Mason, M. F., Banfield, J. F., & Macrae, C. N. (2004). Thinking about actions: The neural substrates of person knowledge. *Cerebral Cortex, 14,* 209–214.

Milne, E., & Grafman, J. (2001). Ventromedial prefrontal cortex lesions in humans eliminate implicit gender stereotypes. *Journal of Neuroscience, 21,* 1–6.

Mitchell, J. P., Heatherton, T. F., & Macrae, C. N. (2002). Distinct neural systems subserve person and object knowledge. *Proceedings of the National Academy of Sciences of the United States of America, 99,* 15238–15243.

Mitchell, J. P., Macrae, C. N., & Banaji, M. R. (2004). Encoding-specific effects of social cognition on the neural correlates of subsequent memory. *Journal of Neuroscience, 24,* 4912–4917.

Moll, J., de Oliveira-Souza, R., Bramati, I. E., & Grafman, J. (2002). Functional networks in emotional moral and nonmoral social judgments. *Neuroimage, 16,* 696–703.

Moll, J., de Oliveira-Souza, R., Moll, F. T., Ignacio, F. A., Bramati, I. E., Caparelli-Daquer, E. M., et al. (2005). The moral affiliations of disgust: A functional MRI study. *Cognitive and Behavioral Neurology, 18,* 68–78.

Morris, J. S., Friston, K. J., Buchel, C., Frith, C. D., Young, A. W., Calder, A. J., et al. (1998). A neuromodulatory role for the human amygdala in processing emotional facial expressions. *Brain, 121,* 47–57.

Ochsner, K. N., Beer, J. S., Robertson, E. A., Cooper, J., Gabrieli, J. D. E., Kihlstrom, J. F., et al. (2005). The neural correlates of direct and reflected self-knowledge. *Neuroimage, 28,* 797–814.

Phillips, M. L., Young, A. W., Senior, C., Brammer, M., Andrew, C., Calder, A. J., et al. (1997). A specific neural substrate for perceiving facial expressions of disgust. *Nature, 389,* 495–498.

Price, B. H., Daffner, K. R., Stowe, R. M., & Marsel-Mesulam, M. (1990). The comportmental learning disabilities of early frontal lobe damage. *Brain, 113,* 1383–1393.

Rahman, S., Sahakian, B. J., Cardinal, R. N., Rogers, R. D., & Robbins, T. W. (2001). Decision making and neuropsychiatry. *Trends in Cognitive Sciences, 5,* 271–277.

Rilling, J. K., Sanfey, A. G., Aronson, J. A., Nystrom, L. E., & Cohen, J. D. (2004). The neural correlates of theory of mind within interpersonal interactions. *Neuroimage, 22,* 1694–1703.

Ruby, P., & Decety, J. (2004). How would you feel versus how do you think she would feel?: A neuroimaging study of perspective-taking with social emotions. *Journal of Cognitive Neuroscience, 16,* 988–999.

Sanfey, A. G., Hastie, R., Colvin, M. K., & Grafman, J. (2003). Phineas gauged: Decision-making and the human prefrontal cortex. *Neuropsychologia, 41,* 1218–1229.

Sato, W., Kochiyama, T., Yoshikawa, S., Naito, E., & Matsumura, M. (2004). Enhanced neural activity in response to dynamic facial expressions of emotion: An fMRI study. *Cognitive Brain Research, 20,* 81–91.

Saver, J. L., & Damasio, A. R. (1991). Preserved access and processing of social knowledge in a patient with acquired sociopathy due to ventromedial frontal damage. *Neuropsychologia, 29,* 1241–1249.

Saxe, R., Carey, S., & Kanwisher, N. (2004). Understanding other minds: Linking developmental psychology and functional neuroimaging. *Annul Reviews of Psychology, 55,* 87–124.

Scott, S. K., Young, A. W., Calder, A. J., Hellawell, D. J., Aggleton, J. P., & Johnson, M. (1997). Impaired auditory recognition of fear and anger following bilateral amygdala lesions. *Nature, 385,* 254–257.

Shamay-Tsoory, S. G., Tomer, R., Berger, B. D., & Aharon-Peretz, J. (2003). Characterization of empathy deficits following prefrontal brain damage: The role of the right ventromedial prefrontal cortex. *Journal of Cognitive Neuroscience, 15,* 324–337.

Shaw, P., Lawrence, E. J., Radbourne, C., Bramham, J., Polkey, C. E., & David, A. S. (2004). The impact of early and late damage to the human amygdala on "theory of mind" reasoning. *Brain, 127,* 1535–1548.

Shin, L. M., Dougherty, D. D., Orr, S. P., Pitman, R. K., Lasko, M., Macklin, M. L., et al. (2000). Activation of anterior paralimbic structures during guilt-related script-driven imagery. *Biological Psychiatry, 48,* 43–50.

Shiv, B., Loewenstein, G., & Bechara, A. (2005). The dark side of emotion in decision-making: When individuals with decreased emotional reactions make more advantageous decisions. *Cognitive Brain Research, 23,* 85–92.

Sprengelmeyer, R., Young, A. W., Schroeder, U., Grossenbacher, P. G., Federlein, J., Buttner, T., et al. (1999). Knowing no fear. *Proceedings of the Royal Society of London: Series B. Biological Sciences, 266,* 2451–2456.

Stone, V. E., Baron-Cohen, S., Calder, A., Keane, J., & Young, A. (2003). Acquired theory of mind impairments in individuals with bilateral amygdala lesions. *Neuropsychologia, 41,* 209–220.

Stone, V. E., Baron-Cohen, S., & Knight, R. T. (1998). Frontal lobe contributions to theory of mind. *Journal of Cognitive Neuroscience, 10,* 640–656.

Stuss, D. T., & Benson, D. F. (1984). Neuropsychological studies of the frontal lobes. *Psychological Bulletin, 1,* 3–28.

Stuss, D. T., Gallup, G. G., & Alexander, M. P. (2001). The frontal lobes are necessary for "theory of mind." *Brain, 124,* 279–286.

Symons, C. S., & Johnson, B. T. (1997). The self-reference effect in memory: A meta-analysis. *Psychological Bulletin, 121,* 371–394.

Takahashi, H., Yahata, N., Koeda, M., Matsuda, T., Asai, K., & Okubo, Y. (2004). Brain activation associated with evaluative processes of guilt and embarrassment: An fMRI study. *Neuroimage, 23,* 967–974.

Tangney, J. P., & Fischer, K. W. (Eds.). (1995). *Self-conscious emotions: The psychology of shame, guilt, embarrassment, and pride.* New York: Guilford Press.

Tooby, J., & Cosmides, L. (1990). The past explains the present: Emotional adaptations and the structure of ancestral environments. *Ethology and Sociobiology, 11,* 375–424.

Tucker, D. M., Luu, P., & Pribram, K. H. (1995). Social and emotional self-regulation. *Annals of the New York Academy of Sciences, 769,* 213–239.

Winston, J. S., Strange, B. A., O'Doherty, J., & Dolan, R. J. (2002). Automatic and intentional brain responses during evaluation of trustworthiness of faces. *Nature Neuroscience, 5,* 192–193.

Wood, J. N. (2003). Social cognition and the prefrontal cortex. *Behavioral and Cognitive Neuroscience Reviews, 2,* 97–114.

Wood, J. N., Romero, S. G., Makale, M., & Grafman, J. (2003). Category-specific representations of social and nonsocial knowledge in the human prefrontal cortex. *Journal of Cognitive Neuroscience, 15,* 236–248.

Young, A. W., Aggleton, J. P., Hellawell, D. J., Johnson, M., Broks, P., & Hanley, J. R. (1995). Face processing impairments after amygdalotomy. *Brain, 118,* 15–24.

Young, A. W., Hellawell, D. J., Van De Wal, C., & Johnson, M. (1996). Facial expression processing after amygdalotomy. *Neuropsychologia, 34,* 31–39.

5

A Social Function
for Self-Conscious Emotions

The Social Self Preservation Theory

TARA L. GRUENEWALD
SALLY S. DICKERSON
MARGARET E. KEMENY

Most theoretical perspectives concerning emotion experience assert that emotions evolved to serve specific adaptive functions (e.g., Ekman, 1992; Frijda, 1986; Johnson-Laird & Oatley, 1992; Levenson, 1994; Oatley & Jenkins, 1992; Tooby & Cosmides, 1990; see Keltner & Gross, 1999). Many theories regarding the elicitors and functions of self-conscious emotions also assert specific functions for these emotions, but theoretical perspectives vary as to whether such functions are basic to human life (e.g., Gilbert, 1997; Scheff, 1988; Tracy & Robins, 2004a). Our social self preservation theory (Dickerson, Gruenewald, & Kemeny, 2004; Kemeny, Gruenewald, & Dickerson, 2004) asserts that self-conscious emotions, in particular, shame-related emotions, are experienced when the fundamental goal of maintaining a positive *social self* is threatened. We argue that situations or circumstances that threaten the social self prompt a coordinated psychobiological response, characterized by the elicitation of shame emotions and physiological processes, which provide signaling and resource mobilization functions to address such threats. As we also argue, since the protection of the social self is essential to life success, shame may be one of the most basic of human emotions.

A SOCIAL FUNCTION FOR SHAME

Although for any given individual shame emotions consist primarily of private, individual experiences, we contend that the elicitation of these emotions occurs in service of an important social function: of signaling a *threat to the social self*. Threat to the social self occurs when there is an actual or likely loss of social esteem, status, or acceptance. Such a devaluation of the social self can often occur in situations in which one's competencies, abilities, or characteristics upon which a positive social image is based are called into question, or situations of potential or explicit exclusion, scorn, or rejection. We assert that shame is the focal emotion experienced under conditions of threat to the social self.

We contend that humans are concerned with the positive or negative character of the social self because it is central for maintaining social relationships essential to survival and reproduction. The positivity of the social self affects the willingness of others to invest in and provide resources to a given individual, which has implications for survival across the lifespan. The positive character of the social self may be especially important for reproductive success: those with higher status have greater access to mating partners and are better able to pass on their genes. A more positive social self may also enable the development of more harmonious and supportive social relationships. A large body of research supports connections between mental and physical well-being and the quantity and quality of individuals' social ties (see Seeman, 2000). Thus, protecting and enhancing the social self enables an individual to survive and to thrive. At the same time, successful communication of an inferior social self within interpersonal interactions may also be essential to survival. This is especially true in circumstances in which acknowledging one's subordinate social status would lead to a deescalation of a conflict and reduced likelihood of being aggressed against by dominant others.

The reproductive and survival advantages associated with protecting the social self may have led to the conservation of this motivation throughout humans' evolutionary history. Shame-related emotions may be experienced when this fundamental goal is threatened and may regulate biobehavioral responses to social-self threat. A common argument for the existence of human emotions is that many emotions serve to regulate biology and behavior designed to address environmental threats to survival and reproduction (Darwin, 1872/1965; Ekman, 1992; see Keltner & Gross, 1999, for an overview). As discussed below, shame appears to be a common emotional response to threat to the social self, the activation of specific physiological systems often accompanies shame responses to social-self threat, and these psychobiological responses are associated with specific behavioral reactions (e.g., appeasement, submission) to such threats.

Our contention that shame serves as an important signaling emotion for threats to the social self is in agreement with a number of theoretical perspectives on the functions or elicitors of shame. Scheff (2003) has argued that shame is the "premier social emotion" and that the experience of shame-related emotions occurs in response to situations or circumstances that pose a threat to a social bond. This proposed function of shame is similar to our assertion that shame acts as a signal of threat to the social self. Our perspective is also in direct accord with the function of shame proposed by Gilbert (1997). According to his social attention holding power (SAHP) hypothesis, shame is the primary emotional response to perceptions of low social attention, low social attractiveness, or declining social status (characteristics of a devalued social self). Leary and associates (Leary, Tambor, Terdal, & Downs, 1995) ascribe a similar role for self-feelings in their sociometer hypothesis, which asserts that self-related emotions and cognitions act as signals of individuals' inclusionary status; however, shame is only one of many emotions and cognitions highlighted in this signaling process.

Phenomenological studies of shame experiences also indicate that this emotion may be a signal of a threatened social self. Individuals have reported that they felt *small and* *inferi*or to others, a sense of *social isolation,* and a *desire to hide* from others in conjunction with shame experiences (e.g., Tangney, Miller, Flicker, & Barlow, 1996; Wicker, Payne, & Morgan, 1983). These feelings highlight perceptions of a damaged or less worthy social self associated with the experience of shame. Kelter and Buswell (1996) found that common antecedents of shame experience were poor performance, hurting others emotionally, failing to meet others' expectations, role-inappropriate behavior, and disappointment in oneself. The majority of these commonly cited antecedents of shame experience share the feature of the self suffering an impaired social status or image.

The centrality of the social self in shame experience also has a long theoretical tradition. Darwin (1872/1965) noted that emotions that excite a blush (shame, shyness, and modesty) were the result of "thinking [about] what others think of us" (p. 324). Cooley (1902/1983) seconded this sentiment:

> There is no sense of "I," as in pride or shame, without its correlative sense of you, or he, or they. . . . The thing that moves us to pride or shame is not the mere mechanical reflection of ourselves, but an imputed sentiment, the imagined effect of this reflection upon another's mind (pp. 182, 184).

Early psychological theorists, such as William James (1890/1955), also identified shame as the result of perceptions of an impaired image in the eyes of others. H. B. Lewis (1971) cited an actual or invoked disapproving other as an important elicitor of shame, and Izard (1977) asserted that shame promotes social cohesion by sensitizing individuals to the opinions of others.

Shame Experience in Response to Threat to the Social Self: Experimental Evidence

Shame experience may be especially sensitive—that is, more so than the experience of other emotions—to the social context of challenging situations, especially situational factors that may increase threat to the social self. In an effort to explore shame experience under conditions of threat to the social self, we have conducted a series of investigations in which aspects of the social environment were manipulated during participants' performance of challenging oral and cognitive activities in the laboratory. Our manipulations typically involve the performance of activities by experimental participants under conditions of critical social evaluation or its absence. Critical social evaluation during display of challenging performance activities is assumed to serve as a potent threat to the social self, as such situations raise concerns about one's social esteem and status. In one investigation (Gruenewald, Kemeny, Aziz, & Fahey, 2004), participants were asked to deliver a speech and participate in a difficult mental arithmetic task either in the presence of a panel of critical evaluators or while alone. Constraints placed on task preparation and performance (e.g., short preparation period, difficulty level of the tasks) made poor performance likely. The performance of these challenging tasks led to an increase in a number of negative emotions and a decrease in positive emotions in both the evaluative and the nonevaluative conditions. However, increases in shame-related emotions were more pronounced in the evaluative condition, indicating that shame experience was more sensitive to social aspects of performance than other emotions (e.g., anxiety-, anger-, or depression-related emotions). Thus, while most negative emotions increased as a result of having to perform difficult and challenging laboratory tasks, only shame increased to a greater degree when performing these tasks under social evaluation. This may be due to threat to the social self that accompanied the experience of critical and unfriendly social evaluation during task performance.

This finding was recently replicated in another laboratory investigation of women employing a similar task performance protocol under conditions of critical social evaluation or its absence (Dickerson, Gable, Kemeny, Aziz, & Irwin, 2005). Compared to other categories of negative emotion experience (e.g., anxiety-related emotions), shame emotions increased to a greater degree in the social evaluation condition. In ongoing research, the experience of shame and other emotions is being investigated in similar laboratory protocols in which positive evaluation and neutral (e.g., mere presence) social conditions are added. This research will allow us to further pinpoint whether shame experience is especially sensitive to social factors that may threaten the social self, such as negative social evaluation, as compared to more neutral or positive social conditions

Other Self-Conscious Emotions: Guilt, Embarrassment, and Pride

Our assertion that threat to the social self elicits the experience of shame naturally begs the question of whether such threats also elicit other negative self-conscious emotions, such as guilt and embarrassment, as well as whether pride is an important component of a system designed to enhance and protect the social self. Although guilt is a social emotion, the elicitation of guilt is thought to arise in response to an *undesirable behavior or action* committed by an individual rather than to arise in response to an *undesirable self*, as in the case of shame (H. B. Lewis, 1971; see Tangney et al., 1996). As previously reviewed, shame appears to be the likely emotional response to situations that threaten social relationships or one's social image (e.g., social role violations, failing to meet the expectation of others, hurting others emotionally), while guilt is the more probable emotional response to behavioral violations of social standards (e.g., lying, cheating, neglecting a responsibility; see Keltner & Buswell, 1996). Individuals report thoughts of undoing aspects of their behavior in thinking of how a guilt experience might have turned out differently, but they more commonly report thoughts of undoing aspects of the self for altering the outcome of a shame experience (Niedenthal, Tangney, & Gavanski, 1994). Compared to shame, guilt is thought to be characterized by a more active and less helpless self and a desire to commit reparative actions. Guilt is also considered to be a less intense and dysphoric emotion than shame (Tangney et al., 1996).

Embarrassment has often been characterized as a mild form of shame (Izard, 1977; Kaufman, 1989; Kroll & Egan, 2004; Scheff, 2003). Some theorists have put embarrassment on the weak and transient end of a shame spectrum with humiliation at the intense and long-lasting other end (with shame falling in between the two extremes; e.g., see Kroll & Egan, 2004; Scheff, 2003). The elicitors of shame and embarrassment are also thought to vary, with embarrassment resulting from trivial social transgressions (e.g., tripping, belching) and shame resulting from more serious transgressions or failures (Tangney et al., 1996; Miller & Tangney, 1994). In comparison with embarrassment, shame is also thought to be the more probable emotion when such events involve the *core self*, while embarrassment is more likely to occur under public exposure of a flaw that the actor does not feel truly represents a core characteristic of the self (Miller & Tangney, 1994; Sabini, Garvey, & Hall, 2001). Tangney and associates (1996) found that embarrassment experiences differed from shame experiences on 22 of 31 phenomenological ratings (e.g., less motivated to hide, perceived others' evaluations as less negative), and found that embarrassment was even more distinct from shame than guilt, which challenges the characterization of embarrassment as a weak form of shame. However, our experimental protocols, which manipulate social-evaluative threat or its absence, typically find that embarrassment experience clusters together with the experience of other shame emotions (feeling ashamed, feeling humiliated). Perhaps a threshold effect may sometimes operate with events that elicit strong shame emotions (shame and humiliation) also eliciting feelings of embarrassment, but the opposite being less likely with more mild events that can elicit embarrassment not eliciting feelings of shame. Two forms of embarrassment have also been suggested, one occurring in response to nonevaluative social attention and another occurring in situations where an actor is the possible target of negative social evaluation (e.g., following failure on laboratory tasks; Lewis & Ramsay, 2002). More empirical research will be needed to differentiate whether embarrassment can be characterized as part of a shame family of emotions or whether there are multiple forms of embarrassment (e.g., social exposure vs. social evaluative).

Pride is perhaps one of the least studied of the self-conscious emotions—a neglect that may be the result of a focus on negative emotions contributing to psychopathology and less historical interest in emotions that might promote positive mental well-being. Thus far, our experimental manipulations of negative social evaluation or its absence have not shown that pride experience is sensitive to the social context of task performance; pride has been found to decrease as a result of challenge performance in both evaluative and nonevaluative conditions. However, cues of *positive* social evaluation may be necessary to elicit pride experience. This is consistent with theoretical positions that characterize pride as the opposite side of shame, occurring in response to positive evaluations of the social self (e.g., Cooley, 1902/1983; Darwin, 1872/1965; James, 1890/1955; Scheff, 1988). Future theoretical and empirical attention needs to be paid to the elicitors of pride and the role of this emotion in protecting and enhancing the social self.

Is Shame a Basic Emotion?

Shame and other self-conscious emotions have often been characterized as complex emotions that occur only in humans, and that are distinct from more basic emotions, such as fear and anger. Whether shame can be considered a basic emotion depends in part on the defining set of characteristics of basic emotions employed in making this distinction, a topic that continues to be debated among emotion researchers. Ekman (1992) proposed a number of characteristics that might be used to separate basic from more complex emotions, including distinctive universal signals (e.g., a universal facial expression), distinctive universals in antecedent events, a distinctive physiology, and presence in other primates. Other defining characteristics cited by Ekman include quick onset and brief duration of emotion experience, an automatic appraisal, coherence among emotion expression and associated physiology, and involuntary experience.

Shame is not commonly featured in most theorists' lists of basic emotions (e.g., Ekman, 1992; Frijda, 1986; Plutchik, 1980), although Tomkins (1962, 1963) included it in his list of innate, hardwired emotions and Ekman has acknowledged that shame is a basic emotion candidate. One reason shame has not been identified as a basic emotion may be due to the relative neglect of this emotion in empirical and theoretical research compared to other emotions (Tracy & Robins, 2004a). A second factor inhibiting the accumulation of reliable data on which to judge shame as a basic emotion includes individuals' unwillingness to discuss shame experiences or inability to correctly identify and/or label shame-related emotions. Shame has been argued to be a taboo topic, especially in North American and other Westernized cultures (Kaufman, 1989; Scheff, 2003). Perhaps the most obvious reason that shame has not been identified as a basic emotion is the reliance on universal facial expressions as a defining characteristic in basic emotion research. Although Ekman (1992) and others have acknowledged that universal expressions can include distinctive vocalizations or bodily movements, most basic emotions have been identified on the basis of cross-cultural consistency in the expression and recognition of facial emotion signals. While shame may not have a universal distinct facial expression, it is characterized by a unique bodily display including gaze aversion, head tilted to the side or downward, and a slumped posture (Gilbert, 1997; Keltner & Buswell, 1996; Keltner, Young, & Buswell, 1997). Recent research also documents a distinctive facial and bodily signal for pride, including the head tilted slightly up with a small smile, a visibly expanded posture, and arms raised above the head or hands on hips (Tracy & Robins, 2004b). The bodily characteristics of shame and pride are similar to many behaviors that denote submission and dominance, respectively, in other animals (see Gilbert, 1997; Keltner & Buswell, 1997; Keltner et al., 1997). Thus, there is some evidence that these emotions may also fulfill the basic emotion characteristic of display in other primates, albeit the experience of shame and pride would be of more rudimentary form in other animals.

More research in which shame experiences are experimentally induced will be needed to determine whether shame fulfills other suggested criteria of a basic emotion including quick onset and brief duration, automatic appraisal, coherence among expression and physiology, and involuntary experience. If threat to the social self elicits a shame response, it would be expected that this emotional reaction should occur automatically and involuntarily in support of physiological and behavioral responses designed to address the threat. Although shame experience likely has a quick onset and a short duration, it would be expected that shame experience might be prolonged by cognitive processes (e.g., rumination or worry about the status of the social self) or constant threat. However, the same can be said of other emotions generally agreed upon to be basic emotions, such as fear and anger.

The hypothesis that basic emotions should be characterized by universal antecedents derives from the idea that basic emotions evolved to address fundamental life tasks. For example, fear is considered to be a basic emotion that serves to signal a threat to physical self-preservation and to coordinate responses to deal with such a threat. Likewise, we assert that shame may be a basic emotion designed to provide signaling and response functions for a threat to preservation of the social self. Cross-cultural research supports the hypothesis that shame experience is associated with threats to the social self (e.g., communication of inferior social status [Fessler, 1999], concerns over saving face [Ho, Fu, & Ng, 2004]. Rudimentary forms of shame, such as the submission and appeasement behaviors of nonhuman social animals, also serve as evidence of the adaptive function of shame across the phylogenetic hierarchy. Submission and appeasement behaviors in social animals are central to the communication of social status position, a function that serves reproductive and survival needs (MacLean, 1990).

Whether shame is characterized by a distinct physiology remains to be determined empirically. However, as we detail below, we believe that threats to the social self elicit specific patterns of neuroendocrine and immune response and that shame may be associated with this pattern of physiological activity. As we discuss, these physiological patterns are also witnessed under conditions of social threat and are associated with dominance/

submission behavior in nonhuman animals, further supporting the hypothesis that shame and its accompanying physiology is evident across human and nonhuman animals.

Taken together, these characteristics of shame elicitors, expression, and experience indicate that shame fulfills many of the criteria considered necessary to be classified as a basic emotion. However, as we have suggested (Kemeny et al., 2004), it may be more appropriate to classify emotions on a continuum from basic to more complex (e.g., so-called secondary or higher-order emotions), rather than making either-or categorizations. Such rigid distinctions may distract attention from more careful study of the elicitors, experience, and function of specific emotions, especially those characteristics that fall outside the boundaries of basic or complex emotion attributes.

PHYSIOLOGICAL RESPONSES TO THREAT TO THE SOCIAL SELF

We propose that events that threaten the social self elicit activation of the hypothalamic–pituitary–adrenal (HPA) and proinflammatory immune systems, leading to the release of the HPA hormone cortisol and inflammatory cytokines. As we review below, there is empirical evidence of activation of these systems in response to social threat in both humans and other animals, and associations between biomarkers of these systems and shame experience. Although we believe these are key physiological systems activated under conditions of threat to the social self, there may be other important patterns of physiological activity associated with social-self threat, including changes in autonomic nervous system activity and changes in other neurotransmitters systems, such as the serotenergic system.

The HPA System

The HPA system is a physiological axis in the body that regulates metabolism and energy production. This system consists of hormonal pathways in the body that include an activation point in the hypothalamus of the brain that leads to the release of corticotropin-releasing hormone (CRH), which travels through a specialized vascular system to the pituitary in the brain, causing the release of adrenocorticotropic hormone (ACTH), which is subsequently released into the general circulation of the body. ACTH can travel to the adrenal glands, which are located above the kidneys, and cause the release of corticosteroids (e.g., the hormone cortisol in humans and other primates, the hormone corticosterone in rodents) into the bloodstream. Cortisol can then travel to numerous sites in the body and exert a number of effects on various physiological systems (e.g., the immune, reproductive, and metabolic systems).

Classic stress theorists, such as Hans Selye (1950), also identified the HPA system as an important stress regulatory system. In terms of stress regulation, one of cortisol's most important functions is that it stimulates gluconeogenesis in the liver, leading to the release of glucose into the bloodstream. This release of glucose into the general circulation is argued to aid in the preparation of physiological systems in the body to combat the stressor, as glucose is the primary metabolic fuel of the body's cells.

The levels and activity of HPA hormones (e.g., CRH, ACTH, and cortisol) have been shown to be sensitive to both chronic stressors (e.g., major life events, bereavement, caretaking) and acute stressors (e.g., short-term naturalistic and laboratory stressors), with elevations in HPA hormones being characteristic in response to both types of stress experience (e.g., Bauer et al., 2000; Dickerson & Kemeny, 2004; Kirschbaum &

Hellhammer, 1989). However, these increases are not uniformly witnessed in all individuals, and the nature of change (i.e., increases, decreases, or no change) is moderated by the characteristics of stressful events (Kirschbaum & Hellhammer, 1989), and by the characteristics of individuals undergoing stressor experience (e.g., Pruessner, Hellhammer, & Kirschbaum, 1999). Accumulating evidence also suggests that threat to the social self may be an important determinant of HPA reactivity to environmental events.

HPA stress reactivity is often examined in experimental investigations in which stressor exposure is manipulated in the laboratory. In a review of 208 laboratory investigations examining cortisol responses to acute stressors, Dickerson and Kemeny (2004) found that cortisol increases were more likely to occur in stressor paradigms that included aspects of social-evaluative threat. Common elements of social-evaluative threat in laboratory stressor protocols included tasks in which an individual's abilities and competencies were on public display or in which a participant received feedback that he or she performed more poorly on laboratory tasks relative to another—characteristics of situations that are likely to threaten the social self. The effect size for cortisol increase in paradigms that included aspects of social-evaluative threat was much greater than in protocols in which social-evaluative threat was absent (effect sizes $d = .67$ and $d = .21$, respectively). Thus, cortisol increases were much more likely to occur in situations with the potential to threaten the social self than in similar stressor protocols where these situational characteristics were absent or minimized. When laboratory stressor tasks included both elements of social-evaluative threat and uncontrollability over task performance, cortisol increases were even larger ($d = .92$). Such situations create the likelihood of poor performance in a highly evaluative context, producing a potent source of threat to one's social self.

The meta-analytic findings provide strong support for the hypothesis that aspects of events that might act to threaten the social self are powerful elicitors of HPA activity. We have also sought to experimentally manipulate the presence or absence of social-evaluative threat in laboratory protocols to better pinpoint effects on HPA reactivity, and to examine shame-related and other emotional responses to social-self threat. As previously reviewed, we found that increases in shame experience were much more likely when challenging oral and cognitive activities were performed in the presence of critical social evaluation than when such evaluation was absent (Gruenewald et al., 2004). In this same investigation, we found large and robust increases in cortisol in the social evaluation condition but an insignificant response in the nonevaluative condition. Participants in both conditions rated the tasks to be equally difficult, suggesting that the significant cortisol increases in the social evaluation condition were not simply the result of participants interpreting task performance as more "stressful" than those in the nonevaluative condition. In addition, among those in the social evaluation condition, we found that cortisol increases were greater in those who showed the largest increases in shame. There was no association between cortisol increases and the magnitude of increase in other classes of emotion, such as anxiety-related emotions.

A concordance between stress-induced increases in shame and cortisol was found in another laboratory investigation. Lewis and Ramsay (2002) exposed children to laboratory tasks in which they were given success and failure feedback on color-matching tasks, and they also exposed the children to a number of nonevaluative public exposure situations (e.g., being complimented, being pointed at and called by name). The investigators coded children's display of shame, embarrassment, and pride during the tasks and also examined changes in cortisol levels from pre- to posttask. The authors found that cortisol increases were correlated with the display of shame and evaluative embarrassment behaviors during task performance.

Levels and activity of HPA hormones are also associated with dominance and submission behavior in nonhuman animals, including species of rats, mice, monkeys, baboons, tree shrews, and fish. Subordinate animals have been shown to have higher levels of basal corticosteroids than their dominant peers (Fox, White, Kao, & Fernald, 1997; Holst, 1997; Sapolsky, 1993; Shively, Laber-Laird, & Anton, 1997). Corticosteroid and ACTH levels also increase in "losers" following social dominance contests but not in "winners" in rodents and hamsters (e.g., Kollack-Walker, Watson, & Akil, 1997; Skutella et al., 1994). The display of submissive postures during such contests is associated with an increase in corticosterone levels following the interaction in rats, while receiving submissive signals from subordinate animals helps to attenuate corticosteroid responses in "winners" (Haller, Kiem, & Makara, 1996). Similar associations between submissive behavior display and corticosteroid levels have been found in other rodent species (see Holst, 1997) and in primates (Shively et al., 1997). Submissive behaviors in nonhuman animals are often considered to represent a primitive analogue of submission and shame behaviors in humans (Gilbert & McGuire, 1998; Keltner et al., 1997). Thus there is evidence for a connection between shame displays and HPA hormone activity in both humans and other animals.

Although preliminary, these investigations in humans and other animals indicate that the level and activity of HPA hormones are responsive to events that threaten the social self (e.g., critical social evaluation in laboratory studies in humans, the outcomes of social dominance contests in animals). Within the context of such threatening events, cortisol activity is correlated with shame experience and shame and submission displays. This concordance suggests that shame and associated submission action tendencies and the HPA system may be important components of a psychobiological system initiated in response to threat to the social self. Further research will be needed to clearly identify the motivational and behavioral response functions served by shame and HPA activation under conditions of threat to the social self, but research in nonhuman animals clearly points to submission and appeasement functions as important possibilities.

Proinflammatory Immune Activity

Another physiological system that may be activated under conditions of threat to the social self is proinflammatory immune activity. Inflammation is a basic immune process that is initiated in response to the recognition of a foreign substance in the body or bodily injury leading to destruction of foreign substances, disposal of damaged tissue, and wound healing. Proinflammatory cytokines (e.g., interleukin-1 [IL-1], interleukin-6 [IL-6], tumor necrosis factor alpha [TNF-α]) are chemical messengers that orchestrate the initiation and regulation of inflammatory processes. Inflammation typically involves a local inflammatory response designed to attract immune cells to the area of damage or foreign exposure, as well as a systemic acute-phase response that includes induction of fever (to inhibit pathogen growth), increased production of white blood cells (to help fight infection), the production of acute-phase proteins in the liver (e.g., C-reactive protein) that aid in immune activities that destroy foreign substances, and activation of the HPA axis. Activation of the HPA axis by proinflammatory cytokines may occur to regulate the inflammatory response, as HPA hormones have been shown to suppress a number of inflammatory activities.

Similar to HPA activity, proinflammatory immune activity is enhanced in socially subordinate animals. Subordinate rodents show increased numbers of granulocyte cells (which may reflect a shift toward inflammatory immune states) following defeat in dominance contests and under situations of chronic social subordination (e.g., Stefanski, 1998; Stefanski & Engler, 1998; Stefanski, Knopf, & Schulz, 2001). Subordinate rodents have also been shown to produce higher levels of the proinflammatory cytokines IL-1B and TNF-α in response to injection of a bacterial mitogen and to produce higher levels of nerve growth factor (NGF), an immune factor involved in inflammation and wound healing, following social dominance contests (Avitsur, Stark, & Sheridan, 2001; Quan et al., 2001; Sheridan, Stark, Avitsur, & Padgett, 2000). An increase in inflammatory immune activity in subordinate animals following social conflicts may seem odd in consideration of the fact that many other components of immune activity are suppressed in socially subordinate animals (e.g., lymphocyte activity [Holst, 1997; Stefanski, 1998; Stefanski & Engler, 1998], tumor resistance [Stefanski & Ben-Eliyahu, 1996]). However, it has been hypothesized that enhanced inflammatory activity might be adaptive for subordinate or "loser" animals that are more likely to be wounded during social confrontations (e.g., see Avitsur et al., 2001; Stefanski & Engler, 1998). Thus, status loss may initiate proinflammatory activity as an adaptive response to help the losing animal physiologically prepare for potential injury.

Proinflammatory cytokines have also been shown to increase in response to performance of stressful activities in the laboratory in humans (e.g., Ackerman, Martino, Heyman, Moyna, & Rabin, 1998; Altemus, Rao, Dhabhar, Din, & Granstein, 2001); however, increases are not uniformly found in all acute stress investigations (e.g., Dugue, Leppanen, Teppo, Fyhrquist, & Grasbeck, 1993; Zakowski, McAllister, Deal, & Baum, 1992). The nature of stressor tasks may be an important determinant of proinflammatory stress responses. A meta-analytic review of the small number of available experimental studies indicates that those with protocols that included elements of social-evaluative threat had higher average increases in proinflammatory cytokines than those with paradigms in which social evaluation was absent or minimized (Dickerson, 2004). Results of a recent investigation in which exposure to social-evaluative threat was experimentally manipulated validates these meta-analytic findings. An investigation by Dickerson and associates (2005) demonstrated increases in mitogen-induced proinflammatory cytokine TNF-α in response to performance of challenging oral and cognitive activities in the laboratory in the presence of unfriendly social evaluation but not when social evaluation was absent. Thus, situational characteristics that may signal threat to the social self may be important elicitors of proinflammatory immune activity under challenge conditions.

We have also found links between proinflammatory cytokines and shame experience. Dickerson and colleagues (Dickerson, Kemeny, Aziz, Kim, & Fahey, 2004) conducted an experiment in which participants were randomly assigned to write either about a personal experience in which they blamed themselves or a neutral topic on three separate occasions over 1 week. Common self-blame events included experiences of rejection and failing to live up to parental expectations, situations that can serve as potent threats to the social self. Individuals in the self-blame condition showed greater increases in shame and guilt than in other negative emotions on each writing day. Self-blame participants also showed increases in a proinflammatory cytokine immune marker (the receptor for TNF-α) from pre- to postwriting each day; such an increase was not observed in those who wrote about a neutral topic. Increases in this proinflammatory immune marker were greater in those who showed larger increases in shame emotions; however, the magnitude of this immune response was not correlated with increases in other negative emotions. These results suggest that there may be a special interconnection among shame emotions and proinflammatory cytokine activity that occurs in response to events with the potential to threaten the social self.

Inflammatory cytokines are also associated with affective and motivational states that may be adaptive under conditions of social threat in humans and other animals. Proinflammatory cytokines underlie the induction of "sickness behavior," which includes reductions in eating, grooming, social exploration and interaction, aggressive displays, sexual behavior, and pleasure felt in response to social and physical stimuli (see Maier & Watkins, 1998, and Yirmiya, 1996, for overviews). During illness, these cytokines are produced to orchestrate immune responses to fight infection; however, animal studies also indicate that they act on the brain to induce the behavioral changes reviewed above. Sickness behavior is thought to represent an adaptive complex of cognitive, affective, and behavioral changes that motivate organisms to withdraw from the social environment and devote metabolic resources to fighting infection and healing. Social disengagement of this type may also be adaptive under conditions of social dominance threat to decrease the likelihood of attack from more dominant animals (i.e., subordinates may produce more proinflammatory cytokines to support withdrawal, submission, and appeasement behavior that may reduce the likelihoood of further attack). This reasoning provides an additional explanation for increased proinflammatory immune activity in animals that lose dominance contests. The release of these molecules in response to social-self threat and in conjunction with the experience of shame in humans, as reviewed above, may also support similar disengagement and appeasement functions that are adaptive in such contexts.

Taken together, this research provides evidence of activation of proinflammatory cytokine activity under conditions of social threat in humans and other animals. There may be an important link between increased shame and proinflammatory activity witnessed under conditions of threat to the social self, and proinflammatory cytokines may also help orchestrate affective and behavioral changes that encourage appeasement and submission behavior during, as well as disengagement from, threatening situations. While the responses of the HPA and inflammatory immune systems we have reviewed may be adaptive in the short term to situations that threaten the social self, chronic exposure to such threats and accompanying affective and physiological changes may have negative consequences for mental and physical health.

MENTAL AND PHYSICAL HEALTH CONSEQUENCES
OF THREAT TO THE SOCIAL SELF

Potential sources of threat to the social self (e.g., negative social evaluation, interpersonal rejection) are common in daily life, but most individuals probably infrequently experience events that act as significant threats to the social self. This may not be true for all individuals, however. Social and personal characteristics, including the possession of a stigmatizing condition (e.g., physical deformity, stigmatized illness) or an undesirable social status position, may operate to increase the frequency of social-self threat experiences for some individuals. In addition, some individuals may possess personality traits that render them more sensitive to perceive threat to the social self in communications with others or in response to life events, and/or to experience more extreme psychological and physiological reactions to social-self threats.

Chronic or Repeated Threat to the Social Self

Occupation of a low social status position can be seen as one form of chronic threat to the social self because humans and other animals in subordinate status positions must continuously acknowledge the devalued status of their social self in comparison to others. A number of theorists have suggested that the chronic occupation of a low social status position may lead to depressed and anxious mood states (e.g., Gilbert & Trower, 1990; Price, Sloman, Gardner, Gilbert, & Rohde, 1994; Wilkinson, 1999). Shame, submission, and disengagement have been identified as important mediating pathways in such relationships (Gilbert, 1997; Gilbert & Allan, 1998; Gilbert, Allan, & Trent, 1995). Perceptions of low social status at school and within social living groups were associated with higher levels of depressed and anxious mood in two studies of college students, and these associations were mediated by feelings of shame (Gruenewald, Kemeny, & Adler, 2001; Gruenewald, 2003). A similar association between low self-perceived status at school and depressed mood was found in a large epidemiological study of over 10,000 adolescents (Goodman et al., 2001). Social status as rated by one's peers has been found to relate to mental well-being in many studies of adolescents, with rejected children faring much worse on measures of mental health than their more popular or average-status peers (see Newcomb, Bukowski, & Pattee, 1993). Whether feelings of shame and associated submission/disengagement tendencies play a role in these associations in adolescents is unknown.

There is also evidence of links between subordinate status position and depression and anxiety in nonhuman animals. Shively and colleagues (1997) found that cynomolgus monkeys (*Macaca fasicuclaris*) that occupied a subordinate social position over a 26-month period exhibited more signs of depression (e.g., collapsed body posture) and anxiety (e.g., vigilant scanning of the environment) than dominant animals. Anxious and depressive behaviors have also been documented in rodents following defeat in social dominance encounters (e.g., Heinrichs, Pich, Miczek, Britton, & Koob, 1992; Meerlo, Overkamp, & Koolhaas, 1997; Skutella et al., 1994). The HPA and proinflammatory immune systems, which we have hypothesized are activated under conditions of social-self threat, may also underlie connections between subordinate social status and depression and anxiety. Alterations in HPA activity were associated with the depressive and anxious behavior more common in subordinate monkeys in Shively and associates' (1997) investigation, and HPA alterations are well documented in depression in many human and animal studies (Gold, Licinio, Wong, & Chrousos, 1995; Maes et al., 1995; Scott & Dinan, 1998). Increased levels of proinflammatory cytokines and enhanced proinflammatory cytokine activity have also been documented in studies of humans with major depression (see Connor & Leonard, 1998, and Maes, 1999, for reviews), and administration of proinflammatory cytokines in rodents produces anxious behavior (Dunn, Antoon, & Chapman, 1991; Lacosta, Merali, & Anisman, 1998, 1999).

There may also be potential physical health consequences of physiological activation associated with chronic or repeated threat to the social self. High cortisol levels are thought to render organisms more susceptible to disease development or progression through the suppressive effects of cortisol on some aspects of the immune system (Munck, Guyre, & Holbrook, 1984). Elevated levels of proinflammatory cytokines are also characteristic in many physical health disorders, including the metabolic syndrome and diabetes (Black, 2003; Pradhan, Manson, Rifai, Buring, & Ridker, 2001), cardiovascular disease (Danesh, Collins, Appleby, & Peto, 1998), and chronic inflammatory diseases (Feldmann, Brennan, & Maini, 1996). It is interesting to note that socially subordinate animals experience some of these health conditions with greater frequency than their dominant peers (Kaplan et al., 1996; Shively & Clarkson, 1994), and that these conditions are also more common in humans of low socioeconomic status (Adler & Ostrove, 1999; Kaplan & Keil, 1993). Perhaps the frequent or prolonged activation of HPA and proinflammatory immune systems underlies these associations.

Individual Sensitivity to Social-Self Threat

Individual difference factors that increase sensitivity to social-self threat may also render some individuals more vulnerable to the experience of negative mental and physical health states. Such effects may occur through shame-related emotions and physiological responses hypothesized to accompany such threats. Women high in rejection sensitivity, a tendency to expect, readily perceive, and overreact to social rejection, were more likely to experience depression following a partner-initiated breakup than women low in rejection sensitivity in one longitudinal investigation (Ayduk, Downey, & Kim, 2001). Adolescent girls with heightened concerns about social evaluation have also been shown to be vulnerable to depression experience and the development of depression (Rudolph & Conley, 2005). Whether shame is an important emotional pathway between these individual vulnerabilities and depression development remains to be investigated. Shame is thought to be a key component of depression (e.g., Lewis, 1971; Scheff, 2001) and social anxiety (Gilbert & Trower, 1990; Schwarzer, 1986), and the tendency to easily experience shame is associated with depression occurrence (e.g., Andrews, Qian, & Valentine, 2002; Tangney, Wagner, & Gramzow, 1992).

Individuals high in fear of failure have been shown to be more likely to experience shame in response to naturalistic and experimentally induced failure experiences than those low in fear of failure (McGregor & Elliott, 2005). High fear of failure individuals have also been shown to have higher levels of shame and cortisol following performance of difficult laboratory tasks under conditions of social evaluation than low fear of failure individuals (Dickerson & Gable, 2004). We have also found that individuals highly fearful of negative social evaluation show larger cortisol increases to performance of stressful laboratory activities but only under conditions of social-evaluative threat; high and low fear of negative evaluation participants do not show differential cortisol reactivity to performance under nonevaluative conditions (Gruenewald & Kemeny, 2007).

A series of research investigations in individuals infected with the human immunodeficiency virus (HIV) indicates that individual difference factors associated with heightened sensitivity to social-self threat or the experience of negative emotional and cognitive states that we believe follow such threats are associated with poorer disease prognosis. Greater rejection sensitivity specific to one's homosexual identity was associated with a faster rate of CD4 T-cell decline (an important marker of HIV disease progression) and quicker progression to an AIDS diagnosis and mortality in a sample of HIV-positive gay and bisexual men (Cole, Kemeny, & Taylor, 1997). In an independent sample of HIV-positive gay men, greater rejection sensitivity predicted poorer response to the induction of highly active antiretroviral therapy (HAART), a common therapy aimed at reducing HIV viral load and disease progression; men high in rejection sensitivity evidenced less pronounced reductions in viral load and smaller increases in CD4 T cells (Cole, Kemeny, Fahey, Zach, & Naliboff, 2003). In a sample of HIV-positive women, an interpersonal rejection factor of depression predicted declines in CD4 T cells over a 2-year period, while depressed affect or vegetative symptoms subfactors of depression did not (Lewis, Kemeny, Myers, & Wyatt, 2003). Taken together, these investigations provide evidence that a heightened sensitivity to social rejection or greater perceived interpersonal rejection predict an accelerated rate of disease progression in individuals affected with HIV.

The persistent experience of shame and guilt surrounding HIV infection also predicted rate of CD4 T-cell decline over a 7-year period in a sample of HIV-positive gay and bisexual men (Weitzman, Kemeny, & Fahey, 2004). However, the persistent experience of other negative emotions regarding HIV infection, such as anger, anxiety, and sadness, was unrelated to CD4 T-cell decline. Thus, this marker of HIV disease progression appeared to be especially sensitive to emotions we believe flow from threat to the social self. Other research has demonstrated that CD4 T-cell decline is associated with negative self-related cognitions that may be associated with a threatened social self. A self-reproach component of depression predicted CD4 T-cell declines in HIV-positive gay men, while other components of depression (depressed affect and vegetative symptoms) did not (Kemeny & Dean, 1995). The tendency to make negative characterological attributions for negative events was associated with a greater rate of CD4 T-cell decline in another sample of HIV-positive gay and bisexual men (Segerstrom, Taylor, Kemeny, Reed, & Visscher, 1996). Men who were less likely to blame themselves for negative events exhibited a slower rate of cell decline.

Altogether, these investigations indicate that individual difference factors that heighten sensitivity to social-self threat or the experience of emotions and cognitions we believe are characteristic of such threats predict poorer immunological and health outcomes in HIV-positive men and women. The physiological mechanisms linking these shame-relevant individual differences to adverse health outcomes have not been fully delineated; however, it is possible that prolonged activation of the proinflammatory and HPA systems could provide one pathway through which these effects could occur. For example, TNF-α, IL-6, and IL-1B have been shown to lead to HIV replication and disease progression (Kedzierska, Crowe, Turville, & Cunningham, 2003). In other research, elevated cortisol levels have also been linked with disease progression (Leserman et al., 2000). Therefore, the proinflammatory and HPA systems, which we argue can be activated under acute social-self threat, could lead to these poorer immunological and health outcomes in HIV if the social threat was chronic and/or these systems were activated over a prolonged period of time.

HIV infection presents an interesting naturalistic model of social-self threat, as infected individuals possess a stigmatizing disease condition and many also face the additional stigmas of gay or bisexual sexual orientation, impoverished socioeconomic status, and accurate or inaccurate perceptions from others regarding routes of disease infection (e.g., prostitution, intravenous drug use). Thus, many of these individuals are subject to multiple sources of social-self threat. The results of studies reviewed here indicate that the addition of individual difference factors that render individuals more sensitive to such threats, the perception of interpersonal rejection, or the experience of shame and negative self-relevant cognitions to the ongoing social threat associated with these stigmatized identities can lead to hastened disease progression. These findings highlight the critical role that social-self threats, their emotional and cognitive consequences, and individual sensitivity to such threats can have for physical health outcomes.

CONCLUSIONS

Shame appears to be part of a psychobiological system designed to alert organisms to the presence of threat to the social self and to support appropriate behavioral responses to these threats. As we have argued that the preservation of the social self is a fundamental human motivation with implications for thriving and surviving, we believe that shame may be one of humans' most basic emotions. The theoretical and empirical research we have reviewed provides evidence that shame is a social emotion that is elicited in situations in which the social self is threatened. Shame experience is also associated with activation of the HPA and proinflammatory immune systems under conditions of social threat; these physiological systems along with shame may organize submission and disengagement behavioral responses that are adaptive in such situations.

Although we believe that the affective and physiological processes of this social-self preservation system represent adaptive responses under conditions of acute threat to the social self, such processes may be maladaptive under conditions of chronic or repeated threat. Frequent or prolonged experience of shame and activation of the HPA and proinflammatory immune systems may render individuals vulnerable to the experience of negative mental and physical health outcomes. This may be especially true for individuals with a heightened sensitivity to perceive such threats in their social environments.

One goal in postulating the social self preservation theory is to draw attention to the fundamental motivation of protecting the social self and to highlight the activation of shame and specific physiological systems when this fundamental goal is threatened. We hope that such attention will provide support for the premise that has existed since the time of Darwin that shame serves an important function essential to social life. We also hope that our theoretical focus will highlight the potential role of shame in negative mental and physical health states, such as those that occur under conditions of prolonged or repeated threat. Thus, our goal is not only to emphasize the central role of shame in social life, but to highlight the centrality of this emotion in mental and physical well-being.

REFERENCES

Ackerman, K. D., Martino, M., Heyman, R., Moyna, N. M., & Rabin, B. S. (1998). Stressor-induced alteration of cytokine production in multiple sclerosis patients and controls. Psychosomatic Medicine, 60(4), 484–491.

Adler, N. E., & Ostrove, J. M. (1999). Socioeconomic status and health: What we know and what we don't. Annals of the New York Academy of Sciences, 896, 3–15.

Altermus, M., Rao, B., Dhabhar, F. S., Din, W., & Granstein, R. D. (2001). Stress-induced changes in skin barrier function in healthy women. Journal of Investigative Dermatology, 117, 309–317.

Andrews, B., Qian, M., & Valentine, J. D. (2002). Predicting depressive symptoms with a new measure of shame: The Experience of Shame Scale. British Journal of Clinical Psychology, 41, 29–42.

Avitsur, R., Stark, J. L., & Sheridan, J. F. (2001). Social stress induces glucocorticoid resistance in subordinate animals. Hormones and Behavior, 39, 1–11.

Ayduk, O., Downey, G., & Kim, M. (2001). Rejection sensitivity and depressive symptoms in women. Personality and Social Psychology Bulletin, 27(7), 868–877.

Bauer, M. E., Vedhara, K., Perks, P., Wilcock, G. K., Lightman, S. L., & Shanks, N. (2000). Chronic stress in caregivers of dementia patients is associated with reduced lymphocyte sensitivity to glucocorticoids. Journal of Neuroimmunology, 103(1), 84–92.

Black, P. H. (2003). The inflammatory response is an integral part of the stress response: Implications for atherosclerosis, insulin resistance, type II diabetes and metabolic syndrome X. *Brain Behavior and Immunity, 17*(5), 350–364.

Cole, S. W., Kemeny, M. E., Fahey, J. L., Zack, J. A., & Naliboff, B. (2003). Psychological risk factors for HIV pathogenesis: Mediation by the autonomic nervous system. *Biological Psychiatry, 54*(12), 1444–1456.

Cole, S. W., Kemeny, M. E., & Taylor, S. E. (1997). Social identity and health: Accelerated HIV progression in rejection-sensitive gay men. *Journal of Personality and Social Psychology, 72*(2), 320–335.

Connor, T. J., & Leonard, B. E. (1998). Depression, stress and immunological activation: The role of cytokines in depressive disorders. *Life Sciences, 62*(7), 583–606.

Cooley, C. H. (1983). *Human nature and the social order.* New Brunswick, NJ: Transaction Books. (Original work published 1902)

Danesh, J., Collins, R., Appleby, P., & Peto, R. (1998). Association of fibrinogen, C-reactive protein, albumin, or leukocyte count with coronary heart disease: Meta-analyses of prospective studies. *Journal of the American Medical Association, 279*(18), 1477–1482.

Darwin, C. (1965). *The expression of the emotions in man and animals.* Chicago: University of Chicago Press. (Original work published 1872)

Dickerson, S. S. (2004, March). *Social-evaluative threat and proinflammatory cytokine responses to acute stress: A preliminary meta-analysis.* Poster session presented at the annual meeting of the American Psychosomatic Society, Orlando, FL.

Dickerson, S. S., & Gable, S. L. (2004, January). *Emotional and physiological effects of avoidance motives and goals following an acute stressor.* Poster session presented at the annual meeting of the Society for Personality and Social Psychology, Austin, TX.

Dickerson, S. S., Gable, S. L., Kemeny, M. E., Aziz, N., & Irwin, M. (2005, March). *Social-evaluative threat and proinflammatory cytokine activity: An experimental laboratory investigation.* Paper presented at the annual meeting of the American Psychosomatic Society, Vancouver, BC.

Dickerson, S. S., Gruenewald, T. L., & Kemeny, M. E. (2004). When the social self is threatened: Shame, physiology, and health. *Journal of Personality, 72*(6), 1191–1216.

Dickerson, S. S., & Kemeny, M. E. (2004). Acute stressors and cortisol responses: A theoretical integration and synthesis of laboratory research. *Psychological Bulletin, 130,* 355–391.

Dickerson, S. S., Kemeny, M. E., Aziz, N., Kim, K. H., & Fahey, J. L. (2004). Immunological effects of induced shame and guilt. *Psychosomatic Medicine, 66*(1), 124–131.

Dugue, B., Leppanen, E. A., Teppo, A. M., Fyhrquist, F., & Grasbeck, R. (1993). Effects of psychological stress on plasma interleukins-1 beta and 6, C-reactive protein, tumour necrosis factor alpha, anti-diuretic hormone and serum cortisol. *Scandinavian Journal of Clinical and Laboratory Investigation, 53*(6), 555–561.

Dunn, A. J., Antoon, M., & Chapman, Y. (1991). Reduction of exploratory behavior by intraperitoneal injection of interleukin-1 involves brain corticotropin-releasing factor. *Brain Research Bulletin, 26*(4), 539–542.

Ekman, P. (1992). An argument for basic emotions. *Cognition and Emotion, 6*(3–4), 169–200.

Feldmann, M., Brennan, F. M., & Maini, R. N. (1996). Role of cytokines in rheumatoid arthritis. *Annual Review of Immunology, 14,* 397–440.

Fessler, D. M. T. (1999). Toward an understanding of the universality of second order emotions. In A. L. Hinton (Ed.), *Biocultural approaches to the emotions* (pp. 75–116). New York: Cambridge University Press.

Fox, H. E., White, S. A., Kao, M. H., & Fernald, R. D. (1997). Stress and dominance in a social fish. *Journal of Neuroscience, 17*(16), 6463–6469.

Frijda, N. H. (1986). *The emotions.* New York: Cambridge University Press.

Gilbert, P. (1997). The evolution of social attractiveness and its role in shame, humiliation, guilt and therapy. *British Journal of Medical Psychology, 70*(Pt 2), 113–147.

Gilbert, P., & Allan, S. (1998). The role of defeat and entrapment (arrested flight) in depression: An exploration of an evolutionary view. *Psychological Medicine, 28*(3), 585–598.

Gilbert, P., Allan, S., & Trent, D. R. (1995). Involuntary subordination or dependency as key dimensions of depressive vulnerability? *Journal of Clinical Psychology, 51*(6), 740–752.

Gilbert, P., & McGuire, M. T. (1998). Shame, status, and social roles: Psychobiology and evolution. In P. Gilbert & B. Andrews (Eds.), *Shame: Interpersonal behavior, psychopathology, and culture* (pp. 99–125). New York: Oxford University Press .

Gilbert, P., & Trower, P. (1990). The evolution and manifestation of social anxiety. In W. R. Crozier (Ed.), *Shyness and embarrassment: Perspectives from social psychology* (pp. 144–177). New York: Cambridge University Press.

Gold, P. W., Licinio, J., Wong, M. L., & Chrousos, G. P. (1995). Corticotropin releasing hormone in the pathophysiology of melancholic and atypical depression and in the mechanism of action of antidepressant drugs. *Annals of the New York Academy of Sciences, 771,* 716–729.

Goodman, E., Adler, N. E., Kawarchi, I., Frazier, A. L., Huang, B., & Colditz, G. A. (2001). Adolescents' perceptions of social status: Development and evaluation of a new indicator. *Pediatrics, 108*(2), E31.

Gruenewald, T. L. (2003). Psychological and physiological correlates of acute and chronic threat to the social self. *Dissertation Abstracts International, 64,* 2984.

Gruenewald, T. L., & Kemeny, M. E. (2007). *Fear of negative evaluation and cortisol responses to social-evaluative threat.* Manuscript in preparation.

Gruenewald, T. L., Kemeny, M. E., & Adler, N. (2001, March). *Subjective social status, social hierarchy/rank and mental health.* Poster session presented at the annual meeting of the American Psychosomatic Society. Monterey, CA.

Gruenewald, T. L., Kemeny, M. E., Aziz, N., & Fahey, J. L. (2004). Acute threat to the social self: Shame, social self-esteem, and cortisol activity. *Psychosomatic Medicine, 66*(6), 915–924.

Haller, J., Kiem, D. T., & Makara, G. B. (1996). The physiology of social conflict in rats: What is particularly stressful? *Behavioral Neuroscience, 110*(2), 353–359.

Heinrichs, S. C., Pich, E. M., Miczek, K. A., Britton, K. T., & Koob, G. F. (1992). Corticotropin-releasing factor antagonist reduces emotionality in socially defeated rats via direct neurotropic action. *Brain Research, 581*(2), 190–197.

Ho, D. Y., Fu, W., & Ng, S. M. (2004). Guilt, shame and embarrassment: Revelations of face and self. *Culture and Psychology, 10*(1), 64–84.

Holst, D. (1997). Social relations and their health impact in tree shrews. *Acta Physiologica Scandinavica, 640*(Suppl.) 77–82.

Izard, C. W. (1977). *Human emotions.* New York: Plenum Press.

James, W. (1955). *The principles of psychology.* Chicago: Encyclopaedia Britannica. (Original work published 1890)

Johnson-Laird, P. N., & Oatley, K. (1992). Basic emotions, rationality, and folk theory. *Cognition and Emotion, 6*(3–4), 201–223.

Kaplan, G. A., & Keil, J. E. (1993). Socioeconomic factors and cardiovascular disease: A review of the literature. *Circulation, 88*(4), 1973–1998.

Kaplan, J. R., Adams, M. R., Clarkson, T. B., Manuck, S. B., Shively, C. A., & Williams, J. K. (1996). Psychosocial factors, sex differences, and atherosclerosis: Lessons from animal models. *Psychosomatic Medicine, 58*(6), 598–611.

Kaufman, G. (1989). *The psychology of shame.* New York: Springer.

Kedzierska, K., Crowe, S. M., Turville, S., & Cunningham, A. L. (2003). The influence of cytokines, chemokines and their receptors on HIV-1 replication in monocytes and macrophages. *Review of Medical Virology, 13,* 39–56.

Keltner, D., & Buswell, B. N. (1996). Evidence for the distinctness of embarrassment, shame and guilt: A study of recalled antecedents and facial expressions of emotion. *Cognition and Emotion, 10*(2), 155–171.

Keltner, D., & Buswell, B. N. (1997). Embarrassment: Its distinct form and appeasement functions. *Psychological Bulletin, 122*(3), 250–270.

Keltner, D., & Gross, J. J. (1999). Functional accounts of emotion. *Cognition and Emotion, 13,* 467–480.

Keltner, D., Young, R. C., & Buswell, B. N. (1997). Appeasement in human emotion, social practice, and personality. *Aggressive Behavior, 23*, 359–374.

Kemeny, M. E., & Dean, L. (1995). Effects of AIDS-related bereavement on HIV progression among New York City gay men. *AIDS Education and Prevention, 7*(5), 36–47.

Kemeny, M. E., Gruenewald, T. L., & Dickerson, S. S. (2004). Shame as the emotional response to threat to the social self: Implications for behavior, physiology, and health. *Psychological Inquiry, 15*(2), 153–160.

Kirschbaum, C., & Hellhammer, D. H. (1989). Salivary cortisol in psychobiological research: An overview. *Neuropsychobiology, 22*(3), 150–169.

Kollack-Walker, S., Watson, S. J., & Akil, H. (1997). Social stress in hamsters: defeat activates specific neurocircuits within the brain. *Journal of Neuroscience, 17*(22), 8842–8855.

Kroll, J., & Egan, E. (2004). Psychiatry, moral worry, and the moral emotions. *Journal of Psychiatric Practice, 10*, 352–360.

Lacosta, S., Merali, Z., & Anisman, H. (1998). Influence of interleukin-1beta on exploratory behaviors, plasma ACTH, corticosterone, and central biogenic amines in mice. *Psychopharmacology, 137*(4), 351–361.

Lacosta, S., Merali, Z., & Anisman, H. (1999). Behavioral and neurochemical consequences of lipopolysaccharide in mice: Anxiogenic-like effects. *Brain Research, 818*(2), 291–303.

Leary, M. R., Tambor, E. S., Terdal, S. K., & Downs, D. L. (1995). Self-esteem as an interpersonal monitor: The sociometer hypothesis. *Journal of Personality and Social Psychology, 68*(3), 518–530.

Leserman, J., Petitto, J. M., Golden, R. N., Gaynes, B. N., Gu, H., Perkins, D. O., et al. (2000). Impact of stressful life events, depression, social support, coping, and cortisol on progression to AIDS. *American Journal of Psychiatry, 157*(8), 1221–1228.

Levenson, R. W. (1994). The search for autonomic specificity. In P. Ekman & R. Davidson (Eds.), *The nature of emotion: Fundamental questions* (pp. 252–257). New York: Oxford University Press.

Lewis, H. B. (1971). Shame and guilt in neurosis. *Psychoanalytic Review, 58*(3), 419–438.

Lewis, M., & Ramsay, D. (2002). Cortisol response to embarrassment and shame. *Child Development, 73*, 1034–1045.

Lewis, T. T., Kemeny, M. E., Myers, H. F., & Wyatt, G. E. (2003, March). *Perceived interpersonal rejection and CD4 decline in a community sample of women infected with HIV.* Symposium presented at the annual meeting of the American Psychiatric Society, Phoenix, AZ.

MacLean, P. D. (1990). *The triune brain in evolution.* New York: Plenum Press.

Maes, M. (1999). Major depression and activation of the inflammatory response system. *Advances in Experimental Medicine and Biology, 461*, 25–46.

Maes, M., Van Gastel, A., Block, P., Martin, M., Cosyns, P., Scharpe, S., et al. (1995). An augmented escape of androstenedione from suppression by dexamethasone in melancholia: Relationships to intact ACTH and cortisol nonsuppression. *Journal of Affective Disoders, 34*, 291–300.

Maier, S. F., & Watkins, L. R. (1998). Cytokines for psychologists: implications of bidirectional immune-to-brain communication for understanding behavior, mood, and cognition. *Psychological Review, 105*(1), 83–107.

McGregor, H. A., & Elliot, A. J. (2005). The shame of failure: Examining the link between fear of failure and shame. *Personality and Social Psychology Bulletin, 31*(2), 218–231.

Meerlo, P., Overkamp, G. J., & Koolhaas, J. M. (1997). Behavioural and physiological consequences of a single social defeat in Roman high- and low-avoidance rats. *Psychoneuroendocrinology, 22*(3), 155–168.

Miller, R. S., & Tangney, J. P. (1994). Differentiating embarrassment and shame. *Journal of Social and Clinical Psychology, 13*(3), 273–287.

Munck, A., Guyre, P. M., & Holbrook, N. J. (1984). Physiological functions of glucocorticoids in stress and their relation to pharmacological actions. *Endocrine Reviews, 5*(1), 25–44.

Newcomb, A. F., Bukowski, W. M., & Pattee, L. (1993). Children's peer relations: A meta-analytic review of popular, rejected, neglected, controversial, and average sociometric status. *Psychological Bulletin, 113*(1), 99–128.

Niedenthal, P. M., Tangney, J. P., & Gavanski, I. (1994). "If only I weren't" versus "If only I hadn't": Distinguishing shame and guilt in counterfactual thinking. *Journal of Personality and Social Psychology, 67*(4), 585–595.

Oatley, K., & Jenkins, J. M. (1992). Human emotions: Function and dysfunction. *Annual Review of Psychology, 43,* 55–85.

Plutchik, R. (1980). *Emotion: A psychoevolutionary synthesis.* New York: Harper & Row.

Pradhan, A. D., Manson, J. E., Rifai, N., Buring, J. E., & Ridker, P. M. (2001). C-reactive protein, interleukin 6, and risk of developing type 2 diabetes mellitus. *Journal of the American Medical Association, 286*(3), 327–334.

Price, J., Sloman, L., Gardner, R., Gilbert, P., & Rohde, P. (1994). The social competition hypothesis of depression. *British Journal of Psychiatry, 164*(3), 309–315.

Pruessner, J. C., Hellhammer, D. H., & Kirschbaum, C. (1999). Low self-esteem, induced failure and the adrenocortical stress response. *Personality and Individual Differences, 27*(3), 477–489.

Quan, N., Avitsur, R., Stark, J. L., He, L., Shah, M., Caligiuri, M., et al. (2001). Social stress increases the susceptibility to endotoxic shock. *Journal of Neuroimmunology, 115*(1–2), 36–45.

Rudolph, K. D., & Conley, C. S. (2005). The socioemotional costs and benefits of social-evaluative concerns: Do girls care too much? *Journal of Personality, 73*(1), 115–137.

Sabini, J., Garvey, B., & Hall, A. L. (2001). Shame and embarrassment revisited. *Personality and Social Psychology Bulletin, 27*(1), 104–117.

Sapolsky, R. M. (1993). Endocrinology alfresco: Psychoendocrine studies of wild baboons. *Recent Progress in Hormone Research, 48,* 437–468.

Scheff, T. J. (1988). Shame and conformity: The deference-emotion system. *American Sociological Review, 53*(3), 395–406.

Scheff, T. J. (2001). Shame and community: Social components in depression. *Psychiatry, 64*(3), 212–224.

Scheff, T. J. (2003). Shame in self and society. *Symbolic Interaction, 26*(2), 239–262.

Schwarzer, R. (1986). Self-related cognitions in anxiety and motivation: An introduction. In R. Schwarzer (Ed.), *Self-related cognitions in anxiety and motivation* (pp. 1–17). Hillsdale, NJ: Erlbaum.

Scott, L. V., & Dinan, T. G. (1998). Urinary free cortisol excretion in chronic fatigue syndrome, major depression, and health volunteers. *Journal of Affective Disorders, 47,* 49–54.

Seeman, T. E. (2000). Health promoting effects of friends and family on health outcomes in older adults. *American Journal of Health Promotion, 14*(6), 362–370.

Segerstrom, S. C., Taylor, S. E., Kemeny, M. E., Reed, G. M., & Visscher, B. R. (1996). Causal attributions predict rate of immune decline in HIV-seropositive gay men. *Health Psychology, 15*(6), 485–493.

Selye, H. (1950). *The physiology and pathology of exposure to stress: A treatise based on the concepts of the general-adaptation-syndrome and the diseases of adaptation.* Montreal: Acta.

Sheridan, J. F., Stark, J. L., Avitsur, R., & Padgett, D. A. (2000). Social disruption, immunity, and susceptibility to viral infection: Role of glucocorticoid insensitivity and NGF. *Annals of the New York Academy of Sciences, 917,* 894–905.

Shively, C. A., & Clarkson, T. B. (1994). Social status and coronary artery atherosclerosis in female monkeys. *Arteriosclerosis and Thrombosis, 14*(5), 721–726.

Shively, C. A., Laber-Laird, K., & Anton, R. F. (1997). Behavior and physiology of social stress and depression in female cynomolgus monkeys. *Biological Psychiatry, 41*(8), 871–882.

Skutella, T., Montkowski, A., Stohr, T., Probst, J. C., Landgraf, R., Holsboer, F., et al. (1994). Corticotropin-releasing hormone (CRH) antisense oligodeoxynucleotide treatment attenuates social defeat-induced anxiety in rats. *Cellular and Molecular Neurobiology, 14*(5), 579–588.

Stefanski, V. (1998). Social stress in loser rats: Opposite immunological effects in submissive and subdominant males. *Physiology and Behavior, 63*(4), 605–613.

Stefanski, V., & Ben-Eliyahu, S. (1996). Social confrontation and tumor metastasis in rats: Defeat and beta-adrenergic mechanisms. *Physiology and Behavior, 60*(1), 277–282.

Stefanski, V., & Engler, H. (1998). Effects of acute and chronic social stress on blood cellular immunity in rats. *Physiology and Behavior, 64*(5), 733–741.

Stefanski, V., Knopf, G., & Schulz, S. (2001). Long-term colony housing in Long Evans rats: Immunological, hormonal, and behavioral consequences. *Journal of Neuroimmunology, 114*(1–2), 122–130.

Tangney, J. P., Miller, R. S., Flicker, L., & Barlow, D. H. (1996). Are shame, guilt, and embarrassment distinct emotions? *Journal of Personality and Social Psychology, 70*(6), 1256–1269.

Tangney, J. P., Wagner, P., & Gramzow, R. (1992). Proneness to shame, proneness to guilt, and psychopathology. *Journal of Abnormal Psychology, 101*(3), 469–478.

Tomkins, S. S. (1962). *Affect, imagery and consciousness, Vol. I: The positive affects.* New York: Springer.

Tomkins, S, S. (1963). *Affect, imagery and consciousness, Vol. II: The negative affects.* New York: Springer.

Tooby, J., & Cosmides, L. (1990). The past explains the present: Emotional adaptations and the structure of ancestral environments. *Ethology and Sociobiology, 11*(4–5), 375–424.

Tracy, J. L., & Robins, R. W. (2004a). Putting the self into self-conscious emotions: A theoretical model. *Psychological Inquiry, 15*(2), 103–125.

Tracy, J. L., & Robins, R. W. (2004b). Show your pride: Evidence for a discrete emotion expression. *Psychological Science, 15*(3), 194–197.

Weitzman, O., Kemeny, M. E., & Fahey, J. L. (2004). *HIV-related shame and guilt predict CD4 decline.* Unpublished manuscript.

Wicker, F. W., Payne, G. C., & Morgan, R. D. (1983). Participant descriptions of guilt and shame. *Motivation and Emotion, 7*(1), 25–39.

Wilkinson, R. G. (1999). Health, hierarchy, and social anxiety. *Annals of the New York Academy of Sciences, 896,* 48–63.

Yirmiya, R. (1996). Endotoxin produces a depressive-like episode in rats. *Brain Research, 711*(1–2), 163–174.

Zakowski, S. G., McAllister, C. G., Deal, M., & Baum, A. (1992). Stress, reactivity, and immune function in healthy men. *Health Psychology, 11,* 223–232.

PART II

DEVELOPMENTAL CONTEXTS AND PROCESSES

6

The Development
of Self-Conscious Emotions

*Cognitive Processes
and Social Influences*

KRISTIN HANSEN LAGATTUTA
ROSS A. THOMPSON

The development of children's ability to experience, recognize, and understand the self-conscious emotions of pride, shame, guilt, and embarrassment is of rising scientific interest (Bosacki, 2000; Heerey, Keltner, & Capps, 2003; Kornilaki & Chlouverakis, 2004; Lewis, Chapter 8, this volume; Olthof, Ferguson, Bloemers, & Deij, 2004; Tracy, Robins, & Lagattuta, 2005). Investigation into the origins of self-conscious emotions is intriguing because it bridges core areas of developmental research: the development of self-awareness, self-evaluation, and social comparison, as well as the growth of a theory of mind—how children come to understand themselves and other people in relation to intentions, desires, beliefs, thoughts, and emotions (see Wellman & Lagattuta, 2000). Moreover, because self-conscious emotions arise from how we evaluate our skills and behaviors in relation to normative standards or to how we imagine other people will appraise us, self-conscious emotions are also inherently about relationships—about connections between self and other (Bretherton, Fritz, Zahn-Waxler, & Ridgeway, 1986; Harris, 1989; Tangney & Fischer, 1995). Indeed, self-conscious emotions play a formative role in the development of self-regulation, compliance, and conscience; in the maintenance of relationships; and in current and long-term achievement motivation, self-esteem, and mental health (Aksan & Kochanska, 2005; Campos, Campos, & Barrett, 1989; Lewis, 1993; Stipek, 1995).

This chapter examines cognitive and social processes underlying the development of self-conscious emotions. We focus on how early concepts about self, mind, and others result in feelings of pride, shame, guilt, and embarrassment in infancy and early childhood.

91

We also review developmental changes in how children come to understand the causes and consequences of these different emotions. Because self-conscious emotions involve relationships between self and other, we also explore how individual differences in the expression, recognition, and understanding of self-conscious emotions arise from the quality and type of interactions children have with significant others in their everyday lives.

THE DEVELOPMENT OF SELF-CONSCIOUS EMOTIONS IN INFANCY AND TODDLERHOOD

One of the foremost questions in research on the development of self-conscious emotions is at what age humans are first capable of experiencing feelings of pride, shame, guilt, and embarrassment. Converging evidence from developmental studies identifies three core conceptual foundations for a person's ability to experience self-conscious emotions (Lewis, 1995, 2001; Stipek, Recchia, & McClintic, 1992; Tangney & Dearing, 2002; Tracy & Robins, 2004a). First, because self-conscious emotions are inherently self-directed, a rudimentary sense of *self-awareness* must develop before these emotions can occur. Second, the person must be able to *recognize an external standard* against which his or her behavior or characteristics can be evaluated. That standard may be a rule, expectation, or goal that has been satisfied or not, or it may be another's evaluation or judgment. Third, the person must *adopt that standard* and be able to evaluate the degree to which he or she meets, exceeds, or fails to match the standard. For example, one does not feel pride unless the accomplished goal is personally meaningful or another's applause is important for self-evaluation. Although these foundations for the emergence of self-conscious emotions are developmentally complex, there is evidence that young children reach these cognitive achievements and begin to experience pride, guilt, shame, and embarrassment at the end of the second year or the beginning of the third year of life. As these conceptual foundations continue to develop throughout childhood, so also does children's experience of and understanding of self-conscious emotions.

Capacity for Self-Awareness

Early capacity for self-awareness is often studied by examining how infants respond to their mirror appearance after a spot of rouge has been surreptitiously applied to their noses. Before 15 to18 months, infants do not touch their noses in response to their mirror images, but between 18 and 24 months there is a significant increase in mark-directed touching, sometimes accompanied by signs of embarrassment (e.g., smiling and looking down and away from the reflection; Lewis & Brooks-Gunn, 1979). This ability to pass the "rouge test" is considered to reflect the emergence of physical self-recognition, and it has been regarded by some as marking the emergence of the "conceptual self" (Howe & Courage, 1997).

Some researchers have questioned whether the rouge test should be considered the "gold standard" for demonstrating the presence or absence of a sense of self. That is, infants may achieve rudimentary forms of self-awareness many months prior to being able to pass the rouge test. For example, 2-month-olds often exhibit "coy" or "shy" behaviors when interacting with an overly stimulating adult or when viewing themselves in the mirror (Reddy, 2001). Moreover, 2- and 3-month-olds can detect contingencies between their own arm and leg movements and the motion of a mobile, they respond differently to mirror images of the self versus another baby, and they discriminate video displays of another infant's legs kicking versus their own legs (see Rochat, 1995, for a review). Moreover, young infants demonstrate sensitivity to socially contingent actions in that they become visibly upset when a responsive partner acts noncontingently toward them or poses a still face (see Trevarthen & Aitken, 2001). These early forms of self-exploration, intentional action, contingency awareness, and attunement to caregivers likely provide basic foundations of self-awareness prior to the consolidation of a sense of self near the second birthday.

Other researchers argue that the rouge test assesses only a limited form of self-awareness—that is, physical self-recognition—but that other concurrent advances better reflect the emergence of conceptual self-awareness at the end of the second year. These include verbal self-referential behavior (e.g., "Me big!"), verbal labeling of internal experiences such as emotions (including comparisons between emotions of self and others), assertions of competence and responsibility as autonomous beings (such as refusing assistance), assertions of ownership ("Mine!"), categorizing the self by gender and in other ways, and young children's growing interest in how their behavior is regarded by others (see Thompson, 2006, for a review). Taken together, this constellation of behaviors by the end of the second year suggests that toddlers are developing a basic awareness of the self that goes beyond simple mirror recognition of outward bodily appearance, and provides a foundation for self-conscious emotions.

Recognition of External Standards

Consider next infants' emerging recognition of external standards for behavior and performance. Between the first and second year, infants become increasingly interested in what other people are looking at, evaluating, and emotionally reacting toward. Indeed, starting around their first birthday, infants become strongly motivated to establish joint attention, they increasingly point and gesture to attract attention to objects and people in their environment, and they engage in social referencing (i.e., looking to adult emotional cues to clarify their own interpretation of an object, person, or event). For example, Moses, Baldwin, Rosicky, and Tidball (2001) found that when 12-month-olds were shown ambiguous objects, they spontaneously looked to the experimenter's emotional reaction and used that as a guide to their own behavior. They avoided objects that experimenters reacted negatively toward and approached objects that adults emoted positively toward (see also Harter, 1998; Trevarthen & Aitken, 2001). This is one way that infants begin to understand others' evaluations and judgments about events of shared interest.

Through their social referencing, efforts to establish joint attention, and gesturing and pointing, infants reveal increasing cognizance that other people have mental lives: perceptions, intentions, evaluations, and emotions *about* things in the world. These early insights precede later, more developed, understandings about mind in the preschool years (see Baldwin & Moses, 1996; Wellman & Lagattuta, 2000), and likely provide a critical foundation for recognizing social standards. That is, referential behaviors not only enable infants to gather information about people and objects in the world, but they also allow them to learn social expectations for behavior and performance. For example, when a mother responds with a loud "Ahhh!" when the baby looks to the mother while reaching sticky fingers toward expensive electronic equipment, the adult imbues that behavior with an affective valence for the infant. The parent's response is even more influential when his or her emotional cues are accompanied by imperative language and action. Likewise, when the parent responds enthusiastically to a toddler's drawing, the activity assumes a positive emotional tone for the child. In these ways, social referencing helps infants to establish the affective valuation of certain actions and to form connections between their own behavior and the emotional reactions of others. These experiences provide a foundation for the development of feelings of guilt, pride, and shame (Thompson, Meyer, & McGinley, 2006).

Accepting Others' Evaluations and Social Standards

The conclusion that pride, shame, guilt, and embarrassment have developmental origins around the second birthday is further supported by evidence that the third foundation of self-conscious emotions—accepting others' standards for oneself—also begins to emerge at this time. Toward the end of the second year, toddlers become *personally sensitive* to normative standards and expectations for achievement and behavior. For example, Kagan (1981, 2005) reports that during this period (but not before) children become visibly concerned when standards of wholeness and intactness have been violated, such as when they notice missing buttons from garments, torn pages from books, trash on the floor, broken toys, or misplaced objects (see also Lamb, 1993). Kagan has interpreted this phenomenon as an emerging moral sense because these events violate the implicit norms or standards that are typically enforced by parents through sanctions on broken, marred, or damaged objects. Similarly, Kochanska, Casey, and Fukumoto (1995) argue that early responses to mishaps, damage, or incompleteness reflect an emerging system of internal standards about right and wrong.

By 2½ years of age, children exhibit concern about personal responsibility in achievement settings. They express greater pride and attention seeking after finishing a task by themselves (e.g., a shape-sorting cube) compared with watching the task completed by an experimenter (Stipek et al., 1992). In both cases, the goal was achieved, but only in the former did the "self" have control over its outcome. Relatedly, 2-year-olds are notorious for rejecting parental assistance and wanting to do things "by themselves" (Geppert & Küster, 1983). This desire for self-competence is so great that, according to Kagan (1981), toddlers of these ages show clear signs of anxiety or distress when an adult models a task that is too difficult for them to achieve by themselves, with this anxiety likely reflecting an internal evaluation that he or she has failed to meet a standard for performance.

Interim Summary

By the end of the second or the beginning of the third year young children achieve, at least on a very basic level, cognitive achievements essential for experiencing self-conscious emotions: self-awareness, attention to the standards against which one's behavior can be evaluated, and personal acceptance of these external standards for oneself. During the infant and toddler years, infants also become increasingly attuned to the psychological lives of other people—they actively reference others' evaluations and emotional reactions to guide their own behavior. Thus, young children not only become more aware of their own "self" but they also develop stronger interest in other people's emotions and evaluations. With these conceptual foundations in place, most 2-year-olds begin to display behavioral indicators of experiencing pride, shame, guilt, and embarrassment.

SELF-CONSCIOUS EMOTIONS IN THE PRESCHOOL YEARS

Between the ages of 3 and 5 children's language rapidly develops, leading to a more extensive vocabulary for talking about feelings, including self-conscious emotions, as well as more frequent parent–child conversations about current, past, and future emotional events (Lagattuta & Wellman, 2002; Saarni, 1999; Thompson, Laible, & Ontai, 2003). Numerous studies reveal that these parent–child conversations significantly shape children's understanding of the causes and consequences of emotions, their knowledge about rules and standards for behavior, and their developing representations of who they are as individuals (see Fivush & Nelson, 2006; Thompson et al., 2003; Thompson & Lagattuta, 2006).

The everyday contexts in which young children learn about these standards are important for how they are likely to be personally applied. That is, because many rules and expectations concern daily routines (e.g., at mealtime or bedtime), household procedures, play, and behavior at familiar locations (e.g., childcare, church), these standards become incorporated into young children's early prototypical knowledge systems and scripts and, as a result, begin to assume normative value (Nelson, 1978). In a sense, then, children's developing understanding of *how things are done* incorporates their grasp for *how one should act* in everyday situations. Therefore, one reason that young children not only comprehend behavioral expectations but also adopt them personally is that these standards have become integrated into their developing knowledge of the normative routines of everyday life. Indeed, young children's interest in normative standards of behavior and achievement develops at the same time that they are discerning normative standards in many other areas, such as personal appearance (recall their embarrassment at finding their rouge-marked noses in the mirror) and language (as they are mastering the meanings of words) (Thompson et al., 2006).

The rising frequency in conversations about emotions and standards coincides with advances in preschoolers' knowledge about self-conscious emotions and self-presentation. For example, Tracy et al. (2005) report that between the ages of 3 and 5 there is a significant increase in children's ability to recognize photographic depictions of pride. Indeed, preschoolers age 4 years and older recognized pride displays significantly above chance and at the same success rate as they identified depictions of happiness and surprise (see also Tracy & Robins, 2004b, for research with adults). Three- to 5-year-olds also know something about the valence of self-conscious emotions: they can readily categorize pride with positive emotions and shame, guilt, and embarrassment with negative emotions (see Bosacki & Moore, 2004; Harris, Olthof, Terwogt, & Hardman, 1987; Russell & Paris, 1994). Moreover, 4- and 5-year-olds demonstrate knowledge about differences between real and apparent emotion (e.g., that a person can look one way but feel a different emotion inside; see Harris, 1989), and they show awareness of social situations that motivate people to engage in such deliberate, deceptive, self-presentational behaviors (Banerjee, 2002).

Self-Conscious Emotions and Theory of Mind

Arguably, young children's experience of and knowledge about self-conscious emotions are also greatly enhanced by their emerging awareness of their own mental states as well as the psychological perspectives of people around them (i.e., theory of mind). Indeed, self-conscious emotions stem from how a person *thinks* about or evaluates him- or herself in relation to standards of what kind of person he or she wants to or should be (e.g., nice, smart, athletic) or in relation to how he or she imagines other people are thinking about or evaluating him or her. Thus developmental changes in children's understanding about the mind, including individual differences in this knowledge, should bear directly on how children come to experience, identify, and understand self-conscious emotions. During the preschool years, children acquire advanced conceptual understanding about desires, intentions, beliefs (including false beliefs), and thoughts (Wellman, Cross, & Watson, 2001; Wellman & Lagattuta, 2000), as well as more sophisticated knowledge about connections between mental states and emotions (Lagattuta & Wellman, 2001; Lagattuta, Wellman, & Flavell, 1997). Moreover, they begin to view mental states as enduring, that is, they acknowledge that people have preferences, desires, beliefs, emotions, personality traits, and ways of acting and behaving that are consistent across time and situations (Heyman & Gelman, 1999).

Evidence for a connection between theory of mind development and self-conscious emotions comes from research by Cutting and Dunn (2002). They examined whether having an earlier, more precocious understanding of mind might lead to greater sensitivity to criticism. That is, the more one knows about what others might be thinking and believing, the more cognizant one might also be that one could be the subject of negative evaluation. This is exactly what they found. Three- and 4-year-olds who demonstrated advanced knowledge about the mind (as assessed through false belief tasks) were more likely as kindergarteners to lower their evaluation of a "student" puppet's performance after it received negative remarks by the "teacher" puppet compared to kindergarteners with low theory of mind knowledge in preschool. Similar findings were also reported by Dunn (1995): children's ability to pass a false belief task at 40 months predicted greater sensitivity to teacher criticism of their *own* work. Relatedly, individuals impaired in theory of mind understanding, notably children with autism, demonstrate more limited knowledge about self-conscious emotions (Heerey et al., 2003). Importantly, then, development in children's understanding of the mind may influence the emergence of a "looking glass self" (Cooley, 1902), or knowledge about the self that incorporates opinions of other people. This could result in increased vulnerability to feelings of shame, guilt, and embarrassment when standards are not met.

Self-Conscious Emotions and Self-Understanding

The development of young children's understanding of self-conscious emotions emerges in concert with advances in self-understanding. Indeed, one reason for their increased sensitivity to others' evaluations of them is that preschoolers are beginning to acquire more psychologically complex views of their personal characteristics. Researchers have shown that, contrary to the traditional view that young children perceive themselves only in terms of physical appearance and behavior (e.g., running fast, having brown hair), preschoolers view themselves also in terms of a range of internal capabilities, dispositions, and traits, including their social characteristics, academic abilities, and emotions (Goodvin, Meyer, Thompson, & Hayes, 2006; Marsh, Ellis, & Craven, 2002; Measelle, Ablow, Cowan, & Cowan, 1998). These self-views can take the form of a cognitive representation—akin to a naïve theory—about the self's individual desires, beliefs, preferences, emotions, and ways of acting (see Epstein, 1973). This developing self-concept also extends to concepts about morality in that children are beginning to perceive themselves in terms of a "moral self" who feels badly about wrongdoing, seeks to make amends, sympathizes with others' distress, and otherwise acts in a morally responsible fashion (Kochanska, 2002). In a simple sense, preschoolers are beginning to regard themselves as competent versus incompetent, as "good" or "bad," in ways that are relevant to their experience of self-conscious emotions.

INDIVIDUAL DIFFERENCES: TEMPERAMENT, PARENTING, AND CULTURE

Although most young children exhibit behaviors indicative of feeling self-conscious emotions—acting coy when they know others are looking at them, showing expanded posture and smiling when adults respond positively to their actions, looking sad or withdrawing after disobeying or receiving negative feedback, and engaging in reparative behaviors after causing harm to others—there are individual differences in the frequency of these early expressions of pride, shame, guilt, and embarrassment and in the situations where they occur (Ferguson & Stegge, 1995; Kochanska, DeVet, Goldman, Murray, & Putnam, 1994; Stipek, 1995; Stipek et al., 1992; Zahn-Waxler & Robinson, 1995). Therefore, before proceeding further in our discussion of age-related developments in children's experience, expression, and understanding of self-conscious emotions, it is critical to consider sources of variability including temperament, parenting, and culture that may significantly shape the timing, progression, and frequency of self-conscious emotions during childhood.

Temperament

Variability in the frequency of self-conscious emotions can arise from individual differences in temperament. For example, Kochanska and her colleagues report that children who exhibit greater guilt in response to wrongdoing are more temperamentally fearful and reactive than those who show less guilt (Kochanska et al., 1994; Kochanska, Gross, Lin, & Nichols, 2002; see also Kagan, 2005). Thus, temperamental qualities may make young children more versus less susceptible to the feelings of shame and guilt from parental criticism or disapproval, another's upset, or their own internal awareness of having acted wrongly.

Early emerging individual differences in proneness to shame and guilt have also been found in young children's responses to "rigged mishap incidents," situations where children are led to believe that they have damaged the experimenter's special toy. Using this paradigm, Barrett, Zahn-Waxler, and Cole (1993) reliably distinguished 2-year-olds who exhibited guilt (whom they called the "amenders" because they tried to repair the toy and told the experimenter what they had done) from children who exhibited shame (whom they called the "avoiders" because they avoided the experimenter, were slow to repair the toy, and slow to confess to the experimenter). Kochanska et al. (2002) also examined young children's affective and behavioral responses to rigged mishaps. Not only were there individual differences in children's concern and distress reactions at 22 months, but these differences remained stable over time and were modestly predictive (especially at 45 months) of assessments of conscience and moral behavior at 56 months.

Parenting and Discipline

The parenting context in which young children learn about standards, norms, and expectations contributes to variability in children's early experiences of pride, shame, guilt, and embarrassment. That is, in comprehending behavioral standards, young children are aided by adults who convey behavioral expectations in everyday experiences. For example, once infants become capable of self-produced locomotion (around 9–12 months of age), caregivers significantly increase their communication of behavioral expectations as they caution, prevent, restrict, and sanction their exploratory forays—often resulting in battles of will (Campos et al., 2000). Moreover, there are dramatic increases during the second year in parental expectations for child compliance with respect to rules about touching dangerous objects; respecting property rights; participation in family routines; expectations for self-care or self-control with respect to waiting, sharing, aggression, and eating; and prohibitions about making messes and breaking things (Dunn & Munn, 1987; Gralinski & Kopp, 1993).

Perhaps the most powerful way in which parents convey standards and evaluations is by how they choose to discipline their child when he or she misbehaves. An extensive research literature has shown that parental disciplinary practices that are coercive and power assertive elicit children's immediate compliance but also the child's frustration, and that long-term internalization of values—including guilt when children misbehave—is often lacking. By contrast, discipline practices that emphasize reasoning and provide justification for compliance are more likely to foster internalized values in young children and spontaneous guilt after wrongdoing (see Grusec & Goodnow, 1994, and Grusec & Kuczynski, 1997, for reviews).

More broadly, parental discipline provides a cognitive structure that explicitly links the parent's response to the child's violation of the external standard ("You know better than to hit your sister!"), invokes salient attributions of responsibility ("Why did you hit her?"), identifies consequences for another ("Look, she's crying!"), and induces the relevant self-conscious emotion ("You should be ashamed of yourself!"). The same is true of situations evoking pride in young children, when the parent's response likewise emphasizes the child's responsibility for creating a desirable outcome and elicits the relevant self-conscious emotion. By inducing feelings of pride, shame, guilt, and other emotions, and providing a verbal response that makes these causal associations explicit, the parent promotes considerable moral and emotional socialization in these contexts (Kochanska & Thompson, 1997).

As children grow older and develop a better understanding of these causal connections, the parent's disciplinary intervention provides a means of inducing a sense of responsibility and relevant self-conscious emotions that motivate apologetic and reparative behavior (or, in the case of pride, enhanced self-esteem and task persistence). In each instance, however, the arousal of appropriate guilt or shame is facilitated by the parent's rational and reasoned response to misbehavior. By contrast, when the parent's intervention is more coercive and punitive, a child of any age is more likely to experience fear, anxiety, or anger rather than guilt (Hoffman, 1970).

As we have reviewed, temperament is associated with children's proneness to guilt and shame. Not surprisingly, then, research has shown that the most constructive discipline practices for the development of guilt depend, in part, on the child's temperamental profile (Kochanska, 1993, 1995, 1997; Thompson et al., 2006). For example, children who are temperamentally fearful or anxious benefit most from noncoercive discipline practices that enlist the child's discomfort without creating overwhelming distress. For these children, the motivation to behave morally derives from efforts to avoid such aversive feelings. In contrast, for temperamentally fearless children, the emotional incentives for compliance arise not from harsh discipline, but rather from the relational incentives of a warm, mutually responsive parent–child relationship. These children are likely to feel badly after wrongdoing because of its threat to the harmony of their relationship or the possibility of parental love withdrawal (see also Hoffman, 1970).

As children internalize parents' evaluative standards for themselves, they increasingly experience pride, guilt, or shame on their own, even in situations where they are unsupervised or parental judgments are not immediately apparent. These internalized evaluations influence children's self-perceptions and help to explain why, over time, children come to perceive their characteristics and competencies in ways that are similar to how parents and teachers evaluate them (Marsh et al., 2002; Measelle et al., 1998). In families where parents are harshly critical or denigrating, this process can contribute to excessive guilt and shame because children come to internalize parental judgments and evaluations that are unreasonably negative.

Parenting in Achievement Contexts

Discipline illustrates only one forum in which parental evaluations of the child's conduct contribute to individual differences in children's proneness to experiencing guilt and shame. As Stipek (1995) has noted, young children's anticipation of parental reactions is one reason for their emotional responses to success or failure. The expectant smile or the averted gaze of a young child in the parent's presence reflects the importance of the adult's response to his or her self-evaluation in achievement situations. Thus, parents who regularly applaud their child's accomplishments, and who respond with dismay, disapproval, or denigration when the child fails to meet expected standards, contribute to the emergence of feelings of pride, guilt, or shame in preschoolers. Kelly, Brownell, and Campbell (2000) found, for example, that mothers' negative evaluations of their toddler's behavior during a challenging task at 24 months predicted children's shame responses during subsequent achievement tasks at age 3.

Parents convey their expectations and evaluations of children's competencies in indirect ways as well. For example, Pomerantz (Pomerantz, 2001; Pomerantz & Eaton, 2001) found that with increasing age, children more often view their parents' efforts to monitor, guide, and provide uninvited help with homework as an indication that their parents have a low evaluation of their competence. This is particularly true for children of low ability, suggesting that these children may be most prone to experience shame in these situations. More recently, however, Bhanot and Jovanovic (2005) found that girls, even those high in ability, were more likely than boys to interpret unsolicited adult intervention with their math homework as an indication that the teacher or parent believed them to be incompetent. Thus, ability perceptions as well as child gender may influence how children interpret and emotionally respond to adult assistance. More generally, then, in the same manner that discipline approaches contribute to children's comprehension of the associations between personal responsibility for misbehavior and feelings of guilt or rule compliance and feelings of pride, parental (and teacher) behaviors also contribute to children's experience as well as understanding of the reasons for feeling pride and shame in achievement situations.

Parental reactions to child success or failure also shape children's developing theories about their own abilities. Indeed, there are individual differences in the kinds of self-directed thoughts preschoolers have during challenging tasks. For example, Heyman, Dweck, and Cain (1992) found that 4- and 5-year-olds who attribute failure to internal, stable causes ("I am stupid, I can't do this") develop a more helpless response to criticism

by others or to failure on a task compared to preschoolers who attribute failure to internal unstable causes ("I didn't try hard enough") or task difficulty ("That test was hard to
do"). These response patterns, including the emotions that go with them (shame tends to
be associated with stable and guilt with unstable attributions for failure; Tangney &
Dearing, 2002; Tracy & Robins, 2006), have significant consequences for learning. Helpless children tend to give up in the face of failure or criticism whereas mastery-oriented
children persist.

Parenting and Attachment

The broader quality of the parent–child relationship is also important to children's experience of guilt, pride, and shame. Attachment theory has provided a conceptually rich
window through which to explore the influence of the parent–child relationship on self-
conscious emotions. According to this approach, the security of the parent–child relationship is a foundation for early psychological development, with children's developing representations of themselves, close partners, and relationships shaped by their experience of
the parent–child relationship (see Thompson, 2006, for a review). The security of attachment also makes children differentially sensitive to self-related information, with securely
attached children more likely to be receptive to positive feedback concerning the self
(consistent with the more positive self-concept generated by the secure attachment), and
insecurely attached children more prone to remember and internalize negative information about the self. However, in the latter case, defensive processes might also impede
insecure children's responsiveness to negative evaluations, making them paradoxically resistant to accepting criticism, for example, even as they have a more negative sense of
their competencies and characteristics.

Research based on this formulation has yielded several conclusions. First, securely
attached preschoolers generally regard themselves more positively than do insecurely
attached children (Cassidy, 1988; Clark & Symons, 2000; Goodvin et al., 2006; Verschueren, Marcoen, & Schoefs, 1996). Colman and Thompson (2002) found, for example, that in problem-solving situations, insecurely attached preschoolers doubted their
ability more, solicited help from their mothers earlier and in more unnecessary circumstances, and exhibited greater frustration than securely attached children on easy as well
as difficult tasks. Second, in assessments of self-concept that directly evaluated children's
capacity to acknowledge negative characteristics about the self, insecurely attached preschoolers are more resistant to admitting faults of any kind compared to securely attached children (Cassidy, 1988; Clark & Symons, 2000; but see Goodvin et al., 2006, for
contrary findings).

In more extreme circumstances, the negative quality of the parent–child relationship
poses a hazard to healthy emotional development. This is especially true when home life
is threatening, troubled, or disorganized and children are directly affected by parental
affective psychopathology, domestic violence, or other problems. A large literature documents the risks to children's emotional health when they are living with a depressed parent, for example, and studies have underscored the heightened vulnerability to guilty feelings and a sense of responsibility that derives from the caregiver's helplessness, irritability,
and blaming others for her or his sad affect (see Zahn-Waxler & Kochanska, 1990, for a
thoughtful review). Similar processes of emotional enmeshment are apparent for children
growing up in maritally conflicted homes (Cummings & Davies, 1994; Davies &
Cummings, 1994; Davies & Forman, 2002). These studies of emotional development in

troubled families highlight the importance of studying the development of self-conscious emotions in settings that may be provocative of undue shame or guilt in children, particularly in families where children are at high risk for developing insecure attachments to caregivers.

Culture

When parents talk and interact with their children during day-to-day events, they also convey cultural beliefs and expectations for behavior and achievement. These cultural values embedded in everyday conversations and routines can influence the development of children's understanding and experience of self-conscious emotions. In one study, for example, Chinese and American mothers were observed talking about their child's misbehavior in the child's presence. Whereas American mothers tended to attribute child misconduct to spunk or mischievousness, Chinese and Chinese American mothers more often emphasized the shame inherent in misbehavior (Miller, Fung, & Mintz, 1996; Miller, Potts, Fung, Hoogstra, & Mintz, 1990). Indeed, Chinese parents readily endorse shaming as a strategy to educate and socialize their children about the proper ways to behave (Fung, Lieber, & Leung, 2003). Children in Western and non-Western cultures also differ in their beliefs about whether anger or shame is the more appropriate emotional response to interpersonal difficulty, as well as in their understanding of the social conventions that govern the display of positive and negative emotions (Cole, Bruschi, & Tamang, 2002).

Cultural differences in whether the self is construed in an individualistic versus an interdependent fashion also influence the frequency and intensity of pride, shame, and guilt, including their precipitating causes and consequences (see Kitayama, Markus, & Matsumoto, 1995; Wong & Tsai, Chapter 12, this volume). For example, experiences of pride, shame, and guilt may result more frequently from the behaviors of *others* in collectivist cultures that have less distinct boundaries between self and other. Supporting data comes from Stipek (1988) who found that Chinese students were more likely than American students to feel guilt or shame in response to a relative's wrongdoing as well as pride for the accomplishments of a relative. More generally, Americans more often express pride for personal accomplishments, whereas Chinese feel pride for achievements that can benefit others. Thus, the development of self-conscious emotions, including children's views on the value of these emotions, must be considered within the larger cultural belief system, particularly the conceptualization of self.

Interim Summary

Taken together, it is apparent that at the same time that their understanding of themselves and their knowledge about the conditions that provoke self-conscious emotions are expanding, young children are also encountering social evaluations of themselves and their actions that contribute to this understanding. Parent–child communications during discipline encounters, achievement situations, and everyday routines interact with the quality of the parent–child relationship and broader cultural values to affect how young children think about themselves and the situations that make them feel good or bad about themselves. Moreover, it appears that when parental practices are both developmentally graded (e.g., helping young children to understand their responsibility for moral violations or achievement successes) and temperamentally sensitive, young children can acquire the balanced sense of self that enlists self-conscious emotions into responsible conduct and personal success. As this occurs, the association between the developing self and the experience of self-conscious emotions continues to evolve.

SELF-CONSCIOUS EMOTIONS IN MIDDLE TO LATE CHILDHOOD

As children enter grade school and interact with peers in more competitive academic, social, and athletic activities, they more frequently compare their own skills, personality attributes, and characteristics to those of their peers as they become increasingly preoccupied with being accepted, valued, and approved by others outside of the family (Higgins, 1991; Ruble & Frey, 1991). During this time, children's internalization of rules and standards for achievement becomes more solidified, enabling them to better anticipate how other people, including peers and parents, will react to their behavioral choices, as well as how they will evaluate their own performance and moral attributes (Harter, 1998). During middle childhood, children also become more thoughtful interpreters of their parents' behaviors, and, as a result, more frequently evaluate parental reactions in light of their own perceptions of appropriate conduct, the emotional effects of the parent's behavior, and the relevance and consistency of the parental message with what else they know (Grusec & Goodnow, 1994).

These changes in children's social lives and relationships coincide with significant advances in cognition that enable the development of more complex knowledge about the causes of self-conscious emotions. That is, although children begin to personally experience self-conscious emotions early in life, their conceptual knowledge about the determinants of these emotions relies on further development during middle to late childhood. Notably, starting around age 7, children become better able to introspect on their thoughts, they more frequently self-reflect on the contents of their minds, and they become more accurate in judging when other people are thinking and what they are thinking about (Flavell, Green, & Flavell, 1995, 2000). Between the ages of 5 and 10 years children also become more skilled at considering multiple dimensions of a problem at the same time (see Case & Okamoto, 1996; Miller & Aloise, 1989; Piaget, 1952). These cognitive achievements are important because in order to assess self-conscious emotions accurately, the child has to consider both the *outcome* of the person's behavior (Was it positive or negative?) and the person's *control* over that behavior (Was it intentional? Was it due to internal vs. external causes?) at the same time (Thompson, 1989; Weiner & Graham, 1985). Indeed, as we will review, during middle childhood children increasingly understand how people's attributions are causally connected to their emotions, and they demonstrate advancing knowledge about the specific causes of pride, shame, and guilt.

Understanding of Pride

One of the first studies to assess children's ability to differentiate pride from happiness was conducted by Thompson (1987). He found that it was not until after 8 years of age that children were able to differentiate between hypothetical situations depicting pride versus happiness. Most difficult for younger children was attention to the characters' role in producing the positive outcome. Thus, for example, young children often predicted that characters felt proud when something good happened even when the character had no personal hand in producing that positive outcome. Graham (1988) also found that children younger than 8–10 years of age attributed pride to success (doing well on a test) regardless of whether it was caused by an internal (studying hard) versus external cause (easy test) (see also Kornilaki & Chloverakis, 2004; Weiner & Graham, 1989). Even in children's spontaneous descriptions of pride-eliciting situations, personal control of the positive outcome is rarely mentioned prior to 8 years of age (Harris et al., 1987; Harter & Whitesell, 1989).

Understanding of Guilt and Shame

Children's understanding of guilt and shame has been studied by presenting scenarios that vary on locus of control for behaviors as well as the possibility of outsider evaluation. Although even 4- and 5-year-olds associate both guilt and shame with negative outcomes, only children older than 8 years take into account whether the person was personally responsible for the negative consequence (see Thompson, 1987; Weiner & Graham, 1989). Related studies have shown that 7- to 9-year-olds (and older children) attribute more shame versus guilt to people who are incompetent or inferior to their peers, and more shame versus guilt to people who commit moral transgressions that lead others to think poorly of them (Ferguson, Stegge, & Damhuis, 1991; Olthof, Schouten, Kuiper, Stegge, & Jennekens-Schinkel, 2000). These findings are consistent with adult conceptions that shame derives from judgments of oneself as a *person,* whereas guilt derives from judgments of one's *behavior* (see Tangney & Dearing, 2002).

More recently, Olthof et al. (2004) studied young children's knowledge of shame versus guilt in illness-related situations. Results showed that children 7 years and older consistently predicted more shame than guilt in people who did something wrong and it reflected badly on them (e.g., intentionally not taking needed medicine and breaking out in a spotted rash) and more guilt versus shame for situations when people did something wrong and it did not lead to negative evaluation of themselves (e.g., sending a pet rabbit away because the rabbit caused an allergic rash). Interestingly, however, children of all ages predicted high shame reactions in protagonists who suffered a seizure without fault of their own in front of a group of children. Thus, children may not only link shame to behaviors that reflect badly on the self, but also to any kind of personal action that makes other people think one is inferior, bad, or incompetent. In doing so, children demonstrate sophisticated reasoning about the sources of shame, reflective of adult concepts (see Lewis, 2001; Tangney & Dearing, 2002; Tracy & Robins, 2004a).

Self-Conscious Emotions in Rule Situations

Other studies have looked at children's understanding of self-conscious emotions in rule situations. For example, Kornilaki and Chlouverakis (2004) found that between the ages of 7 and 11 children increasingly attribute pride in discretionary moral situations, such as offering one's food to a hungry person, even though one has to make a personal sacrifice. Relatedly, Lagattuta (2005a) found a significant increase between 4 and 7 years of age in children's attributions of negative emotions for transgressors and of positive emotions for rule abiders (see also Arsenio & Lover, 1995). Here, positive affect in compliance situations is closely aligned with pride (being a good person, avoiding harm to self and others, or doing the right thing) and negative affect in transgression situations is reflective of shame and guilt (for being a bad person, violating a standard, or putting oneself or others at risk for harm). Indeed, the developmental shift toward predicting emotions that *mis-*

match desire fulfillment (i.e., feeling good after inhibiting a desire to abide by a rule) was accompanied by a more frequent focus on norms, obligations, and future consequences in children's explanations for emotions. Interestingly, however, all age groups more frequently predicted positive emotions to rule abiders who exhibited willpower in the absence versus the presence of parental monitoring. Thus, children may develop implicit understanding of the importance of personal control for emotions in rule situations prior to being cognizant of these connections in achievement settings (as with Thompson, 1987).

More recently, Lagattuta (2007) again presented 4- to 7-year-olds with scenarios featuring characters who wanted to do an activity but the behavior conflicted with a prohibitive rule. This time, however, participants were asked to predict the character's behavioral decision as well as the *specific* resulting emotion (happy, proud, surprised, OK, mad, sad, afraid, ashamed). Results showed a developmental shift between 4 and 7 years from consistently predicting that people will do what they *want to* at 4 years to consistently predicting that people will do what they *should do* at 7 years. These age-related changes were reflected in emotion attributions as well: 7-year-olds were also more likely than 4-year-olds to predict that story characters felt positive emotions after compliance despite desire inhibition. Girls predicted self-conscious emotions more frequently than boys (see also Bosacki & Moore, 2004), and there was a trend for attributions of pride and shame to increase with age. Replicating Lagattuta (2005a), young children again showed sensitivity to locus of control in rule situations by more frequently predicting positive emotions, especially pride, when characters chose to abide by a standard in the *absence* of authority figures.

Self-Understanding

As with the preschool years, advances in children's experience of and knowledge about self-conscious emotions during middle childhood are propelled by, as well as reflected in, advances in their understanding of self. During middle childhood, children's self-evaluations and social comparisons become more accurate—resulting in more realistic self-appraisals that acknowledge both strengths and faults (see Ruble & Frey, 1991). Their self-evaluations also become more differentiated, as young people distinguish their strengths and weaknesses in different areas of competence, such as athletic, social, academic, and so forth. Self-esteem also becomes based on how competent children perceive themselves to be in the areas that are *personally important* to them. Thus, it may not engender feelings of shame, for example, to be a poor athlete if athletic prowess is not personally meaningful, but it makes a difference to be a poor trumpet player if the child aspires to play in a jazz band (see Harter, 1999). These assessments of self-worth, as well as personal attributions for success or failure, influence children's experience of self-conscious emotions, their motivation to engage in or avoid certain activities, and their persistence in the face of failure or difficulty (Stipek et al., 1992).

Finally, although even young children appreciate that they do not always behave, look, or perform like others desire them to, these differences between "real" (what you are) versus "ideal" (what you or others want you to be) and "ought selves" (what you or others think you should be like) become more salient during middle childhood (Higgins, 1991; Rogers & Dymond, 1954). The development of these internal guides for what one should be like coincides with middle schoolers' greater need for being approved and accepted by others. This need for approval can have both positive and negative emotional consequences. For example, Rudolph, Caldwell, and Conley (2005) report that fourth through eighth graders who cared more strongly about how others evaluated them experienced enhanced self-worth when others liked them and diminished self-worth when others disapproved of them or evaluated them negatively. More generally, children who are more preoccupied with what others think are more easily threatened by others' negative evaluations, and make themselves more vulnerable to more frequent experiences of shame.

Interim Summary

Converging evidence from numerous studies points to 7–8 years of age as a significant transition in children's developing knowledge about the causal determinants of specific self-conscious emotions. Indeed, starting at this age, children become better able to simultaneously consider outcomes, rules, locus of control, and possible future consequences when determining what kind of emotion a person is experiencing. Moreover, they increasingly introspect on their own emotions, evaluations, and beliefs as well as their imaginings about what others may be thinking about them. Such thoughts and introspections coincide with increased differentiation and sophistication in their self-views. Changes in the social environment during middle childhood—most notably, a substantial increase in children's participation in social settings where their skills, characteristics, and behaviors are frequently compared to those of others as well as evaluated by peers and adults outside of the family—propel these cognitive advances.

CONCLUSIONS

Empirical studies on the development of self-conscious emotions have provided revealing insights into how children come to experience, identify, and understand pride, shame, guilt, and embarrassment. However, we still have much to learn. We have identified four directions that may be particularly informative for further research.

Improving Methodology to Assess Young Children's Knowledge

Numerous studies report that preschoolers have more limited knowledge about the causes of self-conscious emotions in comparison to children 7 years and older and adults. Some of this difficulty, however, may arise from the methods used to assess young children's knowledge. That is, because self-conscious emotions involve thoughts (about the self, about standards, about locus of control or responsibility), they can be difficult for young children to comprehend due to their more limited knowledge about and attention to thought processes (see Wellman & Lagattuta, 2000). Arguably, making story characters' thoughts or attributions more explicit and concrete through the use of pictorial thought bubbles may be effective in eliciting more sophisticated responses in young children. Children as young as 3 readily interpret thought bubbles as pictures in the head (Wellman, Hollander, & Schult, 1996), and even children with autism are significantly aided by the use of thought bubbles in experimental tasks involving people's mental states (Wellman et al., 2002).

Lagattuta (2005b) used thought-bubble methodology to investigate the flexibility of young children's reasoning about emotions in situations where desires conflict with rules.

She told and showed preschoolers (using pictorial thought bubbles) that child protagonists were thinking most about rules (that they did or did not do what they were supposed to do), potential outcomes (negatives consequences that might happen next or that had been successfully avoided), or desires (whether they did or did not get what they wanted) after deciding to comply with or break a rule. Results showed that 4- and 5-year-olds, just like adults, attributed positive emotions to rule abiders and negative emotions to rule breakers at high rates ($Ms > 70\%$ trials) when characters were thinking most about rules or potential outcomes, and predicted significantly lower rates of feel good for willpower and feel bad for transgression when characters were thinking most about desires. Indeed, 4- and 5-year-olds predicted positive emotions for compliance and negative emotions for transgression on the think-rule and think-future trials at more than double the rate of their performance on previous studies using identical (Lagattuta, 2005a) or similar scenarios with no thoughts specified (see Arsenio, Gold, & Adams, 2006 for a review). Thus, the inclusion of specific details about the focus of characters' thoughts may be a useful technique for enabling children to demonstrate more advanced reasoning about emotions.

New methodologies are also needed to tap into even younger children's knowledge about self-conscious emotions, as well as their more general attention to rules and standards. For example, numerous studies have successfully used the social referencing paradigm to assess whether infants will modify their affect or behavior in response to an adult's emotional evaluation of an ambiguous *object*. Reasonably, the social referencing paradigm could be used to assess developmental changes in how infants spontaneously reference others' emotional appraisals of *them* (e.g., skills, behaviors) and use that as a guide to future behavior. That is, are infants more likely to repeat or engage in a prior behavior to which an adult responded positively versus negatively? This could be extended to "observer" situations as well. That is, are infants more likely to imitate the novel actions of a person who is praised (and looks proud) versus a person who is denigrated (and looks ashamed) by an outside observer? Indeed, the social referencing paradigm seems a very promising route for assessing early attention to external evaluations and standards (including violations of these standards), as well as early reasoning about what is "good," "bad," "praiseworthy," and "shameful."

Theory of Mind and Self-Conscious Emotions

Future research should also focus more on connections between theory of mind development and children's experience, identification, and knowledge about self-conscious emotions. Because self-conscious emotions are elicited from a person's thoughts or beliefs about the self and about external standards, as well as ideas about other people's thoughts, beliefs, and emotions, children's knowledge about mental states must contribute to the emergence and understanding of self-conscious emotions. Surprisingly, this has not been a widely studied topic in developmental research. As we have reviewed, there are several pieces of evidence pointing to a significant connection between theory of mind and self-conscious emotion development: young children with greater understanding of mental states demonstrate more sensitivity to criticism, and autistic children impaired in theory of mind knowledge demonstrate low knowledge about causes of self-conscious emotions. Moreover, advances in causal understanding of self-conscious emotions between the ages of 5 and 10 years coincide with significant achievements in children's knowledge about the mind including understanding of introspection, sources of thoughts, and stream of consciousness. Obviously, there is much more to explore here.

Attachment and Self-Conscious Emotions

Relationship quality, particularly security of attachment, is strongly connected to how children process information and evaluations about the self. Still, it is unknown whether securely and insecurely attached young children are differentially prone to experiencing guilt, pride, shame, or embarrassment. This is a topic meriting further investigation. A close parent–child relationship can support the growth of pride and self-confidence, for example, but it can also make young children more sensitive to parental criticism or disapproval.

In addition, further study is warranted into the possibility that the security of attachment moderates the influence of other parental practices related to the development of self-conscious emotions. Kochanska, Aksan, Knaack, and Rhines (2004) assessed attachment security at 14 months, parental disciplinary practices at 14–45 months, and conscience development at 56 months. For securely attached children, there was a significant positive longitudinal association between the parent's responsiveness and mild disciplinary procedures and later conscience. For insecurely attached children, there was no such association. Other research groups have also reported that attachment security moderates the influence of parental practices on children's socioemotional development (see Laible & Thompson, 2000; Ontai & Thompson, 2002) and, with respect to self-conscious emotions, this possibility is worth exploring further.

Criteria for Attributing Self-Conscious Emotions to Infants and Toddlers

Finally, it is worth raising the need to develop standard criteria for reliably and validly measuring the experience of self-conscious emotions in preverbal children. That is, when is it valid to identify the gaze aversion of a toddler in response to causing harm to another person, or his or her smile following success on a task, to be indicative of the experience of self-conscious emotions? How do we know it is not simply feeling sad instead of guilty or feeling happy instead of proud, or that the child's behavior reflects an anticipated parental response rather than an internal self-conscious emotion? There are, in short, alternative explanations for these behavioral responses besides that they reflect the experience of self-conscious emotions. Moreover, different studies use different criteria for identifying displays of pride, guilt, shame, and embarrassment. Similar methodological issues plague research with adults (i.e., determining the specific facial and postural behaviors for self-conscious emotions), but at least with adults supplementary measures can be included to verify or confirm the emotional experience, such as self-report (Robins, Noftle, & Tracy, Chapter 24, this volume).

Unfortunately, we do not have a resolution to this problem, aside from the need for researchers to explicitly outline the specific criteria they use to identify displays of self-conscious emotions in very young children so that, at the very least, data can be more easily compared across studies. Promising in this direction is recent research demonstrating that adults (Tracy & Robins, 2004b) as well as children 4 years and older (Tracy et al., 2005) can reliably identify displays of pride (expanded posture, slightly tilted head, small smile) and distinguish it from other positive emotions including happiness. As evidence accumulates for identifiable display markers of self-conscious emotions, researchers will be better equipped to apply standardized criteria for measuring self-conscious emotion displays in young children.

Final Thoughts

Young children's experience, recognition, and conceptual understanding of self-conscious emotions provide a revealing window into the dynamic interplay between social experiences and cognitive development in early development. That is, self-conscious emotions arise from children's self-perceptions and their awareness and adoption of external standards; however, these cognitive achievements are founded in, and informed by, children's everyday experiences, social relationships, and cultural belief systems. As these social connections continue to change and transform as the child develops (e.g., greater parental pressure for achievement and compliance, increased social comparison and extrafamilial evaluation), children's cognitions about themselves and about the situations that elicit feelings of pride, shame, guilt, and embarrassment continue to evolve.

REFERENCES

Aksan, N., & Kochanska, G. (2005). Conscience in childhood: Old questions, new answers. *Developmental Psychology, 41*(3), 506–516.

Arsenio, W. F., Gold, J., & Adams, E. (2006). Children's conceptions and displays of moral emotions. In M. Killen & J. G. Smetana (Eds.), *Handbook of moral development* (pp. 581–609). Mahwah, NJ: Erlbaum.

Arsenio, W., & Lover, A. (1995). Children's conceptions of sociomoral affect: Happy victimizers, mixed emotions, and other expectancies. In M. Killen & D. Hart (Eds.), *Morality in everyday life: Developmental perspectives* (pp. 87–128). New York: Cambridge University Press.

Baldwin, D. A., & Moses, L. J. (1996). The ontogeny of social information gathering. *Child Development, 67*(5), 1915–1939.

Banerjee, R. (2002). Children's understanding of self-presentational behavior: Links with mental-state reasoning and the attribution of embarrassment. *Merrill–Palmer Quarterly, 48*(4), 378–404.

Barrett, K. C., Zahn-Waxler, C., & Cole, P. M. (1993). Avoiders vs. amenders: Implications for the investigation of guilt and shame during toddlerhood? *Cognition and Emotion, 7*(6), 481–505.

Bhanot, R., & Jovanovic, J. (2005). Do parents' academic gender stereotypes influence whether they intrude on their children's homework? *Sex Roles, 52*, 597–607.

Bosacki, S. L. (2000). Theory of mind and self-concept in preadolescents: Links with gender and language. *Journal of Educational Psychology, 92*(4), 709–717.

Bosacki, S. L., & Moore, C. (2004). Preschoolers' understanding of simple and complex emotions: Links with gender and language. *Sex Roles, 50*, 659–675.

Bretherton, I., Fritz, J., Zahn-Waxler, C., & Ridgeway, D. (1986). Learning to talk about emotions: A functionalist perspective. *Child Development, 57*(3), 529–548.

Campos, J. J., Anderson, D. I., Barbu-Roth, M. A., Hubbard, E. M., Hertenstein, M. J., & Witherington, D. (2000). Travel broadens the mind. *Infancy, 1*(2), 149–219.

Campos, J. J., Campos, R. G., & Barrett, K. C. (1989). Emergent themes in the study of emotional development and emotion regulation. *Developmental Psychology, 25*(3), 394–402.

Case, R., & Okamoto, Y. (1996). The role of central conceptual structures in the development of children's thought. *Monographs of the Society for Research in Child Development, 61*(1–2, Serial No. 246).

Cassidy, J. (1988). Child–mother attachment and the self in six-year-olds. *Child Development, 59*(1), 121–134.

Clark, S. E., & Symons, D. K. (2000). A longitudinal study of Q-sort attachment security and self-processes at age 5. *Infant and Child Development, 9*(2), 91–104.

Cole, P. M., Bruschi, C. J., & Tamang, B. L. (2002). Cultural differences in children's emotional reactions to difficult situations. *Child Development, 73,* 983–996.

Colman, R. A., & Thompson, R. A. (2002). Attachment security and the problem-solving behaviors of mothers and children. *Merrill–Palmer Quarterly, 48*(4), 337–359.

Cooley, C. H. (1902). *Human nature and the social order.* New York: Scribner's.

Cummings, E. M., & Davies, P. (1994). *Children and marital conflict: The impact of family dispute and resolution.* New York: Guilford Press.

Cutting, A. L., & Dunn, J. (2002). The cost of understanding other people: Social cognition predicts young children's sensitivity to criticism. *Journal of Child Psychology and Psychiatry, 43*(7), 849–860.

Davies, P. T., & Cummings, E. M. (1994). Marital conflict and child adjustment: An emotional security hypothesis. *Psychological Bulletin, 116*(3), 387–411.

Davies, P. T., & Forman, E. M. (2002). Children's patterns of preserving emotional security in the interparental subsystem. *Child Development, 73*(6), 1880–1903.

Dunn, J. (1995). Children as psychologists: The later correlates of individual differences in understanding of emotions and other minds. *Cognition and Emotion, 9,* 187–201.

Dunn, J., & Munn, P. (1987). Development of justification in disputes with mother and sibling. *Developmental Psychology, 23*(6), 791–798.

Epstein, S. (1973). The self-concept revisited or a theory of a theory. *American Psychologist, 28,* 405–416.

Ferguson, T. J., & Stegge, H. (1995). Emotional states and traits in children: The case of guilt and shame. In J.P. Tangney & K. W. Fischer (Eds.), *Self-conscious emotions: The psychology of shame, guilt, embarrassment, and pride* (pp. 174–197). New York: Guilford Press.

Ferguson, T. J., Stegge, H., & Damhuis, I. (1991). Children's understanding of guilt and shame. *Child Development, 62*(4), 827–839.

Fivush, R., & Nelson, K. (2006). Parent–child reminiscing locates the self in the past. *British Journal of Developmental Psychology, 24*(1), 235–251.

Flavell, J. H., Green, F. L., & Flavell, E. R. (1995). Young children's knowledge about thinking. *Monographs of the Society for Research in Child Development, 60* (1, Serial No. 243), v–96.

Flavell, J. H., Green, F. L., & Flavell, E. R. (2000). Development of children's awareness of their own thoughts. *Journal of Cognition and Development, 1*(1), 97–112.

Fung, H. E., Lieber, E., & Leung, P. W. L. (2003). Parental beliefs about shame and moral socialization in Taiwan, Hong Kong, and the United States. In K. S. Yang & K. K. Hwang (Eds.), *Progress in Asian social psychology: Conceptual and empirical contributions* (pp. 83–109). Westport, CT: Praeger/Greenwood Press.

Geppert, U., & Küster, U. (1983). The emergence of "wanting to do it oneself": A precursor of achievement motivation. *International Journal of Behavioral Development, 6*(3), 355–369.

Goodvin, R., Meyer, S., Thompson, R. A., & Hayes, R. (2006). *Self-understanding in early childhood: Associations with attachment security, maternal perceptions of the child, and maternal emotional risk.* Manuscript submitted for publication.

Graham, S. (1988). Children's developing understanding of the motivational role of affect: An attributional analysis. *Cognitive Development, 3,* 71–88.

Gralinski, J. H., & Kopp, C. B. (1993). Everyday rules for behavior: Mothers' requests to young children. *Developmental Psychology, 29*(3), 573–584.

Grusec, J. E., & Goodnow, J. J. (1994). Impact of parental discipline methods on the child's internalization of values: A reconceptualization of current points of view. *Developmental Psychology, 30*(1), 4–19.

Grusec, J., & Kuczynski, L. (1997). *Parenting and children's internalization of values: A handbook of contemporary theory.* Hoboken, NJ: Wiley.

Harris, P. (1989). *Children and emotion.* Oxford, UK: Blackwell.

Harris, P. L., Olthof, T., Terwogt, M. M., & Hardman, C. E. (1987). Children's knowledge of the situations that provoke emotion. *International Journal of Behavioral Development, 10*(3), 319–343.

Harter, S. (1998). The development of self-representations. In W. Damon & N. Eisenberg (Eds.), *Handbook of child psychology* (5th ed., Vol. 3, pp. 553–618). New York: Wiley.

Harter, S. (1999). *The construction of the self: A developmental perspective.* New York: Guilford Press.

Harter, S., & Whitesell, N. R. (1989). Developmental changes in children's understanding of single, multiple, and blended emotion concepts. In C. Saarni & P. L. Harris (Eds.), *Children's understanding of emotion* (pp. 81–116). New York: Cambridge University Press.

Heerey, E. A., Keltner, D., & Capps, L. M. (2003). Making sense of self-conscious emotion: Linking theory of mind and emotion in children with autism. *Emotion, 3*(4), 394–400.

Heyman, G. D., Dweck, C. S., & Cain, K. M. (1992). Young children's vulnerability to self-blame and helplessness: Relationship to beliefs about goodness. *Child Development, 63*(2), 401–415.

Heyman, G. D., & Gelman, S. A. (1999). The use of trait labels in making psychological inferences. *Child Development, 70*(3), 604–619.

Higgins, E. T. (1991). Development of self-regulatory and self-evaluative processes: Costs, benefits, and tradeoffs. In M. R. Gunnar & A. L. Sroufe (Eds.), *Self processes and development: The Minnesota Symposia on Child Development* (Vol. 23, pp. 125–166). Hillsdale, NJ: Erlbaum.

Hoffman, M. L. (1970). Moral development. In P. H. Mussen (Ed.), *Carmichael's manual of child psychology* (3rd ed., Vol. 2, pp. 261–360). New York: Wiley.

Howe, M. L., & Courage, M. L. (1997). The emergence and early development of autobiographical memory. *Psychological Review, 104*(3), 499–523.

Kagan, J. (1981). *The second year: The emergence of self-awareness.* Cambridge, MA: Harvard University Press.

Kagan, J. (2005). Human morality and temperament. In G. Carlo (Ed.), *Moral motivation through the lifespan: Nebraska Symposium on Motivation* (Vol. 15, pp. 1–32). Lincoln: University of Nebraska Press.

Kelley, S. A., Brownell, C. A., & Campbell, S. B. (2000). Mastery motivation and self-evaluative affect in toddlers: Longitudinal relations with maternal behavior. *Child Development, 71*(4), 1061–1071.

Kitayama, S., Markus, H. R., & Matsumoto, H. (1995). Culture, self, and emotion: A cultural perspective on "self-conscious" emotions. In J. P. Tangney & K. W. Fischer (Eds.), *Self-conscious emotions: The psychology of shame, guilt, embarrassment, and pride* (pp. 439–464). New York: Guilford Press.

Kochanska, G. (1993). Toward a synthesis of parental socialization and child temperament in early development of conscience. *Child Development, 64*(2), 325–347.

Kochanska, G. (1995). Children's temperament, mother's discipline, and security of attachment: Multiple pathways to emerging internalization. *Child Development, 66*, 597–615.

Kochanska, G. (1997). Multiple pathways to conscience for children with different temperaments: From toddlerhood to age 5. *Developmental Psychology, 33*(2), 228–240.

Kochanska, G. (2002). Committed compliance, moral self, and internalization: A mediational model. *Developmental Psychology, 38*(3), 339–351.

Kochanska, G., Aksan, N., Knaack, A., & Rhines, H. M. (2004). Maternal parenting and children's conscience: Early security as moderator. *Child Development, 75*(4), 1229–1242.

Kochanska, G., Casey, R. J., & Fukumoto, A. (1995). Toddlers' sensitivity to standard violations. *Child Development, 66*(3), 643–656.

Kochanska, G., DeVet, K., Goldman, M., Murray, K., & Putnam, S. P. (1994). Maternal reports of conscience development and temperament in young children. *Child Development, 65*(3), 852–868.

Kochanska, G., Gross, J. N., Lin, M.-H., & Nichols, K. E. (2002). Guilt in young children: Development, determinants, and relations with a broader system of standards. *Child Development, 73*(2), 461–482.

Kochanska, G., & Thompson, R. A. (1997). The emergence and development of conscience in toddlerhood and early childhood. In J. E. Grusec & L. Kuczynski (Eds.), *Parenting and children's internalization of values: A handbook of contemporary theory* (pp. 53–77). Hoboken, NJ: Wiley.

Kornilaki, E. N., & Chloverakis, G. (2004). The situational antecedents of pride and happiness: Developmental and domain differences. *British Journal of Developmental Psychology, 22*(4), 605–619.

Lagattuta, K. H. (2005a). When you shouldn't do what you want to do: Young children's understanding of desires, rules, and emotions. *Child Development, 76*(3), 713–733.

Lagattuta, K. H. (2005b, April). *Children's knowledge about the influence of thoughts on emotions in prohibitive rule situations.* Paper presented at the biennial meeting of the Society for Research in Child Development, Atlanta, GA.

Lagattuta, K. H. (2007, March). *Desire psychology meets prohibition: Children's understanding of thoughts, decisions, and emotions in rule situations.* Poster presented at the biennial meeting for the Society for Research in Child Development, Boston, MA.

Lagattuta, K. H., & Wellman, H. M. (2001). Thinking about the past: Early knowledge about links between prior experience, thinking, and emotion. *Child Development, 72*(1), 82–102.

Lagattuta, K. H., & Wellman, H. M. (2002). Differences in early parent–child conversations about negative versus positive emotions: Implications for the development of psychological understanding. *Developmental Psychology, 38*(4), 564–580.

Lagattuta, K. H., Wellman, H. M., & Flavell, J. H. (1997). Preschoolers' understanding of the link between thinking and feeling: Cognitive cuing and emotional change. *Child Development, 68*(6), 1081–1104.

Laible, D. J., & Thompson, R. A. (2000). Mother–child discourse, attachment security, shared positive affect, and early conscience development. *Child Development, 71*(5), 1424–1440.

Lamb, S. (1993). First moral sense: An examination of the appearance of morally related behaviours in the second year of life. *Journal of Moral Education, 22*, 97–109.

Lewis, M. (1993). *Self-conscious emotions: Embarrassment, pride, shame, and guilt.* New York: Guilford Press.

Lewis, M. (1995). Embarrassment: The emotion of self-exposure and evaluation. In J. P. Tangney & K. W. Fischer (Eds.), *Self-conscious emotions* (pp. 198–218). New York: Guilford Press.

Lewis, M. (2001). Origins of the self-conscious child. In W. Crozier & L. Alden (Eds.), *International handbook of social anxiety: Concepts, research and interventions relating to the self and shyness* (pp. 101–118). New York: Wiley.

Lewis, M., & Brooks-Gunn, J. (1979). *Social cognition and the acquisition of self.* New York: Plenum Press.

Marsh, H. W., Ellis, L. A., & Craven, R. G. (2002). How do preschool children feel about themselves?: Unraveling measurement and multidimensional self-concept structure. *Developmental Psychology, 38*(3), 376–393.

Measelle, J. R., Ablow, J. C., Cowan, P. A., & Cowan, C. P. (1998). Assessing young children's views of their academic, social, and emotional lives: An evaluation of the self-perception scales of the Berkeley Puppet Interview. *Child Development, 69*(6), 1556–1576.

Miller, P. H., & Aloise, P. A. (1989). Young children's understanding of the psychological causes of behavior: A review. *Child Development, 60*(2), 257–285.

Miller, P. J., Fung, H., & Mintz, J. (1996). Self-construction through narrative practices: A Chinese and American comparison of early socialization. *Ethos, 24*(2), 237–280.

Miller, P. J., Potts, R., Fung, H., Hoogstra, L., & Mintz, J. (1990). Narrative practices and the social construction of self in childhood. *American Ethnologist, 17*(2), 292–311.

Moses, L. J., Baldwin, D. A., Rosicky, J. G., & Tidball, G. (2001). Evidence for referential understanding in the emotions domain at twelve and eighteen months. *Child Development, 72*(3), 718–735.

Nelson, K. (1978). *Event knowledge: Structure and function in development.* Hillsdale, NJ: Erlbaum.

Olthof, T., Ferguson, T. J., Bloemers, E., & Deij, M. (2004). Morality- and identity-related antecedents of children's guilt and shame attributions in events involving physical illness. *Cognition and Emotion, 18*(3), 383–404.

Olthof, T., Schouten, A., Kuiper, H., Stegge, H., & Jennekens-Schinkel, A. (2000). Shame and guilt in children: Differential situational antecedents and experiential correlates. *British Journal of Developmental Psychology, 18,* 51–64.

Ontai, L. L., & Thompson, R. A. (2002). Patterns of attachment and maternal discourse effects on children's emotion understanding from 3 to 5 years of age. *Social Development, 11*(4), 433–450.

Piaget, J. (1952). *The origins of intelligence in children.* Oxford, UK: International Universities Press.

Pomerantz, E. M. (2001). Parent × child socialization: Implications for the development of depressive symptoms. *Journal of Family Psychology, 15*(3), 510–525.

Pomerantz, E. M., & Eaton, M. M. (2001). Maternal intrusive support in the academic context: Transactional socialization processes. *Developmental Psychology, 37*(2), 174–186.

Reddy, V. (2001). Positively shy! Developmental continuities in the expression of shyness, coyness, and embarrassment. In W. R. Crozier & L. E. Alden (Eds.), *International handbook of social anxiety: Concepts, research and interventions relating to the self and shyness* (pp. 77–99). New York: Wiley.

Rochat, P. (1995). Early objectification of the self. In P. Rochat (Ed.), *The self in infancy: Theory and research* (pp. 53–71). Amsterdam, The Netherlands: Elsevier Science.

Rogers, C., & Dymond, R. (1954). *Psychotherapy and personality change.* Chicago: University of Chicago Press.

Ruble, D. N., & Frey, K. S. (1991). Changing patterns of comparative behavior as skills are acquired: A functional model of self-evaluation. In J. Suls & T. Wills (Eds.), *Social comparison: Contemporary theory and research* (pp. 79–113). Hillsdale, NJ: Erlbaum.

Rudolph, K. D., Caldwell, M. S., & Conley, C. S. (2005). Need for approval and children's well-being. *Child Development, 76*(2), 309–323.

Russell, J. A., & Paris, F. A. (1994). Do children acquire concepts for complex emotions abruptly? *International Journal of Behavioral Development, 17*(2), 349–365.

Saarni, C. (1999). *The development of emotional competence.* New York: Guilford Press.

Stipek, D. (1988). Differences between Americans and Chinese in the circumstances evoking pride, shame, and guilt. *Journal of Cross-Cultural Psychology, 29,* 616–629.

Stipek, D. (1995). The development of pride and shame in toddlers. In J. Tangney & K. Fischer (Eds.), *Self-conscious emotions: The psychology of shame, guilt, embarrassment, and pride* (pp. 237–252). New York: Guilford Press.

Stipek, D., Recchia, S., & McClintic, S. (1992). Self-evaluation in young children. *Monographs of the Society for Research in Child Development, 57*(1, Serial No. 226), 100.

Tangney, J., & Dearing, R.L. (2002). *Emotions and social behavior.* New York: Guilford Press.

Tangney, J., & Fischer, K. (Eds). (1995). *Self-conscious emotions: The psychology of shame, guilt, embarrassment, and pride.* New York: Guilford Press.

Thompson, R. A. (1987). Development of children's inferences of the emotions of others. *Developmental Psychology, 23*(1), 124–131.

Thompson, R. A. (1989). Causal attributions and children's emotion understanding. In C. Saarni & P. L. Harris (Eds.), *Children's understanding of emotion* (pp. 117–150). New York: Cambridge University Press.

Thompson, R. A. (2006). The development of the person: Social understanding, relationships, self, conscience. In W. Damon & R. M. Lerner (Eds.) & N. Eisenberg (Vol. Ed.), *Handbook of child psychology, Vol. 3. Social, emotional, and personality development* (6th ed., pp. 24–98). New York: Wiley.

Thompson, R. A., & Hoffman, M. L. (1980). Empathy and the development of guilt in children. *Developmental Psychology, 16*(2), 155–156.

Thompson, R., & Lagattuta, K.H. (2006). Feeling and understanding: Early emotional development. In K. McCartney & D. Phillips (Eds.), *Blackwell handbook of early childhood development.* (pp. 317–338). Malden, MA: Blackwell.

Thompson, R. A., Laible, D. J., & Ontai, L. L. (2003). Early understanding of emotion, morality, and the self: Developing a working model. In R. V. Kail (Ed.), *Advances in child development and behavior* (Vol. 31, pp. 137–171). San Diego, CA: Academic Press.

Thompson, R. A., Meyer, S., & McGinley, M. (2006). Understanding values in relationship: The development of conscience. In M. Killen & J. Smetana (Eds.), *Handbook of moral development* (pp. 267–297). Mahwah, NJ: Erlbaum.

Tracy, J. L., & Robins, R. W. (2004a). Putting the self into self-conscious emotions: A theoretical model. *Psychological Inquiry, 15,* 103–125.

Tracy, J. L., & Robins, R. W. (2004b). Show your pride: Evidence for a discrete emotion expression. *Psychological Science, 15,* 194–197.

Tracy, J. L., & Robins, R. W. (2006). Appraisal antecedents of shame and guilt: Support for a theoretical model. *Personality and Social Psychology Bulletin, 32*(10), 1339–1351.

Tracy, J. L., Robins, R. W., & Lagattuta, K. H. (2005). Can children recognize pride? *Emotion, 5*(3), 251–257.

Trevarthen, C., & Aitken, K. J. (2001). Infant intersubjectivity: Research, theory, and clinical applications. *Journal of Child Psychology and Psychiatry, 42*(1), 3–48.

Verschueren, K., Marcoen, A., & Schoefs, V. (1996). The internal working model of the self, attachment, and competence in five-year-olds. *Child Development, 67*(5), 2493–2511.

Weiner, B., & Graham, S. (1985). An attributional approach to emotional development. In C. Izard, J. Kagan, & R. Zajonc (Eds.), *Emotions, cognition, and behavior* (pp. 167–191). New York: Cambridge University Press.

Weiner, B., & Graham, S. (1989). Understanding the motivational role of affect: Lifespan research from an attributional perspective. *Cognition and Emotion, 3*(4), 401–419.

Wellman, H. M., Baron-Cohen, S., Caswell, R., Gomez, J. C., Swettenham, J., Toye, E., et al. (2002). Thought-bubbles help children with autism acquire an alternative to a theory of mind. *Autism, 6*(4), 343–363.

Wellman, H. M., Cross, D., & Watson, J. (2001). Meta-analysis of theory-of-mind development: The truth about false belief. *Child Development, 72*(3), 655–684.

Wellman, H. M., Hollander, M., & Schult, C. A. (1996). Young children's understanding of thought bubbles and of thoughts. *Child Development, 67*(3), 768–788.

Wellman, H. M., & Lagattuta, K. H. (2000). Developing understandings of mind. In S. Baron-Cohen, H. Tager-Flusberg, & D. Cohen (Eds.), *Understanding other minds: Perspectives from developmental cognitive neuroscience* (2nd ed., pp. 21–49). Oxford, UK: Oxford University Press.

Zahn-Waxler, C., & Kochanska, G. (1990). *The origins of guilt.* In R. A. Thompson (Ed.), *Nebraska Symposium on Motivation* (Vol. 36, pp. 183–257). Lincoln: University of Nebraska Press.

Zahn-Waxler, C., & Robinson, J. (1995). Empathy and guilt: Early origins of feelings of responsibility. In J. P. Tangney & K. W. Fischer (Eds.), *Self-conscious emotions* (pp. 143–173). New York: Guilford Press.

7

The Development of Pride
and Moral Life

DANIEL HART
M. KYLE MATSUBA

Holy Scripture proclaims to us brothers: "Everyone who exalts
himself shall be humbled, and he who humbles himself shall be
exalted" (Lk. 14:11). It tells us that all self-exaltation is a form
of pride, against which, the prophet tells us, be guarded. . . .
—St. Benedict (cited in Meisel & del Mastro [1975, pp. 56–57])

There are many beautiful aspects of our conscientiousness, like
faith, humility, self-respect, non-craving, non-anger, non-
ignorance, diligence, ease, care, equanimity, and nonviolence.
Unwholesome mental formations, on the other hand, are like a
tangled ball of string. When we try to untangle it, we only wind
it around ourselves until we cannot move. . . . The basic
unwholesome mental formations are greed, hatred, ignorance,
pride, doubts, and views.
—Hanh (1998, pp. 73–74)

Christianity, Buddhism—the two religious traditions represented by the excerpts above—
and other religious traditions admonish us to guard against the dangers of pride. Chris-
tians have traditionally believed pride to be a cardinal sin that undermines membership in
the community of God. Pride is an indication that the focus of worship has been displaced from God onto the self. Among Buddhists, pride is considered to be harmful because it interferes with the attainment of "right-mindfulness," which is a prerequisite to
discovering true happiness (Hanh, 1998). Indeed, these two epigraphs illustrate a common belief that pride reflects an *immoral*—selfish, egoistic—perspective on oneself and
the world. These epigraphs, and the traditions they represent, suggest that humanity can
become more moral by banishing experiences that lead to pride.

Our view is quite different. We believe that developmental transformations in pride
occurring over childhood and adulthood sustain commitment to long-term moral action.

This perspective grows out of our previous research on sustained moral activity (Hart & Fegley, 1995; Matsuba & Walker, 2004) and volunteering (Matsuba, Hart, & Atkins, in press). We have observed in this work that commitment to sustained, voluntary moral activity is rarely observed prior to adolescence (Hart, 2005; Hart & Fegley, 1995; Matsuba & Walker, 2004), an observation consistent with theoretical expositions of moral behavior offered by Kohlberg (1984), Colby and Damon (1992), and many others. The emergence of sustained moral action in adolescence reflects, in part, the elaboration of a moral identity (Hart, 2005), but, in addition, it may reflect the developmental transformation of pride into an emotion that can sustain voluntary ethical behavior.

We believe this perspective is relatively novel principally because (1) only a few psychologists (e.g., Tangney, 2002) and philosophers (e.g., Kristjánsson, 2002) have examined the relation of pride to moral life, and (2) there has been little research on the development of pride (a computerized search of the literature found only a handful of studies). Our goals in this chapter are to (1) sketch a role for pride in moral life, (2) use the extant literature to outline the development of pride in childhood and adolescence, and (3) present new data concerning pride and moral action.

EMOTIONS AND MORALITY

Although the relation of pride to moral behavior has rarely been studied by psychologists or philosophers, there is an enormous body of work on morality, moral action, and moral emotions. We present an overview of this work as the backdrop to our discussion on the role of pride in motivating and sustaining moral commitments.

Empathy and Sympathy

Hume (1740/1978) claimed that morality is best understood as motivated by emotions. According to Hume (1740/1978), "Morality, therefore, is more properly felt than judged of" (p. 278). That is, initial experiences of pain or pleasure lead to moral judgments and actions, and that reason only serves to bring to light this preexisting cause-and-effect relationship. A great deal of research has followed in this tradition. While there are exceptions (e.g., Freud, 1936; Gilligan, 1976; Kagan, 1984), research on moral emotions and its development over the last 40 years has largely focused on empathic distress (Hoffman, 1991) and empathy-related responding (Eisenberg, 2000, 2005). For Hoffman (1991), "empathic distress," which is the tendency to experience another's expressed emotions, is at the heart of moral behavior and moral development. Hoffman asserted that infants are predisposed to experiencing empathic distress, and that this distress motivates moral action. Empathic distress is transformed over the course of development as children's understanding of themselves and others is elaborated.

Eisenberg (2000, 2005) has also emphasized empathy-related responding as the key for understanding morality. "Empathy-related responding" refers to behavior originating from the apprehension of others' emotional state. Typically, empathy-related responding is expressed either through sympathy (i.e., feelings of concern for another person), personal distress (i.e., self-focused, adverse emotional reaction to others' emotion), or a combination of both. Moreover, there is substantial evidence demonstrating significant relationships between empathy-related responses and moral thinking and moral behavior (Eisenberg, 2000, 2005). For example, Eisenberg and her colleagues have found that sympathetic responding to the needs of others was positively related to helping behavior and to moral reasoning. In contrast, personal distress responding was negatively correlated to helping behavior. These results are robust, holding true under different contexts and over time (Eisenberg, 2000, 2005).

Furthermore, researchers have clearly demonstrated that empathy can motivate prosocial behavior (Batson, 1991; Weiner, 1980). For example, recent work by Batson and his colleagues (Batson et al., 1995) has found that manipulating the level of empathy toward a target person in need can cause people to allocate more resources to that person, thereby reducing the amount of resources available to the larger collective group. In another study, Batson, Turk, Shaw, and Klein (1995) showed that manipulating levels of empathy toward a target person in need can affect the extent to which people value the welfare of that person. Those who experienced a high level of empathy toward a person in need tended to increase their valuing of that person, thus demonstrating that people can gain insight into their values system based on their emotional responses to events.

Contempt, Anger, and Disgust

In the last decade researchers investigating moral emotions have expanded their focus beyond empathy to include a broad range of emotions that have relevance for understanding moral life. Rozin and his colleagues have recently focused on *other-condemning emotions* as important for regulating moral life. Other-condemning emotions include contempt, anger, and disgust, and are labeled "moral" because they are often experienced when people witness third parties engaging in behaviors that are in violation of the moral order within the culture (Rozin, Lowery, Imada, & Haidt, 1999). Rozin and his colleagues claim that the specific other-condemning emotion experienced depends, to some extent, on the kind of ethical breach observed. Some breaches result in contempt, others in anger, and still others in disgust. By employing Shweder's ethical model (Shweder, Much, Mahapatra, & Park, 1997), Rozin et al. were able to draw links between type of ethical breach and type of emotion experienced. According to Shweder, there are three types of ethics: community (e.g., social conventions), autonomy (e.g., individual rights), and divinity (e.g., religious, sacred laws). Specifically, Rozin et al. predicted that when people witnessed violations to the ethics of community, autonomy, and divinity, they tended to experience contempt, anger, and disgust (the CAD triad of emotions), respectively.

Shame and Guilt

The third cluster of moral emotions we consider is the self-conscious emotions which include shame, guilt, embarrassment, and pride (Eisenberg, 2000; Lewis, 2000a; Tangney, 1999). Shame, guilt, and embarrassment may be experienced when a person behaves in ways that fail to meet some standard, rule, or goal. In the case of shame, this failure is attributed to the "global" self—that is, in the case of shame, the failure is treated like a dispositional flaw in character spanning across contexts. Guilt, on the other hand, is experienced when the failure is attributed to the self and is isolated to the specific situation in which it occurred, not generalized to other contexts. In the case of guilt, the failure is not assumed to be indicative of a problem with the "global" self. Embarrassment is experienced when a person fails to meet some social convention. Because embarrassment is experienced as lighthearted, and as a less negative emotion than guilt or shame, many see it, at best, as playing only a minor role in moral behavior (Eisenberg, 2000).

Summary of Moral Emotions

The existing traditions have contributed enormously to our understanding of moral functioning and its development. Our overview suggests that this body of work has identified the emotions that motivate moral responses to those in distress (empathy, sympathy) and those that inhibit actions that violate social norms (shame, guilt, disgust, contempt, anger). These are important achievements.

However, one area of moral life that has escaped illumination by research in this tradition is sustained, voluntary moral action on behalf of others. Individuals who show high levels of commitment to others have sometimes been found to be slightly higher in sympathy and empathy than others (e.g., Penner, 2002), but other investigations have found no difference in sympathy between altruists and others (e.g., Monroe, 1991). This pattern suggests that empathy and sympathy by themselves are insufficient to explain sustained voluntary moral action. Moreover, efforts to explain sustained altruism in terms of sophisticated moral reasoning have likewise been disappointing (e.g., Colby & Damon, 1992; Hart & Fegley, 1995). Voluntary and sustained moral action is poorly understood within the popular research traditions of moral life.

Pride and Moral Action

Generally ignored by theorists of moral life—and when discussed usually scorned as an impediment to ethical action—pride deserves consideration as a motivator of altruistic behavior. In particular, we believe that the inclusion of pride into accounts of moral life can contribute to the resolution of two problems in our understanding of moral commitment: (1) *How* is voluntary, planned, moral action sustained over time when it is not triggered by the immediate context?; and (2) *Why* is voluntary, planned, sustained moral action not evident until late childhood and early adolescence? In the sections that follow we review some of the philosophical and psychological literature relevant to these questions.

Pride in Philosophical Accounts of Moral Life

Philosophy, like theology, tends to view pride as resulting from character deficits and motivating unethical and even evil behavior. However, this view may result as much from overly broad connotations of pride as from a careful inspection of pride and its role in moral life. As Dillon (2003) has noted, pride is often used as if it were synonymous with self-esteem, self-confidence, and self-love, and perhaps current usage allows for a certain degree of interchangeability among these terms. Nonetheless, colloquial use may obscure more than it illuminates the unique aspects of a term by making it identical to others. In particular, pride can be understood to be a distinct emotional reaction to an action or event that (1) brings the self closer to goals and standards, and (2) is the product of the self's efforts. Given these qualities, how does pride relate to morality?

Kristjánsson (2002) presents an Aristotelian-influenced account of pride's relation to moral life. According to Kristjánsson, a person with moral virtue "incorporates the episodic emotions of simple pride and shame as acute signals of success or failure, and provides in itself a strong source of motivation: Shame is the ultimate turn-off for the prideful personal and must be avoided at all cost, whereas simple pride becomes a highly-prized end" (p. 106). This model suggests that moral virtue is partly based upon an emotional system that is responsive both to the individual's actions and to the social environment that informs the individual about the success and value of these actions. Individuals who perform actions valued in their social networks experience simple pride, a powerfully pleasant emotion that is a "highly-prized end." Altruistic behavior can be understood to have these qualities: it is a line of action initiated and controlled by the individual and deeply valued by most societies. Moreover, because sustained altruistic behavior—for example, repeated volunteering in a food kitchen—allows the individual to discover that his or her actions are endorsed and supported by the social judgments of others, it is more likely to be reinforced by the experience of pride than are actions that are performed only once. Experiences of pride, then, can be a powerful motivator for sustained altruistic behavior.

Kristjánsson (2002) suggests that another facet of pride, which he calls "pridefulness," also supports moral behavior. Pridefulness means to feel "proud of [one's] good moral character and its results" (p. 105). Pridefulness is a product of reflection on oneself and discerning one's value as a moral actor. To some extent, Kristjánsson's use of pridefulness reflects Hume's notion that self-reflection can induce self-respect as well as respect for others: "This constant habit of surveying ourselves, as it were, in reflection.. . . begets, in noble creatures, a certain reverence for themselves as well as others; which is the surest guardian of every virtue" (Hume, 1748/1972, p. 276). What Kristjánsson and Hume seek to introduce into the analysis of moral life is the idea that self-reflection on moral actions and the character traits from which they emanate can deepen commitment to moral life.

Pride in Psychological Accounts of Moral Life

Much of the research on pride has focused on the *appraisals*, or interpretations, that individuals make about an event and its causes in order for pride to be experienced. This work elaborates the rather basic ideas about pride forming the foundations for the philosophical explorations of morality discussed in the preceding section. Tracy and Robins (2004) posit the following sequence of appraisals in the elicitation of self-conscious emotions like pride. First, there must be triggering events that lead the person to focus on the self, thereby activating specific self-representations. Second, the event needs to be goal-relevant and goal-congruent. That is, the event must be important and meaningful to the person and what he or she wishes to achieve. Third, the cause of the event must be attributed to the self. There is a substantial body of experimental research that demonstrates that this set of attributions is consistent with the experience of pride. Researchers have asked individuals to report how they would feel if they were to make various combinations of appraisals about events, and the findings from a variety of investigations are generally consonant with the predictions made by Tracy and Robins (2004). However, to the best of our knowledge, virtually no research has examined the kinds of appraisals people make about the kinds of sustained moral actions that we have been discussing throughout this chapter.

Not only do philosophers and psychologists posit broadly similar patterns of appraisals as underlying the experience of pride, they share common ground in their understanding of how pride motivates moral action. Borrowing from the work of Dovidio and Penner (2004), we find two possible pathways that explain how pride motivates prosocial behavior. On the one hand, experiencing pride in one's self may motivate people to act in order to help people improve their image of self that others see—this is the *image im-*

provement hypothesis. A second pathway may be that pride motivates people to prosocial action so that they feel better about themselves—this is the *positive state improvement* hypothesis. This latter route of influence is similar to Tangney's (1999) claim that "pride serves to enhance people's self-worth and, perhaps more importantly, to encourage future behavior that conforms to social standards of worth or merit" (p. 395). Both notions of pride are consonant with Kristjánsson's (2002) model of the role of pride in morality discussed in the previous section, and both notions help explain how individuals may become committed to voluntary lines of altruistic behavior.

THE DEVELOPMENT OF PRIDE

If our account to this point is correct, then the *development* of pride ought to influence moral life. There is virtually no research that closely examines the connections between the development of pride and moral cognition or moral action. Nor is there much research that has focused on developmental transformations in pride. Consequently, our account of the development of pride and its effects on moral life will rely on a synthesis of research literatures rather than on a review of a body of directly relevant studies. One goal in this synthesis is to highlight developmental transformations in pride that occur in childhood and early adolescence. A second goal is to suggest that these transformations are the groundwork upon which voluntary, sustained, altruistic behavior is based.

Self-Conscious Emotions

Pride is one of a family of self-conscious emotions (emotions that necessarily require a sense of self). The development of any member of this family of emotions can provide insights into the development of pride. Researchers generally agree that self-conscious emotions emerge later than the more basic emotions (e.g., happiness, sadness), and appear sometime in the second year of life (Lewis, 2000b). At least two sets of cognitive processes, which infants do not possess at birth, seem to be required in order to experience the self-conscious emotions. First, to experience emotions like shame or guilt, children must be able to appraise their failed actions against some standard. These abilities are believed to emerge around age 2–3 years (Lewis, 2000b). This finding is consistent with work by Kagan (2005), who claimed that shame following the violation of a standard is typically observed in the third year, and by Smetana (2006), who stated that by age 3 children are able to distinguish between moral and social-conventional rules. Hence, by around age 3, children have internalized some moral and conventional standards, and are able to evaluate their behavior against these standards.

Moreover, Stipek (1995; Stipek, Recchia, & McClintic, 1992) distinguished between self-conscious emotions that are expressed as a result of meeting internal versus external standards. According to Stipek, young children first experience autonomous pleasure from having some autonomous effect on their environment, and are not concerned about others' reactions. Initial awareness of others' reactions and its link to self-conscious emotions is believed to emerge around the age of 2 years. Sometimes the period between 3 and 3½ years, as children begin to internalize social standards and judge their own performance, the expression of self-conscious emotions becomes more independent from the appraisal of others.

In addition to changes associated with the "standards" that are applied, there are also cognitive developmental changes in the appraisal "structure" (Lewis, 2001). According to Lewis, three dimensions—goal conduciveness, coping potential, and norm (standard) compatibility—are important in understanding the developmental changes to the appraisal structure. At each structural stage, children are faced with evaluating situations that affect their goals, determining how they are going to respond to these situations in order to meet their goals, and examining themselves to see if their behavior meets some standard. However, how they appraise and respond to the situation differs between stages. Lewis provides the example of his 3½-year-old daughter experiencing shame as a result of her evaluating herself against a "schematic" norm of a "good girl" (i.e., goal potential), which at this age remains impervious to "reflection and manipulation." Moreover, this experience of shame may be strong due to his daughter's perceived inability to control the beliefs of other people (i.e., low coping potential). Alternately, the child may try to remove herself from the situation.

As children develop, they enter into a broader social arena that comes with specific norms and expectations associated with peer acceptance (Lewis, 2001). Behaviors that meet or violate these norms will influence the kinds of emotions experienced by children. Fortunately, children are also gaining in cognitive maturity. Thanks to this maturity, they are better equipped to reflect upon situations, to devise effective strategies to accomplish their goals, and to navigate through those situations when they fail to achieve their goals (i.e., high coping potential).

Second, to experience self-conscious emotions also requires that children have a sense of self. Possessing a sense of self is crucial in that it allows children to causally connect the successful or failed outcome to their action. Hart and Karmel (1996) claimed that a sense of self is made up of two experiences: self-awareness and self-understanding. "Self-awareness" refers to people's ability to focus attention on the self as an object distinct from other objects, and being able to uniquely identify with that object. Based on linguistic and cognitive-behavioral research, there seems to be consensus that self-awareness emerges somewhere around 2 years of age in human development (Hart & Karmel, 1996). For example, between the second and third year of life children are able to use pronouns to refer to the self, reference the self in mother–child discourse, and verbally describe the self. In addition, they are able to recognize themselves in a mirror and imitate others' actions. Hence, since 2 years is the age when self-awareness begins to emerge, we would expect self-conscious emotions to emerge no earlier than around this age.

The Development of Self

If the expression of self-conscious emotions is determined, in part, by an event's relevance and congruence with the self, then how the self changes over time is likely to influence the process. As Damon and Hart (1982, 1988) have shown, the self changes over the course of childhood. In early childhood, children define the self in physical and concrete ways. This self-understanding changes as they enter into adolescence, when they are able to integrate social and psychological characteristics. Moreover, over time children understand that the self is not static, but changes and evolves. Therefore, what makes the self unique shifts from an emphasis on physical attributes and single concrete experiences to internal psychological attributes and subjective, private experiences that are "storied."

Furthermore, the facets of the sense of self associated with agency and self-reflection evolve as well (Damon & Hart, 1988). Over time, the individual judges the self to gain in volitional power. Children initially understand that they have control over their physical abilities. As they grow into adolescence, they develop awareness that the self controls its thoughts and feelings. Finally, adolescents are able to construct theories of themselves that integrate different aspects of the self—physical, active, social, and psychological— and different experiences into a whole.

Pride in Childhood and Adolescence

The general developmental transformations evident in the sense of self—from an action-based view to one in which dispositions, beliefs, and agency are prominent—can be discerned in the development of the sense of pride. To begin with, recent research by Tracy, Robins, and Lagattuta (2005) showed that children as young as age 4 were able to distinguish pride expressions from happiness and surprise expressions, and that this ability to discriminate between these emotional expressions generally improved as the cohort of children increased in age up to 7 years. Thus, even at an early age, children are able to recognize pride.

Rosenberg (1979) provided evidence that children not only recognize pride but are able to experience it. In his study, Rosenberg asked children ranging in age from 8 to 18 years questions about experiences of shame and pride. Rosenberg found that, compared to children, adolescents' experiences of pride were less likely to be associated with physical characteristics (e.g., my skin, being bigger), and more likely to be associated with interpersonal traits (e.g., being friendly, well respected, and helpful). Moreover, when questioned about the experience of shame (not pride, but nonetheless in the family of self-conscious emotions), compared to children, adolescents' experiences of shame were less likely to be associated with physical characteristics, and more likely to be associated with impulse control-type traits (e.g., getting mad at my sister over nothing). For Rosenberg, the experiences of pride and shame, along with other aspects of the self, change as a result of the shift from the social exterior conception of self in childhood to the psychological interior conception of self in adolescence.

Further evidence that pride develops through the lifespan derives from the work of Graham and Weiner (1991). They examined the relations among appraisals theoretically linked to pride at different points in the lifespan. Children as young as age 5 and adults as old as 90 were asked to imagine themselves in the role of the protagonist in a series of vignettes, and to rate how proud they would feel if they were to experience a variety of events, with the events varying in the degree to which they were caused by the protagonist. The results showed that the experience of pride varied directly with the extent to which the event was caused by the self for the oldest children and adolescents, but not for the younger children. This finding suggests that for younger children, pride is not bound tightly to the sense that the self is responsible for an event. Graham and Weiner also asked participants in their roles as the protagonists in the vignettes to take the number of rewards (raffle tickets, movie passes) that the positive events depicted in the vignettes warranted. Among younger children, the number of rewards, ratings of pride, and judgments concerning the self's responsibility in producing the positive event were not closely related. In contrast, among older children and adults, these measures were all substantially correlated with each other.

In a study complementing that of Graham and Weiner (1991), Kornilaki and Chlouverakis (2004) studied the effects of a story protagonist's responsibility for a positive outcome on children's judgments of pride. Kornilaki and Chlouverakis found that only the oldest children in the study (11-year-olds) judged that pride would vary according to whether the positive events were caused by the self or by the other. This finding suggests that while younger children can distinguish expressions of pride from other emotional expressions (Tracy et al., 2005), they may have difficulties in the cognitive appraisal process. For instance, the fact that younger children have greater difficulty understanding the reasoning regarding sequences of event (Lewis, 2001) could explain Graham and Weiner's (1991) finding that distinguishing among sources of responsibility for an event may not be a dimension children focus on when rewards are to be had. Furthermore, within these studies, young children may have a difficult time distinguishing their own perspective from those of hypothetical selves and others. While these explanations are speculative, the point we wish to emphasize is that the experience and understanding of pride changes over development and appears to be influenced by cognitive developmental factors (Lewis, 2001; Rosenberg, 1979).

The Development of Hubris and Narcissism

The confluence of developmental transformations that differentiate early childhood pride from the forms of pride found in adolescence is likely to contribute to the development of *hubris* and *narcissism*. "Hubris" refers to excessive pride; individuals who see themselves as god-like may feel boundless pride that is not tempered by awareness of shortcomings and failures in some of the self's pursuits. "Narcissism" connotes excessive self-love and in the psychiatric literature a belief that the self is powerful and omnipotent. Like pride, narcissism is related to the tendency to view the self as all good and deserving (Horowitz, 1988). As we noted in previous sections, in comparison to younger children, for older children and adolescents trait psychological dispositions and agency figure prominently in appraisals of positive events and consequently are central to the experience of pride. Hubris and narcissism are magnified by the same kinds of appraisals: the individual experiencing hubris believes that a positive event is attributable to the self's actions that emanate from a stable disposition in the self. It is questionable whether hubris or narcissism characterize young children, for whom stable traits and inferences of agency are largely absent in self-definitions.

In addition to dispositional influences in the genesis of narcissism and hubris, environmental factors have also been suggested as shaping their development (Robins, Tracy, & Shaver, 2001; Wink, 1992). Specifically, researchers have suggested that childhood experiences of rejection, high parental demand, and lack of parental warmth may create an environment where people, given their trait predisposition, may respond by adopting coping strategies (i.e., ones considered to have high coping potential) that serve not only to protect the ego, but to inflate it. Thus, narcissistic behaviors can be seen as adaptive mechanisms. As Robins et al. (2001) state, narcissists pursue "the most adaptive strategy they could have adopted under the conditions in which they grew up" (p. 12). Furthermore, this theorizing on the importance of childhood context is consistent with general work on cognitive appraisal theories of emotions and emotional understanding, which have emphasized the importance of family and peer influences in their development (Harris, 2000; Lewis, 2001).

In terms of what distinguishes hubris from pride, the appraisals associated with hubris are not differentiated—all positive events are caused by a powerful self with broad, stable, positive traits—while the appraisals associated with pride are specific to events and traits. Hubris is only possible when the individual fails to recognize that the self's efforts have produced worthy accomplishments in some domains of life but not in others. The failure to construct a differentiated sense of self that integrates positive and negative traits as well as an awareness of failures in, and limits to, volition is likely to be associated with psychopathology. For example, hubris and its associated grandiose, undifferentiated sense of self may exist because the individual cannot tolerate the shifts in affective tone that result from a succession of appraisals of failure and success. Individuals unable to endure periods of negative affect—guilt and shame, for example—may invest considerable psychological resources in avoiding the recognition that the self has failed in its efforts to reach a goal, and thus preserving the sense of pride even when the context does not warrant it.

While pride can motivate and sustain moral behavior (as we have argued in preceding sections) hubris and narcissism—close cousins to pride—may undermine it. Ward (2003) has argued that the narcissist's fundamental principle is that a positive self-image must be protected at all costs. Similarly, Baumeister (2001) has suggested that aggression can result from a narcissistic or hubristic individual's realization that the self is not as perfect and powerful as typically imagined, an insight that makes the individual angry with the people who are associated with the insight. Men who abuse women, for example, may do so when their positive images of themselves are threatened.

Summary

Only a sketchy portrait of the development of pride has been presented in the preceding sections because there is too little research available to provide more detail. Pride in early childhood—age 18 months to age 4—is best understood because there are compelling experimental paradigms that reveal the emergence of the sense of self and pride in this age range. Moreover, there are solid findings on the development of pride in early childhood (e.g., Stipek, 1995).

For anchoring voluntary altruistic behavior in childhood transformations in pride, as we seek to do in this chapter, the research base is very thin. The available studies indicate that by the beginning of adolescence, but not before, pride is (1) associated with the sense that the self is the source of the event that is associated with the emotion, (2) linked to self-rewards, and (3) correlated with personality traits and psychological characteristics of the self.

Finally, we have suggested that the developmental transformations in pride that provide the foundation for the emergence of dedicated prosocial behavior in adolescence are also implicated in the antisocial cousins of pride, hubris and narcissism.

Our synthesis of pride, its underlying appraisals, hubris, and moral behavior is largely speculative. As we have noted throughout the first two sections of this chapter, there is remarkably little research on the components or their relations to each other. There is no research on the relation of pride to sustained moral action; no research on the kinds of appraisals that contribute to pride in the context of voluntary moral action; no research on the relation of hubris to voluntary action; and no indication that the developmental transformations we have discussed are prerequisites to sustained moral action. Our chapter therefore is a sketch for a program of research rather than a review of what is well established.

A RESEARCH EXAMPLE

To illustrate how the issues and questions in preceding sections can be addressed empirically, we present analyses of data from the *Mid*life in the *U*nited *S*tates (MIDUS) survey

(MacArthur Foundation Research Network on Successful Midlife Development, n.d.). No single study can address every issue, and this empirical illustration is no exception. In particular, we do not address developmental issues in this section, as the data we use are from a sample of adults.

Our goal was to provide preliminary assessments of four hypotheses. The first of these is that pride in moral projects is associated with heightened participation in them. Specifically, we examine whether individuals who have a great deal of pride in their community service volunteer more hours than do individuals who have less pride in their activities. Second, we propose that pride in moral endeavors is *independent* of related constructs such as generativity (McAdams & de St. Aubin, 1992) and personality dimensions (Extraversion, Conscientiousness, Neuroticism, Agreeableness, Openness; Goldberg, 1990). To add to our understanding of sustained moral action, moral pride must be independent of these other constructs known to predict moral action (Hart et al., 2005). We test for this independence by assessing the extent to which pride predicts hours spent volunteering and helping one's family while controlling statistically for personality-type variables. Third, we test the relation of pride to the theoretically related notions of control and internal standards. As described in the previous section on appraisal theories, people should feel the greatest pride in their behavior when they (1) believe that they control their own behavior and (2) the behavior is relevant to standards that are self-relevant. Fourth, we assess the possibility that pride can be distinguished from hubris.

Methods

Participants

In this research example, we used the MIDUS survey data set (MacArthur Foundation Research Network on Successful Midlife Development, n.d.). The MIDUS survey was completed by a large sample of U.S. adults in 1995. The sampling strategy for the MIDUS was intended to obtain a representative sample of English-speaking U.S. adults between the ages of 25 and 74 residing in households with telephones in the 48 contiguous states. Participants were contacted by phone, and those agreeing to participate in a study of health and well-being in midlife completed both phone and mail-in surveys. Approximately 60% of those contacted by phone agreed to participate (for sampling details, see MacArthur Foundation Research Network on Successful Midlife Development, n.d.). Out of the 4,242 participants who completed the measures, approximately 1,400 were doing volunteer work in their communities and consequently were able to judge the extent to which they felt pride in their volunteer work. Because we are particularly interested in volunteer work, it was these 1,400 individuals (701 males, median household income of $54,000, half of whom had 2-year college degrees or higher levels of educational attainment, with an average age of 46) who composed the sample for the analyses we report below.

Measures

Participants were asked to judge the self-descriptiveness using a 4-point scale (a lot/extremely true to not at all/not at all true) of four items concerning *pride*: (a) "When I think about the work I do in the community, I feel a good deal of pride," (b) "When I think about the work I do at home, I feel a good deal of pride," (c) "When I think about the work I do on my job, I feel a good deal of pride," and (d) "I feel a lot of pride about what I have been able to do for my children." Participants responded to these items only if they were relevant (i.e., 1,150 responded to a; 1,442 responded to b; 1,081 had jobs and responded to c; and 1,226 responded to d).

We computed two summary measures for the four items. First, we averaged the scores (925 participants had scores for the four pride items) for a mean pride score. Second, we calculated the standard deviation of the scores of the four items to measure the differentiation of pride.

Hours per month spent volunteering reflected commitment to volunteering. Participants were asked "How many hours per month do you spend doing formal volunteer work of any of the following types?" The four types of volunteer work included "health-care-oriented," "school or other youth-related," "political organizations or causes," and "any other organization, cause or charity." Hours volunteered across the four types were summed. A few (less than 1%) participants reported donating hundreds of hours a month; to reduce skew, we truncated scores at 80 hours a month.

Generativity (McAdams & de St. Aubin, 1992) was measured with a seven-item scale (representative item: "Many people come to you for advice"). Scores for each of the dimensions of the five-factor model of personality were derived from self-ratings on 30 personality adjectives (Goldberg, 1990). Household income, educational attainment, and age were self-reported.

As we noted in the previous section of the chapter, pride should be related to the perceptions (1) that the self controls an action and (2) that the action corresponds to an internal standard. Participants judged their *control,* using a 10-point scale, by responding to the question "How would you rate the amount of control you have over your contribution to the welfare and well-being of other people these days?" The extent to which participants believed that they had *civic obligations* to contribute to their communities was assessed with a 10-item scale (sample item: "How much obligation would you feel to serve on a jury if called?"). We infer that people who believe that they have civic obligations will perceive volunteering on behalf of others as consistent with their internal standards for themselves.

Results

In the first analysis, we regressed commitment to volunteering on pride, variables related to pride, personality constructs, attribution variables, and demographic variables. The results are presented in Table 7.1. Several facets of Table 7.1 are noteworthy. First, only *community pride* from among the pride items predicted the number of hours volunteered per month. This is reasonable and expected; for the reasons outlined in the previous section of the chapter, pride should be focused on the activity that gives rise to it. Pride related to one's activities in one domain of life should not predict one's actions in another, and the results in Table 7.1 are consistent with this expectation.

Second, community pride is predictive of commitment to volunteering even with scores for generativity and the five dimensions of personality in the equation. This finding suggests that pride contributes uniquely to the prediction of volunteering.

In the second analysis, we regressed community pride on volunteering, variables related to pride, generativity and personality dimensions, and demographic variables. These results are presented in Table 7.2. Table 7.2 suggests that pride is highest among those who (1) volunteer many hours, (2) believe that their contributions to the community are

TABLE 7.1. Regression of Commitment to Volunteering on Pride, Personality, and Demographic Factors

	B	SE	Beta
Intercept	22.26	9.59	
Types of pride			
Community pride	2.32	.83	.12*
Family pride	−.86	.63	−.05
Job pride	−1.21	.87	−.06
Home pride	.80	.86	.04
Attributions affecting pride			
Civic obligation	.15	.43	.01
Control	.37	.27	.06
Personality constructs			
Generativity	4.25	1.20	.16*
Neuroticism	1.34	.90	.06
Agreeableness	−1.25	1.49	−.04
Extraversion	−.31	1.34	−.01
Conscientiousness	1.41	1.45	.04
Openness	−1.13	1.36	−.04
Demographics			
Gender	1.10	1.18	.04
Age	−.04	.06	−.03
Educational attainment	−.49	.24	−.08*
Household income	−.44	.72	−.02

Note. $n = 696$.
* $p < .05$.

under their own control, and (3) believe themselves to be obligated to contribute to their communities. This cluster of findings is exactly what the theory and review in the first half of this chapter predicted.

In the final set of analyses we examined the relationship of mean levels of pride and pride differentiation to the personality dimensions. We reasoned that hubris would be indicated by a lack of differentiation in pride. In other words, individuals who experience equivalent levels of pride across the domains of community, home, children, and work seem to believe that they are succeeding in every area of life—manifesting hubris.

To test this analysis, we correlated differentiation in pride with scores for generativity and the five personality dimensions, while controlling for mean level of pride. Because differentiation in pride and mean level of pride are necessarily correlated—for example, individuals with a mean level of pride of 4 could have no differentiation among their pride scores (a mean level of pride of 4 required that individuals judge themselves to be at the highest level possible for pride in each of the four domains)—we computed correlations of pride differentiation to the personality scores for each of the mean levels of pride. There were only 100 or more participants at mean levels of pride of 3 and higher, suggesting that adults in the United States are generally prideful—manifesting hubris. Because we wanted to calculate correlations between pride differentiation and personality variables, we selected only mean levels of pride for which there was variability in the pride differentiation variable. Among mean levels of pride of 3 and higher, the standard deviation of pride differentiation scores was greater than .2 only for mean pride levels of 3 and

TABLE 7.2. Regression of Pride in Community Contributions
on Volunteering, Personality, and Demographic Factors

	B	SE	Beta
Intercept	1.67	.34	
Volunteering			
Hours per month	.01	.00	.11*
Attributions affecting pride			
Civic obligation	.04	.02	.08*
Control	.04	.01	.12*
Personality constructs			
Generativity	.19	.04	.15*
Neuroticism	.03	.03	.03
Agreeableness	.08	.05	.06
Extraversion	.12	.05	.09*
Conscientiousness	.10	.05	.06*
Openness	.09	.05	.06
Demographics			
Gender	−.07	.04	−.05
Age	.00	.00	.03
Educational attainment	−.01	.01	−.04
Household income	−.44	.72	−.02

Note. n = 1,122.

* p < .05.

3.25. Consequently, we used only participants (n = 225) with mean pride levels of 3 and 3.25 in the correlational analysis.

Generally, our results suggest that low pride differentiation (reflecting high hubris scores) is associated with undesirable personality characteristics. Pride differentiation was positively correlated with generativity (r = .31), openness (r = .20), agreeableness (r = .14), and conscientiousness (r = .20). Pride differentiation was negatively correlated with neuroticism (r = −.16).

Discussion of Empirical Analyses

The purpose of our research example was to test four questions. First, is pride associated with volunteer work? Second, if pride is related to community volunteer work, is the relationship significant once other constructs known to be related to volunteering are controlled? Third, are appraisal variables related to the emotional expression of pride? Fourth, can pride be distinguished from hubris? We present responses to each of these questions below.

Pride as a Motivator

While past research has shown a robust relationship between empathy-related emotional expressions and prosocial action (Eisenberg, 2000), few other emotions have been considered as a potential motivator for such behavior. One purpose of our research was to show that pride may be an important emotion in moral life by serving to motivate people toward prosocial action. Our regression analysis revealed that community pride was a significant predictor of volunteering even when other personality-type variables known to relate to volunteering were controlled. Hence, our results are significant in demonstrating that other moral emotions besides empathy may be serving as additional and/or alternative motivators to moral action.

While our results have demonstrated a link between pride and prosocial action, in reality we have no clear evidence of the actual causal direction of this link. If future research discovers a causal connection from pride to prosocial action, a follow-up study would be to investigate the underlying pathway. As mentioned earlier, two potential pathways have been proposed to explain such a connection (Dovidio & Penner, 2004). One pathway has the experience of pride functioning to bolster people's perceived image in the community. In this scenario, people are motivated to volunteer in order to maintain or increase their community status in the eyes of others. A second pathway has the experience of pride functioning to make people feel good about themselves. In this case, people are motivated to volunteer so that they may feel good about themselves for having helped others through volunteer service.

In either case, each pathway is egoistic in nature, causing one to ask whether acts considered to be prosocial, moral acts can still be self-serving. Applying this question to our study, can volunteer actions be considered both altruistic and egoistic at the same time? We believe actions can. If an individual is initially motivated solely out of empathic concern for others, then that individual is acting out of interest for the other. Once the altruistic act is completed, the individual may evaluate the event in such a way that pride is expressed. In this case, one cannot challenge the underlying motive for the initial action as being self-interested. Moreover, in subsequent action where pride in addition to empathy may act as motivators to action, it seems to us that as long as the action is motivated by a concern for others, the action should still be considered prosocial.

Appraisals and Pride

A second focus of this study was to gain insight into the processes that lead to the expression of pride. Through our study, we were able to find support for those cognitive appraisal theories that consider internal attribution and evaluation by internal standards as important processes in the expression of emotions. Both of these variables were found to be significant and independent predictors of community pride, even after controlling for volunteering and personality-type variables. Thus, in the context of community service work, our results are consistent with appraisal theorists who would claim that community pride is dependent on people's understanding of their control over their volunteer work, and on whether people perceive their work as meeting their internal standards. Unfortunately, our study only supports parts of Tracy and Robin's (2004) cognitive appraisal model of self-conscious emotions. Two important predictors in the expression of self-conscious emotions that remain to be verified in future work are identity congruence and identity relevance.

Pride, Hubris, and Narcissism

Finally, we attempted to distinguish hubris from pride. In this study, hubris was represented by participants' high levels of pride in four domains (community, home, children, and work). We found that hubris was negatively correlated with generativity, openness to experience, agreeableness, and conscientiousness, and positively correlated with neuroticism. That is, people who experience hubris are those who tend to be less concerned about socializing with and helping others, considering novel ideas and experiencing new events, and fulfilling one's commitments and responsibilities. Moreover, these individuals also lack emotional stability. In many ways, our findings are consistent with past research on hubris. Tracy and Robin (2004) highlight research showing the different behavioral outcomes associated with pride and hubris. On the one hand, pride has been found to contribute to prosocial investments. On the other hand, hubris has been found to contribute to "aggression and hostility, interpersonal problems, relationship conflict, and a host of self-destructive behaviors" (p. 116). Thus, the experience of hubris is associated with a number of negative outcomes.

One possible explanation for these negative associations could be that many people who experience hubris also suffer from narcissism. Current thinking on narcissism suggests that narcissists become aggressive and violent when their perception of self is threatened—this is known as threatened egoism theory (Baumeister, 2001). In his work, Baumeister found that narcissists generally show no more aggressive tendencies than nonnarcissists. The exception to this general finding was when narcissists were insulted and criticized. Under such conditions, narcissists showed high levels of aggression. According to Baumeister, when narcissists' grandiose self-concept is challenged in any way, their response is often aggressive in nature.

Moreover, Wink's (1991) research finding on adult women is consistent with our findings. In his initial work within this study, he had nine judges (e.g., clinical psychologists) identify items on the California Q-set that characterized a narcissistic prototype (i.e., self-directed items) and items that reflected the opposite of the narcissistic prototype (i.e., other-directed items). These items were factor-analyzed to reveal three narcissistic dimensions—hypersensitivity, willfulness, and autonomy—and two "contranarcissistic" dimensions: straightforwardness and givingness. When he collected information on these dimensions from adult women, he found the three narcissistic dimensions to generally correlate positively with such measures as aggression and exhibition, and negatively with self-control, nurturance, and well-being. The opposite effects were generally found for the two contranarcissistic dimensions. Hence, our results on hubris and recent work on narcissism suggest that these two concepts are highly related in being self-directed as opposed to other-directed.

Recent work on adolescent bullying has found similar pattern of results as the adult narcissist literature. A recent study on bullying has found that bullies experience a sense of hubris-type pride in their aggressive behavior toward others (Menesini et al., 2003). In another study, Salmivalli, Kaukiainen, Kaistanienmi, and Laerspetz (1999) reported that boys' need for attention, positive self-evaluation, and difficulty with criticism were associated with bullying behavior. Finally, a study of 10-year-old narcissistic children reported that they too lacked empathy, struggled with self and identity stability, and had poor impulse control (Weise & Tuber, 2004). Thus, even in childhood and adolescence, there is evidence that hubris and lack of empathy are associated with antisocial, immoral behaviors.

CONCLUSION

If the central theses in this chapter are right—that the emergence of the experience of pride linked to the sense of self and volition in late childhood and adolescence can motivate and sustain prosocial behavior—then the broad-brush depiction of pride as immodest and immoral must be abandoned in favor of a nuanced picture in which pride is distinguishable from hubris and narcissism. In our view, hubris, close to but not identical with pride, is the emotional state to which ancient religious scriptures generally refer when condemning pride as a character flaw. Indeed, in our research, individuals who exhibit high levels of hubris (undifferentiated pride in the self) do appear to be higher in neuroticism—a generally undesirable trait associated with poor adjustment—than individuals low in hubris.

While hubris and narcissism are associated with poor adjustment and consequently may constitute character deficits, we have argued that there are grounds for hypothesizing that pride can motivate moral behavior. Philosophers such as Kristjánsson (2002) and psychologists such as Dovidio and Penner (2004) have suggested that individuals who are able to feel pride when performing moral actions—and to feel shame and guilt when acting unethically—are appropriately tuned to the standards of behavior in their social groups and to the standards that they hold for themselves. By binding moral actions to an individual's standards and efforts, pride deepens the propensity to act on behalf of others even in the absence of instrumental reward. The results of our analyses provide considerable support for this argument. We found that people who experienced pride in their volunteering were more committed than were others who felt less pride. Importantly, the experience of pride contributed uniquely to commitment to volunteering, and was distinct from broad personality traits and from prosocial personality characteristics such as generativity. Lastly, we found that the experience of pride in volunteering was related to the individual's perception that volunteering directly reflected the self's volition and the self's values.

Finally, we suggested in this chapter that the developmental transformations that occur in pride across childhood contribute to the explanation for the emergence of voluntary, planned, sustained altruism in adolescence. We argued that young children lack the ability to fuse volition, values, and action so as to motivate autonomous moral behavior. Once this fusion occurs—in late childhood and early adolescence—individuals are able to derive satisfaction in behaving ethically, even in the absence of explicit rewards.

All parts of our account for the interplay of development, pride, and moral action blend fact with large doses of speculation. We know far too little about the intersections among these constructs. However, the expanding interest in the nexus of development, pride, and moral action among psychologists and philosophers, in combination with the promising findings reviewed and presented in this chapter, suggest that ignorance and speculation will be displaced by an accumulation of facts and theory. As our understanding deepens, we believe that the appreciation of pride's role in sustaining moral behavior, and in the importance of the development of pride in making such behavior possible, will grow.

REFERENCE

Batson, C. D. (1991). *The altruism question: Toward a social-psychological answer.* Hillsdale, NJ: Erlbaum.

Batson, C. D., Batson, J. G., Todd, R. M., Brummett, B. H., Shaw, L. L., & Aldeguer, C. M. R. (1995). Empathy and the collective good: Caring for one of the others in a social dilemma. *Journal of Personality and Social Psychology, 68,* 619–631.

Batson, C. D., Turk, C. L., Shaw, L. L., & Klein, T. R. (1995). Information function of empathic emotion: Learning that we value the other's welfare. *Journal of Personality and Social Psychology, 68*, 300–313.

Baumeister, R. F. (2001). Violent pride: Do people turn violent because of self-hate, or self-love? *Scientific American, 284*, 96–101.

Colby, A., & Damon, W. (1992). *Some do care: Contemporary lives of moral commitment.* New York: Free Press.

Damon, W., & Hart, D. (1982). The development of self-understanding from infancy through adolescence. *Child Development, 53*, 841–864.

Damon, W., & Hart, D. (1988). *Self-understanding in childhood and adolescence.* New York: Cambridge University Press.

Dillon, R. S. (2003). Respect. In E. N. Zalta (Ed.). *The Stanford encyclopedia of philosophy* (Fall 2003 ed.) Retrieved October 19, 2005, from *plato.stanford.edu/archives/fall2003/entries/respect/*.

Dovidio, J. F., & Penner, L. A. (2004). Helping and altruism. In M. B. Brewer & M. Hewstone (Eds.), *Emotion and motivation* (pp. 247–280). Malden, MA: Blackwell.

Eisenberg, N. (2000). Emotion, regulation, and moral development. *Annual Review of Psychology, 51*, 665–697.

Eisenberg, N. (2005). The development of empathy-related responding. In G. Carlo & C. P. Edwards (Eds.), *Nebraska Symposium on Motivation: Vol. 51. Moral motivation through the lifespan: Theory, research and application* (pp. 73–117). Lincoln: University of Nebraska Press.

Freud, S. (1936). *The problem of anxiety* (H. A. Bunker, Trans.). New York: Norton. (Original work published 1926)

Gilligan, J. (1976). Beyond morality: Psychoanalytic reflections on shame, guilt, and love. In T. Lickona (Ed.), *Moral development and behavior* (pp. 144–158). New York: Holt, Rinehart, & Winston.

Goldberg, L. R. (1990). An alternate "description of personality": The Big-Five factor structure. *Journal of Personality and Social Psychology, 59*, 1216–1229.

Graham, S., & Weiner, B. (1991). Testing judgments about attribution–emotion–action linkages: A lifespan approach. *Social Cognition, 9*, 254–276.

Hanh, T. N. (1998). *The heart of the Buddha's teaching: Transforming suffering into peace, joy, and liberation.* New York: Broadway Books.

Harris, P. L. (2000). Understanding emotions. In M. Lewis & J. M. Haviland-Jones (Eds.), *Handbook of emotions* (2nd ed., pp. 281–292). New York: Guilford Press.

Hart, D. (2005). The development of moral identity. In G. Carlo & C. P. Edwards (Eds.), *Nebraska Symposium on Motivation: Vol. 51. Moral motivation through the lifespan* (pp. 165–196). Lincoln: University of Nebraska Press.

Hart, D., & Fegley, S. (1995). Prosocial behavior and caring in adolescence: Relations to self-understanding and social judgment. *Child Development, 66*, 1346–1359.

Hart, D., & Karmel, M. P. (1996). Self-awareness and self-knowledge in humans, apes, and monkeys. In A. E. Russon & K. A Bard (Eds.), *Reaching into thought: The minds of the great apes* (pp. 325–347). New York: Cambridge University Press.

Hoffman, M. L. (1991). Empathy, social cognition, and moral action. In W. M. Kurtines & J. L. Gewirtz (Eds.), *Handbook of moral behavior and development: Vol. 1. Theory* (pp. 275–301). Hillsdale, NJ: Erlbaum.

Horowitz, M. J. (1988). *Introduction to psychodynamics.* New York: Basic Books.

Hume, D. (1972). *Enquiries concerning the human understanding and concerning the principles of morals.* Oxford, UK: Clarendon Press. (Original work published 1748)

Hume, D. (1978). *A treatise of human nature* (2nd ed.). New York: Oxford University Press. (Original work published 1740)

Kagan, J. (1984). *The nature of the child.* New York: Basic Books.

Kagan, J. (2005). Human morality and temperament. In G. Carlo & C. P. Edwards (Eds.), *Nebraska*

Symposium on Motivation: Vol. 51. Moral motivation through the lifespan: Theory, research and application (pp. 1–32). Lincoln: University of Nebraska Press.

Kohlberg, L. (1984). *Essays on moral development: The psychology of moral development* (Vol. 2). San Francisco: Harper & Row.

Kornilaki, E. N., & Chlouverakis, G. (2004). The situational antecedents of pride and happiness: Developmental and domain differences. *British Journal of Developmental Psychology, 22,* 605–619.

Kristjánsson, K. (2002). *Justifying emotions: Pride and jealousy.* New York: Routledge.

Lewis, M. (2000a). Self-conscious emotions: Embarrassment, pride, shame, and guilt. In M. Lewis & J. M. Haviland-Jones (Eds.), *Handbook of emotions* (2nd ed., pp. 623–636). New York: Guilford Press.

Lewis, M. (2000b). The emergence of human emotions. In M. Lewis & J. M. Haviland-Jones (Eds.), *Handbook of emotions* (2nd ed., pp. 265–280). New York: Guilford Press.

Lewis, M. D. (2001). Personal pathways in the development of appraisal: A complex systems/stage theory perspective. In K. R. Scherer, A. Schorr, & T. Johnstone (Eds.), *Appraisal processes in emotion: Theory, methods, research* (pp. 205–220). New York: Oxford University Press.

MacArthur Foundation Research Network on Successful Midlife Development. (n.d.). *Methodology of the National Survey of Midlife Development in the United States.* Retrieved November 17, 2004, from *midmac.med.harvard.edu./mstech.exe.*

Matsuba, M. K., Hart, D., & Atkins, R. (in press). Psychological and social-structural influences on commitment to volunteering. *Journal of Research in Personality.*

Matsuba, M. K., & Walker, L. J. (2004). Extraordinary moral commitment: Young adults involved in social organizations. *Journal of Personality, 72,* 413–436.

McAdams, D. P., & de St. Aubin, E. (1992). A theory of generativity and its assessment through self-report, behavioral acts, and narrative themes in autobiography. *Journal of Personality and Social Psychology, 62,* 1003–1015.

Meisel, A. C., & del Mastro, M. L. (Eds. and Trans.). (1975). *The rule of Saint Benedict: Translated, with introduction and notes.* New York: Image Books.

Menesini, E., Sanchez, V., Fonzi, A., Ortega, R., Costabile, A., & Lo Feudo, G. (2003). Moral emotions and bullying: A cross-national comparison of differences between bullies, victims and outsiders. *Aggressive Behavior, 29,* 515–530.

Monroe, K. R. (1991). John Donne's people: Explaining differences between rational actors and altruists through cognitive frameworks. *Journal of Politics, 53,* 394–435.

Penner, L. A. (2002). Dispositional and organizational influences on sustained volunteerism: An interactionist perspective. *Journal of Social Issues, 58,* 447–467.

Robins, R. W., Tracy, J. L., & Shaver, P. R. (2001). Shame into self-love: Dynamics, roots, and functions of narcissism. *Psychological Inquiry, 12,* 230–236.

Rosenberg, M. (1979). *Conceiving the self.* New York: Basic Books.

Rozin, P., Lowery, L., Imada, S., & Haidt, J. (1999). The CAD triad hypothesis: A mapping between three moral emotions (contempt, anger, disgust) and three moral codes (community, autonomy, divinity). *Journal of Personality and Social Psychology, 76,* 574–586.

Salmivalli, C., Kaukiainen, A., Kaistaniemi, L., & Lagerspetz, K. M. J. (1999). Self-evaluated self-esteem, peer-evaluated self-esteem, and defensive egotism as predictors of adolescents' participation in bullying situations. *Personality and Social Psychology Bulletin, 25,* 1268–1278.

Shweder, R. A., Much, N. C., Mahapatra, M., & Park, L. (1997). The "Big Three" of morality (autonomy, community, divinity) and the "Big Three" explanations of suffering. In A. Brandt & P. Rozin (Eds.), *Morality and health* (pp. 119–169). New York: Routledge.

Smetana, J. G. (2006). Social-cognitive domain theory: Consistencies and variations in children's moral and social judgments. In M. Killen & J. G. Smetana (Eds.), *Handbook of moral development* (pp. 119–153). Mahwah, NJ: Erlbaum.

Stipek, D. (1995). The development of pride and shame in toddlers. In J. P. Tangney & K. W. Fischer (Eds.), *Self-conscious emotions: The psychology of shame, guilt, embarrassment, and pride* (pp. 237–252). New York: Guilford Press.

Stipek, D., Recchia, S., & McClintic, S. (1992). Self-evaluation in young children. *Monographs of the Society for Research in Child Development, 57*(1, Serial No. 226).

Tangney, J. P. (1999). The self-conscious emotions: Shame, guilt, embarrassment and pride. In T. Dalgleish & M. Power (Eds.), *Handbook of cognition and emotion* (pp. 541–568). New York: Wiley.

Tangney, J. P. (2002). Self-conscious emotions: The self as a moral guide. In A. Tesser, D. A. Stapel, & J. V. Wood (Eds.), *Self and motivation: Emerging psychological perspectives* (pp. 97–117). Washington, DC: American Psychological Association.

Tracy, J. L., & Robins, R. W. (2004). Putting the self into self-conscious emotions: A theoretical model. *Psychological Inquiry, 15,* 103–125.

Tracy, J. L., Robins, R. W., & Lagattuta, K. H. (2005). Can children recognize pride? *Emotion, 5,* 251–257.

Ward, D. E. (2003). Explaining evil behavior: Using Kant and M. Scott Peck to solve the puzzle of understanding the moral psychology of evil people. *Philosophy, Psychiatry, and Psychology, 9,* 2–12.

Weiner, B. (1980). A cognitive (attribution)–emotion–action model of motivated behavior: An analysis of judgments of help-giving. *Journal of Personality and Social Psychology, 39,* 186–200.

Weise, K. L., & Tuber, S. (2004). The self and object representations of narcissistically disturbed children: An empirical investigation. *Psychoanalytic Psychology, 21,* 244–258.

Wink, P. (1991). Self- and object-directedness in adult women. *Journal of Personality, 59,* 769–791.

Wink, P. (1992). Three types of narcissism in women from college to mid-life. *Journal of Personality, 60,* 7–30.

8

Self-Conscious Emotional Development

MICHAEL LEWIS

This chapter has as one of its central themes the idea that the development of emotional life requires changes in cognitive ability. These changes in cognitive ability facilitate and are facilitated by changes in emotional development. This view suggests that cognitions, especially cognitions about the self, are an integral part of emotional and social development (M. Lewis, 2003). While some have argued for a one-to-one correspondence between events in the world (stimulus elicitors) and emotional responses, such an analysis is difficult to understand, especially in regard to the class of emotions called "self-conscious emotions." Darwin (1872/1965), for one, argued that self-conscious emotions were produced by peoples' ideas and, in particular, that they were the focus of the attention of others. If it is true that cognitions underlie these emotions, there are likely to be no simple one-to-one elicitors of these emotions since they involve ideas, especially ideas or cognitions about the self. For example, in discussing blushing, a measure of self-consciousness, Darwin argued that blushing was caused by how we appear to others, or, as he said, "the thinking about others thinking about us . . . excites a blush" (p. 325).

In my model of emotional development, schematized in Figure 8.1, I (M. Lewis, 1992a, 2000) have suggested that cognitions and emotions follow a fugue-like pattern in which emotions lead to cognitions, which in turn lead to new emotions. In this model of emotional development, the earliest emotions, called "primary" or "basic" emotions, those that can be seen in facial expressions, emerge at birth and require relatively little cognition (Bridges, 1932). But even for these basic emotions it is difficult to think of the elicitors–expression connection without invoking some cognition—if nothing more than the cognition necessary for perception. As the model suggests, at around 15 to 18 months, a critical cognition, that involving the idea of "me" (M. Lewis, 2003) or what I have called "self-awareness" or "consciousness," emerges (James, 1884; M. Lewis, 1992b; Lewis & Brooks-Gunn, 1979; Lewis & Michalson, 1983a). The emergence of this cognition gives rise to a set of self-conscious emotions that *at this time do not have* evaluation of self as their basis (M. Lewis, 2000). I have called these "self-conscious exposed emotions." They include embarrassment, empathy, and envy. They are based on cogni-

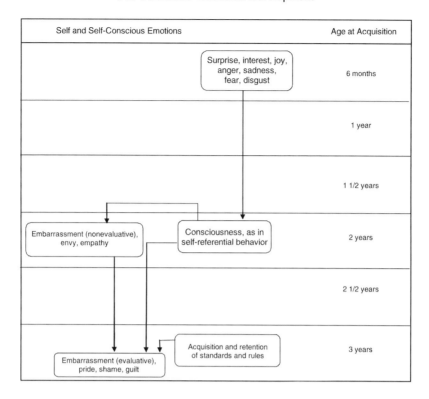

FIGURE 8.1. A model of emotional development.

tions about the self but are not based on evaluation. *Embarrassment* is the result of the self being observed (M. Lewis, 1995b), and *empathy* is the ability to place one's self in the place of the other in order to gather information about how the other thinks or feels. *Envy* is wanting what another has. These self-conscious nonevaluative emotions emerge in the second half of the second year, at the same time that cognition about the self emerges. I have suggested that they are supported by the cognition "I know I know" (M. Lewis, 1995a).

Somewhere around the third birthday, a second set of cognitions emerges. These include standards, rules, and goals; the ability to evaluate one's behavior against those standards; the rise of attributions about the self; and the ability to focus on the self or on the task requirements (Stipek, Recchia, & McClintic, 1992). These cognitions involving the self give rise to a new set of emotions, the "self-conscious evaluative emotions," which do require the child to have these evaluative capacities. Such a developmental sequence of emotional development, therefore, has as its center the development of cognitions, especially those involving the self. The end point of this early developmental sequence is a connection of emotions, cognitions, and social behavior (M. Lewis, 2003).

THINKING AND FEELING

The term "feeling" is most often used when talking about emotional behavior. "Feelings" appear to denote two meanings that affect our understanding of the relation between cognition and emotion. When we say "I am feeling happy," we mean, first, that "I am in a state of happiness" and, second, that "I am aware that I am in this state" (see James, 1884). When we consider the early emerging emotions, those called "primary" or "basic," it is not uncommon to attribute to these emotions little cognition (Zajonc, 1980). This idea is supported by the belief that there may be some direct one-to-one correspondence between certain stimuli and a particular emotional state.

While such a theoretical approach, one that does not invoke cognitive processes, may be possible for some classes of emotion, the difficulty with such an analysis becomes apparent when we consider the more complex emotions, called here "self-conscious emotions." The problem of deciding which emotions are primary and which are complex, and therefore may require more cognition, is not easily solved (Ortony & Turner, 1990). Darwin (1872/1965) suggested that self-conscious emotions (he made little distinction between them) were elicited by thoughts about the self. Later, Plutchik (1980) offered several decision rules to separate the emotions, one of which is relevant for the current discussion. He suggested that the basic emotions are *not* dependent on introspection—in other words, they are not dependent on cognitions—while the other class is dependent on cognitions. Elsewhere, I have proposed a division of emotions based on the concept of self-conscious versus non-self-conscious emotions. I argue that those emotions often considered to be primary—such as fear, interest, anger, disgust, sadness, and joy—do not involve self-consciousness, and therefore do not involve elaborate cognitive processes, as, however, the more complex emotions do (Lewis & Michalson, 1983a).

In the case of jealousy, envy, empathy, embarrassment, shame, pride, and guilt, it is very difficult to think of some one-to-one correspondence between specific environmental elicitors and the production of such emotions. These emotions generally require the organism to make a comparison or to evaluate its behavior vis-à-vis some standard, rule, or goal. Thus, for example, pride occurs when one's evaluation of one's behavior is compared to a standard and indicates that one has succeeded, whereas shame or guilt follows when such evaluation leads to the conclusion that one has failed. The cognitions that give rise to this class of emotions involve elaborate cognitive processes, and these elaborate cognitive processes all involve the notion of the self. While some authors—for example, the psychoanalytic theorists Freud (1936) and Erickson (1950)—argued for some universal elicitors of shame such as failure at toilet training or exposure of the backside, the idea of an automatic noncognitive elicitor does not seem to make much sense. Cognitive processes *must* be the elicitors of these complex emotions (Darwin, 1872/1965; M. Lewis, 1992a). It is the way we think or what we think about that becomes the elicitor. There may still be a one-to-one correspondence between thinking certain thoughts and experiencing particular emotions, but the elicitor remains a cognition. Cognitive processes, therefore, play a vital role in eliciting these types of emotions (see also Tomkins, 1963). While some have argued that primary emotions also are elicited by appraisal (Lazarus, 1982), attributions involve the self and thus a distinction needs to be made between them. Attributions are cognitions about the self, appraisals are not.

THE ROLE OF SELF IN SELF-CONSCIOUS EMOTIONS

There exists a wide range of emotions that, by definition, involve the concept of self (see M. Lewis, 2003). Those specific aspects of self that are involved in the self-conscious emotions can be highlighted by considering the specific emotions of shame, guilt, and pride. Figure 8.2 presents a schematization of the self-attributional process. To begin with, the self-evaluative emotions involve a set of standards, rules, and goals (SRGs) that are inventions of the culture and that are transmitted to the child. As Stipek and her colleagues (1992) have shown, by age 2 children are able to demonstrate that they have incorporated, in some fashion, the SRGs of their parents. By "incorporation" we mean simply that the child knows these SRGs and, at the same time, does not need the support of the actual presence of a parent or someone else in order to react to them. Although the reaction may at first anticipate what parents might say or do, it is still the case that the child is able to build a representation that he or she alone possesses about these SRGs and about what will happen if they are violated or successfully fulfilled. Incorporation is nothing more than the ability of the organism to take the view of the other into the self and make it the view of the self. What is intriguing is that this process appears to start at an extremely early age (see Stipek et al., 1992).

The second point to stress is that the child must be capable of "owning" his or her behavior; if children are unable to perceive that they are the actors or the producers of a particular set of behaviors, then, in fact, they would have no basis for evaluation. Self-evaluation, therefore, implies not only a standard, rule, or goal but also the realization that it is one's own action. This ability also emerges at this time (see, e.g., Kagan, 1981). The self also enters into the comparison between its action and its standard in terms of responsibility. I can, for example, evaluate my behavior against my SRGs and conclude that I have succeeded or failed. However, this will not lead me to either pride or shame unless I am prepared to believe that I am responsible for that success or failure. In the attributional literature, this has been considered as the distinction between an internal and an external attribution (Weiner, 1986). Consider the following example: I take an exam and do not perform well, but I believe that my failure was due to the fact that I was kept awake all night by construction noise next door. If this was my attribution, then it is unlikely that I would feel shame. The same holds for pride. Thus, only when I attribute a responsible self in the comparison between my action and the SRG does my comparison result in specific emotions.

Still another cognition to consider has to do with the evaluation of one's self in terms of specific or global attribution. "Global" refers to the focus on the self and indicates "all of

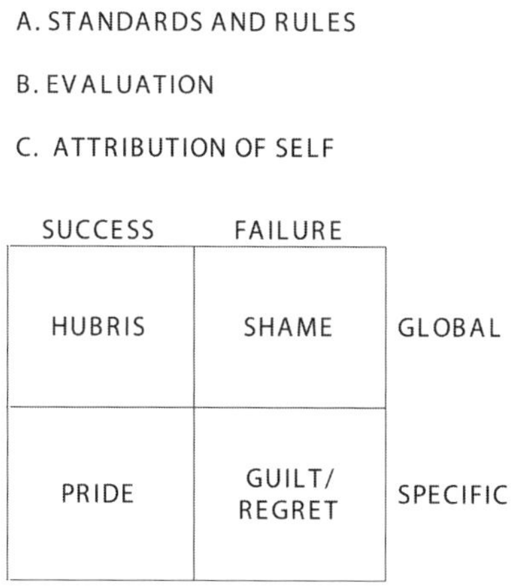

A. STANDARDS AND RULES

B. EVALUATION

C. ATTRIBUTION OF SELF

	SUCCESS	FAILURE	
GLOBAL	HUBRIS	SHAME	
SPECIFIC	PRIDE	GUILT/ REGRET	

FIGURE 8.2. Structural model for the elicitation of self-conscious evaluative emotions.

me." "Specific" refers to a focus on my action (see Dweck & Leggett, 1988; Weiner, 1986). This distinction has been described in various ways. Of particular usefulness is Dweck's distinction between task focus and self- or performance focus. If one internalizes (i.e., accepts) the fact that one has failed a particular standard, rule, or goal and makes a global attribution or self-focus, one is likely to feel shame. However, if the attribution, or focus, is about the task, one is apt to feel guilt or regret (Lewis & Sullivan, 2005; Tracy & Robins, 2004).

Let me give an example of this difference. Imagine that you have written a short story and submitted it for publication. It is rejected. You can assume that the reviewer did not know what she was talking about, and thus refuse to accept the rejection as a failure having to do with you. Alternatively, you can accept the rejection as a failure for which you are responsible. If you do not accept the rejection as failure on your part, you may simply send the story off to another publisher. If you do accept it as failure, you still have a second attribution to make, namely, to determine whether this reflects a global self-focus or a specific task focus about your failure. If you make a global/self-evaluation, such as "I am not a good writer," you are much more likely to feel shame than if you make a specific/task attribution, such as "I should have developed the central character more than I did." The response of global/self-attribution, and therefore shame, is likely to lead to the cessation of activity—that is, the body collapse (H. B. Lewis, 1971), as well as a lack of repair and reparation (see Barrett & Zahn-Waxler, 1987).

In the case of you as a fiction writer, under a global/self internal attribution of failure, you are likely to take the manuscript and put it in a drawer, and never look at it again or at least not for a long time. In contrast, failure that is internalized and specific/task-focused is likely to lead to reparation since a specific feature in need of repair has been identified. In such a case, you are likely to revise the story and send it off again (Tangney & Dearing, 2002).

We can see, therefore, that the role of self-cognitions in this class of emotions is quite elaborate, involving (1) knowledge of SRGs; (2) incorporation of these SRGs; (3) evaluation of one's behavior vis-à-vis the SRGs; (4) distribution of the blame to oneself or to others; and (5) attribution and focus, either global/self-focus or specific/task focus. In each one of these processes, a concept of the self and of self-processes needs to be considered. I (M. Lewis, 1992a) have characterized this process as depicted in Figure 8.2.

Given these three sets of cognitive activities—(1) the establishment of one's SRG, (2) the evaluation of success or failure of one's actions, and (3) the attributions about the self—we can see in these combinations the four self-conscious emotions of shame, guilt, hubris, and pride. The model provides a framework for understanding some of the self-conscious evaluative emotions, in particular shame. Shame is the product of a complex set of cognitions including attributions about the self. The phenomenological experience is a wish to hide, disappear, or die, and it is often accompanied by the physical action of body and facial collapse. It is these physical behaviors that we use to index shame when we work with children (Lewis, Alessandri, & Sullivan, 1992). Guilt has been distinguished from shame because its focus is not on a failed self but on a failed task. While with shame there is a body collapse, guilt appears to be more characterized by the child's attempt to repair or correct a failure (Barrett & Zahn-Waxler, 1987). The characterization of the other evaluative self-conscious emotions, such as hubris, pride, shyness, and evaluative embarrassment, has been explored elsewhere (M. Lewis, 1993, 1995b), so I will not discuss them here. Other chapters in this volume also elaborate on the distinction between pride and hubris (Tracy & Robins, Chapter 15, this volume; Bosson & Prewitt-Freilino, Chapter 22, this volume).

WAYS OF FOCUSING ON THE SELF

It seems obvious that self- or performance versus task focus refers to our attention toward our selves. In self-focus the attention is drawn toward our global selves and the stable attributes by which we define ourselves. Task focus, on the other hand, refers to attention drawn toward the task; it may refer to our selves through our actions vis-à-vis a specific task but not to the stable attributes by which we define ourselves.

Adults have the capacity to direct their attention inward toward themselves or outward toward the task. Even without directing their attention inward toward themselves (e.g., their actions and emotional states), they are capable of performing highly complex and demanding tasks. In fact, the example of solving complex mental problems without focusing on them directly is well known. Solutions to mental problems often "come to us" as if someone inside our heads has been working on them while we go about attending to other problems.

While the term "consciousness" could be used to talk about attention directed inward toward the self as well as outward to the world, I will try to specify some difference between them. Hilgard (1977) and before him Janet (1929), for example, talked about divided consciousness; others have talked about subconsciousness or unconsciousness (Freud, 1960). More recently, work on the modularity of brain function has demonstrated that areas of the brain are quite capable of carrying out complex tasks or learning complex problems without other areas having knowledge of them. As only one example, Gazzaniga (1985) has shown that patients with their corpus callosum ablated (usually to reduce epileptic seizures) are capable of haptically having knowledge in their right hands; for example, they can show by raising their fingers that they know they are feeling the number "3." However, they are unable to report verbally what that number is. Work by LeDoux (1989) with animals and Damasio (Bechara et al., 1995) with humans has demonstrated that both perceptual processes as well as complex learning can take place in the amygdala and hippocampus without cortical involvement or without knowledge of that learning.

Such findings lend support to the idea of *modularity of brain function*—that is, for the involvement of some brain areas without the involvement of others—as well as the idea that complex mental operations can take place without the subject's own knowledge or self-attention (what I wish to call "consciousness") of these operations. These findings about brain function fit with our own well-known experiences of sudden insight or spontaneous solution to complex mental problems, as well as a set of common phenomena that require intrapsychic differentiation and even conflict. These well-known phenomena include hypnotism, perceptual defenses, self-deception, active forgetting, acts of loss of will or akraxia, and multiple personality. These processes, although receiving some attention, have not been given the study they need. Hilgard (1977), for one, called the underlying processes involved in each of them "disassociation," a term once in favor but now not used. This is because Freud (1960) argued for an active process of repression rather than a splitting off of consciousness, a concept favored by Charcot (1889) and Janet (1929). Each of these phenomena appears to rest on a process involving the idea of our ability of divided consciousness which may be supported by the modularity of brain functions.

The ability to direct attention both toward ourselves and toward the outer world is an adaptive strategy. Divided consciousness's adaptive significance is that it allows us to check on our own internal responses in addition to our behavior in the world (self-focus), and quite separately to act in the world (outer or task focus). It is obvious from observations of animals or even cells that it is possible to behave in a highly complex fashion in the world as a function of internally generated plans and programs. This action-in-the-world does not require that we pay attention to ourselves. Paying attention to ourselves allows us to modify action-in-the-world and enables us to modify this action by thinking about our actions rather than by the use of trial and error. Thus, when I want to cross a busy street, it is probably adaptive not to be thinking about how well I am doing but instead coordinating my actions in context. On the other hand, if I have almost had an accident, then thinking about myself and my fear at being almost hit allows me to modify my plans for the future. Both directions of focus are important (see Leary, Chapter 3, this volume).

DEVELOPMENT OF SELF

It is clear that adult humans possess the capacity of directed self-focus or attention. A question, then, is raised: Does this capacity develop? My colleagues and I have been addressing this problem for over 30 years (M. Lewis, 1992a, 1995a, 1995b; Lewis & Brooks, 1974; Lewis & Brooks-Gunn, 1979; Lewis, Goldberg, & Campbell, 1969; Lewis & Michalson, 1983b). I have suggested that there may be some advantage in considering that the self is made up of two systems (M. Lewis, 2003), the first of which I call the "machinery of the self." This consists of complex capacities that are part of the operating rules of the species. One possible such capacity has recently been studied. Although more data are needed, the evidence points to the fact that the amygdala is capable of learning through environmental interaction and this learning may not involve other areas of the brain such as the cortex (LeDoux, 1989). This machinery is made up of many features including built-in, but open to, learning sensory and perceptual capacities. This machinery of the self itself develops through interaction with the environment.

The second system is that of ideas and in particular what I call the "idea of me." This aspect is what I have referred to as "consciousness." While people use the idea of consciousness in a broader sense, often to include the "machinery of the self" system, I wish to restrict my usage of the term "consciousness" to include *only* this "idea of me" (M. Lewis, 1999).

This aspect, the "idea of me," is a metacognition. It is like the memory of a memory, as in "I remember that as I get older I am likely to forget a person's name." Parenthetically, as we age, we increasingly forget things. Pathology of brain function (e.g., senility) is when we forget that we forget; this is a higher-order process involving self-focus. It is also like R. D. Laing's (1970) *Knots*: "I know that you know that I know that today is Saturday." This "idea of me" develops. Recent work suggests regions of the brain that appear to be involved in this cognition and which themselves develop (Carmody & Lewis, 2006; Lewis & Carmody, 2007). Elsewhere, I have argued that the development of the cognition "the idea of me" (or what I call consciousness) occurs in the middle of the second year of life (M. Lewis, 1995a). Such a conclusion is supported by a variety of data, notably the emergence of the personal pronoun "me," self-recognition, and pretend play (Lewis & Ramsay, 2004), as well as the relation between self-recognition and the onset of empathy and embarrassment (see Bischof-Kohler, 1991; Lewis, Sullivan, Stanger, & Weiss, 1989). A self-representation is necessary for emotional development. Work showing that increases in imitative play are associated with self-recognition supports this view (Asendorpf, 2002).

From a developmental perspective, the problem of focused attention on the self or on the self's action in the world has been addressed most noticeably by Dweck (Dweck, Hong, & Chiu, 1993). Dweck's data indicate that children, at least by 6–8 years, differentially use task or self-performance focus (Smiley & Dweck, 1994). Moreover, their differential use is related to achievement motivation. Thus, for example, children who are performance- or self-focus-oriented show poor social and academic achievement (Dweck & Leggett, 1988) as well as low persistence at academic tasks (Dweck, 1991).

There has been little work looking at these strategies in younger children, in part because younger children do not have the verbal abilities necessary to demonstrate these strategies. Recently, my colleague Margaret Sullivan and I have begun to explore whether it is possible to obtain data on attentional focus in children who are 3–6 years of age. Children of this age might well possess such focus-of-attention differences since there is now sufficient data to indicate that 3-year-old children's response to success and failure on tasks is dependent on their perceptions of whether the tasks are easy or difficult to complete (Lewis et al., 1992; Stipek et al., 1992).

In order to measure attentional orientation, children were given four tasks, two easy ones and two difficult ones. On one easy and one difficult task, they succeeded, and on the other easy and difficult tasks they failed. In this way, four conditions were created for each child: easy-fail, easy-succeed, difficult-fail, and difficult-succeed. In the first phase of the study, we measured children's emotional responses to these four conditions. The findings are quite consistent across age and studies: children show shame when they fail, especially when they fail easy tasks, and they show pride when they succeed, especially when they succeed in difficult tasks (Lewis et al., 1992).

After each of the four tasks, children were asked a series of questions about the task and about why they succeeded or failed. Each child was asked if the task was easy or difficult. The responses to the "easy-fail" task present the possibility to look at attentional focus. The task itself was easy; however, all children failed it. We reasoned that if they focused on the task itself, they would say the task was easy; if they focused on their performance, they would say it was hard.

Data on over 100 children's responses on the easy-fail task revealed a significant relation to the children's emotion behavior, including facial and bodily actions. Figure 8.3 presents the percentage of children showing shame, embarrassment, and pride as a function of individual differences in self-performance versus task focus. The pride responses are to success while the shame/embarrassment responses are to failure. Across studies, the findings remain quite consistent. For the self-conscious evaluative emotions, self- or performance-focused children (i.e., children who labeled the easy task difficult after failing at it) showed more embarrassment and shame when they failed and more pride when they succeeded than children who were specific- or task-focused. There are no group differences in either sadness or joy, suggesting that self-focus does not lead to a general increase in emotional behavior but rather only affects those emotions that are elicited by thinking about the self (M. Lewis, 1992a).

SOURCES OF INDIVIDUAL DIFFERENCES IN SELF-CONSCIOUS EMOTIONS

Individual differences in self-conscious evaluative emotions appear as early as self-referential behavior emerges. There are at least two major sources of individual differences in the self-evaluative emotions. The first is constitutional and has to do with temperament,

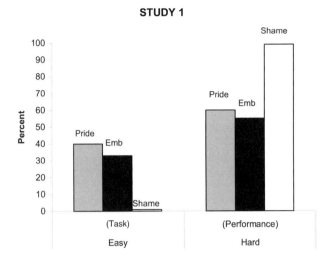

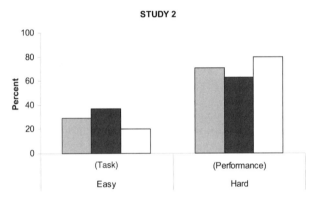

FIGURE 8.3. Self-conscious emotions as a function of task judgments of preschoolers following a "failed" easy task in two studies. The percentage of children showing pride, evaluative embarrassment, and shame is shown for those who said the task was "easy" despite the failure (task focus) and for those who said the task was "hard," congruent with their failure (performance focus).

while the second source of difference is in the socialization process itself. Of course both may be involved.

Temperament

Temperament involves biological tendencies to regulate the latency, duration, and intensity of emotional responses (M. Lewis, 1989; Rothbart & Goldsmith, 1985). Recent analyses suggest that temperament involves individual differences in the tendency to express positive as well as negative emotion, and differences in reactivity level (Ramsay & Lewis, 2001; Rothbart, Ahadi, & Hershey, 1994). These aspects of temperament are related to self-conscious evaluative emotions. For example, higher anger and fearfulness are associated with later guilt (Rothbart et al., 1994). Exposure embarrassment at 13 months is related to having a difficult or more negative temperament in infancy (Lewis & Ramsay, 1997).

Reactivity to stress is an important aspect of temperament that is related to negative self-evaluation, such that higher cortisol responses to stress are associated with greater expression of evaluative embarrassment and shame (Lewis & Ramsay, 1997, 2002). That greater stress reactivity is related to greater levels of evaluative embarrassment and shame may be due to its relation to self-focus. Individual differences in self- or performance focus may arise because of a lower threshold for pain and an inability to gate or block internal physiological signals, resulting in more attention directed toward the self and thus more consciousness (Csikszentmihalyi, 1990). Similarly, Lewis and Ramsay (1997) proposed that greater stress reactivity leads to greater attention to the self. Following failure, greater self-attention increases the likelihood that children will attribute negative outcomes internally to the self, rather than externally to the task or situation, thereby increasing the tendency toward shame and/or evaluative embarrassment. Thus, aspects of temperament influence the tendency toward self-attention, which in turn is likely to promote self-conscious evaluative emotions.

Socialization

Socialization can influence individual differences in the self-conscious emotions through influencing the acquisition of SRGs, internal focus of responsibility, and self- or performance versus task focus of attention. The methods used to teach SRGs, that is, how children are rewarded and punished, influence children's style of self-evaluation and therefore their proneness to self-conscious evaluative emotion (M. Lewis, 1992a).

Learning SRGs

The nature of SRGs themselves—and what constitutes success or failure—varies with individuals. Exactly how one comes to evaluate an action, thought, or feeling as a success or a failure is not well understood. Yet this aspect of self-evaluation is particularly important because the same SRG can result in radically different emotions, depending on whether success or failure is perceived and attributed to the self. Differences in SRGs within a societal group and between cultures will occur because groups within a society and different cultures value some SRGs more than others. The initial evaluation of one's behavior in terms of success and failure is also a very important aspect of the organization of plans and the determination of new goals and future expectations of success and failure. Many factors are involved in producing idiosyncratic, unrealistic evaluations of performance relative to SRGs. High standanrds, however, may not themselves necessarily be bad. Instead, extremes of punishment and the quality of the discipline produce individual differences. Harsh socialization experiences, especially high levels of physical punishment for failure and the use of scorn, humiliation, or contempt as discipline techniques, may also affect the quality of SRGs and how behaviors that meet or violate them are viewed (Gold, Sullivan, & Lewis, 2006).

Acquiring an Attribution Style

Among adults as well as children, people may differ in the tendency to attribute failure or success to themselves. Instead, they may explain their performance in terms of chance or the actions of others (Weiner, 1972). The tendency to make internal as opposed to external attribution is a function of both learning and individual characteristics. Certain inductive parenting styles are related to greater internal attributions (Ferguson & Stegge, 1995). However, there are some individuals who are more likely to blame themselves for failure (or, alternatively, to take credit for success) no matter what happens. Dweck and Leggett (1988) found that many children attributed their academic successes and failures to external forces, although there were some who were likely to evaluate their success and failure in terms of their own personal actions even at young ages. In fact, the tendency to make internal attributions may be greater in young children generally, due to their greater egocentrism.

Individual differences in evaluative style can be observed even in young children. Dweck, Chiu, and Hong (1995) showed that somewhere between ages 3 and 6 differences in perceptions of personal performance emerge and are consistent. Once learned, these early motivational dispositions eventually may become entrenched as a personality or attribution style, especially in response to negative events (Kaslow, Rehm, Pollack, & Siegal, 1988). Strong negative events occurring early in children's lives seem to push children toward a global attribution style in a kind of one-trial learning—that is, children exposed to such events will more consistently make global attributions than others under most conditions of failure. Their attributions made in response to success are less likely to be predictable. The intensity and power of negative events acting on a child with still limited coping skills may promote this development. Strong negative emotion swamps any cognitive processing that might override the child's egocentric perceptions about the event. Because the child cannot separate him- or herself from the failure, the child internalizes blame and focuses on the global self. The range of negative life events that lead to global attributions is in need of further investigation. These may include negative experiences with parents, with others in the immediate social environment, or with general calamities that impact the self, family, or others. However, a reasonable working hypothesis is that the performance or self-attribution style of failure is created in the cauldron of stress (M. Lewis, 1992a).

CONSCIOUSNESS, SELF-FOCUS, AND PATHOLOGY

As adults we are capable of directing our attention both inward toward ourselves and outward toward our action-in-the-world (M. Lewis, 1997). This ability to focus attention differentially is a human capacity. Moreover, it is apparent that adults differ in their focus, some showing too great a self-focus and some too little. Too great a focus toward the outside world results in the loss of self-evaluation and therefore the inability to correct a problem; too great a self-focus also results in problems. One of the major problems is in the increase in the self-conscious evaluative emotions, especially the negative ones of shame, guilt, and embarrassment (M. Lewis, 1992a). The increase in these emotions has been linked to many of the major disassociative disorders (H.B. Lewis, 1987; M. Lewis, 1992a).

We have been exploring the relation between children's trauma, self-cognition, and emotional well-being. Alessandri and Lewis (1996) looked at young children's emotional responses as a function of whether or not they were maltreated. Using the paradigm we have described elsewhere (Lewis et al., 1992), we were interested in seeing whether maltreated children were more likely to make self-cognitions that led to shame and embarrassment when they failed a task and less likely to lead to pride when they succeeded. While we did not collect data on their attributions, our study revealed that the trauma of maltreatment, at least for 3- to 5-year-olds, has important consequences on their self-conscious evaluative emotions. For example, maltreated girls showed more shame when they failed and less pride when they succeeded than nonmaltreated girls. Maltreated boys, on the other hand, showed less emotional responses of all kinds than did nonmaltreated boys, suggesting that girls' attributions are thrown toward internal blame and global/self-focus while boys' attributions are thrown toward external blame and emotional suppression. Such an example indicates that early emotional trauma impacts on self-cognitions which in turn impact on their emotional responses.

While working on the problem of sexual abuse and symptom formation, my colleague Candice Feiring and I found that while severity of abuse is related to shame, it is shame and the changes in shame that predict such symptoms as depression or hypereroticism (Feiring, Taska, & Lewis, 1998). This approach also is relevant for other forms of psychopathology, including acting-out disorders in children (Dodge & Frame, 1982), depression (Beck, 1979), and posttraumatic stress disorder (Foa, Zinbarg, & Rothbaum, 1992). Such findings as these indicate that the relation between self-cognitions and emotion are useful for our understanding of development as well as for our understanding of developmental psychopathology.

More recently we have been looking at the role of shame and attribution style as it relates to (1) how parents punish children and (2) how this affects children's delinquent or acting-out behavior. Based on previous research, we hypothesized a relation between maltreatment (how parents treat their children) and delinquency (acting-out behavior) as mediated by emotional factors. This model is seen in Figure 8.4A. The participants in this study were adolescents who were incarcerated in a juvenile detention facility pending criminal charges. Participants completed measures of child maltreatment, a measure of emotional functioning (the TOSCA-2), and measures of delinquency (self-reports); institutional disciplinary reports were also employed. As seen in Figure 8.4B, subjects exposed to high levels of harsh parental discipline showed higher rates of delinquency. Maltreatment was related to lower levels of shame and guilt, and to an increased reliance on blaming others or avoiding blame in conflict situations. Subjects who engaged in more violent delinquent behavior were less prone to the emotions of shame and guilt and used strategies of blaming others and avoiding blame. While maltreatment may directly relate to delinquent behavior, emotional factors within the child also have a strong effect. Thus we can see that the self-conscious emotions or their lack play an important role in developmental pathology.

The role of cognition plays a critical role in the self-conscious emotions. They are the elicitors of these emotions. While they are the elicitors of these emotions, our experiences of shame or embarrassment are not just cognitions. Rather, these cognitions are elicitors of internal processes, often referred to as "emotional states," which, while not as yet identified, are likely to exist. It is difficult to imagine that we "learn" shame. While we may learn about the elicitors of these emotions or about what responses are culturally appropriate, the emotion itself is not learned. The developmental process appears to take place in the first 3 years of life. The development of emotional life occurs quickly in tandem with cognitive development. This process takes place within a social context and thus influences and is influenced by the children's caregivers.

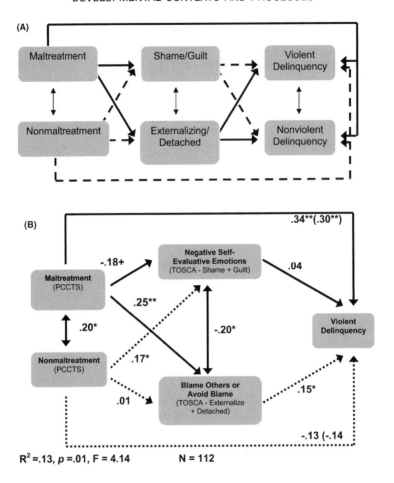

FIGURE 8.4. The effects of harsh parenting on adolescents' emotions, attributions, and delinquent behavior. (A) General mediation model between maltreatment, emotions/attributions, and delinquency. (B) Model of relations between maltreatment, emotions/attributions, and delinquency.

REFERENCES

Alessandri, S. M., & Lewis, M. (1996). Differences in pride and shame in maltreated and nonmaltreated preschoolers. *Child Development, 67,* 1857–1869.

Asendorpf, J. B. (2002). Self-awareness, other-awareness, and secondary representation. In A. N. Meltzoff & W. Prinz (Eds.), *The imitative mind: Development, evolution, and brain bases* (pp. 63–73). New York: Cambridge University Press.

Barrett, K. C., & Zahn-Waxler, C. (1987, April). *Do toddlers express guilt?* Paper presented at the annual meeting of the Society for Research in Child Development, Toronto.

Bechara, A., Tranel, D., Damasio, H., Adolphs, R., Rockland, C., & Damasio, A. R. (1995). Double dissociation of conditioning and declarative knowledge relative to the amygdala and hippocampus in humans. *Science, 269,* 1115–1118.

Beck, A. T. (1979). *Cognitive therapy and emotional disorders.* New York: Times Mirror.

Bischof-Kohler, D. (1991). The development of empathy in infants. In M. E. Lamb & H. Keller (Eds.), *Infant development: Perspectives from German-speaking countries* (pp. 245–273). Hillsdale, NJ: Erlbaum.

Bridges, K. M. B. (1932). Emotional development in early infancy. *Child Development, 3,* 324–334.

Carmody, D. P., & Lewis, M. (2006). Brain activation when hearing one's own and others' names. *Brain Research, 116,* 153–158.

Charcot, J. M. (1889). *Clinical lectures on diseases of the nervous system.* London: New Sydenham Society.

Csikszentmihalyi, M. (1990). *Flow: The psychology of optimal experience.* New York: Harper & Collins.

Darwin, C. (1965). *The expression of emotion in animals and man.* Chicago: University of Chicago Press. (Original work published 1872)

Dodge, K. A., & Frame, C. L. (1982). Social cognitive biases and deficits in aggressive boys. *Child Development, 53,* 630–635.

Dweck, C. S. (1991). Self-theories and goals: Their role in motivation, personality and development. In R. A. Dienstbier (Ed.), *Nebraska Symposium on Motivation, 1990: Perspectives on motivation* (pp. 643–691). New York: Wiley.

Dweck, C. S., Chiu, C., & Hong, Y. (1995). Implicit theories and their role in judgments and reactions: A world from two perspectives. *Psychological Inquiry, 6*(4), 267–285.

Dweck, C. S., Hong, Y., & Chiu, C. (1993). Implicit theories: Individual differences in the likelihood and meaning of dispositional inference. *Personality and Social Psychology Bulletin, 19,* 644–656.

Dweck, C. S., & Leggett, E. L. (1988). A social-cognitive approach to motivation and personality. *Psychological Review, 95,* 256–273.

Erickson, E. H. (1950). *Childhood and society.* New York: Norton.

Feiring, C., Taska, L., & Lewis, M. (1998). The role of shame and attribution style in children's and adolescents' adaptation to sexual abuse. *Child Maltreatment, 3*(2), 129–142.

Ferguson, T. J., & Stegge, H. (1995). Emotional states and traits in children: The case of guilt and shame. In J. P. Tangney & K. W. Fischer (Eds.), *Self-conscious emotions: The psychology of shame, guilt, embarrassment, and pride* (pp. 174–197). New York: Guilford Press.

Foa, E. B., Zinbarg, R., & Rothbaum, B. O. (1992). Uncontrollability and unpredictability in post-traumatic stress disorder: An animal model. *Psychological Bulletin, 112*(2), 218–238.

Freud, S. (1936). *The problem of anxiety.* New York: Norton.

Freud, S. (1960). *The psychopathology of everyday life* (A. Tyson, Trans.). New York: Norton.

Gazzaniga, M. S. (1985). *The social brain: Discovering the networks of the mind.* New York: Basic Books.

Gold, J., Sullivan, M. W., & Lewis, M. (2006). *Shame and blaming others: Relations to parental discipline practices in incarcerated juveniles.* Manuscript in preparation.

Hilgard, E. R. (1977). *Divided consciousness.* New York: Wiley.

James, W. (1884). What is emotion? *Mind, 19,* 188–205.

Janet, P. (1929). *Major symptoms of hysteria.* New York: Hafner.

Kagan, J. (1981). *The second year: The emergence of self-awareness.* Cambridge, MA: Harvard University Press.

Kaslow, N. J., Rehm, L. P., Pollack, S. L., & Siegal, A. W. (1988). Attributional style and self-control behavior in depressed and nondepressed children and their parents. *Journal of Abnormal Child Psychology, 16*(2), 163–175.

Laing, R. D. (1970). *Knots.* New York: Pantheon Books.

Lazarus, R. S. (1982). Thoughts on the relationship between emotion and cognition. *American Psychologist, 37,* 1019–1024.

LeDoux, J. (1989). Cognitive and emotional interactions in the brain. *Cognition and Emotion, 3,* 265–289.

Lewis, H. B. (1971). *Shame and guilt in neurosis.* New York: International Universities Press.

Lewis, H. B. (1987). *The role of shame in symptom formation.* Hillsdale, NJ: Erlbaum.

Lewis, M. (1989). What do we mean when we say emotional development? In L. Cirillo, B. Kaplan, & S. Wapner (Eds.), *Emotions in ideal human development* (pp. 53–76). Hillsdale, NJ: Erlbaum.

Lewis, M. (1992a). *Shame: The exposed self.* New York: Free Press.

Lewis, M. (1992b). The self in self-conscious emotions. A commentary on D. Stipek, S. Recchia, & S. McClintic (Eds.), "Self-evaluation in young children." *Monographs of the Society for Research in Child Development, 57* (1, Serial No. 226).

Lewis, M. (1993). Self-conscious emotions: Embarrassment, pride, shame, and guilt. In M. Lewis & J. Haviland (Eds.), *Handbook of emotions* (pp. 563–573). New York: Guilford Press.

Lewis, M. (1995a). Aspects of self: From systems to ideas. In P. Rochat (Ed.), *The self in early infancy: Theory and research* (pp. 95–115). Amsterdam: Elsevier.

Lewis, M. (1995b). Embarrassment: The emotion of self-exposure and evaluation. In J. P. Tangney & K. W. Fischer (Eds.), *Self-conscious emotions: The psychology of shame, guilt, embarrassment, and pride* (pp. 198–218). New York: Guilford Press.

Lewis, M. (1997). *Altering fate: Why the past does not predict the future.* New York: Guilford Press.

Lewis, M. (1999). Social cognition and the self. In P. Rochat (Ed.), *Early social cognition* (pp. 81–98). Mahwah, NJ: Erlbaum.

Lewis, M. (2000). Self-conscious emotions: Embarrassment, pride, shame, and guilt. In M. Lewis & J. Haviland-Jones (Eds.), *Handbook of emotions* (2nd ed., pp. 623–636). New York: Guilford Press.

Lewis, M. (2003). The role of self in shame. *Social Research, 70*(4), 1181–1204.

Lewis, M., Alessandri, S., & Sullivan, M. W. (1992). Differences in shame and pride as a function of children's gender and task difficulty. *Child Development, 63,* 630–638.

Lewis, M., & Brooks, J. (1974). Self, others and fear: Infants' reactions to people. In M. Lewis & L. Rosenblum (Eds.), *The origins of fear: The origins of behavior* (pp. 195–227). New York: Wiley.

Lewis, M., & Brooks-Gunn, J. (1979). *Social cognition and the acquisition of self.* New York: Plenum Press.

Lewis, M., & Carmody, D. (2007). *Self representation in brain development.* Manuscript in preparation.

Lewis, M., Goldberg, S., & Campbell, H. (1969). A developmental study of information processing within the first three years of life: Response decrement to a redundant signal. *Monographs of the Society for Research in Child Development, 34*(9, Serial No. 133).

Lewis, M., & Michalson, L. (1983a). *Children's emotions and moods: Developmental theory and measurement.* New York: Plenum Press.

Lewis, M., & Michalson, L. (1983b). From emotional state to emotional expression: Emotional development from a person–environment interaction perspective. In D. Magnusson & V. L. Allen (Eds.), *Human development: An interactional perspective* (pp. 261–275). New York: Academic Press.

Lewis, M., & Ramsay, D. S. (1997). Stress reactivity and self-recognition. *Child Development, 68,* 621–629.

Lewis, M., & Ramsay, D. S. (2002). Cortisol response to embarrassment and shame. *Child Development, 73*(4), 1034–1045.

Lewis, M., & Ramsay, D. S. (2004). Development of self-recognition, personal pronoun use, and pretend play during the second year. *Child Development, 75*(6), 1821–1831.

Lewis, M., & Sullivan, M. W. (2005). The development of self-conscious emotions. In A. Elliott & C. Dweck (Eds.), *Handbook of competence and motivation* (pp. 185–201). New York: Guilford Press.

Lewis, M., Sullivan, M. W., Stanger, C., & Weiss, M. (1989). Self-development and self-conscious emotions. *Child Development, 60,* 146–156.

Ortony, A., & Turner, T. J. (1990). What's basic about basic emotions? *Psychological Review, 97,* 315–331.

Plutchik, R. (1980). *Emotion: A psychoevolutionary synthesis.* New York: Harper & Row.

Ramsay, D., & Lewis, M. (2001). Temperament, stress, and soothing. In T. D. Wachs & G. A. Kohnstamm (Eds.), *Temperament in context* (pp. 23–41). Mahwah, NJ: Erlbaum.

Rothbart, M. K., Ahadi, S. A., & Hershey, K. L. (1994). Temperament and social behavior in childhood. *Merrill–Palmer Quarterly, 40,* 21–39.

Rothbart, M. K., & Goldsmith, H. H. (1985). Three approaches to the study of infant temperament. *Developmental Review, 5*(3), 237–260.

Smiley, P. A., & Dweck, C. S. (1994). Individual differences in achievement goals among young children. *Child Development, 65,* 1723–1743.

Stipek, D., Recchia, S., & McClintic, S. (1992). Self-evaluation in young children. *Monographs of the Society for Research in Child Development, 57*(1), (Serial No. 226).

Tangney, J. P., & Dearing, R. L. (2002). *Shame and guilt.* New York: Guilford Press.

Tomkins, S. S. (1963). *Affect imagery consciousness: Vol. 2. The negative affects.* New York: Tavistock/Routledge.

Tracy, J. L., & Robins, R. W. (2004). Putting the self into self-conscious emotions: A theoretical model. *Psychological Inquiry, 5*(2), 103–125.

Weiner, B. (1972). *Theories of motivation: From mechanism to cognition.* Chicago: Rand McNally.

Weiner, B. (1986). *An attributional theory of motivation and emotion.* New York: Springer-Verlag.

Zajonc, R. B. (1980). Feeling and thinking: Preferences need no inferences. *American Psychologist, 35,* 151–175.

PART III

CULTURAL INFLUENCES

9

Shifting Meanings of Self-Conscious Emotions across Cultures

A Social-Functional Approach

JENNIFER L. GOETZ
DACHER KELTNER

Claims about the universality and cultural variations of self-conscious emotions vary dramatically. On the one hand, certain affective scientists argue that self-conscious emotions have evolutionary origins in the status and appeasement-related processes of other mammals (e.g., de Waal, 1996; Gilbert, 2003; Keltner & Buswell, 1997). The clear implication of this evolutionary analysis is that the core elements of self-conscious emotions should involve genetically encoded biological processes that are universal across the broad swath of human cultures (e.g., Eibl-Eibesfeldt, 1989). On the other hand, observations about how self-conscious emotions vary across cultures, often found in anthropology and cultural psychology, are robust and compelling. Across cultures, self-conscious emotions vary in their lexical representation (Edelstein & Shaver, Chapter 11, this volume), their nonverbal display (Haidt & Keltner, 1999), the degree to which they are valued (Eid & Diener, 2001), the pleasantness of their experience (Wallbott & Scherer, 1995), and their consequences for self-esteem and relationship functioning (Fischer, Manstead, & Mosquera, 1999). These claims find inspiration in analyses of cultural variation in self-representation (e.g., Markus & Kitayama, 1991), the structure of social relations (e.g., Fiske, 1992), and the prominence of values like modesty and humility (e.g., Abu-Lughod, 1986). To the extent that cultures vary in self-evaluative processes, in the structure of relationships, or in terms of the values individuals chronically evaluate themselves against, members of different cultures should clearly vary in their experience of self-conscious emotions.

In this chapter, we bring together evolutionary and cultural insights regarding the universals and cultural variations of self-conscious emotions. We argue that the evolutionary and cultural forces that give rise to self-conscious emotions are complementary rather than contrary; both work in response to common problems of social living. Patterns of universality and variation in self-conscious emotions are consistent with this argument, suggesting that cultures have come to utilize the self-conscious emotion systems that evolved long ago to help individuals navigate group living. Through display and feeling rules, through moralization and valuation of the self-conscious emotions, culture has created profound variation in emotion processes that are, at their core, universal. Research shows that self-conscious emotion concepts exist in virtually all languages, have similar appraisal profiles across cultures, and may have cross-culturally recognizable facial displays. However, self-conscious emotions serve to help the individual act according to group norms, and these group norms vary greatly across cultures. These norms result in variation in the specific events that tend to elicit self-conscious emotions, in the elaborate concepts around particular self-conscious emotions, and in the functional value and normative beliefs associated with self-conscious emotions.

We use a social-functional approach to theorize about where we should find universality and where we should find variation in self-conscious emotions. This approach nicely integrates the influence of evolutionary and cultural forces.

A SOCIAL-FUNCTIONAL APPROACH TO SELF-CONSCIOUS EMOTIONS

In this chapter we rely on a social-functional account of self-conscious emotions, which integrates the viewpoints of evolutionary and social constructivist approaches to emotion (Frijda & Mesquita, 1994; Keltner & Haidt, 2001; Keltner, Haidt, & Shiota, 2006). A social-functional account rests on the assumption that emotions have evolved through natural selection to help humans meet the problems and opportunities related to gene replication (Ekman, 1992; Keltner et al., 2006; Tooby & Cosmides, 1990). Emotions, therefore, have been shaped by evolutionary forces: they are genetically encoded and embedded in the human psyche, linked to biological maturation, and involve coordinated physiological, perceptual, communicative, and behavioral processes that are meant to produce specific changes in the individual's interaction with the social and physical environments (Keltner & Haidt, 2001).

In thinking about the functions emotions serve, we have proposed that distinct emotions help meet the problems and opportunities related to three general domains (Keltner & Haidt, 2001). A first pertains to the problems of physical survival—for example, avoiding predators or dangerous microbes—and involves emotions like fear, anger, disgust, and contentment (i.e., the savoring of resources that improve the chances of survival and reproduction). A second domain has to do with reproduction and the demands of raising vulnerable offspring to the age of viability. Emotions like sexual desire, romantic love, filial love, and sympathy help motivate sexual contact, commitment to long-term bonds, and caregiving for offspring, with obvious benefits to the chances of gene replication (Bowlby, 1969; Buss, 1992; Diamond, 2003; Gonzaga, Keltner, Londahl, & Smith, 2001; Hazan & Shaver, 1987). Finally, given their highly social nature, humans face numerous problems and opportunities related to functioning within social groups, so definitive of human culture. These are the problems of group governance. Self-conscious emotions like pride and shame have likely evolved as solutions to them.

In more concrete terms, we argue that self-conscious emotions have evolved in response to two subclasses of problems in group governance. The first is the problem of *regulating cooperative alliances,* in particular protecting against the problems of cheating and defection in reciprocal exchange. Reciprocity is a universal human norm (Gouldner, 1960) and helps individuals exchange reciprocal benefits with kin and nonkin to increase their chances of survival (Trivers, 1971). It is likely that a family of emotions have developed to establish, maintain, and strengthen reciprocity norms and obligations (Nesse, 1990). As Trivers (1971) put it, "Given the universal . . . practice of reciprocal altruism among humans . . . it is reasonable to assume that it has been an important factor in recent human evolution and that the underlying emotional dispositions affecting altruistic behavior have important genetic components" (p. 48). In particular, Trivers suggests that guilt has been selected to motivate the cheater to compensate for cheating and to behave reciprocally in the future, which will help to prevent the rupture of beneficial reciprocal relationships (see also Nesse, 1990).

Consistent with this analysis, research on guilt in the United States shows that it occurs following violations of reciprocity and that it is typically expressed in remedial behavior that reestablishes reciprocity (Baumeister, Stillwell, & Heatherton, 1994; Keltner & Buswell, 1996). Guilt promotes other-oriented behavior, such as cooperation in iterative interactions (e.g., Ketelaar & Au, 2003), altruistic action (Regan, Williams, & Sparling, 1972), and forgiveness (McCullough, Worthington, & Rachal, 1997; McCullough et al, 1998), all of which enhance the likelihood of cooperative bonds.

The second major problem of group governance is that of *group organization,* or how group members fall into specific roles and positions within social hierarchies (Keltner & Haidt, 2001). Status hierarchies are universal throughout human and nonhuman organisms (Keltner, Gruenfeld, & Anderson, 2003). They provide ways of negotiating the distribution of resources such as mates, food, and labor (de Waal, 1986; Fiske, 1992). Hierarchies are not fixed; they are dynamic processes that must be continually negotiated, redefined, and reinforced (de Waal, 1996; Ohman, 1986). Self-conscious emotions like embarrassment and shame serve to help establish and maintain status hierarchies by appeasing dominant individuals and signaling submissiveness, which reduce aggressive tendencies and increase social approach (Keltner & Buswell, 1996; Kemeny, Greunewald, & Dickerson, 2004). They should result from a decrease in one's social status and social regard (Kemeny et al., 2004).

Pride, on the other hand, probably results from an increase in social status and standing. Pride may serve to alert an individual that his or her behavior (or self) is valued by others. It may also indicate to the individual that he or she is part of a high-status group (Gilbert, 2003). The expression of pride may serve a complementary adaptive function, drawing attention to the individual and alerting the social group that he or she merits increased acceptance and status (Tracy & Robins, 2004a). It may also serve to solidify the individual's place in the group through pride in the group. In combination, emotions like shame and pride help us navigate and negotiate our place in a hierarchy.

A social-functional analysis, therefore, highlights how self-conscious emotions help humans form and maintain cooperative, dyadic interactions and negotiate places and roles within dynamic, ever-changing social hierarchies. Given that these problems are defining characteristics of human sociality, in the most general sense we would expect emotions like guilt, shame, embarrassment, and pride to be universal. We would expect, for example, that across different cultures failure to reciprocate or cooperate will elicit guilt (e.g., see Vasquez, Keltner, Ebenbach, & Banaszynski, 2001), decreases in social status will elicit shame, and actions that enhance social status will elicit some degree of pride. How can we arrive, though, at more nuanced predictions about likely universals and cultural variations in self-conscious emotions? To do so, we rely on another insight from social-functional approaches to emotion: that a comprehensive treatment of emotion must recognize that emotions are multilevel constructs.

Multiple Levels of Analysis

We have proposed that the social functions of emotions can be classified at four levels of analysis (Keltner & Haidt, 1999; see also Averill, 1980, and Frijda & Mesquita, 1994, for similar approaches). Evolutionary approaches to emotion have tended to focus on the two levels at which the individual or the dyad is the unit of analysis, whereas social constructivist approaches have more systematically considered the two higher levels, at which the group or the culture is the unit of analysis. The characteristics that make emotions functional at the individual and dyadic levels, we suggest, are likely to be fairly constant across cultures, whereas the social functions of emotions at the group and cultural levels are likely to vary more across cultures.

At the individual level of analysis, researchers focus on emotion-specific changes in experience, cognition, and physiology (Clore, 1994; Clore, Gasper, & Garvin, 2001; Davidson, Pizzagalli, Nitschke, & Kalin, 2003; LeDoux, 1996; Levenson, 1992; Schwarz, 1990). At this level of analysis, emotions are thought to inform the individual about specific social events or conditions, typically those presenting a significant opportunity or threat (Campos, Campos, & Barrett, 1989; Lerner & Keltner, 2001; Loewenstein & Lerner, 2003; Schwarz, 1990). Emotions, in particular their physiological and motivational components, are also thought to prepare the individual for action in his or her best interest (e.g., Frijda, Kuipers, & ter Schure, 1989; Levenson, 1999). As one illustration, sympathetic arousal produced during guilt-like states (e.g., Strauman & Higgins, 1987) is likely to enable the individual to engage in metabolically demanding remedial behavior.

At the dyadic level of analysis, the focus is on communication of emotion through facial, vocal, and postural channels (Ekman, 1992; Keltner et al., 2003; Juslin & Laukka, 2003; Dimberg & Öhman, 1996; Scherer, 1986; Scherer, Johnstone, & Klasmeyer, 2003). At this level of analysis, emotions signal information about current feelings, intentions, and dispositions to conspecifics (Ekman, 1993; Fridlund, 1992; Keltner et al., 2003). Emotional communication evokes complementary and reciprocal emotions in others that help individuals respond to significant social events (Dimberg & Öhman, 1996; Keltner & Kring, 1998). For example, specific displays of embarrassment and shame act as apologies, signaling submissiveness and the commitment to social norms critical to reconciliation processes between group members (e.g., Keltner, Young, & Buswell, 1997).

At the group level of analysis, researchers examine how emotions help collectives of interacting individuals meet shared goals (Clark, 1990; Collins, 1990; de Waal, 1996). Emotions help define group members and negotiate group-related roles and statuses (e.g., Clark, 1990; Collins, 1990). For example, several cultures have a word that includes the feeling related to shame, embarrassment, and gratitude, as well as deferential action directed at high-status individuals (e.g., *lajya* in the Oriya language [Haidt & Keltner, 1999], *hasham* in the Bedouin language [Abu-Lughod, 1986]). The experience and display of this emotion accompanies the recognition of one's place in a social hierarchy. The individual experience of emotion is thought to help each group member engage in collective goal-directed behavior, thereby benefiting the entire group.

At the cultural level of analysis, researchers have focused on the shaping of emotions by historical factors, and on the embedding of emotions in cultural institutions, practices, norms, and discourse (Lutz & Abu-Lughod, 1990). Emotions at this level of analysis help individuals assume cultural identities. Embarrassment (Goffman, 1967) motivates conformity and the proper playing of one's roles, while sociomoral disgust motivates the avoidance and shunning of people who violate key values within a culture (Rozin, Haidt, & McCauley, 2000). Emotions embedded in family conflicts, parental reactions, and socialization practices help children learn the norms and values of their culture (Bretherton, Fritz, Zahn-Waxler, & Ridgeway, 1986; Dunn & Munn, 1985; Shweder, Mahapatra, & Miller, 1987; White, 1990). Emotions interpreted through the lens of cultural values may also reify cultural ideologies and power structures (e.g., Hochschild, 1990). For example, Lutz (1990) has argued, drawing on stereotypes of the emotions of subordinated groups, that cultural discourses about female emotionality relegate women to positions of subordinate status. In experiencing emotions that help the individual take on cultural values and roles, or espouse culturally specific ideologies or moral values, emotions can acquire broader meanings as sensibilities or virtues (e.g., the experience of compassion within a culture that prioritizes the ethic of caring can be felt and perceived as an indicator of an individual's virtue). We propose that this analysis helps explain how members of collectivist and individualist cultures differ in the moralization, and valence, of the experience of self-conscious emotions.

Emotions, then, serve different kinds of functions at each of these four levels of analysis. They inform and orient the individual, coordinate dyadic interactions, signal group identities and values, and transmit culture-related practices, identities, and ideologies. A single emotion may have multiple functions, depending on the level of analysis one considers. A brief episode of shame, for example, can inform the individual of transgressions to avoid; signal others a sense of remorse for the transgression, evoking forgiveness; communicate the individual's position within a group; and convey commitments to cultural mores and standards. This multilevel analysis of the functions of emotions helps generate several predictions concerning the universals and cultural variations of self-conscious emotions, to which we now turn.

SELF-CONSCIOUS EMOTIONS AT THE INDIVIDUAL AND DYADIC LEVEL

As suggested by the social-functional framework, we expect self-conscious emotions to be largely universal across cultures at the individual and dyadic levels of analysis. Emotions at the intra- and interpersonal levels have been shaped by age-old problems of negotiating status and cooperation. Cognitive, experiential, and physiological systems at the individual level should be universal. Displays of facial expression and bodily behavior that communicate intentions and beliefs at the dyadic level should be consistent across cultures. However, culture-specific displays and means of communication may emerge. The basic systems underlying the self-conscious emotions should be universal in relation to broad concerns of status and cooperation. However, cultures also create complex meanings of social practice, norms, and institutions around emotions (Lutz, 1988; Lutz & Abu-Lughod, 1990). These meaning and value systems change the environment in which emotions function and inevitably have influence at the individual and dyadic levels. Thus the self-conscious emotions that evolved through natural selection are also shaped by social discourse and interaction, and by concepts of the self, morality, and the social order (Markus & Kitayama, 1991; Shweder, Much, Mahapatra, & Park, 1997).

Cultures differ dramatically in their conceptions of the self (Markus & Kitayama,

1991). Individualistic societies are best characterized by their conception of an *independent self* that is bounded, unique, and generally autonomous. As found in the United States, a prototypical individualistic society, social behavior is generally judged to be driven from within and attributed to an individual's internal attributes (Morris & Peng, 1994). Personal autonomy values are elevated over concerns related to the community and obligation to a larger in-group (Shweder et al., 1997). By contrast, an interdependent sense of self is more characteristic of non-Western cultures. An *interdependent self* is seen as part of an encompassing social relationship, recognizing that one's "self" is determined by one's relationship with others and the group (Markus & Kitayama, 1991). Likewise, the criteria upon which social status and social standing are based vary by culture (Fiske, 1992). An independent conception of a bounded and autonomous self is related to conceptions of social status based upon internal and personal characteristics. In contrast, an interdependent conception of self is related to a broader conception of social status implicating one's in-groups in both increases and decreases of status.

At the individual and dyadic level of analysis, self-conscious emotions should be broadly consistent across cultures. They should be generally concerned with the self in relation to overall status hierarchies and relationship roles. However, variations in conceptions of the self will shift attention to specific elicitors. For example, cultures that emphasize an interdependent conception of self should encourage individuals to feel more pride and shame for in-group members than cultures that emphasize an independent conception of self. In addition, as discussed in Wong and Tsai (Chapter 12, this volume) inclusive conceptions of self and social status suggest that appraisals of internal versus external locus of control will not be as important in East Asian cultures in the elicitation of self-conscious emotions.

Universal Appraisal Themes and Cultural Variation in the Objects of Emotion

Within the debate over the universality of moral judgment, there is some consensus indicating that certain abstract judgments are universal (e.g., "Harm is wrong," "It is important to keep promises and honor social obligations"), although cultures vary in the more concrete actions that are categorized in such fashion and the extent to which they moralize different domains (Haidt, 2001; Vasquez et al., 2001). This state of affairs—universality in general themes, but variation in specific elicitors and degree of moralization—applies to studies of the antecedents and appraisals of self-conscious emotions, although it is clear that more systematic work is needed.

We would expect the general themes, or appraisal profiles, of self-conscious emotions to be universal. That is, pride should result from an appraisal of congruence with societal standards and an increase in social status. In contrast, appraisal of failure to live up to societal standards or norms should lead consistently to negative self-conscious emotions, such as embarrassment, shame, and guilt. It is unclear whether embarrassment, guilt, and shame are universally distinct emotions with divergent appraisals, as has been suggested by theory and research in the United States (Keltner & Buswell, 1996; Tangney, Miller, Flicker, & Barlow, 1996).

In a study on the antecedents of guilt, shame, and embarrassment, eliciting events clearly differed in the United States (Keltner & Buswell, 1996). Embarrassment tended to follow relatively innocuous social violations, such as losing control over one's body, a cognitive shortcoming, or deviations in one's appearance. Shame followed failure to perform according to personal standards, either one's own or those of others. Finally, the antecedents of guilt involved direct harm to another, brought about by lying, cheating, neglecting another, failing to reciprocate, overt hostility, infidelity, or not helping others. These findings are corroborated by a separate study in which participants described and rated events that led to embarrassment, shame, and guilt (Tangney et al., 1996). Participants rated events that precipitated embarrassment as less negative, less morally charged, and more surprising than events that led to guilt and shame. Both shame and guilt were judged to be serious and negative, and individuals felt more responsible for them.

It is unclear to what extent these distinctions among the appraised antecedents of self-conscious emotions hold up across cultures, although in the most general sense we would expect them to. One study that compared situational descriptions of facial expressions in the United States and India found that embarrassment and shame were consistent in the two samples (Haidt & Keltner, 1999). The embarrassment expression elicited descriptions of situations in which individuals felt awkward social exposure, but had not necessarily violated a social or moral rule. Although the situations associated with the shame display were different in the two cultures, they were all much more negative and relevant to social and moral rules than were the situations associated with embarrassment. This differentiation in situational descriptions occurred despite the fact that embarrassment and shame are labeled using the same word (*lajya*) in the local Oriya language (see Menon & Shweder, 1994).

Members of different cultures differ systematically with respect to the types of elicitors that are relevant to self-conscious emotions. Emotions like pride, guilt, and shame are about the self's relation to group norms, and thus cultural differences in conceptions of self should influence antecedents and appraisals related to these emotions. For example, people with an independent sense of self should experience pride when they appraise a positive situation as being the result of their own actions or attributes. Consistently, individuals who appraise a negative situation as being the result of their own efforts should experience guilt or shame. In cultures where an interdependent sense of self is more prevalent, close in-group members such as family members and friends are considered an extension of the self (Markus & Kitayama, 1991), and thus members of these cultures should be more likely to feel pride and shame in response to the achievements and failures of close others.

In one of the first tests of these hypotheses, Stipek (1998) asked Chinese and American participants to rate the degree of shame and guilt they would feel if they themselves were caught cheating. They also rated how they would feel if their brother was caught cheating. Both Chinese and Americans felt less shame and guilt for their brother than for themselves, suggesting universality in a core appraisal theme of self-conscious emotions: they are most closely linked with self-relevant actions. However, consistent with an interdependent sense of self, Chinese respondents felt more shame when imagining their brother's immoral action than did Americans. For pride, Americans reported that they would be equally proud if they themselves or their child were accepted at a prestigious university. Chinese participants said they would be more proud for their child than for themselves.

Another study asked people from Spain and the Netherlands to describe situations that lead to shame and pride (Fischer et al., 1999). Spanish culture emphasizes a relatively interdependent self. Therefore Spanish individuals should experience shame and pride more in relation to close others than individuals from the Netherlands. In the Netherlands, which emphasizes an independent self, individuals should experience pride and shame more in relation to their sense of unique self. Consistent with these hypotheses,

Spanish participants were more likely to mention enhancement of the honor of intimate others as an elicitor of pride than did Dutch participants. In contrast, Dutch participants more often referred to events that were related to enhancement of self-esteem than did Spanish participants.

These two studies strongly suggest that the specific elicitors of shame, guilt, and pride are likely to vary across cultures according to the culturally valued self-construal. We would likewise expect other kinds of cultural differences to lead to cultural variation in the specific elicitors of self-conscious emotions. Cultures vary dramatically in what is considered morally offensive (Haidt, Koller, & Dias, 1993) and harmful (Shweder et al., 1997). For example, in many cultures impure acts are thought of as more morally offensive than they are in the United States, and it is likely that in these cultures impure acts are more likely to generate shame than in the United States. In addition to individualism and collectivism, it is likely that the degree of hierarchy in a culture is linked to the experience of shame. For example, cultures that value social hierarchy should have more shame experiences related to role violations than those that do not value social hierarchy.

Universal Displays of Self-Conscious Emotions, Cultural Variation in Ritualized Displays

The self-conscious emotions were largely ignored in early studies of emotion-related communication (for exceptions, see Izard, 1977). The past 10 years, however, have seen a burst of interest in the study of displays of self-conscious emotions. The evidence suggests that embarrassment, shame, and pride have universal displays.

The evidence for a distinct and universal display of embarrassment is convincing. In studies of spontaneous and posed expressions, U.S. participants have consistently identified a prototypical expression as embarrassment. Unlike other emotions that have quick, almost instantaneous, displays, the embarrassment display unfolds over a short time (4–5 seconds). It begins with gaze aversion, followed by smile control, a non-Duchenne smile, a second smile control, head movements down, and sometimes face touching (Keltner, 1995). Subsequent research found that a still-photograph version of this expression was consistently labeled as embarrassment in the United States (Keltner & Buswell, 1996).

Recognition of a similar embarrassment display has been studied in the United States and India (Haidt & Keltner, 1999). Embarrassment was tested along with many other emotional expressions, including sadness, amusement, happiness, and shame (see Figure 9.1). Participants identified the expressions using a forced-choice label, an open-ended description of what the person in the photograph was feeling, and an open-ended description of the situation that may have caused them to feel that way. The embarrassment expression elicited similar patterns of responses in both groups across all three methods. The label chosen most often was *lajya* ("embarrassment") in India and *embarrassment* in the United States. Perhaps more convincingly, the situations mentioned most often in both groups had to do with awkward social exposure in which one had not necessarily violated a social or moral rule. Both groups gave examples of being praised in front of others, or being in an awkward social situation, particularly the awkwardness of male–female interactions (flirting in the United States, the first meeting in an arranged marriage in India). Together, these findings suggest that embarrassment has a display that is interpreted as different from shame, sadness, and amusement across cultures.

The results for displays of shame are less consistent and clear (for a review, see Keltner & Harker, 1998). A study by Keltner (1995) found that spontaneous dynamic ex-

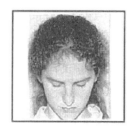
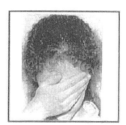

 EMBARRASSMENT   SHAME   FACE COVER

FIGURE 9.1. Self-conscious emotion displays tested by Haidt and Keltner (1999).

pressions with head and gaze down were labeled as shame in the United States. Further study of a posed photograph of this expression found that Americans recognized it most often as shame (Keltner & Buswell, 1996). A replication of this study found that the shame display was labeled most often as shame in the United States, but as sadness in India (Haidt & Keltner, 1999). The situational causes of the display were also different in the two cultures. In the United States, the modal situation types were failure and setback, and material loss, followed by violation of a social or moral rule, both of which are consistent with theories of shame and guilt. In India, the modal situation types were the loss of a valued person or attachment relationship, violation of a social or moral rule, and harm or insult done to the self by another. This suggests that the shame expression reflected concepts of sadness, shame, and anger to the Indian participants. The researchers tested another possible expression of shame: the face cover. Participants in both cultures also labeled this expression with self-conscious emotion words and antecedents. Both of the facial expressions tested have a likeness to nonhuman appeasement displays. Many species use gaze aversion, smiling behavior, head movements down, reduced physical size, and even self-touching or grooming to appease more powerful others (Keltner & Buswell, 1997).

Finally, reliable facial displays for guilt have yet to be found. One study by Keltner and Buswell (1996) tested three possible displays of guilt in the United States: a display of self-contempt, a display of sympathy, and a display of pain. None of these displays were labeled most often as guilt. This suggests that while shame and embarrassment have reliable facial signals, guilt does not.

The displays associated with the negative self-conscious emotions signal weakness, submission, and desire for appeasement through postural constriction and reduction of physical size. It has been hypothesized that pride displays are meant to show the opposite of weakness—for example, expansive postures and head movements up and back. A study tested recognition for photographs of people displaying postural expansion as well as a backward head tilt and a slight smile in the United States (see Tracy & Robins, Chapter 15, this volume). Observers reliably judged these displays as pride (Tracy & Robins, 2004a). A replication of this study in Burkina Faso with nonliterate participants found that this display was reliably labeled as pride. Recognition rates of pride were similar or better than displays such as fear, anger, and sadness (Tracy & Robins, 2006). Finally, recent research has found that children as young as 4 years old can recognize pride and reliably distinguish it from other positive emotions like happiness (Tracy, Robins, & Lagattuta, 2005).

How do cultures vary in the display of self-conscious emotion? One might expect variation in ritualized displays of emotion, which are stylized ways of expressing particular emotions. Each emotional display has numerous actions involved in it. The anger expression, for example, involves the furrowed brow, the glare, the lip tighten, and the lip press as prototypical actions. The embarrassment display involves gaze down, head turns and movements down, a controlled smile, and face touches. In ritualized displays, cultures take elements of an emotion display and elaborate upon it, dramatize it, or make it more stereotypical and exaggerated to express an emotion. Throughout much of Southeast Asia, for example, the combined tongue bite and shoulder shrug is a ritualized display of embarrassment. It involves exaggerated versions of two elements of the embarrassment display: inhibitory muscle actions around the mouth (the tongue bite) and constricted, size-reducing posture (the shoulder shrug). This display might only signal embarrassment in Southeast Asian cultures. To explore this possibility, Haidt and Keltner (1999) presented participants with photos of the tongue bite/shoulder shrug. Indian participants also readily perceived the expressions that included the tongue bite as embarrassment. In contrast, U.S. college students were bewildered by this expression, and achieved little consensus in identifying the emotion communicated by the display. One might hypothesize that ritualized displays of other self-conscious emotions would work similarly. For example, the postural expansion found to be universally recognized as a sign of pride could be exaggerated in ritualized displays of victory, such as the celebratory chest bumping often seen between teammates in U.S. athletic events. Although such ritualized expressions have not been documented, it is likely that they exist.

SELF-CONSCIOUS EMOTIONS AT THE GROUP AND CULTURAL LEVELS

We expect dramatic cultural variation of self-conscious emotions at the group and cultural levels of analysis. There are two major pathways through which cultures change the relationship between emotions and the social problems they were designed to solve (Keltner & Haidt, 2001). The first is that cultures find new solutions to ancient problems, which may involve formalizing emotion functions in social institutions or may involve creating institutions that render old emotions less necessary. Such formalization has resulted in a highly elaborated conception, or hypercognition, of shame in East Asian cultures. The second pathway is that cultures find new uses for old emotions that have little to do with their "original" function. We expect variation in self-conscious emotions based on the degree to which cultures apply them to problems of hierarchy and cooperation. For example, cultures that emphasize shame to reinforce group norms and social status will underemphasize pride. East Asian cultures place a positive value on the experience of shame and see it as a useful and appropriate emotion. In contrast, East Asian cultures devalue pride, suggesting that shame has supplanted pride to some degree. These differences in valuation appear to be closely related to the motivational and behavioral implications of self-conscious emotions. Finally, differences in the moralization of self-conscious emotions and their elicitors may be an indication of cultural variation in the function of self-conscious emotions. As we discuss below, traditional cultural analyses using collectivism and individualism fall short in explaining these patterns of variation and suggest that more research is needed.

Focal Events and Hypercognition of Shame

Event types that correspond to central cultural values and concerns draw attention and become focal event types (Mesquita & Frijda, 1992). For example, concerns over individual rights, central ideological concerns in the United States, show a tighter association with a rights-based emotion, anger, in the United States than in collectivist cultures (Vasquez et al., 2001). Because focal events for emotions relate to central cultural values, focal event types are well structured with clear norms for how to interpret and respond to them. They are also highly salient, with many events recognized as instances of the focal event type.

This analysis has clear implications for cultural variation in the elicitors of self-conscious emotions, as well as for the lexical representation of self-conscious emotion. For example, in cultures where face and honor concerns are important, situations bearing on one's dignity are focal (e.g., Mesquita & Frijda, 1992). These situations are numerous and highly salient, and emotions related to shame and pride are very likely elicited by them. For example, when Spanish and Dutch participants were asked to rate the importance of certain values in their cultures, Spanish participants reported valuing honor, humility, social power, social recognition, and success more highly than Dutch participants. In addition, Spanish respondents reported a broader range of events that led to shame, consistent with the thesis that focal event types are highly salient (Fischer et al., 1999).

However, focal event types do not necessarily occur more frequently. They may be highly salient, but considered as situations to be avoided. In the case of Bedouin culture (Abu-Lughod, 1986), concerns about one's honor are paramount and situations in which one may lose dignity are avoided. In their study of Chinese shame concepts, Li, Wang, and Fischer (2004) also found an entire category related to fear and avoidance of shameful experiences.

While culture-specific values can give rise to emotion-specific focal events, culture may also over- or underemphasize certain emotions in describing the realms of experience. The concept of hypercognition has been discussed in the social constructivist literature (Levy, 1984; Lutz & White, 1986). When hypercognition occurs, concepts for a particular emotion may become highly elaborated (e.g., more words, more phrases) and scripts around the emotion are also elaborated (e.g., more ways of expressing it, and more responses to expressions of the emotion). For example, in studies of emotion categorization, shame emerges as an emotion family in China, but not for other collectivistic cultures such as Indonesia or Italy (Shaver, Wu, & Schwartz, 1992). It appears that China's emphasis on honor, respect, and face has led to a highly articulated script around the expression of and reactions to shame (Li et al., 2004).

Although most languages have words in their lexicon for self-conscious emotions (Hupka, Lenton, & Hutchison, 1999), languages differ in the number of emotion words they use and in the distinctions they make between emotions (Russell, 1991). Using information derived from ethnographic interviews with Taiwanese informants, Bedford (2004) argued that although the distinctions found between guilt and shame "may be sufficient for those with a Western background, they are not necessarily adequate for describing the Asian experience of guilt and shame" (p. 29). She describes three distinct forms of guilt and four forms of shame in Mandarin. These are mostly distinguished by their antecedents and appraisals, such as *diu lian* (丟臉), which involves a loss of reputation or face in the eyes of others, versus *xiu kui* (羞愧), which is brought about by personal failure, and *xiu chi* (羞恥), which is brought about by social failure. Personal shame (*xiu kui*) is not nearly as negative as social shame (*xiu chi*), and the behavioral tendencies associated with these states are very different. Whereas social failure leads to feelings of deep shame (*xiu chi*) from which one can only long for impossible escape, personal failure (*xiu kui*) motivates thoughts about how to improve oneself and resolve to change for the better in the future.

In contrast, the Oriya language contains a single word, *lajya*, to cover a large area of emotion-space that encompasses the English words *shame, embarrassment, shyness,* and *modesty* (Menon & Shweder, 1994). In their study of emotional expression, Haidt and Keltner (1999) found that *lajya* was the closest translation of the English words *shame* and *embarrassment*. Interestingly, the lack of lexicalized emotion terms did not prevent participants from making conceptual distinctions. Indian participants distinguished between two forms of *lajya* in their responses to two different expressions: prototypical embarrassment and a face-cover expression (see Figure 9.1). The embarrassment display was labeled by participants most often as *lajya*, followed by happiness, love, and amusement. The face cover was labeled with *lajya* as well as with words for sadness, worry, and fear. These two expressions seemed to represent different versions of *lajya*. As one participant stated when looking at the embarrassment expression, "This is not the *lajya* felt when you do something wrong. This is *lajya* on hearing one's own praises being spoken" (p. 259).

Valuation and Normative Beliefs: When Pride Is Negative and Shame Is Positive

In addition to influencing the emotion process within individuals, cultures vary greatly in the degree to which they value the experience and function of self-conscious emotions as appropriate emotions within social groups. Emotions that are considered negative in one culture may be considered more positive and desirable in another. Although in the United States shame is a highly negative emotion, Abu-Lughod (1986) observed that a similar emotion in Bedouin culture, *hasham*, has positive associations. While living with the Bedouins, Abu-Lughod observed that *hasham* incorporates the concept of shame with feelings of embarrassment, humility, and modesty. For a woman in Bedouin culture, these are highly valued characteristics, so the experience of *hasham* is considered desirable and even pleasurable.

The implications of these ethnographic observations are supported by quantitative evidence for variation in the value of self-conscious emotions. In fact, norms for experiencing self-conscious emotions may be more influenced by culture than the norms for experiencing emotions like anger or sadness. A study about the appropriateness of normative beliefs found that norms regarding self-conscious emotions of pride and guilt varied the most compared to other emotions across cultures (Eid & Diener, 2001). The researchers examined norms for experiencing eight emotions, including pride and guilt, across four cultures (United States, Australia, Taiwan, and China). In the United States and Australia, positive emotions, including pride, were considered both acceptable and desirable. In contrast, the pattern of norms in China and Taiwan were indifferent and even negative toward pride. In addition, guilt was very undesirable in all countries except for China. Consistent with these findings, Chinese participants in another study consistently rated the experience and expression of pride as less valuable than participants in the United States, except in the case of achievements that benefited close others (Stipek, 1998).

From a Western perspective, it is difficult to understand shame as a desirable emotion. Within a wide array of contexts, from childrearing to interactions between leaders and subordinates, the elicitation and utilization of shame is considered inappropriate. However, in cultures such as China, a sense of shame is considered a healthy part of an individual's life (Li et al., 2004). Admitting one's misconduct and mistakes is considered a courageous and desirable act. Thus shame is not merely an emotion in Chinese culture, but a moral and virtuous sensibility to be pursued. Having a sense of shame is considered essential to moral development, and children are instilled with it from an early age (Fung, 1999). In this framework, a shameless person is considered more shameful than a shamed person. Shamelessness and reactions to people who fail to show appropriate shame appear prominently in Chinese lay conceptions of shame (Li et al., 2004). People who do not show an appropriate sense of shame are seen as outside the constraints of the moral order. They are less predictable and trustworthy. Thus, the expression of shame is valued as an indicator of adherence to social norms and collective values.

Findings about variation in normative beliefs regarding shame and pride are not limited to East–West comparisons. Similar ambivalence about experiencing shame and pride has been found in comparisons of Spanish and Dutch participants (Fischer et al., 1999). In particular, Spanish participants reported that pride had fewer positive implications for themselves and was less socially approved of than did Dutch participants. They reported sharing their experiences of pride less often compared to the Dutch subjects. On the other hand, pride was socially acceptable and even desirable in the Netherlands. Dutch respondents mentioned more overt expressions, such as telling everyone about and sharing their pride experiences. The opposite pattern was found with respect to normative beliefs about shame; Spanish participants were more likely to express positive beliefs about shame. In addition, Spanish participants reported sharing shame or shameful events with others more than Dutch participants.

Cultural Variation in the Function of Self-Conscious Emotions

Normative beliefs are strongly related to the regulation strategies and implications of the self-conscious emotions. If a particular emotion is considered useful and valuable, there will be more positive outcomes associated with its experience and expression. If an emotion is considered undesirable, however, there will be more negative outcomes associated with its experience. This may be due to the individual's response to his or her own feelings (i.e., emotions about emotions) or it may be due to other people's responses to their expression. In turn, we expect cultural variation in socialization and scripts around self-conscious emotions.

Shame is a good example of such a case. Wallbott and Scherer (1995) analyzed self-reported experiences of shame across 37 cultures. They found that experiences of shame in more collectivistic countries had less negative influences on self-esteem and on relationships. Shame experiences in collectivistic cultures were also associated with more smiling and laughing, suggesting that the experience was less negative. This is consistent with the Confucian conceptualization of shame as an emotion that directs a person's focus inward for self-examination and motivates the person toward change (Li et al., 2004). In Japan and China, shame and self-criticism are used as strong socializing forces in childrearing (Fung, 1999; Lewis, 1995). This early training may help to familiarize and regulate shame so that its experience and resulting behaviors differ across cultures.

Cross-cultural findings examining intrinsic motivation suggest that pride and shame may have dramatically different personal outcomes (Heine, Kitayama, Lehman, Takata,

& Ide, 1999, as cited in Heine, Lehman, Markus, & Kitayama, 1999). Japanese and Canadian participants were told that they either succeeded or failed on a creativity test.
They were then left alone in the room with a related task. Canadian participants persisted
significantly longer on the second task when they thought they had succeeded on the first
task than when they thought they had failed. Japanese participants, on the other hand,
persisted longer when they thought they had failed. Although the researchers did not
measure pride or shame experiences, task performance would be a valid elicitor in both
cultures. We can infer that Japanese participants were more motivated by shame and that
Canadians were more motivated by pride.

Another study looked specifically at the effects of experiencing shame on subsequent
behavior (Bagozzi, Verbeke, & Gavino, 2003). Dutch and Filipino salespersons were presented with scenarios in which they were shamed by customers. Emotional responses to
the shameful experiences were of similar intensity and physiological reactions in the
Netherlands and in the Philippines. However, self-regulation and the final behavioral outcomes of shame were dramatically different in the two cultures. For Dutch salespeople,
shame was related to engaging in more protective actions such as withdrawal from conversation with customers and related to less adaptive use of resources. In contrast, shame
did not relate to protective actions or adaptive resource utilization in Filipino salespersons.
Instead, shame was positively related to Filipino salespeople increasing their relationship-
building efforts, degree of courtesy, and general efforts on the job. It appears that for the
Filipino salespeople, shame was a signal that social harmony had been disrupted and personal action was needed to restore that harmony. Instead of motivations to hide from
others in whose presence they felt ashamed, the Filipino salespeople felt the need to
approach those who were the source of shame and repair the damage to the relationship
(Bagozzi et al., 2003). Thus the behavioral and emotional implications of feeling self-
conscious emotions may vary dramatically depending on the cultural beliefs, values, and
scripts surrounding them.

Cultural Variation in the Moralization of Self-Conscious Emotions

Self-conscious emotions, in particular shame, guilt, and forms of pride, are intimately intertwined with moral judgments of harm, character, and responsibility (e.g., Haidt, 2003;
Tangney et al., 1996). They are moral emotions (Haidt, 2003). Here we suggest that these
emotions are likely to vary in their moral connotations across cultures—a thesis for
which there is modest yet suggestive empirical support.

This idea of the moralization of self-conscious emotions traces back to Scherer
(1997), who in a review of studies of culture and emotion-related appraisal reasoned that
cultures should vary little in the activation of more "primitive" or automatic dimensions
of appraisal, such as pleasantness, attentional activity, certainty, coping ability, and goal–
need conduciveness. Variation should be more likely, however, in "complex" dimensions
like attribution of agency or responsibility, fairness or legitimacy, and norm compatibility
or morality.

These speculations, in combination with studies of cultural variation in causal attribution, suggest some interesting predictions regarding the moralization of self-conscious
emotions. Judgments of agency and responsibility are central to moral judgment (e.g.,
Haidt, 2001), as well as the occurrence of self-conscious emotions (Tracy & Robins,
2004b; Weiner, Graham, & Chandler, 1982). Judgments of agency and responsibility also
vary dramatically across different cultures, with the typical study finding that members of

collectivistic, interdependent cultures place less of an emphasis on individual responsibility in explaining pro- and antisocial actions (e.g., Miller, 1985; Morris & Peng, 1994). Taken together, these notions suggest that members of different cultures should vary in the extent to which they "moralize" self-conscious emotions, that is, consider them matters of right and wrong, and as implicating punishment or sanctions.

Findings from research by Scherer (1997) are consistent with these claims. In this study, participants from 37 different cultures rated the antecedents and appraisal patterns of seven emotions: joy, anger, fear, sadness, disgust, shame, and guilt. The results showed that, of all of the appraisal dimensions, immorality judgments for emotional events varied the most across countries. The emotions that showed the most variation on this dimension were shame and guilt. In particular, individuals from African countries rated shame and guilt situations as more immoral than did participants from other regions. In contrast, Latin American and Asian participants rated shame events as less immoral than did individuals from other regions.

In a similar fashion, Stipek, Weiner, and Li (1989) found that Chinese participants were less likely to mention violations of social laws and moral principles as determinants of guilt and shame than were U.S. participants. They were also less likely to mention physical harm—a prototypical moral infraction—as an elicitor of shame. These findings likewise suggest that self-conscious emotions are less moralized in collectivistic Asian cultures.

What is one to make of these differences? Certainly, cultural differences in attributional processes may have had a hand in producing these results. Given that members of Asian cultures tend to attribute the responsibility of morally relevant actions more to situational factors than members of other cultures (e.g., Morris & Peng, 1994), it is likely that shameful and guilt-inducing actions in these cultures implicate less the moral worthiness of the individual's character. It is also possible that the range of shameful eliciting events in individualistic cultures is more restricted than in collectivistic cultures, as Fischer and colleagues (1999) found in their comparative study of Spain and the Netherlands. The inclusion of more antecedent events, not simply morally relevant ones, may dampen average immorality ratings of shameful events. However, Scherer (1997) found that people from countries in Africa, a region that is especially collectivistic (Oyserman, Coon, & Kemmelmeier, 2002), also rated shameful events as more immoral than did people from any other region. This finding suggests that collectivism is not the only factor influencing ratings of morality. Perhaps other factors, such as culture-specific theories or normative beliefs, are at work. Clearly, further study is needed.

CONCLUSIONS AND FUTURE DIRECTIONS

We have outlined a social-functional approach to self-conscious emotions that suggested patterns of both universality and variation across cultures. The empirical data, though sparse, suggests that those general patterns hold true. Consistent with evolutionary forces, self-conscious emotions are associated with problems of social status, cooperation, and reciprocity across cultures. Pride is clearly different from its negative counterparts, and is generally elicited in response to increased social status or standing. Embarrassment, shame, and guilt are all elicited in response to decreases in social status or standing. The data do not yet show a consistent distinction between concepts related to embarrassment, shame, and guilt across cultures. Nevertheless, people in different cultures clearly differentiate between the antecedent events that elicit self-conscious emotions. Whether these differentiations follow similar patterns across cultures remains to be seen. More research is needed to examine self-conscious emotion concepts at a deep level within cultures. It appears the story may be more complex than the one the English lexicon (of guilt, shame, embarrassment, and pride) indicates. Research that goes beyond the limits of the English language and the emotion terms suggested by it (e.g., Kitayama, Markus, & Matsumoto, 1995) can enlighten new areas of self-conscious emotion that will otherwise be left in the dark.

Early data suggest that self-conscious emotions have displays that are somewhat recognizable across cultures. There are submissive appeasement gestures that are clearly recognized as signals of shame and embarrassment, and dominant gestures that are clearly recognized as pride, across cultures. In addition, it appears that there are culture-specific displays and behaviors. These displays provide interesting points of departure for research to examine the cultural elaborations of basic emotions processes. Indeed, exploring natural displays across cultures could be a fruitful research route, rather than recognition approaches that have been used in traditional cross-cultural studies of emotional expression. Such an approach could allow room for patterns of variation in expression to follow patterns of expression in language and appraisals.

If the self-conscious emotions are, as we believe, based in evolutionary roots, there should be systematic commonality and differentiation underlying the systems. Analysis of universal social problems suggests that failure to uphold norms of reciprocity versus failure to uphold hierarchy may result in different self-conscious emotions. To our knowledge, little research has examined such a hypothesis. In general, the degree of differentiation in the self-conscious emotion systems is unclear. Further research is needed to reach across cognitive, neural, physiological, and behavioral systems.

Finally, the bulk of the research summarized here suggests that cultures differentially value and utilize shame and pride to reinforce the social order. Research on the mechanisms involved in these differences could elucidate the extent to which culture permeates the emotion process. Is it possible that culture influences the function of self-conscious emotions at the dyadic and individual levels? In addition, more research is needed to clarify the underlying cultural factors that influence self-conscious emotions. Conceptions of self and values related to collectivism and individualism are clearly an issue, though not the whole story, as evidenced in our discussion of the moralization of self-conscious emotions. We propose that any variation in the basis of social status in a culture is likely to have an influence on the function and valuation of self-conscious emotions. Conceptions of self are a clear example of this, but so are concepts like honor, face, or bloodline that influence one's place in a hierarchy. We believe that research in a broader array of cultures will be necessary to understand the full range of this variation.

REFERENCES

Abu-Lughod, L. (1986). *Veiled sentiments.* Berkeley and Los Angeles: University of California Press.

Averill, J. R. (1980). A constructivist view of emotion. In R. Plutchik & H. Kellerman (Eds.), *Emotion: Theory, research, and experience* (pp. 305–339). New York: Academic Press.

Bagozzi, R. P., Verbecke, W., & Gavino, J. C. Jr. (2003). Culture moderates the self-regulation of shame and its effects on performance: The case of salespersons in the Netherlands and the Philippines. *Journal of Applied Psychology, 88*(2), 219–233.

Baumeister, R. F., Stillwell, A. M., & Heatherton, T. F. (1994). Guilt: An interpersonal approach. *Psychological Bulletin, 115,* 243–267.

Bedford, O. A. (2004). The individual experience of guilt and shame in Chinese culture. *Culture and Psychology, 10*(1), 29–52.

Bowlby, J. (1969). *Attachment.* New York: Basic Books.

Bretherton, I., Fritz, J., Zahn-Waxler, C., & Ridgeway, D. (1986). Learning to talk about emotions: A functionalist perspective. *Child Development, 57,* 529–548.

Buss, D. (1992). Male preference mechanisms: Consequences for partner choice and intrasexual competition. In J. H. Barkow, L. Cosmides, & J. Tooby (Eds.), *The adapted mind* (pp. 267–288). New York: Oxford University Press.

Campos, J. J., Campos, R. G., & Barrett, K. C. (1989). Emergent themes in the study of emotional development and emotion regulation. *Developmental Psychology, 25,* 394–402.

Clark, C. (1990). Emotions and the micropolitics in everyday life: Some patterns and paradoxes of "place." In T. D. Kemper (Ed.), *Research agendas in the sociology of emotions* (pp. 305–334). Albany: State University of New York Press.

Clore, G. L. (1994). Why emotions are felt. In P. Ekman & R. J. Davidson (Eds.), *The nature of emotion* (pp. 103–111). New York: Cambridge University Press.

Clore, G. L., Gasper, K., & Garvin, E. (2001). Affect as information. In J. P. Forgas (Ed.), *Handbook of affect and social cognition* (pp. 121–144). Mahwah, NJ: Erlbaum.

Collins, R. C. (1990). Stratification, emotional energy, and the transient emotions. In T. D. Kemper (Ed.), *Research agendas in the sociology of emotions* (pp. 27–57). Albany: State University of New York Press.

Davidson, R. J., Pizzagalli, D., Nitschke, J. B., & Kalin, N. H. (2003). Parsing the subcomponents of emotion and disorders: Perspectives from affective neuroscience. In R. J. Davidson, K. Scherer, & H. H. Goldsmith (Eds.), *Handbook of affective sciences* (pp. 8–24). New York: Oxford University Press.

de Waal, F. B. M. (1986). The integration of dominance and social bonding in primates. *Quarterly Review of Biology, 61,* 459–479.

de Waal, F. B. M. (1996). *Good natured.* Cambridge, MA: Harvard University Press.

Diamond, L. M. (2003). What does sexual orientation orient?: A biobehavioral model distinguishing romantic love and sexual desire. *Psychological Review, 110*(1), 173–192.

Dimberg, U., & Öhman, A. (1996). Behold the wrath: Psychophysiological responses to facial stimuli. *Motivation and Emotion, 20*(2), 149–182.

Dunn, J., & Munn, P. (1985). Becoming a family member: Family conflict and the development of social understanding in the second year. *Child Development, 56,* 480–492.

Eibl-Eibesfeldt, I. (1989). *Human ethology.* New York: Aldine de Gruyter.

Eid, M., & Diener, E. (2001). Norms for experiencing emotions in different cultures: Inter and intranational differences. *Journal of Personality and Social Psychology, 81*(5), 869–885.

Ekman, P. (1992). An argument for basic emotions. *Cognition and Emotion, 6,* 169–200.

Ekman, P. (1993). Facial expression and emotion. *American Psychologist, 48,* 384–392.

Fischer, A. H., Manstead, A. S. R., & Mosquera, P. M. R. (1999). The role of honour-related vs. individualistic values in conceptualizing pride, shame, and anger: Spanish and Dutch cultural prototypes. *Cognition and Emotion, 13*(2), 149–179.

Fischer, K. W., & Tangney, J. P. (1995). Self-conscious emotions and the affect revolution: Framework and overview. In J. P. Tangney & K. W. Fischer (Eds.), *Self-conscious emotions: The psychology of shame, guilt, embarrassment, and pride* (pp. 465–487). New York: Guilford Press.

Fiske, A. P. (1992). Four elementary forms of sociality: Framework for a unified theory of social relations. *Psychological Review, 99,* 689–723.

Fridlund, A. J. (1992). The behavioral ecology and sociality of human faces. In M. S. Clark (Ed.), Emotion [special issue], *Review of Personality and Social Psychology, 13,* 90–121.

Frijda, N. H., Kuipers, P., & ter Schure, E. (1989). Relations among emotion, appraisal, and emotional action readiness. *Journal of Personality and Social Psychology, 57*(2), 212–228.

Frijda, N. H., & Mesquita, B. (1994). The social roles and functions of emotions. In S. Kitayama & H. R. Marcus (Eds.), *Emotion and culture: Empirical studies of mutual influence* (pp. 51–87). Washington, DC: American Psychological Association.

Fung, H. (1999). Becoming a moral child: The socialization of shame among young Chinese children. *Ethos, 27*(2), 180–209.

Gilbert, P. (2003). Evolution, social roles, and the differences in shame and guilt. *Social Research, 70*(4), 1205–1230.

Goffman, E. (1967). *Interaction ritual: Essays on face-to-face behavior.* Garden City, NY: Anchor Books.

Gonzaga, G. C., Keltner, D., Londahl, E. A., & Smith, M. D. (2001). Love and the commitment problem in romantic relationships and friendship. *Journal of Personality and Social Psychology, 81,* 247–262.

Gouldner, A. (1960). The norm of reciprocity: A preliminary statement. *American Sociological Review, 25,* 161–179.

Haidt, J. (2001). The emotional dog and its rational tail: A social intuitionist approach to moral judgment. *Psychological Review, 108*(4), 814–834.

Haidt, J. (2003). The moral emotions. In R. J. Davidson, K. R. Scherer, & H. H. Goldsmith (Eds.), *Handbook of affective sciences* (pp. 852–870). London: Oxford University Press.

Haidt, J., & Keltner, D. (1999). Culture and facial expression: Open-ended methods find more expression and a gradient of recognition. *Cognition and Emotion, 13,* 225–266.

Haidt, J., Koller, S., & Dias, M. (1993). Affect, culture, and morality, or is it wrong to eat your dog? *Journal of Personality and Social Psychology, 65,* 613–628.

Hazan, C., & Shaver, P. (1987). Romantic love conceptualized as an attachment process. *Journal of Personality and Social Psychology, 52,* 511–524.

Heine, S. J., Lehman, D. R., Markus, H. R., & Kitayama, S. (1999). Is there a universal need for positive self-regard? *Psychological Review, 106*(4), 766–794.

Hochschild, A. R. (1990). Ideology and emotion management. In T. D. Kemper (Ed.), *Research agendas in the sociology of emotions* (pp. 117–142). Albany: State University of New York Press.

Hupka, R. B., Lenton, A. P., & Hutchison, K. A. (1999). Universal development of emotion categories in natural language. *Journal of Personality and Social Psychology, 77*(2), 247–278.

Izard, C. E. (1977). *Human emotions.* New York: Plenum Press.

Juslin, P. N., & Laukka, P. (2003). Communication of emotions in vocal expression and music performance: Different channels, same code? *Psychological Bulletin, 129*(5), 770–814.

Keltner, D. (1995). Signs of appeasement: Evidence for the distinct displays of embarrassment, amusement, and shame. *Journal of Personality and Social Psychology, 68*(3), 441–454.

Keltner, D., & Buswell, B. N. (1996). Evidence for the distinctness of embarrassment, shame, and guilt: A study of recalled antecedents and facial expressions of emotion. *Cognition and Emotion, 10*(2), 155–171.

Keltner, D., & Buswell, B. N. (1997). Embarrassment: Its distinct form and appeasement functions. *Psychological Bulletin, 122*(3), 250–270.

Keltner, D., Gruenfeld, D. H., & Anderson, C. (2003). Power, approach, and inhibition. *Psychological Review, 110*(2), 265–284.

Keltner, D., & Haidt, J. (1999). Social functions of emotions at four levels of analysis. *Cognition and Emotion, 13*(5), 505–521.

Keltner, D., & Haidt, J. (2001). Social functions of emotions. In T. J. Mayne & G. A. Bonanno (Eds.), *Emotions: Current issues and future directions* (pp. 192–213). New York: Guilford Press.

Keltner, D., Haidt, J., & Shiota, M. N. (2006). Social functionalism and the evolution of emotions. In M. Schaller, J. A. Simpson, & D. T. Kenrick (Eds.), *Evolution and social psychology* (pp. 115–142). New York: Psychology Press.

Keltner, D., & Harker, L. (1998). The forms and functions of the nonverbal signal of shame. In P. Gilbert & B. Andrews (Eds.), *Shame: Interpersonal behavior, psychology, and culture* (pp. 78–98). New York: Oxford University Press.

Keltner, D., & Kring, A. M. (1998). Emotion, social function, and psychopathology. *Review of General Psychology, 2*(3), 320–342.

Keltner, D., Young, R. C., & Buswell, B. N. (1997). Appeasement in human emotion, social practice, and personality. *Aggressive Behavior, 23,* 359–374.

Kemeny, M. E., Gruenewald, T. L., & Dickerson, S. S. (2004). Shame as the emotional response to threat to the social self: Implications for behavior, physiology, and health. *Psychological Inquiry, 15*(2), 153–159.

Ketelaar, T., & Au, W. T. (2003). The effects of feelings of guilt on the behaviour of uncooperative individuals in repeated social bargaining games: An affect-as-information interpretation of the role of emotion in social interaction. *Cognition and Emotion, 17*(3), 429–453.

Kitayama, S., Markus, H. R., & Matsumoto, H. (1995). Culture, self, and emotion: A cultural perspective on "self-conscious" emotions. In J. P. Tangney & K. W. Fischer (Eds.), *Self-conscious emotions: The psychology of shame, guilt, embarrassment, and pride* (pp. 439–464). New York: Guilford Press.

Le Doux, J. (1996). *The emotional brain.* New York: Simon & Schuster.

Lerner, J. S., & Keltner, D. (2001). Fear, anger, and risk. *Journal of Personality and Social Psychology, 81*(1), 146–159.

Levenson, R. W. (1992). Autonomic nervous system differences among emotions. *Psychological Science, 3,* 23–27.

Levenson, R. W. (1999). The intrapersonal functions of emotion. *Cognition and Emotion, 13*(5), 481–504.

Levy, R. I. (1984). Emotion, knowing, and culture. In R. A. Shweder & R. A. LeVine (Eds.), *Culture theory: Essays on mind, self, and emotion* (pp. 214–237). New York: Cambridge University Press.

Lewis, C. C. (1995). *Educating hearts and minds.* Cambridge, UK: Cambridge University Press.

Li, J., Wang, L., & Fischer, K. W. (2004). The organization of Chinese shame concepts. *Cognition and Emotion, 18*(6), 767–797.

Loewenstein, G., & Lerner, J. S. (2003). The role of affect in decision making. In R. J. Davidson, K. R. Scherer, & H. H. Goldsmith (Eds.), *Handbook of affective sciences* (pp. 619–642). New York: Oxford University Press.

Lutz, C. A. (1988). *Unnatural emotions.* Chicago: University of Chicago Press.

Lutz, C. A. (1990). Engendered emotion: Gender, power, and the rhetoric of emotional control in American discourse. In C. A. Lutz & L. Abu-Lughod (Eds.), *Language and the politics of emotion* (pp. 69–91). New York: Cambridge University Press.

Lutz, C. A., & Abu-Lughod, L. (1990). Introduction: Emotion, discourse, and the politics of everyday life. In C. A. Lutz & L. Abu-Lughod (Eds.), *Language and the politics of emotion* (pp. 1–23). New York: Cambridge University Press.

Lutz, C., & White, G. (1986). The anthropology of emotions. *Annual Review of Anthropology, 15,* 405–436.

Markus, H. M., & Kitayama, S. (1991). Culture and the self: Implications for cognition, emotion, and motivation. *Psychological Review, 98,* 224–253.

McCullough, M. E., Rachal, K. C., Sandage, S. J., Worthington, E. L. Jr., Brown, S. W., & Hight, T. L. (1998). Interpersonal forgiving in close relationships: II. Theoretical elaboration and measurement. *Journal of Personality and Social Psychology, 75,* 1586–1603.

McCullough, M. E., Worthington, E. L. Jr., & Rachal, K. C. (1997). Interpersonal forgiving in close relationships. *Journal of Personality and Social Psychology, 73,* 321–336.

Menon, U., & Shweder, R. A. (1994). Kali's tongue: Cultural psychology, cultural consensus and the meaning of "shame" in Orissa, India. In H. Markus & S. Kitayama (Eds.), *Culture and the emotions* (pp. 241–284). Washington, DC: American Psychological Association.

Mesquita, B., & Frijda, N. H. (1992). Cultural variations in emotions: A review. *Psychological Bulletin, 112*(2), 179–204.

Miller, J. G. (1984). Culture and the development of everyday social explanation. *Journal of Personality and Social Psychology, 46,* 961–978.

Morris, M. W., & Peng, K. (1994). Culture and cause: American and Chinese attributions for social and physical events. *Journal of Personality and Social Psychology, 67*(6), 949–971.

Nesse, R. (1990). Evolutionary explanations of emotions. *Human Nature, 1,* 261–289.

Ohman, A. (1986). Face the beast and fear the face: Animal and social fears as prototypes for evolutionary analysis of emotion. *Psychophysiology, 23,* 123–145.

Oyserman, D., Coon, H. M., & Kemmelmeier, M. (2002). Rethinking individualism and collectivism: Evaluation of theoretical assumptions and meta-analysis. *Psychological Bulletin, 128,* 3–72.

Regan, D. T., Williams, M., & Sparling, S. (1972). Voluntary expiation of guilt: A field experiment. *Journal of Personality and Social Psychology, 24*(1), 42–45.

Rozin, P., Haidt, J., & McCauley, C. R. (2000). Disgust. In M. Lewis & J. M. Haviland-Jones (Eds.), *Handbook of emotions* (2nd ed., pp. 637–653). New York: Guilford Press.

Russell, J. A. (1991). Culture and the categorization of emotions. *Psychological Bulletin, 110,* 426–450.

Scherer, K. R. (1986). Vocal affect expression: A review and a model for future research. *Psychological Bulletin, 99*(2), 143–165.

Scherer, K. R. (1997). The role of culture in emotion-antecedent appraisal. *Journal of Personality and Social Psychology, 73*(5), 902–922.

Scherer, K. R., Johnstone, T., & Klasmeyer, G. (2003). Vocal expression of emotion. In R. J. Davidson, K. R. Scherer, & H. H. Goldsmith (Eds.), *Handbook of affective sciences* (pp. 433–456). New York: Oxford University Press.

Schwarz, N. (1990). Feelings as information: Informational and motivational functions of affective states. In E. T. Higgins & R. M. Sorrentino (Eds.), *Handbook of motivation and cognition* (Vol. 2, pp. 527–561). New York: Guilford Press.

Shaver, P. R., Wu, S., & Schwartz, J. C. (1992). Cross-cultural similarities and differences in emotion and its representation: A prototype approach. In M. S. Clark (Ed.), Emotion [Special issue], *Review of Personality and Social Psychology, 13,* 175–213.

Shweder, R. A., Mahapatra, M., & Miller, J. (1987). Culture and moral development. In J. Kagan & S. Lamb (Eds.), *The emergence of morality in young children* (pp. 1–83). Chicago: University of Chicago Press.

Shweder, R. A., Much, N. C., Mahapatra, M., & Park, L. (1997). The "Big Three" of morality (autonomy, community, and divinity), and the "Big Three" explanations of suffering. In A. Brandt & P. Rozin (Eds.), *Morality and health* (pp. 119–169). New York: Routledge.

Stipek, D. (1998). Difference between Americans and Chinese in the circumstances evoking pride, shame, and guilt. *Journal of Cross-Cultural Psychology, 29*(5), 616–630.

Stipek, D., Weiner, B., & Li, K. (1989). Testing some attribution–emotion relations in the People's Republic of China. *Journal of Personality and Social Psychology, 56*(1), 109–116.

Strauman, T. J., & Higgins, E. T. (1987). Automatic activation of self-discrepancies and emotional syndromes—When cognitive structures influence affect. *Journal of Personality and Social Psychology, 53*(6), 1004–1014.

Tangney, J. P., Miller, R. S., Flicker, L., & Barlow, D. H. (1996). Are shame, guilt, and embarrassment distinct emotions? *Journal of Personality and Social Psychology, 70*(6), 1256–1269.

Tooby, J., & Cosmides, L. (1990). The past explains the present: Emotional adaptations and the structure of ancestral environments. *Ethology and Sociobiology, 11,* 375–424.

Tracy, J. L., & Robins, R. W. (2004a). Show your pride: Evidence for a discrete emotion expression. *Psychological Science, 15,* 194–197.

Tracy, J. L., & Robins, R. W. (2004b). Putting the self into self-conscious emotions: A theoretical model. *Psychological Inquiry, 15*(2), 103–125.

Tracy, J. L., & Robins, R. W. (2006). *The nonverbal expression of pride: Evidence for cross-cultural recognition.* Manuscript submitted for publication.

Tracy, J. L., Robins, R. W., & Lagattuta, K. H. (2005). Can children recognize pride? *Emotion, 5*(3), 251–257.

Trivers, R. L. (1971). The evolution of reciprocal altruism. *Quarterly Review of Biology, 46,* 35–57.

Vasquez, K., Keltner, D., Ebenbach, D. H., & Banaszynski, T. L. (2001). Cultural variation and similarity in moral rhetorics: Voices from the Philippines and the United States. *Journal of Cross-Cultural Psychology, 32*(1), 93–120.

Wallbott, H. G., & Scherer, K. R. (1995). Cultural determinants in experiencing shame and guilt. In J. P. Tangney & K. W. Fischer (Eds.), *Self-conscious emotions: The psychology of shame, guilt, embarrassment, and pride* (pp. 465–487). New York: Guilford Press.

Weiner, B., Graham, S., & Chandler, C. (1982). Pity, anger, and guilt: An attributional analysis. *Personality and Social Psychology Bulletin, 8*(2), 226–232.

White, G. M. (1990). Moral discourse and the rhetoric of emotions. In C. A. Lutz & L. Abu-Lughod (Eds.), *Language and the politics of emotion* (pp. 46–68). New York: Cambridge University Press.

10

From Appeasement to Conformity

Evolutionary and Cultural Perspectives on Shame, Competition, and Cooperation

DANIEL M. T. FESSLER

Like all living things, humans are the product of natural selection. By gradually modifying existing features over many generations, this process leads to divergence between related species. While many attributes of human morphology and psychology closely parallel those of our closest relatives, the nonhuman primates, in addition to such obvious traits as an upright stance and larger brains, we also differ from our primate kin with regard to several fundamental aspects of behavior. First, to an unprecedented degree, our species relies on socially transmitted information (i.e., culture) to adapt to local physical and social environments (see Richerson & Boyd, 2004). Second, only humans routinely cooperate with unrelated individuals—among other creatures, cooperative behavior, to the extent that it occurs at all, is usually restricted to close relatives (Richerson & Boyd, 2004). Focusing on shame, in this chapter I argue that these two attributes are key to understanding the existence and functioning of self-conscious emotions.

I begin by describing the panprimate substrate upon which human shame is built. Arguing that this primordial facet of shame operates in hierarchical social relationships, I then suggest that our species' reliance on culture and cooperation favored the evolution of a new motivational system, one oriented not toward relationships between superiors and inferiors, but rather toward relationships among prospective cooperative partners. It is this orientation, I suggest, that lies at the heart of most human shame experiences, as shame functions to enhance conformity to cultural standards for behavior that form the basis for much cooperation; this perspective sheds light on the relationship between shame, the self, and decision making.

Taking seriously the notion that cultural information is central to human functioning, in the second portion of this chapter I explore how the experience of shame may be influenced by cross-cultural variation in the importance, and conceptualization, of this emotion. A comparison of the cultural construction of shame in a Western and a non-Western society illustrates the range of variation in this domain, and raises questions regarding the relationship between shame and guilt, and the origins of the latter. This comparison also draws attention to the larger societal consequences of employing shame as a mechanism of social control, a topic of importance given recent attempts to reintroduce shame-based sanctions into U.S. public life.

EVOLUTIONARY PERSPECTIVES ON SHAME

Reconstructing the Evolution of Shame

Phylogenetic Origins

Darwin (1872) was among the first to recognize that the display behaviors accompanying many human emotions provide clues to their evolutionary origins. As a number of investigators have noted, the patterned and largely involuntary actions frequently seen in association with shame resemble the appeasement displays of many nonhuman primates (Fessler, 1999; Gilbert, 1989, 1992, and Chapter 16, this volume; Keltner & Harker, 1998; Weisfeld, 1997, 1999). When experiencing shame, people often lower their faces, avert their gaze, slump their shoulders, and adopt a stooped posture and bent-kneed gait. Conversely, pride, the opposite of shame, involves the inverse pattern of behavior, namely, an elevated face, direct gaze, squared shoulders, erect posture, and stiff-legged gait (see Tracy & Robins, 2004a). Direct gaze is a central element in the stereotyped behaviors evinced when primates challenge rivals. Thus, consistent with what Darwin termed the "principle of antithesis" (the notion that antithetical messages are best communicated using inverse forms), the clearest way of signaling that one acquiesces to a subordinate position is to avert one's gaze. Similarly, whereas animals adopt an expansive posture when threatening rivals so as to appear maximally intimidating, subordinate individuals employ a shrinking posture, making themselves appear small and nonthreatening, in order to appease those who threaten them. With remarkable fidelity, human shame and its opposite, pride, preserve the respective features of primate appeasement and threat displays, suggesting that shame and pride evolved from earlier emotions present in the common ancestors of humans and primates. Against this ethological backdrop, it is possible to infer the evolutionary development of human shame by exploring the circumstances in which shame is experienced.

Together with others' ethnographic and psychological investigations, my research in California and Sumatra (Fessler, 2004) suggests that, at the grossest level of analysis, a substantial fraction of shame-eliciting events can be divided into two categories. First, shame is prototypically elicited by situations in which (1) the actor has failed to live up to some cultural standard for behavior, (2) others are aware of this failure, and (3) the actor is aware of others' knowledge in this regard.[1] Cultures differ in the extent to which they highlight or ignore aspects of human emotional propensities, and this is notably true with regard to shame, as many Western cultures attend exclusively to the aforementioned class of elicitors. Nevertheless, both in the United States and, more dramatically, in Southeast Asia, where this event is often lexically marked, the subjective state and display behaviors associated with shame can also be elicited by events in which the actor is subordinate to another person independent of any failure to adhere to social standards—simply occupying a lower position in a social hierarchy can cause individuals to experience this aversive state and display the corresponding behavioral pattern. This latter class of elicitors is congruent with the message of appeasement communicated by the panprimate shame-like display—viewed ethologically, when humans occupy a subordinate position, they often behave much like other primates in low-ranking positions do. This suggests that the feeling of shame elicited by subordinate status is the original or ancestral form of the emotion.

The conclusion that subordinance shame is evolutionarily ancient is bolstered by the fact that recognizing that one occupies an inferior position in a social hierarchy requires far less cognitive complexity than does recognizing that others know that one has failed. To achieve the latter, actors must be able to see themselves through observers' eyes and to understand what observers do or do not know about their behavior (cf. Tracy & Robins, 2004b). While humans engage in such inferences effortlessly, the ability to assess others' knowledge and mental states, commonly referred to as the capacity to manipulate a theory of mind, is either absent or severely limited in nonhuman primates (Povinelli & Bering, 2002; but see also discussion in Tracy & Robins, 2004b). It is therefore likely that the common ancestor of humans and primates likewise lacked the cognitive capacity for a theory of mind, and hence that any emotions experienced by this species were not dependent on this capacity, making it all the more plausible that subordinance shame is the original or primordial aspect of this emotion.

Prestige Has Replaced Dominance as the Basis of Social Hierarchies

To summarize, human shame is a bipartite emotion consisting of an ancient, or ancestral, component that is shared with nonhuman primates, and a novel, or derived, component that is likely unique to our species. These two aspects of shame, which can operate both in isolation and simultaneously, differ in that the former (1) is cognitively simpler, (2) focuses exclusively on questions of social rank, and (3) does not intrinsically revolve around questions of conformity to cultural standards for behavior. With regard to the latter, it is noteworthy that, compared to human societies, nonhuman primates are largely devoid of culture, meaning that they lack the rich and parochial socially transmitted rules and expectations that govern much of human behavior (see Fragaszy & Perry, 2003). Correspondingly, lacking cultural criteria whereby success is measured, for nonhuman primates social position is principally a function of dominance, the ability to forcibly displace a rival from a resource. Natural selection has presumably favored the evolution of the capacity to experience emotions that motivate animals to strive for dominance because access to resources (e.g., food, mates, refuge) is a primary determinant of survival and reproductive success. Viewed in this light, the aversive shame-like emotion experienced by subordinate individuals is part of a motivational system that leads actors to fight for higher rank. As any victim of schoolyard bullying can attest, dominance still plays a role in some human relationships and, correspondingly, our species maintains the propensity to experience an aversive emotion when placed in a subordinate position. However, while the biological significance of human dominance hierarchies is nontrivial, in most societies these relations are overshadowed by prestige hierarchies. Whereas in *dominance hierarchies* a superordinate social position is obtained through force or the threat thereof, in *prestige hierarchies* select individuals are elevated to superordinate positions by observers—in short, a dominant position is *taken from* others, but a prestigious position is *given by* others.

Prestige hierarchies are an outgrowth of the human reliance on socially transmitted information. We elevate individuals who perform exceptionally well in a culturally valued domain in part because, by deferring to them, we gain opportunities to observe, and learn from, their successful behavior (Henrich & Gil-White, 2001). Much human social competition thus takes the form of attempts to excel at culturally defined activities—hierarchical social position is awarded by observers rather than wrested by force from adversaries. This difference, while profound, does not change the fundamental adaptive utility of the hedonic aspects of shame and pride.[2] As is true of dominance, those who achieve high prestige have greater access to the resources that contributed to survival and, prior to the advent of contraception, reproductive success; it is thus understandable that natural selection has preserved in humans the motivational system that makes it aversive to occupy a subordinate position in the social hierarchy and rewarding to occupy a superordinate position.

The Shame Display in Nondominance Contexts: Vestigial Behavior or Functional Signal?

While the evolutionary shift from dominance hierarchies to prestige hierarchies has not altered the adaptive utility of the hedonic component of shame, the same is not true of the functional consequences of the associated display behaviors. In a dominance system, individuals who assess themselves as possessing inferior fighting ability relative to a rival benefit by signaling this assessment to the competitor—natural selection favors the evolution of appeasement displays because it is less costly to signal acquiescence than to engage in a fight that one is likely to lose. In contrast, in a prestige system, individuals who signal their inferiority do not gain the benefit of avoiding injury, since prestige competitions generally do not involve physical aggression. Moreover, such a signal often inflicts costs on the signaler because it advertises the individual's acknowledgment of inferiority to the larger audience, and it is observers who bestow or withhold prestige—we admire the competitor who, though bested, bravely vows to return to win another day, but we lose respect for the loser who slinks away from a contest in an inferior pose. Why, then, has natural selection not eliminated the largely involuntary shame display from all but dominance-related social interactions? One possibility is that selection cannot eliminate the display without altering other key aspects of shame. While this cannot be ruled out, a more compelling possibility is that the panprimate appeasement display acquired additional utility in the course of the evolution of human shame, utility that outweighs the costs of acknowledging inferiority during prestige competitions. The key here is that, while shame can be elicited by subordinance or defeat in social contests, competition is by no means necessary for shame elicitation. Below, I argue that we can understand many shame experiences in light of their implications not for competition, but rather for cooperation.

Conformist Shame, a Uniquely Human Emotion

To gain insight into the types of situations that elicit shame, I asked 281 Southern Californian native speakers of English to recount an event in which someone felt shame (for details of this and the material summarized below, see Fessler, 2004). Over half of the resulting stories involved situations in which the actor knows that others know that the actor has failed to live up to some cultural standard for behavior. Consistent with the argument developed above, some of these stories involved prestige competition (e.g., losing a public athletic contest, being unable to keep up in the conspicuous consumption of prestige goods). However, at just over 6%, prestige competitions accounted for only a fraction of the stories in this category. Far more common, constituting over three-quarters of the stories, were situations in which no competition was evident (indeed, often no rival was present at all); instead, people reported feeling shame simply because they had failed to live up to some minimum standard for social acceptability (e.g., being caught cheating on an exam, failing during a public ritual or performance). A similar pattern was present in my observations, collected in a Malay fishing village in Bengkulu, Indonesia, of 305 naturally occurring events in which people spontaneously described themselves or someone else as feeling *malu*, "ashamed." Again, over half of the cases involved an actor's recognition of others' knowledge of the actor's failure, and again only a portion of these (12.8%) concerned prestige competition (many examples directly parallel those described earlier); the majority of events simply involved failure without overt competition (again, many examples parallel those in California, with the prominent addition of pregnancy out of wedlock). Hence, although shame can be elicited by subordinance or defeat, the prototypical eliciting situation is not a competitive one, but rather a situation in which the actor has failed to conform to some cultural standard—rather than addressing issues of hierarchical ranking, shame often revolves around failing to meet some threshold for social acceptability.

Although any aspect of culturally shaped behavior can become an arena for social competition, most human behavior is not competitive. In every society people spend most of their time engaged in economic, social, or leisure activities that do not focus on comparisons premised on hierarchical ranking. These activities are shaped by cultural understandings concerning the normal, appropriate, or reasonable way to behave. While competition is absent from such domains, social evaluation is not: humans constantly observe one another and measure each other's behavior in light of cultural standards.[3] Correspondingly, while its prominence in consciousness varies considerably depending on the situation, we are aware of the presence of others who are, or could be, monitoring our own actions.

Attention is a finite cognitive resource: the more that is devoted to one task, the less that is available for other tasks. Why, then, do humans expend so much of this important resource in both (1) monitoring the extent to which others conform to cultural standards, and (2) monitoring the extent to which our own behavior is being monitored? Competitive concerns play a role here, yet it is likely that attending to the actions and social position of one's rivals constitutes only a small fraction of all social monitoring, since (1) monitoring occurs even in many domains and activities that are not competitive, and (2) actors are cognizant of the presence of observers even when, due to their age, gender, or social position, the observers could not possibly be the actor's rivals. The key to understanding our obsession with watching one another's behavior lies in the fact that ours is a cooperative species. In the next section, I consider how the combination of opportunities and dangers presented by cooperative activities favored the evolution of a uniquely human form of shame, the emotion behind our attention to others' attention to our behavior.

Human Cooperation, the Problem of Defection, and the Role of Shame in Motivating Conformity

Cooperative interactions are those in which two or more individuals incur some cost, whether by investing time, energy, or resources, or by forgoing other opportunities, in order to behave in a fashion that will benefit all involved. When efforts, energy, and knowledge are pooled, the results are often not merely additive, but multiplicative. However, the fact that other parties invest in the interaction creates opportunities for exploitation. Often, unscrupulous individuals can withhold all or some of their own contributions, freeriding on others' efforts. Defection of this sort inflicts costs on cooperators—at best, their efforts must increase to achieve the same success obtained in the absence of defection, and, at worst, the venture collapses completely.

Because cooperative ventures entail the potential for both rewards and exploitation, natural selection can be expected to have crafted the mind so as to maximize the likelihood of obtaining the former and minimize the likelihood of suffering the latter (Cosmides & Tooby, 1992). Monitoring others' behavior during cooperative ventures furthers these goals, as it often pays to be aware of how much each individual contributes to the activity (such monitoring is advantageous even when the observer is not a participant, as it is useful to gather information about prospective partners in anticipation of future endeavors). Results from experimental economic games in which participants invest real money in cooperative relationships demonstrate that the opportunity to evaluate others' behavior is a crucial determinant of the level of cooperation: people are more willing to behave cooperatively when their observations of one another give them reason to believe that others will do likewise (Fehr & Gächter, 2000). Correspondingly, it pays to be cognizant of the presence of others who are monitoring one's own behavior, since maintaining a reputation as a trustworthy cooperator enhances the likelihood that others will enter into cooperative relationships with one. The power of the psychological mechanisms regulating reputation management is illustrated by the facts that (1) looking obliquely into another person's eyes prior to participation in an economic experiment enhances cooperation (Kurzban, 2001), (2) the presence of a robotic face increases such cooperation (Burnham & Hare, in press), and (3) stylized eyespots suffice to induce individuals to behave more generously in economic games (Haley & Fessler, 2005). These effects presumably occur because, in ancestral populations, eyes facing in one's direction were a reliable indicator that one was being monitored, hence natural selection crafted the mind so as to enhance prosocial actions in the presence of this cue—we are so attuned to the possibility that someone might be watching us that we increase our cooperation in response to even a hint of the presence of an observer.

While the results discussed above do not speak directly to the question of whether cues of observability lower the threshold for the elicitation of shame, they do suggest that motivational systems influencing cooperative behavior, of which, I argue, shame is a part, are sensitive to the presence of social monitoring. However, as I explore below, the relationship between shame and cooperation is more extensive than the simple decision as to whether to cooperate or defect.

Cooperation and the Problem of Coordination

Cultures vary enormously in how cooperative relationships are defined and what is expected of the participants. Nevertheless, it is likely that all cultures condemn shirking, freeriding, or otherwise defecting in such a relationship, particularly when it is longstanding and involves members of the local group. Arguably, an important function of shame is thus to motivate reputation management behavior with regard to culturally constituted cooperative relationships. However, results from both California and Bengkulu (Fessler, 2004) indicate that, while defection in a cooperative relationship is central to some shame events, this category is dwarfed by a larger one in which the cultural standard at issue does not concern cooperation.

Earlier, I argued that two features that distinguish our species from closely related primates are the importance of cultural standards in shaping behavior and the extent of cooperation among unrelated individuals. While a key aspect of the connection between these two features is the existence of cultural understandings that define the nature and content of cooperative interactions, the effect of culture on cooperation extends far beyond overt rules governing how and when to cooperate. Although coping with the possibility of defection is a necessary condition for the maintenance of cooperation, cooperation itself can only take place after a more elementary problem, that of coordination, has been surmounted. Cooperative activities are contingent on the actor's ability to engage in actions that complement those of other participants: each actor must know both what to do and when to do it. The more individuals involved, and the more indirect their interactions, the more challenging coordination becomes.

Cultural information makes cooperation possible in part by defining the nature and timing of cooperative behavior. A determinant of an individual's attractiveness as a prospective cooperative partner is therefore the extent to which he or she possesses and is motivated to conform to relevant cultural understandings. However, because there are many forms of cooperative activity, with new permutations always possible, it is often difficult to assess others' adequacy in this regard. One solution is to gauge the target individual's conformity to diverse cultural understandings in order to assess familiarity with, and motivation to adhere to, the cultural standards of the given group. Cultural standards are often baroque, with many rules being rarely, if ever, articulated. Standards are sufficiently extensive and difficult to acquire that only individuals possessing intimate familiarity with many aspects of the culture will be able to successfully conform to appropriate standards across the myriad domains of daily life. Likewise, only individuals who are deeply motivated to conform will expend the mental resources needed to maintain conformity across domains, whether through overt attention or through automatization following extensive repetition. Observing that someone consistently behaves appropriately in a variety of activities thus provides an initial indication that the individual likely both (1) possesses the cultural knowledge relevant to a given cooperative enterprise, and (2) is motivated to adhere to cultural standards in a manner that facilitates coordination.

The above argument sheds light on why we both monitor others' behavior and attend to the presence of others who can monitor our behavior. Evaluating the degree of conformity to cultural standards provides valuable information to the observer: by updating one's assessment of others' command of, and motivation to conform to, social standards of behavior, social monitoring facilitates evaluating others' current potential as a partner in cooperative ventures. Equally important, humans are unique in that they not only hold cultural standards for behavior, they also enforce them, incurring costs in order to punish wrongdoers even when the violation does not impinge on them. Such costly prosocial behavior is itself explicable in terms of the strategic importance of reputation management. Cultures contain not only rules for behavior, but also rules about *enforcing* rules for behavior. Incurring costs to punish wrongdoers is thus a form of conspicuous cultural conformity, a way of advertising that the actor both knows and adheres to local standards. Fitness-enhancing punitive behavior is motivated by a discrete emotion: moral outrage (Fessler & Haley, 2003). Consistent with the above argument, subjects report more moral outrage at norm violations when observers are present than when they are alone (Haley, 2006). The fact that people are motivated to punish those who violate cultural standards explains the survival of the ancestral appeasement display as a component of shame: there is considerable value in signaling to observers that one does not contest their moralistic aggression. In Bengkulu, individuals who fail to exhibit shame when others become aware of their wrongdoing are termed "thick-eared," as they are unaffected by gossip or excoriation. Being thick-eared is a form of higher-order norm violation, as it indicates both that one does not value cultural standards and that one does not care about others' valuation of these standards. Not surprisingly, given that shaming is a principal social sanction in Bengkulu, thick-eared people are viewed as dangerous and, if they persist in violating important standards, may even be killed. Hence, whereas recalcitrance simply adds fuel to the fire of moralistic punishment, acknowledgment of the wrongness of the violation, and the correspondingly deserved nature of the reduction in social status, is likely to have the opposite effect. Paralleling work by others (de Jong, 1999; Keltner & Harker, 1998; Keltner, Young, & Buswell, 1997), this perspective generates the prediction that the appropriate and timely presentation of the shame display should reduce the costs that morally outraged witnesses seek to inflict on those who violate important cultural standards. Moreover, this approach provides a solution to the puzzle raised earlier, namely, why, if prestige hierarchies have largely replaced dominance hierarchies in human societies, and if shame's appeasement display is costly in prestige competitions, both the display and the attendant behavioral tendencies have nevertheless been retained—in a world in which norm violations evoke moralistic punishment, the appeasement facets of shame are an effective means of communicating acquiescence to moralistically hostile others.

Whereas the value of the shame display derives from its in-the-moment effects on others, the value of the hedonic component of shame stems from its prospective effects. The aversive nature of shame provides an anticipatory incentive to conform to cultural standards, and to be cognizant of the extent to which others are aware of any digressions. Because degree of conformity to moralized standards for behavior is likely predictive of both the probability that an actor will not defect in a cooperative relationship and the probability that the actor will behave in a predictable manner facilitating coordination, in ancestral populations, adherence to such rules will have often influenced an individual's survival and reproductive success; natural selection can thus be expected to have given particular weight to conformity to highly moralized cultural standards. While there is debate about the exact relationship between shame and embarrassment (see Keltner, 1995; Keltner & Buswell, 1996), it is plausible that selection created a division of labor, with shame motivating conformity to the most moralized cultural standards, and embarrassment motivating conformity to many cultural rules that hold less moral import.

Determinants of the Intensity of Shame

To summarize the argument thus far, in parallel with the rise of our species' reliance on cultural information, natural selection modified an existing motivational system, one that initially evolved to further rank-striving behavior, in order to drive individuals to behave in ways that advertise to others that they will constitute reliable cooperative partners. This suggests that a number of factors should govern the intensity of the experience of shame. While some of these entailments are consistent with obvious characteristics of shame (and hence the theory adds little other than explanation), others are more subtle.

First, all else being equal, the more serious the rule violation at issue, the more it damages the actor's reputation as a cooperator, and hence the greater the aversive experience of shame that should accompany others' learning of it. Second, the greater the number of people who know of a given transgression, the larger the number of opportunities for cooperation that may be lost, and hence the more intense the experience of shame that should follow. Next, the identities of observers should affect the intensity of shame. The costliness of the reputational damage entailed by a given transgression is in part a function of the extent to which those who learn of it are attractive as prospective cooperative partners. At the grossest level, due to the problem of coordination described above, members of the actor's cultural group are more attractive as potential partners than are members of other groups; shame should therefore be more intense when observers are members of one's own group. Within the cultural group, opportunities for cooperation are generally greatest with those nearest at hand, hence geographical proximity should be a determinant of shame intensity. Likewise, because opportunities for cooperation are greatest among individuals who interact often, the frequency with which the actor interacts with those who know of the transgression should affect shame intensity. Similarity often shapes the extent of cooperation between individuals, as those who are similar with respect to age, gender, and so on often face similar tasks and have similar objectives. The extent of similarity between the actor and those who know of the transgression can thus be expected to influence shame intensity. Individuals who excel in domains relevant to the actor's objectives are valuable prospective partners; hence knowledge of the transgression by such individuals is costly to the actor, and therefore likely to exacerbate shame intensity.

Overlapping with, but separate from, the attractiveness of observers as potential cooperation partners is the extent to which those who know of the transgression can influence others' assessments of the actor. Condemnation by a prominent figure may disproportionately increase the intensity of shame because such individuals are in a position to both disseminate information about the transgression to others and enhance the weight assigned to it by others. Lastly, even among those who lack social prominence, the capacity to disseminate information varies; because this attribute affects the reputational costs associated with a given transgression, the intensity of shame felt should be influenced by the density of the social network in which a given observer is embedded, the observer's ability and propensity to communicate with diverse members of the community, and so on.

Shame and the Self

The above discussion sheds light on differences between shame and guilt, the emotion with which, in individualistic cultures such as those of the West, shame is frequently conflated. Phenomenologically, guilt focuses on the actions that elicited it, while shame focuses on the actor: one feels guilt over what one has done, but feels shame over who one is (Tangney, 1995). The latter is an outgrowth of the fitness consequences that attend reputation management. To see why, consider the role of self-assessment in decision making.

In many domains, determining which course of action is optimal is contingent on one's future prospects. Individuals whose prospects are dim have little to lose, and much to gain, by extensive risk taking; conversely, those whose prospects are bright benefit from a more conservative strategy (Daly & Wilson, 1988). Optimization thus requires an index of future prospects. Future prospects are a function of the consequences of past and current successes and failures; hence we can expect the mind to maintain a running tally in which, weighted for their potential impacts on fitness, past and current events are summed. Self-esteem functions in this manner, and can be conceptualized as a constantly updated subjective index of the actor's future fitness prospects (Fessler, 2001; Kirkpatrick, Waugh, Valencia, & Webster, 2002; Leary, Tambor, Terdal, & Downs, 1995). In ancestral populations, access to resources would have been contingent on inclusion in co-operative ventures, and such inclusion would, in turn, have been in part a function of the individual's reputation as someone who both knows and conforms to social norms. It therefore would have been adaptive to experience an intimate association between self-esteem and events impacting the actor's reputation. Consistent with this logic, the same motivational system that ties negative social evaluation to an aversive affective state also diminishes the individual's self-assessment of success to date—shame entails both pain and a reduction in subjective self-worth, simultaneously providing an hedonic incentive to avoid additional social disapproval and a recalibration of that index of future prospects that is vital to optimal decision making (Fessler, 2001; see also Leary, Chapter 3, this volume).

Shame and Risk Taking

Because the optimal level of risk taking is in part a function of an individual's future prospects, the above argument entails the prediction that, in many situations, the experience of shame will increase risk taking.[4] Although this proposition is potentially clinically important, to date few studies have attended to this possibility. Previously (Fessler, 2001), I applied this reasoning to a case in which a trivial altercation escalated into murder. However, one difficulty with this and similar accounts is that intimate associations exist between, on the one hand, shame and anger, and, on the other hand, anger and risk taking. Shame and anger often both co-occur and exacerbate one another (Tangney, 1995), a pattern understandable in light of shame's role in social competition. "Humiliation" refers to a social state wherein others either cause the actor to fail or intentionally draw attention to the actor's failure, leading, in both instances, to shame (cf. Gilbert, 1997). Humiliation seems to involve an awareness that others have benefited at the actor's expense, often by reducing the actor's standing in a social hierarchy. Experiencing harm at the hands of another is the prototypical elicitor of anger, the emotion that functions to truncate or deter transgressions by motivating the actor to inflict costs on the transgressor (reviewed in Fessler, Pillsworth, & Flamson, 2004). Because inflicting costs on others is risky, the functional objectives of anger are achieved by increasing the propensity to take risks, a pattern that is both readily observed and experimentally demonstrable (Fessler et al., 2004). In light of the effects of anger on risk taking, increases in risk taking following humiliation or similar conjunctions of shame and anger cannot be taken as evidence that shame enhances risk taking in and of itself.

To date, only a limited number of experiments have investigated the effects of shame on risk taking. Leith and Baumeister (1996) show that anticipating revelation of inability increases risk taking (although the authors interpret this as an effect of embarrassment, the elicitor is potentially congruent with shame). Likewise, Baumeister, Heatherton, and Tice (1993) demonstrate that ego threats (events plausibly interpreted as shame-inducing) increase risk taking in individuals with high self-esteem.

CULTURAL PERSPECTIVES ON SHAME

The Relationship between Culture and Experience

I have emphasized the importance of our species' reliance on cultural information when examining self-conscious emotions. However, nowhere in the above discussion have I examined how the nature of such information can itself influence the experience, and motivational importance, of self-conscious emotions and facets thereof. It is to this topic that I now turn.

If the mind contains evolved mechanisms dedicated to the acquisition and use of socially transmitted information, cross-cultural comparison should reveal both marked differences in the experience and conceptualization of emotions and notable underlying similarities. Work in cognitive anthropology (reviewed in D'Andrade, 1995) and cognitive linguistics (cf. Levinson, 2003) indicates that, particularly when encoded in language, cultural information shapes the ease with which ideas or perceptions are processed. Because cultures address the nature, form, and expression of emotions, cultural information thus not only shapes the normative value of particular forms of emotion or emotion display but, more profoundly, also influences individuals' propensity to experience particular facets of emotions. In the following section, I illustrate this phenomenon by exploring shame in two disparate cultures.

Comparing Shame across Two Cultures

The findings referred to earlier concerning Bengkulu culture derive from 32 months of anthropological fieldwork conducted between 1990 and 1993. Bengkulu is particularly relevant to the present discussion because shame is markedly elaborated in this culture and, correspondingly, is a common and salient element in discourse. When Bengkulu participants rated the frequency with which 52 emotion terms were used in everyday conversation, averaging across 80 participants, the term *malu*, readily translated as "shame," ranked second; in contrast, when 75 Southern Californians performed a similar task using 52 common English emotion terms, *shame* was ranked 49th (Fessler, 2004). Although language is not a rigid determinant of experience, nevertheless, together, the existence of lexical labels for particular emotions and the culturally conceptualized relationships between such labels likely have substantial impact on subjective experience. To compare cultural conceptions of shame across two disparate cultures, I therefore explored the synonymic relationships among shame-related emotion terms in Bengkulu and Southern California (see Fessler, 2004, for the complete study).

Using focus groups in Bengkulu and California, I composed large (over 400 items) lists of locally recognized emotion terms. I then asked literate individuals to provide a synonym for each term. Following Heider (1991), I generated maps of the relationships between emotion terms by pooling responses across participants within each culture, counting the number of times that a given word was used as a synonym for another term, and then linking synonymic terms using a numerical indicator of this connection strength. Results reveal that Californians have a relatively impoverished cognitive/lexical "landscape of shame." Consistent with earlier research (e.g., Crozier, 1990; Gilbert, 1997), there are intimate links between *shame, embarrassment,* and *humiliation.* However, beyond the additional term *red-faced,* this cluster of items has no further links, with the exception of a strong connection between *shame* and *guilt.* Moreover, whereas *shame* is not highly productive of first- and higher-order associations, *guilt* is part of a large complex of terms, anchored by *remorse,* focusing on regret over past actions and concern about harm suffered by others. The landscape of Californian shame is thus one in which this emotion is overshadowed by guilt and, consistent with existing work on the subject (see Lickel, Schmader, Curtis, Barquissau, & Ames, 2005; Tangney, 1995), the latter can be differentiated from shame in that guilt, but not shame, is prototypically associated with issues of harm to others.

In contrast to the Californian case, results from Bengkulu support the contention that this culture attends extensively to shame. The connections branching off of the term *malu* form two elaborate clusters, each distinct from the other. One cluster concerns feelings of failure and social unacceptability, as well as the contemptuous reactions of others toward individuals who are in such a position. This rich set of terms simultaneously encompasses the social events and subjective experience associated with an awareness that others know of some grave misdeed on the actor's part, that is, the same general set of circumstances as those prototypically associated with the English term *shame*. However, consistent with my earlier claim that Bengkulu speakers also use *malu* to describe the emotion experienced when occupying a position of inferiority independent of any failing, *malu* is also linked to a second large cluster of terms revolving around shyness and a reticence to act in the presence of others who are more important than oneself. Hence, whereas the first cluster of terms captures a culturally constituted landscape that expresses the derived form of shame, the second cluster of terms captures an analogous landscape that expresses the ancestral form, the emotion likely shared with nonhuman primates.

Because cultures differentially elaborate on or ignore features of the panhuman emotional spectrum, no single culture provides a privileged window into that underlying spectrum. Nevertheless, it is likely that Bengkulu culture, with its extensive focus on shame, presents a more complete portrait of this emotion than does Californian (and, more broadly, Western) culture, as the latter is relatively impoverished in comparison. Many non-Western cultures explicitly link shame, subordinance, respect, and shyness (Fessler, 2004), suggesting that this is a core aspect of shame. Given that Californians are capable of understanding this association, this raises the question why some cultures ignore subordinance shame. One possibility is that subordinance shame is incompatible with the Californian ethos that combines ideals of a meritocracy with an individualistic, even libertarian, orientation—society is hierarchical, but it is (or should be) a prestige hierarchy in which everyone is free to compete for the admiration of others; individuals, who are of equal basic worth, are to achieve high status through others' freely granted deference, not through their involuntary subordination. In such a culture, an aversive feeling of inadequacy in the presence of a superior individual is an anathema—one should admire those who are superior, not feel subordinated by them.

The most marked feature of the Californian landscape of shame is the extent to which guilt and related affects are elaborated, to the point that they overshadow shame.[5] In the analysis of self-reported shame events mentioned earlier, guilt-like features (e.g., concern over having harmed another, remorse, and a lack of focus on the opinions of observers) played an important role in over one-third of the cases. In contrast, not only were such features not present in any of the cases in which Bengkulu speakers referred to someone as feeling *malu*, but, moreover, guilt is largely absent from Bengkulu culture—there is no simple means of translating the concept into the Bengkulu dialect of Malay, and Bengkulu participants often expressed uncertainty when the concept was discussed in detail (see Fessler, 2004). In the following sections, I first discuss the implications of cultural variation in the relative importance of shame and guilt for an understanding of the origins of the latter emotion, and then turn to the question of the broader implications for society of relying on shame as a means of regulating behavior.

Implications of the Relative Predominance of Shame or Guilt

The patterns evident in the Bengkulu–California comparisons, namely, the relatively rich conceptualization of shame in the former, and the predominance of guilt in the latter, are consistent with Wallbott and Scherer's (1995) finding that participants from collectivistic cultures like that of Bengkulu report shame experiences that are central to the profile of this emotion, while participants from individualistic cultures like that of California often report shame experiences that resemble guilt experiences. People from individualistic cultures thus seem more likely to conflate, equate, or blend shame and guilt than are people from collectivistic cultures. Correspondingly, although early anthropological efforts to dichotomize "shame cultures" and "guilt cultures" (e.g., Benedict, 1946) were rightly abandoned as overly simplistic, cultures nevertheless appear to differ substantially in the extent to which they attend to shame versus guilt and the roles played by these two emotions in regulating social behavior.

The observation that guilt or guilt-like concepts are markedly absent from some cultures can be explained in two ways. First, it is possible that, although the propensity to experience guilt is a feature of our evolved human nature, this affect is nonetheless ignored by some cultures for reasons of history or ethos analogous to those proposed with regard to subordinance shame in California. Second, the propensity to experience guilt may not be an intrinsic part of the panhuman emotional architecture, but rather may derive from culturally particular combinations of sympathy, empathy, regret, and sadness. Congruent with the first explanation, a number of evolutionists (e.g., Frank, 1988; Trivers, 1971) note that guilt is a potentially highly adaptive emotion. Guilt is often elicited by harm inflicted on a valued partner, ally, or relative. The prototypical outcome behavior, an attempt to compensate the harmed party, thus potentially preserves valuable relationships by mitigating damage to the relationship stemming from the eliciting action. If this action tendency is blocked, guilt often results in self-punishment, behavior that may have value as an honest signal of the desire to maintain the damaged relationship. Lastly, the aversive nature of guilt prospectively deters actors from repeating the costly error of damaging valuable relationships. However, congruent with the second explanation, whereas (1) evolved social emotions generally are accompanied by stereotypic involuntary displays, and (2) such a display would be particularly valuable in an emotion aimed at repairing damaged relationships (since the involuntary nature of the display would signal sincerity), no such display exists for guilt (Keltner & Buswell, 1996). Evidence to date is thus insufficient to determine whether guilt is a discrete, evolved emotion or a cultural construct cobbled together out of more elementary universal components.

The Social Benefits and Costs of a Cultural Emphasis on Shame

The degree to which shame is overshadowed by guilt in cultures such as Southern California appears to have increased over the last century. Literary and historical accounts suggest there was previously a greater concern with public reputation and a greater reliance on institutionalized shaming, ranging from the dunce cap to the stockade, as a means of punishing wrongdoers. Today's commentators bemoan the reduced concern with this emotion and the decline in its use as a means of regulating behavior (cf. Davies, 2002; Hamill, 2003; Jackson, 2003; Karen, 1992; O'Neill, 2002). Underlying these arguments is the intuition that enhancing the attention paid to the experience of shame and increasing the use of shaming as a sanction will result in greater social cohesion and more cooperation, as people will be motivated to engage in fewer self-interested actions and more group-beneficial behaviors. Paralleling this movement, a number of legal scholars argue for reinstating so-called scarlet letter punishments, judicial sanctions that punish miscreants by publicizing their wrongdoing (cf. Kahan, 1996; Kahan & Posner, 1999). These scholars argue that scarlet letter sentences are inexpensive, appropriately express society's moral condemnation, and effectively deter certain classes of crime. Correspondingly, some judges and state and local governments increasingly employ sentences and enforcement tactics explicitly or implicitly aimed at causing shame. Judges have ordered thieves to advertise their convictions using T-shirts or signs, and drunk drivers to do likewise via bumper stickers; a number of municipalities maintain web sites or broadcast television programs identifying individuals who are guilty of soliciting prostitutes or are delinquent in child support payments; and prosecutors increasingly employ the "perp walk" wherein suspects in white-collar crimes are arrested at work and paraded in handcuffs before co-workers and television cameras (see Fessler, 2006).

Studies of everyday behavior suggest that the motivational salience of shame can be reinvigorated in Western cultures. In addition to the economic experiments described earlier, studies indicate that people are more likely to wash their hands after using a restroom when an observer is present (Munger & Harris, 1989), and that drivers of convertible automobiles are quicker to honk, and honk more frequently, when the convertible top is up, providing the illusion of anonymity, than when the top is down, exposing the driver to observers (Ellison, Govern, Petri, & Figler, 1995).[6] Moreover, the pathway to social change is not difficult to discern, as increased use of scarlet letter sentences may create a ripple effect extending beyond the judicial system.

In contrast to incarceration or fines, scarlet letter sentences not only expose the public to the punitive process but, more importantly, invite the public to participate in it. Such punishments paint a target on convicted individuals, inviting others to hurl invective at them. These sentences thus convey the message that not only are public expressions of moral outrage or contempt in response to wrongdoing acceptable but, moreover, that they are the mark of a good citizen. Indeed, consistent with the argument outlined earlier regarding the reputation-management aspects of moral outrage, it is dangerous not to react in such a fashion, since to display indifference is to risk giving the impression that one condones the misdeed, placing one in the same moral category as the convicted individual. Scarlet letter punishments thus not only familiarize the public with the use of shaming, they both legitimate and encourage, perhaps even demand, active participation in it. By normalizing this experience, scarlet letter punishments make it more likely that people will view the application of shaming in nonjudicial contexts as acceptable, and hence that the dunce cap and its ilk will return to U.S. culture.

The above suggests that social engineers could revitalize shame as a principal feature of behavior regulation in Western societies. Importantly, however, popular, academic, and judicial movements to increase both the cultural prominence of shame and the institutionalized use of shaming are taking place in the absence of any assessment of the long-term societal consequences of assigning shame a more central role in personal experience and behavior regulation. Although a systematic evaluation is beyond the scope of this chapter, in order to initiate a discussion of this topic, I briefly review some factors worthy of consideration.

Shame and its opposite, pride, are quintessentially other-oriented emotions, as how one feels about oneself is contingent on others' assessments. Advocates of efforts to increase the prominence of both shame and shaming are therefore likely correct in arguing that such changes would increase civility, cooperation, and prosociality in the United States, since these behaviors are linked with both attention to others and the desire to make a positive impression.[7] Cross-cultural comparisons are an imperfect source of insight in this regard, as many factors vary across cultures in addition to the prominence of shame. Nevertheless, observations support a link between shame and prosociality, at least at the local level. In Bengkulu, largely as a result of concern with others' assessments, social interactions are highly cordial and hospitality is profuse. More broadly, Bengkulu villagers rely on others' sensitivity to shame to ensure participation in a variety of community maintenance and improvement projects. Shirkers become the target of gossip, and may be shamed via public announcements, a highly effective sanction. However, the effects of shame sensitivity need not be so overt—for example, in Japan, participation in recycling programs is enhanced through the use of transparent garbage bags that allow neighbors to discern whether one has diligently separated one's various recyclables.

Limits on the extent of prosociality engendered through enhanced sensitivity to shame stem primarily from the factors described earlier as determinants of the intensity of shame. Bengkulu villagers endorse the Japanese aphorism that, when traveling, one should "leave one's shame at home": the opinions of strangers living far from one's home community carry little weight, and hence behavioral pre- and proscriptions can easily be disregarded. Qualified thusly, it is reasonable to conclude that resurrecting shame in U.S. public life would increase prosociality, with commensurate increases in security, social cohesion, and harmony. However, such benefits are not free, but rather are accompanied by costs that, I believe, outweigh them.

In Bengkulu, the prominence of shame in personal experience and the frequency of shaming as a method of behavior regulation frequently lead individuals to focus not on achieving excellence, but rather on avoiding failure—people are often more concerned with avoiding punishments than with reaping the benefits of social action. During intercommunity competitions for village tidiness, leaders exhort their followers to work hard not so their village can be proclaimed the cleanest, but so that they can avoid the ignominy of having it named the dirtiest. At the end of each school year, children wait with anticipation to hear not whether they have excelled in their studies, but rather whether they have managed to avoid the disgrace of failing to advance to the next grade. Indeed, the concern with avoiding shame pervades educational and intellectual domains. Schoolchildren sit passively in class. They do not answer the teacher's questions for fear of shame: if they are wrong, the teacher shames them, and if they are right, their peers shame them for being a know-it-all. This extends to the highest levels of academia—rather than featuring spirited debate, or even open discussion, academic panels, policy meetings, and conferences are often characterized by a wooden reiteration of the least controversial position or perspective.

The systematic application of shaming sanctions makes conformism the safest option. As a result, not only do people not seek to excel, they often do not innovate. Bengkulu villagers typically adopt new economic activities or medical or hygienic practices only after a majority of people in neighboring areas have done so. New inventions or business opportunities are forsaken out of concern with what people might say about unconventional behavior. These constraints impose real costs on the people of Bengkulu, as their health, welfare, and ability to compete economically all suffer due to a conservatism that is social, not personal, in nature.

Life in a rural Southeast Asian fishing village differs from life in the United States along so many axes that skeptics might complain that it is impossible to garner insight from cases such as the above into changes that might occur in the West were shame to be elevated in motivational prominence. Consider, therefore, the case of Japan. While early anthropological characterizations of Japan as a pure shame culture proved inaccurate, shame nevertheless holds greater motivational and social significance in Japan than in the United States (cf. Lebra, 1983). On the positive side, the intense attention to shame and social comparison in part contributes to a phenomenally low crime rate (Komiya, 1999). However, a high price is paid for security and prosociality. Consistent with the above description, Japanese education often does not foster innovation and creativity, but rather stifles it (Ramirez, 1999; Saeki, Fan, & Van Dusen, 2001; Yamada, 1991). Together with the overall depressive effects on innovation stemming from an emphasis on conformity, this has created a modern economic efflorescence that is largely based on developing ideas originated elsewhere—as a percentage of its gross domestic product, Japan's creative economy, that portion of a nation's productivity composed of intellectual property and patents, is among the smallest of the world's economic giants (Howkins, 2002). In the postindustrial era, ideas are often more valuable than labor or materials; it therefore remains to be seen whether, in the absence of substantial cultural changes, the Japanese economic miracle of rapid growth can be maintained. While it is unlikely that, in the United States, shame will ever again achieve the cultural prominence that it held in the past, cases such as this should give both pundits and jurists reason to pause before seeking to enhance the propensity to experience shame and the frequency with which it is intentionally induced in others as a means of regulating behavior.

As exemplified by Southern California, U.S. culture fosters free-spirited innovation and experimentation, features that are vital to the economic and political success of the United States. In comparison to at least one small-scale community in a semitraditional society, the cultural prominence and, arguably, the motivational significance of shame are greatly attenuated in Southern California. Likewise, both U.S. society in general, and Southern Californian society in particular, are characterized by huge metropolitan areas and substantial social and geographical mobility, features that differ markedly from the types of social groupings that predominated for most of human history. One of the most important lessons to be drawn from the systematic investigation of shame is therefore that, while this emotion likely played a central role in the evolution of human cooperation in small-scale groups, in today's world of globalized and hypercompetitive markets, there are intrinsic costs to relying on shame as a mechanism of social regulation. Caution should therefore be exercised before advocating what amounts to increased conformism in the name of civility and prosociality: the era of shame may be passing.

ACKNOWLEDGMENTS

I thank Jessica L. Tracy and Richard W. Robins for their many helpful suggestions.

NOTES

1. There is debate as to whether an audience is a prerequisite for shame experience (cf. Tangney, Miller, Flicker, & Barlow, 1996). Two factors may have contributed to mixed reports in this regard. First, possessing a theory of mind, humans are capable of anticipating others' reactions to events, allowing for the autoelicitation of shame via scenario running wherein the actor envisions how others would evaluate the actor were they to learn of the actor's failings. Subjects may

therefore report feeling shame in the absence of publicity not because publicity is not a key factor in shame elicitation, but because they recall powerful autoelicited shame events. Second, much research on shame employs Western subjects. Western cultures likely deemphasize shame relative to guilt (see text); because publicity is irrelevant to guilt elicitation, its role in shame may be clouded in research involving Western subjects.

2. The term "adaptive" is used here in the biological sense, that is, as enhancing the probability of survival and reproduction; this differs from the clinical notion of enhancing individual happiness or social harmony.

3. While we are often unaware that we are actively monitoring those around us, this nevertheless must be true given that we readily detect deviations from normative patterns of behavior—consider, for example, how starkly the staggering drunkard, the gauche foreigner, or the muttering mentally ill individual stands out from the crowd.

4. This does not contradict my conclusion, discussed in the final section of this chapter, that employing shame as a mechanism of social control inhibits innovation and other forms of risk taking. The key to this apparent paradox is the recognition that the active experience of a shame state is predicted to increase the propensity to take risks, while the desire to prospectively avoid such a state leads to increased conformism, and thus to decreased risk taking.

5. This observation does not conflict with clinicians' claims that, in the West, shame is an important factor in psychological distress and psychopathology (Lewis, 1987; Tangney, 1999; Tangney & Dearing, 2002). Indeed, these circumstances may actually contribute to the pathogenicity of shame in the West, as the absence of elaborate cultural models means that few institutional or conventional processes are likely to exist to assist individuals in coping with the experiences that elicit the problematic emotion (cf. Levy, 1973).

6. The fact that these differences in driving behavior occur despite the ready identification provided by the vehicle's license plate is consistent with the argument, advanced earlier, that the evolved psychological mechanisms underlying much prosocial behavior are sensitive to cues that once accurately indexed the extent to which an actor's behavior was observable, but which are often inaccurate in today's evolutionarily novel environments.

7. A reviewer of this chapter noted that this prediction seems to be at odds with published findings indicating that, unlike guilt, shame does not promote behavioral change in response to wrongdoing (see Tangney & Dearing, 2002). However, holding aside the question of the generalizability of such findings, it is important to distinguish between the effects of a particular shame experience and the deterrent power of shame as an aversive event. Individuals reason prospectively, and the knowledge that violations of norms governing cooperation will entail shame can often serve as a powerful incentive motivating prosociality.

REFERENCES

Baumeister, R. F., Heatherton, T. F., & Tice, D. M. (1993). When ego threats lead to self-regulation failure: Negative consequences of high self-esteem. *Journal of Personality and Social Psychology*, 64(1), 141–156.

Benedict, R. (1946). *Patterns of culture.* New York: New American Library.

Burnham, T., & Hare, B. (in press). Engineering cooperation: Does involuntary neural activation increase public goods contributions? *Human Nature.*

Cosmides, L., & Tooby, J. (1992). Cognitive adaptations for social exchange. In J. Barkow, L. Cosmides, & J. Tooby (Eds.), *The adapted mind: Evolutionary psychology and the generation of culture* (pp. 163–228). New York: Oxford University Press.

Crozier, W. R. (1990). Social psychological perspectives on shyness, embarrassment, and shame. In W. R. Crozier (Ed.), *Shyness and embarrassment: Perspectives from social psychology* (pp. 19–58). New York: Cambridge University Press.

Daly, M., & Wilson, M. (1988). *Homicide.* New York: Aldine de Gruyter.

D'Andrade, R. G. (1995). *The development of cognitive anthropology.* New York: Cambridge University Press.

Darwin, C. (1872). *The expression of the emotions in man and animals.* London: Murray.

Davies, J. (2002, November 10). Have we no shame?: Actions that were once unthinkable are now the stuff of every-day exploits. *San Diego Union-Tribune,* p. E-1.

de Jong, P. J. (1999). Communicative and remedial effects of social blushing. *Journal of Nonverbal Behavior, 23*(3), 197–217.

Ellison, P. A., Govern, J. M., Petri, H. L., & Figler, M. H. (1995). Anonymity and aggressive driving behavior: A field study. *Journal of Social Behavior and Personality, 10*(1), 265–272.

Fehr, E., & Gächter, S. (2000). Cooperation and punishment in public goods experiments. *American Economic Review, 90*(4), 980–994.

Fessler, D. M. T. (1999). Toward an understanding of the universality of second order emotions. In A. L. Hinton (Ed.), *Biocultural approaches to the emotions* (pp. 75–116). New York: Cambridge University Press.

Fessler, D. M. T. (2001). Emotions and cost/benefit assessment: The role of shame and self-esteem in risk taking. In R. Selten & G. Gigerenzer (Eds.), *Bounded rationality: The adaptive toolbox* (pp. 191–214).Cambridge, MA: MIT Press.

Fessler, D. M. T. (2004). Shame in two cultures: Implications for evolutionary approaches. *Journal of Cognition and Culture, 4*(2), 207–262.

Fessler, D. M. T. (2006). *Maybe not such a bargain after all: The potential hidden social costs of scarlet letter punishments.* Manuscript in preparation.

Fessler, D. M. T., & Haley, K. J. (2003). The strategy of affect: Emotions in human cooperation. In P. Hammerstein (Ed.), *The genetic and cultural evolution of cooperation* (pp. 7–36). Cambridge, MA: MIT Press.

Fessler, D. M. T., Pillsworth, E. G., & Flamson, T. J. (2004). Angry men and disgusted women: An evolutionary approach to the influence of emotions on risk taking. *Organizational Behavior and Human Decision Processes, 95*(1), 107–123.

Fragaszy, D. M., & Perry, S. (Eds.). (2003). *The biology of traditions: Models and evidence.* New York: Cambridge University Press.

Frank, R. H. (1988). *Passions within reason: The strategic role of the emotions.* New York: Norton.

Gilbert, P. (1989). *Human nature and suffering.* Hillsdale, NJ: Erlbaum.

Gilbert, P. (1992). *Depression: The evolution of powerlessness.* New York: Guilford Press.

Gilbert, P. (1997). The evolution of social attractiveness and its role in shame, humiliation, guilt and therapy. *British Journal of Medical Psychology, 70*(2), 113–147.

Haley, K. J. (2006). *Strangers in familiar lands: Reputational psychology and moralistic responses to norm violations.* Manuscript in preparation.

Haley, K. J., & Fessler, D. M. T. (2005). Nobody's watching?: Subtle cues affect generosity in an anonymous economic game. *Evolution and Human Behavior, 26*(3), 245–256.

Hamill, P. (2003, May 11). The death of shame: From crusading Bill Bennett to "Top Gun" George Bush, our leaders have lost a vital value. *Daily News* (New York), p. 41.

Heider, K. G. (1991). *Landscapes of emotion: Mapping three cultures of emotion in Indonesia.* New York: Cambridge University Press.

Henrich, J., & Gil-White, F. J. (2001). The evolution of prestige: Freely conferred deference as a mechanism for enhancing the benefits of cultural transmission. *Evolution and Human Behavior, 22*(3), 165–196.

Howkins, J. (2002). *The creative economy: How people make money from ideas.* London: Penguin Books.

Jackson, T. (2003, May 20). The death of shame is a real shame. *Tampa Tribune,* p. 1.

Kahan, D. M. (1996). What do alternative sanctions mean? *University of Chicago Law Review, 63,* 591–653.

Kahan, D. M., & Posner, E. A. (1999). Shaming white-collar criminals: A proposal for reform of the federal sentencing guidelines. *Journal of Law and Economics, 42*(1), 365–391.

Karen, R. (1992, February). Shame. *Atlantic Monthly,* pp. 40–70.

Keltner, D. (1995). Signs of appeasement: Evidence for the distinct displays of embarrassment, amusement, and shame. *Journal of Personality and Social Psychology, 68*(3), 441–454.

Keltner, D., & Buswell, B. N. (1996). Evidence for the distinctness of embarrassment, shame, and guilt: A study of recalled antecedents and facial expressions of emotion. *Cognition and Emotion, 10*(2), 155–171.

Keltner, D., & Harker, L. (1998). The forms and functions of the nonverbal signal of shame. In P. Gilbert & B. Andrews (Eds.), *Shame: Interpersonal behavior, psychopathology, and culture* (pp. 78–98). New York: Oxford University Press.

Keltner, D., Young, R. C., & Buswell, B. N. (1997). Appeasement in human emotion, social practice, and personality. *Aggressive Behavior, 23*(5), 359–374.

Kirkpatrick, L. A., Waugh, C. E., Valencia, A., & Webster, G. D. (2002). The functional domain specificity of self-esteem and the differential prediction of aggression. *Journal of Personality and Social Psychology, 82*(5), 756–767.

Komiya, N. (1999). A cultural study of the low crime rate in Japan. *British Journal of Criminology, 39*(3), 369–390.

Kurzban, R. (2001). The social psychophysics of cooperation: Nonverbal communication in a public goods game. *Journal of Nonverbal Behavior, 25*(4), 241–259.

Leary, M. R., Tambor, E. S., Terdal, S. K., & Downs, D. L. (1995). Self-esteem as an interpersonal monitor: The sociometer hypothesis. *Journal of Personality and Social Psychology, 68*(3), 518–530.

Lebra, T. S. (1983). Shame and guilt: A psychocultural view of the Japanese self. *Ethos, 11*(3), 192–209.

Leith, K. P., & Baumeister, R. F. (1996). Why do bad moods increase self-defeating behavior?: Emotion, risk tasking, and self-regulation. *Journal of Personality and Social Psychology, 71*(6), 1250–1267.

Levinson, S. C. (2003). *Space in language and cognition: Explorations in linguistic diversity.* New York: Cambridge University Press.

Levy, R. I. (1973). *Tahitians: Mind and experience in the Society Islands.* Chicago: University of Chicago Press.

Lewis, H. B. (1987). *The role of shame in symptom formation.* Hillsdale, NJ: Erlbaum.

Lickel, B., Schmader, T., Curtis, M., Barquissau, M., & Ames, D. R. (2005). Vicarious shame and guilt. *Group Processes and Intergroup Relations, 8*(2), 145–157.

Munger, K., & Harris, S. J. (1989). Effects of an observer on handwashing in a public restroom. *Perceptual and Motor Skills, 69*(3, Pt. 1), 733–734.

O'Neill, T. (2002, November 18). What popular culture needs is a good strong dose of mortification. *Canadian Business and Current Affairs, 29,* 17.

Povinelli, D. J., & Bering, J. M. (2002). The mentality of apes revisited. *Current Directions in Psychological Science, 11*(4), 115–119.

Ramirez, J. A. (1999). Assessing the effects of higher education on the creative thinking abilities of future Japanese teachers. *Korean Journal of Thinking and Problem Solving, 9*(1), 5–23.

Richerson, P. J., & Boyd, R. (2004). *Not by genes alone: How culture transformed human evolution.* Chicago: University of Chicago Press.

Saeki, N., Fan, X., & Van Dusen, L. (2001). A comparative study of creative thinking of American and Japanese college students. *Journal of Creative Behavior, 35*(1), 24–36.

Tangney, J. P. (1995). Shame and guilt in interpersonal relationships. In J. P. Tangney & K. W. Fischer (Eds.), *Self-conscious emotions: The psychology of shame, guilt, embarrassment, and pride* (pp. 114–139). New York: Guilford Press.

Tangney, J. P. (1999). The self-conscious emotions: Shame, guilt, embarrassment and pride. In T. Dalgleish & M. J. Power (Eds.), *Handbook of cognition and emotion* (pp. 541–568). Chichester, UK: Wiley.

Tangney, J. P., & Dearing, R. L. (2002). *Shame and guilt.* New York: Guilford Press.

Tangney, J. P., Miller, R. S., Flicker, L., & Barlow, D. H. (1996). Are shame, guilt, and embarrassment distinct emotions? *Journal of Personality and Social Psychology, 70*(6), 1256–1269.

Tracy, J. L., & Robins, R. W. (2004a). Show your pride: Evidence for a discrete emotion expression. *Psychological Science, 15*(3), 194–197.

Tracy, J. L., & Robins, R. W. (2004b). Putting the self into self-conscious emotions: A theoretical model. *Psychological Inquiry, 15*(2), 103–125.

Trivers, R. L. (1971). The evolution of reciprocal altruism. *Quarterly Review of Biology, 46*(1), 35–57.

Wallbott, H. G., & Scherer, K. R. (1995). Cultural determinants in experiencing shame and guilt. In J. P. Tangney & K. W. Fischer (Eds.), *Self-conscious emotions: The psychology of shame, guilt, embarrassment, and pride* (pp. 465–487). New York: Guilford Press.

Weisfeld, G. (1997). Discrete emotions theory with specific reference to pride and shame. In N. L. Segal, G. E. Weisfeld, & C. C. Weisfeld (Eds.), *Uniting psychology and biology: Integrative perspectives on human development* (pp. 419–443). Washington, DC: American Psychological Association.

Weisfeld, G. (1999). Darwinian analysis of the emotion of pride/shame. In J. M. G. van der Dennen, D. Smillie, & D. R. Wilson (Eds.), *The Darwinian heritage and sociobiology* (pp. 319–333). Westport, CT: Praeger/Greenwood Press.

Yamada, K. (1991). Creativity in Japan. *Leadership and Organization Development Journal, 12*(6), 11–14.

11

A Cross-Cultural Examination of Lexical Studies of Self-Conscious Emotions

ROBIN S. EDELSTEIN
PHILLIP R. SHAVER

Researchers have long disagreed about the extent to which aspects of human emotions, including cognitive, linguistic, and cultural representations of the emotion domain, are cross-culturally universal, perhaps for biological reasons, or culturally variable and socially constructed. Studies of emotional phenomena, including facial expressions of emotion, dimensions underlying emotion categories, and the representation of emotions in language, have generally supported the claim that there is a core set of emotions that are expressed and recognized in all cultures (see Shaver, Murdaya, & Fraley, 2001, for a brief overview). But there have also been many challenges to this view. Several philosophers and anthropologists have maintained that some cultures have no name for, and thus no conception of, particular emotions recognized in other cultures (e.g., Lutz & White, 1986), that different cultures place different emphases on particular emotions (e.g., Levy, 1984), and that different cultures have devised new emotions and non-Western conceptions of emotion (e.g., Lutz, 1988).

In recent years, the rigid distinction between "universalism" and "relativism" has been breaking down. Wierzbicka (1999), who conducts detailed qualitative studies of emotions named in different languages, for example, has presented cross-linguistic evidence for both universality and cultural specificity. Ekman (1992) has labeled his own approach "neurocultural" to indicate that although there is a hardwired neural substrate for some emotions and emotional expressions, these emotions and expressions are contextualized within cultures and regulated by cultural "display rules." Shaver and colleagues (2001; see also Alonso-Arbiol et al., 2006; Shaver, Schwartz, Kirson, & O'Connor, 1987; Shaver, Wu, & Schwartz, 1992) have found both substantial cross-cultural similarities and noteworthy cross-cultural differences in the linguistic categorization of emotions, suggesting an underlying commonality augmented and shaped by local cultural emphases. These authors have argued that emotion researchers should conduct more studies in different cultures, based on languages with different historical roots, so that the issue of universality versus difference, at least with respect to cognitive and linguistic representations of the emotion domain, can be evaluated in light of a more extensive database.

In the present chapter we examine the relatively small literature on lexical approaches to four self-conscious emotions: shame, guilt, embarrassment, and pride. We are particularly interested in discovering whether these emotions have been included in major lexical studies and, if so, where these emotions are located in multidimensional or hierarchical representations of the emotion domain. We begin by describing the goals of the lexical approach to emotions and emotion concepts, placing special emphasis on the prototype approach we have adopted when studying emotion concepts. We then turn to the empirical evidence, such as it is, concerning lexical and prototype approaches to shame, guilt, embarrassment, and pride. In the final section of the chapter we offer tentative conclusions about the self-conscious emotions gleaned from existing lexical studies and suggest possible avenues for further research.

EMOTIONS AND THEIR COGNITIVE REPRESENTATION

It has been notoriously difficult for researchers and theorists to agree on a definition of "emotion." This difficulty exists despite the ability of ordinary people in every culture with which we personally have come in contact to talk about the mental and behavioral states that psychologists have studied under the name "emotion"—for example, love, joy, anger, fear, and sadness, as well as more specifically designated states such as disappointment, hatred, and pride. In many languages there is a single name for this category of psychological states. In other languages there are (to our way of thinking) more metaphorical names for the category, such as "feelings of the heart" (e.g., *perasaan hati* in Indonesian; Shaver et al., 2001). (Of course, the word *emotion,* in its Latin roots, means to "be moved," which is also metaphorical.)

One way to get around initial linguistic barriers between cultures is to show people pictures of facial expressions of possible emotions or to provide them with examples of situations that typically evoke emotional reactions, such as being badly cheated, having one's most important goal achieved or impeded, or watching one's child die of illness. Usually, these states can be encompassed by a single term or two that can easily be agreed upon by multiple speakers of a particular language. Once the category name itself has been established, people are typically given a list of potential emotional states and asked to rate the extent to which they consider each to be an emotion. This is what Shaver and colleagues have done in numerous studies. Responses to such questions provide an index of the emotion-prototypicality of a given mental state name (i.e., the degree to which the state exemplifies "emotion"). In other studies, measures of emotion-prototypicality have been obtained by asking participants to list (by name) states they consider to be emotions (e.g., van Goozen & Frijda, 1993) and by recording the time it takes participants to determine whether or not a particular word names an emotion (e.g., Niedenthal et al., 2004).

Many people reading the literature on emotion names or cognitive representations of emotions think the authors are talking about "words" rather than emotions (e.g., Sabini & Silver, 2005), but no one who listens to a baseball game on the radio or attends a university lecture about modern cosmology thinks he or she is hearing only about words used to describe baseball games or the universe. Most people think they are hearing about an actual event that unfolds in reality pretty much as described (in the case of the baseball game) or an actual universe filled with galaxies and gravitational forces that developed over time (in the case of the cosmology lecture). Of these two ways of thinking about people's everyday discourse about emotions (i.e., as a discourse about words or as a rough characterization of the actual emotion domain), we prefer the latter.

THE PROTOTYPE APPROACH TO EMOTION CONCEPTS AS AN EXAMPLE

We are most familiar with the methods used by Shaver and colleagues (based on pioneering work by Fehr & Russell, 1984) in studies conducted in the United States, China, Indonesia, Italy, and Spain to examine the lexical representation of emotions. The theory behind those methods, called the "prototype approach to categorization," was first proposed by Rosch (1978; Rosch, Mervis, Gray, Johnson, & Boyes-Braem, 1976) in her writings about "fuzzy categories" in everyday language and cognition—categories for which there are no clear "classical" definitions based on necessary and sufficient features. Despite their inherent fuzziness, such categories can be roughly defined in terms of prototypes and central features, and arranged hierarchically according to conceptual levels, which Rosch (1978) called the *superordinate,* the *basic,* and the *subordinate* levels. This approach to categorization has continued to prove useful in studies of perceptual and linguistic development, memory, and social categorization.

An example of a fuzzy superordinate category is *animal,* which includes diverse category members and is difficult to define using necessary and sufficient features. Within that category are diverse creatures, such as dogs, birds, and snakes, that share few identical physical features but nonetheless are all members of the animal kingdom. Within the fuzzy basic-level category "birds," for example, there are subordinate-level categories—parrots, canaries, penguins, and so on—which differ as well but can be summarized in terms of a list of largely shared, though not universally shared, prototypical features (e.g., having feathers, flying, living in trees or other high places, and laying eggs in nests).

When Rosch's (1978) approach is applied to the domain of emotions, with emotions conceptualized as psychological or behavioral "objects" or "events"—that is, as subjectively experienced and objectively observable events that unfold in regular, script-like (though variable and context-sensitive) ways within particular episodes—it is possible to conceptualize their mental representations as event prototypes or scripts. (The nature of the scripts themselves was explored by Shaver et al. [1987].) Like other fuzzy categories, emotion categories can be arrayed hierarchically, in terms of superordinate, basic, and subordinate levels.

A formal picture of the underlying category system can be obtained by applying hierarchical cluster analysis to people's judgments about similarities and differences between differently named emotional states (e.g., anger, sadness, embarrassment). When this technique has been used in our studies, a fairly simple picture has arisen in each of the languages studied: At the top of the category hierarchy one finds a major split between what many psychologists call "hedonically positive" and "hedonically negative" emotions, indicating that this common distinction in academic psychology, like the common distinction between emotions and other psychological states, is a carryover from ordinary, everyday knowledge.

Moreover, there is usually a handful of what can be considered "basic-level" categories below the superordinate level, and these categories typically include love, happiness, anger, sadness, and fear. In particular cultures and languages, there are sometimes additional basic-level categories, including shame (e.g., in Chinese; Shaver et al., 1992). A separate surprise cluster emerges in Basque, Italian, and English; however, this cluster is considerably smaller and less differentiated than the other basic-level clusters, making its status as a basic-level category questionable. For present purposes, it makes no difference whether surprise is or is not considered to be a cognitively basic emotion because most of our attention will be focused on shame, guilt, embarrassment, and pride.

Theoretically, concepts at each level should function psychologically like the corresponding concepts in the domains of buildings, furniture, dramas, sports, and animals. People should tend to make preliminary "cuts" of the emotion domain at the basic level, they should be faster when categorizing basic-level emotions, and children should learn basic-level emotion concepts first during language acquisition. The existing empirical evidence supports these hypotheses (Bretherton & Beeghley, 1982; Bretherton, Fritz, Zahn-Waxler, & Ridgeway, 1986; Shaver et al., 1992; Zammuner, 1998). To the extent that different languages and cultures create different emotion category systems, people who live in different cultures and speak the associated languages should make different intuitive judgments about emotions in social situations, which might sometimes lead to different understandings, behaviors, and social outcomes.

Indices of emotion-prototypicality are generally consistent with hierarchical cluster analyses: Basic-level emotions tend to be rated as most emotion-prototypical; they are most likely to be nominated as emotions in free-listing tasks, and they are judged most quickly to be emotions. Below this level, and within each of the basic-level categories, there are many more explicitly named emotions (the number depending on the language and the associated culture), such as tenderness, relief, hatred, disappointment, and anxiety.

It is noteworthy that the five largest basic-level emotion categories identified in lexical studies overlap considerably with the emotions proposed by emotion researchers to be "basic" in a biological sense (e.g., Ekman, 1992; Izard, 1991). Although there is some variation across theorists, the list of biologically basic emotions typically includes joy, anger, fear, and sadness, as well as surprise, disgust, and possibly contempt. Interestingly, love is not generally considered to be a basic emotion (see Shaver, Morgan, & Wu, 1996), perhaps because it lacks a unique facial signal (but see Gonzaga, Keltner, Londahl, & Smith, 2001, for preliminary evidence regarding such signals). On the other hand, in lexical studies, disgust, surprise, and contempt seem less "basic" than love; they typically receive lower ratings of emotion-prototypicality, are more slowly recognized as emotions, and are less likely to be nominated as emotions in free-listing tasks. With the possible exception of surprise, these emotions tend to appear as subordinate categories in the hierarchical lexical structure.

For the purpose of the present chapter, which is descriptive, exploratory, tentative, and eclectic, we need not adopt any particular stance toward the meaning of the empirical results obtained with different abstract analytic procedures. We want mainly to understand where self-conscious emotions are situated in structural representations of the emotion domain, or the domain of emotion names and concepts, whichever domain one believes the results represent. Although the self-conscious emotions are less commonly included in taxonomies of basic emotions, they are sometimes considered "potential" candidates for basic status (e.g., Ekman, 1992; Izard, 1991; Kemeny, Gruenewald, & Dickerson, 2004). In the following sections, we discuss the status of shame, guilt, embarrassment, and pride in the hierarchical structure of emotion terms across languages and the extent to which these emotions are considered emotion-prototypical.

SHAME

Hierarchical Organization

Across languages, shame-related words are consistently found within the superordinate negative emotion cluster, often side by side with guilt (e.g., Brandt & Boucher, 1986; Church, Katigbak, Reyes, & Jensen, 1998). In Italian, for instance, shame and guilt appear together within the sadness cluster (along with remorse; Shaver et al., 1992), and these terms join the sadness cluster high in the hierarchy, suggesting the potential for a separate basic-level category if additional shame-related terms had been included in the analysis. In English, shame and guilt are also clustered closely together within the sadness category (along with remorse and regret; Shaver et al., 1987). However, there is no indication that either term would ever form a basic-level cluster in English. (Examining an English-language thesaurus confirms that there are very few words with similar but slightly different meanings compared with *shame*, unlike the case for words like *love*, *happiness*, and *anger*.)

Although Shaver et al. (2001) similarly located shame within the sadness cluster in Indonesian (along with hurt), Fontaine, Poortinga, Setiadi, and Markam (2002), using similarity ratings rather than a sorting procedure, found that shame fell into a larger fear cluster in both Indonesian (along with embarrassment, but not guilt) and Dutch (along with guilt). Shame also appears within the fear cluster in Basque (Alonso-Arbiol et al., 2006) and, along with guilt/discomfort, in Ifaluk (Lutz, 1982).

In fact, Wierzbicka (1986) claimed that, in some languages (e.g., Gidjingali, spoken in Aboriginal Australia), shame is not distinguished lexically from fear. The closest translation of shame, *kunta*, is associated with a desire to retreat or run away, as distinct from the desire to hide or disappear that is typically associated with shame in the North American psychological literature on emotion. In a similar vein, in some languages the equivalent of shame is an emotion that occurs *before* one commits an immoral act, in the way that fear occurs prior to a potentially threatening event, rather than as a response to committing an immoral or socially inappropriate act (e.g., Bilimoria, 1995; Wierzbicka, 1986). Indian philosophy, for instance, describes a shame-like emotion, *hri*, as the fear of social disapproval experienced before committing a misdeed, which may prevent the immoral behavior (Bilimoria, 1995).

Interestingly, in both Chinese (Shaver et al., 1992) and Japanese (Brandt & Boucher, 1986; Kobayashi, Schallert, & Ogren, 2003), shame-related emotions form a separate basic-level cluster (which includes guilt) within the superordinate negative emotion category. Shame-related terms also appear within other basic-level clusters in Chinese (e.g., rage from shame and shame/resentment in the anger cluster). In a more extensive analysis of 113 Chinese shame-related concepts (Li, Wang, & Fischer, 2004), at least two distinct subclusters were identified: "shame self-focus," which included guilt, and "reactions to shame, other-focus," which included embarrassment. The abundance and elaboration of shame terms in Chinese suggests that shame is discussed more frequently and in more detail (i.e., is "hypercognized"; Levy, 1973) in China than in other places. Consistent with this idea, Shaver et al. (1992) found that shame was among the first words learned by Chinese children: By age 2, approximately 70% of Chinese children (according to parental report) knew the Chinese word for shame, whereas even by age 3, only 10% of U.S. children were thought by their parents to know the English equivalent (Ridgeway, Waters, & Kuczaj, 1985).

The differential placement of shame and guilt in different lexical studies—sometimes within a large "sadness" category, sometimes within a large "fear/anxiety" category, and sometimes within its own basic-level category—demonstrates the subtleties inherent in everyday conceptions of emotion. It also shows why it will always be difficult to pin emotion concepts down to certain words or to substitute a technical vocabulary in the psychology of emotions for the everyday language of emotion. In cultures or situations where shame is associated with anxiety or ambivalence about committing a particular action or transgression, it is similar to other forms of anxiety, apprehension, and fear. But in cultures or situations where shame is conceptualized as an emotion that arises when a person has done something inappropriate, despicable, or regrettable, the emotion is viewed, appropriately, as akin to regret, remorse, and—more broadly—sadness. This suggests that the emotion itself partakes of, or blends with, other emotions, depending on the situation (either an actual situation or a culturally prototypical situation).

It is common on the listserv for the International Society for Research on Emotion for researchers to advocate moving away from everyday language and creating a technical language so that emotions such as shame, self-esteem, and love can be operationalized more precisely. This is similar to Cattell's (1957) early efforts to give names like "sizothymia/affectothymia," "threctia/parmia," "harria/premsia," and "praxernia/autia" to basic personality traits, and Ainsworth's (Ainsworth, Blehar, Waters, & Wall, 1978) efforts to call the three major attachment patterns in infancy "A," "B," and "C," rather than give them more natural English-language names. Present-day theorists and researchers retain these authors' ideas but now use terms like "warmth," "dominance," and "openness" for some of Cattell's personality trait dimensions and "avoidant," "secure," and "anxious" for Ainsworth's infant attachment categories. The same thing is likely to occur in studies of emotion because so much of our knowledge of emotion is wrapped up with the nuances of everyday experience, language, and social interaction that we would quickly lose our intellectual bearings if we attempted to abandon what we already know, albeit somewhat intuitively and implicitly, in favor of a technical language whose connections to reality are unclear to everyone except the language's inventor.

Forms of Cognitive and Linguistic Elaboration in the Emotion Domain

Shaver et al. (1987) noted, when discussing the relatively small number of cognitively "basic" emotion categories within the large English emotion lexicon, that there seem to be two main reasons for lexical elaboration. One is to mark *degrees of intensity*. For example, in English one can be "slightly embarrassed," "embarrassed," or "mortified"; one can be "annoyed," "angry," or "enraged"; one can be "apprehensive," "frightened," or "terrified." The other reason for creating new emotion words is to indicate something special or specific about the *situation* in which the emotion arises. For example, in English one could be "disappointed," which implies that one is sad or unhappy about having expected more than reality delivered; one could be "homesick," which implies that one is sad because of being away from home; and so on. The fact that Li et al. (2004) could find 113 shame-related words in Chinese is an indication that there are many designated levels of shame in China, and many specific kinds of situations in which shame arises.

This expectation is confirmed when we see the following attempts to translate some of the Chinese shame terms into English: "losing face," "truly losing face," and "losing face terribly." There is "being ashamed," but also "being ashamed to death." As if that were not sufficient, one can be "so ashamed that even the ancestors of eight generations can feel it." Beyond these remarkably specific designations of degrees of shame, there are many situation-specific shame words, which (when translated into English by Li et al., 2004) mean "hushing up a scandal (to avoid shame)," "family shame should not be made public," and "hiding one's illness from doctors (trying to hide shameful things)." There are specific words for being "afraid of being gossiped about" and "looking for a hole to climb into." There are also many fascinatingly graphic words for being shameless: "thick-skinned face without shame," "one's facial skin is even thicker than the corner of the city wall (absolutely no sense of shame)."

In contrast, English and Indonesian appear to have very few salient shame-related words. In Indonesian, among the 124 emotion-prototypical words examined by Shaver et al. (2001), only *malu* (shame, disgrace, mortification) qualified. Yet anthropological observations suggest that shame plays an important role in Indonesian social life, particularly in comparison with Western culture (Fessler, 1999, 2004). Consistent with such observations, Fessler (2004) found that the term *malu*, which was included in Shaver et al.'s (2001) study, is used considerably more often in Indonesia than the word *shame* is used in Southern California, and the situations associated with shame in Indonesia were somewhat different and more elaborately linked to other kinds of feelings than those in California. In Indonesian, the concept of shame was centered on inadequacy and social rejection and, consistent with Shaver et al.'s (2001) findings based on cluster analysis, was not closely linked with guilt (see also Brandt & Boucher, 1986). Also consistent with previous findings (Shaver et al., 1987; Brandt & Boucher, 1986), Fessler's shame cluster in English included only guilt, embarrassment, and humiliation, and was not linked to social rank or shyness. In Indonesia, shame was related to being "reluctant to approach someone of higher status," "embarrassed by others' importance," "feeling inferior," and feeling "stained" or "dirty."

Despite these differences, it is easy to imagine North American parallels to the situations implied by the Indonesian words in Fessler's (2004) study. People in North America can certainly be ashamed of their worn or dirty clothes, their less than polished manners, or their "uneducated" language; they can feel awkward and out of place at cocktail parties with famous or high-status individuals. Thus, as with most cross-cultural comparisons we have seen in the emotion literature, there is no indication that people in different cultures, or people speaking different languages, have wildly different experiences or conceptions of emotion (see also Frank, Harvey, & Verdun, 2000). It is likely, however, that certain emotions occur more often in one culture than another, are noticed more often and in more detail, matter more, and can be spoken about with greater precision and more easily. We agree with anthropologists and cross-cultural psychologists that these differences are likely to be important and worth understanding much better than we currently do.

Is Shame Ever Positive?

Although there is good evidence for the hypercognition of shame in some cultures (e.g., Chinese culture, as just mentioned), there is little support for the claim made by some emotion theorists that, in some societies, shame is a phenomenologically positive experience, or that shame is associated with positive emotions (e.g., Mesquita & Karasawa, 2004; Wallbott &

Scherer, 1995). Scheff (1994) argues that the English language is unique in that there is no distinction between positive and negative aspects of shame: In his view, most languages include a word (roughly translated as "humility"—e.g., *pudor* in Spanish) that emphasizes "everyday shame," which is "always a positive attribute" (p. 40). However, in the languages examined here, shame was consistently located within the superordinate *negative* emotion cluster, and even when more extensive analyses of shame-related words were conducted (Fessler, 2004; Li et al., 2004) the semantic domain of shame was always negatively valenced, at least in the minds of people who experienced shame.

This does not mean, however, that shame has no social value and is not looked upon favorably by people who would like to induce it in others. In English we can say, "He's shameless," and when we do, it means the person *should* be ashamed but is either too ignorant or too morally insensitive to realize it. We can say, "Have you no shame?," which means "Surely you *should* be ashamed," and so on. In the study by Li et al. (2004), there are many ways to say in Chinese "Even a devil would be scared of one who doesn't want to maintain his/her face (a shameless person is hopeless)." Li et al. (2004) mention other studies of Asian cultures that indicate that shame is viewed as a desirable state when it encourages people to behave properly. For example, "In Orissa, India, shame also indicates a heightened awareness and is seen and experienced both as a healthy emotion and an antidote to rage" (p. 768).

In fact, Menon and Shweder (1994) reported that Indian participants tended to associate shame with happiness, whereas U.S. participants were more likely to associate shame with anger. These findings could be taken as evidence that shame is positively valenced in India. However, in a replication of Menon and Shweder's study, Rozin (2003) found that the two cultures differed not in the *valence* attributed to shame, but in their means of classifying emotions: U.S. participants tended to classify emotions based on valence, whereas Indian participants were more likely to classify them based on their social effects. Because both shame and happiness are perceived to have positive effects on the social order, they were classified together. When asked to make classifications based on valence, both Indian and U.S. participants associated shame with anger. Conversely, when asked to make classifications based on the social effects of the emotion, both groups associated shame with happiness. Taken as a whole, these findings suggest that shame feels bad everywhere in the world when one experiences it oneself, but the capacity to experience shame in culturally appropriate situations is likely to be viewed everywhere as a socially desirable trait.

Measures of Prototypicality

In most samples in which prototypicality ratings have been obtained, shame is perceived as more prototypical of the emotion category than are the other self-conscious emotions (Alonso-Arbiol et al., 2006; Fontaine et al., 2002; Niedenthal et al., 2004; Smith & Smith, 1995; Zammuner, 1998). In fact, in several languages the prototypicality ratings of shame closely approximated those of the basic-level emotions (e.g., in Basque [Alonso-Arbiol et al., 2006]; in Italian [Zammuner, 1998]), and in most languages shame prototypicality ratings exceeded those for disgust, surprise, and contempt. There were a few exceptions: In Indonesia, pride received the highest rating, followed by shame (Shaver et al., 2001), and in English there was little difference among the ratings of guilt, shame, and embarrassment, although pride received the lowest emotion-prototypicality ratings of the four emotions (Shaver et al., 1987).

Other indices similarly suggest that shame is considered more emotion-prototypical than the other self-conscious emotions: Compared to guilt and embarrassment, shame was more likely to be nominated in free-listing tasks (Smith & Smith, 1995; van Goozen & Frijda, 1993; Zammuner, 1998; but see Fehr & Russell, 1984) and was recognized more quickly and accurately as an emotion (Niedenthal et al., 2004). In fact, shame was more likely to be nominated than some of the basic emotions (e.g., more so than surprise in Turkish, according to Smith and Smith [1995]; more so than disgust and contempt in Italian, according to Zammuner [1998]). It was recognized more quickly than disgust, contempt, and surprise in French (Niedenthal et al., 2004) and was more likely than disgust and surprise to be classified as an emotion in Filipino (Church et al., 1998).

These findings highlight the importance of shame across languages and the central role of this emotion in human social life. Together with anthropological evidence that a shame-like emotion is present across cultures (Fessler, 1999) and research suggesting that there is a unique behavioral shame display (e.g., Keltner & Buswell, 1996), such findings indicate that shame shares many qualities with the basic-level emotions (Kemeny et al., 2004). It may have been left off the "basic" lists in U.S. psychology partly because it is not as salient as other basic emotions in North America, and partly because its display is not limited to the face and is easier to detect when seen developing over time, in a social context. (Love has been neglected for similar reasons [Gonzaga et al., 2001; Shaver et al., 1996].)

GUILT

In several studies of emotion terms, guilt was not included because it received low emotion-prototypicality ratings in initial studies (e.g., in Basque [Alonso-Arbiol et al., 2006], in Indonesian [Shaver et al., 2001], and in Turkish [Smith & Smith, 1995]). In cases where it was included, guilt often clustered with shame and, at times, with embarrassment. In English and Italian, these three emotions are clustered together within the sadness cluster. In Dutch, guilt and shame also appear together, but within the fear cluster, and in Chinese, guilt falls within the basic-level shame cluster. (An equivalent of embarrassment was not included in either the Dutch or the Chinese studies.)

Thus, at least from a lexical perspective, findings regarding guilt and shame provide little support for social scientists' distinctions between these two emotions. Some have proposed that guilt is more important in individualistic cultures, whereas shame is more important in collectivistic cultures (e.g., Triandis, 1994). However, as described earlier, shame is generally perceived as a more prototypical emotion than guilt, with little variation across cultures. Even the dictionary (*American Heritage Dictionary of the English Language*, 2000) suggests close connections between shame and guilt, defining *shame* as "a painful emotion caused by a strong sense of guilt, embarrassment, unworthiness, or disgrace." *Guilt* is defined as a "remorseful awareness of having done something wrong," and "self-reproach for supposed inadequacy or wrongdoing." This might be a case where science *can* create more precise and scientifically useful distinctions than people make in their everyday conversations.

In fact, we believe this is precisely what Tangney (1990; see also Tangney & Dearing, 2002) has done. She retained the ordinary language terms "shame" and "guilt," but gave each word a technical definition and then operationalized her definitions in a carefully designed questionnaire. Pursuing that strategy, she was able to identify important correlates and consequences of shame and guilt, showing that the two constellations are quite different. In essence, guilt is "good," is associated with high self-esteem, and can result in improved social behavior; shame is "bad" and is associated with low self-esteem and destructive personal consequences. Perhaps, as has occurred with the distinction between "ordinary sadness" and "clinical depression," science will eventually influence everyday language and cause ordinary people to draw a sharper distinction between guilt and shame.

EMBARRASSMENT

Like guilt, embarrassment was not always included in studies of emotion terms because of low initial emotion-prototypicality ratings. When included, embarrassment was often located close to shame, either within the sadness cluster (in English [Shaver et al., 1987], in Italian [Shaver et al., 1992]) or the fear cluster (Indonesian [Fontaine et al., 2002]). In fact, several languages (e.g., Ifaluk [Lutz, 1982], Oriya of eastern India [Haidt & Keltner, 1999]) appear not to have a distinct term for embarrassment, possibly because of the high degree of semantic overlap between shame and embarrassment. Both intuition and the dictionary suggest that embarrassment is less serious and less deeply painful than shame: "feeling self-conscious or ill at ease, disconcerted." Most thesauruses list *awkwardness, humiliation, mortification,* and *shame* as substitutes for *embarrassment,* suggesting that *intense* embarrassment is similar to, or the same as, shame. If so, this may be a case where English has marked degrees of intensity within the shame category rather than naming two completely distinct emotions.

PRIDE

In most languages, pride falls within the positive emotion superordinate category and the joy/happiness category at the cognitively basic level. It is accompanied in this cluster by triumph in English (Shaver et al., 1987; Storm & Storm, 1987); by amazement, courage, and anticipation in Dutch (Fontaine et al., 2002); by boastful and surprise in Japanese (Brandt & Boucher, 1986); and by tranquil in Sinhalese (Brandt & Boucher, 1986). In Ifaluk, *bagbeg,* which is translated as "pride/love," falls into a cluster that Lutz labels "emotions of good fortune," which includes happiness and excitement and is indistinguishable from joy/happiness in other studies.

Several of the studies reviewed here included two (or more) words for pride, differing in their evaluative implications. In Indonesian, for instance, *besar hati* implies pride and elation, whereas *tinggi hati* is translated as "conceit" or "arrogance." French includes both *fierté* (pride) and *orgueil* (arrogant pride; Niedenthal et al., 2004). In Italian, *orgoglio* and *fierezza* correspond to justified and arrogant pride, respectively (although only *orgoglio* was included by Zammuner, 1998). As might be expected from this distinction, these two kinds of pride appear in different clusters in the emotion hierarchies. Justified or morally acceptable forms of pride are typically clustered with other positive emotions (e.g., triumph, pleasure). Arrogant pride tends to fall into a large anger cluster, which also includes envy, jealousy, disgust, and contempt (Alonso-Arbiol et al., 2006; Shaver et al., 1992, 2001). However, in an analysis of English emotion words, Storm and Storm (1987) found that all pride-related words were clustered together within the superordinate positive emotion category. Within this pride cluster, two distinct sub-clusters were evident: One included terms such as "triumph" and "victorious" and the other included terms such as "smug," "superior," and "arrogant." In this case, the tendency of some research participants to put multiple pride words into the same category, with many of them implying a positive emotional state, caused all of the pride words to end up on the positive side of the superordinate distinction between positively and negatively valenced emotions. A more extensive analysis of 20 pride-related words similarly revealed two dimensions of pride, one including words such as *confident, achieving,* and *victorious,* and another including words such as *haughty, arrogant,* and *pompous* (Tracy & Robins, 2007).

The Ifaluk language (Lutz, 1982) also appears to contain words for undesirable pride-like emotions: *gatinap* describes someone who is boastful about skills or intelligence, and *gabosbos* refers to a person who shows off material possessions. But these terms, which are typically used to describe someone else's behavior, not one's own feelings, were not included in Lutz's (1982) analysis of emotion words. This situation raises an important issue: We (North Americans and Ifalukians) tend to use different words when describing our own emotions than when describing someone else's emotions or emotional behavior, especially when we think another person's emotions or behaviors are reprehensible. If we ourselves accomplish something important, we are likely to view ourselves as justifiably proud; when our children perform well in school or athletics, our parental pride seems natural, very positive, and morally sensible. But when we see someone else "gloating" over a success, especially one we consider minor or undeserved, the words "arrogant," "smug," "boastful," and "self-satisfied" come to mind. This suggests that the term "negative emotion" has two meanings: negative in valence as experienced by oneself and negative in its effects on other people, no matter how good it may feel from the inside.

Tracy and Robins (2004, 2007) have argued, however, that both forms of pride, which they refer to as "authentic" and "hubristic" pride, can be used in a self-descriptive manner. Further, according to their model, authentic and hubristic pride are distinguished not only by their effects on others, but also by the extent to which pride-eliciting experiences are attributed to global, stable characteristics of the self (e.g., intelligence) versus specific, unstable factors (e.g., hard work). In this framework, global, stable attributions for success lead to hubristic pride, whereas specific, unstable attributions lead to authentic pride. In support of these ideas, Tracy and Robins (2007) found that some participants did rate words such as *arrogant* and *conceited* as self-descriptive when recalling past pride-eliciting experiences. People who rated these hubristic words highly were more likely to attribute their success to stable characteristics of the self, and they also scored higher on a measure of narcissism. These findings suggest that hubristic pride may not depend entirely on the evaluations of others. However, the idea that hubristic pride is a negative emotion primarily from an evaluative perspective has two further implications that have not yet, to our knowledge, been addressed. First, hubristic pride should be attributed more often to others than to oneself and, second, it should be a phenomenologically positive emotion for the person who experiences it.

CONCLUDING COMMENTS

We can draw several tentative conclusions from our examination of the sparse literature on shame, guilt, embarrassment, and pride in lexical studies of emotion terms. First, these emotions have been relatively neglected in lexical studies. Most lexical studies have been initiated and conducted by North American English speakers, in a part of the world where, until recently, scant attention has been paid to self-conscious emotions in psychology. Moreover, even if researchers had paid attention to words designating these emotions, English seems to be somewhat lacking in single-word names for them. For instance, although many languages make clear distinctions between two forms of pride (i.e., justified pride vs. smugness or arrogance), only "pride" in English was considered emotion-prototypical enough to qualify for inclusion in subsequent analyses. (This may be due in part to the fact that smugness and arrogance are not "feelings," but rather are ways of acting.) In addition, in the few lexical studies of English emotion terms, guilt, shame, and embarrassment all cluster closely together, suggesting that typical English speakers, even those attending college, do not draw clear distinctions among these emotions. Moreover, as we mentioned briefly, English dictionaries seem to draw the different emotions together in readers' minds rather than distinguish among them. This paucity of terms is certainly not a problem in languages like Chinese, but even there, where shame forms a basic-level category, guilt and embarrassment terms reside within the shame cluster, suggesting strong similarity. Thus, if psychologists wish to distinguish among shame, guilt, and embarrassment, as Tangney and her associates have done, they must refine or go beyond the distinctions embedded in everyday language.

Second, shame, guilt, and embarrassment are hedonically negative emotions, at least as experienced by people who are ashamed, guilt-ridden, or embarrassed, even though other people—including guilty, ashamed, and embarrassed people at times when they are not feeling these negative emotions—may view such states as socially desirable and useful. These "self-conscious" emotions play a role in social control and interpersonal relations, and are therefore unlikely to be ignored or eliminated by any society.

In contrast, although pride is a hedonically positive emotion, it may have negative connotations when it is expressed in an excessive, inconsiderate, or arrogant way. Terms related to arrogance were often placed in the anger category along with envy, jealousy, and contempt. Such classifications may reflect participants' perceptions of the source of arrogance, or simply the co-occurrence of these different emotions. This may also be a case of observers having a negative emotion in response to seeing another person experience what is for him or her a presumably positive emotion. Languages make this distinction in ways that research participants in lexical studies may not clearly understand. This may be one reason why, at least in English, emotions similar to arrogant pride were not considered prototypical emotions (e.g., vanity, superiority; Shaver et al., 1987), or were not included in initial lists of potential emotion terms. Such terms may also have been excluded because they often refer to trait-like behavior patterns (e.g., conceit, smugness) rather than emotional states.

Third, lexical studies conducted to date suggest that shame is the most distinctive and salient of the self-conscious emotions. It seems to play a larger role in some cultures and languages than either guilt or embarrassment, and at least in Chinese there are many words and ideas associated with it. It would be worthwhile to understand the reasons for shame's special status. One possibility, which is inherent in Tangney's work (e.g., Tangney & Dearing, 2002), is that guilt occurs when a person misbehaves in relation to specific rules, laws, or moral prescriptions. This can obviously be a serious matter for society, but it can often be handled by appropriate punishment or rectified in fairly straightforward ways (apologizing, paying restitution to the injured party, paying a fine to society, or serving a prison sentence). Shame involves a violation of something broader and deeper: society's definition of what it means to be a worthy, competent, good, and respectable person. Here, the implication seems to be that society can no longer count on a person to meet minimal standards for membership. Because of the strong links between perceived acceptance and social status, on the one hand, and one's feelings of self-worth, optimism, and self-confidence, on the other hand, entering a state of shame can do profound damage to a person's overall sense of well-being, safety, and self-respect. Embarrassment, by comparison, typically deals with much less serious violations of social standards, and can usually be erased by admitting a mistake or faux pas and showing a sincere wish to be admitted immediately back into a local group's good graces.

If this analysis is on the right track, it suggests that shame needs and deserves more linguistic concepts to cover its various forms and degrees of intensity. In Chinese, the requisite linguistic work appears to have been done, but in English it has not. This has made it necessary for English-speaking theorists like Lewis (1971) and Scheff (1994; Scheff & Retzinger, 1991) to analyze shame in great detail, for both clinical and research purposes. It might be worthwhile for psychologically trained speakers of Chinese to work with North American, English-speaking psychologists to flesh out our technical language for dealing with self-conscious emotions, especially shame. It is possible that this would speed our advancement toward an appropriately complex analytic framework for thinking about and assessing self-conscious emotions. It might also take the individualistic edge off our typical social behavior, making us more comfortable fellow citizens in an increasingly shrinking world.

REFERENCES

Ainsworth, M. D. S., Blehar, M. C., Waters, E., & Wall, S. (1978). *Patterns of attachment: A psychological study of the Strange Situation.* Hillsdale, NJ: Erlbaum.

Alonso-Arbiol, I., Shaver, P. R., Fraley, R. C., Oronoz, B., Unzurrunzaga, E., & Urizar, R. (2006). Structure of the Basque emotion lexicon. *Cognition and Emotion, 20,* 836–865.

American Heritage Dictionary of the English Language, The (4th ed.). (2000). New York: Houghton Mifflin.

Bilimoria, P. (1995). Ethics of emotion: Some Indian reflections. In J. Marks & R. T. Ames (Eds.), *Emotions in Asian thought: A dialogue in comparative philosophy* (pp. 65–90). Albany: State University of New York Press.

Brandt, M. E., & Boucher, J. D. (1986). Concepts of depression in emotion lexicons of eight cultures. *International Journal of Intercultural Studies, 10,* 321–346.

Bretherton, I., & Beeghley, M. (1982). Talking about internal states: The acquisition of an explicit theory of mind. *Developmental Psychology, 18,* 906–912.

Bretherton, I., Fritz, J., Zahn-Waxler, C., & Ridgeway, D. (1986). Learning to talk about emotions: A functionalist perspective. *Child Development, 57,* 529–548.

Cattell, R. B. (1957). *Personality and motivation structure and measurement.* Yonkers-on-Hudson, NY: World Book.

Church, A. T., Katigbak, M. S., Reyes, J. A. S., & Jensen, S. M. (1998). Language and organisation of Filipino emotion concepts: Comparing emotion concepts and dimensions across cultures. *Cognition and Emotion, 12,* 63–92.

Ekman, P. (1992). An argument for basic emotions. *Cognition and Emotion, 6,* 169–200.

Fehr, B., & Russell, J. A. (1984). Concept of emotion viewed from a prototype perspective. *Journal of Experimental Psychology: General, 113,* 464–486.

Fessler, D. M. T. (1999). Toward an understanding of the universality of second order emotions. In A.

L. Hinton (Ed.), *Biocultural approaches to the emotions* (pp. 75–116). New York: Cambridge University Press.

Fessler, D. M. T. (2004). Shame in two cultures: Implications for evolutionary approaches. *Journal of Cognition and Culture, 4,* 207–262.

Fontaine, J. R. J., Poortinga, Y. H., Setiadi, B., & Markam, S. (2002). Cognitive structure of emotion terms in Indonesia and the Netherlands. *Cognition and Emotion, 16,* 61–86.

Frank, H., Harvey, O. J., & Verdum, K. (2000). American responses to five categories of shame in Chinese culture: A preliminary cross-cultural construct validation. *Personality and Individual Differences, 28,* 887–896.

Gonzaga, G. C., Keltner, D., Londahl, E. A., & Smith, M. D. (2001). Love and the commitment problem in romantic relations and friendship. *Journal of Personality and Social Psychology, 81,* 247–262.

Haidt, J., & Keltner, D. (1999). Culture and facial expression: Open-ended methods find more faces and a gradient of recognition. *Cognition and Emotion,13,* 225–266.

Izard, C. E. (1991). Basic emotions, relations among emotions, and emotion–cognition relations. *Psychological Review, 99,* 561–565.

Keltner, D., & Buswell, B. N. (1996). Evidence for the distinctness of embarrassment, shame, and guilt: A study of recalled antecedents and facial expressions of emotion. *Cognition and Emotion, 10,* 155–171.

Kemeny, M. E., Gruenewald, T. L., & Dickerson, S. S. (2004). Shame as the emotional response to threat to the social self: Implications for behavior, physiology, and health. *Psychological Inquiry, 15,* 153–160.

Kobayashi, F., Schallert, D. L., & Ogren, H. A. (2003). Japanese and American folk vocabularies for emotions. *Journal of Social Psychology, 143,* 451–478.

Levy, R. I. (1973). *Tahitians: Mind and experience in the Society Islands.* Chicago: University of Chicago Press.

Levy, R. I. (1984). The emotions in comparative perspective. In K. R. Scherer & P. Ekman (Eds.), *Approaches to emotion* (pp. 397–412). Hillsdale, NJ: Erlbaum.

Lewis, H. B. (1971). *Shame and guilt in neurosis.* New York: International Universities Press.

Li, J., Wang, L., & Fischer, K. W. (2004). The organization of Chinese shame concepts. *Cognition and Emotion, 18,* 767–797.

Lutz, C. A. (1982). The domain of emotion words on Ifaluk. *American Ethnologist, 9,* 113–128.

Lutz, C. A. (1988). *Unnatural emotions: Everyday sentiments on a Micronesian atoll and their challenge to Western theory.* Chicago: University of Chicago Press.

Lutz, C. A., & White, G. M. (1986). The anthropology of emotions. *Annual Review of Anthropology, 15,* 405–436.

Menon, U., & Shweder, R. A. (1994). Kali's tongue: Cultural psychology and the power of shame in Orissa, India. In S. Kitayama & H. R. Markus (Ed.), *Emotion and culture: Empirical studies of mutual influence* (pp. 241–282). Washington, DC: American Psychological Association.

Mesquita, B., & Karasawa, M. (2004). Self-conscious emotions as dynamic cultural processes. *Psychological Inquiry, 15,* 161–166.

Niedenthal, P. M., Auxiette, C., Nugier, A., Dalle, N., Bonin, P., & Fayol, M. (2004). A prototype analysis of the French category "émotion." *Cognition and Emotion, 18,* 289–312.

Ridgeway, D., Waters, E., & Kuczaj, S. A. (1985). Acquisition of emotion-descriptive language: Receptive and productive vocabulary norms for ages 18 months to 6 years. *Developmental Psychology, 21,* 901–908.

Rosch, E. (1978). Principles of categorization. In E. Rosch & B. B. Lloyd (Eds.), *Cognition and categorization* (pp. 27–48). Hillsdale, NJ: Erlbaum.

Rosch, E., Mervis, C. B., Gray, W. D., Johnson, D. M., & Boyes-Braem, P. (1976). Basic objects in natural categories. *Cognitive Psychology, 8,* 392–439.

Rozin, P. (2003). Five potential principles for understanding cultural differences in relation to individual differences. *Journal of Research in Personality, 37,* 273–283.

Sabini, J., & Silver, M. (2005). Why emotion names and experiences don't neatly pair. *Psychological Inquiry, 16,* 1–10.

Scheff, T. J. (1994). *Bloody revenge: Emotions, nationalism, and war.* Boulder, CO: Westview Press.

Scheff, T. J., & Retzinger, S. M. (1991). *Emotions and violence: Shame and rage in destructive conflicts.* Lexington, MA: Lexington Books.

Shaver, P. R., Morgan, H. J., & Wu, S. (1996). Is love a basic emotion? *Personal Relationships, 3,* 81–96.

Shaver, P. R., Murdaya, U., & Fraley, R. C. (2001). Structure of the Indonesian emotion lexicon. *Asian Journal of Social Psychology, 4,* 201–224.

Shaver, P. R., Schwartz, J., Kirson, D., & O'Connor, C. (1987). Emotion knowledge: Further exploration of a prototype approach. *Journal of Personality and Social Psychology, 52,* 1061–1086.

Shaver, P. R., Wu, S., & Schwartz, J. C. (1992). Cross-cultural similarities and differences in emotion and its representation: A prototype approach. In M. S. Clark (Ed.), *Review of personality and social psychology: Vol. 13. Emotion* (pp. 175–212). Newbury Park, CA: Sage.

Smith, S. T., & Smith, K. D. (1995). Turkish emotion concepts: A prototype approach. In J. A. Russell & J. Fernandez-Dols (Eds.), *Everyday conceptions of emotion: An introduction to the psychology, anthropology, and linguistics of emotion* (pp. 103–119). New York: Kluwer Academic/Plenum Press.

Storm, C., & Storm, T. (1987). A taxonomic study of the vocabulary of emotions. *Journal of Personality and Social Psychology, 53,* 805–816.

Tangney, J. P. (1990). Assessing individual differences in proneness to shame and guilt: Development of the Self-Conscious Affect and Attribution Inventory. *Journal of Personality and Social Psychology, 59,* 102–111.

Tangney, J. P., & Dearing, R. L. (2002). *Shame and guilt.* New York: Guilford Press.

Tracy, J. L., & Robins, R. W. (2004). Putting the self into self-conscious emotions: A theoretical model. *Psychological Inquiry, 15,* 103–125.

Tracy, J. L., & Robins, R. W. (2007). The psychological structure of pride: A tale of two facets. *Journal of Personality and Social Psychology, 92,* 506–525.

Triandis, H. C. (1994). Major cultural syndromes and emotion. In S. Kitayama & H. R. Markus (Eds.), *Emotion and culture: Empirical studies of mutual influence* (pp. 285–308). Washington, DC: American Psychological Association.

van Goozen, S., & Frijda, N. H. (1993). Emotion words used in six European countries. *European Journal of Social Psychology, 23,* 89–95.

Wallbott, H. G., & Scherer, K. R. (1995). Cultural determinants in experiencing shame and guilt. In J. P. Tangney & K. W. Fischer (Eds.), *Self-conscious emotions: The psychology of shame, guilt, embarrassment, and pride* (pp. 465–487). New York: Guilford Press.

Wierzbicka, A. (1999). *Emotions across languages and cultures: Diversity and universals.* Cambridge, UK: Cambridge University Press.

Zammuner, V. L. (1998). Concepts of emotion: "Emotionness," and dimensional ratings of Italian emotion words. *Cognition and Emotion, 12,* 243–272.

12

Cultural Models of Shame and Guilt

YING WONG
JEANNE TSAI

Sin hath the devil for its father, shame for its companion, and
death for its wages.

—Thomas J. Watson Sr. (founder of IBM)

Men cannot live without shame. A sense of shame is the
beginning of integrity.

—Mencius (Chinese philosopher)

In the anthropological and cross-cultural literatures, much attention has been paid to
cultural differences in shame and guilt. Indeed, as early as the 1940s, Benedict (1946)
famously described Japanese culture as a "shame culture" and U.S. culture as a "guilt culture." Since then, several empirical studies have documented significant cultural variation
in the valuation, elicitors, and behavioral consequences of shame and guilt (e.g, Crystal,
Parrott, Okazaki, & Watanabe, 2001; Fischer, Manstead, & Mosquera, 1999; Kitayama,
Markus, & Masumoto, 1995; Li, Wang, & Fischer, 2004; Menon & Shweder, 1994;
Romney, Moore, & Rusch, 1997; Stipek, 1998). The majority of mainstream emotion research, however, has ignored these empirical findings. In this chapter, we argue that current models of shame and guilt would benefit by incorporating cross-cultural research
findings not only to achieve a more comprehensive understanding of shame and guilt, but
also to reveal how these models are embedded in Western cultural ideas and practices. We
first present the dominant model of shame and guilt in the emotion literature. Then we
demonstrate how this model reflects a view of the self that pervades many individualistic
cultural contexts, including the United States. Next we show how shame and guilt may
differ in cultures that promote a different view of the self. We present findings from the
cross-cultural literature supporting this argument. Finally, we discuss future research directions as well as practical implications of existing findings. But first we define our
terms.

DEFINITIONS

At their core, "shame" and "guilt" are feelings associated with being negatively evaluated (either by the self or others) because one has failed to meet standards and norms regarding what is good, right, appropriate, and desirable (H. B. Lewis, 1974). For this reason, shame and guilt are often referred to as "moral" emotions (Tangney & Stuewig, 2004). In addition, shame and guilt are referred to as "self-conscious" emotions because they require a concept of the self, or an ability to see the self as an object of evaluation (Tracy & Robins, 2004). Indeed, developmental research suggests that shame and guilt emerge only after children are able to recognize themselves in the mirror (M. Lewis, 1997).

We use the term "culture" to refer to historically derived and socially transmitted ideas (e.g., symbols, language, values, and norms) and practices (e.g., rituals, mores, laws), as well as artifacts (e.g., tools, media) and institutions (e.g., family structure) that are simultaneously products of human action and producers of future action (Kroeber & Kluckhohn, 1952, p. 181). For example, religious beliefs and practices created by individuals who lived centuries ago now guide and shape the thoughts and behaviors of individuals living today, just as religious beliefs and practices created today will shape the thoughts and behaviors of generations to come. Anthropologists and cultural psychologists have recently used the term "cultural model" to describe organized patterns of ideas and practices related to specific social, physical, and psychological phenomena, including the self and emotion (Fryberg & Markus, in press; Shore, 1996; Strauss, 1992).

DOMINANT MODELS OF SHAME AND GUILT

According to the dominant model of shame and guilt, people experience these emotions when they have done something "bad" or "wrong" in their own eyes or in the eyes of others. Thus, Tomkins, Sedgwick, and Frank (1995) described shame as "the affect of indignity, of defeat, of transgression, and of alienation . . . [it] is felt as an inner torment, a sickness of the soul" (p. 133). For this reason, as the epigraph by Thomas Watson Sr., the founder of IBM, suggests, shame and guilt are emotions that are devalued and that should be actively avoided.

However, in mainstream emotion research, scholars have also distinguished between shame and guilt. Some researchers have argued that although both emotions occur when someone has committed a transgression that results in being negatively evaluated by others, the emotions differ in the origin of the transgression. When people attribute their transgressions to their global and stable self ("I can't believe *I* did that"), they experience shame, but when people attribute their transgressions to transient actions or states ("I can't I believe I did *that*"), they experience guilt (H. B. Lewis, 1987; Tangney, 1991, 1998; Tracy & Robin, 2004). For example, if a person hits a tree while driving, the person feels guilt if she attributes her accident to being sick while driving, whereas the person feels shame if she attributes the accident to her own incompetence. Thus, shame is often viewed as more devastating to people's self-concepts and self-esteem than guilt.

Emotion researchers have differentiated between shame and guilt in other ways as well. For example, some scholars argue that the emotions differ in their orientation to self or others. While shame typically involves being negatively evaluated by *others* (real or imagined), guilt typically involves being negatively evaluated by *oneself* (e.g., Smith, Webster, Parrott, & Eyre, 2002). In other words, whereas shame has an "external" orientation (i.e., being oriented to others), guilt has an "internal" orientation (i.e., being oriented to the self).[1] Shame, therefore, is associated with the fear of exposing one's defective self to others. Guilt, on the other hand, is associated with the fear of not living up to one's own standards (Benedict, 1946; Kitayama et al., 1995). Consistent with this distinction, studies have found that compared to guilt, shame occurs more frequently in the presence of others (Smith et al., 2002). Similarly, Helen Block Lewis, an early leader in shame research, argued that people who experience shame are more sensitive to contextual cues and pay more attention to others than are those who experience guilt (H. B. Lewis, 1985; Tangney & Dearing, 2002).

Finally, in the dominant models of shame and guilt, guilt leads to reparative action, whereas shame does not. For instance, empirical findings suggest that in U.S. contexts, unlike experiencing shame, experiencing guilt leads to higher self-esteem and increases in empathy and perspective taking (e.g., Leith & Baumeister, 1998; Tangney, 1998). Moreover, shame-prone individuals are more likely to engage in avoidance and withdrawal, to experience inward anger, and to blame others than are guilt-prone individuals (e.g., Lutwak, Panish, Ferrari, & Razzino, 2001; Tangney, 1991; Tangney & Fischer, 1995). This pattern of results may explain why in U.S. samples high levels of shame have been linked to mental illness (see Ferguson, Stegge, Miller, & Olsen, 1999; H. B. Lewis, 1987; Scheff, 1998; Tantam, 1998; Tracy & Robin, 2004) and physiological stress (Dickerson, Gruenewald, & Kemeny, 2004; Gruenewald, Kemeny, Aziz, & Fahey, 2004).

In summary, according to the mainstream emotion literature, people experience shame and guilt when they have violated standards or norms (e.g., see Hoblitzelle, 1987; H. B. Lewis, 1987; Tangney, 1991). However, whereas shame occurs when one is negatively evaluated by others for behaving inappropriately, involves global and stable attributions for transgressions, and is associated with maladaptive consequences, guilt occurs when one negatively evaluates one's own self for behaving inappropriately, involves specific and temporary attributions for transgressions, and is associated with adaptive consequences.

Assumptions of Prevailing Models of Shame and Guilt

This view of shame and guilt, however, rests on assumptions that may not apply to other cultural contexts. For example, the notion that global, stable attributions lead to shame and specific, temporary attributions lead to guilt assumes that there is a stable self that can be differentiated from one's temporary actions. Similarly, the notion that shame has an external orientation (i.e., is oriented to others' standards or social norms) whereas guilt has an internal orientation (i.e., is oriented to one's own standards) assumes that internal and external orientation can be easily separated, and that internal orientation is more powerful and genuine than external orientation. These assumptions reflect a view of the self that is bounded, separate from others, and defined by stable personal characteristics, or what Markus and Kitayama (1991) refer to as an "independent" self-construal. Finally, the dominant model assumes that being negatively evaluated by others or by oneself is bad and should be "actively avoided." This assumption may reflect the value placed on feeling good in many North American contexts (Heine, Lehman, Markus, & Kitayama, 1999).

Given the significant body of research that has demonstrated that U.S. culture promotes the independent self (e.g., Markus & Kitayama, 1991; Triandis, 1995), and given that most models of shame and guilt are based on Western samples, it is likely that the view of shame and guilt that pervades mainstream emotion research is an individualistic, or, even more specifically, an American one. Thus, if we look to other cultures rooted in other philosophical traditions that have different views of the self, it is possible that different views of shame and guilt will emerge (Mesquita & Karasawa, 2004; Camras & Fatani, 2004; Kitayama et al., 1995).

For example, in contrast to "individualistic" countries such as the United States that emphasize "independent" concepts of the self, "collectivistic" countries such as China, Japan, and Korea, promote "interdependent" concepts of the self. Individuals with "interdependent" conceptions of the self view themselves in terms of their connections with others (Markus & Kitayama, 1991; Triandis, 1995). Thus, external influences (i.e., other people's thoughts and feelings) are as important and meaningful as internal ones (i.e., one's own thoughts and feelings). In these cultural contexts, selves are contextually and situationally dependent, and therefore situational changes in concepts of the self are viewed as normative (Kondo, 1990). For instance, in cultures influenced by Confucian values where individuals are encouraged to constantly cultivate and improve themselves, changes in the self are explicitly valued and expected (Cho, 2000). Moreover, few, if any, aspects of the self are seen as immutable (Li & Wang, 2004). Thus, in these contexts, feeling bad about the self is not only normal, but to some degree expected because it serves the larger goal of self-improvement. In the next section, we illustrate how having an "interdependent" self-construal may result in different models of shame and guilt.

COLLECTIVISTIC MODELS OF SHAME AND GUILT

Given the importance of the self in the emotions of shame and guilt, we hypothesize that having an "interdependent" self-construal should alter the valuation, elicitors, and behavioral consequences of these emotions. Having an interdependent self-construal may even render the distinction between shame and guilt less clear than having an independent self-construal. We discuss this point first.

Distinction between Shame and Guilt

As discussed above, dominant models of shame and guilt clearly differentiate between these two emotions. However, this distinction may apply less in cultures that promote interdependent selves. For instance, Li et al. (2004) produced a list of terms related to shame in the Chinese lexicon by consulting the dictionary and by asking research subjects to generate terms related to shame. Another set of research subjects then grouped the terms into different categories on the basis of how similar or different the terms were to each other. Hierarchical cluster analyses revealed that participants viewed guilt as a component of shame rather than as a separate construct. Indeed, when translated into English, some Chinese terms that are related to shame are often translated as guilt (e.g., *kui* 愧), or as a combination of shame and guilt (e.g., *xiucan* 羞惭 and *xiukui* 羞愧) in English (Li et al., 2004).

Interestingly, research has also revealed that European Americans view shame and guilt as closely related. For example, in a study by Shaver, Schwartz, Kirson, and O'Conner (1982), guilt, shame, regret, and remorse clustered together as a subfactor of sadness. However, this study broadly examined the similarity of 135 emotions, and therefore, compared to the other emotions, it may not be surprising that guilt and shame were seen as similar to each other. In contrast, the Li et al. (2004) study looked more specifically at the structure of shame and guilt only. In this context, there was little difference between guilt and shame. Therefore, research that examines the structure of shame compared specifically to guilt in European American samples is needed.

In many collectivistic cultures, the differences in the attributions associated with shame and guilt appear less pronounced. Whereas in individualistic contexts shame is associated with global and stable attributions, and guilt is associated with specific and temporary attributions, in collectivistic contexts Wikan (1984) found that shame is associated with temporary and specific actions rather than their global and stable characteristics. Swartz (1988) also argues that among the Swahili of Mombasa, shame may result from the actor's belief that others view his *actions* negatively. These findings suggest that in some cultural contexts shame is associated with the same attributions that are associated with guilt in U.S. contexts.

There is other evidence that shame and guilt may be more similar than different in collectivistic contexts. For instance, when Bedford (2004) interviewed Taiwanese Chinese subjects, she found three subtypes of "guilt" and four subtypes of "shame" in Chinese that are not distinguishable from each other in English. Although most subtypes of shame involved violations of others' expectations and being negatively evaluated by others, one subtype of shame did not involve others' judgments, and therefore resembled U.S. guilt. In addition, many subtypes of shame prompted increases in prosocial behavior, again making it more similar to than different from U.S. guilt. For instance, Bedford argued that *can kui*, a form of Chinese shame, "functions to prompt people to try their best possible" (p. 46) and the fear of *xiu kui*, which one feels when one discovers deficiencies in oneself, is usually enough to deter shame-inducing actions.

In the few instances when the distinction between shame and guilt has been made in collectivistic contexts, the basis of this distinction is also different from that of many individualistic, Western contexts. For instance, in describing shame and guilt in Chinese culture, Bedford and Hwang (2003) argue that guilt is more effective as a regulatory emotion in individualistic cultures because it is associated with a general code of ethics (held by oneself and others), but shame is more effective in collectivistic cultures because it associated with a code of ethnics that varies by situation and relationship (again, held by oneself as well as others). Thus, in Chinese culture, people experience guilt when they feel an absolute standard is violated, whereas people experience shame when a situation-specific standard is violated. In Western cultures, shame and guilt are not distinguished in this way. Because Confucianism focuses more on situations and relations, and Confucianism is a dominant philosophical tradition in many East Asian contexts, experiencing shame in these contexts is more appropriate than experiencing guilt (Cho, 2000; Bedford & Hwang, 2003).

Recently, Breugelmans and Poortinga (2006) argued that the distinctions between guilt and shame hold across cultures, even when cultures do not have a word for "guilt." They presented Rarámuri and Javanese subjects with scenarios of shame and guilt generated by another group of Rarámuri and Javanese subjects, and asked subjects to rate the scenarios on different attributes associated with shame and guilt, such as "powerless and small," "sweating," and "will change behavior." They then conducted multidimensional scaling analyses on subjects' responses and compared the results to responses provided by Dutch and Indonesian students. A similar guilt–shame dimension emerged in all three samples, leading the authors to argue that guilt is distinct from shame. However, a number of the attributes clustered differently in Rarámuri and Javanese samples when compared to Dutch and Indonesian samples. For instance, "change behavior," an attribute that has been viewed as a defining feature of guilt according to dominant models of emotion, is associated with shame in Rarámuri and Javanese cultures, suggesting some overlap between the two.

In summary, shame and guilt may be less differentiated in collectivistic contexts because in these contexts people do not view themselves as separate from their relationships with others, their contexts, or their actions. Consequently, there is less emphasis placed on having an "internal" orientation in collectivistic than in individualistic contexts (Morling, Kitayama, & Miyamoto, 2002; Weisz, Rothbaum, & Blackburn, 1984). Therefore, the differences between shame and guilt in individualistic cultures, which largely rest on this distinction, may be less pronounced in collectivistic cultures. Future research is needed to test this hypothesis.

Valuation of Shame

As suggested by the Chinese proverb that opened this chapter, in many non-Western cultural contexts shame is not only valued, but is also viewed as an appropriate emotional response to failure. Indeed, according to the anthropologist David Jordan (n.d.), shame in Chinese cultures is "the ability or tendency to . . . *take delight in the performance of one's duty*" (see also Bedford, 2004). The positive value placed on shame in many non-Western cultural contexts is consistent with the interdependent goals of self-effacement, adjustment to group standards and norms, and self-improvement. Research supports this point. For example, in a study by Kitayama, Markus, Matsumoto, and Norasakkunkit (1997), Japanese were found to view failure events that induced self-criticism as more relevant to their self-esteem than did Americans, whereas Americans viewed success situations that enhanced their self-views as more relevant to their self-esteem than did Japanese. These findings suggest that negatively evaluating the self, a core component of shame, is not universally viewed as harmful to psychological well-being. Indeed, negative views of the self may have informational and motivational significance in collectivistic contexts.

For these reasons, shame may be viewed more positively in collectivistic contexts. Indeed, in Indian culture, a popular Hindu story describes how the diety Kali's shame saved the world (Menon & Shweder, 1994). In addition, Menon and Shweder (1994) presented Hindu and American participants with a list of three emotions (shame, happiness, and anger), and asked them to identify the emotion that was the most different from the other two. Whereas Americans viewed happiness as being the most different from shame and anger, the Hindu Indians viewed anger as being the most different from happiness and shame. These findings suggest that the Hindu Indians viewed shame more positively than did their European American counterparts. In a subsequent study, Rozin (2003) replicated these findings and found that Americans viewed shame and anger as more similar to each other because they are both viewed as negatively valenced, whereas Hindu Indians viewed shame and happiness as more similar to each other because they are both viewed as socially constructive.

Studies conducted in other collectivistic contexts corroborate this point. For instance, Fischer et al. (1999) found that Spanish individuals held more positive beliefs about shame and therefore were more likely to express shame and share their experiences of shame with others compared to their Dutch counterparts. In a survey study of European American, Asian American, and Hong Kong Chinese college students conducted in our lab, we observed that Hong Kong Chinese valued shame more (or devalued it less) than Asian Americans and European Americans, even after controlling for differences in how much shame they actually felt (Tsai, 2006). And in a study comparing the semantic structure of various emotions, Romney et al. (1997) found that shame was viewed as more similar to positive states such as excitement, love, and happiness for Japanese speakers than for English speakers, for whom shame was more similar to negative emotions such as anguish and fear.

Research also demonstrates that parents in Chinese culture are more likely to use shaming techniques in their educational strategies than are parents in U.S. culture (Fung, 1999; Fung & Chen, 2001; Fung, Lieber, & Leung, 2003). Chinese parents readily discuss and disclose children's transgressions in front of strangers to induce shame and to socialize children to behave properly. Consequently, Chinese children learn the word *shame* at an earlier age than do children in the United States and England (Shaver et al., 1992).

Given the greater valuation (or lesser devaluation) of shame in collectivistic cultures compared to individualistic ones, it should not be surprising that in many East Asian and other collectivistic contexts shame plays a more salient role in everyday life (e.g., Crystal et al., 2001). For instance, Wikan (1984) observed that in the Egyptian and Omani cultures, "everyone is judged by *some* significant others to be blemished by shame" (p. 636). Similarly, Kilborne (1992) argues that in many societies where anthropologists conduct their fieldwork, the possibility of experiencing shame is omnipresent and salient during interpersonal interactions. Moreover, compared to U.S. culture, Chinese culture has more elaborate models of shame and guilt. For example, Shaver et al. (2002) found that shame and guilt, along with remorse and regret, jointly formed a separate category of emotions for Chinese, whereas these emotions were part of the sadness category for U.S. culture. Similarly, Russell and Yik (1996) argue that shame is hypercognized in the Chinese language. Li et al. (2004) found 83 shame-related terms in a Chinese dictionary, and their Chinese subjects were able to provide even more terms and phrases that described shame—in total, they came up with a list that contained 113 shame-related terms. Such an abundance of shame terms suggests that the Chinese conception of shame may be more complex than that of English-speaking cultures.

These findings also suggest that shame is a "focal" emotion (Frijda & Mesquita, 1994) in many collectivistic contexts, or an emotion that is salient and commonly experienced. Indeed, in a study by Cole, Bruschi, and Tamang (2002), children from two South Asian cultures—Tamang and Brahman—and U.S. culture were asked how they would feel in certain hypothetical situations. These children were asked to read scenarios and think about what emotions they would feel. Tamang children were more likely to endorse shame as the emotion they would feel in difficult situations compared to Brahman and U.S. children. In contrast, Brahman and U.S. children were more likely to endorse anger as the emotion they would feel than were Tamang children. These findings suggest that shame is viewed as a more appropriate response than anger among certain cultural groups, even among young children. In another line of research, Tinsley and Weldon (2003) found that Chinese managers in Hong Kong are more likely to use shame to resolve conflicts than are U.S. managers. In contrast, U.S. managers are more likely to use shame to punish their employees than are Hong Kong Chinese managers (Tangney & Dearing, 2002). More direct comparisons, however, are needed to confirm this cultural difference.

Elicitors of Shame

The elicitors or triggers of shame and guilt also differ in individualistic versus collectivistic contexts. Because Western cultural contexts assume a self that is separate from others, only the individual who committed the transgression typically feels shame or guilt. However, collectivistic cultural contexts assume a self that is connected to and exists in relationship with others. Therefore, in collectivistic models of shame and guilt, these emotions may be induced by others' actions (Camras & Fatani, 2004). Some research evidence supports this hypothesis. In another study, participants were presented with scenarios in which either they or a close family member was responsible for hypothetical transgressions. Compared to European American participants, Chinese were more likely to report feeling ashamed and guilty in response to a family member's (e.g., mother, brother) transgressions (Stipek, 1998). Similarly, we found that when we asked participants to describe different shame episodes in their lives, compared to European Americans, Hmong Americans were more like to describe actions committed by another person (e.g., "someone in my clan"). In other words, European Americans experience shame in response to something that they themselves did, whereas East Asians experience shame in response to something that someone close to them did (Tsai, 2006). Consistent with this finding, in his interviews with European American and Asian American college students, Liem (1997) found that when asked to describe a past shame event, Asian American students were more likely to talk about events experienced by close others than were European Americans.

Moreover, although shame may include some degree of public exposure across contexts, individuals with interdependent selves might be more likely to experience shame in the presence of others because they are more attentive to others. In support of this hypothesis, Chinese American and European American dating couples were brought into a lab and asked to discuss an area of conflict in their relationships. Half of these couples discussed the conflict in a room by themselves, while the other half discussed the conflict in the presence of an authority figure. Tsai (1996) found that while European American couples who discussed the conflict in private reported more shame than those who discussed the conflict in public (i.e., in front of the authority figure), Chinese American couples in public reported more shame than those in private (i.e., in a room by themselves). This finding supports Morisaki and Gudykunst's (1994) claim that the relationship between the ashamed person and the people with whom he or she is ashamed is a particularly important facet of the experience of shame for East Asians.

Behavioral Consequences of Shame

Western models of shame and guilt view shame as the "bad" and guilt as the "good" moral emotion, in part because of their different psychological, social, and physical consequences. Cross-cultural studies, however, suggest that shame may have better and more adaptive consequences in collectivistic contexts. For instance, Bagozzi, Verbeke, and Gavino (2003) found that although salespersons in the Netherlands and the Philippines experience shame when they have a painful experience that is threatening to the self, feelings of shame led Dutch salespersons to take self-protective actions, such as disengaging from customers and devoting fewer mental resources to the immediate task at hand. In contrast, feelings of shame led Philippino salespersons to engage in more relationship building and to be more courteous to their customers. In another study, Wallbott and

Scherer (1995) asked members of 37 different countries to describe episodes of shame and guilt. They found that shame caused less disruption in collectivistic cultures than in individualistic cultures. As stated earlier, we believe this is because in cultures that promote interdependent selves the experience of shame is consistent with cultural norms.

To summarize, these findings suggest that the valuation, elicitors, and behavioral consequences, as well as the distinction between shame and guilt, varies systematically across individualistic and collectivistic cultures. These findings suggest that some of the core assumptions about shame and guilt held by dominant models in the emotional literature may not apply to more collectivistic contexts. Consequently, they may motivate emotion researchers to consider further the aspects of shame and guilt that may be universal and those that may be culturally constituted. Clearly, much more research needs to be done in this area, especially with other cultural samples. In the next section, we outline some obvious and promising avenues for future research.

FUTURE RESEARCH DIRECTIONS

First, more research is needed to differentiate among the various types of shame and guilt observed in different cultural settings. As mentioned earlier, in the Chinese language, there are over 100 terms for shame (Li et al., 2004; Russell & Yik, 1996; Bedford, 2004). In addition to assessing whether these variations of shame and guilt exist in the United States or other individualistic contexts, it would also be important to examine how they differ from each other and why they exist. One possibility is that they reflect different types of the self. For example, researchers who study "face" (i.e., "public self," or the positive aspects of the self that people want others to see) have identified at least three kinds of face: face concerning one's own image ("self face," or presenting positive aspects of the individual), face concerning another person ("other face," or presenting positive aspects of another person), and face that is shared between people ("mutual face," or presenting positive aspects of the relationship) (see Ting-Toomey & Kurogi, 1998). Since loss of face elicits intense shame in Chinese culture, it is possible that variation in the types of shame reflect these different types of public self. Another relevant distinction is between people who view the self as fixed ("entity theorists") versus those who view the self as malleable ("incremental theorists") (Dweck, 1999). It is possible that in Western cultural contexts, incremental theorists may be more likely to experience guilt than shame (see Tracy & Robin, 2006). However, when they experience shame, they may be more likely to engage in self-improving rather than in self-defeating behaviors. Thus, even in Western cultural contexts, there may be a form of shame that leads to adaptive behaviors as well as one that leads to maladaptive behaviors. Again, examining different forms of shame and guilt should address this and other questions.

Second, although we argue that cultural variation in the valuation, eliciting events, and behavioral consequences of shame are due to different self-construals, no studies have actually demonstrated this link. Therefore, future studies are needed to illustrate that the differences described by many scholars are in fact due to differences between individualistic and collectivistic conceptions of the self.

Third, more studies are needed that measure the physiological and behavioral components of shame and guilt. This is particularly important when studying shame and guilt across cultures because of the difficulty of accurately translating emotion terms (Wierzbicka, 1999). Unfortunately, most cross-cultural studies of shame have relied on self-reports, despite the fact that physiological and behavioral indices of shame exist (Keltner, 1995; Kemeny, Gruenewald, & Dickerson, 2004). For example, we found that Chinese American couples expressed more shame than did European American couples while discussing an area of conflict in their relationships, despite the fact that there were no group differences in how much shame couples reported feeling (instead, the groups differed in terms of the context in which they reported feeling shame, as mentioned above) (Tsai, 1996). Chinese American couples may have behaviorally expressed more shame because shame is the appropriate emotion to show in collectivistic contexts in response to transgressions. These findings suggest that cultural values may have a differential impact on the reported experience and behavioral expression of shame and guilt. Indeed, in a previous study, we found that cultural factors shaped positive and negative expressive behavior even more than reports of positive and negative emotional experience (Tsai, Levenson, & McCoy, 2006). Thus, whereas participants' reports of shame may have more strongly reflected how they were actually feeling, their behavioral expressions of shame may have more strongly reflected how they thought they *should* or how they *would like* to feel.

Fourth, future research should examine the development of shame and guilt across cultural contexts. As suggested by previous research, the development of shame and guilt are closely linked to the development of the self (H. B. Lewis, 1974). Thus, in U.S. contexts, children may learn to avoid shame at the same time that they are learning to value feeling good about themselves (i.e., having high self-esteem) (Kitayama, Markus, & Kurokawa, 2000; Twitchell, 1997). Similarly, in collectivistic contexts, the value placed on shame may emerge at the same time children are learning to adjust to group norms. Consistent with this hypothesis, Miller, Wiley, Fung, and Liang (1997) found that while U.S. personal storytelling focused on entertainment (and elicited positive emotions), Chinese personal storytelling focused on morality (and elicited shame). Moreover, by examining the development of shame and guilt across the lifespan, researchers can begin to identify the specific ways in which values and beliefs regarding shame and guilt are socially transmitted.

Fifth, within each culture there exists variation in models of shame and guilt. For example, although the model of shame and guilt that dominates U.S. culture is the one we started this chapter with, less popular models of shame and guilt also exist. Indeed, while Thomas Watson's quote represents the dominant model of shame and guilt in Western cultural contexts, George Bernard Shaw (1903/1987) also expressed a model of shame that resembles the collectivistic cultural model of shame: "The more things a man is ashamed of, the more respectable he is." We predict that variation within cultural contexts may be due to the within-culture variation in self-construals. Future research is needed to test this hypothesis.

Finally, more theories of shame and guilt that incorporate cultural factors are needed. At a broader level, more work is needed to integrate different perspectives on cultural similarities and differences in emotion. As Goetz and Keltner (Chapter 9, this volume) argue, different levels of analyses (e.g., at the level of individuals or cultures) might lead to different conclusions about cultural universality versus cultural specificity for self-conscious emotions. They also argue that different components of self-conscious emotions, because of their different functions, vary on the cultural universality continuum. Thus, more theoretical work is needed to achieve a unified understanding about evolutionary and sociocultural influences on emotion.

PRACTICAL IMPLICATIONS

Because our worlds are becoming increasingly multicultural, cross-cultural research on shame and guilt is becoming increasingly significant in a variety of applied settings. For example, in educational settings, U.S. teachers place great emphasis on promoting their students' self-esteem (Reasoner, 1992). While such gestures may be motivating for students from individualistic cultural contexts, they may be less motivating for students from collectivistic ones. Similarly, while U.S. teachers may find that students from individualistic cultural contexts are harmed when shamed, students from collectivistic cultural contexts may actually be helped when shamed (e.g., motivated to improve their performance). Similarly, in Western clinical practice, therapists are trained to look for and then remove their patients' shame and/or guilt (Kaufman, 1989). Obviously, this is appropriate in cultural contexts for which shame has maladaptive effects. However, in contexts in which shame has adaptive effects, eradicating shame may have negative psychological and social consequences. While more research in the educational and mental health domains are clearly needed, the existing research findings suggest that cultural differences in shame and guilt must be taken into account in these settings.

CONCLUSION

Although words for shame and guilt exist in various languages (Casimir & Schnegg, 2002), an increasing body of literature suggests that the valuation, elicitors, and behavioral consequences of shame differ across cultural contexts. Indeed, the epigraphs at the beginning of this chapter suggest vastly different conceptions of shame. In this chapter, we have proposed that the valuation, elicitors, and behavioral consequences of shame vary as a function of the type of self-construal that is promoted in one's cultural context. In contexts that promote an independent self, shame and guilt are both devalued emotional states; they are experienced by people who commit transgressions, and there are clear distinctions between the two states. Because guilt is based on internal standards and leads to adaptive consequences, it is preferred to shame, which is based on external standards and leads to maladaptive consequences. However, in contexts that promote an interdependent self, shame and guilt are viewed more positively; people can feel shame and guilt for actions that they themselves did not commit, and there is less of a distinction between shame and guilt. Most importantly, in these contexts, experiencing shame is associated with adaptive consequences. These findings suggest that current models of shame and guilt—which assume an independent self—may be incomplete when applied to other cultural contexts. It is our hope that by providing a review of the cross-cultural literature on shame and guilt, we will prevent future models of shame and guilt from suffering the same fate.

NOTE

1. The terms "internal" and "external" have been used in numerous—and sometimes opposing—ways in the literature (e.g., see Kilborne, 1992).

REFERENCES

Bagozzi, R. P., Verbeke, W., & Gavino, J. C. Jr. (2003). Culture moderates the self-regulation of shame and its effects on performance: The case of salespersons in the Netherlands and the Philippines. *Journal of Applied Psychology, 88*, 219–233.

Bedford, O. A. (2004). The individual experience of guilt and shame in Chinese culture. *Culture and Psychology, 10*, 29–52.

Bedford, O. A., & Hwang, K. K. (2003). Guilt and shame in Chinese culture: A cross-cultural framework from the perspective of morality and identity. *Journal for the Theory of Social Behaviour, 33*, 127–144.

Benedict, R. (1946). *The chrysanthemum and the sword: Patterns of Japanese culture.* Boston: Houghton Mifflin.

Breugelmans, S. M., & Poortinga, Y. H. (2006). Emotion without a word: Shame and guilt among Raramuri Indians and rural Javanese. *Journal of Personality and Social Psychology, 91*, 1111–1122.

Camras, L. A., & Fatani, S. S. (2004). Development, culture, and alternative pathways to self-conscious emotions: A commentary on Tracy and Robins. *Psychological Inquiry, 15*, 166–170.

Casimir, M. J., & Schnegg, M. (2002). Shame across cultures: The evolution, ontogeny and function of a "moral emotion." In H. Keller & Y. H. Poortinga (Eds.), *Between culture and biology: Perspectives on ontogenetic development* (pp. 270–300). New York: Cambridge University Press.

Cho, H. (2000). Public opinion as personal cultivation: A normative notion and a source of social control in traditional China. *International Journal of Public Opinion Research, 12*, 299–325.

Cole, P. M., Bruschi, C. J., & Tamang, B. L. (2002). Cultural differences in children's emotional reactions to difficult situations. *Child Development, 73*, 983–996.

Crystal, D. S., Parrott, W. G., Okazaki, Y., & Watanabe, H. (2001). Examining relations between shame and personality among university students in the United States and Japan: A developmental perspective. *International Journal of Behavioral Development, 25*, 113–123.

Dickerson, S., Gruenewald, T., & Kemeny, M. (2004). When the social self is threatened: Shame, physiology, and health. *Journal of Personality, 72*, 1191–1216.

Dweck, C. S. (1999). *Self-theories: Their role in motivation, personality, and development.* Philadelphia: Taylor & Francis/Psychology Press.

Ferguson, T. J., Stegge, H., Miller, E. R., & Olsen, M. E. (1999). Guilt, shame, and symptoms in children. *Developmental Psychology, 35*, 347–357.

Fischer, A. H., Manstead, A. S. R., & Mosquera, P. M. R. (1999). The role of honour-related vs. individualistic values in conceptualising pride, shame, and anger: Spanish and Dutch cultural prototypes. *Cognition and Emotion, 13*, 149–179.

Frijda, N. H., & Mesquita, B. (1994). The social roles and functions of emotions. In S. Kitayama & H. Markus (Eds.), *Emotion and culture: Empirical studies of mutual influence* (pp. 51–87). Washington, DC: American Psychological Association.

Fryberg, S. A., & Markus, H. R. (in press). Cultural models of education in American Indian, Asian American, and European American contexts. *Social Psychology of Education.*

Fung, H. (1999). Becoming a moral child: The socialization of shame among young Chinese children. *Ethos, 27*, 180–209.

Fung, H., & Chen, E. C. H. (2001). Across time and beyond skin: Self and transgression in the everyday socialization of shame among Taiwanese preschool children. *Social Development, 10*, 420–437.

Fung, H., Lieber, E., & Leung, P. W. L. (2003). Parental beliefs about shame and moral socialization in Taiwan, Hong Kong, and the United States. In K. S. Yang & K. K. Hwang (Eds.), *Progress in Asian social psychology: Conceptual and empirical contributions* (pp. 83–109). Westport, CT: Praeger/Greenwood Press.

Gruenewald, T. L., Kemeny, M. E., Aziz, N., & Fahey, J. L. (2004). Acute threat to the social self: Shame, social self-esteem, and cortisol activity. *Psychosomatic Medicine, 66*, 915–924.

Heine, S. J., Lehman, D. R., Markus, H. R., & Kitayama, S. (1999). Is there a universal need for positive self-regard? *Psychological Review, 106,* 766–794.

Hoblitzelle, W. (1987). Differentiating and measuring shame and guilt: The relation between shame and depression. In H. B. Lewis (Ed.), *The role of shame in symptom formation* (pp. 207–235). Hillsdale, NJ: Erlbaum.

Jordan, D. (n.d.). Terms particularly stressed by Confucianism. Retrieved January 31, 2007, from *http://weber.ucsd.edu/~dkjordon/chin/hbphiloterms-u.html#part2.*

Kaufman, G. (1989). *The psychology of shame: Theory and treatment of shame-based syndromes.* New York: Springer.

Keltner, D. (1995). Signs of appeasement: Evidence for the distinct displays of embarrassment, amusement, and shame. *Journal of Personality and Social Psychology, 68,* 441–454.

Kemeny, M. E., Gruenewald, T. L., & Dickerson, S. S. (2004). Shame as the emotional response to threat to the social self: Implications for behavior, physiology, and health. *Psychological Inquiry, 15,* 153–160.

Kilborne, B. (1992). Fields of shame: Anthropologists abroad. *Ethos, 20,* 230–250.

Kitayama, S., Markus, H. R., & Kurokawa, M. (2000). Culture, emotion, and well-being: Good feelings in Japan and the United States. *Cognition and Emotion, 14,* 93–124.

Kitayama, S., Markus, H. R., & Matsumoto, H. (1995). Culture, self, and emotion: A cultural perspective on "self-conscious" emotions. In J. P. Tangney & K. W. Fischer (Eds.), *Self-conscious emotions: The psychology of shame, guilt, embarrassment, and pride* (pp. 439–464). New York: Guilford Press.

Kitayama, S., Markus, H. R., Matsumoto, H., & Norasakkunkit, V. (1997). Individual and collective processes in the construction of the self: Self-enhancement in the United States and self-criticism in Japan. *Journal of Personality and Social Psychology, 72,* 1245–1267.

Kondo, D. K. (1990). *Crafting selves: Power, gender, and discourses of identity in a Japanese workplace.* Chicago: University of Chicago Press.

Kroeber, A., & Kluckhohn, C. (1952). *Culture.* New York: Meridian Books.

Leith, K. P., & Baumeister, R. F. (1998). Empathy, shame, guilt, and narratives of interpersonal conflicts: Guilt-prone people are better at perspective taking. *Journal of Personality, 66,* 1–37.

Lewis, H. B. (1974). *Shame and guilt in neurosis.* Oxford, UK: International Universities Press.

Lewis, H. B. (1985). Depression vs. paranoia: Why are there sex differences in mental illness? *Journal of Personality, 53,* 150–178.

Lewis, H. B. (1987). The role of shame in depression over the life span. In H. B. Lewis (Ed.), *The role of shame in symptom formation* (pp. 29–50). Hillsdale, NJ: Erlbaum.

Lewis, M. (1997). The self in self-conscious emotions. In J. G. Snodgrass & R. L. Thompson (Eds.), *The self across psychology: Self-recognition, self-awareness, and the self concept* (pp. 119–142). New York: New York Academy of Sciences.

Li, J., Wang, L., & Fischer, K. W. (2004). The organization of Chinese shame concepts. *Cognition and Emotion, 18,* 767–797.

Li, J., & Wang, Q. (2004). Perceptions of achievement and achieving peers in U.S. and Chinese kindergartners. *Social Development, 13,* 413–436.

Liem, R. (1997). Shame and guilt among first- and second- generation Asian Americans and European Americans. *Journal of Cross-Cultural Psychology, 28,* 365–392.

Lutwak, N., Panish, J. B., Ferrari, J. R., & Razzino, B. E. (2001). Shame and guilt and their relationship to positive expectations and anger expressiveness. *Adolescence, 36,* 641–653.

Markus, H. R., & Kitayama, S. (1991). Culture and the self: Implications for cognition, emotion, and motivation. *Psychological Review, 98,* 224–253.

Menon, U., & Shweder, R. A. (1994). Kali's tongue: Cultural psychology and the power of shame in Orissa, India. In S. Kitayama & H. R. Markus (Eds.), *Emotion and culture: Empirical studies of mutual influence* (pp. 241–282). Washington, DC: American Psychological Association.

Mesquita, B., & Karasawa, M. (2004). Self-conscious emotions as dynamic cultural processes. *Psychological Inquiry, 15,* 161–166.

Miller, P. J., Wiley, A. R., Fung, H., & Liang, C. H. (1997). Personal storytelling as a medium of socialization in Chinese and American families. *Child Development, 68,* 557–568.

Morisaki, S., & Gudykunst, W. B. (1994). Face in Japan and the United States. In S. Ting-Toomey (Ed.), *The challenge of facework: Cross-cultural interpersonal issues* (pp. 47–94). New York: State University of New York Press.

Morling, B., Kitayama, S., & Miyamoto, Y. (2002). Cultural practices emphasize influence in the United States and adjustment in Japan. *Personality and Social Psychology Bulletin, 28,* 311–323.

Reasoner, R. (1992). Pro: You can bring hope to failing students. What's behind self-esteem programs: Truth or trickery? *School Administrator, 49,* 23–24, 26, 30.

Romney, A. K., Moore, C. C., & Rusch, C. D. (1997). Cultural universals: Measuring the semantic structure of emotion terms in English and Japanese. *Proceedings of the National Academy of Sciences, 94,* 5489–5494.

Rozin, P. (2003). Five potential principles for understanding cultural differences in relation to individual differences. *Journal of Research in Psychology, 37,* 273–283.

Russell, J. A., & Yik, M. S. M. (1996). Emotion among the Chinese. In M. H. Bond (Ed.), *The handbook of Chinese psychology* (pp. 166–188). Hong Kong: Oxford University Press.

Scheff, T. J. (1998). Shame in the labeling of mental illness. In P. Gilbert & B. Andrews (Eds.), *Shame: Interpersonal behavior, psychopathology, and culture* (pp. 191–205). New York: Oxford University Press.

Shaver, P. R., Schwartz, J., Kirson, D., & O'Connor, C. (1987). Emotion knowledge: Further exploration of a prototype approach. *Journal of Personality and Social Psychology, 52*(6), 1061–1086.

Shaver, P. R., Wu, S., & Schwartz, J. C. (1992). Cross-cultural similarities and differences in emotion and its representation: A prototype approach. In M. S. Clark (Ed.), *Review of Personality and Social psychology* (pp. 175–212). Newbury Park, CA: Sage.

Shaw, G. B. (1987). *George Bernard Shaw's "Man and Superman"* (H. Bloom, Ed.), New York: Chelsea House. (Original work published 1903)

Shore, B. (1996). *Culture in mind: Cognition, culture, and the problem of meaning.* New York: Oxford University Press.

Smith, R. H., Webster J. M., Parrott, W. G., & Eyre, H. L. (2002). The role of public exposure in moral and nonmoral shame and guilt. *Journal of Personality and Social Psychology, 83,* 138–159.

Stipek, D. (1998). Differences between Americans and Chinese in the circumstances evoking pride, shame, and guilt. *Journal of Cross-Cultural Psychology, 79,* 616–629.

Strauss, C. (1992). Models and motives. In R. D'Andrade & C. Strauss (Eds.), *Human motives and cultural models* (pp. 1–20). New York: Cambridge University Press.

Swartz, M. J. (1988). Shame, culture, and status among the Swahili of Mombasa. *Ethos, 16,* 21–51.

Tangney, J. P. (1991). Moral affect: The good, the bad, and the ugly. *Journal of Personality and Social Psychology, 61,* 598–607.

Tangney, J. P. (1998). How does guilt differ from shame? In J. Bybee (Ed.), *Guilt and children* (pp. 1–17). San Diego, CA: Academic Press.

Tangney, J. P., & Dearing, R. L. (2002). *Shame and guilt.* New York: Guilford Press.

Tangney, J. P., & Fischer, K. W. (Eds.). (1995). *Self-conscious emotions: The psychology of shame, guilt, embarrassment, and pride.* New York: Guilford Press.

Tangney, J. P., & Stuewig, J. (2004). A moral-emotional perspective on evil persons and evil deeds. In A. G. Miller (Ed.), *The social psychology of good and evil* (pp. 327–355). New York: Guilford Press.

Tantam, D. (1998). The emotional disorders of shame. In P. Gilbert & B. Andrews (Eds.), *Shame: Interpersonal behavior, psychopathology, and culture* (pp. 161–175). New York: Oxford University Press.

Ting-Toomey, S., & Kurogi, A. (1998). Facework competence in intercultural conflict: An updated face-negotiation theory. *International Journal of Intercultural Relations, 22,* 187–225.

Tinsley, C. H., & Weldon, E. (2003). Response to a normative conflict among American and Chinese managers. *International Journal of Cross Cultural Management, 3*, 183–194.

Tomkins, S. S., Sedgwick, E. K., & Frank, A. (Eds.). (1995). *Shame and its sisters: A Silvan Tomkins reader*. Durham, NC: Duke University Press.

Tracy, J. L., & Robins, R. W. (2004). Putting the self into self-conscious emotions: A theoretical model. *Psychological Inquiry, 15*, 103–125.

Tracy, J. L., & Robins, R. W. (2006). Appraisal antecedents of shame and guilt: Support for a theoretical model. *Personality and Social Psychology Bulletin, 32*, 1339–1351.

Triandis, H. (1995). *Individualism and collectivism*. Boulder, CO: Westview Press.

Tsai, J. L. (1996). *Cultural and contextual influences on the emotional responding of Chinese-American and European-American couples during conflict*. Unpublished doctoral dissertation, University of California, Berkeley.

Tsai, J. L. (2006). *Cultural differences in the valuation of shame and other complex emotions*. Manuscript in preparation.

Tsai, J. L., Levenson, R. W., & McCoy, K. (2006). Cultural and temperamental variation in emotional response. *Emotion, 6*, 484–497.

Twitchell, J. B. (1997). *For shame: The loss of common decency in American culture*. New York: St. Martin's Press.

Wallbott, H. G., & Scherer, K. R. (1995). Cultural determinants in experiencing shame and guilt. In J. P. Tangney & K. W. Fischer (Eds.), *Self-conscious emotions: The psychology of shame, guilt, embarrassment, and pride* (pp. 465–487). New York: Guilford Press.

Weisz, J. R., Rothbaum, F. M., & Blackburn, T. C. (1984). Standing out and standing in: The psychology of control in America and Japan. *American Psychologist, 39*, 955–969.

Wierzbicka, A. (1999). *Emotions across languages and cultures: Diversity and universals*. Paris: Cambridge University Press.

Wikan, U. (1984). Shame and honour: A contestable pair. *Man, 19*, 635–652.

13

Respect as a Positive Self-Conscious Emotion in European Americans and Chinese

JIN LI
KURT W. FISCHER

The last decade has witnessed a growing interest in self-conscious emotions. For example, guilt, shame, and embarrassment have been studied both within and across cultures (Casimire & Schnegg, 2003; Lewis, 1993; Lindsay-Hartz, de Rivera, & Mascolo, 1995; Scheff, 2003; Tangney, 1998; Tangney & Fischer, 1995; Schneider, 1977). As a result, our knowledge in this area is not limited to the West as was most past psychological research, but our understanding is enriched from many researchers studying people from diverse cultural backgrounds (Abu-Lughod, 1996; Fischer, Manstead, & Rodriguez Mosquera, 1999; Fontaine, Poortinga, Setiadi, & Markam, 2002; Fung, 1999; Heider, 1991; Li, Wang, & Fischer, 2004; Menon & Shweder, 1994; Rodriguez Mosquera, Manstead, & Fischer, 2002). However, the field mostly focuses on negative self-conscious emotions. In contrast, very little research exists on positive self-conscious emotions. Except for the growing research on pride (Tracy & Robins, 2004; Tracy, Robins, & Lagattuta, 2005), little research exists on other positive self-conscious emotions such as honor, respect, gratitude, humility, and, probably, the now well-known concept of "face" (Ting-Toomey, 1994).

As Tangney (2002) points out, positive self-conscious emotions may be viewed as part of the emerging field of positive psychology, which has gained recognition in mainstream psychology since the American Psychological Association presidential address by Seligman (1999). Indeed, while the field continues to strive to understand mental illnesses, deviant behaviors, transgressions, and personal failures, it is essential that we study what enables human beings to function positively in life (Linley, Joseph, Harrington, & Wood, 2006; Selgiman & Csikszentmihalyi, 2000). Researchers focusing on positive self-conscious emotions have unique contributions to make in this new direction of psychology.

In this chapter, we discuss respect as a positive self-conscious emotion. Our discussion is grounded in two important perspectives: Frijda's (1986) appraisal theory of emotion and Mesquita and Frijda's (1992; see also Mesquita, 2003) cultural perspective on emotion. Accordingly, we first discuss Frijda's appraisal theory briefly. We then introduce two particular cultures, European American and Chinese, by presenting a description of each culture's basic value system in order to provide a framework for understanding respect. Next, we outline our conceptualization of respect as a self-conscious emotion and use Frijda's theory to describe how respect may occur in the two cultures' people. We offer an analysis of the functions that respect may serve for Westerners and Chinese people. To the extent possible, we draw on existing research to refine our conceptualization of respect. We conclude with a set of suggestions for future research on this positive self-conscious emotion.

At this juncture, we find it important to point out that the cultural perspective is indispensable in research on emotions, particularly self-conscious emotions. Examining emotions cross-culturally affords several important advantages. First, according to Mesquita (2003) and Mesquita and Frijda (1992), virtually every aspect of emotion is under cultural influence; this is particularly true of the self-conscious emotions due to their social nature. Second, research on negative self-conscious emotions has already made great strides in adopting the cross-cultural perspective and as a result has enriched our understanding in ways never before found in mainstream psychology. Research on positive self-conscious emotions has much to benefit from this achievement, which can only lead to greater insights. Third, and relatedly, this perspective avoids the pitfall of setting the Western cultures as the norm of human psychological functioning and then measuring other non-Western cultures against this norm. As the history of psychology attests, this outdated perspective has proven to be a liability rather than an asset. Fourth, cross-cultural analysis enables us to identify patterns that are common across as well as specific to cultures. If common patterns do emerge, they are more likely to be valid. And the culture-specific patterns must then be studied and understood in their own right. Last, but not least, a cross-cultural perspective promotes mutual understanding of positive self-conscious emotions among the world's peoples, a goal that psychology in general ought to strive to achieve.

APPRAISAL THEORY

Human emotions are generally understood as episodes that take place temporally. Simply put, emotions come and go. Buck (1999) notes that we tend to notice our emotions (and are often noticed by others around us) when they become relatively strong even though our emotional system is always turned on under normal circumstances. Thus, any emotional episode can be seen as having three basic components that unfold in time: a cause or antecedent, a response/reaction, which is frequently physiological in nature, and then coping afterward (Shaver, Schwartz, Kirson, & O'Connor, 1987). Frijda (1986) advanced this basic description of emotions into a sequence of seven components: (1) *antecedent events* that generate emotions, (2) *event coding* where one characterizes the event in reference to event types as recognized by one's culture (e.g., insult), (3) *appraisal* where one evaluates the implications of the event to the self (e.g., "Am I responsible?"), (4) *physiological reaction patterns* where a given emotion is linked to a set of autonomic reactions (e.g., shame leads to blushing and gazing away; Casimire & Schnegg, 2003), (5) *action readiness* where the person selects the next course of actions from a repertoire of possible actions (e.g., fear promotes the impulse to run away), (6) *emotional behavior* where one takes action (e.g., actual running away in fear), and finally (7) *regulation* where the person selects ways to deal with the emotion and the action taken (e.g., stay engaged with the event when feeling happy).

Frijda's theory is referred to as an "appraisal theory" because it pays a great deal of attention to the perception of preceding causes, coding of events, personal appraisal, and so forth. The mere fact that our emotions are a result of how we perceive events in our environments points to the indispensable role sociocultural context plays in our emotional experience (Frijda & Mesquita, 1995; Mesquita & Frijda, 1992). Although Frijda did not develop his theory based on self-conscious emotions, this theory applies readily to self-conscious emotions.

A Cultural Perspective on Appraisal Theory

Mesquita and Frijda (1992) and Mesquita (2003) have advanced a cultural perspective on Frijda's appraisal theory of emotion. They maintain that culture is involved in all seven phases because human emotional experience is a result of the combination of autonomic responses and regulated responses according to specific cultural models. Levy (1973) studied Tahitians and found that some emotions in that culture were elaborated and fully expressed whereas others were almost not visible. Anger in Tahitian culture is an example of the former and sadness is an example of the latter due to the norms concerning the function of these emotions in Tahitian social life. Levy proposed the distinction between "hypercognized" and "hypocognized" emotions to capture culturally shaped emotional experiences. While hypercognization has more terms, indicating a great deal more conceptual differentiation of a given emotion, hypocognization has few terms, indicating less conceptual differentiation. Drawing on this framework, Mesquita (2003) argues that cultures can differ in frequency of appraisals, action readiness, expression and behavior, and regulatory processes. The high or low frequencies of these processes indicate consistency or inconsistency within a given cultural model.

Frijda and Mesquita (1995) further suggest three aspects of emotion that are particularly subject to cultural influence: (1) social consequences of emotions that regulate expression and suppression of emotions, (2) importance of norms for expressing different emotions, and (3) social-cohesive functions of emotions. Although the first concerns event coding and appraisal, the second addresses issues of display rules. Based on this framework, we show that respect is a self-conscious emotion that may be appraised, displayed, and regulated differently in European Americans and Chinese people because of their very different cultural models.

European American and Chinese Cultural Models as Guides for Emotional Life

Cultural models structure, frame, and constrain what is desirable and undesirable, allowed and sanctioned, and rewarded and punished. Cultural models thus influence thinking, emotion, goals and motives, and social behavior (D'Andrade, 1992, 1995; Harkness & Super, 1996; Quinn & Holland, 1987; Shweder, Much, Mahapatra, & Park, 1997). However, the existence of cultural models does not automatically turn all cultural members into copies of their cultural models. Instead, individual members vary in their degree and form of appropriation of their cultural models (Spiro, 1987; Strauss, 1992). How much a given person internalizes his or her cultural model depends on many factors including the person's characteristics, proclivities, and upbringing experiences.

In our discussion of respect, we focus on the United States as a typical Western culture and China as a typical Asian culture to discuss respect. We chose to examine these cultures because they still have very different traditions and cultural systems despite recent political, economic, scientific/technological, and educational adaptation on the part of Asia to the West. These cultural differences are likely to persist, as the cases of Japan, Korea, and Hong Kong have demonstrated; basic cultural values endure in spite of these countries' Westernized economic and political systems. Moreover, these cultures have been subject to ongoing comparative psychological research in recent decades, which provides a good basis for a comparative analysis of respect in European Americans and Chinese people.

Western Cultures and Respect

Research generally portrays Western cultures as promoting individual autonomy, independence, and rights. Westerners purportedly seek personal uniqueness and distinction rather than trying to be like others or to fit into their social group (Markus & Kitayama, 1991; Fiske, Kitayama, Markus, & Nisbett, 1998). They pursue their personal goals and express their personal sense of agency more than the goals of their group. Individualism seems prominent in the West, particularly in European American (EA) culture. Individual rights are strongly emphasized and protected based on political, moral, and social practices. Therefore, people are expected to, and often do, assert their rights and associated entitlements. This cultural imperative may make people feel that they should be respected simply for who they are, their backgrounds, choices, styles, and preferences. When people show respect, their attitude and feelings may also stem from this cultural model that recognizes people's dignity, deservingness, acknowledgment, and entitlement (Barreto & Ellemers, 2002; De Cremer, 2002; Heuer, Blumenthal, Douglas, & Weinblatt, 1999). Violations of this model may lead to anger, indignation, and, in some cases, legal action.

Other than this common feeling of respect, Westerners show a somewhat different kind of respect for people they admire, appreciate, revere, and/or hold in awe. This feeling of respect can be seen when fans meet a rock star or when admirers meet their great political or moral leaders. This kind of respect is not rights-based but personally generated and expressed.

Chinese Culture and Respect

Chinese culture has traditionally been characterized as collectivist (Hofstede, 1980; Leung & Bond, 1984; Markus & Kitayama, 1991; Triandis, McCusker, & Hui, 1990). Confucianism promotes social relations and harmony as the foundation for human lives. Accordingly, Chinese people are defined not as separate and independent but as interdependent selves. Social positions, hierarchy, roles, and relationships, but not their personal uniqueness and distinction, assume essential significance (Ho, 1986; Hsu, 1981; K. S. Yang, 1997). Thus, Chinese people are said to be principally motivated to pursue group goals rather than their own goals. Therefore their sense of agency is also socially defined (Menon, Morris, Chiu, & Hong, 1999). Children are socialized early on to focus on social connections within their kin and community by following adults' instructions. Children are taught to obey teachers and to cooperate with, instead of challenge, their teachers and peers at school (Tweed & Lehman, 2002). Due to their strong concerns about social harmony and respect for related social order, Chinese people may be deferential toward authority.

However, recent research suggests that the collectivistic aspect of Chinese culture may be overstated. Neglected in this research is the Confucian emphasis on individuality, particularly in the person's own moral striving and development of personal virtues (Chang, 1997; de Bary, 1983; King, 1985; Li, 2003b; C. F. Yang, 1993). A revised view is that, despite their noted sociocentric tendency, Chinese people emphasize self-reliance, individual responsibility (Chang & Hue, 1991; Ho & Chiu, 1994), success, ambition, personal capability (Schwartz, 1994), personal agency (Chen & Fung, 2004; Fung, Miller, & Lin, 2004; Wink, Gao, Jones, & Chao, 1997), and even autonomy in decision making and parent–child relationships (Helwig, Arnold, Tan, & Boyd, 2003; Yau & Smetana, 2003). Most recent research (Li, 2006a) on Chinese adolescents' goals and agency in learning reveals that Chinese have many more individual learning goals, such as developing their own ability and ambition, than social learning goals (e.g., honoring parents). These adolescents also expressed a great deal more personal agency (e.g., exerting utmost effort to learn, self-discipline, and humility) than social agency (e.g., listening to parents and teachers).

Thus, while Chinese people may generally be more socially oriented, they appear to display a high level of personal aspiration and agency in the domain of learning. This dual orientation is unlikely to be due to recent influence from the West. Rather, it appears to reflect an important side of Confucian teaching, which has been in existence for millennia but has hitherto been neglected in research (Lee, 1996; Tu, 1979). It is the Confucian concept of *ren*, a lifelong striving for self-perfection that everyone is believed able to seek through the process of learning. This self-perfecting process is a general moral striving and is not limited to academic learning. For the Chinese, this approach to life constitutes an ideal self because it is open-ended, creative, aesthetic, deeply fulfilling, and lies in the hand of the individual (Ames & Rosemont, 1999; de Bary, 1991; Kupperman, 2004; Tu, 1979). Recent research indeed documents moral self-perfection as the most significant learning goal among Chinese people (Li, 2001, 2003a, 2003b; Li & Fischer, 2004; Watkins & Biggs, 1996). Chinese children as young as age 4 already show rudimentary awareness of similar learning goals and related virtues (Li, 2004a, 2004b). Chinese people thus may be particularly tuned to people who are exemplary in achieving these elements of their ideal life model. They may feel strong respect for such people, not because they are obedient or docile toward them, but because learning from and emulating these models can help people perfect themselves.

RESPECT IN AMERICAN AND CHINESE CULTURES

Respect is a positive emotion in both Westerners and Chinese people (Cohen, Hsueh, Zhou, Hancock, & Floyd, 2006; Hsueh, Zhou, Cohen, Hundley, & Deptula, 2005). The opposite of respect is disrespect or, as Gottman (1994) argued, contempt, in the West, and quite likely also in Chinese culture. Although it is a common concept in both cultures that occurs in political, legal, and academic discourse as well as in people's daily communication, respect as a psychological construct has, surprisingly, been seldom studied.

We propose that respect qualifies as a self-conscious emotion. This emotion arises when one recognizes the good qualities of another, such as moral, intellectual, athletic, artistic, and other personal qualities and achievement that the self either desires, is in the process of acquiring, or already possesses to some degree. The self-conscious part resides in the likelihood that the self may identify with such a person and be reminded of self's own good qualities. However, the self may not regard the level and degree of his or her own qualities as being as high or as extensive as those of the target. The recognition of this gap may be the foundation for one to long for, to approach (rather than to avoid), and to emulate the target. We suggest that respect may be an emotion that promotes positive self-development, which we call "self-Pygmalion." Therefore, there may be different kinds of respect. One kind may emphasize people's rights; another may acknowledge qualities of others that one may not want to acquire (e.g., grandparents); and yet another may be more involved in the self-Pygmalion process. We will address different kinds of respect in more detail later.

The limited research on Western respect is found in the literatures on social psychology (Barreto & Ellemers, 2002; De Cremer, 2002; Heuer et al., 1999) and character education and development (Chapman, 1986; Kohlberg, 1984; Lawrence-Lightfoot, 2000; Piaget, 1932/1962, 1941/1995). Most of the social psychology research views respect as a social construct rather than as an emotion, and this research examines it with regard to group perceptions, interactions, and dynamics in group-based psychological functioning such as group identity, resource allocation, attribution of power, cooperation, and conflict generation and resolution. The psychologists who focus on moral and social development regard respect as a relational skill and attitude toward peers among individual children.

Recently, Kellenberg (1995) distinguished four kinds of respect: (1) respect for persons, (2) respect for persons based on their accomplishments and ability, (3) respect for the rights of others, and (4) respect for duty or moral law. Whereas the first three kinds bear on individuals, the last does not. However, empirical research is generally lacking. Most research in psychology appears to focus on adult close relationships such as romantic love and marriage. Here respect has also been only tangentially touched on instead of being the focal point of investigation. In general, respect is viewed as an attitude toward or quality of a person—for example, as the "admired" characteristics of another, a part of liking and loving of one's partner, for the value and worth of the other (Gottman, 1996; Markman, Stanley, & Blumberg, 1994; Rubin, 1973), and a central feature of love, commitment, and intimacy (Aron & Westbay, 1996; Fehr, 1988; Tzeng, 1993).

A study by Frei and Shaver (2002) sheds some light on the affective nature of respect. They found 22 features that define respect. Inspection of these features reveals six groups of features: (1) moral and virtuous qualities (e.g., honest, trustworthy, loyal, and caring), (2) sensitivity toward others (e.g., considerate, accepting others, and understanding and empathic), (3) members of a respectworthy social category, (4) admirable talents/skills, (5) inspiring/motivating, and (6) mutuality. Because their open-ended probes did not produce an episode-like description of respect, the authors concluded that respect is not an emotion but "an attitude or a disposition toward a particular person based on his or her perceived good qualities" (p. 125). They also used the term "respect-worthy" person or behavior to address respect as an attitudinal/dispositional construct.

However, we maintain that, although respect may be viewed as a social/attitudinal construct, it clearly possesses some hard-to-dismiss affect. To begin with, all of the above cited researchers and theorists in psychology considered respect a component of emotions such as liking, love, empathy, and admiration (even Piaget [1941/1995] discussed respect as a feeling of valorization between two individuals), and other strongly affective manifestations such as commitment, intimacy, caring, loyalty, showing interest, sensitive to feelings, and inspiring/motivating among Frei and Shaver's features. Second, Frei and Shaver, in their attempt to identify the unique contribution of respect in adult close relationships, found strong correlations among their respect features and other common variables with strong affect that are characteristic of such relationships: liking, loving, positive valence, negative valence, and relationship satisfaction. Although they found distinct explanatory power of respect, these important correlational findings for respect compel us to consider respect as a construct with a strong emotional component. Third, as will be seen, respect in Chinese people may lean even more toward the affective side including a clear feeling state and a set of distinct physical gestures and expressions (Li, 2006b). We disagree with Frei and Shaver's conclusion that respect is categorically not an emotion. Their instructions for generating respect features did not ask their participants to describe an incident where they felt respect toward another person as was done on other basic emotions by Shaver et al. (1987). Therefore, they did not have relevant data to rule out respect as an emotion. We argue that we stand to gain important understanding by looking at respect as a self-conscious emotion in addition to its social and attitudinal nature in both cultures.

Distinguishing Ought-Respect and Affect-Respect in Westerners

Respect is an important concept in the West. Consulting word frequency in modern English (Francis & Kucera, 1982) reveals that *respect* has a token index of 22, indicating highly frequent usage. Kellenberg's (1995) three-sided distinction of respect (excluding respect for duty or moral law for our purposes) provides some conceptual clarification. Respect for persons and respect for persons based on their accomplishments and ability are quite different from respect for the rights of others. Before elaborating on respect as a self-conscious emotion, it may be conceptually profitable to further distinguish these two kinds of respect as *ought-respect* and *affect-respect* both extended to another person.

"Ought-respect" refers to the kind of respect everyone deserves based on political, moral, and legal considerations in the West. However, ought-respect is not generated in a specific social context or relationship because it is for everyone. This kind of respect does not vary due to temporal or contextual particularities. Therefore, it is not, under normal circumstances, expressed as an emotion. Nor does ought-respect generate specific physical/bodily gestures and behaviors as do typical emotions, despite some of the attitudinal and behavioral manifestations of ought-respect, such as listening, respecting other's views, and accepting others, as noted by Frei and Shaver (2002). Given that ought-respect is tied to a rights-based moral principle and mandated by law, and it is not person- or relationship-specific, ought-respect is unlikely to be a prototypical emotion, but a more reason-based social, moral, and attitudinal construct.

Respect for authority is also common in the West. We argue that this kind of respect is also ought-respect for two reasons. First, it is directed at the *notion* of authority, not at a given person, even though authority is usually embodied and occupied by persons. However, respect is still more for the position and power that gives the person authority, not vice versa. Second, emotionality is minimal in the respect for authority (perhaps involving more fear if emotion is involved at all), again because authority has institutions, laws, and policies underlying it.

Quite differently, "affect-respect" is mostly an emotion that is generated in a specific social context or relationship. This kind of respect occurs when an individual genuinely recognizes, acknowledges, and admires another for his or her merit, achievement, moral qualities, and/or status/position/role/power. Affect-respect necessarily rests on the awareness that the self is either of lesser quality than the other or shares a similar quality. This self-awareness, particularly of the gap between oneself and the other, is the basis for our consideration of affect-respect as a self-conscious emotion. The recognition of such a gap necessarily presupposes that the self values and desires the qualities of the other. The realization that one values/desires the quality, which the self should and can acquire but has not yet achieved, may be the very foundation for respect. The awareness of the gap is likely to have further implications for the self.

Affect-respect can be observed when a baseball fan meets his beloved player (e.g., Roger Clemens), or when a college student who has been studying Toni Morrison's novels since sixth grade finally meets her, or when an admirer meets Nelson Mandela. Affect-respect is not limited to the extreme experience with the greatest individuals in the world: people can feel affect-respect toward a teenager who is on the high school honor roll or is dedicated to volunteer work. Affect-respect does not require mutuality as a condition, as Piaget would argue for respect among peers. We do not feel this kind of respect toward certain people because we expect them to extend equivalent respect back to us. In fact, our self-awareness of our lesser qualities prevents us from expecting such mutuality (mutuality as part of respect, as found by Cohen et al. [2006], Frei and Shaver [2002], and Hsueh et al. [2005], may be necessary for marital or peer relationships). This kind of respect is self-conscious, whereas ought-respect need not be.

Other forms of affect-respect include holding someone in awe, admiring someone, and, simply, loving someone. It is important to point out that admiration and love, but not awe, are the two common terms that occur frequently in the previously reviewed research that studies close (specific) relationships. It is this affect-respect that led Gottman (1994) to consider contempt, a clearly negative self-conscious emotion, as the opposite of respect. Because affect-respect is not necessarily tied to a moral principle (although a good moral character is a feature defining respect; Frei & Shaver, 2002) or mandated by law, we do not extend this kind of respect to everyone. We feel affect-respect only toward certain persons in a temporal sense (e.g., we generate and therefore begin to feel) respect when we recognize the good qualities of a person, but we also lose (i.e., end) respect for a person previously admired if, for example, that person's moral character becomes questionable later. Therefore, affect-respect is unlikely to be a disposition as claimed by Frei and Shaver that the respect-showing/giving person possesses, for a disposition is a trait-like quality that persists over time. But affect-respect can come and go and rise and fall as our appraisal of the person changes. The person-specific nature coupled with temporality as well as a set of distinct bodily expressions (evident from Chinese data) of affect-respect compels us to conceptualize affect-respect as an emotion. Finally, the fact that the English term *respect* denotes both ought-respect and affect-respect may have impeded conceptualization and empirical research concerning respect in the West.

According to Keltner and Haidt (2003), awe is an emotion that may overlap with admiration and respect due to two distinct attributes: felt vastness and the need to accommodate. It seems that awe is a term people feeling respect may use. However, we argue, respect is not awe according to the definition employed by Keltner and Haidt. Affect-respect is directed mostly toward a person in a specific social context/relationship, not toward events, objects, and supernatural phenomena as the authors included. Moreover, awe is frequently associated with threat, fright, and fear due to vastness and shock-like experience that the mind cannot grasp, but prototypical respect is not. Awe may cause submission in a person, which is more associated with the unfathomable power of the target rather than identification with the target's good qualities that is predominantly involved in respect.

Experience of Affect-Respect in Westerners

Given that there is virtually no research documenting actual episodes of affect-respect, we apply Frijda's (1986) appraisal theory to map this process. We propose that antecedent events of affect-respect are the presence of persons recognized as possessing valued qualities such as moral character, courage (e.g., cultural heroes), knowledge (e.g., scholars), wisdom, merit (e.g., Olympic champions), achievement, and talent (e.g., artists), and often also people in high ranks (e.g., CEOs) with high status, with great power, or in particular roles (e.g., great teachers). Such a presence is then recognized/coded as greatness (but typically not unfathomable) or worthy of admiration. This recognition is generally based on and consistent with cultural values (therefore respect-eliciting persons are not typically regarded as mysterious or threatening). This event-coding process also reminds one of one's lesser or shared quality, yet this realization does not lead one to feel ashamed or inadequate, as is typically the case with shame-eliciting events, because the focus is on the target. This event-coding process likely makes one long for such qualities. As hinted previously, it is quite possible that people who respect the other already possess, or are in the process of acquiring, or have committed themselves to the acquisition of the good qualities the respected person has. If this is the case, then some sort of identification with the respected person may be at work. For example, beginning basketball players recognize Michael Jordan because they aspire to be great players themselves. Likewise, young physicists admire Einstein because they themselves want to be like Einstein.

The ensuing appraisal process alerts one that the respected person has positive implications for the self, either because one has learned/read/heard about his or her good qualities, or has formed high opinions of the person, or has been desiring to meet, study/work with, learn from, or emulate the person. This positivity for the self may stem from the fact that one is reminded of one's own good qualities, aspirations, and hopes, therefore generating a sense of direction for possible selves (Markus & Nurius, 1986), possibly because of a process of identification, as discussed earlier. It is important to note that the young basketball player's respect for Jordan is the self-conscious kind. But the respect for Jordan by an ordinary person who recognizes Jordan's achievement, but does not aspire to be like him, may not be self-conscious.

We propose that the bodily/behavioral reaction pattern for affect-respect may include smile while having wider-opened eyes, dropped jaw, raised eyebrows, and lowered and contracted bodily gestures (Fiske & Haslam, 2005), with slightly bent legs, a hunched back, a bow, and a self-effacing/agreeable facial expression as well as honoring words. One may simply become speechless, for one may feel that no words can express the respect he or she feels toward the person. When respect is felt, one will approach, not avoid, the person, drawing his or her attention to the self so that the self gets ready to express/show respect to the target. Affect-respect may be fully expressed and displayed in both gestures and words. Respect-related regulation may direct one into sharing one's felt respect with one's social circles and at seeking ways to be like, to follow, to connect with, and to acquire qualities as exemplified by the person. In other words, the self may experience increased motivation in these self-regulatory processes. It is important to point out that affect-respect may not require the target to be physically present. One may feel this kind of respect at any time or in any context when the self is made aware of the person, such as by reading, hearing, or otherwise learning about the target, or even when one merely thinks about the target person.

In light of the emphasis the West places on individual distinctions, qualities, merit, and achievement, Westerners' affect-respect may be felt and expressed only to those who earn or deserve their respect, that is, those who are found respect-worthy (Frei & Shaver, 2002). Preexisting conditions such as age, role, or seniority alone that are not associated with individual moral character, merit, and achievement may not be regarded as respect-worthy. This cultural tendency may differ markedly from the Chinese/Asian cultural model for respect where certain people may not need to earn or to acquire worthiness for respect through their own individual efforts and achievements.

Function of Affect-Respect in Westerners

We propose that affect-respect is likely to do a great deal of psychological good to the self. First, it may account for the function of role models. A role model is necessarily someone whom the self admires and desires to emulate, and it is one positive possible self (Markus & Nurius, 1986). When a person has identified a role model, that person has a clear, concrete, tangible, real human figure in mind. The fact that a person is identified as a role model for the self indicates that the self has some understanding of the basic quality, merit, and achievement that role model has (unlike awe elicitors). The identification of a role model also necessarily indicates at least some self-awareness of the *discrepancy* between the self and the role model and quite possibly also awareness of ways to narrow this discrepancy. Second, each time the self is made aware of the target, the self may experience affect-respect, a highly positive emotion that also makes the self feel good about him- or herself, as discussed earlier. Third, because it is often directed at people with strong moral characters, affect-respect may be an essential emotion that underlies our moral understanding and growth. Whereas the same process applies to excellence in other domains, affect-respect may be particularly important in the moral domain. Finally, affect-respect may generate strong motivation for action and behavior that propels the self toward acquiring the qualities that the respected person possesses. In sum, feeling affect-respect for a person may make the self eventually become such a person. This may be called the "self-Pygmalion process" (named after the sculptor in Greek mythology whose sculpture came to life).

However, there is some evidence that ought-respect may be more prevalent in the West than in Asia, while affect-respect is less commonly experienced among Westerners than Asians. For example, Hsueh e al. (2005) found that whereas 19% of EA children also named authority as a definition of respect, only 6% of Chinese children did so. Australian schoolchildren expressed less respect for their parents (affect-respect is assumed in this parent–child relationship) than their Japanese peers (Mann, Mitsui, Beswick, & Harmoni, 1994). Moreover, Hsueh et al. (2005) found that the highest number of EA schoolchildren (74%) identified reciprocity as their definition of respect (compared with only 38% of their Chinese peers who identified reciprocity, while 44%, the highest percentage, identified admiration as their definition of respect). Reciprocity is a feature similar to the mutuality that Frei and Shaver (2002) found, and it indicates social exchange more than emotionality. Finally, given that few EA children (2%) named admiration as their definition of respect, Cohen et al. (2006) examined whether peer respect mediated peer liking, related peer social competence, and mutual friends. They found that peer respect mediated these factors among EA children much less than among their Chinese counterparts. These findings are consistent with our view that because respect is more defined and experienced in the West as ought-respect than as affect-respect, EA children's social competence and friendship may be less affected by respect than Asian children's social competence and friendship.

Description of Ought-Respect and Affect-Respect in Chinese People

Respect is a significant concept in Chinese culture. The distinction between ought-respect and affect-respect also applies to respect in Chinese people. Significantly, there are two Chinese terms, *zunzhong* (尊重) and *zunjing* (尊敬), that denote the two kinds of respect that we have distinguished. Consulting word frequency in modern Chinese (Wang et al., 1986) reveals that *zunzhong* has a token index of 50 and *zunjing* an index of 27, indicating highly frequent usage for both terms. Both terms have the highest frequency among their synonyms and are among the 8,000 most frequently used of all Chinese words. These empirical indices provide support for the importance of respect in Chinese culture. The two terms have some affiliation because both share the common character *zun*, a term referring since ancient times to "elder," "senior," "respect," and honorable titles and addresses used to differentiate social positions, statuses, and roles according to the *Chinese–English Dictionary* (Wu et al., 1978). However, the fact that the Chinese language has two highly used terms is indicative of the significant distinction between the two.

Zunzhong seems to resemble the English term *respect*. Despite scarce research on respect in any culture, there is, fortunately, empirical evidence that *zunzhong* and *respect* are the closest equivalents based on a translation procedure conducted by Hsueh et al. (2005). Basically, *zunzhong* denotes (1) the recognition, agreement with, and obeying of law, regulations, and social order; (2) people's basic rights (to education, spouses of their own choice, housing, education, health care, etc.); (3) valuing different cultures, traditions, customs, and social conventions; and (4) accepting or considering the other's opinion, viewpoints, choices, and preferences within daily social interactions. It seems reasonable to state that *zunzhong* is also a social/attitudinal construct. Underlying *zunzhong* are basic social/moral principles that guide people's social interactions, exchanges, and transactions similar to those principles in the West. But it is important to point out that *zunzhong* is not a concept or practice imported or derived from the Western type of rights that stress individual autonomy and independence (Ihara, 2004; Rosemont, 2004). Nevertheless, *zunzhong* is a social/attitudinal construct that functions similarly in regulating people's social and moral lives within Chinese culture.

Quite differently, *zunjing* has a clearly emotional tone. It is this kind of respect that we are scrutinizing more carefully because we believe that it qualifies as a self-conscious emotion. It has more affinity to, though it is not identical with, affect-respect in the West. In order to gain some understanding of *zunjing*, we draw on Li's (2006b) recent collection of 159 terms in Chinese that were generated with the priming term *zunjing*. These terms are yet to be rated for typicality and centrality and sorted for organizational structure. Therefore, we can only offer a preliminary analysis of these meanings.

Experience of Affect-Respect in Chinese People

There are 116 terms in at least five discernible categories of antecedent events/persons that elicit *zunjing* in people. The first category contains 39 terms about (1) high moral character and (2) virtues. Within the former, examples include noble people, moral self-perfection, integrity, honesty, kindness, and sincerity. Within the latter, examples include generosity, magnanimity, being considerate, and carefulness in handling affairs. The second category, with 31 terms, refers to high ability, knowledge, and achievement, which also consists of two subcomponents: (1) intellectual excellence and (2) personal greatness/charisma. Whereas the first subcomponent contains terms such as strong ability and breadth and depth of knowledge, the second subcomponent has items referring to unmatched greatness, dignified persons, heroes, and persons standing on a pedestal. The third category, with 15 terms, includes elders in one's kinship group such as parents and grandparents, old age itself, significant peers such as schoolmates and apprentice peers (particularly older ones) who study with the same mentor. The fourth category, with 11 terms, concerns persons in high political, social, and institutional positions such as the president of the country, school principals, and evaluative committee members. Finally, the fifth category, with six terms, refers to one's teachers, mentors, and admired scholars.

If we juxtapose these five Chinese categories of antecedents with the features found by Frei and Shaver (2002), it becomes clear that the first two also exist on their list. Most striking is the large number (12, or 55%, in our tally of 22 features) of what we term "virtues" (13 Chinese items) within the moral domain that also exist on their list. Moreover, they listed a feature termed "member of a respectworthy social category." Because they did not specify what kind of people this feature included, it is not clear whether it referenced kin members, elders, teachers/mentors, and persons in high political/social positions as referred to by the Chinese items. These latter three Chinese categories have a total of 32 terms, which is fairly large.

We propose that when one recognizes or is made aware of the presence (physical or in thought) of any of these categories of people, one is likely to code this presence as *zunjing*-relevant. For the first two kinds (people with high moral/virtuous qualities and high ability/achievement), the event-coding and appraisal processes are similar to those in Westerners. However, in Chinese individuals, these processes may also apply to one's teachers, mentors, and scholars. Yet, for kinship elders/old age and leaders, identification may not be at work because one cannot be the elder to an elder. One may be made aware of one's younger age, generational status, and lower position instead. This realization may also be linked to the idea that one is a beneficiary of the care and nurture that one's older kin provides to oneself. The same feeling also applies to community leaders, for one is also a beneficiary of their work and care. There are 25 terms that describe the entire reaction pattern or the feeling state: awe, admiration, love, appreciation, worship, longing, favoring, submission, even caution with the person and fear (similar to awe). There are many words that express nuanced feelings, but they are difficult to translate into English. It is likely that feelings of admiration, awe, worship, surrendering oneself, and longing are more linked to those from the first three categories, whereas love, caring, and caution are linked more to kin elders, old age, and leaders.

With regard to emotional expression and behavior, there are three interrelated types: (1) physically looking up to the person, with five terms (raising one's head to peek at the height of the person), for example, "look up to the highness of the mountain" and "look up longingly"; (2) physically lowering one's body, with seven terms ("prostrate oneself before the person"), "listening attentively," "following," and "feeling oneself small"; and (3) exhibiting humble behavior before the person, with six terms (e.g., polite and yielding). Finally, there are two terms referring to identification with and motivation for emulating the target, which may indicate regulation of *zunjing*.

Function of Affect-Respect in Chinese People

Despite a near absence of research on respect, there is some data indicating how affect-respect may function in Chinese people. Although some terms of *zunzhong* (ought-respect) emerged when Chinese adults were primed with *zunjing* (affect-respect), they were much smaller in quantity (23 out of a total of 159 terms, or 14%). The majority of Chinese *zunjing* terms (Li, 2006b) indicate emotional processes in accordance with Frijda's appraisal theory. Thus, affect-respect may be more, and ought-respect less, prevalent in Asia than in the West (Mann et al., 1994) because Asian cultures may emphasize affect-respect more. The recent pioneering comparative research on respect in EA and Chinese schoolchildren by Hsueh et al. (2005) and Cohen et al. (2006) indeed reveals that most Chinese but not EA children nominated admiration as a defining attribute of respect even when Chinese children were primed with *zunzhong*, that is, ought-respect. Moreover, peer respect as defined in this way mediated Chinese children's social competence and mutual friends (but peer respect as defined more in terms of reciprocity did not mediate the same outcomes among EA children). These findings are sensible considering that children's social competence and friendship making depend strongly on their emotional bonding with other children. If respect is mostly experienced as peer admiration, affect-respect should be linked to Chinese children's social competence and friendship making. By contrast, it should not be surprising that respect construed and experienced with a lack of emotionality by Western children does not predict their social outcomes.

Li's (2006b) *zunjing* terms are worth further discussion with regard to the Chinese cultural value system, particularly in the three additional categories (beyond those with moral qualities and high talent/skills, as identified for EAs by Frei and Shaver [2002]). These people are inherently respect-worthy for one's own benefit. Respect for one's elder kin is of paramount importance in Confucian filial piety (Wu & Lai, 1992). One owes his or her own life to their love and nurture and is explicitly socialized to express respect to them. Old age in general also signals wisdom, which one is encouraged to acquire. Respect for one's community leaders rests on the assumption that a person does not become such a leader without exemplary moral character and intellectual achievement. Along with leadership positions comes the fiduciary trust from the community in Chinese tradition (Tu, 1989). Respect for one's teachers/mentors continues to be an expression of one's aspirations as well as an expression of gratitude toward those who nurture one's intellectual and moral growth (Hsueh et al., 2005; Li, 2003a; Li & Wang, 2004). All in all, respect for all five kinds of people may guide the self in forming high aspirations in life, to lead the self to identify with these people as role models, to be motivated to emulate them, and eventually to become like them (Li & Wang, 2004; Munro, 1975). The process of self-Pygmalion may be even stronger and more prevalent.

Summary of Respect in Westerners and Chinese People

Based on the forgoing discussion, respect includes both ought-respect and affect-respect. Whereas the former is mostly a social/attitudinal construct with little emotionality, the latter is much more emotionally charged. People in the West may experience more ought-respect than affect-respect because Western ought-respect is deeply rooted in the moral and social notions of justice, fairness, and equality for everyone regardless of people's particularities and diversity in origin and culture. Nevertheless, affect-respect is also experienced by Westerners when they meet those who are deemed respect-worthy. These people possess good qualities that lie in the moral/social and talent/achievement domains. Chinese culture distinguishes ought-respect and affect-respect by using two different terms. Although not originating from Western moral conceptions, Chinese ought-respect, too, tends to be directed at following law/social order, people's basic rights to resources and opportunities, valuation of different cultures and peoples, and sensitivity to one's social world. Chinese affect-respect may be less accurately constrained by the notion of earned respectworthiness. Their affect-respect is extended to five categories of people with the first two similar to those in the West (therefore perhaps more aligned with earned respectworthiness). But the three additional kinds of people are family and elders, persons in high political and social positions, and teachers/mentors/scholars. Earned respectworthiness may not apply to these categories of individuals. Finally, affect-respect is likely to benefit the self in both cultures (see Figure 13.1).

Future Research on Respect as a Self-Conscious Emotion

It has become apparent through our literature review that there is a dearth of research on respect as a positive self-conscious emotion in both cultures. Here we suggest some promising directions for future research. First, we need more research on the meaning of respect in European American and Chinese culture. Until we know what "respect" means to people in their own cultures, we are handicapped in our attempt to analyze the specific processes. Well-established methods to map out the meaning of respect can be found in studies such as Shaver et al. (1987) and Li et al. (2004). Once we have gained a basic un-

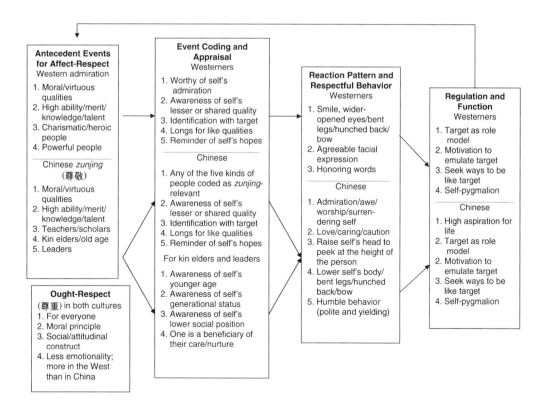

FIGURE 13.1. Diagram for respect as a self-conscious emotion in Westerners and Chinese people.

derstanding of the meaning of respect, the typical experience of respect as well as specific elements of each of Frijda's (1986) appraisal processes can be described. Shaver et al. (1987), Fischer et al. (1999), and Kitayama, Mesquita, and Karasawa (2006) offer a useful set of methods to collect and analyze such data. Further research could test specific hypotheses regarding the functions of respect in both cultures as has been done by researchers (Higgins et al., 2001; Ross, Heine, Wilson, & Sugimori, 2005). Finally, developmental research (Mascolo, Fischer, & Li, 2002) may focus on how respect develops in children with a broad range of methods such as those used by Aksan and Kochanska (2005) to study preschoolers' guilt and those used by Fung (1999) to study Taiwanese caregivers' socialization of moral learning with shaming techniques.

Research has come a long way toward recognizing the importance of human respect. Our inquiries will undoubtedly enlighten us about respect as a positive self-conscious emotion in lives across cultures.

REFERENCES

Abu-Lughod, L. (1996). Honor and shame. In M. Jackson (Ed.), *Things as they are: New directions in phenomenological anthropology* (pp. 51–69). Bloomington: Indiana University Press.

Aksan, N., & Kochanska, G. (2005). Conscience in childhood: Old questions, new answers. *Developmental Psychology, 41*(3), 506–516.

Ames, R. T., & Rosemont, H. Jr. (1999). *The "Analects" of Confucius: A philosophical translation.* New York: Ballantine.

Aron, A., & Westbay, L. (1996). Dimensions of the prototype of love. *Journal of Personality and Social Psychology, 70,* 535–551.

Barreto, M., & Ellemers, M. (2002). The impact of respect versus neglect of self-identities on identification and group loyalty. *Personality and Social Psychology Bulletin, 28*(5), 629–639.

Buck, R. (1999). The biological affects: A typology. *Psychological Review, 106*(2), 301–336.

Casimire, M. J., & Schnegg, M. (2003). Shame across cultures: The evolution, ontogeny, and function of a "moral emotion." In H. Keller, Y. H. Poortinga, & A. Scholmerich (Eds.), *Between culture and biology: Perspectives on ontogenetic development* (pp. 270–300). Cambridge, UK: Cambridge University Press.

Chang, H. C. (1997). Language and words: Communication in the *Analects* of Confucius. *Journal of Language and Social Psychology, 16,* 107–131.

Chang, Y.-C., & Hue, C.-W. (1991). Chinese college students' spontaneous self-concept: Configurations of content and order effects. *Chinese Journal of Psychology, 33,* 11–21.

Chapman, M. (1986). The structure of exchange: Piaget's sociological theory. *Human Development, 29,* 181–194.

Chen, E. C. H., & Fung, H. (2004, July). Crafting selves through everyday storytelling: A follow-up study of Taiwanese and Euro-American children. In Q. Wang, J. Li, & H. Fung (Chairs), *Narrative self-making in cultural contexts.* Poster symposium presented at the Conference of the International Society for the Study of Behavioral Development, Ghent, Belgium.

Cohen, R., Hsueh, Y., Zhou, Z.-K., Hancock, M. H., & Floyd, R. (2006). Respect, liking, and children's social competence in China and the United States. In D. W. Shwalb & B. J. Shwalb (Eds.), *Respect and disrespect: Cultural and developmental origins* (New Directions in Child and Adolescent Development Series, No. 114, pp. 53–65). San Francisco: Jossey-Bass.

D'Andrade, R. G. (1992). Schemas and motivation. In R. G. D'Andrade & C. Strauss (Eds.), *Human motives and cultural models* (pp. 23–44). New York: Cambridge University Press.

D'Andrade, R. G. (1995). *The development of cognitive anthropology.* New York: Cambridge University Press.

de Bary, W. T. (1983). *The liberal tradition in China.* New York: Columbia University Press.

de Bary, W. T. (1991). *Learning for one's self.* New York: Columbia University Press.

De Cremer, D. (2002). Respect and cooperation in social dilemmas: The importance of feeling included. *Personality and Social Psychology Bulletin, 28*(10), 1335–1341.

Fehr, B. (1988). Prototype analysis of the concepts of love and commitment. *Journal of Personality and Social Psychology, 55,* 557–579.

Fischer, H. A., Manstead, A. S. R., & Rodriguez Mosquera, P. M. (1999). The role of honor-related vs. individualist values in conceptualizing pride, shame, and anger: Spanish and Dutch cultural prototypes. *Cognition and Emotion, 13*(2), 149–179.

Fiske, A. P., & Haslam, N. (2005). The four basic social bonds: Structures for coordinating interaction. In M. W. Baldwin (Ed.), *Interpersonal cognition* (pp. 267–298). New York: Guilford Press.

Fiske, A. P., Kitayama, S., Markus, H. R., & Nisbett, R. E. (1998). The cultural matrix of social psychology. In G. T. Gilbert, S. T. Fiske, & G. Lindzey (Eds.), *Handbook of social psychology* (4th ed., Vol. 2, pp. 915–981). Boston: McGraw-Hill.

Fontaine, J. R. J., Poortinga, Y. H., Setiadi, B., & Markam, S. S. (2002). Cognitive structure of emotion terms in Indonesia and the Netherlands. *Cognition and Emotion, 16,* 61–86.

Francis, N. W., & Kucera, H. (1982). *Frequency analysis of English usage: Lexicon and grammar.* Boston: Houghton Mifflin.

Frei, J. R., & Shaver, P. R. (2002). Respect in close relationships: Prototype definition, self-report assessment, and initial correlates. *Personal Relationships, 9,* 121–139.

Frijda, N. H. (1986). *The emotions.* Cambridge, UK: Cambridge University Press.

Frijda, N. H., & Mesquita, B. (1995). The social roles and functions of emotions. In S. Kitayam & H. R. Markus (Eds.), *Emotion and culture: Empirical studies of mutual influence* (pp. 51–88). Washington, DC: American Psychological Association.

Fung, H. (1999). Becoming a moral child: The socialization of shame among young Chinese children. *Ethos, 27,* 180–209.

Fung, H., Miller, P. J., & Lin, L. C. (2004). Listening is active: Lessons from the narrative practices of Taiwanese families. In M. W. Pratt & B. E. Fiese (Eds.), *Family stories and the life course: Across time and generations* (pp. 303–323). Mahwah, NJ: Erlbaum.

Gottman, J. M. (1994). *Why marriages succeed or fail . . . and how you can make yours last.* New York: Simon & Schuster.

Gottman, J. M. (1996). *The heart of parenting: How to raise an emotionally intelligent child.* New York: Simon & Schuster.

Harkness, S., & Super, C. M. (Eds.). (1996). *Parents' cultural belief systems: Their origins, expressions, and consequences.* New York: Guilford Press.

Heider, K. (1991). *Landscapes of emotion: Mapping three cultures of emotion in Indonesia.* New York: Cambridge University Press.

Helwig, C. C., Arnold, M. L., Tan, D.-.L., & Boyd, D. (2003). Chinese adolescents' reasoning about democratic and authority-based decision making in peer, family, and school contexts. *Child Development, 74*(3), 783–800.

Heuer, L., Blumenthal, E., Douglas, A., & Weinblatt, T. (1999). A deservingness approach to respect as a relationally based fairness judgment. *Personality and Social Psychology Bulletin, 25*(10), 1279–1292.

Higgins, E. T., Friedman, R. S., Harlow, R. E., Idson, L. C., Adyuk, O. N., & Taylor, A. (2001). Achievement orientations from subjective histories of success: Promotion vs. prevention pride. *European Journal of Social Psychology, 31*(1), 3–23.

Ho, D. Y. F. (1986). Chinese patterns of socialization: A critical review. In M. Bond (Ed.), *The psychology of the Chinese people* (pp. 1–37). Hong Kong: Oxford University Press.

Ho, D. Y. F., & Chiu, C. Y. (1994). Component ideas of individualism, collectivism, and social organization: An application in the study of Chinese culture. In U. Kim, H. C. Triandis, Ç. Kagitçibasi, S. C. Choi, & G. Yoon (Eds.), *Individualism and collectivism: Theory, method, and applications* (pp. 137–156). Thousand Oaks, CA: Sage.

Hofstede, G. (1980). *Culture's consequences: International differences in work-related values.* Thousand Oaks, CA: Sage.

Hsu, F. L. K. (1981). *Americans and Chinese: Passage to difference* (3rd ed.). Honolulu: University of Hawaii.

Hsueh, Y., Zhou, Z.-K., Cohen, R., Hundley, R. J., & Deptula, D. P. (2005). Knowing and showing respect: Chinese and U.S. children's understanding of respect and its association to their friendships. *Journal of Psychology in Chinese Societies, 6*(2), 89–120.

Ihara, C. K. (2004). Are individual rights necessary?: A Confucian perspective. In K.-L. Shun & D. B. Wong (Eds.), *Confucian ethics: A comparative study of self, autonomy, and community* (pp. 11–30). New York: Cambridge University Press.

Kellenberg, J. (1995). *Relationship morality.* University Park: Pennsylvania State University Press.

Keltner, D., & Haidt, J. (2003). Approaching awe: A moral, spiritual, and aesthetic emotion. *Cognition and Emotion, 17*(2), 297–314.

King, A. Y. C. (1985). The individual and group in Confucianism: A relational perspective. In D. H. Munroe (Ed.), *Individualism and holism: Studies in Confucian and Taoist values* (pp. 57–70). Ann Arbor: University of Michigan Press.

Kitayama, S., Mesquita, B., & Karasawa, M. (2006). Cultural affordances and emotional experience: Socially engaging and disengaging emotions in Japan and the United States. *Journal of Personality and Social Psychology, 91*(5), 890–903.

Kohlberg, L. (1984). *Essays on moral development: Vol. 2. The psychology of moral development.* San Francisco: Harper & Row.

Kupperman, J. J. (2004). Tradition and community in the formation of character and self. In K.-L. Shun & D. B. Wong (Eds.), *Confucian ethics: A comparative study of self, autonomy, and community* (pp. 103–123). New York: Cambridge University Press.

Lawrence-Lightfoot, S. (2000). *Respect: An exploration.* Cambridge, MA: Perseus Books.

Lee, W. O. (1996). The cultural context for Chinese learners: Conceptions of learning in the Confucian tradition. In D. A. Watkins & J. B. Biggs (Eds.), *The Chinese learner* (pp. 45–67). Hong Kong: Comparative Education Research Centre.

Leung, K., & Bond, M. H. (1984). The impact of cultural collectivism on reward allocation. *Journal of Personality and Social Psychology, 4,* 793–804.

Levy, R. I. (1973). *Tahitians.* Chicago: University of Chicago Press.

Lewis, M. (1993). The emergence of human emotions. In M. Lewis & J. M. Haviland (Eds.), *Handbook of emotions* (pp. 223–235). New York: Guilford Press.

Li, J. (2001). Chinese conceptualization of learning. *Ethos, 29,* 111–137.

Li, J. (2003a). The core of Confucian learning. *American Psychologist, 58,* 146–147.

Li, J. (2003b). U.S. and Chinese cultural beliefs about learning. *Journal of Educational Psychology, 95*(2), 258–267.

Li, J. (2004a). "I learn and I grow big": Chinese preschoolers' purposes for learning. *International Journal of Behavioral Development, 28*(2), 116–128.

Li, J. (2004b). Learning as a task and a virtue: U.S. and Chinese preschoolers explain learning. *Developmental Psychology, 40*(4), 595–605.

Li, J. (2006a). Self in learning: Chinese adolescents' goals and sense of agency. *Child Development, 77*(2), 482–501.

Li, J. (2006b). [Chinese terms referring to positive self-conscious emotions of pride, honor, respect, face, gratitude, and humility]. Unpublished raw data.

Li, J., & Fischer, K. W. (2004). Thoughts and emotions in American and Chinese cultural beliefs about learning. In D. Y. Dai & R. Sternberg (Eds.), *Motivation, emotion, and cognition: Integrative perspectives on intellectual functioning and development* (pp. 385–418). Mahwah, NJ: Erlbaum.

Li, J., & Wang, L.-Q. (2004). Perceptions of achievement and achieving peers in U.S. and Chinese kindergartners. *Social Development, 13*(3), 413–436.

Li, J., Wang, L.-Q., & Fischer, K. W. (2004). The organization of Chinese shame concepts. *Cognition and Emotion, 18*(6), 767–797.

Lindsay-Hartz, J., de Rivera, J., & Mascolo, M. F. (1995). Differentiating guilt and shame and their effects on motivation. In J. P. Tangney & K. W. Fischer (Eds.), *Self-conscious emotions: The psychology of shame, guilt, embarrassment, and pride* (pp. 274–300). New York: Guilford Press.

Linley, P. A., Joseph, S., Harrington, S., & Wood, A. M. (2006). Positive psychology: Past, present, and (possible) future. *Journal of Positive Psychology, 1*(1), 3–16.

Mann, L., Mitsui, H., Beswick, G., & Harmoni, R. (1994). A study of Japanese and Australian children's respect for others. *Journal of Cross-Cultural Psychology, 25,* 133–145.

Markman, H., Stanley, S., & Blumberg, S. L. (1994). *Fighting for your marriage: Positive steps for preventing divorce and preserving a lasting love.* San Francisco: Jossey-Bass.

Markus, H. R., & Kitayama, S. (1991). Culture and the self: Implications for cognition, emotion and motivation. *Psychological Review, 98*(2), 224–253.

Markus, H. R., & Nurius, P. (1986). Possible selves. *American Psychologist, 41,* 954–969.

Mascolo, M. J., Fischer, K. W., & Li, J. (2002). Dynamic development of component systems of emotions: Pride, shame, and guilt in China and the United States. In R. J. Davidson, K. Scherer, & H. H. Goldsmith (Eds.), *Handbook of affective sciences* (pp. 375–408). Oxford, UK: Oxford University Press.

Menon, T., Morris, M. W., Chiu, C.-Y., & Hong, Y.-Y. (1999). Culture and construal of agency: Attribution to individual versus group dispositions. *Journal of Personality and Social Psychology, 76,* 701–717.

Menon, U., & Shweder, R. A. (1994). Kali's tongue: Cultural psychology and the power of shame in Orissa, India. In S. Kitayama & H. R. Markus (Eds.), *Emotion and culture: Empirical studies of mutual influence* (pp. 241–284). Washington, DC: American Psychological Association.

Mesquita, B. (2003). Emotions as dynamic cultural phenomena. In N. Davidson, K. Scherer, & H. Goldsmith (Eds.), *Handbook of affective science* (pp. 871–890). New York: Oxford University Press.

Mesquita, B., & Frijda, N. H. (1992). Cultural variations in emotions: A review. *Psychological Bulletin, 112,* 179–204.

Munro, D. J. (1975). The Chinese view of modeling. *Human Development, 18,* 333–352.

Piaget, J. (1962). *The moral judgment of the child* (M. Gabain, Trans.). New York: Collier Books. (Original work published 1932)

Piaget, J. (1995). Essay on the theory of qualitative values in static sociology. In J. Piaget, *Sociological studies* (L. Smith, Ed., T. Brown et al., Trans., pp. 97–133). London: Routledge. (Original work published 1941)

Quinn, N., & Holland, D. (1987). Introduction. In D. Holland & N. Quinn (Eds.), *Cultural models in language and thought* (pp. 3–40). New York: Cambridge University Press.

Rodriguez Mosquera, P. M., Manstead, A. S. R., & Fischer, H. A. (2002). The role of honour concerns in emotional reactions to offences. *Cognition and Emotion, 16*(1), 143–163.

Rosemont, H. Jr. (2004). Whose democracy? Which rights?: A Confucian critique of modern Western liberalism. In K.-L. Shun & D. B. Wong (Eds.), *Confucian ethics: A comparative study of self, autonomy, and community* (pp. 49–71). New York: Cambridge University Press.

Ross, M., Heine, S. J., Wilson, A. E., & Sugimori, S. (2005). Cross-cultural discrepancies in self-appraisals. *Personality and Social Psychology Bulletin, 31*(9), 1175–1188.

Rubin, Z. (1973). *Liking and loving: An invitation to social psychology.* New York: Holt, Rinehart, & Winston.

Scheff, T. J. (2003). Shame in self and society. *Symbolic Interaction, 26*(2), 239–262.

Schneider, C. D. (1977). *Shame, exposure, and privacy.* Boston: Beacon Press.

Schwartz, S. H. (1994). Beyond individualism/collectivism: New cultural dimensions of values. In U. Kim, H. C. Triandis, Ç. Kagitçibasi, S.-C. Choi, & G. Yoon (Eds.), *Individualism and collectivism: Theory, method, and applications* (pp. 19–40). Thousand Oaks, CA: Sage.

Seligman, M. E. (1999). The president's address. *American Psychologist, 54,* 559–562.

Seligman, M. E., & Csikszentmihalyi, M. (2000). Positive psychology: An introduction. *American Psychologist, 55,* 5–14.

Shaver, P., Schwartz, J., Kirson, D., & O'Connor, C. (1987). Emotion knowledge: Further exploration of a prototype approach. *Journal of Personality and Social Psychology, 52,* 1061–1086.

Shweder, R. A., Much, N. C., Mahapatra, M., & Park, L. (1997). The "Big Three" of morality (autonomy, community, and divinity), and the "Big Three" explanations of suffering. In A. Brandt & R. Rozin (Eds.), *Morality and health* (pp. 119–169). New York: Routledge.

Spiro, M. E. (1987). Collective representations and mental representations in religious symbol systems. In B. Kilborne & L. L. Langness (Eds.), *Culture and human nature: Theoretical papers of Melford E. Spiro* (pp. 161–184). Chicago: University of Chicago Press.

Strauss, C. (1992). Models of motives. In R. G. D'Andrade & C. Strauss (Eds.), *Human motives and cultural models* (pp. 1–20). New York: Cambridge University Press.

Tangney, J. P. (1998). How does guilt differ from shame? In J. Bybee (Ed.), *Guilt and children* (pp. 1–17). San Diego, CA: Academic Press.

Tangney, J. P. (2002). Humility. In C. R. Snyder & S. J. Lopez (Eds.), *Handbook of positive psychology* (pp. 411–419). New York: Oxford University Press.

Tangney, J. P., & Fischer, K. W. (Eds.). (1995). *Self-conscious emotions: The psychology of shame, guilt, embarrassment, and pride.* New York: Guilford Press.

Ting-Toomey, S. (Ed.). (1994). *The challenge of facework: Cross-cultural and interpersonal issues.* Albany: State University of New York.

Tracy, J. L., & Robins, R. W. (2004). Show your pride: Evidence for a discrete emotion expression. *Psychological Science, 15*(3), 194–197.

Tracy, J. L., Robins, R. W., & Lagattuta, K. H. (2005). Can children recognize pride? *Emotion, 5*(3), 251–257.

Triandis, H., McCusker, C., & Hui, C. (1990). Multimethod probes of individualism and collectivism. *Journal of Personality and Social Psychology, 54,* 323–338.

Tu, W. M. (1979). *Humanity and self-cultivation: Essays in Confucian thought.* Berkeley, CA: Asian Humanities Press.

Tu, W. M. (1989). *Centrality and commonality: An essay on Confucian religiousness.* Albany: State University of New York Press.

Tweed, R. G., & Lehman, D. R. (2002). Learning considered within a cultural context: Confucian and Socratic approaches. *American Psychologist, 57*(2), 89–99.

Tzeng, O. C. S. (1993). *Measurement of love and intimate relations: Theories, scales, and application for love development, maintenance, and dissolution.* Westport, CT: Praeger.

Wang, H., Chang, B.-R., Li, Y.-S., Lin, L.-H., Liu, J., Sun, Y.-L., et al. (1986). *Xiandai hanyu pinlu cidian* [Dictionary of the frequency of vocabulary in modern Chinese]. Beijing, China: Beijing Languages Institute Press.

Watkins, D. A., & Biggs, J. B. (Eds.). (1996). *The Chinese learner: Cultural, psychological, and contextual influences.* Hong Kong: Comparative Education Research Centre.

Wink, P., Gao, B., Jones, S., & Chao, F. (1997). Social values and relationships with parents among American college women of Chinese and European descent. *International Journal of Psychology, 32,* 169–179.

Wu, S.-P., & Lai, C.-Y. (1992). *Complete text of the four books and five classics in modern Chinese* [in Chinese]. Beijing, China: International Culture Press.

Wu, J.-R., Wang, Z.-L., Liu, S.-M., Wei, D.-Y., Wang, B., Ying, M.-R., et al. (1978). *Chinese–English dictionary.* Beijing, China: Business Press.

Yang, C. F. (1993). Are Chinese people really "collectivist"?: On Chinese cultural value system. In K. S. Yang (Ed.), *Chinese values from the perspective of social science* (pp. 321–433). [in Chinese]. Taipei, Taiwan: Guiguan.

Yang, K. S. (1997). Theories and research in Chinese personality: An indigenous approach. In H. S. R. Kao & D. Sinha (Eds.), *Asian perspectives on psychology* (Cross-cultural research and methodology series, Vol. 19, pp. 236–264). New Delhi, India: Sage.

Yau, J., & Smetana, J. G. (2003). Conceptions of moral, social-conventional, and personal events among Chinese preschoolers. *Child Development, 74*(3), 647–658.

PART IV

SPECIFIC EMOTIONS

Function and Conceptualization

14

Is Embarrassment a Blessing or a Curse?

ROWLAND S. MILLER

Embarrassment is an unpleasant emotion. On occasion, when we have done something merely goofy—such as making an innocent malapropism—our small miscues may be entertaining and amusing to everyone present. But even mild embarrassments cause unwelcome chagrin and abashment, and we are rarely glad that they have occurred. And there is nothing delightful about the crushing discombobulation and mortification that stronger embarrassment can bring; intense embarrassment can be humiliating, ruining interactions and reputations and causing substantial distress.

Why should such a disagreeable emotion exist? As we will see, functional analyses of embarrassment note its social, self-conscious nature and generally assert that embarrassment evolved to maintain social order. In becoming embarrassed, people communicate to others that they recognize and regret their misbehavior and can be trusted to (try to) do better in the future. And to the extent that embarrassment provides an automatic and effective way to avoid painful rejection and exclusion by others, embarrassment often serves us well. In many instances, embarrassment reassures others of our good intentions and elicits from them kindly, supportive reactions that help us quickly overcome our missteps.

There is, however, a dark side to embarrassment's effects on social life. Fueled by overactive imaginations, enduring egocentrism, and misunderstanding of embarrassment's ameliorative effects, people often respond to embarrassing events with undue anxiety and woe. In addition, they may go to lengths to avoid potential embarrassment that can be risky and self-destructive. Instead of being beneficial, embarrassment sometimes operates not as a personal blessing, but as a harmful curse.

In what follows, I address embarrassment's disadvantages and trace them to sources that are maladaptive but avoidable. After delineating the nature of embarrassment and its interactive effects, I draw on Mark Leary's (2004b, and Chapter 3, this volume) provocative analysis of the liabilities of human self-consciousness to ponder whether embarrassment is more often a blessing or a curse.

THE NATURE OF EMBARRASSMENT

Embarrassment is an acute state of startled, flustered abashment and chagrin that results from events that increase the threat of unwanted evaluations from real or imagined audiences (Miller, 1996, 2001a). It is involuntary, and it usually strikes without warning, being created by abrupt changes of fortune that cause unanticipated predicaments. These surprises bring self-conscious feelings of exposure and ungainly awkwardness; embarrassed people typically feel painfully conspicuous and clumsy, and their discomfiture can make them maladroit. And pervading these feelings is sheepish regret and chagrin; embarrassed people rue their circumstances and may be abashed, mortified, or even humiliated by the unwanted impressions they feel they have made on others (Parrott & Smith, 1991).

In being a social-evaluative emotion, embarrassment is a cousin of both shyness and shame, but it is clearly different from either one (Harris, 2003; Miller, 2001b). Importantly, embarrassment is clearly an *emotion* (Ekman, 1992) that strikes quickly and automatically but lasts only a short time, whereas shyness operates as a *mood* that lingers for longer periods. Shyness is also characterized by conscious worry and trepidation over disapproval that has not yet occurred—it is a *"future-oriented* mood state" (Barlow, Chorpita, & Turovsky, 1996, p. 253)—whereas embarrassment is a stronger unbidden reaction to real current threats (Mosher & White, 1981). Shame also emerges from actual transgressions, but it is a darker, angrier, and more intense emotion (Elison & Harter, 2004) that, unlike embarrassment, occurs now and then when people are alone, contemplating their misbehavior in private (Tangney, Miller, Flicker, & Barlow, 1996). Embarrassment engenders sheepish discombobulation, whereas shame produces spiteful disgust and disdain for one's flaws (Miller & Tangney, 1994). Thus, embarrassment, shyness, and shame are all self-conscious states that depend, in part, on people's concern for what others may be thinking of them, but they are phenomenologically distinct, they emerge from different events, and they have different effects on social interaction (Miller, 1996, 2001b). In particular, shyness and shame are typically much less desirable than embarrassment can be; whereas the inhibited disaffiliation of shyness and the antagonistic self-disgust of shame motivate aloof or obnoxious social behavior, embarrassment makes people conciliatory and eager to please, as we will see shortly.

Antecedents

Most embarrassments occur when someone violates a norm of deportment, civility, self-control, or gracefulness by making a mental error, behaving clumsily, or losing control of possessions such as cars, clothes, and pets. In such instances, "people may trip and fall, spill their drinks, rip their pants, stall their cars, fart inadvertently, and forget others' names" (Miller, 2001b, p. 283), and these sorts of individual misbehavior cause about two-thirds of the embarrassments people encounter (Miller, 1992). Importantly, however, embarrassment only results from such missteps *when other people are present*. Embarrassment almost never occurs when people are alone (Tangney et al., 1996), and when it does, discovery of one's misbehavior by others usually seems imminent. Thus, people may unabashedly choose to engage in private conduct that nevertheless causes a flash of embarrassment when they hear an unexpected car in the drive or footsteps in the hall.

Embarrassment may also occur through no fault of one's own when interactions take awkward turns (Miller, 1992), one is the innocent butt of a practical joke (Sharkey, Kim,

& Diggs, 2001), or even when teammates or partners misbehave and one is sullied by association (Curtis, Lickel, & Schmader, 2005). The common element in these events is that, fairly or unfairly, they all convey to others surprising, undesired information that makes an unwanted impression. Embarrassing events all (threaten to) portray their targets in an unwelcome and usually unfavorable manner to others, and they thereby raise the prospect of negative evaluation and interpersonal rejection (Sabini, Siepmann, Stein, & Meyerowitz, 2000).

It is also noteworthy that embarrassment appears to operate similarly around the world. Formal studies of embarrassment have been undertaken in Sweden, Hungary, India, Yemen, Iran, and Japan, as well as in North America (e.g., Hashimoto & Shimizu, 1988; Stattin, Magnusson, Olah, Kassin, & Reddy, 1991), and the events that discombobulate those in Western cultures befuddle those in the East as well. Across cultures, embarrassment occurs when events suddenly increase the threat of unwanted evaluations from others.

Physiology

Particular events cause embarrassment and particular physical reactions result. When embarrassment strikes, a rather distinctive pattern of sympathetic nervous system activation unfolds (Gerlach, Wilhelm, & Roth, 2003). Systolic and diastolic blood pressures both increase, rising gradually and continuously throughout the embarrassing episode. Heart rate increases, too, but only for the first minute of a predicament; after its initial rise, heart rate returns to its baseline level another minute or so later (Harris, 2001). The adrenal gland also releases cortisol into the blood, further preparing embarrassed actors to deal with their threatening circumstances (Dickerson, Gruenewald, & Kemeny, 2004). Embarrassing events clearly have autonomic impact. Altogether, these reactions seem to be unique to embarrassment, distinguishing it from other emotional states (Herrald & Tomaka, 2002).

These reactions may also be accompanied by an even more singular physical response, the visible reddening of the face known as a "blush" (Edelmann, 2001). When an imposing threat occurs, veins in other areas of the skin constrict (to direct more blood to muscles). However, the veins in our necks and cheeks are supplied with unusual β-adrenergic receptors that lead them to behave differently (Mellander, Andersson, Afzelius, & Hellstrand, 1982): They dilate in response to social threat (Drummond, 1997), bringing more blood closer to the surface of the skin and causing coloration that can be readily distinguished from the facial flushing that sometimes occurs with intoxication or exercise (Leary, Britt, Cutlip, & Templeton, 1992). Blushing is uniquely associated with embarrassment (Edelmann, 2001), and with individual differences in susceptibility to embarrassment (Leary & Meadows, 1991), around the world; it has been observed in every country and in every ethnic group in which it has been studied (e.g., Edelmann & Iwawaki, 1987; Simon & Shields, 1996), and those who are prone to embarrassment blush more readily and more intensely than do those who are harder to embarrass. It is also remarkable that this response occurs only in areas of the body that are routinely visible to others. Indeed, the visibility of this response may underlie its evolutionary origins, as we shall see.

None of these reactions occur if one is unaware of one's social peril. Notably, people who lack the self-conscious ability to understand what other people may be thinking of them are relatively immune to embarrassment. Studies of the brain employing fMRI have demonstrated that medial regions of the prefrontal cortex are active when people recognize and react to violations of social norms (Berthoz, Armony, Blair, & Dolan, 2002). Significantly, these are the areas of the brain that allow us to comprehend others' judgments of us (Beer, Heerey, Keltner, Scabini, & Knight, 2003). Young children who incur damage to the prefrontal cortex never fully learn the conventions and moral rules that govern the social behavior of the rest of us (Anderson, Bechara, Damasio, Tranel, & Damasio, 1999), and adults with orbitofrontal lesions sometimes lose their capacity for embarrassment altogether (Beer et al., 2003; Devinsky, Hafler, & Victor, 1982). Embarrassment is evidently closely tied to the momentous human ability to take others' perspectives and to judge ourselves as others do; when this normal ability is impaired, susceptibility to embarrassment is diminished (Heerey, Keltner, & Capps, 2003).

Nonverbal Behavior

Embarrassment also elicits a distinctive pattern of nonverbal behavior that makes one's chagrin plain to others whether or not blushing occurs (Keltner, 1995; Keltner & Buswell, 1997). When a predicament begins, people avert their gazes (typically looking down and to the left) and try to keep from smiling by compressing their lips or pulling down the corners of their mouths. These efforts usually fail, and embarrassed actors typically break into abashed, sheepish grins that are recognizably different from the smiles that accompany real amusement (Asendorpf, 1990). Then, they may cover their smiles with one hand, bow their heads, restlessly shift their postures, and gesture broadly, and, if they try to speak, they may stutter and stammer (Edelmann & Hampson, 1979, 1981). This entire sequence takes about 5 seconds to unfold (Keltner, 1995).

The social situations people inhabit can influence their nonverbal responses (Costa, Dinsbach, Manstead, & Ricci Bitti, 2001), and not all of these actions always occur. In addition, there is no particular facial expression (as is the case with several other emotions) that signals embarrassment to others (Keltner & Ekman, 2000). Nevertheless, the nonverbal behavior that springs from embarrassment usually presents a tableau that is coherent and characteristic enough to allow others to correctly identify embarrassment in their midst. David Marcus and I demonstrated in two studies that observers generally agree among themselves about the extent of a target's embarrassment, and these judgments are reliably correlated with the target's self-reports of actual abashment and chagrin. In the first investigation, groups of women watched from an observation room as, one by one, each of them performed an embarrassing task: dancing for 60 seconds to recorded music (Marcus, Wilson, & Miller, 1996). In the second study, men and women giving presentations to their college classes provided reports of their embarrassment as their classmates rated their awkwardness and chagrin (Marcus & Miller, 1999). Both in the lab and in the field, embarrassment was dependably detected, and audiences could tell how embarrassed others were.

Thus, embarrassment may feel disorganized and chaotic, but nonverbal expressions of embarrassment nonetheless emerge in a patten that is discernable and readily recognizable. And when the flustered nonverbal signals of abashment or mortification are coupled with a blush, embarrassment is positively unmistakable (Keltner, 1995). When people become embarrassed, their distress is usually visible to others, and this appears to be true around the world (Consedine, Strongman, & Magai, 2003).

Individual Differences

Of course, some people respond more intensely to social predicaments than others do. Individuals differ in *embarrassability,* or susceptibility to embarrassment, and the correlates of this trait shed further light on the nature of embarrassment (Miller, 1995). Highly embarrassable people get embarrassed more frequently than other people, but that is not because they are especially maladroit or inept; there is no link between embarrassability and one's global level of social skill (Miller, 1995). Instead, embarrassable people labor under the weight of two interrelated burdens: They pay particular attention to cues that indicate what others are thinking about them, and they fear that others' evaluations are more negative and rejecting than they really are.

First, embarrassability is related to the need to belong (Leary & Cottrell, 2001). Embarrassable people want to be accepted by others. They tend to be high in rejection sensitivity (Sabini et al., 2000), and they are highly motivated to avoid social exclusion (Sharkey & Kim, 2000). As a result, they heed social norms with more diligence than most (Miller, 1995), and they probably assess others' implicit reactions to them more alertly and perceptively than less embarrassable people do (Edelmann, 1985; Pickett, Gardner, & Knowles, 2004).

A desire to be included and accepted by others that is coupled with attentiveness to decorum and propriety may actually be a desirable disposition, all by itself. However, embarrassability is also positively correlated with neuroticism (Maltby & Day, 2000). Highly embarrassable people are prone to fretfulness and worry, and, in particular, they brood about what others are thinking of them. They exhibit high fear of negative evaluation (Miller, 1995): They dread potential disapproval, and they worriedly anticipate more displeasure from others than they actually receive.

So acute susceptibility to embarrassment seems to depend, at least in part, on exaggerated sensitivity to social evaluation. People who are less attuned to the evaluative whims of others, and who are less prone to dread trivial disregard when it occurs, experience milder embarrassments than more fearful people do. Please keep this conclusion in mind; it is central to our consideration of whether embarrassment is more a blessing than a curse.

Interactive Responses

Several studies have examined self-reports of recent embarrassments (e.g., Cupach & Metts, 1992; Miller, 1996; Sharkey & Stafford, 1990). When they are flustered by embarrassment, people respond in various ways. They sometimes find themselves in such disarray that they simply flee the scene, abandoning the situation and running away. This desperate response occurs about a tenth of the time (Miller, 1996), and it usually makes a bad impression on any onlookers, compounding one's peril (Levin & Arluke, 1982). More often, however, in a third of all cases, embarrassed actors behave in conciliatory ways that are likely to assuage disgruntled audiences (Miller, 1996): They apologize for their misbehavior and take action to repair any damage or redress any inconvenience they have caused. If no harm is done to others, they may resort to humor, acknowledging their gaffe with a lighthearted remark; this approach is employed about a sixth of the time (Miller, 1996).

Thus, half of the time, people are agreeable or contrite (or both) when they respond to embarrassment. On other occasions, usually when minor disruptions occur, people make no mention of their missteps and continue with their interactions as if nothing had happened. This, too, can be a good-natured response that is not at all brusque or impolite because belabored apologies for minor social misdemeanors can create more commotion than they resolve. A brief nonverbal display of chagrin that is followed by a return to the interaction is often a fitting, efficacious response to small miscues (Cupach & Metts, 1994).

Finally, people do sometimes behave angrily when they are embarrassed, but this occurs rarely (only 5% of the time), and only when someone else has intentionally caused one's embarrassing predicament (Miller, 1996). Anger and aggression almost never occur when one's embarrassment is self-imposed.

In general, then, embarrassment leads people to behave in an amiable, conciliatory manner. Embarrassed people are also more helpful and generous than they would otherwise be; they volunteer more help than usual to those in need, even when the recipients are unaware of the prior predicament (Apsler, 1975). Embarrassment is unpleasant, but it engenders agreeable conduct: "Most of the time when we're embarrassed, we are contrite, humble, and eager to please" (Miller, 1996, p. 175).

Others' Reactions

How, then, do onlookers respond to an actor's obvious embarrassment? This is a key element of embarrassment's influence on social life, and it is widely misunderstood (Savitsky, Epley, & Gilovich, 2001), perhaps because of the lessons we learn as children. When we were youngsters, our embarrassing missteps may have routinely resulted in harsh treatment. When I asked fifth-graders to keep track of their embarrassments, I found that *most* of the time peer audiences responded with laughter, derision, or ridicule to any gaffe or slip that made one conspicuous (Miller, 1996). Jeers and mockery were frequent, and merely witnessing others' predicaments—much less encountering such ridicule ourselves—probably taught many of us to dread any departure from accepted behavior (Janes & Olson, 2000).

Adolescence is a developmental period of novelty and change in which relations with one's peers become exceptionally important (Csikszentmihalyi & Larson, 1984), and that may account in part for the harsh treatment audiences dish out to those who clumsily misbehave (Buss, 1980). However, things are different now that we are adults. Surveys consistently show that, among adults, obvious embarrassment is ordinarily greeted by empathy and support from others (e.g., Metts & Cupach, 1989; Miller, 1996). Abashed actors are routinely provided comfort and consolation ("It's okay, it's no big deal"), understanding ("I know how you feel—it happens to me all the time"), and encouragement ("Don't worry about it"). Instead of encountering hostility and rejection, embarrassed adults are often explicitly reassured that their audiences continue to hold them in high esteem. Smiling and laughing does sometimes occur, but they are rarely derisive; instead, they are usually jocular and affable. Even if laughter increases the target's embarrassment, it demonstrates that the circumstances *are* laughable rather than grave.

Adult audiences are agreeable rather than critical because, importantly, embarrassment in response to a public predicament *makes a good impression* on observers. If some transgression occurs, people who become abashed by their public pratfalls receive more favorable evaluations than do those who remain unruffled and unperturbed by their misbehavior. Gün Semin and Tony Manstead (1982) provided a clever demonstration of this pattern when they showed research participants videotapes of a man who inadvertently knocked over a large display of toilet paper rolls in a grocery store. Four different versions of the tape were prepared, depicting the shopper reacting with evident embarrassment or cool aplomb and either picking up the rolls or leaving them scattered on the floor. Observers liked the shoppers who were abashed by their predicaments more than those who remained calm. A sheepish shopper who cleaned up his mess received the kindest evaluations, but even the obviously mortified actor who just fled the scene was liked somewhat better than the unflappable fellow who calmly picked up the rolls. After a clumsy miscue, when it was appropriate, embarrassment engendered more social acceptance than imperturbableness did.

Blushing has similar effects. Peter de Jong (1999) manipulated the presence or absence of a visible blush in written descriptions of other shopping mishaps (with someone knocking bakery rolls to the floor in one version, or knocking jars of vegetables off a shelf in another), and found that blushing also deflected disapproval. Readers considered shoppers who blushed to be more trustworthy, sympathetic, and likable than those who did not blush, and, in particular, an errant protagonist who blushed seemed a more moral and decent person than one who did not.

These and other data (Edelmann, 1982; Semin & Papadopoulou, 1990) converge on the conclusion that, when we encounter social predicaments, "*others will like us and treat us better if we do become embarrassed* than they will if we remain unruffled, cool, and calm" (Miller, 1996, p. 152). Moreover, people seem to be aware of this fact: When they are embarrassed by laboratory tasks, they *wish* their chagrin to be known to observers (Leary, Landel, & Patton, 1996). This is a sensible desire, because embarrassment that follows sticky situations mollifies observers and elicits more social approval than would otherwise occur.

There is, however, an important qualification to all of this: The interactive influence of signs of embarrassment depends on the context in which they occur. Blushing that occurs in ambiguous circumstances or in the absence of a known predicament may signify that its owner has a guilty conscience, and it can undermine, rather than improve, one's public image (de Jong, Peters, De Cremer, & Vranken, 2002). Consider this scenario: A friend asks for a special favor so that she can leave town early the next morning, and you grant the request, but you run into her in the mall the following afternoon and she blushes deeply when she sees you. In this instance, the presence of a blush causes poorer evaluations than would occur without one, probably because it demonstrates that the actor *has* misbehaved and knows it (de Jong, Peters, & De Cremer, 2003); the blush belies the possibility that an innocent misunderstanding has occurred.

In a similar fashion, embarrassment that seems extreme, being disproportional to one's predicament, does not impress audiences favorably. Levin and Arluke (1982) demonstrated this reality in a procedure in which a young woman visited several college classes to recruit volunteers for a research project. In one condition in their design, she presented her appeal calmly and without incident, but in another she dropped her sign-up sheets and appeared to be embarrassed as she made her request. Finally, in a third condition, she exclaimed, "Oh, my god! I can't continue," when she dropped the sheets, and she scurried from the room (and the class's instructor distributed the sheets for her). Consistent with embarrassment's potentially beneficial effects, the students offered her more help when she flubbed and was abashed than when a predicament did not occur. However, the students were quite unhelpful when she overreacted to her rather innocuous blunder. Instead of helping the situation and improving her outcomes, disproportionate discombobulation evidently made a poor impression on her audience.

The take-home message here is that, when it is calibrated to its context—and thereby appropriate to the circumstances in which it occurs—embarrassment is a *desirable* response to social misdemeanors that portray a person in an unwanted manner. Audiences generally respond to such embarrassment with sympathy and support, and the actor receives more favorable evaluations than those that would have followed had the embarrassment been absent. In contrast, exaggerated embarrassment that seems excessive and overstated does not make a good impression, likely making one seem inept or anxious. And embarrassment that occurs in the absence of any apparent predicament is suspicious; it, too, is either overstated or founded in a previously unknown transgression that it may bring to light.

THE FUNCTIONS OF EMBARRASSMENT

Altogether, then, the characteristics of embarrassment—including the public pitfalls that elicit it, the visible reactions it engenders, and the conciliatory responses it promotes—are distinctive. Embarrassment emerges from social peril, takes a recognizable form, and motivates desirable remedial behavior. It is involuntary, and its physical manifestations (e.g., a blush) cannot be faked.

Why does such a singular set of reactions exist? Theorists' reasoning usually begins with the assumption that, because nature is parsimonious, emotions like embarrassment must be (or once must have been) advantageous: Such an elaborate system would never have evolved if it were not in some way adaptive (Fridlund, 1994; Plutchik, 1980). Then, noting embarrassment's public nature and its beneficial interactive effects, theorists have suggested that embarrassment arose to serve several particular useful social functions (Miller, 2004).

First, an embarrassing wash of flustered chagrin interrupts any misbehavior and focuses one's attention on one's predicament. Moreover, because embarrassment is aversive, it readies one for corrective action that will address one's peril and reduce one's discomfort (Keltner & Haidt, 2001; Leary, 2000). Embarrassment thus acts in this regard as an interactive, social counterpart to physical pain that alerts us to threats to our bodily well-being; it informs us that dangerous rebuke and rejection may be imminent (Miller & Leary, 1992). Without this information, we might misbehave more persistently. In fact, people who are incapable of experiencing embarrassment blithely violate social norms without realizing that they are doing so (Beer et al., 2003).

In addition, because it is readily recognizable, embarrassment is a reliable *signal* to others that one both realizes and regrets one's predicament (Bless, 2002). And in being uncontrollable, embarrassment may serve as a nonverbal apology that demonstrates that one is genuinely contrite:

> Those who are blushing are somehow saying that they know, care about, and fear others' evaluations and that they share those values deeply; they also communicate their sorrow over any possible faults or inadequacies on their part, thus performing an acknowledgment, a confession, and an apology aimed at inhibiting others' aggression or avoiding social ostracism. (Castelfranchi & Poggi, 1990, p. 240)

It is likely that embarrassment thus reassures observers of one's good intentions, and that may be a key reason why adults respond with more kindness and approval to embarrassed actors than to implacable malefactors after some predicament occurs.

Thus, as a social emotion rooted in our concern over what others are thinking of us, embarrassment provides us with a useful mechanism with which to overcome the inevitable small miscues of social life. It presumably evolved because it forestalls punishment or rejection that would otherwise occur (Semin & Papadopoulou, 1990). Early hominids who developed such a mechanism probably lived with others (and reproduced) more successfully than did those who were heedless of their fellows' evaluations of them (Leary, 2004a; Turner, 1996). Justifiable embarrassment that is proportional to a predicament mollifies and reassures one's critics, motivates remedial action, and generally resolves social perils, and we would likely be much worse off without it.

THE DOWNSIDE OF EMBARRASSMENT

Our species is thus equipped with a desirable emotional system that leaves us attuned to social evaluation and that provides us a propitious means of managing inadvertent misbehavior (Baldwin & Baccus, 2004; Leary, 2004a). Its useful social functions make embarrassment adaptive, and although it is unpleasant, it aids and abets social life. Indeed, I think that embarrassment is usually accorded less respect and admiration than it deserves. It may seem trivial, and it is sometimes laughable, but embarrassment almost certainly exists because it afforded evolutionary advantages to our ancient ancestors.

That is the upside of embarrassment. It is a hardwired, natural offshoot of human self-consciousness that affords us a handy, effective mechanism with which to forestall social rejection. And, if it always operated as it was designed, becoming active only when needed and then operating at fitting levels, embarrassment would unquestionably be a blessing.

Unfortunately, the system sometimes misfires. Embarrassment occurs too readily and too intensely in too many of us. We care too much about what others are thinking of us, and we believe that our actions are more conspicuous and salient to others than they really are. In addition, unnecessary and exaggerated desires to avoid embarrassment lead to timidity and passivity that can put us in harm's way. And, when it is extreme, susceptibility to embarrassment has pathological effects, significantly impairing our sociality. Embarrassment is a desirable emotion, but disadvantage results when it occurs when it is not needed or warranted. Interestingly, it is much like other aspects of human self-consciousness in this regard.

The Curse of the Self

In his notable analysis of the potential problems that can result from our human capacity for self-reflection—a work entitled *The Curse of the Self*—Mark Leary (2004b) acknowledged that self-consciousness is an extraordinary capability. Our remarkable ability to think consciously about ourselves allows us to plan for the future, and to set intentional goals and to monitor our progress toward achieving them. We can contemplate and evaluate our own thoughts and behaviors, and we can imagine others' points of view, including what they may be thinking of us. Self-consciousness underlies self-control and makes civilization possible.

However, Leary asserted, self-consciousness can be surprisingly costly too. We worry about improbable events that never occur, making mountains out of entirely imaginary molehills. We construct and then work to defend egotistical self-concepts that magnify the impact of any imperfection. And, motivated by the wish to favorably impress others, we forgo seat belts, condoms, and sun screen and take other foolhardy risks while we drink, tan, and diet imprudently. According to Leary (2004b, p. 24), "The same ability to self-reflect that makes us wonderfully human and underlies the best features of civilization also creates havoc with people's lives, leading to suffering, . . . disastrous decisions," and maladaptive behavior.

Thus, for Leary, self-consciousness is both a great ally and, on occasion, a fearsome foe. I contend that the self-conscious emotion of embarrassment is a good example of Leary's point.

The Spotlight Effect

One influence that leads to disproportionate embarrassment when we commit some gaffe is our tendency to assume that our actions are more prominent and salient to others than they really are. Our successes and failures are usually very interesting and notable to us, and because most people are rather egocentric, we expect that our conduct will be conspicuous to others as well. We naively expect that others will be as aware of our missing buttons, cold sores, and bad hair days as we are. But others neither care about nor notice our actions or appearances as much as we think they do, a misperception known as the *spotlight effect* (Gilovich, Medvec, & Savitsky, 2000).

In their demonstrations of the spotlight effect, Tom Gilovich and his colleagues have asked research participants to wear odd T-shirts, engage in group discussion of touchy topics, or play volleyball, and in each case, the participants' perceptions of what their colleagues or audiences would think of them were compared to the observers' actual judgments. Every time, onlookers found the participants' actions less noteworthy and memorable than the participants thought they would. For instance, audiences were six times less likely to take note of the T-shirts than the wearers expected (Gilovich et al., 2000), and teammates noticed fewer ups and downs in each other's play than the individual players reported (Gilovich, Kruger, & Medvec, 2002). People also expected to be missed when they left a group (they were not), and they believed that their absence would change the group (it did not); individuals' presence or absence was clearly less striking to others than the individuals expected (Savitsky, Gilovich, Berger, & Medvec, 2003).

Obviously, "others are seldom as focused on us as we are on ourselves" (Savitsky et al., 2003, p. 391). This can be disappointing when we want others to note and celebrate our successes. (I remember, in this regard, how excited I was to arrive at school the day after my braces were removed; I expected everyone to marvel at my new dazzling smile, but it was 2 days before anyone noticed that the braces were gone. Clearly, no one else cared as much as I did.) However, the spotlight effect also guarantees that others are routinely less aware of our missteps than we believe. We are painfully aware of our many lapses of poise and grace, but we are less likely to notice similar behavior in others, and they, in turn, are less likely than we expect to notice it in us (Epley, Savitsky, & Gilovich, 2002). Further, if observers do note our missteps, they consider them less significant than we think them to be (Epley et al., 2002). Our self-conscious preoccupation with ourselves can make our embarrassing misbehaviors seem momentous, but they are simply less salient and important to others than we suppose.

Excessive Social-Evaluative Concern

Embarrassing circumstances are also more dreadful when they are magnified by unwarranted fear of negative evaluation. Some regard for others' evaluations of us is clearly sensible; those who remain unperturbed when they misbehave risk rejection from others, and a healthy respect for appropriate norms of social conduct is clearly adaptive (Baumeister & Tice, 1990). However, needless worry about others' opinions, like that found in highly embarrassable people, is both pointless and counterproductive. Excessive fear of negative evaluation leads to timidity and inhibition in social settings and makes people unwilling to engage in public performances that could be quite rewarding (Larkin & Pines, 2003). Over time, it also leads to psychological distress; for instance, it accounts entirely for sex differences in the incidence of depression in adolescent boys and girls (Rudolph & Conley, 2005). And when it is extreme, social-evaluative concern becomes debilitating social phobia that leaves sufferers unable to engage in public actions that the rest of us find unremarkable (Miller, 2001a).

Arguably, a major reason why self-awareness evolved was "to provide a way for people to make reasoned guesses about other people's thoughts and feelings, including their thoughts and feelings about us" (Leary, 2004a, p. 131). The ability to anticipate and comprehend others' judgments made survival much more likely. However, too many of us are *too* concerned with what others think of us, and we are unnecessarily apprehensive—and unduly susceptible to embarrassment—as a result. Our fears are out of proportion to the threats we face; they cause useless and needless distress. That is why therapies for the treatment of social phobia often encourage their clients to try to care less about others' judgments of them (Cohn & Hope, 2001).

The Illusion of Transparency

Possessed of potent phenomenologies and insufficient perspective taking, we also tend to overestimate how obvious our feelings are to others. We generally assume that others can discern what we are feeling, and we believe that our emotions are more plain than is really the case. Studies of this *illusion of transparency* have demonstrated that nervous public speakers overestimate how anxious they appear (Savitsky & Gilovich, 2003), liars misjudge how detectable their deception is, and revolted people sipping foul drinks misapprehend how disgusted they seem (Gilovich, Savitsky, & Medvec, 1998).

Embarrassed people also overestimate how flustered and discombobulated they appear to be (Endo, 2002). This matters because feelings of conspicuousness fuel embarrassment, and believing that one's flustered confusion is obvious can add to one's woes and actually make one's embarrassment worse (Drummond & Lim, 2000). In particular, people who believe that they blush readily are often unduly sensitive about their blushing—probably because of the teasing and mockery they received as adolescents—and they become more embarrassed and blush even harder when their blushes are mentioned by others (Drummond et al., 2003).

Given embarrassment's useful role in managing awkward situations, it does not make much sense to become (even more) embarrassed about being embarrassed when some predicament occurs. But, egoistically misapprehending others' points of view, too many people seem to believe that their internal discomfiture is patently plain and that others must disapprove. The illusion of transparency feeds this misunderstanding: Notably, people who fear blushing believe that they are blushing more obviously and conspicuously than others even when they are not. When researchers asked women to watch a goofy video of themselves singing "Happy Birthday" in the presence of male strangers, their fear of blushing did not predict the actual intensity of their blushes; those who feared blushing did not display more facial coloration or warmer cheeks than those who were more relaxed (Mulkens, de Jong, Dobbelaar, & Bögels, 1999). Thus, their fear of blushing evidently did not stem from stronger physiological responses to embarrassing predicaments. Instead, they were probably prone to misconstrue how conspicuous they seemed, and wrongly disposed to perceive disapproval where there was none. Convincing them that their discomfort is not overly obvious to others when awkward situations arise would likely reduce their fear of blushing, and perhaps their susceptibility to embarrassment, over time (Drummond et al., 2003; Savitsky & Gilovich, 2003).

Undue Fears of Embarrassment

Coupled with aversive past experiences with embarrassment, the spotlight effect, excessive social-evaluative concern, and the illusion of transparency lead most of us to misperceive the damage done to our reputations when we blunder in public. In fact, however, embarrassing circumstances simply are not as damning as we think they are. Savitsky et al. (2001) assessed research participants' reactions to embarrassing scenarios and actual lab predicaments and found that "observers' judgments were consistently more charitable than actors expected" (p. 54). We misunderstand embarrassment's effects, and we do so in part because we routinely underestimate how empathic others are (Epley et al., 2002). If we more correctly understood just how we are perceived and judged by others when we become embarrassed, our natural tendencies to become embarrassed by social predicaments would provide us with interactive benefits at less personal cost.

Indeed, our misapprehensions of others' perceptions of us appear to be a common element in the patterns that can make embarrassment disadvantageous. We believe that others are monitoring our actions more closely than they are, and that our flustered disarray, when it occurs, is plain to them. Then, too many of us assume that others are prone to pejorative evaluations that, in truth, are rather rare. All of this stems from failures to comprehend others' perspectives accurately and effectively; suffused with our own chagrin, we do not properly adjust our perceptions to account adequately for others' dispassion and generosity, and we assume that their judgments fit the discomfiture we feel (Epley, Keysar, Van Boven, & Gilovich, 2004).

The result is that we too often fear undesirable interactive consequences that never occur. As marvelous as it is, self-consciousness is egocentric, and our perceptions of the world are too much influenced by our own self-concepts (Leary, 2004b). When embarrassment comes, we inadequately understand what others are thinking, and we envision self-centered, self-important—but entirely imaginary—outcomes that fit our feelings but that misjudge the social harm that is actually done. As it turns out, "people's fears over others' harsh recriminations are generally exaggerated. Not only are people less inclined than we think to see the worst in us, they are also less inclined to see us at all" (Epley et al., 2002, p. 300).

Thus, an overactive, egocentric self makes embarrassing episodes seem more dreadful than they actually are. Most embarrassments would be less phenomenologically costly were we able to experience them from the more detached, less ego-involved perspectives of external observers. We would more often recognize our missteps, acknowledge them, and then get over them without exaggerated and unnecessary worry and concern. Our responses to awkward social situations would be less overstated and more effectual.

In particular, we would engage in fewer foolhardy efforts to avoid imagined future embarrassments. Because we care overmuch about what others are thinking of us, we too often fail to take actions that, although prudent, could be awkward. Seeking to avoid potential embarrassment, people sometimes fail to seek medical care for sexually transmitted infections (Hook & Sharma, 2005), urinary incontinence (Horrocks, Somerset, Stoddart, & Peters, 2004), sexual dysfunction (Brown & Haaser, 2005), colorectal cancer (Hou, 2005), and mental illness (Outram, Murphy, & Cockburn, 2004). They fail to buy and use condoms (Moore, Dahl, Gorn, & Weinberg, 2006), get mammograms (Pakenham, 2004), and report sexual assaults (Dussich, 2001). In all of these instances people are situationally shy; they are cowed by the possibility that, if they do what they should, awkwardness, mortification, and negative evaluations will follow. Objectively, however, the social disapproval they fear almost never occurs. The prospect of humiliation emerges entirely from an overactive, egocentric imagination. They would behave more adaptively in such situations if that self-process were switched off.

Poor perspective taking also fuels undue fears of embarrassment. We underestimate the reticence with which others face potentially embarrassing situations, believing that they are relatively immune to the concerns that beset us (Van Boven, Loewenstein, & Dunning, 2005), and that misperception makes our own social qualms seem more acute. Because "the self is the gravitational center of social cognition" (Van Boven et al., 2005, p. 139), too many of us are unable to adequately discern that others are equally susceptible to embarrassment and that they are glad to help us through awkward interactions.

Overall, then, were we able to dispassionately witness others' actions toward us without filtering them through the egoistic lenses of our overactive self-consciousness, we would find that, now that we are adults, observers are usually heedless or unconcerned about many of the missteps that cause us chagrin. Moreover, if they do notice, they are usually supportive and sympathetic, and any disregard resides entirely in our heads and not in their actual treatment of us. However, we do tend to misjudge others' reactions to our embarrassing predicaments, and those misperceptions cause considerable undue social stress and strain.

CONCLUSION

When it is proportional to the predicaments it follows, embarrassment is a productive emotion that engenders conciliatory behavior, elicits favorable evaluations from others, and generally resolves sticky social situations. It probably exists because it is a handy way to reassure others, to forestall potential exclusion, and to overcome the inevitable pitfalls of social life. It becomes less advantageous when it is excessive or out of place, however, and several consequences of human self-consciousness can cause embarrassment to occur when it is unnecessary or inappropriate. We believe that our behavior is more salient and interesting to others than it actually is, and we overestimate the extent to which others are carefully monitoring, and critically judging, our public actions.

Then, when we do become embarrassed, too many of us are excessively prone to dread negative social evaluations that never occur. We presume that others must be judging us harshly, and that is a fear that is usually quite unwarranted. Moreover, our misplaced and needless concerns can lead us to approach with undue timidity and trepidation situations in which awkward or sensitive information about us is made known to others. Over time, pointless, excessive fear of embarrassment can lead us to behave maladaptively, leading to unnecessary, preventable harm.

Thus, if embarrassment routinely operated in our species as it was designed to do, it would be a mixed, but unquestionable, blessing, an aversive experience that serves desirable social ends. Appropriate sensitivity to others' evaluations of us is adaptive, and an alarm mechanism that both alerts us to social threats and forestalls rejection by others is clearly beneficial. However, the same consequences of our remarkable self-consciousness that lead us to worry about imaginary perils and to work too hard to impress others also influence our reactions to embarrassing circumstances. Our overactive imaginations and egocentrism often make embarrassments more disruptive and costly than they would be were we better able to dispassionately appreciate embarrassment's real interactive effects. Ordinary and inevitable miscues of social life result in counterproductive and futile disquiet and dread that are exaggerated and needless in too many of us. Human self-consciousness is the wellspring of embarrassment, but it can, and too often does, make embarrassment a curse.

REFERENCES

Anderson, S. W., Bechara, A., Damasio, H., Tranel, D., & Damasio, A. R. (1999). Impairment of social and moral behavior related to early damage in human prefrontal cortex. *Nature Neuroscience, 2,* 1032–1037.

Apsler, R. (1975). Effects of embarrassment on behavior toward others. *Journal of Personality and Social Psychology, 32,* 145–153.

Asendorpf, J. (1990). The expression of shyness and embarrassment. In W. R. Crozier (Ed.), *Shyness and embarrassment: Perspectives from social psychology* (pp. 87–118). Cambridge, UK: Cambridge University Press.

Baldwin, M. W., & Baccus, J. R. (2004). Maintaining a focus on the social goals underlying self-conscious emotions. *Psychological Inquiry, 15,* 139–144.

Barlow, D. H., Chorpita, B. F., & Turovsky, J. (1996). Fear, panic, anxiety, and disorders of emotion. In D. A. Hope (Ed.), *Perspectives on anxiety, panic, and fear* (pp. 251–328). Lincoln: University of Nebraska Press.

Baumeister, R. F., & Tice, D. M. (1990). Anxiety and social exclusion. *Journal of Social and Clinical Psychology, 9,* 165–195.

Beer, J. S., Heerey, E. A., Keltner, D., Scabini, D., & Knight, R. T. (2003). The regulatory function of self-conscious emotion: Insights from patients with orbitofrontal damage. *Journal of Personality and Social Psychology, 85,* 594–604.

Berthoz, S., Armony, J. L., Blair, R. J. R., & Dolan, R. J. (2002). An fMRI study of intentional and unintentional (embarrassing) violations of social norms. *Brain, 125,* 1696–1708.

Bless, H. (2002). Where has the feeling gone?: The signal function of affective states. *Psychological Inquiry, 13,* 29–31.

Brown, G. R., & Haaser, R. C. (2005). Sexual disorders. In J. L. Levenson (Ed.), *American Psychiatric Publishing textbook of psychosomatic medicine* (pp. 359–386). Washington, DC: American Psychiatric Publishing.

Buss, A. H. (1980). *Self-consciousness and social anxiety.* San Francisco: Freeman.

Castelfranchi, C., & Poggi, I. (1990). Blushing as a discourse: Was Darwin wrong? In W. R. Crozier (Ed.), *Shyness and embarrassment: Perspectives from social psychology* (pp. 230–251). Cambridge, UK: Cambridge University Press.

Cohn, L. G., & Hope, D. A. (2001). Treatment of social phobia: A treatments-by-dimensions review. In S. G. Hofmann & P. M. DiBartolo (Eds.), *From social anxiety to social phobia: Multiple perspectives* (pp. 354–378). Boston: Allyn & Bacon.

Consedine, N. A., Strongman, K. T., & Magai, C. (2003). Emotions and behaviour: Data from a cross-cultural recognition study. *Cognition and Emotion, 17,* 881–902.

Costa, M., Dinsbach, W., Manstead, A. S. R., & Ricci Bitti, P. E. (2001). Social presence, embarrassment, and nonverbal behavior. *Journal of Nonverbal Behavior, 25,* 225–240.

Csikszentmihalyi, M., & Larson, R. (1984). *Being adolescent: Conflict and growth in the teenage years*. New York: Basic Books.

Cupach, W. R., & Metts, S. (1992). The effects of types of predicament and embarrassability on remedial responses to embarrassing situations. *Communication Quarterly, 40*, 149–161.

Cupach, W. R., & Metts, S. (1994). *Facework*. Thousand Oaks, CA: Sage.

Curtis, M. H., Lickel, B., & Schmader, T. (2005, January). *Vicarious emotion: Examining the experience of shame or guilt due to the wrongdoings of a romantic partner*. Paper presented at the meeting of the Society for Personality and Social Psychology, New Orleans.

de Jong, P. J. (1999). Communicative and remedial effects of social blushing. *Journal of Nonverbal Behavior, 23*, 197–217.

de Jong, P. J., Peters, M. L., & De Cremer, D. (2003). Blushing may signify guilt: Revealing effects of blushing in ambiguous social situations. *Motivation and Emotion, 27*, 225–249.

de Jong, P. J., Peters, M. L., De Cremer, D., & Vranken, C. (2002). Blushing after a moral transgression in a prisoner's dilemma game: Appeasing or revealing? *European Journal of Social Psychology, 32*, 627–644.

Devinsky, O., Hafler, D. A., & Victor, J. (1982). Embarrassment as the aura of a complex partial seizure. *Neurology, 32*, 1284–1285.

Dickerson, S. S., Grunewald, T. L., & Kemeny, M. E. (2004). When the social self is threatened: Shame, physiology, and health. *Journal of Personality, 72*, 1191–1216.

Drummond, P. D. (1997). The effect of adrenergic blockade on blushing and facial flushing. *Psychophysiology, 34*, 163–168.

Drummond, P. D., Camacho, L., Formentin, N., Heffernan, T. D., Williams, F., & Zekas, T. E. (2003). The impact of verbal feedback about blushing on social discomfort and facial blood flow during embarrassing tasks. *Behaviour Research and Therapy, 41*, 413–425.

Drummond, P. D., & Lim, H. W. (2000). The significance of blushing for fair- and dark-skinned people. *Personality and Individual Differences, 29*, 1123–1132.

Dussich, J. P. J. (2001). Decisions not to report sexual assault: A comparative study among women living in Japan who are Japanese, Korean, Chinese, and English-speaking. *International Journal of Offender Therapy and Comparative Criminology, 45*, 278–301.

Edelmann, R. J. (1982). The effect of embarrassed reactions upon others. *Australian Journal of Psychology, 34*, 359–367.

Edelmann, R. J. (1985). Individual differences in embarrassment: Self-consciousness, self-monitoring, and embarrassability. *Personality and Individual Differences, 6*, 223–230.

Edelmann, R. J. (2001). Blushing. In W. R. Crozier & L. E. Alden (Eds.), *International handbook of social anxiety: Concepts, research and interventions relating to the self and shyness* (pp. 301–323). Chichester, UK: Wiley.

Edelmann, R. J., & Hampson, R. J. (1979). Changes in non-verbal behaviour during embarrassment. *British Journal of Social and Clinical Psychology, 18*, 385–390.

Edelmann, R. J., & Hampson, R. J. (1981). The recognition of embarrassment. *Personality and Social Psychology Bulletin, 7*, 109–116.

Edelmann, R. J., & Iwawaki, S. (1987). Self-reported expression and consequences of embarrassment in the United Kingdom and Japan. *Psychologia, 30*, 205–216.

Ekman, P. (1992). An argument for basic emotions. *Cognition and Emotion, 6*, 169–200.

Elison, J., & Harter, S. (2004, May). *Facets of shame, embarrassment, and humiliation*. Paper presented at the annual meeting of the American Psychological Society, Chicago.

Endo, Y. (2002, June). *Mechanisms of social anxiety in terms of the illusion of transparency*. Paper presented at the annual meeting of the American Psychological Society, New Orleans.

Epley, N., Keysar, B., Van Boven, L., & Gilovich, T. (2004). Perspective taking as egocentric anchoring and adjustment. *Journal of Personality and Social Psychology, 87*, 327–339.

Epley, N., Savitsky, K., & Gilovich, T. (2002). Empathy neglect: Reconciling the spotlight effect and the correspondence bias. *Journal of Personality and Social Psychology, 83*, 300–312.

Fridlund, A. J. (1994). *Human facial expression: An evolutionary view*. San Diego, CA: Academic Press.

Gerlach, A. L., Wilhelm, F. H., & Roth, W. T. (2003). Embarrassment and social phobia: The role of parasympathetic activation. *Journal of Anxiety Disorders, 17,* 197–210.

Gilovich, T., Kruger, J., & Medvec, V. H. (2002). The spotlight effect revisited: Overestimating the manifest variability of our actions and appearance. *Journal of Experimental Social Psychology, 38,* 93–99.

Gilovich, T., Medvec, V. H., & Savitsky, K. (2000). The spotlight effect in social judgment: An egocentric bias in estimates of the salience of one's own actions and appearance. *Journal of Personality and Social Psychology, 78,* 211–222.

Gilovich, T., Savitsky, K., & Medvec, V. H. (1998). The illusion of transparency: Biased assessments of others' ability to read one's emotional states. *Journal of Personality and Social Psychology, 75,* 332–346.

Harris, C. R. (2001). Cardiovascular responses of embarrassment and effects of emotional suppression in a social setting. *Journal of Personality and Social Psychology, 81,* 886–897.

Harris, N. (2003). Reassessing the dimensionality of the moral emotions. *British Journal of Psychology, 94,* 457–473.

Hashimoto, E., & Shimizu, T. (1988). A cross-cultural study of the emotion of shame/embarrassment: Iranian and Japanese children. *Psychologia, 31,* 1–6.

Heerey, E. A., Keltner, D., & Capps, L. M. (2003). Making sense of self-conscious emotion: Linking theory of mind and emotion in children with autism. *Emotion, 3,* 394–400.

Herrald, M. M., & Tomaka, J. (2002). Patterns of emotion-specific appraisal, coping and cardiovascular reactivity during an ongoing emotional episode. *Journal of Personality and Social Psychology, 83,* 434–450.

Hook, E. W., III, & Sharma, A. K. (2005). Public tolerance, private pain: Stigma and sexually transmitted infections in the American Deep South. *Culture, Health, and Sexuality, 7,* 43–57.

Horrocks, S., Somerset, M., Stoddart, H., & Peters, T. J. (2004). What prevents older people from seeking treatment for urinary incontinence?: A qualitative exploration of barriers to the use of community continence services. *Family Practice, 21,* 689–696.

Hou, S. (2005). Factors associated with intentions for colorectal cancer screenings in a Chinese sample. *Psychological Reports, 96,* 159–162.

Janes, L. M., & Olson, J. M. (2000). Jeer pressures: The behavioral effects of observing ridicule of others. *Personality and Social Psychology Bulletin, 26,* 474–485.

Keltner, D. (1995). Signs of appeasement: Evidence for the distinct displays of embarrassment, amusement, and shame. *Journal of Personality and Social Psychology, 68,* 441–454.

Keltner, D., & Anderson, C. (2000). Saving face for Darwin: The functions and uses of embarrassment. *Current Directions in Psychological Science, 9,* 187–192.

Keltner, D., & Buswell, B. N. (1997). Embarrassment: Its distinct form and appeasement function. *Psychological Bulletin, 122,* 250–270.

Keltner, D., & Ekman, P. (2000). Facial expression of emotion. In M. Lewis & J. M. Haviland-Jones (Eds.), *Handbook of emotions* (2nd ed., pp. 236–249). New York: Guilford Press.

Keltner, D., & Haidt, J. (2001). Social functions of emotions. In T. J. Mayne & G. A. Bonanno (Eds.), *Emotions: Current issues and future directions* (pp. 192–213). New York: Guilford Press.

Larkin, J. E., & Pines, H. A. (2003). Gender and risk in public performances. *Sex Roles, 49,* 197–210.

Leary, M. R. (2000). Affect, cognition, and the social emotions. In J. P. Forgas (Ed.), *Feeling and thinking: The role of affect in social cognition* (pp. 331–356). Cambridge, UK: Cambridge University Press.

Leary, M. R. (2004a). Digging deeper: The fundamental nature of "self-conscious" emotions. *Psychological Inquiry, 15,* 129–131.

Leary, M. R. (2004b). *The curse of the self: Self-awareness, egotism, and the quality of human life.* New York: Oxford University Press.

Leary, M. R., Britt, T. W., Cutlip, W. D., II, & Templeton, J. L. (1992). Social blushing. *Psychological Bulletin, 112,* 446–460.

Leary, M. R., & Cottrell, C. A. (2001, February). *Individual differences in the need to belong.* Paper presented at the annual meeting of the Society for Personality and Social Psychology, San Antonio.

Leary, M. R., Landel, J. L., & Patton, K. M. (1996). The motivated expression of embarrassment following a self-presentational predicament. *Journal of Personality, 64,* 619–636.

Leary, M. R., & Meadows, S. (1991). Predictors, elicitors, and concomitants of social blushing. *Journal of Personality and Social Psychology, 60,* 254–262.

Levin, J., & Arluke, A. (1982). Embarrassment and helping behavior. *Psychological Reports, 51,* 999–1002.

Lichtenstein, B., Hook, E. W., III, & Sharma, A. K. (2005). Public tolerance, private pain: Stigma and sexually transmitted infections in the American Deep South. *Culture, Health and Sexuality, 7,* 43–57.

Maltby, J., & Day, L. (2000). The reliability and validity of a susceptibility to embarrassment scale among adults. *Personality and Individual Differences, 29,* 749–756.

Marcus, D. K., & Miller, R. S. (1999). The perception of "live" embarrassment: A social relations analysis of class presentations. *Cognition and Emotion, 13,* 105–117.

Marcus, D. K., Wilson, J. R., & Miller, R. S. (1996). Are perceptions of emotion in the eye of the beholder?: A social relations analysis of embarrassment. *Personality and Social Psychology Bulletin, 22,* 1220–1228.

Mellander, S., Andersson, P., Afzelius, L., & Hellstrand, P. (1982). Neural beta-adrenergic dilatation of the facial vein in man: Possible mechanism in emotional blushing. *Acta Physiologica Scandinavia, 114,* 393–399.

Metts, S., & Cupach, W. R. (1989). Situational influence on the use of remedial strategies in embarrassing predicaments. *Communication Monographs, 56,* 151–162.

Miller, R. S. (1992). The nature and severity of self-reported embarrassing circumstances. *Personality and Social Psychology Bulletin, 18,* 190–198.

Miller, R. S. (1995). On the nature of embarrassability: Shyness, social evaluation, and social skill. *Journal of Personality, 63,* 315–339.

Miller, R. S. (1996). *Embarrassment: Poise and peril in everyday life.* New York: Guilford Press.

Miller, R. S. (2001a). Embarrassment and social phobia: Distant cousins or close kin? In S. G. Hofmann & P. M. DiBartolo (Eds.), *From social anxiety to social phobia: Multiple perspectives* (pp. 65–85). Boston: Allyn & Bacon.

Miller, R. S. (2001b). Shyness and embarrassment compared: Siblings in the service of social evaluation. In W. R. Crozier & L. E. Alden (Eds.), *International handbook of social anxiety: Concepts, research and interventions relating to the self and shyness* (pp. 281–300). Chichester, UK: Wiley.

Miller, R. S. (2004). Emotion as adaptive interpersonal communication: The case of embarrassment. In L. Z. Tiedens & C. W. Leach (Eds.), *The social life of emotions* (pp. 87–104). Cambridge, UK: Cambridge University Press.

Miller, R. S., & Leary, M. R. (1992). Social sources and interactive functions of emotion: The case of embarrassment. In M. S. Clark (Ed.), *Review of personality and social psychology* (Vol. 14, pp. 202–221). Newbury Park, CA: Sage.

Miller, R. S., & Tangney, J. P. (1994). Differentiating embarrassment and shame. *Journal of Social and Clinical Psychology, 13,* 273–287.

Moore, S. G., Dahl, D. W., Gorn, G. J., & Weinberg, C. B. (2006). Coping with condom embarrassment. *Psychology, Health and Medicine, 11,* 70–79.

Mosher, D. L., & White, B. B. (1981). On differentiating shame and shyness. *Motivation and Emotion, 5,* 61–74.

Mulkens, S., de Jong, P. J., Dobbelaar, A., & Bögels, S. M. (1999). Fear of blushing: Fearful preoccupation irrespective of facial coloration. *Behaviour Research and Therapy, 37,* 1119–1128.

Outram, S., Murphy, B., & Cockburn, J. (2004). Factors associated with accessing professional help for psychological distress in midlife Australian women. *Journal of Mental Health, 13,* 185–195.

Pakenham, K. I. (2004). Mammography screening distress and pain: Changes over time and relations with breast symptoms, implants and cancer detection concerns. *Psychology, Health and Medicine, 9,* 403–410.

Parrott, W. G., & Smith, S. F. (1991). Embarrassment: Actual vs. typical cases, classical vs. prototypical representations. *Cognition and Emotion, 5,* 467–488.

Pickett, C. L., Gardner, W. L., & Knowles, M. (2004). Getting a cue: The need to belong and enhanced sensitivity to social cues. *Personality and Social Psychology Bulletin, 30,* 1095–1107.

Plutchik, R. (1980). *Emotion: A psychoevolutionary synthesis.* New York: Harper & Row.

Rudolph, K. D., & Conley, C. S. (2005). The socioemotional costs and benefits of social-evaluative concerns: Do girls care too much? *Journal of Personality, 73,* 115–137.

Sabini, J., Siepmann, M., Stein, J., & Meyerowitz, M. (2000). Who is embarrassed by what? *Cognition and Emotion, 14,* 213–240.

Savitsky, K., Epley, N., & Gilovich, T. (2001). Do others judge us as harshly as we think?: Overestimating the impact of our failures, shortcomings, and mishaps. *Journal of Personality and Social Psychology, 81,* 44–56.

Savitsky, K., & Gilovich, T. (2003). The illusion of transparency and the alleviation of speech anxiety. *Journal of Experimental Social Psychology, 39,* 618–625.

Savitsky, K., Gilovich, T., Berger, G., & Medvec, V. H. (2003). Is our absence as conspicuous as we think?: Overestimating the salience and impact of one's absence from a group. *Journal of Experimental Social Psychology, 39,* 386–392.

Semin, G. R., & Manstead, A. S. R. (1982). The social implications of embarrassment displays and restitution behavior. *European Journal of Social Psychology, 12,* 367–377.

Semin, G. R., & Papadopoulou, K. (1990). The acquisition of reflexive social emotions: The transmission and reproduction of social control through joint action. In G. Duveen & B. Lloyd (Eds.), *Social representations and the development of knowledge* (pp. 107–125). Cambridge, UK: Cambridge University Press.

Sharkey, W. F., & Kim, M. (2000). The effect of embarrassability on perceived importance of conversational constraints. *Human Communication, 3,* 27–40.

Sharkey, W. F., Kim, M., & Diggs, R. C. (2001). Intentional embarrassment: A look at embarrassors' and targets' perspectives. *Personality and Individual Differences, 31,* 1261–1272.

Sharkey, W. F., & Stafford, L. (1990). Responses to embarrassment. *Human Communication Research, 17,* 315–342.

Simon, A., & Shields, S. A. (1996). Does complexion color affect the experience of blushing? *Journal of Social Behavior and Personality, 11,* 177–188.

Stattin, H., Magnusson, D., Olah, A., Kassin, H., & Reddy, N. Y. (1991). Perception of threatening consequences of anxiety-provoking situations. *Anxiety Research, 4,* 141–166.

Tangney, J. P., Miller, R. S., Flicker, L., & Barlow, D. H. (1996). Are shame, guilt, and embarrassment distinct emotions? *Journal of Personality and Social Psychology, 70,* 1256–1264.

Turner, J. H. (1996). The evolution of emotion in humans: A Darwinian–Durkheimian analysis. *Journal for the Theory of Social Behavior, 26,* 1–33.

Van Boven, L., Loewenstein, G., & Dunning, D. (2005). The illusion of courage in social predictions: Underestimating the fear of embarrassment in other people. *Organizational Behavior and Human Decision Processes, 96,* 130–141.

15

The Nature of Pride

JESSICA L. TRACY
RICHARD W. ROBINS

> In so far as a man amounts to anything, stands for anything, is
> truly an individual, he has an ego about him to which his
> passions cluster, and to aggrandize which must be a principal aim
> within him.
>
> —Cooley (1902, p. 216)

As the epigraph illustrates, feeling pride in oneself, or having one's "passions" "cluster about the ego," is a central part of human nature. Scheff (1988, p. 399) went so far as to claim, "We are virtually always in a state of pride or shame." Although this statement may be somewhat extreme, Scheff made a prescient observation: our everyday lives are frequently infused with a sense of mastery and achievement, or conversely, frustration and failure, and we react to these self-relevant events with often intense self-conscious emotions.

Yet, despite the importance of pride to everyday social life, this emotion has received relatively little research attention, particularly compared with fear, joy, and other so-called basic emotions. Like all self-conscious emotions, pride is generally viewed as a "secondary" emotion (Lewis, Sullivan, Stanger, & Weiss, 1989), and even compared with other self-conscious emotions pride is something of an underdog. A PsycINFO search found only 208 publications with the words "pride" or "proud" in their title, compared with 1,633 publications with the words "guilt" or "guilty," and 1,312 with the words "shame" or "ashamed." Similarly, in Tangney and Fischer's (1995) volume on self-conscious emotions, not a single chapter provided a review of the extant research or theory on pride, and only four of the 20 chapters discussed it.

However, a growing body of research may change all this: new theory and findings support the views of Cooley and Scheff, and suggest that pride is a psychologically important and evolutionarily adaptive emotion. The pleasurable subjective feelings that accompany a pride experience may reinforce the prosocial behaviors that typically elicit the emotion, such as achievement and caregiving (Hart & Matsuba, Chapter 7, this volume;

Herrald & Tomaka, 2002; Stipek, 1983; Weiner, 1985). Over the long term, these same feelings may contribute to the development of a genuine and deep-rooted sense of self-esteem. Pride is the emotion (along with shame) that gives self-esteem its affective kick (Brown & Marshall, 2001; Tracy & Robins, 2007b), and self-esteem in turn influences a wide range of intrapsychic and interpersonal processes. Meanwhile, the loss of pride, in the form of humiliation or ego threats, can provoke aggression and other antisocial behaviors (Bushman & Baumeister, 1998).

Since the publication of Tangney and Fischer's (1995) volume, a small body of research and theory on pride has emerged. Studies have begun to explore the structure, antecedents, expression, and function of this important emotion. In this chapter, we review these studies and highlight a central implication of their findings: that pride is likely to be an adaptive part of human nature. The chapter is divided into five sections. First, we describe a recent set of studies that explore the structure of pride and provide the first systematic empirical evidence for the long-standing claim that pride has two distinct facets. Second, we briefly review research on the development of pride (see also Lagattuta & Thompson, Chapter 6, this volume). Third, we describe a recent line of research testing whether pride has a recognizable nonverbal expression. Fourth, we discuss the extent to which pride and its expression may generalize across cultures (see also Edelstein & Shaver, Chapter 11, this volume; Fessler, Chapter 10, this volume; Goetz & Keltner, Chapter 9, this volume). Fifth, we describe a functionalist, or evolutionary, perspective on pride. Finally, we close by proposing several directions for future research. Our overarching goals for this chapter are to lay the foundation for continued programmatic research on pride and to convince our readers that there is a reason for pride's ubiquity in social life: it is part of what makes us human.

A TALE OF TWO PRIDES

Theoretical and Historical Perspectives Pointing to Two Facets of Pride

"Pride or arrogance . . . has been recognized since early times as a root cause of cruelty and evil" (Schimmel, 1997, p. 29). Both ancient Greek and biblical thought condemned what they referred to as "excessive pride" or "hubris" (Schimmel, 1997), and these prevalent early philosophical and religious views led Dante to refer to pride as the deadliest of the Seven Deadly Sins. Yet, in Western culture, "pride has been transformed from a vice into a virtue" (Schimmel, 1997, p. 37). Much like self-esteem, pride is generally perceived as something to be sought out, with its acquisition rewarded and encouraged in children and adults. This raises a perplexing question: Is pride good or bad?

Several researchers have addressed this apparent incongruity by arguing that pride is too broad a concept to be considered a single, unified emotion, and may be better viewed as two or more distinct emotions (Ekman, 2003; M. Lewis, 2000; Tangney, Wagner, & Gramzow, 1989). Consistent with this perspective, pride has been theoretically linked to markedly divergent outcomes. On the one hand, pride in one's successes and relationships is assumed to promote future positive behaviors in the achievement domain and to contribute to further prosocial investments such as relationship maintenance and altruism. On the other hand, the "hubristic," "sinful," or "defensive" pride that is more associated with narcissism may contribute to aggression and hostility, interpersonal problems, relationship conflict, and a host of maladaptive behaviors (Bosson & Prewitt-Freilino, Chapter 22, this volume; Kernberg, 1975; M. Lewis, 2000; McGregor, Nail, Marigold, & Kang, 2005; Morf & Rhodewalt, 2001).

We recently developed a theoretical model that addresses this paradox by distinguishing between two facets of pride: "authentic" and "hubristic" (Tracy & Robins, 2004a; see also Tracy & Robins, Chapter 1, this volume). Psychologists have long noted that pride occurs in response to internal attributions—that is, when the self is credited as the cause of the event (Ellsworth & Smith, 1988; M. Lewis, 2000; Roseman, 1991; Smith & Lazarus, 1993; Weiner, 1985). In our model, two facets of pride are distinguished by subsequent attributions. Specifically, authentic pride ("I'm proud of what I did") may result from attributions to internal, unstable, controllable causes ("I won because I practiced"), whereas hubristic pride ("I'm proud of who I am") may result from attributions to internal, stable, uncontrollable causes ("I won because I'm always great"). This distinction parallels the distinction frequently made between guilt and shame, where guilt involves a focus on negative aspects of one's behavior—the "*thing* done or undone"— whereas shame involves a focus on negative aspects of one's self—the *self* who did or did not do it (H. B. Lewis, 1971, p. 30; M. Lewis, 2000; Tangney, Stuewig, & Mashek, Chapter 2, this volume; Tangney & Dearing, 2002). We labeled the first facet "authentic" to emphasize that it is based on actual accomplishments and is likely accompanied by genuine feelings of self-worth; in contrast, hubristic pride may be a genuine emotional experience that is fueled by a more inauthentic sense of self (i.e., distorted and self-aggrandized self-views).[1]

If pride is indeed characterized by these two distinct facets, then each facet should be associated with unique concepts, subjective feelings, and personality correlates, and the two facets should be elicited by distinct cognitive attributions. We conducted a series of studies to test these ideas (Tracy & Robins, 2007b).

The Semantic Structure of Pride

In our first study, we examined people's conceptualizations of pride. That is, what kinds of meaning do people infer from pride words and concepts? We asked research participants to rate the semantic similarity of pride-related words, which were derived from an open-ended study of the pride nonverbal expression (i.e., words were participant-generated labels for the pride expression; Tracy & Robins, 2004b). Analyses of participants' ratings supported a two-cluster structure that converged with our theoretical distinction between authentic and hubristic pride. Specifically, words in the first cluster, such as "accomplished," "triumphant," and "confident," described feelings about a controllable, typically effort-driven achievement. In contrast, words in the second cluster, such as "arrogant," "cocky," and "conceited," connoted feelings associated with narcissistic self-aggrandizement. This study thus suggested that people conceptualize pride in terms of two distinct semantic categories, which correspond to authentic and hubristic pride.

Experiencing Pride

We next examined whether the pride experience—the way that pride subjectively feels— is also characterized by two distinct facets. It is possible that, although people think of pride in terms of the two facets, only a single facet of feelings actually occur during a pride experience. For example, given that many hubristic pride words have a negative connotation, individuals may exclusively use authentic pride words to describe their own subjective feelings; hubristic pride words may exist in the lexicon only to describe pride felt by others. To test this possibility, we asked participants to write, in a narrative fashion, about a time when they had felt pride, and to rate the extent to which a set of pride-related words (including words from both clusters) characterized their feelings. Factor analyses of their ratings suggested that a two-factor structure provided the best fit to the data.

Furthermore, the content of the words that loaded on each factor replicated the conceptual clusters found previously, such that an "authentic" pride factor emerged, with words like "achieving" and "confident" loading highly; and a hubristic pride factor emerged, with words like "arrogant" and "pompous" loading highly. We replicated these findings in five subsequent studies, two of which used the same method to assess momentary, state pride, and three of which assessed pride as a trait-like dispositional tendency (i.e., proneness to pride). Regardless of whether pride was measured as a trait or a state, we found two factors corresponding to authentic and hubristic pride. Moreover, these two factors were only weakly correlated (.22–.30 across studies), suggesting that they are relatively independent facets of pride.

We next tested whether the two factors could be accounted for by distinctions in evaluative valence (i.e., Do the authentic and hubristic pride factors simply reflect positively and negatively valenced words for a unitary pride emotion?), activation (i.e., Do the authentic and hubristic pride factors simply reflect high vs. low activity words for pride?), or a temporal distinction (i.e., Do the authentic and hubristic pride factors simply reflect state vs. trait words for pride?). We found that the factors replicated even when evaluative variance (i.e., ratings of pleasure and displeasure) and activation (i.e., ratings of activation and deactivation; Feldman-Barrett & Russell, 1998) were partialled out, suggesting that the two factors are not simply a statistical artifact of the tendency to distinguish between positive and negative valences or between activated and deactivated states. We also found that the two factors did not differ substantially in the degree to which the words defining each factor reflect stable traits versus transient states.

Based on these studies, we now believe that pride is best conceptualized in terms of two distinct facets, one reflecting authentic feelings surrounding achievement and mastery, and the other reflecting hubristic feelings of arrogance, grandiosity, and superiority. To facilitate future research, we developed brief, reliable measures of each facet (see Robins, Noftle, & Tracy, Chapter 24, this volume). These scales tend to be either weakly or not significantly correlated, suggesting that they assess relatively independent aspects of pride.

Correlates of Pride

We next set out to test whether the two facets of pride have distinct personality correlates. If they do, then the two-facet perspective could resolve the long-standing question of whether pride is a psychologically healthy or a "sinful" emotion. Contradictory ideas about the consequences of pride may exist because one facet is associated with a positive personality profile and prosocial behaviors, whereas the other is associated with a more negative profile and antisocial behaviors.

As expected, we found that authentic pride is positively related to self-esteem, whereas hubristic pride is negatively related to self-esteem and positively related to narcissism. Interestingly, these correlations become even stronger when self-esteem and narcissism are partialled out of each other. We also found that authentic pride is negatively related, and hubristic pride positive related, to shame-proneness. This pattern is consistent with theories of narcissism as a defensive process in which explicit self-aggrandizement and hubris are used to protect the self from deep-seated feelings of shame and inadequacy (Kernberg, 1975; Kohut, 1977; Tracy & Robins, 2003a). Finally, we found that authentic pride was positively correlated with the socially desirable and generally adaptive Big Five traits of Extraversion, Agreeableness, Conscientiousness, and Emotional Stability, whereas hubristic pride was negatively correlated with Agreeableness and Conscientiousness—two traits that reflect a prosocial orientation, or what Digman (1997) referred to as "socialization."

Together, these findings support the claim that authentic pride is the adaptive, prosocial, achievement-oriented facet of the emotion, which likely promotes the development of a deep-rooted and stable sense of self-esteem. In contrast, hubristic pride is uniquely related to narcissistic self-aggrandizement, and may, in part, be a defensive response to underlying feelings of shame. In addition, the correlations between hubristic pride and the Big Five suggest that hubristic pride is the less prosocial facet of pride. Importantly, for each of the Big Five traits except Openness, correlations with authentic and hubristic pride differed significantly, suggesting that individuals who tend to experience authentic pride have a markedly divergent personality profile from those who tend to experience hubristic pride.

Antecedents of Authentic and Hubristic Pride

We next explored whether the two facets are elicited by distinct cognitive antecedents. Based on our theoretical model (Tracy & Robins, 2004a, and Chapter 1, this volume), attributing positive events to internal, unstable, controllable causes (e.g., effort) should lead to authentic pride, whereas attributing those same events to internal, stable, uncontrollable causes (e.g., ability) should lead to hubristic pride.

Across three studies, we found support for our theory that the two facets have distinct cognitive antecedents. First, based on content coding of narrative descriptions of pride experiences, we found that positive events with internal, unstable causes tended to promote authentic pride, whereas positive events caused by an individual's stable ability, but not by any efforts made, and by "the self" (as opposed to unstable behaviors or actions), tended to promote hubristic pride. Second, we experimentally manipulated participants' attributions for a hypothetical success, and found that they reported feeling greater authentic pride when success was attributed to internal, unstable, controllable causes (e.g., effort) than when success was attributed to internal, stable, uncontrollable causes (e.g., ability). Reports of hubristic pride showed the opposite pattern. Third, we examined participants' dispositional attributional styles, and found that individuals who generally attribute outcomes to their own effort tend to experience authentic pride, whereas those who generally attribute outcomes to their own ability tend to experience hubristic pride.

Importantly, we also found that the two facets of pride are not distinguished by the *kinds* of events that elicit them. When we examined participants' narratives about their pride experiences, we found no differences between the two facets in the degree to which the eliciting events involved success in academics, romantic relationships, family, athletics, or any other dimension, suggesting that people experience authentic and hubristic pride in response to all kinds of successes. Thus, it is not the event, but the way in which the event is *appraised*, that determines which facet is experienced.

As a whole, these studies provide empirical support for the claim that pride is not a unitary construct, and that, instead, there are distinct authentic and hubristic facets. In many ways, the relation between the two dimensions of pride seems similar to the relation between shame and guilt, the two major negative self-conscious emotions. Shame and guilt tend to be positively related yet have divergent and statistically independent correlations with other relevant variables. As with shame and guilt, there are reliable and measurable individual differences in people's tendencies to experience each of the pride dimensions. Both pairs are also distinguished by the same causal attributions; shame and hubristic pride tend to be elicited by internal, stable, uncontrollable attributions, whereas guilt and authentic pride tend to be elicited by internal, unstable, controllable attributions (Tangney & Dearing, 2002; Tracy & Robins, 2006a). Finally, like shame and guilt, one facet of pride—hubristic—seems to have maladaptive correlates, whereas the other facet—authentic—seems to have adaptive correlates. One remaining question, which constitutes an important direction for future research, is whether the two facets are two forms of the same emotion or two distinct emotions.

THE DEVELOPMENT OF PRIDE

Like all self-conscious emotions, pride emerges later in the course of development than basic emotions like fear and joy (Izard, 1971). Previous research suggests that most basic emotions emerge within the first 9 months of life (e.g., Campos, Barrett, Lamb, Gold-smith, & Stenberg, 1983), but that pride does not emerge until close to the end of a child's third year (Belsky & Domitrovich, 1997; Heckhausen, 1984; Lewis, Alessandri, & Sullivan, 1992; Stipek, 1995; Stipek, Recchia, & McClintic, 1992). These studies, which have examined toddlers' responses to success, have typically given young children a task they can accomplish and compared their behavioral and verbal responses after successful completion versus failure. For example, Stipek (1995) found that 2½- to 3-year-olds who successfully completed a puzzle tended to smile and look up (i.e., tilt their heads back, part of the pride nonverbal expression) more frequently than children who observed the experimenter complete the puzzle. The looking-up response was not observed in younger children, suggesting the later development of pride (Stipek et al., 1992). Lewis and colleagues (1992) and Belsky and Domintrovich (1997) observed 3-year-olds additionally display an erect posture (expanded chest, shoulders back), and make positive self-evaluative verbal statements after success; neither of these behaviors were seen in unsuccessful children of the same age, and all of these displays were more frequent when children succeeded on difficult, as compared with easy, tasks, suggesting that even young children feel pride only from a true accomplishment.

The capacity to understand pride emerges somewhat later than its experience. The form of understanding that seems to emerge first is the ability to recognize the pride nonverbal expression. At age 3, children cannot reliably distinguish the pride expression from expressions of happiness or surprise, but by age 4 pride recognition is significantly greater than chance and comparable to recognition of the more basic emotions (Tracy, Robins, & Lagattuta, 2005). In contrast to pride recognition, the ability to understand the situations and contexts in which pride is elicited seems to develop later. Harris, Olthuf, Terwogt, and Hardman (1987) reported that children under the age of 7 cannot spontaneously generate appropriate situations that would elicit pride. Thompson (1989) found that even 7-year-olds often attribute pride to individuals whose successful task completion is due to external (e.g., luck) rather than internal (e.g., effort) factors (see also Graham, 1988; Graham & Weiner, 1986). Similarly, Kornilaki and Chlouverakis (2004) found that 7-year-olds were unable to distinguish between the situations that elicit pride versus happiness. In several of these studies, it was also shown that by age 9 or 10 children can make the appropriate attributional distinctions, and become more likely to grant pride only to individuals who are the cause of their own success (Kornilaki & Chlouverakis, 2004; Thompson, 1989).

This developmental trajectory is consistent with the theoretical perspective that certain cognitive capacities are prerequisites for the elicitation of any self-conscious emotion: self-awareness, the formation of stable self-representations, comparisons between one's own behavior and external standards, and internal attributions (Lagattuta & Thompson, Chapter 6, this volume; M. Lewis, 2000; Tracy & Robins, 2004a). By the age of 3, children begin to acquire these abilities and display pride-like responses to success, but even at this age children cannot identify pride in others. The ability to recognize pride emerges at age 4, but this capacity is not accompanied by a full understanding of the situations and attributions that elicit pride and distinguish it from happiness. This complex understanding of pride is apparently not mastered until children have reached the age of 9 or 10.

THE NONVERBAL EXPRESSION OF PRIDE

One of the major findings in the behavioral and social sciences is the discovery that a small set of "basic" emotions—anger, disgust, fear, happiness, sadness, and surprise—have distinct, universally recognized, nonverbal expressions (Ekman, Sorenson, & Friesen, 1969; Ekman & Friesen, 1971; Izard, 1971). These findings emerged from studies demonstrating agreement on the emotions conveyed by each of these expressions across a wide range of nations and cultures, including highly isolated, preliterate tribal groups. Based on this research, many scientists came to accept Darwin's (1872) claim that emotions and their expressions evolved through natural selection. Within the emotion literature, the knowledge that certain emotions could be assessed through quantifiable, observable behaviors led to a strong research emphasis on those emotions known to have expressions, and to a corresponding lack of attention on more complex emotions thought to not have expressions—such as the self-conscious emotions.

However, Darwin (1872) also suggested that pride should have a recognizable display, writing: "Of all the . . . complex emotions, pride, perhaps, is the most plainly expressed" (p. 263). In fact, research on the development of pride supports this claim: preverbal toddlers show a specific set of nonverbal behaviors in response to success that are not seen when they fail (Lewis et al., 1992; Stipek, 1995). Furthermore, linguistically based folk models of pride tie behavioral elements to basic conceptions of the emotion, such as erect posture, chest out, head held high (Kovecses, 1986). Despite these varying sources of evidence, however, there was, until recently, no systematic test of whether pride is associated with a distinct, recognizable nonverbal expression.

Building on findings from the developmental literature, we tested whether the movements shown by successful toddlers might represent an early version of a pride expression. In a series of studies using forced-choice (i.e., asking participants to match expressions with specific emotion-word options) and open-ended (i.e., allowing participants to label expressions with any word they chose) response methods, we found that pride is associated with a distinct, recognizable, nonverbal expression (see Figure 15.1; Tracy & Robins, 2004b).

We began our research by instructing actors to pose expressions similar to those seen in young children after a success. We then manipulated potentially relevant components of these expressions (e.g., extent of head tilt, arm position) to determine the set of components that produced the highest level of agreement. Results demonstrated that the best

Expression A   Expression B

FIGURE 15.1. Prototypical pride expressions. Expression A is slightly better recognized than Expression B, but both are identified as pride. From Tracy and Robins (2004b). Copyright 2004 by Jessica L. Tracy. Reprinted by permission.

recognized, or, most prototypical, pride expression includes the body (i.e., expanded posture, head tilted slightly back, arms akimbo with hands on hips) as well as the face (i.e., small smile; Tracy & Robins, 2004b, 2007a). This expression is reliably recognized and distinguished from similar emotions (e.g., happiness) by adults from the United States and Italy, and, as was mentioned above, by children as young as 4 years old (Tracy & Robins, 2003b; Tracy et al., 2005). Pride recognition rates (typically around 80–90%) are comparable to recognition rates found for the basic emotions, and, like the basic emotions, pride can be recognized from a single snapshot image, both quickly and efficiently (Tracy & Robins, 2004b, 2004c).

One unique feature of the pride expression is that, unlike basic emotion expressions, it is not limited to facial musculature. The fact that pride recognition requires inclusion of at least the upper body (face-only pride expressions are equally likely to be identified as happiness) may be informative about the expression's unique evolutionary course. A nonverbal expression that involves the body as well as the face is more complex than face-only expressions, and this complexity may be more ideally suited to the complex message sent by pride. It is also possible that the bodily component makes the pride expression more easily regulated, which would be beneficial in a number of circumstances (Kemeny, Gruenewald, & Dickerson, 2004; Tracy & Robins, 2004a). Facial expressions are more difficult to regulate than body movements and posture because many of the facial muscle contractions involved are involuntary responses. Thus, although we may wish we could control the expression of all of our emotions, in our evolutionary history it was likely adaptive that our basic emotions be involuntarily expressed. The expression of pride, however, may be less directly linked to survival, and in some cases may be detrimental to fitness. As we explain below, in many cultures it is considered unacceptable to openly display pride, and such displays may lower a person's likeability (Eid & Diener, 2001;

Mosquera, Manstead, & Fischer, 2000; Paulhus, 1998; Zammuner, 1996). We may have evolved to show a pride expression that can be quickly suppressed when appropriate.

More broadly, the importance of the body in the pride expression is consistent with a growing number of studies suggesting that the body may be utilized in the recognition of all emotion expressions (e.g., Slaughter, Stone, & Reed, 2004). These studies have shown, for example, that similar neurological patterns occur during the perception of bodies and faces, whereas the recognition of ordinary objects recruits a different neurological process. Together, these findings suggest that it might be fruitful to focus more attention on the body in emotion research.

Much of the research on the pride expression, like the large majority of research on basic emotion expressions, has taken the form of judgment studies demonstrating that a posed version of the expression is highly recognizable (Tracy & Robins, 2004b, 2006b; Tracy et al., 2005). However, several studies have used encoding methods—assessing behaviors shown during actual pride experiences. These studies address the important question of whether the expression reliably identified by observers as pride is displayed when people feel proud. In addition to the developmental studies examining the spontaneous displays shown by toddlers after success, Weisfeld and Beresford (1982) found that high school students' performance on an exam was positively correlated with the increased erectness of their posture, suggesting that students who did well (and likely felt pride) expanded their posture more than those who did poorly. In another study, examining proprioceptive responses (i.e., how body movements influence perceptions and feelings) to success, Stepper and Strack (1993) found that individuals who were instructed to expand their posture while successfully completing a task reported greater pride than those who succeeded but did not make the corresponding postural movement.

In addition, in the only cross-cultural, naturalistic encoding study, Tracy and Matsumoto (2007) found that Olympic judo winners of medal (i.e., gold, silver, bronze) and nonmedal competitions tended to show aspects of the pride expression immediately after a match was completed. Winners typically displayed a head tilted back, expanded chest, torso pushed out, arms outstretched from the body, and hands in fists—all components of the recognizable pride expression—and these findings held across the wrestlers' gender and culture. Losers of these matches were much less likely to show pride. This research suggests that the well-replicated finding of accurate pride recognition is due to the fact that the pride expression *is* displayed during real-life pride evocative experiences.

CROSS-CULTURAL RESEARCH ON PRIDE

A Universal Pride Expression

Perhaps the strongest evidence for the pride expression is the recent finding that it is recognized across highly diverse cultures that have little or no contact with each other (Tracy & Robins, 2006b). Researchers since Darwin (1872) have suspected that the pride expression may be universal. Ethnographic accounts support this view. For example, Fessler (1999) noted that a pride-like emotion discussed among the Malay people of Indonesia is thought to be associated with an erect posture, and Lindholm (1982) made a similar observation of the Swat Pukhtun of northern Pakistan. Until recently, however, these descriptive reports had not been empirically tested. In fact, a 2002 study, using meta-analyses to analyze the results of all judgment studies of emotion expressions conducted, found studies examining recognition of 36 different possible emotional states—none of which included pride (Elfenbein & Ambady, 2002).

However, in a recent study conducted in rural villages near Bobo Dioulasso, Burkina Faso, we examined whether preliterate individuals could accurately identify the pride expression (Tracy & Robins, 2006b). We chose to collect data in Burkina Faso because, as the third-least developed country in the world (United Nations Human Development Report, 2005), it is highly isolated from the rest of the world's shared cultures and media, making our Burkinabe participants unlikely to have learned the pride expression through exposure to Western media. The participants in our study live in mud huts in rural villages, have had no formal education, speak only their native African language, and cannot read or write. As a result, these individuals have virtually no exposure to Western media (e.g., television, film, magazines, newspapers), a fact evidenced by their inability to recognize photographs of George Bush, Tony Blair, Tom Cruise, or several other well-known Western figures. Similar to the Fore tribe in Papua New Guinea, who, in Ekman and colleagues' (1969, 1971) seminal studies were found to recognize the basic emotion expressions, our participants' lack of exposure to foreign cultures made them an ideal sample to test the universality of pride.

To assess emotion recognition in Burkina Faso, we photographed male and female Caucasian Americans and West Africans posing emotion expressions, and asked participants to choose from a list of emotion words (spoken aloud in their native language) the word that best matched the expression shown by each individual. Participants were also given the option to say "I don't know" and "other emotion." The mean pride recognition rate, 57%, was significantly greater than chance, $p < .05$, and comparable to the recognition rates found for the six basic emotions in this study ($M = 50\%$) and in previous studies of preliterate cultures (Ekman et al., 1969). The pride recognition rate did not differ for male versus female participants or targets. There was a small but significant tendency for American targets to be better recognized than African targets—but given that only four targets were used, this effect was likely due to the posing ability of these specific individuals.

These findings suggest that pride is reliably recognized and distinguished from related emotions, even by non-Western, culturally isolated, nonliterate individuals. Pride thus meets the primary criterion for universality that exists within the emotion literature (Ekman, 1992). It has previously been assumed that self-conscious emotions differ from basic emotions because they lack universally recognized expressions (Ekman, 1992), but our research challenges this assumption and suggests that even a highly social, cognitively complex, self-evaluative emotion like pride may be universal.

Cross-Cultural Views of Pride

Despite universal recognition, it is nonetheless likely that there are cultural differences in the expression and experience of pride. Beyond its isolation, Burkina Faso is an ideal place to test the universality of pride because African countries tend to have highly collectivistic cultural values (Hofstede, 1984), which contrast sharply with the more individualistic values of most Western cultures (Wong & Tsai, Chapter 12, this volume). Perceptions of emotions and self processes relevant to pride (e.g., self-esteem) differ dramatically across these two types of cultures (Eid & Diener, 2001; Heine, 2004; Markus & Kitiyama, 1991). In particular, collectivistic cultures tend to promote the group over the individual, such that individuals are more prone to accept status differences rather than try to change them and assert the self (Hoffstede, 2001; Rossier, Dahourou, & McCrae, 2005). Such values seem inconsistent with pride, an emotion geared toward enhancing and affirming the self. Thus, evidence for similarities in the recognition of pride across Burkina Faso and the United States suggests that, at least to some extent, the emotion transcends a fundamental cultural difference.

However, evidence for a cross-culturally recognized pride expression does not preclude the possibility that there are cultural differences in other aspects of pride, such as the situational elicitors, display rules, and societal value placed on the emotion. In fact, several studies have found that pride is viewed more negatively in collectivistic versus individualistic cultures. In a study comparing views of emotions in two individualistic (United States, Australia) versus two collectivistic (China, Taiwan) cultures, Eid and Diener (2001) found that pride was one of the few emotions valued differently across the cultural groups. In both collectivistic cultures, pride (along with contentment) was one of only two positive emotions not considered desirable, whereas among the two individualistic cultures pride was fairly highly valued. Similarly, Mosquera and colleagues (2000) compared the experience and expression of pride in Spain (a collectivistic, "honor-related valuing" culture) and the Netherlands (a more individualistic culture), and found that Dutch participants expressed more positive feelings in their descriptions of pride and were more likely to tell others about the pride-eliciting situation, as compared with Spanish participants. Finally, Scollon, Diener, Oishi, and Biswas-Diener (2004) assessed daily reports of pride and other emotions in five cultures (Asian American, European American, Hispanic American, Indian, and Japanese), and found the single largest cultural difference in reports of pride. Hispanic Americans reported feeling the most pride, and the three Asian cultures reported the least. Furthermore, cluster analyses showed that in India pride clustered with the negative emotions, but in Japan pride clustered with the positive emotions. These findings raise new complexities concerning the individualist/collectivistic distinction because Hispanic and Japanese cultures are both considered collectivistic. Nonetheless, all of these studies converge on the finding that the experience of pride is culturally variant.

The presence of two distinct facets of pride may make it particularly vulnerable to diverging cultural views. It is possible, for example, that in collectivistic cultures the predominant conceptualization of pride is tilted toward the hubristic facet. If this is the case, it could account for the more negative view of pride found in several collectivistic cultures. Alternatively, pride may be well accepted and valued in collectivistic cultures—as long as it is pride about one's group instead of one's individual self. In a study comparing pride in China and the United States, Chinese participants reported more positive views of pride that resulted from others' accomplishments than from their own (Stipek, 1998). Recent research suggests that group pride can be authentic or hubristic, but it must be elicited by the activation of collective, rather than personal, self-representations (i.e., when the individual's social group succeeds; Pickett, Gonsalkorale, Tracy, & Robins, 2006).

Furthermore, in addition to conceptualizations and subjective reports of pride, even the universally recognized pride expression may be influenced by culture. Research suggests that that the in-group bias typically found in emotion recognition (i.e., higher levels of recognition when expressions are derived from the same culture as the research participants), which has emerged in our pride expression research, may be the result of "cultural dialects" in expressions (Elfenbein & Ambady, 2002). According to this perspective, cultural influences produce small but noticeable changes in otherwise universal expressions, such that expressions are best recognized when individuals view them in the precise way that they are displayed within their own culture. In other words, although Burkinabes can recognize the American version of the pride expression, there may be some other, slightly different, version that they would identify with greater accuracy. Of note, the in-group bias could also be explained by culturally divergent display rules for showing pride (Matsumoto, 2002). According to this perspective, if Burkinabe culture prohibits the experience or expression of pride, as some collectivistic cultures seem to do (Eid & Diener, 2002; Zammuner, 1996), then Burkinabe individuals would openly display the expression only infrequently. If viewing the pride expression is an uncommon experience in everyday social life, a lack of familiarity with it could promote the lower levels of recognition found in Burkina Faso. It is noteworthy, however, that in our Olympic judo competition study, cultural differences were not found in the tendency to display pride after success, suggesting that Asian, Latin American, European, and North American judo wrestlers were equally likely to display the expression in response to a victory (Tracy & Matsumoto, 2007).

In general, to the extent that pride is an adaptive emotion that functions to maintain and enhance social status, it is likely to be universal. Culture may influence the way it is displayed, regulated, and experienced, but not the core environmental contingencies that elicit it (i.e., its evolutionarily programmed cognitive antecedents) or the behavioral responses it generates (i.e., its adaptive outcomes).

PRIDE AS A FUNCTIONAL EMOTION

In this section, we build on Darwin's (1872) claim about pride to present a functionalist account of the emotion. We first describe the potential adaptive value of the pride experience, and then turn to the likely adaptive benefits of its expression. We conclude by considering whether the two facets of pride might serve distinct functions.

Adaptive Benefits of Experiencing Pride

Emotions are likely to have evolved through natural selection to serve two primary functions: promoting the direct attainment of survival and reproductive goals, and promoting the attainment of social goals (e.g., getting along and getting ahead) which are more distally related to survival and reproduction. According to Kemper (1984), "when we examine the biological survival value of emotions, we see that [it] entails not merely the survival of organisms, but the preservation of patterns of social organization. Hence . . . emotions have not simply biological, but social survival value" (p. 373). As social creatures, social goals are essential for our survival, but their attainment represents a more intermediary step toward adaptive fitness than the direct attainment of survival goals. Whereas basic emotions clearly serve both survival and social functions, self-conscious emotions, like pride, seem to promote the attainment of specifically social goals (Keltner & Buswell, 1997; Tracy & Robins, 2004a).

Humans evolved to navigate within a social structure that has complex layers of multiple, overlapping, and sometimes nontransitive social hierarchies (e.g., the highest status hunters were not always the highest status warriors). These complex social contexts likely promoted the unique ability to hold complex self-representations and use self-awareness to coordinate and motivate behaviors essential to these social dynamics (Robins, Norem, & Cheek, 1999). Self-conscious emotions may have evolved to provide information about one's current self-representations (i.e., self-evaluations), and to motivate the functional behaviors (e.g., achievement and caregiving) that allow individuals to maintain a positive self-concept and the respect and liking of others. Self-conscious emotions guide individual behavior by compelling us to do things that are socially valued and to avoid doing things that lead to social approbation (Tangney & Dearing, 2002). We strive to achieve, to be a "good person," or to treat others well because doing so makes us proud of ourselves. Put simply, society tells us what kind of person we should be; we internalize these beliefs in the form of actual and ideal self-representations; and pride motivates behavioral action toward the goals embodied in these self-representations. Thus, although we might know cognitively that we should help others in need, it takes the psychological force of the desire to feel pride to make us act in altruistic ways (Hart & Matsuba, Chapter 7, this volume). Similarly, we strive to achieve in school and work not only because we think that doing so will promote our status, but because the pride we experience when we succeed *feels* good. The reinforcement properties of pride are supported by a study showing that pride (at least as experienced by European Canadians) may facilitate memory for pride-eliciting events and make these events seem temporally more recent (Ross, Heine, Wilson, & Sugimori, 2005). In one of the few other studies examining the effects of pride, Herrald and Tomaka (2001) found that participants manipulated to experience pride showed higher task performance during and immediately following the pride experience.

Self-esteem may play an important role in this motivational process. Researchers have suggested that self-esteem functions as a social barometer, or "sociometer," to inform individuals of their social status and ensure that they behave in ways that will maintain their status and the acceptance of others, and avoid group rejection (Leary, Tambor, Terdal, & Downs, 1995). Given that pride (along with shame) is the emotion most strongly related to self-esteem (Brown & Marshall, 2001), it may be the affective motivator behind the maintenance and enhancement of self-esteem, and thus a key component of an individual's sociometer. Specifically, when individuals experience a success, they feel pride in response, and over time and with repetition, these feelings may promote positive feelings and thoughts about their global self, leading to the high self-esteem that informs individuals of their social value. This longitudinal process is somewhat speculative, however, and the precise nature of the relation between pride and self-esteem is an important direction for future research.

Adaptive Benefits of Expressing Pride

In the previous section, we discussed how the experience of pride can motivate adaptive behaviors. Here we consider how the pride expression may serve a complementary adaptive function: alerting others that the proud individual merits increased group acceptance and social status. The cross-cultural generalizability of the pride expression is consistent with the possibility that it is an evolved response. Furthermore, similar displays (e.g., standing upright, pilo-erected fur, a "cocky" gait) have been observed in dominant nonhuman primates, suggesting that the expression may have evolved directly from earlier "protopride" displays in our evolutionary ancestors (de Waal, 1989; Maslow, 1936). In human research, studies have found that high-status individuals are assumed to feel more pride than lower status individuals working on the same task; if this link works bidirectionally, high status would likely be inferred from the pride expression (Tiedens, Ellsworth, & Mesquita, 2000).

Guilford and Dawkins (1991) have argued that the evolutionary "design" of social signals should reflect cues that perceivers will be best able to detect and interpret. According to the theory of ritualization, emotion signals begin as purely functional displays, and over time become simplified and exaggerated to the highly obvious expressions we see in everyday life (Eibl-Eisenfeldt, 1989). Thus, it may be fruitful to examine the components of a universal signal for insights into its possible original functions, bearing in mind that each component may be somewhat different than its original form.

One necessary component of the pride expression is expanded posture (Tracy & Robins, 2006b), which makes the individual showing pride look larger. Increased size conveys dominance, and might also attract attention. This would promote greater recognition from peers at the moment when such recognition is most desired: after an achievement. Another critical feature of the pride expression is the small smile. The fact that the smile is small helps observers distinguish pride from happiness, but the necessary presence of a smile in the expression (Tracy & Robins, 2004b) may reveal another function. Smiles convey friendship or alliance, and displaying a smile after an achievement sends the message "I'm dominant, but I'm still your friend; do not attack." Without the smile, the pride display could promote hostility from others, as well as a desire to conspire against a person who has become too dominant.

Do the Two Facets Serve Distinct Functions?

Our functionalist account of pride raises a perplexing question: Why does pride have a dark side? If pride evolved to promote status, why would a hubristic facet, which could foment coalitions against the proud individual, have evolved?

One possibility is that the two facets solve unique adaptive problems regarding the acquisition of status. For example, authentic pride might motivate behaviors geared toward the long-term attainment and maintenance of status, whereas hubristic pride might be a "shortcut" solution, providing status that is more immediate but fleeting. A related possibility, suggested by the correlations between the facets and the Big Five factors of personality, is that authentic pride promotes status through relationship-oriented, prosocial means (i.e., "getting along"), whereas hubristic pride promotes status by eliciting the admiration, if not the liking, of others (i.e., "getting ahead"). In fact, the personality correlates, as well as the correlations with self-esteem and narcissism, suggest that hubristic pride may be associated with psychopathy or Machiavellianism—two personality dispositions that may have short-term adaptive benefits despite causing long-term interpersonal problems (Paulhus & Williams, 2002). More generally, the likely outcomes of hubristic pride (e.g., boastfulness, competitiveness) may be adaptive in situations where it is advantageous to display one's relative superiority to an adversary in order to intimidate an opponent. In contrast, authentic pride may be more tailored toward the formation and stabilization of longer term relationships and social bonds. Future studies are needed to disentangle the potentially unique functions of the two facets.

A broader question for future research in this area is whether pride is one emotion with two facets, as we have been assuming, or whether there are two distinct pride-related emotions. Our research to date suggests that, in terms of the way people conceptualize and experience pride, there are two facets so distinct as to have unique cognitive antecedents and entirely opposite personality correlates. However, in other research (Tracy & Robins, 2007b) we have found that both facets are reliably associated with the *same* nonverbal expression, suggesting that, from a behavioral perspective at least, there is only one pride. Future studies addressing this complicated issue might test whether both facets exist across cultures, and whether the two facets are associated with distinct behavioral responses and interpersonal reactions—that is, whether each facet might, in fact, serve an independent function.

CONCLUSIONS AND FUTURE DIRECTIONS

In this chapter, we have reviewed the small but growing literature on pride. Recent research and theory suggest that this emotion (1) has two conceptually and experientially distinct facets with distinct cognitive antecedents and personality correlates; (2) develops somewhat later than the more biologically basic emotions, but is experienced and recognized by the time children reach the age of 4 years; (3) has a cross-culturally recognizable nonverbal expression; and (4) evolved to promote dominance and status. Despite this emerging understanding of the nature and function of pride, much work remains to be done on this fundamental emotion.

We would like to highlight several directions for future research, inspired by linguist Noam Chomsky, neuroscientist David Marr, and ethologist Nico Tinbergen's proposed levels of analysis for understanding a faculty of the mind. These researchers have independently argued that a faculty of the mind needs to be understood in terms of: (1) "its real-time operation (how it works proximately, from moment to moment)"; (2) "how it is implemented in neural tissue"; (3) "how it develops in the individual"; (4) "its function (what it accomplishes in an ultimate, evolutionary sense)"; and (5) "how it evolved in the species" (Pinker, 2002, p. 70).

Real-Time Operation

Regarding the first level of analysis, the "real-time operation" of pride, more research is needed on the pride expression to establish that the spontaneous display of pride corresponds to the recognizable posed display. Our study on Olympic judo wrestlers addressed this issue by demonstrating that elements of the recognizable expression are shown in response to a success experience (Tracy & Matsumoto, 2007), but future research should test whether individuals in these kinds of situations report feeling pride, make pride-eliciting cognitive attributions (i.e., internal), and show physiological responses that might be associated with the emotion (e.g., low cardiac and/or vascular activity; Herrald & Tomaka, 2001).

Also relevant to the real-time operation of pride is its connection to stable individual difference variables such as self-esteem and narcissism. Our research suggests that the two facets of pride show predicted correlations with these pride-related dispositions, but the process underlying the connection remains unclear. Is self-esteem simply the trait-like dispositional tendency to experience pride with great frequency across situations and over time? How does a pride experience boost one's self-esteem? And how might the dynamic interplay between (hubristic) pride and shame promote narcissism?

Neural Level

To date, we know of no research on the neural bases of the experience, expression, or recognition of pride. Evidence for distinct prefrontal cortex activity in response to task-contingent (i.e., pride-eliciting) versus noncontingent (i.e., happiness-eliciting) reward suggests that the pride experience, at least, may have a distinct neural signature (Davidson & van Reekum, 2005; see also Beer, Chapter 4, this volume), but considerably more work is required before we can begin to develop a neurobiological model of pride.

Development

Developmental research on pride has provided insights into the age at which children first experience, recognize, and understand pride. However, we know little about the development of pride beyond childhood, and research is needed on later periods of life including adolescence, adulthood, and old age. One important direction is to explore the link between pride and self-esteem development. Studies suggest that self-esteem is at its highest during childhood but drops dramatically during adolescence and again in old age (Robins, Trzesniewski, Tracy, Gosling, & Potter, 2002); developmental changes in pride experiences (e.g., less frequent pride in adolescence and old age) may influence these normative changes.

Function

Based on the research reviewed in this chapter, we have formulated hypotheses about pride's function. In our view, pride likely evolved to serve several distinct functions. The *experience* of pride reinforces prosocial and achievement-oriented behaviors and informs the individual that he or she has done something to increase his or her status and group acceptance. At the same time, the *expression* of pride may serve a third function: informing other group members that the individual deserves higher status and acceptance. All three functions seem ideally suited toward the overarching function of promoting social status, and suggest that humans may have evolved to communicate social messages about status, in part, through transitory emotions.

To test this functional account, we plan to examine the status implications of the pride expression (e.g., Does it convey dominance and promote higher status in those who show it?) and the pride experience (e.g., Is it associated with prosocial and achievement-oriented behaviors that might enhance the individual's status over the long term?) Additional cross-cultural studies are also needed to test whether the conceptual and experiential components of pride found in our research are universal. For example, do Burkinabes infer the same meaning from the pride expression as Westerners? Do they agree about the situations and contexts that elicit pride?

Evolutionary Level

Finally, future studies should begin to tackle the last level of analysis: the evolutionary level. The functional level of analysis asks about the purpose of pride, but the evolutionary level asks a broader question: Given our evolutionary history, *how* did humans come to experience and express pride in the ways that we do? This level may be the most important for the functionalist view of pride because it addresses the critical "how" and "why" of pride's existence. Extant research provides few answers to these questions, but researchers might begin with the comparative literature and the growing evidence that humans, and possibly the great apes, are the only animals that experience pride (Hart & Karmel, 1996; Tracy & Robins, 2004a). Combined with the fact that pride and other self-conscious emotions share a small set of features that distinguish them from other emotions and that seem relevant to some of the psychological characteristics unique to humans (e.g., self-awareness, self-representations, causal attributions; Tracy & Robins, 2004a), understanding the evolution of pride may provide important clues toward understanding humans' unique phylogenetic history. We hope that future researchers begin to address this issue, and, in doing so, reinvigorate the perspective on pride adopted over a century ago by psychologists such as Cooley, James, and others. Part of what it means to be human is to seek out the pride experience, and, perhaps, to show it to others.

NOTE

1. In a previous paper, we labeled authentic pride with the somewhat narrower descriptor "achievement-oriented" (Tracy & Robins, 2004a).

REFERENCES

Belsky, J., & Domitrovich, C. (1997). Temperament and parenting antecedents of individual difference in three-year-old boys' pride and shame reactions. *Child Development, 68,* 456–466.

Brown, J. D., & Marshall, M. A. (2001). Self-esteem and emotion: Some thoughts about feelings. *Personality and Social Psychology Bulletin, 27,* 575–584.

Bushman, B. J., & Baumeister, R. F. (1998). Threatened egotism, narcissism, self-esteem, and direct and displaced aggression: Does self-love or self-hate lead to violence? *Journal of Personality and Social Psychology, 75,* 219–229.

Campos, J. J., Barrett, K. C., Lamb, M. E., Goldsmith, H. H., & Stenberg, C. (1983). Socioemotional development. In M. M. Haith & J. J. Campos (Eds.), *Handbook of child psychology: Vol. 2. Infancy and developmental psychobiology* (4th ed., pp. 783–915). New York: Wiley.

Cooley, C. H. (1902). *Human nature and the social order.* New York: Scribner's.

Darwin, C. (1872). *The expression of the emotions in man and animals* (3rd ed.). New York: Oxford University Press.

Davidson, R., & van Reekum, C. M. (2005). Emotion is not one thing. *Psychological Inquiry, 16,* 16–18.

de Waal, F. B. M. (1989). *Chimpanzee politics: Power and sex among apes.* Baltimore: Johns Hopkins University Press.

Digman, J. M. (1997). Higher-order factors of the Big Five. *Journal of Personality and Social Psychology, 73,* 1246–1256.

Eibl-Eibesfeldt, I. (1989). *Human ethology.* New York: Aldine de Gruyter.

Eid, M., & Diener, E. (2001). Norms for experiencing emotions in different cultures: Inter- and intranational differences. *Journal of Personality and Social Psychology, 81,* 869–885.

Ekman, P. (1992). An argument for basic emotions. *Cognition and Emotion, 6,* 169–200.

Ekman, P. (2003). *Emotions revealed.* New York: Times Books.

Ekman, P., & Friesen, W. V. (1971). Constants across cultures in the face and emotion. *Journal of Personality and Social Psychology, 17,* 124–129.

Ekman, P., Sorenson, E. R., & Friesen, W. V. (1969). Pan-cultural elements in facial displays of emotion. *Science, 164,* 86–88.

Elfenbein, H. A., & Ambady, N. (2002). On the universality and cultural specificity of emotion recognition: A meta-analysis. *Psychological Bulletin, 128,* 203–235.

Ellsworth, P. C., & Smith, C. A. (1988). Shades of joy: Patterns of appraisal differentiating pleasant emotions. *Cognition and Emotion, 2,* 301–331.

Feldman-Barrett, L., & Russell, J. A. (1998). Independence and bipolarity in the structure of current affect. *Journal of Personality and Social Psychology, 74,* 967–984.

Fessler, D. M. T. (1999). Toward an understanding of the universality of second-order emotions. In A. L. Hinton (Ed.), *Biocultural approaches to the emotions: Publications of the Society for Psychological Anthropology* (pp. 75–116). New York: Cambridge University Press.

Graham, S. (1988). Children's developing understanding of the motivational role of affect: An attributional analysis. *Cognitive Development, 3,* 71–88.

Graham, S., & Weiner, B. (1986). From an attributional theory of emotion to developmental psychology: A round-trip ticket? *Social Cognition, 4,* 152–179.

Guilford, T., & Dawkins, M. S. (1991). Receiver psychology and the evolution of animal signals. *Animal Behavior, 42,* 1–14.

Harris, P. L., Olthof, T., Terwogt, M. M., & Hardman, C. E. (1987). Children's knowledge of the situations that provoke emotion. *International Journal of Behavioral Development, 10,* 319–343.

Hart, D., & Karmel, M. P. (1996). Self-awareness and self-knowledge in humans, apes, and monkeys. In A. E. Russon, K. A. Bard, & S. T. Parker (Eds.), *Reaching into thought: The minds of the great apes* (pp. 325–347). Cambridge, UK: Cambridge University Press.

Heckhausen, H. (1984). Emergent achievement behavior: Some early developments. In J. Nicholls (Ed.), *Advances in motivation and achievement: Vol. 3. The development of achievement motivation* (pp. 1–32). Greenwich, CT: JAI Press.

Heine, S. J. (2004). Positive self-views: Understanding universals and variability across cultures. *Journal of Cultural and Evolutionary Psychology, 21,* 109–122.

Herrald, M. M., & Tomaka, J. (2002). Patterns of emotion-specific appraisal, coping, and cardiovascular reactivity during an ongoing emotional episode. *Journal of Personality and Social Psychology, 83,* 434–450.

Hofstede, G. (1984). National cultures revisited. *Behavioral Science Research, 18,* 285–305.

Hoftstede, G. (2001). *Culture's consequence: Comparing values, behaviors, institutions, and organizations across nations* (2nd ed.). Thousand Oaks, CA: Sage.

Izard, C. E. (1971). *The face of emotion.* East Norwalk, CT: Appleton-Century-Crofts.

Keltner, D., & Buswell, B. N. (1997). Embarrassment: Its distinct form and appeasement functions. *Psychological Bulletin, 122,* 250–270.

Kemeny, M. E., Gruenewald, T. L., & Dickerson, S. (2004). Shame as the emotional response to threat to the social self: Implications for behavior, physiology, and health. *Psychological Inquiry, 15,* 153–160.

Kemper, T. D. (1984). Power, status, and emotions: A sociological contribution to a psychophysiological domain. In K. R. Scherer & P. Ekman (Eds.), *Approaches to emotion* (pp. 369–383). Hillsdale, NJ: Erlbaum.

Kernberg, O. F. (1975). *Borderline conditions and pathological narcissism.* New York: Jason Aronson.

Kornilaki, E. N., & Chlouverakis, G. (2004). The situational antecedents of pride and happiness: Developmental and domain differences. *British Journal of Developmental Psychology, 22,* 605–619.

Kovecses, Z. (1986). *Metaphors of anger, pride, and love: A lexical approach to the structure of concepts.* Amsterdam: Benjamins.

Kohut, H. (1977). *The restoration of the self.* New York: International Universities Press.

Leary, M. R., Tambor, E. S., Terdal, S. K., & Downs, D. L. (1995). Self-esteem as an interpersonal monitor: The sociometer hypothesis. *Journal of Personality and Social Psychology, 68,* 518–530.

Lewis, H. B. (1971). *Shame and guilt in neurosis.* New York: International Universities Press.

Lewis, M. (2000). Self-conscious emotions: Embarrassment, pride, shame, and guilt. In M. Lewis & J. M. Haviland-Jones (Eds.), *Handbook of emotions* (2nd ed., pp. 623–636). New York: Guilford Press.

Lewis, M., Alessandri, S. M., & Sullivan, M. W. (1992). Differences in shame and pride as a function of children's gender and task difficulty. *Child Development, 63,* 630–638.

Lewis, M., Sullivan, M. W., Stanger, C., & Weiss, M. (1989). Self development and self-conscious emotions. *Child Development, 60*, 146–156.

Lindholm, C. (1982). Swat Pukhtun family as a political training ground. *South Asia Occasional Papers and Theses, 8*, 51–60.

Markus, H. R., & Kitayama, S. (1991). Culture and the self: Implications for cognition, emotion, and motivation. *Psychological Review, 98*, 224–253.

Maslow, A. H. (1936). The role of dominance in the social and sexual behavior of infra-human primates: I. Observations at Vilas Park Zoo. *Journal of Genetic Psychology, 48*, 261–277.

Matsumoto, D. (2002). Methodological requirements to test a possible in-group advantage in judging emotions across cultures: A comment on Elfenbein and Ambady (2002) and evidence. *Journal of Personality and Social Psychology, 128*, 236–242.

McGregor, I., Nail, P. R., Marigold, D. C., & Kang, S. (2005). Defensive pride and consensus: Strength in imaginary numbers. *Journal of Personality and Social Psychology, 89*, 978–996.

Morf, C. C., & Rhodewalt, F. (2001). Unraveling the paradoxes of narcissism: A dynamic self-regulatory processing model. *Psychological Inquiry, 12*, 177–196.

Mosquera, P. M., Manstead, A. S. R., & Fischer, A. H. (2000). The role of honor-related values in the elicitation, experience, and communication of pride, shame, and anger: Spain and the Netherlands compared. *Personality and Social Psychology Bulletin, 26*, 833–844.

Paulhus, D. L. (1998). Interpersonal and intrapsychic adaptiveness of trait self-enhancement: A mixed blessing? *Journal of Personality and Social Psychology, 74*, 1197–1208.

Paulhus, D. L., & Williams, K. M. (2002). The dark triad of personality: Narcissism, Machiavellianism, and psychopathy. *Journal of Research in Personality, 36*, 556–563.

Pickett, C., Gonsalkorale, K., Tracy, J. L., & Robins, R. W. (2006). *Two facets of collective pride.* Manuscript in preparation, University of California, Davis.

Pinker, S. (2002). *The blank slate: The modern denial of human nature.* New York: Penguin Books.

Robins, R. W., Norem, J. K., & Cheek, J. M. (1999). Naturalizing the self. In L. A. Pervin & O. P. John (Eds.), *Handbook of personality: Theory and research* (2nd ed., pp. 443–477). New York: Guilford Press.

Robins, R. W., Trzesniewski, K., Tracy, J. L., Gosling, S., & Potter, J. (2002). Global self-esteem across the lifespan. *Psychology and Aging, 17*, 423–434.

Roseman, I. J. (1991). Appraisal determinants of discrete emotions. *Cognition and Emotion, 5*, 161–200.

Ross, M., Heine, S. J., Wilson, A. E., & Sugimori, S. (2005). Cross-cultural discrepancies in self-appraisals. *Personality and Social Psychology Bulletin, 31*, 1175–1188.

Rossier, J., Dahourou, D., & McCrae, R. R. (2005). Structural and mean-level analyses of the five-factor model and locus of control: Further evidence from Africa. *Journal of Cross-Cultural Psychology, 36*, 227–246.

Scheff, T. J. (1988). Shame and conformity: The deference-emotion system. *American Sociological Review, 53*, 395–406.

Schimmel, S. (1997). *The seven deadly sins: Jewish, Christian, and classical reflections on human psychology.* New York: Oxford University Press.

Scollon, C. N., Diener, E., Oishi, S., & Biswas-Diener, R. (2004). Emotions across cultures and methods. *Journal of Cross-Cultural Psychology, 35*, 304–326.

Slaughter, V., Stone, V. E., & Reed, C. (2004). Perception of faces and bodies: Similar or different? *Current Directions in Psychological Science, 13*, 219–223.

Smith, C. A., & Lazarus, R. S. (1993). Appraisal components, core relational themes, and the emotions. *Cognition and Emotion, 7*, 233–269.

Stepper, S., & Strack, F. (1993). Proprioceptive determinants of emotional and nonemotional feelings. *Journal of Personality and Social Psychology, 6*, 211–220.

Stipek, D. J. (1983). A developmental analysis of pride and shame. *Human Development, 26*, 42–54.

Stipek, D. (1995). The development of pride and shame in toddlers. In J. P. Tangney & K. W. Fischer

(Eds.), *Self-conscious emotions: The psychology of shame, guilt, embarrassment, and pride* (pp. 237–252), New York: Guilford Press.

Stipek, D. (1998). Differences between Americans and Chinese in the circumstances evoking pride, shame, and guilt. *Journal of Cross-Cultural Psychology, 29*(5), 616–629.

Stipek, D., Recchia, S., & McClintic, S. (1992). Self-evaluation in young children. *Monographs of the Society for Research in Child Development, 57*(1, Serial No. 226).

Tangney, J. P., & Dearing, R. L. (2002). *Shame and guilt.* New York: Guilford Press.

Tangney, J. P., & Fischer, K. W. (Eds.). (1995). *Self-conscious emotions: The psychology of shame, guilt, embarrassment, and pride.* New York: Guilford Press.

Tangney, J. P., Wagner, P., & Gramzow, R. (1989). *The Test of Self-Conscious Affect (TOSCA).* Fairfax, VA: George Mason University.

Thompson, R. A. (1989). Causal attributions and children's emotional understanding. In C. Saarni & P. Harris (Eds.), *Children's understanding of emotion* (pp. 117–150). Cambridge, UK: Cambridge University Press.

Tiedens, L., Ellsworth, P. C., & Mesquita, B. (2000). Sentimental stereotypes: Emotional expectations for high- and low-status group members. *Personality and Social Psychology Bulletin, 26,* 560–575.

Tracy, J. L., & Matsumoto, D. (2007). *More than a thrill: Cross-cultural evidence for spontaneous displays of pride in response to victory at the Olympic Games.* Manuscript submitted for publication.

Tracy, J. L., & Robins, R. W. (2006a). Appraisal antecedents of shame and guilt: Support for a theoretical model. *Personality and Social Psychology Bulletin, 32,* 1339–1351.

Tracy, J. L., & Robins, R. W. (2006b). *The nonverbal expression of pride: Evidence for cross-cultural recognition.* Manuscript submitted for publication.

Tracy, J. L., & Robins, R. W. (2007a). *The prototypical pride expression: Development of a nonverbal behavior coding scheme.* Manuscript submitted for publication.

Tracy, J. L., & Robins, R. W. (2007b). The psychological structure of pride: A tale of two facets. *Journal of Personality and Social Psychology, 92,* 506–525.

Tracy, J. L., Robins, R. W., & Lagattuta, K. H. (2005). Can children recognize the pride expression? *Emotion, 5,* 251–257.

Tracy, J. L., & Robins, R. W. (2004a). Putting the self into self-conscious emotions: A theoretical model. *Psychological Inquiry, 15,* 103–125.

Tracy, J. L., & Robins, R. W. (2004b). Show your pride: Evidence for a discrete emotion expression. *Psychological Science, 15,* 194–197.

Tracy, J. L., & Robins, R. W. (2004c, January). *The automaticity of emotion recognition.* Poster presented at the annual meeting of the Society for Personality and Social Psychology, Austin, TX.

Tracy, J. L., & Robins, R. W. (2003a). "Death of a (narcissistic) salesman": An integrative model of fragile self-esteem. *Psychological Inquiry, 14,* 57–62.

Tracy, J. L., & Robins, R. W. (2003b). Does pride have a recognizable expression? In P. Ekman, J. J. Campos, R. J. Davidson, & F. B. M. de Waal (Eds.), *Emotions inside out: 130 years after Darwin's "The expression of emotions in man and animals."* Annals of the New York Academy of Sciences, 1000, 1–3.

United Nations Human Development Report. (2005). Available online at *hdr.undp.org/reports/global/2005/pdf/presskit/HDR05_PKE_HDI.pdf.*

Weiner, B. (1985). An attributional theory of achievement motivation and emotion. *Psychological Review, 92,* 548–573.

Weisfeld, G. E., & Beresford, J. M. (1982). Erectness of posture as an indicator of dominance or success in humans. *Motivation and Emotion, 6,* 113–131.

Zammuner, V. L. (1996). Felt emotions and verbally communicated emotions: The case of pride. *European Journal of Social Psychology, 26,* 233–245.

16

The Evolution of Shame
as a Marker for Relationship Security

A Biopsychosocial Approach

PAUL GILBERT

Evolution has designed us to be exquisitely social from the first days of our lives. Babies respond to human faces and voice tones within hours of birth (Trevarthen & Aitken, 2001). They will grow and develop complex competencies for linguistic communications, and become capable of operating in culturally transmitted meaning-making and knowledge systems that give rise to art, science, and cultural diversities (Mithen, 1996). As we mature, a suite of evolved, social motivational systems come on line. These include seeking and responding to attachment to carers (Bowlby, 1969; Cassidy & Shaver, 1999) and groups (Baumeister & Leary, 1995), and concern with our relative social place (e.g., being treated by others as inferior, equal, or superior; Gilbert, 1992, 2000). In addition, there are unfolding competencies for social understanding (such as theory of mind; Byrne, 1995) and self-conscious awareness (Duval & Wicklund, 1972; Lewis, 2003; Tracy & Robins, 2004). All of these make us very sensitive, focused, and responsive to "what others think and feel about us." Conscious and nonconscious processing systems monitor self-in-relationship-to-others, influencing both social behavior and self-evaluation (Baldwin, 2005).

So powerful are social relationships in shaping our minds and brains that there is now good evidence that the quality of early care/affection we receive significantly impacts on brain maturation, especially affect regulation systems (Gerhardt, 2004; Schore, 2001; Siegel, 2001; Teicher, 2002). Indeed, throughout life social relationships are powerful biological regulators (Cacioppo, Berston, Sheridan, & McClintock, 2000; Carter, 1998). Hence although shame emerges with complex cognitive systems for self-consciousness and self-evaluation (Tracy & Robins, 2004), these are intimately linked to processing systems focusing on what is going on in, and expressed from, "the mind of the other." Thus, shame, is related to negative evaluation *by others*, has complex physiological effects (Dickerson & Kemeny, 2004), and is associated with specific personal and cultural meanings, and narrative discourses (see, e.g., Mack's [2003] special issue of the journal *Social Research* on shame).

Understanding that evolution has lead humans to be highly regulated within social relationships sets the context for a *biopsychosocial* approach to shame. In this approach shame may be a price we pay for becoming such self-aware social beings. Shame emerges from our complex evolved abilities to be aware of "how we exist for others," and make predictions of what they think and feel about us. Thus shame is commonly defined as an experience linked to having deficits, failures, and flaws *exposed*; shame is a response to feeling an unattractive and undesired self (Lewis, 1992; Tangney & Dearing, 2002). Outlined below is the suggestion that such exposures matter because of our needs to *compete* for our social places via creating positive images of our "selves" in the mind of others and thus advance our chances for inclusion, belonging, and being wanted, and for being chosen as a friend, lover, or team member (Etcoff, 1999; Gilbert, 1997). Failure or rejections in these domains not only makes the world a dangerous place, but also can significantly undermine a variety of reproductive strategies, such as attracting sexual partners, allies, and kin support (Gilbert, 2003; Gilbert & McGuire, 1998). Shame emotions can act as warnings that we "live in the minds of others" as a person with negative characteristics, or lack of positive ones, and thus are at risk of their rejection, exclusion, being passed by, or even persecution.

Given the evolved power of relationships to regulate our physiological and psychological systems, it is not surprising that many authors to this volume outline how, "being shamed," "feeling ashamed," and the process of "shaming others" are powerful social experiences that have far-reaching impacts on people's physical and mental health and social behavior (Gilbert, 2002; Gilbert & Andrews, 1998; Tangney & Dearing, 2002). In addition, shame (and the avoidance of being shamed) may underpin compliance to authorities (Kelman & Hamilton, 1989; Milgram, 1974); honor killings (Lindsfarne, 1998); violence (Cohen, Vandello, & Rantilla, 1998; Gilligan, 2003; Retzinger, 1991); cruelty, as acted out in atrocities (Gilbert, 2005a; Kelman & Hamilton, 1989); and difficulties in escaping violent relationships (Buchbinder & Eisikovits, 2003). To seek insight into the multifarious nature of shame requires exploration of the evolved power and importance of *positive* social relationships, and of the drive to be "accepted and well thought of by others." Hence this topic is a focus for this chapter.

WHY WE NEED (TO KNOW IF) OTHERS LOVE, LIKE, OR ACCEPT US

Recognition of the human drive for social approval, acceptance, positive reputations, and prestige has been part of philosophical thought for many centuries (Fukuyama, 1992), and have been key elements in anthropological, sociological, and psychological models of human behavior (Barkow, 1989; Scheff, 1988). Nearly all theories of shame view shame as intimately linked to these challenges of courting positive relationships with others and creating good impressions in the minds of others (e.g., Barrett, 1995; Lewis, 1992; Nathanson, 1994; Scheff, 1988, 1998; Schore, 1994, 1998). This chapter cannot review these theories (see Mills, 2005, and Tracy & Robins, 2004, for comprehensive reviews) but will explore some evolutionary and psychosocial aspects that build on this general premise. A central idea is that it is only when disruption in relationships conveys information that the *self is unattractive* to others in some way that shame will be a possible felt consequence. Thus disruptions to interpersonal relationships via (say) death may ignite grief (and loss of positive affect) but not shame. Shame, then, is about exposure of that deemed unattractive (Lewis, 1992, 2003). If this is so, then evolutionary questions focus on (1) the human need to be valued and to court good feelings about the self in the mind of "the other," in, and for, a variety of roles (see Gilbert, 1989, 2005b; Gilbert & McGuire, 1998; Greenwald & Harder, 1998) and (2) the evolved special processing systems underpinning self-processing competencies that tract our social standing and how we think others think about us (Gilbert & McGuire, 2003; Tracy & Robins, 2004). Although shame is often linked to global negative self-evaluations (Tangney & Dearing, 2002), shame can be role-focused. For example, one might feel shame when in the role of sexual engagement but not public speaking. Shame can also be focused on specific attributes of the self such as one's body or (perceived lack of) intellectual abilities. Presumably the degree to which shame becomes spread to a global sense of self depends on the meaning and values of the roles and attributes that are deemed important for self-definition and identity (Tracy & Robins, 2004).

Creating "positive feelings in the mind of the others about the self" not only increases the chances of engaging others in fitness-conducive roles (e.g., eliciting care from and engaging friends and sexual partners, and finding acceptance in groups) but importantly makes the world *safe*(r). The reason for this is that being cared for, liked, desired, and valued goes with being supported and chosen for role enactments with others, which has salient effects on various physiological mediators of health such as the immune and stress systems (Cacioppo et al., 2000; Carter, 1998) and promotes resilience to threats and negates life events (Masten, 2001). Being rejected, shunned, or expelled, or even being allocated an unwanted low social position in a social group, not only compromises reproductive chances (one may not be able to attract desirable sexual partners or form bonds with them) but can activate stress systems and seriously compromise health-regulating social relationships and survival (Cacioppo et al., 2000). Dickerson and Kemeny (2004) have shown that social, evaluative threats, especially those that involve negative exposures, are among the most powerful activators of the stress-cortisol response. It is therefore in the competitive dynamics of being loved, valued, and chosen, where audiences make choices over whom they will associate with, care for, and form intimate, caring, or cooperative relationships with, prefer and favor, include or exclude and stigmatize, that shame exerts its power. Competing for positive social relationships, trying to work out how to impress others, and being sensitive to shifts of feeling in "them about us," may have fueled the evolution of various cognitive processes (such as empathy, mind reading, and competencies for types of self-awareness and self-identities; Byrne, 1995; Gilbert, 2005a). Thus to create negative emotions in the mind of the other (e.g., anger or contempt) renders the social world unsafe and calls forth some defensive maneuvers—with shame as one possible automatic defense (Gilbert, 2002).

THREAT AND SAFENESS

The importance of "others" for making the world safe for oneself is set against the fact that the struggles for life and procreation are highly risky. For example, it is estimated that of all species that have evolved on this planet, over 99% are now extinct. Hence, all organisms and animals are confronted with selective pressures/challenges to their survival and reproduction in their domain of existence. It is now understood that the mechanism(s) for attachment formation between parents and infants/children evolved because it was a solution to threat (Bowlby, 1969, 1973, 1980). For species without early attachment, after birth offspring need to be mobile and able to disperse and hide to cope with the risk from predation (sometimes even from their own parents; MacLean, 1985). The genes of the parents are represented in subsequent generations because of the large numbers (hundreds and sometimes thousands) of offspring produced, with perhaps only 1–2% surviving to adulthood to reproduce. The evolution of parental investment and care (that has many different aspects) was to change that (Geary, 2000). In species that provide parental investment, offspring evolved to stay close to parent(s) (rather than to disperse) and do not have to be mobile or self-sufficient the moment they are born. This was to have enormous implications on the possibilities for subsequent evolution, including evolution of cognitive competencies (Bjorklund, 1997). In addition, belonging to and being accepted by peer and other groups, mutual support, cooperating, and sharing have been vital to human success and survival (Baumeister & Leary, 1995). For many mammals (and especially early humans), those excluded or rejected by a group would have a poor survival rate.

For Bowlby (1969, 1973; see also Cassidy & Shaver, 1999), the crucial element of parental care was that it provides a *safe base* for the infant. Not only does access to a parent offer protection, but parent–child interactions can sooth and calm an infant. For an infant to be calmed and feel secure, via interactions with others, implies the evolution of mental mechanisms that are sensitive and responsive to such care-providing behaviors. Hence, Gilbert (1989, 1993, 2005a) suggested that what has evolved in mammals, and especially humans, is a *social safeness* system that is specifically attuned to certain social cues (e.g., touch, voice tone, facial expressions, access to care) from others. Such cues are not just signals of an absence of threat but are linked to a specific type of positive affect system. Indeed, as noted below, work in neuroscience suggests that we have different types of positive affect systems, one of which is especially linked to social soothing.

Positive Affect and Safeness

One form of positive affect is linked to a pattern of neurohormones (e.g., oxytocin and endorphins) that mediate *affiliative and affectionate* behavior and provide a neural basis for soothing and feeling soothed (Carter, 1998; Depue & Morrone-Strupinsky, 2005; Panksepp, 1998; Uväns-Morberg, 1998; Wang, 2005). The powerful role of oxytocin on social behavior and stress regulation evolved in part as the physiological substrate for attachment (Carter, 1998; Uväns-Morberg, 1998). Recent research has shown that oxytocin and social support interact, and both have inhibiting effects on the stress system as measured by cortisol, especially in evaluative situations (Heinrichs, Baumgartner, Kirschbaum, & Ehlert, 2003). It is now known that from the first days of life, safeness-via-warmth (Rohner, 1986) is not simply the absence of threat but is also *conferred* and stimulated by others. The specific signals that stimulate this safeness soothing system include the caregiver signals of, touching, stroking, and holding (Field, 2000); voice tone, the "musicality" of the way a mother speaks to her child; facial expressions; feeding and mutually rewarding interchanges that form the basis for the emergence of an attachment *bond* (Trevarthen & Aitken, 2001); and various signals of support and friendliness (Heinrichs et al., 2003). Depressed mothers, who may not directly threaten their infants, can nevertheless have detrimental effects on their infants' maturation because of the relative *absence* of (positive) forms of communication such as eye gaze, smiling, positive facial expressions, holding, talking to and stroking, that stimulates positive affects in the infant and creates experiences of safeness and soothing (Murray & Cooper, 1997).

The importance of an infant's/child's evolved ability to recognize and respond to safeness/soothing signals and human warmth, together with cognitive competencies such as theory of mind, have implications for considering the social experiences of people with autism. They appear to have difficulties in coding social signals or maternal warmth, such as eye gaze, smiling, and physical closeness, as "safe and rewarding," but instead respond to them as if they are threats that trigger withdrawal, eye gaze aversion, and distress. Donna Williams (1999), who herself suffers from autism, discusses her fear of being touched or hugged and explains how other people were always felt as threats. In a moving passage toward the end of her book she writes:

> I believe that autism is the case where some sort of mechanism which controls emotion does not function properly, leaving an otherwise relatively normal body and a normal mind unable to express itself with the depth that it would otherwise be capable of. Perhaps before an autistic child is even born it is unable to receive or make sense of any message that there is a connection between itself and its mother or rejects these messages as overwhelming and painful. *This would result in an inability to comprehend closeness central to forming attachments and make meaning of one's environment in infancy.* Without this, perhaps the child creates within itself what it perceives as missing and in effect becomes a world within itself to which all else is simply irrelevant, external and redundant. . . . (pp. 175–176, emphasis added)

One can only speculate on how a brain that struggles to distinguish signals of warmth and safeness from those of threat may mature, and thus if and how they experience shame and its meaning for them.

The attachment system, however, is only one of a number of social-relational processing systems where the creation of safeness, through social interaction, plays a prominent role in the physiological organization of participants (Cacioppo et al., 2000; Uväns-Morberg, 1998). For example, as children mature, there are important new audiences to engage with as they enter a social world of competitors for social place. Children and adults seek to form friendships and peer group alliances both within and outside their kinship networks (Bailey, 2002), learning that their acceptance is dependent on the choices made for or against them by others (e.g., peers).

There were a variety of evolutionary pressures that made "concern to create positive feelings and thoughts in the mind of others about the self" central to human evolution (Barkow, 1989). Baumeister and Leary (1995) reviewed evidence for a need to belong, to be accepted, and to be valued by others, and how belonging creates a sense of safeness for the self. Clearly, a sense of "being safe" derived from a sense of belonging may suffer if one feels vulnerable to shame, condemnation, and rejection. In another domain, Boehm (1999) suggests that humans gradually evolved abilities that enabled subordinates to communicate and work together to depose feared dominants and to shun aggressive, nonsharing, or disruptive individuals, and those who threatened the social order. Social group formation moved away from typical primate "dominant male"-based hierarchies to more egalitarian social structures because survival depended on mutual support. Cooperation on activities (e.g., hunting), learning from others, and sharing of resources required that participating individuals be seen as trustworthy and able to make a contribution. Those perceived as cheaters/untrustworthy, morally corrupt, lazy, or diseased, and those who threatened the social order, could be excluded and shunned (Kurzban & Leary, 2001). Thus, to be included in such (group-sharing) relations required individuals to monitor the thoughts and feelings of their colleagues and ensure that they (as individuals) were (1) able to understand others sufficiently to make meaningful and useful contributions; and (2) not behave in ways that could result in developing a reputation of being bad or inferior, and thereby risk "the collective" shaming/shunning them. Hence, when one's peers and potential sexual partners are free to make choices about whom they associate with and form cooperative or sexual relationships with, the most advantageous strategy is to display qualities of self that are attractive and useful to others; one seeks to be chosen for roles by them (Gilbert, 1997; Gilbert & McGuire, 1998).

Attracting sexual partners has long been recognized as requiring the displays of characteristics about the self that a potential partner finds "attractive," and thus individuals will work hard to cultivate and display such qualities (Etcoff, 1999). There have also been some suggestions in the literature that female choice, away from brawny males in favor of more altruistic males, especially those who were good at forming alliances they could call on for help, may have affected the evolution of male characteristics (Buss, 2003). The more females could form their own alliances against aggressive males and thus not be coerced by them, the more they would be able to "chose" altruistic males who would form bonds with them. Taylor et al. (2000) suggest that because women carry their offspring, are responsible for their care, and are dependent on kin support, they cannot risk injury from fighting and are more orientated to "tend and befriend" as stress-controlling strategies. This may make women especially susceptible to loss of affiliative relationships via shame and stigma.

The point is that it is likely there have been *a number* of evolutionary pressures that operate on the desire to create positive feelings about the self in the mind of others—from early attachment through to cooperative, emotionally supportive, and sexual relationships. Securing these relationships is associated with positive affect and feelings of safeness, while their loss constitute threats. Being (and knowing that one is) loved, accepted, respected, and valued by others—be these friends, allies, group peers, lovers, or one's superiors—provides contexts for the deactivation of threat systems, provides major resources for coping with adversity, and organizes physiological systems that are conducive to health and well-being (Wang, 2005). In fact, as noted, there is now much evidence that throughout life, caring, supportive, and affiliative relationships are powerful regulators of a number of physiological systems that are conducive to health and well-being (Cacioppo et al., 2000; Heinrichs et al., 2003; Masten, 2001).

THREAT AND SAFENESS IN RELATION
TO INTERSUBJECTIVITY AND THEORY OF MIND

The importance of parental care has evolved to a profound degree in humans, making human infants exquisitely sensitive to communications from others, especially the mother. Being loved and cared for early in life matters greatly to one's capacity for and success in maturing a sense of self that is able to regulate emotions and feel safe (and lovable/valued) in the world, and capable of developing supportive and committed relationships (Baldwin, 2005; Gilbert, 1993; Schore, 1994). The mental state and motives of a mother (what is going on in her mind) is translated into a range of behaviors such as how she talks/sings, looks at, strokes, and holds her infant, and her ability to empathically reflect and resonate with her infant's feelings and mental states. The process by which the mind of the mother is able to influence the mind of the infant, through a process of empathic resonance, is called *intersubjectivity* (Trevarthen & Aitken, 2001)—that is, intersubjectivity is related to the moment-by-moment coregulation of participants as they experience the feelings of others directed at them (Stern, 2004). These coregulating "dances" of mother and infant have important effects on the infant's mind/brain, helping to choreograph the infant's brain maturation as it forms new neuronal connections at a rate of many thousands a day (Gerhardt, 2004; Schore, 1994; Siegel, 2001). Later, the way others (especially the primary carer), as socializing agents, understand and empathize with the child's emotions and behaviors has major impacts on the child's ability to understand and regulate his or her own emotions, behaviors, and personal characteristics and link these to self-processing and self-defining systems (Schore, 1994).

As noted by Gray (1987) and Saplosky (1994), the absence or withdrawal of a needed positive stimulus acts as a threat and stimulates the threat system. A number of authors have suggested that both lack of a positive "attuned" facial expression (e.g., the mother presents a blank face in interaction with her infant) or a facial expression, body posture, or voice tone that indicates a negative affect (e.g., anger, disgust) in the mind of the mother can stimulate threat systems and produce a distress-withdrawal response in the infant. This response may be a precursor for later shame responses (Schore, 1998; although see Mills, 2005, for alternative views). However, intersubjectivity, and the subtle way we remain sensitive to verbal and nonverbal communications from others that convey information about how we "exist in the mind of the other," remains salient throughout life and is especially important in psychotherapy (Stern, 2004). It is the key process in shame.

Hence, to experience self as "positive in the mind of the other" means three things: (1) the other is safe and thus one can relax in his or her presence; (2) the other will be positively disposed to help and sooth the self if needed; and (3) the other will cooperate in the coconstruction of various social roles and mutually beneficial activities. In consequence, self-regulation systems emerge in contexts of safeness and thus are less threat-focused, primed for defensive maneuvers. In feeling safe with others we can relax and be more open to the flow of interactions and their rewarding and helpful aspects (Gilbert, 1993, 2005a). If safeness and acceptance are so important to humans, and this comes from seeing that we exist positively for others, then we can begin to build a model that suggests that shame is an affect that warns us we are in danger of losing or have lost this protective shield. The idea that shame is related to loss of positive (valuing and acceptance) feelings for self by others is actually an old idea (Scheff, 1998), although it has rarely been linked to our basic evolved safeness and threat-processing systems (Gilbert, 2002).

New Cognitive Abilities for Understanding the Minds of Others

What competencies have we evolved to monitor what others might feel and think about us? Animals can pick up on threat or rejection cues, but they cannot locate symbolic reasons for being ignored, rejected, or experiencing hostility from others—that is, they probably can't appreciate that one can be attacked or rejected *because* one is judged by others to be ugly, untrustworthy, immoral, stupid, or lazy. Humans, however, have evolved high-level cognitive, metacognitive, and symbolic abilities that not only give rise to a sense of self (Tracy & Robins, 2004) but that can also *attribute* intentions and feelings governing the actions of others (e.g., "I believe she does not like me *because* she sees me as bad, ugly, untrustworthy"; Byrne, 1995). Thus humans need to know (or at least have reasons for) why others accept or reject them, and evaluate themselves such that they can predict the qualities of self that others will like or value, or reject or attack. Indeed, Santor and Walker (1999) found that it is believing one has personal traits/abilities *that others value* that is especially linked to self-esteem.

With maturation there are a host of evolved cognitive competencies that come on line that are specifically focused on understanding the mind of others and our relation to other minds. These include theory of mind (Byrne, 1995; Suddendorf & Whitten, 2001), symbolic self–other representations (Sedikides & Skowronski, 1997), and metacognition (Bjorklund, 1997; Wells, 2000). All these abilities play a crucial role in social interactions and self-regulation (Suddendorf & Whitten, 2001). With theory of mind abilities we can think about someone else—what motivates *their* behavior, what *they* might value, what *they* know and what *they* don't know, who *they* may like and why—and we can also *think* how to manipulate them to like us or be wary of us. Whitten (1999) argues that "reading others' minds makes minds deeply social in that those minds *interpenetrate* each other" (p. 177). Trevarthen and Aitken (2001) suggest that theory of mind abilities emerge from neonate abilities for intersubjectivity—that is, the neonate's innate sensitivities to the feelings of others, mediated by verbal and nonverbal cues directed at him or her, are key early elements for later theory of mind competencies.

We can also think of linked inferences: "I believe that you believe, that she believes 'X' about me." The ability to think like this clearly puts developing a social reputation central to social interactions, especially in contexts where there is increased freedom of choice over whom one will favor or associate with. In seeking sexual partners we hope our friends will put in a good word for us. Often it is gaining good reputations and prestige (creating positive views of self in the mind of others), not aggression, that will advantage our social claims (Barkow, 1989).

Sedikides and Skowronski (1997) have explored some of the possible origins and earlier precursors for a capacity to symbolize "a self." *Symbolic* self–other awareness is the ability to imagine the self (or other) as *an object* and to judge and give value to self and other; to have self-esteem, pride, or shame; or to allocate positive or negative values to others (good and able, or worthless and useless). Metacognition enables us to think about our thinking, feelings, and behavior; to evaluate their implications and consequences; and judge them to be good or bad (Wells, 2000). These competencies interact, giving rise to a complex of self–other processing sequences in interactions (and in imagination) and capacities for self-focused feelings (Lewis, 2003; Tracy & Robins, 2004). Thus children become able to recognize that they exist as "objects" for others, that others have feelings about them and are judging their behavior. They are able to understand social roles and rules, to engage in pretend play, and to learn the symbolic meanings of behaviors. Many of these abilities have been implicated in shame (Lewis, 2003; Mills, 2005). Parents not only indicate their own displeasure with a child's behavior directly but also the displeasure of those not present—for example, "your father [others, God] will be angry at what you did." It is these social interactions, and the cognitive abilities to understand them, that blend with primary emotions (e.g., anger, anxiety, and disgust), and give rise to self-conscious emotions such as shame and pride, and thus texture self-conscious emotions (Lewis, 2003; Tracy & Robins, 2004). Hence, shame can be infused with anger, anxiety, and/or disgust, making it a rich and multifaceted experience that can vary in form between people (e.g., one person may experience more disgust and another more anger in the shame episode).

The cognitive competencies that enable us to understand social interactions and communications also enable a crucial ability to inwardly construct *imaginary audiences* (Kaufman, 1989) and interpersonal schemas that contain memories that guide expectations of how others will view and respond to the self (Baldwin, 1997; Baldwin & Holmes, 1987). Thus, according to this view, self-conscious emotions emerge from the unfolding of complex cognitive competencies that help to construct self-identities that blend and texture primary emotions (Lewis, 2003; Tracy & Robins, 2004). These self-identities are key to the presentation of self in social relationships and to what kind of self one seeks to become.

Nonetheless, while there is no doubt that our social and self-evaluative competencies shape emotions into experiences like shame, there is debate as to whether the *defensive responses* of infants to interpersonal disruptions (such as parasympathetic arousal, slumped posture, eye gaze avoidance, and distress) can be seen as the early precursors of shame (Draghi-Lorenz, Reddy, & Costall, 2001; Schore, 1998). The question here is whether we should view the evolution of a human infant's extraordinary sensitivities to "the mind of the other" and intersubjectivity as the primary focus for the origins of shame (Trevarthen & Aitken, 2001) or reserve this emotion label for later cognitive-based experiences (Lewis, 2003; Tracy & Robins, 2004). Further, as noted below, shame responses can be activated outside conscious awareness (Baldwin, 2005).

Implicit and Explicit Processing

These various, recently evolved cognitive abilities are complex and lay down a powerful implicit regulating process that can operate outside of consciousness. There is increasing evidence that nonconscious decision making plays a significant role in our emotional reactions to situations and shapes our personal values (Haidt, 2001). Although evaluations underpin emotions, they can be made rapidly, automatically, and outside conscious control (e.g., via fast routes to the thalamus and amygdala; LeDoux, 1998), and this includes self-relevant evaluations (Koole, Dijksterhuis, & van Knippenberg, 2001; Lerner & Keltner, 2001).

Both conscious and nonconscious information processing can follow an "if–then" rule (Baldwin, 1992, 1997). For example, *if* others express disapproval, *then* respond with withdrawal or shame/submissive defenses. Such automatic rules have been explored in a research program by Baldwin and colleagues (for reviews, see Baldwin & Dandeneau, 2005). For example, in one early study students were asked to generate research ideas and were then subliminally primed (outside of conscious awareness) with either the approving or the disapproving face of the department professor. Those primed with the disapproving face rated their ideas more unfavorably than those primed with the approving face. *Self*-evaluation was nonconsciously linked to approval/disapproval of another (see Baldwin & Dandeneau, 2005, for reviews of this work).

Consciously priming people into caring roles also impacts in shame-related processes. For example, Baldwin and Holmes (1987) found that people who were primed with a highly evaluative relationship, and who then failed at a laboratory task, showed depressive and shame-like responses of blaming themselves for their failure and drawing broad negative conclusions about their personality (i.e., a typical shame response). Conversely, individuals who were instead primed with a warm, supportive relationship were much less upset by the failure and attributed the negative outcome to situational factors rather than personal shortcomings. People can cope better with failures if they have access to schemas of others as warm and supportive.

Kumashiro and Sedikides (2005) gave students a difficult intellectual test. They were then asked to visualize either a close negative, close neutral, or close positive relationship. Those who visualized the close positive relationship had the highest interest in obtaining feedback on the test even when that feedback reflected unfavorably on them. Baldwin and his colleagues (e.g., Baldwin, 1994; Baldwin & Holmes, 1987; Baldwin & Sinclair, 1996) have demonstrated that a key variable determining self-evaluative styles in certain contexts is the cognitive accessibility of other-to-self (e.g., others as critical or reassuring) schemas and role relationships that are activated. Attachment theorists have also shown that the way people respond to various interpersonal threats (i.e., the degree of anxiety and anger they may feel) is related to internal working models of attachment security (see Baldwin, Keelan, Fehr, Enns, & Koh-Rangarajoo, 1996, and also Mikulincer & Shaver, 2005, for reviews). These studies suggest that the degree to which people are able to access warm and supportive (in contrast to condemning and critical) other-to-self and self-to-self scripts and memories has a central bearing on emotional and social responses to negative, self-defining events and abilities to cope with (shame-linked) failures.

STRATEGIES OF SOCIAL ENGAGEMENT

So far we have explored the nature of threat and safeness systems for humans, our high sensitivity to others as safe (or not), some physiological mediators of safeness-creating support and affiliation (e.g., oxytocin and opiates), and the accessibility of internal representations of others in relation to self. Hence, as Baldwin (1992, 1997) suggests, self-organization revolves around interpersonal schemas that can operate at implicit levels. Such ideas also fit with those of shame theorists that focus on the role of interpersonal scripts, coded in the activation of recall of interpersonal episodes and scenes (e.g., Kaufman, 1989).

A key premise is therefore that the adaptive advantages of various *positive* relationships meant that the use of aggression/threatening to dominate others, to subdue threat from them, and/or to get what one wants was tempered by the need to compete for social place and elicit support by stimulating positive feelings in and eliciting helpful behaviors from others. If we can do that, then others will engage and cocreate sharing, supportive relationships with us. The competitive dynamic to this is rooted in the fact that an audience can chose whom they will associate with. Aggression may still be useful if one can limit the choices of others and/or in some way enforce compliance out of fear—this, of course, is far from uncommon in human relationships. Aggression is risky, however, in that it can increase the chances of conflict and injury and also the likelihood of withdrawal and defection by others. An alternative strategy is to display qualities of the self that attract others and stimulate their approach behaviors toward the self. These two social systems for social engagements are presented in Table 16.1.

Gilbert (1989, 1997, 2003) suggested that people have evolved mechanisms to monitor their attractiveness to others, called their *social attention holding potential* (SAHP). SAHP can be positive (e.g., "I am attractive to others because I have these aspects/characteristics, and people have a positive interest in me") or negative (e.g., "I am unattractive to others because I have these aspects/characteristics and people have a disin-

TABLE 16.1. Strategies for Gaining and Maintaining Rank–Status in Social Roles

Strategy	Aggression	Attractiveness
Tactics used	Coercive Threatening Authoritarian	Show talent Show competence Affiliative
Outcome desired	To be obeyed To be reckoned with To be submitted to	To be valued To be chosen To be freely given to
Purpose of strategy	To inhibit others To stimulate fear	To inspire, attract others To stimulate positive affect

Note. From Gilbert and McGuire (1998, p. 112). Copyright 1998 by Oxford University Press. Reprinted by permission.

terest in me or negative opinion of me"). SAHP can be role-focused; thus it can be high in one role but negative in another (e.g., friends like my helpfulness, but academic colleagues think my work is seriously flawed). The more I wish to compete in a certain domain (e.g., seek academic acceptance), the more vulnerable to shame in that domain I might be. From a different paradigm Leary, Tambor, Terdal, and Downs (1995) suggested that people have a mechanism for evaluating their relative social position (called a sociometer) that underpins self-esteem and is thus (presumably) a mechanism for shame. Whether we call such evaluative mechanisms SAHP or a sociometer, they are built from the various cognitive competencies outlined above and serve the enactment of strategies for social engagement via attraction, with efforts to impress others so that one will be chosen and desired for roles by others; that is to say, we monitor how we are stimulating *liking* in our friends, *desire* in our sexual partners, and *admiration* of our talents or skills in our bosses.

In this scheme of things "shaming" acts as a social signal from another to the self that the self is not attractive to the other; in the mind of the other, one is not stimulating positive affect but rather a negative affect of anger, dislike, disgust, or contempt. Hence, for both reasons of making the social world safe and for engaging others to chose in one's favor for advantageous roles (such as mating or alliance formation), it is our abilities to stimulate positive affects and beliefs about the self in the minds of others that are crucial for our social success.

Learning that we have not or cannot stimulate positive affects in the minds of others about ourselves is curial to shame vulnerabilities. It is well known that various forms of child abuse (physical, sexual, and verbal) are linked to vulnerabilities to shame. These are associated with fear of the other, being treated as an object, lack of felt care from the other, and sense of powerlessness to defend against harm from others (Andrews, 2002). However, people can become highly shame-sensitive in the absence of such experiences. Possible alternative routes to developing shame include parental favoritism (Gilbert & Gelsma, 1999; Mills, 2005), parental neglect (that leaves children feeling unsafe and needing to compete for social place), and high parental expectations that promotes socially orientated perfectionism (Wyatt & Gilbert, 1998). It is also known that high expressed emotion, which is a combination of intrusiveness and criticalness, is linked to a range of psychopathologies (Wearden, Tarrier, Barrowclough, Zastowny, & Rahil, 2000). Although not fully researched, it is likely that high expressed emotion in families increases stress in interactions, offers few(er) opportunities for developing memories of others as accepting and soothing, and increases vulnerabilities to threat focused-shame, even in the absence of other forms of abuse. There may also be cultural processes that elevate shame-proneness through, for example, the way social groups objectify, rate, and ascribe values to female body shapes (Etcoff, 1999; Fredrickson & Roberts, 1997), bodily functions (Roberts, 2004), or male aggressive/competitive behavior (Gilmore, 1990).

Social Comparison

One process that helps us work out how well we might do in engaging others to chose in our favor (our SAHP) is social comparison (Gilbert, Price, & Allan, 1995). We can, for example, compare how much attention and (say) praise is bestowed on us compared to others. In families, sibling rivalries for parental attention, and feelings that siblings were favored over self, are linked to feelings of shame (Gilbert, Allan, & Goss, 1996; Mills, 2005). Insofar as shame can be linked to feeling inferior to others (Kaufman, 1989), shame is also associated with problems of envy and jealousy (Gilbert, 1992). Moreover, there is evidence that shame is highly linked to making unfavorable comparisons with others and feeling that, compared to others, one is lacking in some way and is (thus) less likely to be chosen for or be able to sustain desired social roles (Gilbert, 2000). Stipek (1995) suggests that social comparisons begin in early childhood and that becoming aware that one is doing less well than others ignites social referencing. Presumably, the ways parents and teachers help children to feel valued, despite doing less well than others, help children feel safe and accepted. Sibling rivalries and parental and social pressures to compete may accentuate vulnerabilities to feelings of shame (Gilbert & Gelsma, 1999). Societal competitive dynamics for social place and inclusion can also be a source for shame and elevated rates of psychopathologies (Gilbert, 2005a).

SHAME AS A RESPONSE TO SOCIAL THREAT OF BEING UNATTRACTIVE

From what has been discussed so far any analysis of shame must link two different types of evaluation: how I think (or experience what) others think about me, and how I think and experience myself as a social agent (Gilbert, 1998). This is not a new view. Indeed, the interactions between "what I think others think about me" and "what I think about me given what I think others think about me" have been understood to be central to social behavior for a considerable time (Baldwin, 1992; Gilbert, 1998; Scheff, 1988).

External and Internal Shame

Theories of shame have tended to follow a similar focus (Mills, 2005). There is a long tradition of distinguishing internally focused (on self) and externally focused (on the other) attention (Arndt & Goldenberg, 2004; Duval & Wicklund, 1972). Gilbert (1997, 1998) suggested that when the focus of shame is on what others are thinking about the self, this can be called *external shame*. Here the attention and monitoring systems are externally directed, focused primarily on what is going on in the minds of others. In this sense it is like other threat defenses (e.g., to an approaching predator) where feelings and actions are highly coordinated to tracking the actions, signals, and intents emanating from others. However, threats in the social domain are significantly modified by the various competencies noted above, such as theory of mind and metacognition, and how we imagine we exist for the other.

Internal shame, however, is linked to complex memory systems—for example, of scenes of previous episodes of being shamed (Kaufman, 1989)—and self-evaluations where attention turns inward to the self and self-feelings and judgments (Tracy & Robins, 2004). Here self-evaluation is partly linked to our *imaginary audiences* that have been created through experiences with others (Baldwin, 1997). Internal shame is also linked to a process of *internal shaming* where individuals can be self-critical and self-persecuting. This dynamic is far more than self-blame for it involves emotions such as anger and contempt in self-to-self relationships (Gilbert & Irons, 2005; Whelton & Greenberg, 2005). In extreme cases patients may say they "hate" themselves and may want to hurt themselves.

Although shame has been linked to failing to meet self-standards, the evidence does not support this view unless these "failures" are seen to render one as an unattractive social agent in some way. Indeed, exploring the idea that shame was about failure to live up to ideals and using qualitative methods Lindsay-Hartz, de Rivera, and Mascolo (1995) note that

> to our surprise we found that most of the participants rejected this formulation. Rather, when ashamed, participants talked about being who they did *not* want to be. That is, they experienced themselves as embodying an anti-ideal, rather than simply not being who they wanted to be. The participants said things like, "I am fat and ugly," not "I failed to be pretty"; or "I am bad and evil," not "I am not as good as I want to be." This difference in emphasis is not simply semantic. Participants insisted that the distinction was important. . . . (p. 277)

It would appear, then, that internal shame requires that there has to be some perception of self as actually "unattractive"—not just a failure to reach a standard (Gilbert, 1992, 1997, 2002); that is to say, it is closeness to an undesired and unattractive self rather than distance from a desired self that is at issue (Ogilive, 1987). Although internal and external shame can be linked, they need not be. For example, a patient who was homosexual did not feel personal/internal shame for his sexual orientation but was terrified of it being discovered at work and "being shamed." Sometimes people will expose themselves to social ridicule and rejection and even persecution in fighting for a cause they believe is just. Another complication is that of dignity, where we might not feel personal shame for (say) a disease, and we do not want others to see our deformities or bodily secretions. External and internal shame must therefore be regarded as different types of experience, with different attention, monitoring, and processing systems that often blend together (Baldwin, 2005) but can also be distinguished (Gilbert, 1998, 2003).

Although external and internal shame are obviously bound together in various ways, there has been little research exploring their differences. However, Gilbert (2000) used a series of self-report questionnaires relating to social anxiety (SA) and fear of negative evaluation by others (FNE), a measure of external shame (called the "Other as Shamer Scale [OAS]) that measures beliefs that "others look down and negatively evaluate the self," and an internal shame scale (focusing on negative self-evaluation) called the Test of Self Conscious Affect (TOSCA; Tangney & Dearing, 2002). In a student group the TOSCA (internal) shame measure correlated $r = .54$ with SA, $r = .43$ with FNE, and $r = .54$ with OAS. In a clinically depressed group the TOSCA (internal) shame measure correlated $r = .54$ with SA, $r = .38$ with FNE, and $r = .65$ with OAS. Although significant, these correlations are not especially high and suggest that the measures are tapping different things. It is also worthy of note that the TOSCA (internal) shame measure correlated with depression at $r = .36$ in students and $r = .35$ in depressed patients. The OAS (an external shame measure) correlated with depression at $r = .56$ in students and $r = .45$ in depressed patients. In other words, it is how one thinks one exists for others that may be more related to depression. Even more intriguing is new work using implicit self-esteem measures that show that depressed people (who can score highly on explicit shame measures) can have *positive* implicit self-esteem (Raedt, Schacht, Franck, & Houwer, 2006). One can, of course, choose to define shame as only related to negative self-evaluation and self-experience. However, given these data, along with the emerging evidence of how negative self-evaluation can be elicited by subliminal presentations of disapproving others (Baldwin & Dandeneau, 2005), and the fact that in many philosophical traditions shame is about how we exist for others (see Gilbert, 1998, for a review), a purely self-focused approach to shame may be limited.

Self-Criticism and Internal Shame

If internal shame is linked to self-criticisms and having negative images of self in one's *own* eyes, then, as noted above, two factors may influence the degree of shame. One is the type and intensity of negative emotions directed at the self (in other words, shame-based self-criticism is not just a set of evaluations or thoughts about the self but comes with powerful emotions of anger or disgust with the self). The other is the ability to activate self-soothing systems when failing. Whelton and Greenberg (2005) measured students' level of self-reported tendencies to be self-critical. They then asked each student to sit in one chair and spend 5 minutes imagining him- or herself sitting in the other chair and to criticize that imagined self. They were then invited to switch chairs and respond to the self-criticism. Those high in self-criticism often submitted to (agreed with) their own self-criticisms, expressed shame and submissive postures (slumbered with head down, eyes averted) and sad faces, and felt weak and unable to counteract their own self-criticisms— in other words shame, submission, and defeat-like profiles were activated by their own attacks. High self-critics had much *contempt* in their own self-attacks. In a self-report study Gilbert, Clarke, Hempel, Miles, and Irons (2004) found that self-hatred and self-disgust, with desires to hurt the self for failures, were particularly pathogenic forms of self-criticism, and more so than self-criticism aimed at self-improvement or correction. These studies suggest that we will need to be more aware of the *emotions* directed at the self and not only focus on self-evaluations or attributions (Whelton & Greenberg, 2005). I suspect the same is true for external shame in that it is not just having a belief that others view us negatively but the emotions (e.g., anger or contempt) that we think others feel about us that is crucial.

In Whelton and Greenberg's (2005) study low self-critics found it easy to dismiss their criticisms. It is possible that low self-critics find it easier to activate self-soothing when confronted by their own failure and criticisms. Some evidence for this has been found in a study showing that self-criticism and depressive symptoms were significantly related to the (in)ability to be self-reassuring (Gilbert, Clarke, et al., 2004). In another study self-criticism was associated with difficulties in forming images of supportive and compassionate aspects of oneself (Gilbert, Baldwin, Irons, Baccus, & Clarke, 2006). In both studies self-criticism was highly associated with external shame. The implications of this work is that the experience of internal shame is linked to both (1) the power of hostile (e.g., contempt and anger) emotions directed at the self *and* (2) the inability to access self-soothing via positive images of, and feelings for, the self.

The Defense of Submissive Behavior: A Shame Complication

It is well known that submissive behavior, associated with the inhibition of aggression and challenging more powerful-hostile individuals, is a powerful defensive strategy seen in a variety of species (Gilbert & McGuire, 1998). Research has also shown that shame is highly associated with tendencies for submissive behavior (Gilbert, 2000). Also anger inhibition is related to social rank, with subordinates inhibiting anger expression to more powerful others (Allan & Gilbert, 2002; Fournier, Moskowitz, & Zuroff, 2002). Self-blame and shame can also be part of a submissive defense in the face of hostile dominant others (Gilbert & Irons, 2005). Trower, Sherling, Beech, Horrop, and Gilbert (1998) asked socially anxious and non-socially anxious students (social anxiety is linked to feeling inferior to others) to engage in a conversation with a lecturer while being videotaped. The lecturer was part of the study and was (unbeknown to the students) instructed to break conversational rules, such as butting in and changing the subject. On viewing the videotape, socially anxious students blamed themselves for the problems in the conversation while non-socially anxious students blamed the lecturer. Forrest and Hokanson (1975) found that depressed people were more self-punitive in a conflict situation than nondepressed people. They suggested that this submissive style was a learnt coping response for dealing with conflicts. Hence some elements of negative self-evaluations may be fuelled by nonconscious submissive strategies to cope with hostile, rejecting others, which then become part of self-processing (Gilbert & McGuire, 1998).

SHAME THREATS

Various types of interpersonal threat can trigger shame. Dugnan, Trower, and Gilbert (2002) explored two types of social threat related to *exclusion* and *intrusion*. In threats of exclusion, fear is focused on displays that *fail* to impress or attract much interest. One would like to be chosen for a role but others prefer someone else; thus others are too distant. Disappointment is the most obvious affect here, but shame could also be prominent if the focus becomes the *deficits* of self (in comparison to others) and ignites self-focused self-blame and self-criticism. Fear of intrusion, however, is where others get too close; one does not want to be seen and revelation of one's negatives is feared (Lewis, 1992). There may be a fear that "the other" can intrude into one's private world, get to know one's thoughts and feelings, and then impose his or her own (negative) definition of self. This can lead to concealment. Apter, Horesh, Gothelf, and Lepkifker (2001) found that being unwilling to engage in self-disclosure distinguished suicide attempters from nonattempters and was significantly linked to the seriousness of the attempt. Smart and Wegner (1999) found that people attempting to conceal an eating disorder had more anxiety and more intrusive negative thoughts than nonconcealers. Major and Gramzow (1999) explored concealment and fear of stigma in relation to having an abortion. Concealers had greater distress, made more efforts at thought suppression, and had more intrusive thoughts. One suspects that the fear of revelation/discovery in contrast to the fear of deficit is linked to a more paranoid focus in shame, especially if people attribute malevolence to others. Although such distinctions are important in psychotherapy, they have yet to texture the discourse and research on forms of shame. They need not be mutually exclusive fears.

Reflected Shame

Another form of shame relates not to self-actions but to those of one's associates. In a study of southern Asian women, Gilbert, Gilbert, and Sanghera (2004) found that self-focused shame was sometimes deemed less important than the shame-honor to one's family and community (see also Rodriguez Mosquera, Manstrad, & Fischer, 2000). Gilbert, Gilbert, and Sanghera (2004) labeled this *reflected* shame (the shame one can cause others and the shame others can cause/reflect onto the self). Gilbert (2002) suggested that the link between external shame and reflected shame may be via the degree to which families and social groups ascribe control of one person over another. Thus, for example, it is when (say) a parent is held responsible for the behavior of his or her child (are in some sense seen to "own" his or her child) that the child's bad behavior can shame a parent with the parental plea "Don't show me up in public." As Lindisfarne (1998) notes, it is in cultures where male honor is constructed around the control of female sexuality that issues of violence (from wife beating to wife killing) emerge. These behaviors are designed to reduce external shame and restore honor.

THE CULTURAL DIMENSIONS OF SHAME

Fukuyama (1992) notes that the themes of social status, competing for social acceptance and recognition, and creating good (attractive) impressions on others have been central to philosophical and political writings for hundreds of years, stretching back to Plato. Within these traditions it has been noted that the drive for recognition can involve desire for control and superiority, but also the need to avoid inferiority and being ignored or rejected (Gilbert, 2005b). The issue of "recognition" is thus itself complex and may come down to being recognized as "being one of us" or of "being good or attractive enough to be chosen or valued" to be able to cocreate helpful and supportive (safeness-conferring) relationships. Indeed, too much "drive to assert oneself" can result in being shamed.

All cultures have their own ways of deciding who should be seen as "one of us," given "value," and rewarded with social status (Barkow, 1989) or punished with its taking away—as in shame (Kaufman, 1989). Evolutionists argue that humans adapt their various strategies for social engagement (e.g., to acquire status, to seek out sexual partners, to share childrearing) in (often) nonconscious ways to fit local physical and social ecologies (see Cohen, 2001; Smith, 2000). In hostile, threat-filled contexts with predators, dangerous hunting, or hostile male groups, male identity takes shape around males as strong and fearless, with various associated rituals and processes for demonstrating courage, strength, and aggressive retaliations to conflicts. However, in more benign ecologies, gendered identities are more androgynous, friendliness and gentleness are valued, and aggressiveness and self-promotion can be shamed (Gilmore, 1990). Pinker (2002) argues similarly that although there are biological and temperamental differences between men and women, noted from childhood, whether men endorse and enhance aggression or affiliation depends on their socialization, that is, the way the social context shapes how reputations are made or lost, processes of shame and prestige giving, and the relative benefits from each way of behaving. To some extent, then, the objectification of the self is a social process that may vary in focus—for example, for women it can be body shape (Fredrickson & Roberts, 1997) and for men their preparedness to risk harm/injury to self in defense of honor (Gilmore, 1990). More research is needed to explore under what ecological and social conditions such objectifications emerge, the forms they take, their gender variations, and how they become part of a self-defining process that opens possibilities for failure and shame.

Cultural variations also impinge significantly on accepted forms of sexuality. While homosexuality has been valued in some cultures (e.g., early Athenian and Spartan), it has brought major condemnation from some Christian groups. Shaming has also been linked to various intrasexual competitive strategies. For example, Baumeister and Twenge (2002) suggest that in some female groups being too open in seeking sexual partners (i.e., promiscuous) can be shamed and derogated. Female-on-female shaming can thus be used to inhibit female competition and keep the "price" of sex high. Male shaming of female sexuality has been linked to desires to control females and not risk investing in another man's offspring (Buss, 2003). Others suggest that it is female competition that pushes women to extremes in body shape-size control, which is done as much to impress other women as to impress men; this can be especially acute in younger women and fed by the modern media and the "selling of products" (Abed, 1998). In low-resource ecologies fatness in women is prized whereas in high-resource cultures fatness is a mark of lack of control, and female forms are competitively pushed toward thinness and youthful appearance (Abed, 1998). In some cultures male honor and shame systems are linked to sexual control over females (to limit their choices) and beatings and killings of a female spouse or daughter may be allowed in defense of male honor and control (Lindisfarne, 1998). Practices such as female circumcision and foot binding are linked to social traditions where change is inhibited by fear of shame (Gilbert, 2002). There are, of course, major debates on the innate verses cultural aspects underpinning shaming practices, but from our point of view shame is *a key process* of social regulation/control. Social control therefore often deliberately links certain behaviors to self-definition ("You are bad if you feel or do X."). Such control will work much better if one can get people to internalize these values—that is, when they themselves come to view some of their own feelings or desires negatively. As traditions and cultural values change, so do our *own* internal experiences of our desires and possibilities.

Another key domain where culture and shame collide is in acknowledgment of harmful and exploitative actions carried out by groups (e.g., acknowledging atrocities in war). Robins (1993) points out that individuals in groups can collude to "keep silent" on their own perpetrations of injustice to avoid shame, and may even engage in denial. Thus shame avoidance can operate at the collective level. We are shamed if we draw attention to our (collective) shame—that is, if we reflect shame back onto our group. As Robins (1993) notes, the media can become instrumental in the evasion of our anxiety and shame, and will stigmatize those who would be critical of our cultural values, double dealings, and actions. Societies are always ambivalent about whistle-blowers or those who draw attention to the politics of poverty or the oppression of certain sections of a society. As Robins (1993) and Postman (1987) suggest, the media supports and shapes our identities (what it means to be British, an American, a Christian, or a Muslim) by its efforts to articulate, mirror, and present core values and role models of citizenship, or of members of a nation-state or other group—that is, what is required of us if we are "to belong." These are based on *positive* values and not acknowledging the darker sides. Group belonging offers personal identities (Baumeister & Leary, 1995) and is held together via validations and shared positives—not negatives. Beware of shaming a group you want to belong to.

When shame and humiliation reside in group conflicts new means of healing those harmed are required. Forcing groups to confront shame may not be helpful for it can lead to defensive maneuvers and efforts to defend self-identities and justify past actions. Here the subtle but important distinctions between shame and guilt are important (Gilbert, 2003; Tangney & Dearing, 2002). Shame focuses on the "badness" and devaluation of self or one's group and the infliction of narcissistic wounds, whereas guilt and remorse focus on empathic identification with victims, sadness/sorrow, and desires for reparation. Perhaps some of the South African efforts at reconciliation, where pain suffered can be given a voice and perpetrators are engaged in awareness of the harm they have done, and opened to possibilities for empathy, sorrow, and remorse (guilt-based processes), can offer new ways forward. However, even here critics have seen a "collusion in silence," especially regarding women's experience of apartheid (Graybill, 2001). Others focus on how the search for a national "reconciled" unity required turning blind eyes to economic injustice. Healing social division thus often requires ways of anticipating and working with shame that can operate on the tendency "not to see" past and current harms/injustice, to shame those who "open wounds" and the rageful defenses of the perpetrator's shame as they seek to restore collective honor and justification for harms done. Processes of social threat, shaming, and responses to being shamed thus reach well beyond our individual psychology and texture and choreograph a range of social, cultural, and political domains.

TOWARD A MODEL

The complex dynamics of shame, as they arise and emerge from our human dispositions to feel safe, fit in, and belong, compete for social place, and engage with others to form advantageous social roles, can be depicted in a simple model (Figure 16.1). From the first days of life we need others to care for us, for not only will that influence our survival but also such inputs (along with genes) will actually shape the kind of brain we will mature and the self we will become. Key to such is the generation of positive feelings in others about us. We are born with unfolding motives and competencies to mature into complex social beings, which evolved to be able to cocreate and navigate our self-identities to fit local, social ecologies. Thus, the social contexts for shame arise from local, historical, cultural, and ecological conditions that influence personal interactions and provide the backdrop on which people seek to mature and satisfy their social needs and shape their identities. Groups emerging in different ecologies vary in the ways they rear their children, engage in sexual activities, compete for material resources, regulate (legitimize or shame) those who have greater or lesser access to those resources, and endorse sharing/altruism over personal accumulations of wealth (or vice versa). They vary as to the kinds of gods, religions, and religiously focused shaming processes they create (Hinde, 1999), and they vary in what is deemed acceptable (sexual and moral) behavior and modes of deference, and they vary in regard to gendered values and roles. These variations set the backgrounds in which relationships between individuals emerge and thus the dynamics of shame, honor, and pride, of acceptance and approval or rejection and condemnation. The variations and complexities of these domains should not obscure the evolution of motives

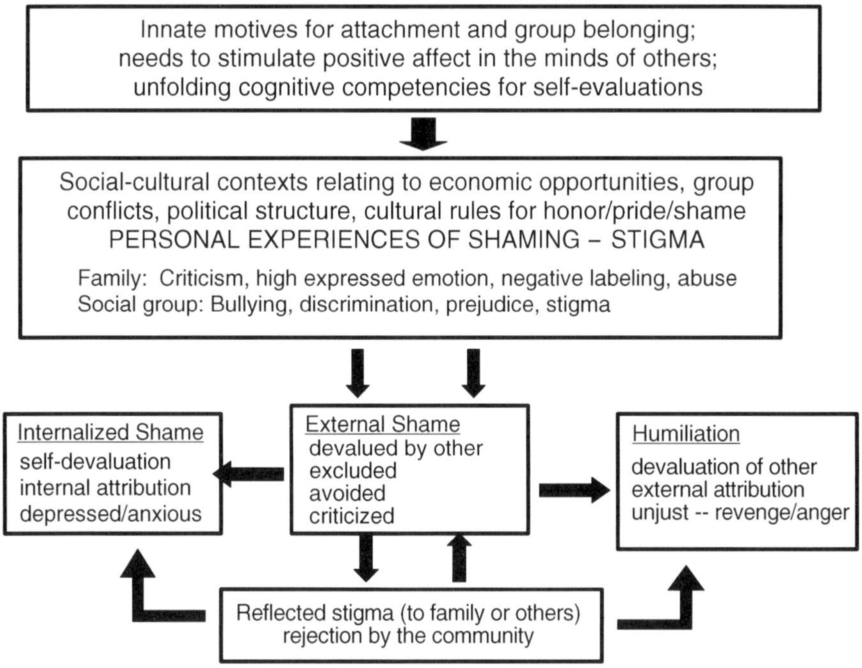

FIGURE 16.1. An evolutionary and biopsychosocial model for shame. Adapted from Gilbert (2002, p. 34). Copyright 2002 by Routledge. Adapted by permission.

(e.g., for acceptance and to compete for social place) and the evolved cognitive competencies on which they depend.

At the next level are the social processes that impinge on *personal* experiences. Within family contexts, children will be subject to parental rearing practices that can be caring, soothing, and loving, or hostile, critical, abusive, or neglectful. These early experiences will lay down affect-based memories of others as helpful or not, caring or threatening (Kaufman, 1989), and interpersonal schemas that will come to regulate self-organizing systems (Baldwin, 2005). Conflicts of interest within intimate relationships may be worked out affectionately or with high levels of shaming and countershaming, and various defenses.

In the wider social domains of peers, individuals may experience their reference groups as accepting and supportive or bullying. Peer bullying can be a common experience for shame, especially when bullying involves exclusion and ridicule, that is, attacks on one's attractiveness and social standing (Hawker & Boulton, 2000). As for group dynamics beyond close peer relationships, the social contexts can be experienced as prejudicial or discriminatory on the basis of ethnicity, gender, physical attributes (e.g., body shape, deformities), desires (e.g., homosexuality), and talents (or lack of talents). Moreover, individuals can fear being shamed and stigmatized not necessarily because of their personal abilities as such, but because of fear of being classed as belonging to a stigmatized group (Pinel, 1999).

The center of this model is therefore *external shame*. Hence, there are a variety of cultural, social, peer, and parental experiences that can funnel down onto individuals and influence how they perceive themselves as "existing in the minds of others" and self-objectification. In other words, individuals can come to believe that because of certain of their characteristics they will or will not be able to create positive/acceptable images in the mind of the other. In addition, they will form expectancies of whether others will be supportive, helpful, and forgiving or harsh and rejecting if they fail in some way, or express certain feelings, desires, or characteristics. It is when the world is seen as unsafe (and others as rejecting) that people will engage in defensive maneuvers. If the chosen defense is submissive, (and this can be triggered in the first instances nonconsciously), this will go with high levels of self-monitoring, self-attribution styles, and efforts to try to regulate expressions and minimize harm from others (Gilbert & Irons, 2005; Gilbert & Miles, 2000; Keltner & Harker, 1998). Such individuals tend to focus on their relative inferiority and relative (lack of) power to resist others, and blaming self can be safer than blaming powerful others (e.g., one's gods or parents) who can retaliate (Gilbert, 2005a). This does not mean that shamed people who adopt submissive defenses do not feel anger. A number of studies have found that shame is associated with anger to self and others, and can be ruminative and destructive (Gilbert & Miles, 2000; Tangney, Wagner, Barlow, Marschall, & Gramzow, 1996). Self-monitoring and self-blame can thus be linked to power dynamics; subordinates tend to self-blame and inhibit anger more than dominants (Fournier et al., 2002; Gilbert & Irons, 2005).

An alternative defense to social threats, however, is to express aggression, particularly in environments where submissiveness is likely to cause even more difficulties and threats. This can be seen as *the humiliation* response, which focuses on "the other as bad," with desires for revenge (Gilbert, 1998). The essence of the humiliation response arises with anger as the automatic defense to a put-down, slur, or rejection. In street language it is to be "dissed," and the need to develop a reputation of someone not to be "messed with" (Ahmed & Braithwaite, 2004). Some authors suggest that the rage related to humiliated fury is a defense against acknowledging shame—acknowledging that one is in the wrong, in error, or is unattractive to others. It has been called "by-passed shame" (Mills, 2005; Retzinger, 1991). To date there has been little work exploring how by-passed shame is different from processes such as repression, denial, or dissociation. And, as noted above, by-passed shame can operate at a sociocultural level where people collectively reinforce and support denial and dissociations.

Another reason for an externalized other-blaming, humiliated response is where there are no grounds for assuming responsibility and it is indeed the aggressive actions of the other that is the only source for an enraged response. Abusive experiences such as rape and torture might fit this category. In humiliation the person does not feel he or she deserves the harsh treatment given to him or her, whereas in shame there is usually some sense of blame-worthiness for such treatment (see Gilbert, 1998, for a review).

We cannot explore the genetic, gendered, conditioning/learning, and social reasons for why people engage different internalizing or externalizing strategic choices, or why a person may choose different strategies with different audiences. Suffice to say that in this model the core sources of shame are experiences of lack of social safeness (experiences or expectations that others will be critical and rejecting rather than forgiving and helpful), with a heightened sense of social threat and an insecure sense of one's social position/acceptance (external shame) and (in some contexts) poor self-soothing abilities. Once a threat from another is detected, be this real or imagined, fueled by conscious or nonconscious memories and interpersonal schemas, then defensive emotions, thoughts, and behaviors are primed. Whether the defensive sequence unfolds as submissive or aggressive humiliation depends on various social, psychological, and biological processes.

Finally, we can note that in cultures where shame and honor systems are intimately linked to the behaviors of one's associates, issues of reflected shame/honor become prominent, and then the defense and repair of shame is linked to the power dynamic of the relationship and cultural scripts for honor and the repair of honor.

So this descriptive process model places center stage the importance of how we have experienced, and currently experience, "the mind of others" and their behavior toward us in various domains, both intimate and social. In this model shame cannot be detextualized from the social dynamics in which it exists, nor from our evolved needs for social safeness and to engage others in various social roles. It has been this kind of thinking that has begun to point to new ways to help highly shame-prone people to develop various aspects of compassion that can be self-soothing in contexts of failure and less-than-optimum performances (Gilbert, 2005c, Gilbert, 2007).

CONCLUSION

Evolution has designed us to be exquisitely social from the first days of our lives, with social-cognitive competencies that are very sensitive and focused on what others think and feel about us. We can understand that not only can others have negative feelings about us, which would lead them to criticize, harm, shun, or even expel us from the relationship, but in addition social life is partly a competition where audiences, and our desired partners, can choose in favor of someone else. Self-identities help us navigate these challenges and threats, but also make us highly sensitive to shame.

If this view has value, then one implication is that shame, although linked to social threat, cannot be understood simply as "threat" but must also be seen as lack of activation of safeness; that is, it is linked to (in)abilities to elicit acceptance and soothing from others and learn how to be self-soothing (e.g., see Mikulincer & Shaver, 2005). Thus, faced with rejection or criticism, we might all experience a first flush of defensive emotion and action tendency (Dickerson & Kemeny, 2004), but it is our ability to activate self-soothing systems and access positive schemas of others that determines the unfolding of a full shame response (Baldwin & Dandeneau, 2005). Such a view has major implications for psychotherapy, for it suggests that some people may be unable to engage with or "heal" shame "material" until they feel safe with others or their therapist and internalize self-soothing abilities (Gilbert, 2005a, 2007; Gilbert & Irons, 2005). So evolution has made us highly social beings, with the consequent nature of shame and defense against it responsible for some our deepest fears, despairs, and complicant immoral behaviors.

ACKNOWLEDGMENT

I would like to thank Jessica Tracy and reviewers for their very helpful comments on earlier drafts of this chapter.

REFERENCES

Abed, R. T. (1998). The sexual competition hypothesis of eating disorders. *British Journal of Medical Psychology, 71,* 525–547.

Ahmed, E., & Braithwaite, V. (2004). "What, me ashamed?": Shame management and school bullying. *Journal of Research in Crime and Delinquency, 41,* 269–294.

Allan, S., & Gilbert, P. (2002). Anger and anger expression in relation to perceptions of social rank, entrapment, and depressive symptoms. *Personality and Individual Differences, 32,* 551–565.

Andrews, B. (2002). Body shame and abuse in childhood. In P. Gilbert & J. N. V. Miles (Eds.), *Body shame: Conceptualisation, research and treatment* (pp. 256–266). London: Brunner-Routledge.

Apter, A., Horesh, N., Gothelf, H., & Lepkifker, E. (2001). Relationship between self-disclosure and serious suicidal behavior. *Comprehensive Psychiatry, 42,* 70–75.

Arndt, J., & Goldenberg, J. L. (2004). From self-awareness to shame proneness: Evidence of causal sequence amongst women. *Self and Identity, 3,* 27–37.

Bailey, K. G. (2002). Recognizing, assessing and classifying others: Cognitive bases of evolutionary kinship therapy. *Journal of Cognitive Psychotherapy: An International Quarterly, 16,* 367–383.

Baldwin, M. W. (1992). Relational schemas and the processing of social information. *Psychological Bulletin, 112,* 461–484.

Baldwin, M. W. (1994). Primed relational schemas as a source of self-evaluative reactions. *Journal of Social and Clinical Psychology, 13,* 380–403.

Baldwin, M. W. (1997). Relational schemas as a source of if–then self-inference procedures. *Review of General Psychology, 1,* 326–335.

Baldwin, M. W. (Ed.). (2005). *Interpersonal cognition.* New York: Guilford Press.

Baldwin, M. W., & Dandeneau, S. D. (2005). Understanding and modifying the relational schemas underlying insecurity. In M. W. Baldwin (Ed.), *Interpersonal cognition* (pp. 33–61). New York: Guilford Press.

Baldwin, M. W., & Holmes, J. G. (1987). Salient private audiences and awareness of the self. *Journal of Personality and Social Psychology, 52,* 1087–1098.

Baldwin, M. W., Keelan, J. P. R., Fehr, B., Enns, V., & Koh-Rangarajoo, E. (1996). Social cognitive conceptualisation of attachment working models: Availability and accessibility effects. *Journal of Personality and Social Psychology, 71,* 94–104.

Baldwin, M. W., & Main, K. J. (2001). The cued activation of relational schemas in social anxiety. *Personality and Social Psychology Bulletin, 27,* 1637–1647.

Baldwin, M. W., & Sinclair, L. (1996). Self–esteem and "if . . . then" contingencies of interpersonal acceptance. *Journal of Personality and Social Psychology, 71,* 1130–1141.

Barkow, J. H. (1989). *Darwin: Sex and status.* Toronto: University of Toronto Press.

Barrett, K. C. (1995). A functionalist approach to shame and guilt. In J. P. Tangney & K. W. Fischer (Eds.), *Self-conscious emotions: The psychology of shame, guilt, embarrassment and pride* (pp. 25–63). New York: Guilford Press.

Baumeister, R. F., & Leary, M. R. (1995). The need to belong: Desire for interpersonal attachments as a fundamental human motivation. *Psychological Bulletin, 117,* 497–529.

Baumeister, R. F., & Twenge, J. M. (2002). Cultural suppression of female sexuality. *Review of General Psychology, 6,* 166–203.

Bjorklund, D. F. (1997). The role of immaturity in human development. *Psychological Bulletin, 122,* 153–169.

Boehm, C. (1999). *Hierarchy in the forest: The evolution of egalitarian behavior.* Cambridge, MA: Harvard University Press.

Bowlby, J. (1969). *Attachment: Vol. 1. Attachment and loss.* London: Hogarth Press.

Bowlby, J. (1973). *Attachment and Loss: Vol. 2. Separation, anxiety and anger.* London: Hogarth Press.

Bowlby, J. (1980). *Attachment and Loss, Vol. 3. Loss: Sadness and depression.* London: Hogarth Press.

Buchbinder, E., & Eisikovits, Z. (2003). Battered women's entrapment in shame: A phenomenological study. *American Journal of Orthopsychiatry, 73,* 355–366.

Buss, D. M. (2003). *Evolutionary psychology: The new science of mind* (2nd ed.). Boston: Allyn & Bacon.

Byrne, R. W. (1995). *The thinking ape.* Oxford, UK: Oxford University Press.

Cacioppo, J. T., Berston, G. G., Sheridan, J. F., & McClintock, M. K. (2000). Multilevel integrative analysis of human behavior: Social neuroscience and the complementing nature of social and biological approaches. *Psychological Bulletin, 126,* 829–843.

Carter, C. S. (1998). Neuroendocrine perspectives on social attachment and love. *Psychoneuroendocrinology, 23,* 779–818.

Cassidy, J., & Shaver, P. R. (Eds.). (1999). *Handbook of attachment: Theory, research and clinical applications* (pp. 115–140). New York: Guilford Press.

Cohen, D. (2001). Cultural variation: Considerations and implications. *Psychological Bulletin, 127,* 451–471.

Cohen, D., Vandello, J., & Rantilla, A. K. (1998). The sacred and the social: Cultures of honor and violence. In P. Gilbert & B. Andrews (Eds.), *Shame: Interpersonal behavior, psychopathology and culture* (pp. 261–282). New York: Oxford University Press.

Depue, R. A., & Morrone-Strupinsky, J. V. (2005). A neurobehavioral model of affiliative bonding. *Behavioral and Brain Sciences, 28,* 313–395.

Dickerson, S. S., & Kemeny, M. E. (2004). Acute stressors and cortisol response: A theoretical integration and synthesis of laboratory research. *Psychological Bulletin, 130,* 335–391.

Draghi-Lorenz, R., Reddy, V., & Costall, A. (2001). Rethinking the development of "nonbasic" emotions: A critical review of existing theories. *Developmental Psychology, 21,* 263–304.

Dugnan, D., Trower, P., & Gilbert, P. (2002). Measuring vulnerability to threats to self construction: The Self and Other Scale. *Psychology and Psychotherapy: Theory, Research and Practice, 75,* 279–294.

Duval, S., & Wicklund, R. A. (1972). *A theory of objective self-awareness.* New York: Academic Press.

Etcoff, N. (1999). *Survival of the prettiest: The science of beauty.* New York: Doubleday.

Field, T. (2000). *Touch therapy.* New York: Churchill Livingstone.

Forrest, M. S., & Hokanson, J. E. (1975). Depression and autonomic arousal reduction accompanying self-punitive behavior. *Journal of Abnormal Psychology, 84,* 346–357.

Fournier, M. A., Moskowitz, D. S., & Zuroff, D. C. (2002). Social rank strategies in hierarchical relationships. *Journal of Personality and Social Psychology, 83,* 425–433.

Fredrickson, B. L., & Roberts, T. A. (1997). Objectification theory: Toward understanding women's lived experiences and mental health risks. *Psychology of Women Quarterly, 21,* 173–206.

Fukuyama, F. (1992). *The end of history and the last man.* London: Penguin Books.

Geary, D. C. (2000). Evolution and proximate expression of human parental investment. *Psychological Bulletin, 126,* 55–77.

Gerhardt, S. (2004). *Why love matters: How affection shapes a baby's brain.* London: Brunner-Routledge.

Gilbert, P. (1989). *Human nature and suffering.* Hove, UK: Erlbaum.

Gilbert, P. (1992). *Depression: The evolution of powerlessness.* New York: Guilford Press.

Gilbert, P. (1993). Defence and safety: Their function in social behaviour and psychopathology. *British Journal of Clinical Psychology, 32,* 131–153.

Gilbert, P. (1997). The evolution of social attractiveness and its role in shame, humiliation, guilt and therapy. *British Journal of Medical Psychology, 70,* 113–147.

Gilbert, P. (1998). What is shame?: Some core issues and controversies. In P. Gilbert & B. Andrews (Eds.), *Shame: Interpersonal behavior, psychopathology and culture* (pp. 3–38). New York: Oxford University Press.

Gilbert, P. (2000). The relationship of shame, social anxiety and depression: The role of the evaluation of social rank. *Clinical Psychology and Psychotherapy, 7,* 174–189.

Gilbert, P. (2002). Body shame: A biopsychosocial conceptualisation and overview, with treatment implications. In P. Gilbert & J. N. V. Miles (Eds.), *Body shame: Conceptualisation, research and treatment* (pp. 3–54). London: Brunner-Routledge.

Gilbert, P. (2003). Evolution, social roles, and differences in shame and guilt. *Social Research: An International Quarterly of the Social Sciences, 70,* 1205–1230.

Gilbert, P. (2005a). Compassion and cruelty: A biopsychosocial approach. In P. Gilbert (Ed.), *Compassion: Conceptualisations, research and use in psychotherapy* (pp. 9–74). London: Routledge.

Gilbert, P. (2005b). Social mentalities: A biopsychosocial and evolutionary reflection on social relationships. In M. W. Baldwin (Ed.), *Interpersonal cognition* (pp. 299–335). New York: Guilford Press.

Gilbert, P. (Ed.). (2005c). *Compassion: Conceptualisations, research and use in psychotherapy.* London: Routledge.

Gilbert, P. (2007). *Psychotherapy and counselling for depression.* London: Sage.

Gilbert, P., Allan, S., & Goss, K. (1996). Parental representations, shame, interpersonal problems, and vulnerability to psychopathology. *Clinical Psychology and Psychotherapy, 3,* 23–34.

Gilbert, P., & Andrews, B. (Eds.). (1998). *Shame: Interpersonal behaviour, psychopathology and culture.* New York: Oxford University Press.

Gilbert, P., Baldwin, M. W., Irons, C., Baccus, J., & Clarke, M. (2006). Self-criticism and self-warmth: An imagery study exploring their relation to depression. *Journal of Cognitive Psychotherapy: An International Quarterly, 20,* 183–200.

Gilbert, P., Clarke, M., Hempel, S., Miles, J. N. V., & Irons, C. (2004). Criticising and reassuring oneself: An exploration of forms, styles and reasons in female students. *British Journal of Clinical Psychology, 43,* 31–50.

Gilbert, P., & Gelsma, C. (1999). Recall of favouritism in relation to psychopathology. *British Journal of Clinical Psychology, 38,* 357–373.

Gilbert, P., Gilbert, J., & Sanghera, J. (2004). A focus group exploration of the impact of izzat, shame, subordination and entrapment on mental health and service use in South Asian women living in Derby. *Mental Health, Religion and Culture, 7,* 109–130.

Gilbert, P., & Irons, C. (2005). Focused therapies and compassionate mind training for shame and self attacking. In P. Gilbert (Ed.), *Compassion: Conceptualisations, research and use in psychotherapy* (pp. 263–325). London: Routledge.

Gilbert, P., & McGuire, M. (1998). Shame, social roles and status: The psychobiological continuum from monkey to human. In P. Gilbert & B. Andrews (Eds.), *Shame: Interpersonal behavior, psychopathology and culture* (pp. 99–125). New York: Oxford University Press.

Gilbert, P., & Miles, J. N. V. (2000). Sensitivity to put-down: Its relationship to perceptions of shame, social anxiety, depression, anger and self–other blame. *Personality and Individual Differences, 29,* 757–774.

Gilbert, P., & Miles, J. N. V. (Eds.). (2002). *Body shame: Conceptualisation, research and treatment.* London: Brunner-Routledge.

Gilbert, P., Price, J. S., & Allan, S. (1995). Social comparison, social attractiveness and evolution: How might they be related? *New Ideas in Psychology, 13,* 149–165.

Gilligan, J. (2003). Shame, guilt and violence. *Social Research: An International Quarterly of the Social Sciences, 70,* 1149–1180.

Gilmore, D. D. (1990). *Manhood in the making: Cultural concepts of masculinity.* New Haven, CT: Yale University Press.

Gray, J. A. (1987). *The psychology of fear and stress* (2nd ed.). Cambridge, UK: Cambridge University Press.

Graybill, L. (2001). The contribution of the Truth and Reconciliation Commission toward the promotion of women's rights in South Africa. *Women's Studies International Forum, 24,* 1–10.

Greenwald, D. F., & Harder, D. W. (1998). Domains of shame: Evolutionary, cultural, and psychotherapeutic aspects. In P. Gilbert & B. Andrews (Eds.), *Shame: Interpersonal behavior, psychopathology and culture* (pp. 225–245). New York: Oxford University Press.

Haidt, J. (2001). The emotional dog and its rational tail: A social intuitionist approach to moral judgment. *Psychological Review, 108,* 814–834.

Hawker, D. S., & Boulton, M. J. (2000). Twenty years' research on peer victimisation and psychosocial maltreatment: A meta-analytic review of cross sectional studies. *Journal of Child Psychology and Psychiatry and Allied Disciplines, 41,* 441–455.

Heinrichs, M., Baumgartner, T., Kirschbaum, C., & Ehlert, U. (2003). Social support and oxytocin interact to suppress cortisol and subjective responses to psychosocial stress. *Biological Psychiatry, 54,* 1389–1398.

Hinde, R. A. (1999). *Why gods persist: A scientific approach to religion.* London: Routledge.

Kaufman, G. (1989). *The psychology of shame.* New York: Springer.

Kelman, H. C., & Hamilton, V. L. (1989). *Crimes of obedience.* New Haven, CT: Yale University Press.

Keltner, D., & Harker, L. A. (1998). The forms and functions of the nonverbal signal of shame. In P. Gilbert & B. Andrews (Eds.), *Shame: Interpersonal behavior, psychopathology and culture* (pp. 78–98). New York: Oxford University Press.

Koole, S. L., Dijksterhuis, A., & van Knipperberg, A. (2001). What's in a name: Implicit self-esteem and the automatic self. *Journal of Personality and Social Psychology, 80,* 669–685.

Kumashiro, M., & Sedikides, C. (2005). Taking on board liability-focused information: Close positive relationship as a self-bolstering resource. *Psychological Science, 16,* 732–739.

Kurzban, R., & Leary, M. (2001). Evolutionary origins of stigmatisation: The functions of social exclusion. *Psychological Bulletin, 127,* 187–208.

Leary, M. R., Tambor, E. S., Terdal, S. K., & Downs, D. L. (1995). Self-esteem as an interpersonal monitor: The sociometer hypothesis. *Journal of Personality and Social Psychology, 68,* 519–530.

LeDoux, J. (1998). *The emotional brain.* London: Weidenfeld & Nicolson.

Lerner, J. S., & Keltner, D. (2001). Fear, anger and risk. *Journal of Personality and Social Psychology, 81,* 146–159.

Lewis, M. (1992). *Shame: The exposed self.* New York: Free Press.

Lewis, M. (2003). The role of the self in shame. *Social Research: An International Quarterly of the Social Sciences, 70,* 1181–1204.

Lindisfarne, N. (1998). Gender, shame, and culture: An anthropological perspective. In P. Gilbert & B. Andrews (Eds.), *Shame: Interpersonal behavior, psychopathology and culture* (pp. 246–260). New York: Oxford University Press.

Lindsay-Hartz, J., de Rivera, J., & Mascolo, M. F. (1995). Differentiating guilt and shame and their effects on motivations. In J. P. Tangney & K. W. Fischer (Eds.), *Self-conscious emotions: The psychology of shame, guilt, embarrassment and pride* (pp. 274–300). New York: Guilford Press.

Mack, A. (Ed.). (2003). Shame [special issue]. *Social Research: An International Quarterly of the Social Sciences, 70,* 1105–1378.

MacLean, P. (1985). Brain evolution relating to family, play and the separation call. *Archives of General Psychiatry, 42,* 405–417.

Major, B., & Gramzow, R. H. (1999). Abortion as stigma: Cognitive and emotional implications of concealment. *Journal of Personality and Social Psychology, 77,* 735–745.

Masten, A. S. (2001). Ordinary magic: Resilience processes in development. *American Psychologist, 56,* 227–238.

Mikulincer, M., & Shaver, P. (2005). Mental representations of attachment security: Theoretical foundations for a positive social psychology. In M. W. Baldwin (Ed.), *Interpersonal cognition* (pp. 233–266). New York: Guilford Press.

Milgram, S. (1974). *Obedience to authority.* New York: Harper & Row.

Mills, R. S. L. (2005). Taking stock of the developmental literature on shame. *Developmental Review, 25,* 26–63.

Mithen, S. (1996). *The prehistory of the mind: A search for the origins of art and religion.* London: Thames & Hudson.

Murray, L., & Cooper, P. J. (1997). *Postpartum depression and child development.* New York: Guilford Press.

Nathanson, D. L. (1994). *Shame and pride: Affect, sex, and the birth of the self.* New York: Norton Paperbacks.

Ogilive, D. M. (1987). The undesired self: A neglected variable in personality research. *Journal of Personality and Social Psychology, 52,* 379–388.

Panksepp, J. (1998). *Affective neuroscience.* New York: Oxford University Press.

Pinel, E. C. (1999). Stigma consciousness: The psychological legacy of social stereotypes. *Journal of Personality and Social Psychology, 76,* 114–128.

Pinker, S. (2002). *The blank slate: The modern denial of human nature.* New York: Lane.

Postman, N. (1987). *Amusing ourselves to death.* New York: Methuen.

Raedt, R., Schacht, R., Franck, E., & Houwer, J. (2006). Self-esteem and depression revisited: Implicit positive self-esteem in depressed patients? *Behaviour Research and Therapy, 44,* 1017–1028.

Retzinger, S. (1991). *Violent emotions: Shame and rage in marital quarrels.* New York: Sage.

Roberts, T. A. (2004). Female trouble: The Menstrual Self-Evaluation Scale and women's self-objectification. *Psychology of Women Quarterly, 28,* 22–26.

Robins, K. (1993). The politics of silence: The meaning of community and the uses of the media in the new Europe. *New Formations, 21,* 80–101.

Rodriguez Mosquera, P. M., Manstead, A. S. R., & Fischer, A. H. (2000). The role of honor-related values in the elicitation, experience, and communication of pride, shame and anger: Spain and the Netherlands compared. *Personality and Social Psychology Bulletin, 26,* 833–844.

Rohner, R. P. (1986). *The warmth dimension: Foundations of parental acceptance–rejection theory.* Beverly Hills, CA: Sage.

Santor, D., & Walker, J. (1999). Garnering the interests of others: Mediating the effects among physical attractiveness, self-worth and dominance. *British Journal of Social Psychology, 38,* 461–477.

Sapolsky, R. M. (1994). *Why zebras don't get ulcers: An updated guide to stress, stress-related disease, and coping.* New York: Freeman.

Scheff, T. J. (1988). Shame and conformity. The deference-emotion system. *American Review of Sociology, 53,* 395–406.

Scheff, T. J. (1998). Shame in the labeling of mental illness. In P. Gilbert & B. Andrews (Eds.), *Shame: Interpersonal behavior, psychopathology and culture* (pp. 191–205). New York: Oxford University Press.

Schore, A. N. (1994). *Affect regulation and the origin of the self: The neurobiology of emotional development.* Hillsdale, NJ: Erlbaum.

Schore, A. N. (1998). Early shame experiences and infant brain development. In P. Gilbert & B. Andrews (Eds.), *Shame: Interpersonal behavior, psychopathology and culture* (pp. 57–77). New York: Oxford University Press.

Schore, A. N. (2001). The effects of early relational trauma on right brain development, affect regulation, and infant mental health. *Infant Mental Health Journal, 22,* 201–269.

Sedikides, C., & Skowronski, J. J. (1997). The symbolic self in evolutionary context. *Personality and Social Psychology Review, 1,* 80–102.

Siegel, D. J. (2001). Toward an interpersonal neurobiology of the developing mind: Attachment relationships, "mindsight" and neural integration. *Infant Mental Health Journal, 22,* 67–94.

Smart, L., & Wegner, D. M. (1999). Covering up what can't be seen: Concealable stigma and mental control. *Journal of Personality and Social Psychology, 77,* 474–486.

Smith, E. A. (2000). Three styles in the evolutionary analysis of human behavior. In L. Cook, N. Chagnon, & W. Irons (Eds.), *Adaptation and human behavior: An anthropological perspective* (pp. 23–46). New York: Aldine de Gruyter.

Stern, D. N. (2004). *The present moment in psychotherapy and everyday life.* New York: Norton.

Stipek, D. (1995). The development of pride and shame in toddlers. In J. P. Tangney & K. W. Fischer (Eds.), *Self-conscious emotions: The psychology of shame, guilt, embarrassment and pride* (pp. 237–252). New York: Guilford Press.

Suddendorf, T., & Whitten, A. (2001). Mental evolutions and development: Evidence for secondary representation in children, great apes and other animals. *Psychological Bulletin, 127,* 629–650.

Tangney, J. P., & Dearing, R. L. (2002). *Shame and guilt.* New York: Guilford Press.

Tangney, J. P., Wagner, P. E., Barlow, D. H., Marschall, D. E., & Gramzow, R. (1996). Relation of shame and guilt to constructive versus destructive responses to anger across the lifespan. *Journal of Personality and Social Psychology, 70,* 797–809.

Taylor, S. E., Klein, L. B., Lewis, B. P., Gruenwald, T. L., Gurung, R. A. R., & Updegaff, J. A. (2000). Biobehavioral responses to stress in females: Tend and befriend, not fight and flight. *Psychological Review, 107,* 411–429.

Teicher, M. H. (2002). Scars that won't heal: The neurobiology of the abused child. *Scientific American, 286*(3), 54–61.

Tracy, J. L., & Robins, R. W. (2004). Putting the self into self-conscious emotions: A theoretical model. *Psychological Inquiry, 15,* 103–125.

Trevarthen, C., & Aitken, K. (2001). Infant intersubjectivity: Research, theory, and clinical applications. *Journal of Child Psychology and Psychiatry, 42,* 3–48.

Trower, P., Sherling, G., Beech, J., Horrop, C., & Gilbert, P. (1998). The socially anxious perspective in face to face interaction: An experimental comparison. *Clinical Psychology and Psychotherapy: An International Journal of Theory and Practice, 5,* 155–166.

Uväns-Morberg, K. (1998). Oxytocin may mediate the benefits of positive social interaction and emotions. *Psychoneuroendocrinology, 23,* 819–835.

Vande Walt, C., Franchi, V., & Stevens, G. (2003). The South African Truth and Reconciliation Commission: "Race," historical compromise and transitional democracy. *International Journal of Intercultural Relations, 27,* 251–267.

Wang, S. (2005). A conceptual framework for integrating research related to the physiology of compassion and the wisdom of Buddhist teachings. In P. Gilbert (Ed.), *Compassion: Conceptualisations, research and use in psychotherapy* (pp. 75–120). London: Routledge.

Wearden, A. J., Tarrier, N., Barrowclough, C., Zastowny, T. R., & Rahil, A. A. (2000). A review of expressed emotion research in health care. *Clinical Psychology Review, 5,* 633–666.

Wells, A. (2000). *Emotional disorders and metacognition: Innovative cognitive therapy.* Chichester, UK: Wiley.

Whelton, W. J., & Greenberg, L. S. (2005). Emotion in self-criticism. *Personality and Individual Differences, 38,* 1583–1595.

Whitten, A. (1999). The evolution of deep social mind in humans. In M. C. Corballis & S. E. G. Lea (Eds.), *The descent of mind: Psychological perspectives on humanoid evolution* (pp. 173–193). New York: Oxford University Press.

Williams, D. (1999). *Nobody nowhere: The remarkable autobiography of an autistic girl.* London: Kingsley.

Wyatt, R., & Gilbert, P. (1998). Perfectionism and social rank. *Personality and Individual Differences, 24,* 71–79.

17

Humiliation

Causes, Correlates, and Consequences

JEFF ELISON
SUSAN HARTER

> Although humiliation figures in the life of almost all scholars, it
> has itself had virtually no scholarly life. As an object of
> intellectual inquiry, humiliation has had a hard time extricating
> itself from its two close cousins, shame and embarrassment.
> —W. I. Miller (1993, p. 131)

Picture Jason, a seventh-grade boy. Jason is small for his age, not at all athletic, and dreads gym class. Unfortunately, gym class is where we find him, waiting with the rest of the students for the teacher to walk in and start class. As they wait the biggest boy in the class sneaks up behind Jason and yanks his gym shorts all the way down to his ankles. *Everyone laughs at him.* Imagine how Jason might feel and how he might react. Jason's situation serves as a prototypical example of humiliation, an intensely painful experience believed to motivate thoughts or acts of revenge (Gilbert, 1997; Klein, 1992; W. I. Miller, 1993; Sarphatie, 1993; Stamm, 1978).

In spite of humiliation's painful nature and association with violence, there is scant empirical attention devoted to humiliation in the emotion literature in general and in the adolescent literature in particular (e.g., see Lewis & Haviland-Jones, 2000; Tangney & Dearing, 2002; Tangney & Fischer, 1995, where humiliation does not appear in the index, nor is it discussed at any length in the chapters). Instead, researchers have primarily focused on shame and guilt, and to a lesser extent embarrassment. We find this lack of data on humiliation surprising given that many children and adolescents are being humiliated every day in school (the most obvious arena) and adults in their social and occupational groups also suffer from humiliation. Thus, our program of research is designed to fill in some of these gaps. Specifically, we have addressed the characteristics that define a situation as humiliating, the relationships between humiliation and other negative self-conscious emotions, and outcomes that follow humiliation such as anger, violent ideation, and suicidal ideation. In this chapter we review the substantial theoretical literature and the nearly nonexistent empirical literature on humiliation, present our own conceptualization of humiliation, and describe the results from our series of three studies.

THEORIES OF HUMILIATION/WHAT IS HUMILIATION?

Although more than 50 articles and book chapters have addressed the causes and correlates of humiliation, only five have provided data beyond informal or clinical observations. Using Shaver's (Shaver, Wu, & Schwartz, 1992) emotion prototype framework, we discuss three themes: common causes, emotional correlates, and behavioral reactions to humiliation.

In terms of causes or antecedents, the first theme is being lowered in the eyes of others: losing esteem, social status, or dignity (Gilbert, 1997, 1998a, 1998b; Hartling & Luchetta, 1999; Kaufman, 1992; Klein, 1991; Lazare, 1987; Lindner, 2002; S. B. Miller, 1988; W. I. Miller, 1993; Sarphatie, 1993; Stamm, 1978; Statman, 2000; Tomkins, 1963). The *Oxford English Dictionary* (OED; Simpson & Weiner, 1989) defines "humiliation" as the "condition of being humiliated" and defines "humiliate" as "to make low or humble in position." Thus, the theoretical emphasis on lowered position is consistent with the OED definitions. The OED reflects a second theme common to conceptualizations of humiliation: the role of the other. The humiliated person is made to feel psychologically lowered by someone else. This is often perceived as an attack reflecting hostile intent to hurt the victim emotionally through put-downs, teasing, mocking, and even torture (Gilbert, 1997, 1998a, 1998b; Hartling & Luchetta, 1999; Kaufman, 1992; Klein, 1991; Lazare, 1987; Lindner, 2002; S. B. Miller, 1988; W. I. Miller, 1993; Sarphatie, 1993; Silver, Conte, Miceli, & Poggi, 1986; Stamm, 1978; Statman, 2000; Tomkins, 1963). Humiliation typically involves more than a dyad; the lowering occurs in the eyes of an audience, a third theme (Klein, 1991; S. B. Miller, 1988; W. I. Miller, 1993; Silver et al., 1986). Fourth, a sense of unfairness is often part of the experience (Gilbert, 1997, 1998a; Hartling & Luchetta, 1999; Silver et al., 1986; Stamm, 1978; Statman, 2000). In other words, is the humiliation related to a characteristic acknowledged by the victim such as incompetence or is it completely undeserved? The role of such trait-like characteristics appears to be equivocal as some writers have suggested that such personal features are not necessary, others contend that ownership of such characteristics increases the intensity of humiliation, and still others assert that their absence (e.g., being bullied for no reason) increases humiliation's intensity.

In terms of emotional correlates, humiliation is frequently associated, if not equated, with shame, embarrassment, or both. Many theorists view humiliation as simply high-intensity embarrassment, or the high-intensity member of a family of emotions grouped under the term "shame" (Kaufman, 1992; Lewis, 1987; W. I. Miller, 1993; Nathanson, 1992; Tomkins, 1963). Second, anger toward others, as an emotional correlate, results from what is seen as an attack (Gilbert, 1997, 1998a; Kaufman, 1992; Klein, 1991, 1992; Lindner, 2002; S. B. Miller, 1988; W. I. Miller, 1993; Sarphatie, 1993; Stamm, 1978; Tomkins, 1963). Third, humiliation is associated with longer term correlates such as sadness and depression (Gilbert, 1997, 1998b; Silver et al., 1986; Stamm, 1978; Tomkins, 1963). Indeed, the majority of theoretical writings on humiliation are written from a clinical perspective.

In terms of behavioral correlates, humiliation due to status attacks is believed to motivate retaliation and revenge (Gilbert, 1997, 1998a, 1998b; Kaufman, 1992; Klein, 1991, 1992; Lindner, 2002; S. B. Miller, 1988; W. I. Miller, 1993; Sarphatie, 1993; Stamm, 1978; Tomkins, 1963). This theme is perhaps the most pervasive. Klein (1991, p. 19) writes, "When it is outwardly directed, humiliated fury unfortunately creates additional victims, often including innocent bystanders as is so often the case in war, civil strife, personal and family vendettas, and terrorist attacks."

In fact humiliation came to the attention of the second author in studying the media accounts of high-profile school-shooting cases where humiliation was a root cause of the violence. An analysis of the media accounts of the 12 high-profile school shootings since 1996 reveals that in every case the shooters described how they had been ridiculed, taunted, teased, harassed, or bullied by peers (because of their inadequate appearance, social or athletic behavior), spurned by someone in whom they were romantically interested, or put down, in front of other students, by a teacher or school administrator, all events that led to profound humiliation (see Harter, Low, & Whitesell, 2003). All of the white, middle-class males eventually sought revenge. "I killed because people like me are mistreated everyday," said pudgy, bespectacled Luke Woodham, age 16, from Pearl, Mississippi, who murdered two students and injured seven others. "My whole life I felt outcasted, alone." In Peducah, Kentucky, 15-year-old Michael Carneal was tired of being teased and picked on by his schoolmates. Another shooter, Mitchell Johnson, observed that "Everyone that hates me, everyone I don't like, is going to die." In his Internet manifesto, Eric Harris, age 18, from Columbine High School in Littleton, Colorado, described how classmates, primarily the jocks, "ridiculed me, chose not to accept me, and treated me like I am not worth their time." A surviving member of the "Trenchcoat Mafia" (the name given pejoratively to Harris, Dylan Klebold, and friends by the jocks at Columbine), described how he, as well as Harris and Klebold—the second shooter—were constantly "cornered, pushed day after day, being ridiculed or bashed against lockers."

In all cases, such a history culminated in violent revenge causing the death of peers and, for certain shooters, adults. In Harris's manifesto, written days before the shooting incident, he described the constant humiliation by peers. As another member of the Trenchcoat Mafia told reporters, "Tell people that we were harassed and sometimes it was impossible to take; eventually someone was going to snap." He noted that the torment often became vicious. He described waking on school days with a knot in his stomach, dreading to face the continual humiliation. Central to the events that the boys described was the presence of an audience who witnessed the harassment, often laughing or joining in the mockery.

Violence may also be directed toward the self in the form of ideation, self-harm, or suicide (Klein, 1991; Tomkins, 1963). In two incidents, Columbine and the 2005 Red Lake shooting, the boys successfully killed themselves. In another case, an attempted suicide was averted by police. Other common reactions include those associated with shame, such as a desire to hide or escape (Klein, 1991; Lazare, 1987; Tomkins, 1963).

EMPIRICAL RESULTS

One prior study empirically addressed the causes of humiliation (Jackson, 2000). Two methodologies were employed. The first methodology was the autobiographical narrative technique, in which participants were asked to write about an incident where they experienced either shame or humiliation, followed by a questionnaire which inquired about details thought to be consistent with experiences of shame and humiliation. The second methodology employed vignettes in which three factors believed to underlie humiliation (excessive overt derogation, deservingness, and publicity) were manipulated. After reading the vignettes, participants responded to the same questionnaire based on how the character would respond. Support was found for several of the hypothesized causes or features of humiliating events. Lowered social status, the active role of the other, and hostile intent were illustrated by what Jackson labeled "excessive overt derogation." An audience was frequently present and the derogation from others was often viewed by the victim as undeserved.

While not an empirical test of the causes of humiliation, Hartling and Luchetta's (1999) Humiliation Inventory is based on a definition incorporating many of the features mentioned above: *"The internal experience of humiliation is the deep dysphoric feeling associated with being, or perceiving oneself as being, unjustly degraded, ridiculed, or put down—in particular, one's identity has been demeaned or devalued"* (p. 264). The self-report scale is comprised of two subscales assessing past experiences of humiliation and fear of future humiliation. Items with the highest factor loadings included being cruelly criticized, laughed at, put down, ridiculed, and excluded. Empirical results with the Humiliation Inventory are limited; however, females reported significantly more past humiliations and fear of future humiliations than males. Of particular interest is the fact that the subscales are significantly correlated, suggesting that one's current fear of humiliation is predicted by one's past history of humiliations.

Regarding the emotional correlates of humiliation, participants in Jackson's (2000) study reported anger toward others and significant levels of shame. Three additional studies (Brown, Harris, & Hepworth, 1995; Farmer & McGuffin, 2003; Kendler, Hettema, Butera, Gardner, & Prescott, 2003) have examined the link between humiliating life events assessed via the Life Events and Difficulty Schedule (Brown et al., 1995) and depression. In all three studies depression was predicted by higher ratings of loss and humiliation. Moreover, in Kendler et al., events involving humiliation and loss were more depressogenic than pure loss events (e.g., death) and in Brown et al. events involving humiliation and entrapment were more depressogenic than pure loss or pure danger events. Finally, in terms of behavioral responses to humiliation, participants in Jackson's (2000) study reported a desire for revenge and a desire to hide or escape.

OUR CONCEPTUALIZATION

Consistent with basic or discrete emotions theories (Ekman, 1972; Izard, 1971; Tomkins, 1963), we view humiliation as a member of a family that includes embarrassment, shame, and guilt (Elison, 2005; Kaufman, 1992; W. I. Miller, 1993; Nathanson, 1992; Tomkins, 1963). Similarly, from the perspective of Shaver's (Shaver et al., 1992) emotion prototype framework, emotions may be grouped into families based on similarities relative to a number of criteria (e.g., common antecedents, feelings, facial expressions, and behavioral reactions). As an identifier for the family, we use the term "shame family." This family consists of all the emotion terms related to perceived devaluation; the family is believed to be an evolutionary adaptation to the threat of social exclusion or loss of status (Elison,

2005). In contrast, everyday usage of the term "shame" is seen as a subset of the shame family domain. Thus, our use of the terms "shame family" and "shame" are not synonymous. Shaver et al. (1992) note that in most cultures members of emotion families denote intensity (e.g., irritation vs. rage), context (e.g., guilt's context is rule violation), or both (e.g., grief). Our conceptualizations of shame, humiliation, embarrassment, and guilt fit within this framework. In many Western cultures everyday usage of *shame* denotes high intensity and a (usually) moral context (i.e., related to an offense, crime, sin, or harm to others), much like guilt (Wallbott & Scherer, 1995). *Humiliation* denotes intensity and context—a highly intense emotional reaction to the context of having been lowered in the eyes of others. *Embarrassment* denotes low-intensity (even humorous) emotional reaction and a public context. *Guilt* denotes moderate to high intensity and the context of a moral violation.

Due to the theoretical and anecdotal links between humiliation and acts of revenge and retaliation, we developed a model linking humiliation with outcomes such as anger, violent ideation, and suicidal ideation. Here we distinguish between the act of attempting to humiliate another person and the emotion associated with *feeling humiliated*. As actions, attempts to humiliate and bullying are nearly synonymous. In either case, we hypothesized that these acts elicit the emotions of humiliation, shame, and embarrassment in the victim. These emotions, in turn, elicit inward- and outward-directed anger and motivate violent ideation, especially in the form of revenge or retaliation. What distinguishes our work from the bullying literature is that bullying is seen by others (e.g., theorists, investigators, educators) as having a direct impact on revenge. In our conception, humiliation is a necessary *mediator*. That is, bullying leads to feelings of humiliation, which in turn lead to acts of aggression or revenge.

Our conceptualization implies two categories of hypotheses that define humiliation: (1) similarities between humiliation, embarrassment, shame, and guilt as members of a single family, and (2) features or causes that characterize each of these emotions and differentiate humiliation from these other emotions. The first category of hypotheses includes presence of the antecedent condition of being viewed as less than one would like to be and a number of hypotheses regarding intensity. Specifically, intensity of humiliation, embarrassment, shame, and guilt should increase when: (1) audience size increases, (2) the audience is more important (e.g., loved ones or friends vs. strangers), (3) the audience intent is hostile (e.g., putdowns) versus friendly or sympathetic, (4) the victim acknowledges a personal characteristic that is devalued (e.g., a person who already views himself as a klutz trips), and (5) the magnitude of the devaluation increases (e.g., rejection vs. a disapproving look).

The second category of hypotheses, regarding which causes or features differentiate humiliation from embarrassment, shame, and guilt, is based on our Western definition of humiliation (as a context), which involves being lowered, typically by someone else. Therefore, we hypothesize that participants will apply the term "humiliation" to events involving a drop in esteem, of high intensity, occurring in public, and that are caused by someone else's purposeful and hostile actions. The type of standard violation (e.g., moral vs. social) should be unrelated to participants' use of the term "humiliation." However, we view the four emotion terms as fuzzy concepts, without sharp boundaries defined by necessary and sufficient conditions (Shaver et al., 1992). Therefore, our hypotheses, as a set, are made in regard to the features of the humiliation prototype; less prototypical instances of humiliation may be labeled as such due to the presence of a subset of these hypothesized features (e.g., public and high intensity).

OVERVIEW OF STUDIES

In Study 1 (Harter, Low, & Whitesell, 2003) our model of the antecedents and correlates of self-worth and depression was expanded to include active peer rejection and aggressive anger (in response to humiliating actions of others) to predict not only suicidal thinking but homicidal ideation in adolescents. In a second phase, vignettes designed to simulate humiliating events such as the school shooters experienced were presented, and the predictions in the model were examined for high and low violent ideators. Study 2 (Harter, Kiang, Whitesell, & Anderson, 2003) was an exploratory attempt to utilize Shaver's (Shaver et al., 1992) emotion prototype theory to identify common causes, common emotional correlates, and common behavioral reactions in the experience of humiliation among college students. Content analyses of responses to open-ended questions on these topics were performed. In Study 3 (Elison & Harter, 2004a, 2004b, 2005) facet theory (Guttman, 1954; Borg & Shye, 1995) and multidimensional scaling (Borg & Groenen, 1997) were employed to examine hypotheses about similarities and differences among humiliation, embarrassment, shame, and guilt, as well as their relationships to violent ideation.

STUDY 1: AN EXTENSION OF OUR MODEL OF THE CAUSES, CORRELATES, AND CONSEQUENCES OF GLOBAL SELF-ESTEEM

A major goal of our past program of research (see Harter, 1999) has been the construction of a theoretically driven model of the causes, correlates, and consequences of "self-esteem," defined as perceptions of one's global worth as a person. The primary correlates have been self-reported affect (cheerful to depressed) and hope versus hopelessness. In the original model, we focused on one particular outcome: suicidal ideation. In identifying potential causes of self-esteem, we drew upon the historical formulations of James (1892) and Cooley (1902). For detailed descriptions of these formulations, see Harter (1999).

Considerable evidence from participants ages 8 and older (see Harter, 1999; Harter & Marold, 1993; Harter, Marold, & Whitesell, 1992) provides support for a model in which competence or inadequacy in one cluster of domains judged important (namely, perceived physical appearance, peer likeability, and athletic competence) not only impacts self-esteem directly but is partially mediated by peer approval. Thus, those who value these domains but express their inadequacy will also report lower levels of peer support that, in turn, leads to lower self-esteem. A cluster of two additional domains (perceived scholastic competence and behavioral conduct) not only directly impact self-esteem but also have an indirect effect on self-esteem that is mediated by parental approval. Those who report weaknesses in these latter two domains do not feel that they garner the support of parents, and both these perceived inadequacies and associated lack of parental approval have been found to erode individuals' self-esteem. It was of interest to us that many of the school shooters were described as incompetent and unattractive, leading to rejection by their peers and to neglect by their parents. Moreover, many of these boys were reported to have low self-esteem.

With regard to the correlates of global self-esteem, we have demonstrated (see Harter, 1999) that it bears strong empirical relationships (r's from .70 to .82) to two other constructs, *affect* (along a continuum of cheerful to depressed) and *hope* on a continuum from (hopeful to hopeless) about one's future (see also Kovacs & Beck, 1977,

1978). These three constructs that we combined into a depression/adjustment composite, in turn, are highly predictive of suicidal ideation, the initial outcome in our model.

There were limitations to this earlier model, however. First, it focuses on only one outcome: suicidal ideation. Second, it identifies only one mediator, represented by the depression/adjustment composite. The psychological literature (see review in Harter, Low, & Whitesell, 2003), as well as the media accounts of the school shooters, informs us that feelings of inadequacy or lack of competence and perceived lack of peer and parental approval can also result in angry and aggressive responses, and in violent ideation, namely, the intent to harm others. Antecedents in our model—specifically, feelings of inadequacy and lack of peer and parental support—have been found by others to be associated with physical aggression, as well as with depression. Several of the school shooters were identified as being both depressed and violent, which is consistent with the clinical literature (Achenbach & Edelbrock, 1983) on the high co-occurrence of anger at others (an externalizing symptom) and depression (an internalizing symptom). Thus, in our revised model, we added aggressive anger (in response to humiliating actions by others) and homicidal ideation (Figure 17.1).

This model was tested employing a sample of 313 sixth-, seventh-, and eighth-grade middle school students (175 males, 138 females). The school is approximately one-third European American, one-third Hispanic, and one-third African American, from lower-middle-class to lower-class families.

Path-modeling techniques revealed that, consistent with the original modeling, the domains of physical appearance and peer likeability contributed to the depression/adjustment composite through a direct path (Figure 17.1). However, their impact on this composite was also partially mediated by peer rejection/humiliation. Findings similar to the original modeling were also obtained given a direct path from the combination of scholastic competence and behavioral conduct to the depression/adjustment composite. Thus, young adolescents who feel that they have inadequacies, with regard to their appearance and their peer likeability, report both peer rejection and depressive reactions. The path from the

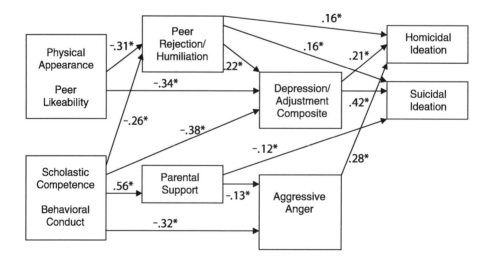

FIGURE 17.1. Path model, revised to include anger-induced aggression and homicidal aggression. $\chi^2(6) = 8.27$, $p > .05$, NFI = .99, NNFI = .99, critical N = 507.

depression/adjustment composite to suicidal ideation is also consistent with the original modeling. There are also direct paths from peer rejection and from parental support to suicidal ideation, revealing that those adolescents who lack supportive social relationships are more likely to engage in suicidal thinking.

What is novel about the extended model are links *to* and *from* aggressive anger as well as *to* homicidal ideation, the two new constructs added in light of our interest in thoughts of violence among adolescents (Figure 17.1). Aggressive anger was predicted by perceptions of poor behavioral conduct and scholastic performance, as well as by low parental support. Thus, those evaluating their conduct and school performance negatively were most likely to report that they were aggressively angry and that they lacked parental support. Homicidal ideation, not surprisingly, was predicted by aggressive anger and by peer rejection/humiliation. Thus, those adolescents who report high levels of aggressive anger in response to humiliation are more likely to have thoughts of killing others, as do those adolescents who experience more rejection and more humiliation at the hands of peers. Interestingly, the depression/adjustment composite was also predictive of homicidal ideation. Adolescents who experience this combination of low self-esteem, depressed affect, and hopelessness are more likely to turn their thoughts not only to suicide but to killing others. Moreover, the fact that homicidal ideation and suicidal ideation were correlated at .55 also attests to the co-occurrence of ideation directed at harming others and harming the self.

Troubled adolescents, therefore, with a history of perceived inadequacies as well as active peer rejection that can be humiliating and low parental support, not only experience depressive and aggressive reactions but become introspective about terminating both their own lives and those of others, putting them in double jeopardy. There is obvious value, therefore, in developing models that address the predictors of homicidal and suicidal ideation, given the common pathways to each of these outcomes. The findings represented in this model give credence to the challenges expressed by experienced clinicians who often, in treating adolescents with such histories, find it difficult to predict whether they will become violent toward *others*, violent toward *self*, or violent toward *both*, as we saw in the cases of the Columbine and Red Lake shootings.

In phase two, to address the experience of humiliation more directly, we crafted hypothetical events that simulated the types of harassment, ridicule, and taunting that the school shooters experienced (see Harter, Low, & Whitesell, 2003). These situations also involved an audience who laughed at the victim. The same adolescents from our normative sample were asked to put themselves in the position of the victim and indicate how humiliated they would feel, as well as what action they would take, along a continuum from doing nothing to planning serious harm or violence. Humiliation ratings were high for all adolescents, as anticipated, because the vignettes were designed to be humiliating. A central research question, therefore, was what predicts who will react with violent thoughts and who will not. Thus, next we identified violent and nonviolent ideators based on the hypothetical actions they would take. Violent ideators were those who endorsed items involving (1) plans for revenge against those who harassed them or laughed at them, or (2) thoughts of seriously harming anyone, regardless of their involvement. Nonviolent ideators were those who endorsed items involving (1) doing nothing, or (2) attempting a constructive solution. These two groups were compared with regard to potential differences in the predictors of our general model, antecedents that represent predisposing factors in their background.

The violent ideators reported significantly greater depressed affect, lower self-worth, and greater hopelessness. In addition, the violent ideators reported greater suicidal ideation, greater homicidal ideation, and higher levels of anger-induced physical aggression. Thus, the pattern is consistent with our framework emphasizing the co-occurrence of internalizing and externalizing reactions, where violent ideators report higher levels of both.

With regard to the *predictors* of these reactions, drawn from the model, we found marked and highly significant differences between the violent and the nonviolent ideators for the self-concept domains of peer likeability, physical appearance, and scholastic competence. With regard to *social rejection,* the other key predictor in the model, the violent ideators also showed significantly more rejection. They also reported less peer support. Thus, the factors that predispose young adolescents to depression, aggression, homicidal ideation, and suicidal ideation in the general model also discriminate between those who do (and do not) report violent ideation in reaction to the hypothetical events in the vignettes involving harassment and humiliation.

STUDY 2: A PROTOTYPE APPROACH TO THE EMOTION OF HUMILIATION IN COLLEGE STUDENTS

As described above, one route to our interest in humiliation was derived from an analysis of the media accounts of the 12 high-profile cases in which suburban, white, male adolescents took weapons to school, shooting and killing classmates and, in some cases, teachers. To review these accounts, the shooters described how they had been ridiculed, taunted, teased, harassed, or bullied by peers; spurned by someone in whom they were romantically interested; or put down in front of other students by a teacher—all events that led to profound humiliation. Central to these experiences was the presence of an audience who laughed and joined in the mockery. This history led to revenge, in the form of violence, resulting in numerous deaths.

Surprisingly, as noted earlier, in the emotion literature in general and in the adolescent literature in particular, there is scant empirical attention devoted to humiliation. This is especially surprising given the fact that the periods of adolescence and emerging adulthood are psychologically fragile periods of development, where youth have heightened levels of self-consciousness and a vulnerable sense of self (see Harter, 1999), making them prone to reactions of humiliation.

Thus, to examine the dynamics underlying the experience of humiliation, we turned to emotion prototype theory (Shaver et al., 1992) as a framework within which to explore the processes that define humiliating reactions (see Harter, Kiang, et al., 2003). Emotion prototype theory, initially applied to the basic emotions of happiness, sadness, anger, and fear, identifies common or prototypic causes of, correlates of, and reactions to, each emotion.

Following the conceptual and methodological lead of Shaver and colleagues (1992), we asked university students to describe their experiences of humiliation with regard to the three categories above. In addition, we were particularly interested in whether it was necessary to have an audience, namely, witnesses to the event, in order to experience humiliation, and what role the audience played.

Ninety-five college students (53 females, 42 males) were given an open-ended survey that asked about the following issues:

1. *Common causes.* One set of questions asked students to generate three different events that would cause them to feel humiliated. We also coded for whether they mentioned that an audience was present and asked whether the number of witnesses would impact the level of humiliation they would experience.
2. *Emotional correlates.* Building upon our own earlier work on multiple emotions (Harter & Whitesell, 1989), another set of questions asked them to generate other emotions that they would also feel in the face of a humiliating event.
3. *Behavioral reactions.* A final set of questions asked what they would do in response to being humiliated, both at the time of the humiliation and after the event was over, looking back on it.

Content analyses were performed on the responses to all of these open-ended questions as an exploratory examination of whether there were commonalities, consistent with a prototype approach.

Prototypical or common causes of humiliation described by students included (1) being teased, harassed, ridiculed, or put down, consistent with the experience of the school shooters. Two other causes were (2) public behaviors or accidents that violate social norms, and (3) incompetence or mistakes observed by others. Critical to the experience of humiliation was the role of an audience, peers who typically *laughed* at the victim. Moreover, students reported that the larger the audience, the greater the level of humiliation.

An examination of spontaneously mentioned emotional correlates of humiliation included anger (86%), embarrassment (66%), sadness (56%), and shame (16%). The relatively high frequency with which participants mentioned embarrassment and the low frequency with which they mentioned shame are consistent with our conceptualization.

The analysis of the behavioral reactions to humiliation revealed that acts of revenge or retaliation were common, as in the case of the school shooters. While the majority indicated that they would direct their revenge toward the perpetrator, some responses revealed that they would act violently toward anyone, a common feature of the school shootings where the targets appeared to be random. Nonviolent reactions included attempts to escape from the perpetrator and the humiliating event, as well as attempts to laugh it off or minimize the insult (more common when looking back on the situation).

One of our future goals is to develop a process model in which we can make direct links between particular causes, emotional correlates, and behavioral reactions. For example, if one is harassed, ridiculed, bullied, or put down, as in the case of the school shooters, is one more likely to report an emotion of anger and to report a behavioral reaction of violence? If one violates a social norm, do people also report embarrassment and turn to minimizing strategies?

STUDY 3: DIFFERENTIATING HUMILIATION FROM EMBARRASSMENT, SHAME, AND GUILT

Given the results from Studies 1 and 2, humiliation may be characterized as an intensely unpleasant emotional experience that often leads to thoughts of, and in some cases acts of, revenge or retaliation. Therefore we felt it was important to understand how humiliation differs from other negative self-conscious emotions. The overarching goal in this investigation (Elison & Harter, 2004a, 2004b, 2005) was to identify what distinguishes humiliation from embarrassment, shame, and guilt, in terms of eliciting conditions, intensity, and correlates. To explore these questions, we employed facet theory (Guttman, 1954; Borg & Shye, 1995) to develop vignettes incorporating variables that were hypothesized to affect emotional intensity and distinguish between emotions. University students rated our three sets of vignettes on a number of emotional and behavioral reactions. The three sets contained approximately 30 vignettes each and were rated by 123–132 students.

Audience size (none, small, large) was of interest for two reasons. First, all four of these emotions were expected to increase in intensity as audience size increased. Second, an audience appears to be present in prototypical instances of embarrassment (R. S. Miller, 1996) and humiliation (Klein, 1991; S. B. Miller, 1988; W. I. Miller, 1993; Silver et al., 1986), but is not necessarily present for shame and guilt (Tangney, Miller, Flicker, & Barlow, 1996). In addition, the type of standard violation was expected to differentiate between particular emotions. We explored three categories of standard violations. Our social violations (trip, spill) were similar to what R. S. Miller (1996) calls *individual behavior*, self-created social dilemmas. We wanted social violations to be distinct from our competence violations (mistakes, stupidity) in that the former did not involve an effortful performance and thus did not reflect directly on one's abilities. Moral violations (cheat, steal, cheat on significant other) involved an offense, crime, or harm to others. Social and competence standard violations were expected to be somewhat more typical of embarrassment (R. S. Miller, 1996) and humiliation, while moral violations were expected to be more typical of shame and guilt (Wallbott & Scherer, 1995). We also examined the intent of the audience, distinguishing between friendly and hostile reactions from others. For instance, friendly intent is evident in joking between friends and in instances where other people smile sympathetically in response to violations of social norms. Hostile intent is exemplified by condescending looks and mocking. Each of the four emotions was expected to be more intense in response to hostile intent. Hostile intent was expected to increase the use of all four emotion terms, but to be especially relevant to humiliation. A sample vignette involving a sympathetic response by an audience to a competence standard violation is, "While discussing a class assignment with a *large group,* you realize you just *said something stupid*. The others notice and *smile sympathetically.*" Due to relationships between self-conscious emotions and self-esteem (Tangney & Dearing, 2002), we also explored self-concept congruence in which the victim acknowledges a characteristic weakness (e.g., "Heather, who already *views herself as a klutz* . . .").

Finally, we were interested in whether the strong relationships between humiliation and violence observed in Studies 1 and 2 would be evident in Study 3. Moreover, we sought to contrast the strength of the relationships between the four emotions and violence, with the expectation that humiliation would be most strongly related to violence.

The results from Study 3 will be discussed by topics: (1) feeling badly about ourselves; (2) characterizing humiliation, embarrassment, shame, and guilt; (3) similarities among these emotions; (4) relative intensities of the four emotions; and (5) humiliation and violence.

Feeling Badly about Ourselves

Our first category of hypotheses was in regard to similarities between humiliation and the other three emotions. We reasoned that the commonality these emotions share is some degree of feeling badly about oneself based on negative self-evaluations or in response to perceived or expected negative judgments from others. Therefore, for each vignette, participants rated how badly they would feel about themselves, ranging from 1 (*Not at all badly*) to 9 (*Very badly*). To examine the effects of the hypothesized variables (i.e., variables manipulated in the vignettes), multidimensional scaling (MDS; Borg & Groenen, 1997) was used to map vignettes into geometric solution spaces based on similarities among vignettes as rated on this badly-about-self variable. Thus, the common badly-about-self variable was important because it allowed us to compare and contrast the four emotions based on common MDS solutions.

The dimensions within the MDS solutions are somewhat like factors. They account for similarities in the data—for instance, correlations among vignettes sharing similar values along a given dimension (e.g., type of standard violation). Dimensions may correspond to quantitative or qualitative similarities among variables; some, but not all, dimensions were hypothesized to correspond to mean differences between groups of vignettes. Because the variables in our vignettes were experimentally manipulated in an a priori fashion, our use of MDS was a confirmatory procedure.

How the Type of Standard Violation Affects How Badly We Feel about Ourselves

Of all the variables we explored, the type of standard violation (social, competence, moral) had the clearest effect on similarities in how badly participants said they would feel about themselves. The MDS solutions clearly reflected three separable groups of vignettes, ordered from social to competence to moral violations. However, these groups of vignettes did not correspond to mean differences on the badly-about-self variable. In other words, in terms of how participants anticipated feeling about themselves, the type of standard violation was associated with qualitatively different reactions. This is analogous to the qualitative differences between intelligence test items; verbal, math, and spatial items are qualitatively different, but none of these groups is inherently more difficult than the others. As discussed in the section "Characterizing Humiliation, Embarrassment, Shame, and Guilt" below, embarrassment and humiliation were reported in response to all types of violations, while shame and guilt were reported almost exclusively in response to moral violations. In sum, we feel badly in different ways in reaction to different classes of violations.

How an Audience Affects How Badly We Feel about Ourselves

Because we believe humiliation, embarrassment, shame, and guilt are inherently social (Elison, 2005), we were particularly interested in effects related to the presence and size of an audience. Between vignettes, a large effect on the badly-about-self variable was observed between the absence and presence of an audience; as predicted, participants anticipated feeling worse when an audience was present. However, a much smaller effect was observed between small and large audiences. In sum, we feel worse about ourselves when an audience is present to witness our standard violations or to witness when someone puts us down.

How the Intent of Others Affects How Badly We Feel about Ourselves

When we violate a standard in public the audience may react in a sympathetic manner, a hostile manner, or not at all. We hypothesized that the perceived intent of others would have an effect on how badly we would feel about ourselves in these situations. As predicted, mean levels of the badly-about-self variable were higher for the vignettes with hostile intent compared to friendly intent. Thus, hostile responses from others magnify how badly we feel in response to our mishaps and violations.

How Self-Concept Congruence Affects How Badly We Feel about Ourselves

Because self-conscious emotions are related to self-esteem (Tangney & Dearing, 2002), we expected their intensity to increase when the standard violation in the vignette was congruent with an individual's perceived self-concept. Among all the variables manipulated in Study 3, the congruence variable had the largest effect in terms of mean differences. As predicted, we feel worse about ourselves when our violations or the negative judgments of others are congruent with our self-concepts. Not surprisingly, negative self-concepts appear to predispose us to the experience of these emotions.

Characterizing Humiliation, Embarrassment, Shame, and Guilt

The second category of hypotheses addressed the features that characterize humiliation, embarrassment, shame, and guilt. The meanings of the four terms are thought to be represented as schemas (Borg, Staufenbiel, & Scherer, 1988) or prototypes (Shaver et al., 1992). Therefore, for each vignette participants rated how *accurately* the emotions (e.g., *humiliation*) described what their initial feeling would be in response to each vignette, ranging from 1 (*Not at all*) to 5 (*Very accurately*). In other words, we assessed how participants label emotional situations, the fit between vignettes, and their implicit emotion prototypes or schemas. For example, the accuracy ratings were high for embarrassment and humiliation for a vignette in which other people mock the protagonist for spilling a soda all over herself; in contrast the accuracy ratings were low for shame and guilt in response to this same vignette. Then vignettes with the highest accuracy ratings (above the scale midpoint) for each emotion were identified as good exemplars of the respective emotions. Finally, the locations of these good exemplars were mapped onto the MDS solutions that were generated from the badly-about-self ratings. This representation allowed us to contrast participants' use of the individual emotion terms and to do so relative to our hypothesized dimensions (e.g., audience presence vs. audience absence). Many vignettes elicited multiple emotions.

Humiliation

Twenty-seven (of 92) vignettes served as good exemplars of humiliation and illustrate its nature. In all 27 vignettes that were judged to be humiliating an audience was present; moreover, in 22 of them the audience was displaying hostile intent in the form of condescending looks or mocking and laughing. Among the vignettes where self-concept congruence was salient, all the humiliating vignettes involved congruence. The humiliating vignettes represented all types of standard violations and even the absence of any violation (e.g., being bullied for no reason); thus, standards did not differentiate humiliating vignettes from nonhumiliating vignettes. In other words, participants' schemas or prototypes for humiliation included presence of a hostile audience and self-concept congruence, but were not limited to certain types of standard violations. In sum, (1) we may feel humiliated over the exposure of any type of violation, and (2) we are most likely to do so when we believe the violation reflects our character, and (3) when other people are putting us down.

Embarrassment

Sixty-three (of 92) vignettes served as good exemplars of embarrassment and illustrate its nature. In all 63 embarrassing vignettes an audience was present. The embarrassing vignettes represented all types of standards and intent; thus, neither standards nor intent differentiated embarrassment-inducing vignettes from non-embarrassment-inducing vignettes. Among the vignettes where self-concept congruence was salient, most of the embarrassing vignettes involved self-concept congruence. Thus, participants' schemas or prototypes for embarrassment included presence of an audience and self-concept congruence, but were not limited to certain types of standard violations or intent on the part of others. In sum, embarrassment implies little more than the presence of an audience witnessing our weak moments, making it the least restrictive of these emotion terms.

Guilt and Shame

All of the vignettes that served as good exemplars of guilt (12) and shame (15) involved moral standard violations, with the exception of a single shame vignette that involved a competency violation (making a stupid mistake). This is consistent with Wallbott and Scherer's (1995) observation that in many Western cultures everyday usage of the term "shame" is nearly identical to usage of the term "guilt"; in fact they refer to this constricted cultural construal as "guilt-shame." It may at first seem surprising that only one of the shame exemplars involved a competency violation. This may have been because the competency violations (mistakes, stupidity) were not central aspects of participants' identities, or because they stood in sharp contrast to the moral violations (cheating, stealing). In addition, due to our method of identifying the good exemplars (i.e., median of *accuracy* ratings), absence of competency violations among the exemplars does not imply that shame was reported to be a completely inaccurate label for vignettes describing competency violations. Vignettes pulling for guilt and shame represented audience presence and absence, friendly and hostile intent; thus, neither audience presence nor intent (friendly vs. hostile) differentiated guilt- or shame-inducing vignettes from vignettes that did not induce shame or guilt. In sum, participants' schemas or prototypes for shame and guilt were very similar to each other; they included a moral standard violation, but were not restricted by audience presence or intent.

Similarities among Humiliation, Embarrassment, Shame, and Guilt

We used multiple methods of assessing similarity between pairs of emotions. First, participants were asked to rate the similarity of each pair of emotions from 1 (*Very similar*) to 4 (*Very different*). These questions appeared before any of the vignettes, so they were asked without reference to any particular event. Second, as an alternate measure of similarity Spearman's rank-order correlations were calculated between the vignettes' means on the accuracy ratings for each pair of emotions. In other words, if participants said a given vignette provoked one emotion, did they also say it provoked other emotions? Humiliation and embarrassment were judged to be most similar by both methods, with correlations greater than, or equal to, .90. Shame and guilt were also judged to be very similar to each other and relatively dissimilar to humiliation and embarrassment.

The similarities between these two pairs of emotions (humiliation/embarrassment, shame/guilt) were also clearly evident in the multidimensional scaling solutions, where many vignettes provoked multiple emotions. In particular, every humiliating vignette was also embarrassing. Similarly, the sets of shame-inducing and guilt-inducing vignettes were almost identical to each other. As described above, almost all of the shame- and guilt-inducing vignettes involved a moral standard violation; however, the humiliating and embarrassing vignettes included violations of all types of standards. As a result, all four sets of emotions overlapped. In fact, several vignettes, which involved being mocked for stealing or cheating, were rated high on humiliation, embarrassment, shame, and guilt.

Intensity of Humiliation, Embarrassment, Shame, and Guilt

Since humiliation is typically viewed as a high-intensity emotion, we wanted to compare its intensity with the intensities of the other emotions. Participants were asked to rate the intensity of each emotion on an abstract scale from 1 (*Very mild*) to 9 (*Very intense*). These questions appeared before any of the vignettes, so they were asked without reference to any particular causal event. The intensity ratings in order were: guilt, 6.69; humiliation, 6.61; shame, 6.57; embarrassment, 5.06. All differences between means were significant at $p < .001$, with the exception of humiliation-guilt and humiliation-shame, neither of which was significant. Among the four emotions, humiliation fell at the high end between shame and guilt, with embarrassment clearly being lower in intensity (but still moderate in absolute terms).

ADDING IT ALL UP: WHAT IS THE STRENGTH OF THE LINK BETWEEN HUMILIATION AND VIOLENCE COMPARED TO OTHER SELF-CONSCIOUS EMOTIONS?

Due to our interest in bullying and previous findings linking humiliation and violence, we focused on violent ideation as a correlate of the four emotions. In response to each vignette, participants rated the number of violent thoughts they would have toward self and others from 1 (*None at all*) to 5 (*Very Many*). Spearman's rank-order correlations were computed between the vignettes' means for the emotion accuracy ratings and their means for violent ideation. Among humiliation, embarrassment, shame, and guilt, humiliation was most highly correlated with violent ideation toward self ($r_s = .72$) and violent ideation toward others ($r_s = .88$). Thus, the association between humiliation and violent ideation toward others, while not unique, was stronger than for embarrassment ($r_s = .74$), shame ($r_s = .37$), and guilt ($r_s = -.01$). In sum, humiliation appears to be a strong motivation for acts of revenge and retaliation.

CONCLUSIONS

After reviewing the humiliation literature above, we presented our conceptualization of what constitutes humiliation and a model linking humiliation and violence. To reiterate, we conceptualize humiliation as an emotion term whose meaning conveys intensity and context—a high-intensity emotional reaction to having been lowered in the eyes of others. This context includes loss of status in the form of threats to the self at the hands of a hostile other, often in public. Our model treats humiliation as a necessary *mediator* of violence. As noted earlier, the existing literature on bullying links bullying directly to violence, without reference to the mediating role of emotions, specifically humiliation. In our model, bullying leads to feelings of humiliation, which in turn leads to acts of aggression or revenge. Data from our three studies provide strong support for both our conceptualization of humiliation and our humiliation-violence model.

So What Is Humiliation?

In defining humiliation, our hypotheses and conclusions fall into two categories. The first category addresses similarities between the term *humiliation* and the terms *embarrassment, shame,* and *guilt* based on our conceptualization in which all of these terms denote members of a basic shame family. Support is evident for a number of the hypotheses in this category. First, in all three studies, the hypothesized effects of audience size (or presence) and hostile intent in eliciting higher intensities for all four emotions are supported. These results regarding audience size are consistent with those of Jackson (2000) and Tangney and colleagues (Tangney et al., 1996). Second, the strong effect of self-concept congruence was demonstrated. When someone who sees herself as a klutz trips, or when a boy who sees himself as unattractive is teased about his looks, participants rate their emotional responses as much more intense in contrast to vignettes where the characters do not see themselves in a negative light. Third, the type of standard violation has a large qualitative effect on the experience of these emotions; we feel differently in response to violating different classes of standards (e.g., social vs. moral).

The positive effect of self-concept congruence at first appears to be contradictory to an observation in Study 1 (i.e., a significant correlation between unfairness and humiliation) and Jackson's (2000) observation that humiliation is associated with unfairness. However, we believe self-concept congruence and unfairness represent two different features of these painful situations. At the same time that others' judgments of us may be congruent with our self-concepts (e.g., lazy), others' treatment of us may be unfair. For instance, a student doing poorly on a test because of her failure to study may see criticism from a teacher as valid, while also seeing its delivery as unfair, possibly because it is excessive, delivered in front of an audience, or personally derogatory in nature. Thus, it appears that negative truths make us feel bad about ourselves, and, when accompanied by unfair treatment, this increases our humiliation and, in turn, increases our anger toward others.

The second category of hypotheses addresses causes or features that differentiate humiliation from embarrassment, shame, and guilt. Support is evident for all of our hypotheses. The intensity ratings from Study 3 support the first hypothesis of high intensity: humiliation hurts. The mappings of the most humiliating vignettes onto the multidimensional scaling solutions strongly support the hypotheses regarding causes. In these mappings, all of the humiliating vignettes involve an audience and most (82%) involve hostile intent, consistent with the data from Jackson's (2000) study. Examination of the individual vignettes suggests that hostile intent in the form of being laughed at and mocked is especially painful. Indeed, the presence of a mocking and laughing audience is the single best predictor of when participants believe they would feel humil-iated. Finally, the humiliating vignettes represent all types of standard violations, in-cluding the absence of a violation; thus, the type of standard violation does not predict humiliation. For example, humiliation was reported when the protagonist tripped, made a mistake, or cheated, and even when a violation was absent, as long as a hostile audience was present. Cases in which violations are absent are particularly interesting because they illustrate the unfairness and pain of being picked on for no reason, or for merely being different.

In characterizing humiliation, it is informative to contrast it with what appears to be its nearest emotional relative, embarrassment. Observations converge in supporting the claim of similarity. Specifically, the humiliating vignettes form a proper subset of the em-barrassing vignettes. Thus, if a person feels humiliated, he or she also feels embarrassed, but if he or she feels embarrassed, he or she does not necessarily feel humiliated. In terms of characteristics, both terms imply presence of an audience and little, if anything, about the standard violation. Humiliation and embarrassment differ only in that hostile intent is an additional condition typically present in humiliation and, apparently as a result, hu-miliation is of higher intensity.

Humiliation and Violence

Support for our model, in which feelings of humiliation act as a mediator between acts of mocking and bullying and outcomes such as anger, violent ideation, and suicidal ideation, is evident in all three studies. First, the best elicitors of humiliation are mocking, laugh-ing, and bullying. In other words, they involve intentional putdowns by a hostile other, usually in front of an audience. Second, feelings of humiliation, in turn, elicit inward- and outward-directed anger and motivate violent ideation. Of all the emotions assessed, humiliation demonstrates the strongest links with violent ideation. Indeed, the magnitude of the relationship is extremely high, $r_s = .88$. This result is consistent with Jackson's (2000) findings of a strong relationship between humiliation and a desire for revenge. In addition, humiliation demonstrated the strongest relationship with violent ideation toward self ($r_s = .72$). Using path modeling, the data from Study 1 demonstrate this link between humiliation/peer rejection and both suicidal and homicidal ideation.

In our epigraph, W. I. Miller (1993) asserts that humiliation, as an object of study, has taken a back seat to shame and embarrassment. Indeed the vast majority of the litera-ture on negative self-conscious emotions, especially the empirical literature, focuses on guilt, shame, and embarrassment. It is surprising that research on humiliation is so sparse, given anecdotal observations that it is common in the lives of both adolescents and adults. We are aware of only one prior study on the causes of humiliation (Jackson, 2000) and three previous studies that found a relationship between humiliation and de-pression (Brown et al., 1995; Farmer & McGuffin, 2003; Kendler et al., 2003). However, our studies indicate that humiliation may be especially important due to its strong rela-tionships with violent ideation, both inward and outward. The notion, widely endorsed in the theoretical literature, that acts that threaten the self and lower psychological status lead to retaliation and revenge enacted by the victim is consistent with our findings. However, our model goes beyond this link in clearly demonstrating that the experience of humiliation as a mediator is critical to this process. The old adage that "sticks and stones can break my bones, but names will never hurt me" is erroneous, as we now know from our programmatic research.

Practical Implications for Interventions

What are the implications of our research for intervention efforts? First and foremost, they alert us to the importance of identifying critical *emotions* that provoke behaviors. Pollack (1998) argues convincingly that boys are socialized into a "boy code" in which feelings of weakness, fear, and vulnerability are unacceptable and therefore are to be suppressed. This boy code continues into adulthood as a "man code." Thus, boys and men are unlikely to reveal feelings of humiliation in public, although our converging methodologies demonstrate that humiliation is a very salient internal reaction to loss of psychological status, particularly where events involve mocking audiences. Understanding such reactions should, we contend, be an important component in programs designed to prevent bullying and victimization in the schools. It should also be important in addressing causes of humiliation during the period of emerging adulthood where college counseling needs to address the young man code that continues to be a product of males' socialization.

What about females? Is humiliation merely a problem for males? No, nor do our findings manifest significant gender differences. Girls and adult females also suffer humiliation at the hands of others. Until very recently, the focus has been on "relational aggression" (Crick & Grotpeter, 1995), namely, a form of indirect aggression, such as spreading rumors behind one's back. However, anecdotal observations and emerging evidence (see Putallaz & Bierman, 2004) describe the increasing levels of physical aggression, antisocial behavior, and violence among girls in our contemporary society. Thus, it behooves us to realize that the dynamics that we have identified apply to both genders. As a result, it is critical that we include psychological mediators such as humiliation and related emotions into our models and methodologies for predicting violence against others as well as against the self. Moreover, we should take these emotions seriously in both prevention and intervention efforts to understand and reduce levels of violence in the new millennium.

REFERENCES

Achenbach, T. M., & Edelbrock, C. S. (1983). *Manual for the Child Behavior Checklist and Revised Child Behavior Profile*. Burlington: University of Vermont.

Borg, I., & Groenen, P. (1997). *Modern multidimensional scaling: Theory and applications*. New York: Springer.

Borg, I., & Shye, S. (1995). *Facet theory: Form and content*. Thousand Oaks, CA: Sage.

Borg, I., Staufenbiel, T., & Scherer, K. R. (1988). On the symbolic basis of shame. In K. R. Scherer (Ed.), *Facets of emotion: Recent research* (pp. 79–98). Hillsdale, NJ: Erlbaum.

Brown, G. W., Harris, T. O., & Hepworth, C. (1995). Loss, humiliation and entrapment among women developing depression: A patient and non-patient comparison. *Psychological Medicine, 25*, 7–21.

Cooley, C. H. (1902). *Human nature and the social order*. New York: Scribner's.

Crick, N. R., & Grotpeter, J. K. (1995). Relational aggression, gender and social psychological adjustment. *Child Development, 66*, 710–722.

Ekman, P. (1972). Universals and cultural differences in facial expressions of emotion. In J. Cole (Ed.), *Nebraska Symposium on Motivation 1971* (pp. 207–283). Lincoln: University of Nebraska Press.

Elison, J. (2005). Shame and guilt: A hundred years of apples and oranges. *New Ideas in Psychology, 23*, 5–32.

Elison, J., & Harter, S. (2004a, April). *Anger and violent ideation as correlates of shame, embarrassment, and humiliation*. Paper presented at the annual meeting of the Rocky Mountain Psychological Association, Reno, NV.

Elison, J., & Harter, S. (2004b, May). *Facets of shame, embarrassment, and humiliation*. Poster session presented at the annual meeting of the American Psychological Society, Chicago, IL.

Elison, J., & Harter, S. (2005, May). *Humiliation and violent ideation predicted by audience presence, hostile intent, and validity*. Poster session presented at the annual meeting of the American Psychological Society, Los Angeles, CA.

Farmer, A. E., & McGuffin, P. (2003). Humiliation, loss and other types of life events and difficulties: A comparison of depressed subjects, healthy controls and their siblings. *Psychological Medicine, 33,* 1169–1175.

Gilbert, P. (1997). The evolution of social attractiveness and its role in shame, humiliation, guilt and therapy. *British Journal of Medical Psychology, 70,* 113–147.

Gilbert, P. (1998a). What is shame?: Some core issues and controversies. In P. Gilbert & B. Andrews (Eds.), *Shame: Interpersonal behavior, psychopathology, and culture* (pp. 3–38). New York: Oxford University Press.

Gilbert, P. (1998b). Shame and humiliation in the treatment of complex cases. In N. Tarrier & A. Wells (Eds.), *Treating complex cases: The cognitive behavioural therapy approach* (pp. 241–271). New York: Wiley.

Guttman, L. (1954). A new approach to factor analysis: The radix. In P. Lazarfeld (Ed.), *Mathematical thinking in the social sciences* (pp. 258–348). New York: Free Press.

Harter, S. (1999). *The construction of the self.* New York: Guilford Press.

Harter, S., Kiang, L., Whitesell, N. R., & Anderson, A. V. (2003, April). *A prototype approach to the emotion of humiliation in college students*. Poster session presented at the biannual meeting of the Society for Research in Child Development, Tampa, FL.

Harter, S., Low, S. M., & Whitesell, N. R. (2003). What have we learned from Columbine: The impact of the self-system on suicidal and violent ideation among adolescents. *Journal of School Violence, 2,* 3–26.

Harter, S., & Marold, D. B. (1993). The directionality of the link between self-esteem and affect: Beyond causal modeling. In D. Cicchetti & S. L. Toth (Eds.), *Rochester Symposium on Developmental Psychopathology: Disorders and dysfunctions of the self* (Vol. 5, pp. 333–369). Rochester, NY: University of Rochester Press.

Harter, S., Marold, D. B., & Whitesell, N. R. (1992). A model of psychosocial risk factors leading to suicidal ideation in young adolescents. *Development and Psychopathology, 4,* 167–188.

Harter, S., & Whitesell, N. R. (1989). Developmental changes in children's understanding of single, multiple and blended emotion concepts. In C. Saarni & P. L. Harris (Eds.), *Children's understanding of emotion* (pp. 81–116). Cambridge, UK: Cambridge University Press.

Hartling, L. M., & Luchetta, T. (1999). Humiliation: Assessing the impact of derision, degradation, and debasement. *Journal of Primary Prevention, 19,* 259–278.

Izard, C. E. (1971). *The face of emotion.* New York: Appleton-Century-Crofts.

Jackson, M. A. (2000). Distinguishing shame and humiliation. *Dissertation Abstracts International, 61* (04), 2272. (UMI No. 9968089)

James, W. (1892). *Psychology: The briefer course.* New York: Holt.

Kaufman, G. (1992). *Shame: The power of caring* (3rd ed.). Rochester, VT: Schenkman Books.

Kendler, K. S., Hettema, J. M., Butera, F., Gardner, C. O., & Prescott, C. A. (2003). Life event dimensions of loss, humiliation, entrapment, and danger in the prediction of onsets of major depression and generalized anxiety. *Archives of General Psychiatry, 60,* 789–796.

Klein, D. C. (1991). The humiliation dynamic: An overview. *Journal of Primary Prevention, 12,* 93–121.

Klein, D. C. (1992). Managing humiliation. *Journal of Primary Prevention, 12,* 255–268.

Kovacs, M., & Beck, A. T. (1977). The wish to die and the wish to live in attempted suicides. *Psychology, 33*(2), 361–365.

Kovacs, M., & Beck, A. T. (1978). Maladaptive cognitive structures in depression. *American Journal of Psychiatry, 135,* 525–533.

Lazare, A. (1987). Shame and humiliation in the medical encounter. *Archives of International Medicine, 147,* 1653–1658.

Lewis, H. B. (1987). Shame and the narcissistic personality. In D. L. Nathanson (Ed.), *The many faces of shame* (pp. 93–132). New York: Guilford Press.

Lewis, M., & Haviland-Jones, J. M. (Eds.). (2000). *Handbook of emotions* (2nd ed.). New York: Guilford Press.

Lindner, E. G. (2002). Peace and conflict. *Journal of Peace Psychology, 8,* 125–138.

Miller, R. S. (1996). *Embarrassment: Poise and peril in everyday life.* New York: Guilford Press.

Miller, S. B. (1988). Humiliation and shame: Comparing two affect states as indicators of narcissistic stress. *Bulletin of the Menninger Clinic, 52,* 40–51.

Miller, W. I. (1993). *Humiliation, and other essays on honor, social discomfort, and violence.* Ithaca, NY: Cornell University Press.

Nathanson, D. L. (1992). *Shame and pride: Affect, sex and the birth of the self.* New York: Norton.

Pollack, W. (1998). *Real boys.* New York: Random House.

Putallaz, M., & Bierman, K. L. (2004). *Aggression, antisocial behavior, and violence among girls.* New York: Guilford Press.

Sarphatie, H. (1993). On shame and humiliation: Some notes on early development and pathology. In H. Groen-Prakken & A. Ladan (Eds.), *Dutch annual of psychoanalysis* (Vol. 1, pp. 191–204). Lisse, The Netherlands: Swets & Zeitlinger.

Shaver, P. R., Wu, S., & Schwartz, J. C. (1992). Cross-cultural similarities and differences in emotion and its representation: A prototype approach. In M. S. Clark (Ed.), *Review of personality and social psychology* (Vol. 13, pp. 175–212). Newbury Park, CA: Sage.

Silver, M., Conte, R., Miceli, M., & Poggi, I. (1986). Humiliation: Feeling, social control, and the construction of identity. *Journal for the Theory of Social Behavior, 16,* 269–283.

Simpson, J. A., & Weiner, E. S. C. (Eds.). (1989). *The Oxford English dictionary* (2nd ed.). Oxford, UK: Oxford University Press.

Stamm, J. L. (1978). The meaning of humiliation and its relationship to fluctuations in self-esteem. *International Review of Psychoanalysis, 5,* 425–433.

Statman, D. (2000). Humiliation, dignity and self-respect. *Philosophical Psychology, 13,* 523–540.

Tangney, J. P. (1996). Conceptual and methodological issues in the assessment of shame and guilt. *Behaviour Research and Therapy, 34,* 741–754.

Tangney, J. P., & Dearing, R. L. (2002). *Shame and guilt.* New York: Guilford Press.

Tangney, J. P., & Fischer K. W. (Eds.). (1995). *Self-conscious emotions: The psychology of shame, guilt, embarrassment, and pride.* New York: Guilford Press.

Tangney, J. P., Miller, R. S., Flicker, L., & Barlow, D. H. (1996). Are shame, guilt, and embarrassment distinct emotions? *Journal of Personality and Social Psychology, 70,* 1256–1269.

Tomkins, S. S. (1963). *Affect/imagery/consciousness: Vol. 2. The negative affects.* New York: Springer.

Walbott, H. G., & Scherer, K. R. (1995). Cultural determinants in experiencing shame and guilt. In J. P. Tangney & K. W. Fischer (Eds.), *Self-conscious emotions: The psychology of shame, guilt, embarrassment, and pride* (pp. 465–487). New York: Guilford Press.

18

Shame and Guilt as Morally Warranted Experiences

TAMARA J. FERGUSON
DANIEL BRUGMAN
JENNIFER WHITE
HEIDI L. EYRE

In Western psychology, as in daily life, there is little disagreement that shame is a painful feeling of inadequacy. In the scientific literature and popular media of the past two decades, shame has gripped center stage as the emotional source of psychological and interpersonal woe, and is often branded a "dark" emotion contrasting starkly with the nobler feeling of guilt (cf. Tangney & Dearing, 2002). Why shame continues to play the starring emotional role in tortuous psychological dramas has long remained a mystery to us. Conversely, guilt's leading role in tales of morality and heroic defeat of a darker, shameful alter ego rings false to our experiences. Equally unclear, moreover, is whether extant findings truly reveal shame's devastating consequences and/or mirror westerners' beliefs and norms regarding shame's aversiveness.

Contrasting portrayals of shame and guilt are overarching themes of this chapter. As our detective story unfolds, we discuss evidence relevant to the contrast's validity and, in so doing, seek answers to questions bearing on the extent to which, and conditions under which, individuals perceive shame and guilt to be warranted feelings and reflect well on an agent's moral virtue or character. By story's end, we hope to have clarified the importance of conducting further research regarding whether the two states' co-experience, rather than either experience in isolation, is a powerful motivating force in moral decision making and behavior. We also seek to address whether the true villains (or heroes) contributing to intrapersonal and interpersonal adjustment are not the states themselves, but facets of the situations in which they are aroused (e.g., perceptions of control) and the methodology frequently employed to measure them.

FOCUS OF THE CHAPTER: WARRANT FOR SHAME AND GUILT

Individuals "make sense" of their own and others' emotions in various ways, including their "fitting," "appropriate," or "intelligible" nature relative to the agent's proximate and ultimate goals. In addition to judgments of intelligibility or fit, individuals judge an emotion as *warranted* or *obligated* (cf. Gibbard, 1990). There are multiple bases for any emotion's perceived warrant (e.g., role appropriateness, aesthetics, morality) and these are subject to conflicting viewpoints (e.g., the agent's or the victim's). In this chapter, we focus largely on when and why *observers and victims* (termed "outsiders") oblige agents to react with guilt or shame to morally significant events, in part because outsiders' perspectives have received less attention in this area and because our research has targeted feelings of guilt and shame primarily in the moral realm. The obligatory warrant for any *emotion*, including guilt and shame as reactions to immoral events, is interesting in many respects. Its particular relevance to this chapter concerns a frequent refrain in the extant literature contrasting guilt with shame. Many authors in this literature seem to accord considerably greater moral warrant to guilt than shame (cf. Tangney & Dearing, 2002). This stance toward the two state's differential warrant is understandable in light of guilt's demonstrated beneficial role in mending relationships with others (e.g., Baumeister, Stillwell, & Heatherton, 1994). To date, however, there is very little noncorrelational evidence pertaining to an equally important assumption being made in this literature, that is, that outsiders, including relationship partners, negatively evaluate and react toward agents who express shame alone or shame in conjunction with guilt. The research reviewed in this chapter was, in fact, meant to explore whether and why outsiders differentiate the two emotions' moral warrant and to discern whether and how these differences impact others' evaluations of agents when they express the (un)warranted emotion. Studying the warrant for these emotions sheds light on whether extant literature has devalued shame as a moral emotion by granting much of the moral credit to guilt (cf. Ausubel, 1955; Baumeister et al., 1994; Greenspan, 1995; Haidt, 2003; Tangney, 1991, 1995).

There are at least two reasons for our interest in outsiders' perceptions of the two emotions' moral warrant. First, these perceptions indirectly convey outsiders' evaluations of the agent's moral status and, second, they can initiate a series of further exchanges affecting the agent's moral orientation. When outsiders warrant either state, this grants them the right and the authority to express complementary *reactive* sentiments (e.g., contempt to shame or angry indignation to guilt). These sentiments convey a wealth of information regarding others' evaluations of the agent (e.g., perceptions of the agent's character, quality of "will," and motivation), and they likely affect the overt change efforts (e.g., preaching, criticism, ridicule, rejection) that others direct toward those who continue to express unwarranted emotional states (cf. Mason, 2003; Strawson, 1962; Weiner, 1994, 1995). These exchanges can, in turn, promote changes in the agents' beliefs or values that may lead agents to actually experience or at least feign the experience of the contextually obliged feelings.

CHARACTERIZING SHAME AND GUILT

Our View

The purpose in this section is to briefly note *our* view of one important difference between the two states. In the past decade, we have proposed guilt's primary elicitor to be self-perceptions of responsibility for an untoward outcome or state of affairs, which we abbreviate with the terms "disadvantaging the self" or "disadvantaging another." In contrast, we have treated the *threat* of the person being held responsible for an *unwanted identity* as shame's central elicitor. Several studies (total $N = 688$) of ours with children, adolescents, or adults support these distinctions (cf. Alberico et al., 1998; Ferguson & Crowley, 1997a; Ferguson, Edmondson, & Gerity, 2000; Edmondson, 2002; Ferguson & Eyre, 2000; Ferguson, Stegge, Eyre, Vollmer, & Ashbaker, 2000; Olthof, Ferguson, Bloemers, & Deij, 2004). In these, we manipulated whether the situations implicated agents as responsible for disadvantaging the self or another (a predicted guilt elicitor—e.g., failing to offer help to another in an emergency). We further manipulated whether the situations portrayed agents as responsible for threats to age-appropriate identities (the predicted shame elicitor—e.g., the failed intervention being due to the agent's unfit physical condition). Ratings of shame and guilt varied as predicted across the four cells in studies with older children and adults. We also found considerable correlational support for the hypothesized shame-unwanted identity and guilt-disadvantaging self/other connections, but only when agents were responsible. We also have traced the traditionally found tendency of women to report greater shame or guilt than men to their disparate perceptions of whether the stimulus situations typically used in this area threatened valued identities or had disadvantaged another (e.g., Ferguson, Eyre, & Ashbaker, 2000).

The Dominant View

The distinctions we have supported contrast with prevailing characterizations of these states' constituents or their phenomenology in contemporary literature (cf. Tangney & Dearing, 2002). In this literature, authors portray shame to be an *all-consuming* experience of the self as *fundamentally flawed or defective* (in H. B. Lewis's [1971] terms, "How could *I* do that?"). Some believe the shame experience to be elicited by attributions of the untoward outcome to internal and uncontrollable self-characteristics (e.g., failure due to low ability; Weiner, 1995), which is intensified when these characteristics are perceived to be global and stable (Tracy & Robins, 2004, 2006). Guilt, in contrast, connotes the person's focus on a specific untoward act negatively affecting the self or another ("How could I do *that*?"), which certain authors believe is aroused by attributions to causes of an internal and controllable nature (e.g., failure due to low effort; Tracy & Robins, 2006).

Characterizations of guilt and shame, respectively, as a focus on the untoward behavior versus a focus on the flawed self are reflected in widely used measures of them. For example, the Test of Self-Conscious Affect (TOSCA; Tangney, Wagner, & Gramzow, 1989), its predecessors (see Tangney, 1995, 1996), and successors (e.g., the TOSCA-2; Tangney, Ferguson, Wagner, Crowley, & Gramzow, 1996) are the "gold standard" in this research area and are ones we frequently use in our own research. To interpret findings in this area, to inform our own predictions and findings regarding the potential moral warrant for feelings of guilt or shame, and for readers to both understand and evaluate others' and our own findings, it is important to provide detail regarding the dominant paradigm and to consider the paradigm's strengths and limitations. The TOSCAs represent each state using descriptors of the thoughts or action tendencies associated with experiences of guilt or shame in response to relatively minor or isolated mishaps. The thoughts or action tendencies used to portray shame or its aftermath involve self-criticism and tendencies to avoid the victim or failures to solve the problem caused. For example, after breaking something at work and then hiding it, the available shame response is

"You would think about quitting." The TOSCAs portray guilt, in contrast, as thoughts or intended behaviors acknowledging the act's or outcome's untoward nature, the victim's plight, and a need to offer apology or make repair. In the "broken object" vignette, for example, the guilt alternative is "This is making me anxious. I need to fix it or get someone else to."

Depicting shame or guilt in the TOSCAs' associative language, rather than simply asking people to rate "how guilty" or "how ashamed" they feel, seems ideal, because it minimizes interpretive problems due to people's confusion of the two terms (cf. Tangney, 1996). Moreover, at first glance, presenting *only* the thought/behavior descriptors seems a perfectly reasonable means of depicting how someone would feel, because these are, after all, the very descriptors people use when narrating experiences of guilt or shame. Readers should carefully consider, however, whether these prevailing distinctions are depicting people's feelings or the emotions of guilt and shame. *Doing x'ly* (actually or in one's imagination) does not necessarily imply *feeling x'ly*; in fact, actually *doing x'ly* (or intending to do so) can imply not feeling anything at all or in particular (Sabini & Silver, 1997). Using the "wine stain" scenario from the TOSCA, for example, anyone who actually would stay late (or think they would) after a party to help remove the stain they made by spilling red wine on a coworker's brand new white carpet need not at all "do this" because he or she felt *guilt* in particular. In contrast, those who specifically avow *feeling* guilty (as opposed to feeling nothing or feeling angry) probably would be more inclined to specifically engage in remedial efforts.

Findings from Ferguson and colleagues' labs show that after having made or seen others' strong endorsements of the TOSCA's "guilty" thought or behavior descriptors, people will judge a hypothetical other or themselves to feel any number of ways (e.g., fearful, anxious), including *nothing* at all, or simply wanting to "get off the hook" (e.g., Ferguson & Barrett, 2003). The same is true of the TOSCA-like shame endorsements (e.g., perceivers judge "thinking about quitting" to equally imply being strongly angry at the self, angry at the other, or afraid of the victim more than being "ashamed of self").

Although a tall order, it is unclear whether the TOSCA-based distinctions between guilt as approach/repair *versus* shame as avoid/self-criticize do validly reflect differences between the two states as "feelings" (cf. Alexandrova, Ferguson, & Crowley, 1996; Aronfreed, 1968; Barrett, 1995; Ferguson, 1996; Ferguson & Crowley, 1997b; Ferguson & Stegge, 1995, 1998; Ferguson, Stegge, & Damhuis, 1991; Ferguson, 2001; Ferguson, Stegge, Miller, & Olsen, 1999; Harder, 1995; Harris, 2003; Kugler & Jones, 1992; Luyten, Fontaine, & Corbeleyn, 2002; Ortony, Clore, & Collins, 1998; Stegge & Ferguson, 2003; Tangney, 1996; Tangney & Dearing, 2002; Tangney et al., 1996). We stress the need to measure *feelings* of guilt and shame, in addition to related behaviors or cognitions, because people perceive feelings as unintentional or involuntary, happening "to" someone, and difficult to turn on or off at will. Whether concerning themselves or others, people often trust feelings *more* than avowed beliefs or behaviors as genuine reflections of character and valid predictors of likely future behavior (cf. Heise & O'Brien, 1993). In our view, the esteem in which others hold agents and the feedback they give to them depend not only on agents' overtly expressed apologetic or withdrawn behavior, but also on whether outsiders *believe* the person genuinely *feels* a corresponding emotion. This, in turn, affects the quality of the relationship and further shapes the agents' future reactions (e.g., by affecting the extent to which the agent apologizes "with feeling"). In fact, one of the research questions on which we focus in this chapter is whether people instill greater trust in *feelings* of either state than in their TOSCA-based depictions as reflections of a person's true character.

WARRANT FOR INTERPERSONALLY ORIENTED GUILT AND SHAME: EXPERIENCE, THOUGHT, ACTION, AND OUTCOME

Thoughts and Action Tendencies or Feelings

The issues raised above led us to imagine four agents who transgressed a moral norm, with each of them then expressing emotion(s) representing one cell in a 2 (high, low magnitude) 2 (guilt, shame) factorial. If forced to choose, whom do we esteem as the most moral or virtuous person? In the sections to follow, we highlight results of several studies tackling this question. Before specifically addressing this question, however, we first ask whether people differentially value the TOSCA-based thought or behavior depictions of "guilt" and "shame" when compared to their feelings of the two states. We predicted that people would differentially *warrant* the thoughts and behaviors frequently associated in the literature with each state's presumed constituents, although we doubted whether people would differentially warrant the two feelings *as such*. In fact, we suspected individuals would equally and positively value *feelings* of shame and guilt when acknowledged in appropriate contexts. People understand these feelings to bring into awareness concerns of vital interest to the agent (an unwanted identity threat, disadvantaging the self or others), thereby also directing the agent's attention to solving them (e.g., Damasio, 2003).

Results of six studies—each involving 124 to 140 (30% men) students enrolled in an introductory psychology course—reveal the warrant perceived for the two states. In four of these, participants never encountered the terms "guilt" or "shame." Instead, they read the TOSCA-2's thought- or behavior-based *descriptors* (D) of guilt, shame, and defensive externalization, which are very similar to those in the original TOSCA (e.g., guilt operationalized as the desire or intent to offer repair; defensive externalization as thinking it was the other person's fault; shame as withdrawal or self-criticism), which they rated after reading the 16 TOSCA-2 situations. Participants rated the descriptions associated with "guilt," "shame," and "externalization" in response to differently framed questions. Specifically, each person rated *one* of how much (1) people, in general, *should* react in this way, (2) the participant *should* react this way, (3) the participant *would* react this way if trying to make the *best impression* on others, or (4) the participant *would* react this way if trying to make the *worst impression* on others. In the remaining two samples, participants rated their feelings (F) in reaction to the 16 TOSCA situations by judging "how much they . . ." *should feel* or *would feel* guilty, ashamed, and angry (an imperfect feeling substitute for externalization).

Effect size computations among the means revealed several interesting results. College students attached considerable warrant to the TOSCA-2's standard-, reparative-, or victim-oriented responses supposedly reflecting experiences of guilt when judged in terms of how people in general should react, how they (the participants) should react, or making the best impression. In contrast, they rejected the warrant for shame-relevant descriptors (e.g., withdrawing from the situation, avoiding the victim, and self-oriented criticism) when judged from these three viewpoints. Whereas they endorsed the TOSCA guilt descriptors more strongly when trying to make the best rather than the worst impression, the same comparison was not statistically significant for judgments of the TOSCA-2 shame descriptors. Finally, participants' judgments of how much they "should" and "would" feel *guilty or ashamed* revealed considerable warrant for both feelings, but less warrant for anger (especially when judged as "should").

As a whole, these results suggest that the TOSCA (and related paradigms) underestimate shame's potential warrant (e.g., Elison, 2003). Of course, one might cry "foul" at these six studies because they support shame's greater warrant only when operationalized as a "feeling" that individuals could easily confuse with guilt. In our view, this concern is unfounded in light of other results showing adults, adolescents, and children to parse these two feeling terms in meaningful and expected ways (Ferguson & Stegge, 1998; Olthof et al., 2004; Olthof, Schouten, Kuiper, Stegge, & Jennekens-Schinkel, 2000). Even 7- to 8-year-old children can accurately categorize a long list of TOSCA-like descriptors as uniquely guilt- or shame-related, as opposed to neither or both (e.g., Ferguson, Stegge, & Damhuis, 1990; Ferguson et al., 1991). Moreover, these results and those presented later do not change when we calculate adjusted scores or part correlation coefficients to identify variance uniquely attributable to guilt or shame (e.g., Tangney, 1995, 1996).

Does Guilt Suffice as Thought/Action or Feeling?

Why would the feeling of shame yield results discrepant from its implied basis in self-critical or avoidant thoughts and behaviors? An answer to this question might be available in the appeasement literature. There are distinctive nonverbal indicators (e.g., gaze or body avert) conveying *that* people *are feeling* ashamed. We would equate our findings regarding shame as a subjectively experienced feeling with those found regarding spontaneously expressed "gaze avert" and other visible shame displays. The latter do lead to greater ratings of forgiveness, or liking, of a person who just failed an achievement task or a person on trial for a misdemeanor (e.g., Keltner & Harker, 1998; Lazowski, 1987). They may do so, because people believe the feeling of shame to reflect the agent's focus of attention on the scripts this feeling primes, for example, scripts related to morality (e.g., what is wrong, why, how this affects others, what the consequences are for the person's own evaluations of the deed), which combine to constitute shame's propositional object and communicate sincere contrition.

Although the TOSCA shame reactions might well be *intended* to convey the same meaning as the gaze/body avert of shame by virtue of their shared basis in avoidance or implied self-criticism, they do not seem to communicate the same message. Consider, for example, the TOSCA shame response "You would think about quitting" after the person first breaks an object and then tries to conceal the mistake. Whether this conveys *any* feeling, including that of shame, which an audience (or the agent) then interprets as an admission of wrongdoing or contrition is debatable. Instead of reflecting these reactions, the TOSCA shame descriptor is easily misconstrued, for example, as one of fear and/or extreme cowardice that further compounds the agent's first two errors (breaking the object and then concealing the damage), suggesting strongly that the agent is the *kind* of person who fails (or even refuses) to respond appropriately to his or her mistakes.

In actuality, a stronger case can be made for a functional similarity between the TOSCA "guilty" responses in this situation ("This is making me anxious. I need to fix it or get someone else to") and nonverbal displays representing "underlying" feelings of shame (such as "gaze avert"), as both are sociomoral signals to others of the person's desire to repair the wrong done and clear the person's moral record. This particular correspondence further acknowledges an already known fact: there are *no* nonverbal signals distinct from shame implying *that* someone does *feel* guilty (e.g., Keltner & Harker, 1998). Should the latter correspondence prove valid (e.g., based on future neurobiological findings), it would be the ultimate irony vis-à-vis the now prevalent insistence on shame's maladaptive functions and "ugly" nature.

The above explanation of differences found in the extent to which people (including the self) reported they would or should feel guilty or ashamed *versus* their endorsements of these states as thoughts, overt actions, and verbal behaviors suggested that *outsiders* who learn of another's experience of guilt or shame will perceive them equally *favorably*. This is a reasonable prediction *not* because people confuse the two states, but because they consider their co-occurrence especially likely in the moral contexts often studied in this literature. Results confirming favorable evaluations of the two states as feelings were found in a college student sample (currently consisting of 26 men, 35 women) in which we rigged the TOSCA to portray four different response patterns, involving a 2 (guilt, shame reaction) × 2 (low, high magnitude) between-subjects design, depicting *agents* who had judged their *feelings* of guilt or shame in response to the TOSCA situations. After receiving for inspection one of the four agent-completed "TOSCAs," accompanied by additional measures the agents had presumably completed (held constant across the four cells), participants then shared their impressions of the agents based on descriptions of 25 traits drawn from the personality literature (including, e.g., conscientiousness, virtue, a mature moral orientation, trustworthiness, and likeability). Analyzed individually and when averaged across the 25 traits, respondents expressed more *unfavorable* impressions of agents who had endorsed feelings of low than high guilt *or* low than high shame, but they esteemed equally greatly agents responding with feelings of high shame *or* high guilt. Of course, these results do not show participants to equally favor the highly guilty or ashamed agents *because* of beliefs that each conveys the unique focus of attention we attribute to them (unwanted identity, disadvantaging others). We do think, however, this is a reasonable inference in light of the results presented earlier.

We turn now to whether similar evaluations were made of agents who "endorsed" the same pattern for the two states when expressed via the TOSCA-based "guilt" and "shame" desriptors. If it *is* true that these convey to outsiders the underlying *feelings* of shame and guilt, then we should replicate the pattern of agent evaluations described above. We addressed this issue in another sample (currently consisting of 51 men, 74 women), again employing the 2 (guilt, shame reaction) × 2 (low, high magnitude) between-subjects design, but presenting these students first with the wrongdoings followed by the agents' purported endorsements of the original TOSCA approach/repair (guilt) and avoid/self-criticize (shame) descriptors. Participants then used the above-mentioned personality descriptions to summarize impressions of the agent. Note that we introduced a new twist in this sample that greatly affected the results obtained. Participants received information that agents repeatedly made the same "mistake" in each of the eight TOSCA situations for which continued errors were plausible (e.g., adjusting the missed lunch appointment scenario to read: "After having missed several lunch appointments with a friend, the student made plans to meet a friend for lunch. At 5 o'clock the student realized: I stood my friend up again"; see Nelsen & Peterson, 2005).

In this study, respondents more *unfavorably* evaluated the traits of actors reacting with *low than high* ratings of approach/repair (guilt). Interestingly, however, they also were more unfavorable regarding the characters of agents who responded with *high than low* avoid/self-criticize (shame); this is precisely the *opposite* of findings reported above regarding shame as a feeling. This main effect for the shame-related thoughts/behaviors suggests that avoid/self-criticize does *not* convey the same information as feelings of shame (or nonverbal indicators of shame), confirming the suspicions detailed above. Yet, and very importantly, participants evaluated agents in the high "shame" *combined with* high "guilt" cell as the *most* likely to worry about failing, the least impulsive, but the most conscientious, moral, and empathic when compared to agents in the other three cells.

Positive evaluations of the agents expressing *high "shame"* + *high "guilt"* directly contradict expectations based on extant findings and conceptualizations of the two states (e.g., Tangney & Dearing, 2002). Why would avoidance or self-criticism coupled with approach/repair actually support *positive* evaluations of the agents' characters? Before entertaining several possible interpretations, we first describe one additional set of findings. In this study, we provided college students with "experts' " detailed evaluations of agents depicting them as morally worthy *or* unworthy characters. After reading these, respondents *predicted* the extent to which each agent would respond with guilt and/or shame to interpersonal mistakes, offering these in the form of either feeling predictions or predictions regarding the TOSCA-like thought/behavior descriptors. Focusing for now on participants' predictions regarding the TOSCA mishaps represented as isolated mistakes, we found respondents to evaluate the worthy agents as likelier to endorse the TOSCA-based "approach/repair" (guilt) than the "avoid/self-criticize" (shame) reactions, suggesting that these shame reactions are not warranted responses to relatively isolated or mild incidents. Respondents also predicted that worthy agents would *feel* both guilt and shame to an equal and greater extent than they would express either behaviorally. Regarding the morally despicable actors, participants thought they were likelier to express the TOSCA-like guilt than shame counterparts; in fact, they thought the despicable agents would *most* strongly endorse the TOSCA-based guilt reactions compared to the remaining three emotion alternatives. They did not expect unworthy agents to feel intense shame or guilt.

Let us now summarize and comment on the entire set of findings pertaining to the impressions formed, or predictions made regarding, feelings of guilt and shame, and expressions of the TOSCA "avoid/self-criticize" ("shame") and TOSCA "approach/repair" ("guilt") reactions. Outsiders formed favorable impressions and expected strong endorsements of guilt as a feeling in general and when judging morally worthy agents. They did not anticipate morally despicable transgressors to feel intensely guilty, but they did expect even the unworthy characters to respond with approach/repair. These results suggest some correspondence between genuinely feeling guilty and this state's purported associations with approach or repair, but *only* in virtuous people. Results regarding the morally unworthy characters further suggest, however, that the TOSCA "approach/repair" descriptors do *not* necessarily reflect genuine feelings of guilt but may be expressed, instead, as an immediate way to remedy the situation and possibly ward off counterattacks. Regarding shame, outsiders also thought feelings of shame were likely in reaction to the TOSCA situations in themselves, in others in general, and in those already known to be morally admirable individuals. They did *not* anticipate morally unworthy people to feel ashamed. In addition, they believed the TOSCA avoid/self-criticize rendition of "shame" to be *unlikely* and *inappropriate* responses in themselves, in others in general, and in others with known praiseworthy or blameworthy characteristics. Combined, these results raise the question of whether the TOSCA "avoid/self-criticize" descriptors of shame reflect underlying genuine feelings of shame.

To answer this question, we focus on a feature *unique* to the study showing positive evaluations of "avoid/self-criticize" in the context of "avoid/repair." Of all studies in this series, this was the only one depicting agents who repeatedly had failed to change or to learn from previous experiences. Imagine outsiders' thoughts concerning these repeat offenses, their victims, and the repeat offenders themselves. Certainly these recurring mistakes come across as more severe than any one in isolation (e.g., missing an appointment for the umpteenth time compared to missing one appointment). They also reflect negatively on agents' characters. Thus, victims have every right to be upset, if not downright livid. Offering an apology or promising to set right the wrong most recently done would seem shallow or insensitive, and these alone certainly seem insufficient to reestablish trust or to affirm one's worthy character. Victims in these situations have every right to call the offender to account and to demand more than an apology or reparative efforts as evidence of agents' commitment to genuinely changing, rendering appropriate self-criticism and even withdrawal.

In a sense, then, one could see outsiders' favorable reactions to avoid/self-criticize in these more extreme contexts to align neatly with results showing that submissive displays (e.g., gaze avert) are ways to appease others or minimize counterattacks and rejection (cf. Gilbert, 1998; Keltner & Harker, 1998; Lazowski, 1987). The nonverbal and short-lived indicators of submissive appeasement (e.g., gaze or body avert) studied in that literature do, however, seem insufficient to guarantee our "slow learners'" true commitment to change efforts. In other words, outsiders may have required the repeat offenders to show even stronger signs of commitment to change in the form of overtly submissive behaviors and self-criticism. Of course, this interpretation seems to suggest that "avoid/self-criticize" *can* signify underlying feelings of shame, which *flatly* contradicts our findings and the interpretations we provided of them. The contradiction is probably more apparent than real, however. We predicted and found "avoid/self-criticize" to be an unwarranted response that also *did not* imply underlying feelings of shame in the *minor, isolated* contexts most often studied in this literature. Fascinating to explore will be whether the very same behaviors (e.g., avoid/self-criticize) undergo changes in affective meaning—from implying *no* feeling at all to implying particular feelings—as a function of contextual changes (such as the repeated offenses we examined).

There remains the tricky question of how to differentiate whether a given co-occurrence of TOSCA guilt with TOSCA shame represents *one of either* "guilt-infused shame" or "shame-infused guilt" (cf. Tangney & Dearing, 2002). This distinction is of tremendous relevance to questions regarding the adaptiveness of either state alone or in conjunction. Stated in the lingo of the contemporary literature, one might argue that participants' favorable evaluations of repeat offenders who manifested "avoid/self-criticize" in the context of "approach/repair" reflected guilt's influence on shame's functionality, that is, shame became adaptive when "fused" with guilt. We already gave reason to dismiss this as a feasible interpretation of the findings. Moreover, if anything, the opposite interpretation seems more plausible, that is, that the guilt of "*shame*-infused guilt" becomes more believable or sincere by virtue of the agents' acknowledgment of serious character flaws requiring equally serious change efforts.

We found evidence favoring the latter interpretation in Ferguson and Eyre's Q factor analysis of 144 college students' self-reports of over 400 items representing facets of guilt and shame (unpublished data). These items included those from all of the TOSCA-2 scales, as well as those from our own instruments measuring ruminative facets of guilt and shame. The two person factors identified accounted for 57% of the variance. Person factor 1 represented a contrast between extremely positive factor scores for the traditionally emphasized "approach/repair" operationalization of guilt versus strong negative factor scores for the tendency to ruminate about being guilty and shame-worthy. Person factor 2 contrasted high positive factor scores for ruminative guilt and shame tendencies versus negative factor scores for affectively laden defensive traits and defensive responses to concrete wrongdoings (the TOSCA-2 detachment, minimization, and externalization alternatives). Importantly, fewer respondents' scores loaded highly on only one of the two person factors (25%) than the number of individuals with combined high (.55 and above) and moderate (.39 and above) loadings on the two person factors. Expressed categorically, one of the combined groups loaded highly on person factor 1, but moderately on person factor 2 (45%), and another group (30%) had the opposite loadings.

Interestingly, independent assessments based either on self-reports and/or on reports by best friends or close family members showed that respondents who loaded highly on person factor 1 but moderately on person factor 2 engaged in the *least* self-deceptive enhancement. They also scored the least extremely of all groups on indices of amorality and defensiveness against shame or guilt, but showed stronger indications of empathy, moral standards, and acknowledgments of their moral responsibility and ability to avoid the negative outcomes. This combined group did manifest somewhat greater problems on MMPI indicators (e.g., depression, anxiety) than the "approach/reparative" guilt only group, but none of the problem scores for any group were in the clinical range. Respondents with extreme loadings *only* on person factor 1, however, scored the least extremely on the MMPI indicators, but they actually were the most shame-defensive, guilt-defensive, and amoral. Furthermore, they showed the least empathy, weaker moral standards, and fewer concerns related to moral responsibility or control. Finally, because the group scoring highly only on person factor 2 was very small (8%), we deemed any comparisons involving this group to be unreliable.

In all, these results suggest that the shame-free guilt known to be most positively associated with well-being or negatively linked with problematic outcomes also reflects an orientation devoid of moral concerns but replete with *genuinely* believed self-serving and defensive tactics (unlike the overt impression management strategies to which TOSCA-based guilt proneness is not strongly related; cf. Tangney & Dearing, 2002). We are not certain regarding the label that most aptly describes the group of individuals with scores loading highly on person factor 1 but moderately on person factor 2. Whether this group best represents individuals with a *guilt*-infused shame as opposed to *shame*-infused guilt is debatable. Nonetheless, it is clear that *joint* tendencies to offer repair and apologies (as opposed to *primarily* ruminating about one's guilt or shame) and genuine acceptance of one's guilt combined with meditations about ourselves and how we could improve (as opposed to externalizing, minimizing, or rationalizing) serves individuals most adaptively in the realm of morality *and* honest self-assessment. The latter confirms our earlier suspicion that qualities of the two emotions combined represent adaptive responses. It also affirms the findings presented earlier pertaining to outsiders' positive evaluations of people expressing both tendencies.

Results from the Q factor analyses revealing a link between defensive tendencies and people's strict emphasis on guilt as the *immediate* repair or resolution of a problem accompanied by little self-criticism are not isolated findings, in either adults or children. In adults, for example, Treadwell (2001) found *no* tendency for them to respond exclusively with guilt as a means of expressing empathy, seeking forgiveness, or manifesting prosocial attitudes. In fact, in his "close relationship" condition, *shame* and its close cousins (e.g., embarrassment), *instead* of guilt, were associated more with the qualities the literature typically attributes to guilt (e.g., seeking forgiveness). In one of Ferguson's studies with children (Ferguson, 2001), results showed that 25% of the 5- to 13-year-old children endorsed almost exclusively "guilt-like" responses to intentionally produced interpersonal transgressions. Their guilt responses involved offers of repair and acknowledgments of proper standards of conduct, but only a moderate to slight expression of empathy or concerns with the victims' plights. The same group did not endorse high-intensity "shame-like" reactions (operationalized primarily as feelings of shame or tendencies to self-criticize) to intentionally harmful incidents, they did not express extreme degrees of shame or guilt to situations in which untoward outcomes were unintentional, nor did they strongly externalize blame for any of the transgressions. Although the children's "guilt-like" responses seem quite morally mature, mothers characterized the same children as *extremely* "morally" *deviant* (e.g., aggressive, irresponsible, dishonest, disrespectful), and they additonally reported the strongest efforts to socialize a morally mature orientation in this group of children.

As a whole, these children's frequent real-life experiences with consequences of their standard violations, and possibly the effects of expressing different emotions in reaction to them, seemed to have taught them to express a "superficial" or "pseudo" guilt for purposes of minimizing adults' negative reactions. This is very unlike the process of internalization usually envisaged, in which discipline encounters promote genuine *feelings* of guilt or shame that ultimately become sufficient motivators to avoid or atone for similar future wrongdoing to minimize these emotional self-punishments. Ferguson (2001) found the strongest evidence of internalization or conscientious behavior in children liable not only to guilt, but also to the shame of appearing to be an immoral agent (21% of sample). For example, they endorsed stopping to help a child in need (instead of continuing their mad dash home to catch their favorite TV program) and they preferred preparing for the next day's "show and tell" presentation (instead of playing with friends) *in order to* avoid negative feelings not only of guilt, but also of shame. We see these findings, and interpret those of others (e.g., Aksan & Kochanska, 2005; Kochanska, 2002), to implicate *combined* tendencies toward guilt and shame in mature moral self-regulation.

White and Ferguson (2004) supported similar conclusions in their analysis of over 400 student narratives detailing the beneficial and detrimental sequelae of their guilt experiences, the involvement of others as important reminders of a behavior's inappropriateness, and their emphasis on shame in what were meant to be exclusively guilt narratives (see Ferguson, Eyre, & Stegge, 1996; Weaver, Miller, & Ferguson, 2005). Briefly, the *dual* presence of guilt and shame in the narratives was associated with the most beneficial consequences (and the fewest detrimental consequences) than either experience in isolation (e.g., reporting greater self understanding and/or resolutions to improve as opposed to continued anger, indifference, or no self-change). Interestingly, co-occurring shame and guilt was more beneficial than either guilt or shame alone primarily when the *other* had *meant* to make them feel guilty. To us, these findings highlight the important role of others as reminders of our moral values and commitments as well as shame's communicative role in affirming these.

WARRANT FOR INTERPERSONALLY ORIENTED GUILT AND SHAME: CAUSALITY AND RESPONSIBILITY

Some of the results highlighted previously were unexpected, particularly those indicating a nexus between shame and perceptions of moral responsibility or control (e.g., the Q factor analysis findings). Lively discussions abound regarding whether appraisals of causality, moral responsibility, or blameworthiness are antecedents, constituents, or afterthoughts of *any* emotion, and regarding whether these are necessary or sufficient to distinguish between guilt and shame (e.g., Baumeister et al., 1994; Malle, 2004; Parkinson, 1995). In Weiner's well-known attribution model of social emotions, the agent presumably feels guilty after attributing failure to an internal/controllable cause (e.g., low effort), but ashamed when failure reflects an internal/uncontrollable cause (e.g., low ability) (see

Weiner, 1995, for an overview). These attribution models make understandable why the emotion of shame readily comes to mind regarding characteristics such as age, physical size, strength, deformities, or attractiveness; dependence on others; gender-inappropriate characteristics; abilities/skills; weaknesses of the "will" (e.g., addictions, perversions); sexual matters (e.g., orientation, infertility or impotence); and even national or ethnic heritage (e.g., Gilbert, Pehl, & Allan, 1994; Lindsay-Hartz, 1984). In attribution terms, these are difficult-to-alter characteristics with potentially far-reaching and long-term negative consequences, particularly when also viewed as global and stable characteristics (see Tracy & Robins, 2004, 2006).

In our view, however, the traditional attributional perspective essentially identifies shame with self-attributed helplessness and ignores people's tendencies to feel as, if not more, ashamed of voluntary choices, intentions, and desires than involuntary characteristics (e.g., Morris, 1971; Williams, 1993). Conversely, although a perceived ability to avoid or undo unwanted outcomes may exacerbate guilt's intensity, guilty experiences certainly are not limited to states of affairs the person perceives to be voluntary, controllable, effortful, or even analyzable in terms of a prior cause and later effect (Greenspan, 1995). One can feel horrifically guilty, and suffer the torment of clinically significant anxiety or depression, even when there is no "event" or specific behavior that the person could have controlled or avoided (cf. Ferguson, 1999, 2006; Ferguson, Stegge, et al., 2000; Olthof et al., 2004; O'Connor, Berry, & Weiss, 1999), as shown by genuinely devastating instances of separation guilt, survivor guilt, traumatic guilt, collective guilt, overbenefited guilt, guilt concerning wishes or desires, and guilt regarding long eschewed beliefs (e.g., cultural prohibitions) or commitments (e.g., religious affiliation). June Tangney (personal communication, May 2006) suggests viewing these as instances of "problematic" guilt fused with shame. This may well be. However, in our view, what renders these instances problematic is not necessarily the feelings as such, but the underlying appraisals. In particular, we suspect that these individuals *ruminate* about their responsibility for the tragic outcome; they focus, for example, on unrealistic perceptions that they should have been able to avoid them. Overestimates of an outcome's controllability might support intense feelings of guilt (for producing avoidable harm) and shame (for being the type of person who produces avoidable harm).

Unconvinced that shame exclusively bodes poorly for individuals because shame is reliably produced by perceptions of uncontrollability, we asked college students in one study to narrate accounts of instances in which feeling ashamed resulted in useful or harmful consequences (see Ferguson, Barrett, et al., 2000). Even after removing the influence of guilt-related content, students typified significantly more of the "good" than "bad" shame incidents as *controllable* experiences motivating personal growth vis-à-vis a second-order *desire* they could and *should* change (Frankfurt, 1987). Consistent with previous findings, however, students associated every single instance of "bad" shame with outcomes they considered wrong and elicitors they characterized as uncontrollable. The perceived inability to control contributors to an unwanted outcome clearly rendered shame a dysfunctional experience, yet shame's association with controllable outcomes also resulted in multiple benefits.

These findings prompted us to reexamine results of published studies regarding the two emotions' association with perceptions of control (e.g., Tangney, Miller, Flicker, & Barlow, 1996; Wicker, Payne, & Morgan, 1983). Two representative examples of studies in this literature suffice to illustrate our concern that shame, like guilt, can be a function of increased rather than decreased perceptions of control. In the frequently cited Wicker et al. (1983) studies, participants rated memories of shame and guilt experiences in terms of multiple items, some of which reflected perceptions of control. For example, their mean ratings on 9-point scales of control-related perceptions such as "I felt my power in this situation was too little" were 5.98 and 5.22 for the guilt and shame experiences, respectively; similarly, the respective means were 5.52 and 5.99 for the item "I was active." Effect sizes for these two comparisons are less than .17, indicating little difference in the extent to which people thought they could control the events leading to their shame versus guilt experiences. Results for these two items are not deviant from trends we generally observed in the literature. They also illustrate that the magnitude of ratings reflecting perceptions of control, even as they pertained to shame, are not infrequently at or near the scale's midpoint, even though participants made use of the entire scale in rating other items. People apparently *do* associate certain experiences of shame with as much control as they associate their guilty experiences.

In this respect, it is interesting to revisit Davitz's (1969) long-ignored volume summarizing a series of studies meant to capture the dimensions underlying different emotions, including guilt and shame. Davitz first identified over 250 statements describing various correlates of a wide range of emotions; these statements depicted, for example, emotions' cognitive-experiential and physiological-experiential components, action tendencies, and coping strategies. Factor analyses revealed that six dimensions (e.g., hypoactivation, inadequacy) differentiated reliably among the various emotions. Although not labeled as such by Davitz, two of these dimensions contained items relevant to perceptions of control's presence or absence. A definite majority of items representing one of these dimensions pertained to beliefs in *control or change* (e.g., "begin to think what I can do to change the situation," "want to hurry up and begin to change"), although certain items were ambiguous in meaning (e.g., "nothing I do is right"). Davitz showed that this "control/change" dimension *far* outweighed—by a factor of seven and greater—the remaining five dimensions in characterizing *both* shame and guilt experiences. Interestingly, however, beliefs in one's future ability to control or change one's outcomes were weighted 12 units *higher* for *shame* than for guilt experiences. Items representing the second dimension of interest reflected precisely the opposite beliefs, that is, that the person *could not exert control or change* (e.g., " . . . being wholly unable to control the situation"; "feel vulnerable and totally helpless"). Importantly, Davitz derived a much *lower* weight for these items and their weights were *similar* in magnitude for guilt *and* shame.

Davitz's series of studies indicate that the perception of control or potential to change, rather than their absence, are characteristic of both experiences; moreover, optimism regarding control and change can even be greater for certain shame than guilt experiences. These results, and others, seem inconsistent with the standard attributional view distinguishing elicitors of shame from elicitors of guilt in terms of *opposing* perceptions representing the controllability dimension (among other dimensions; cf. Tracy & Robins, 2004). Of course, we have not done justice to a large body of literature confirming the standard view. We do not doubt, moreover, that controllability perceptions *can* be shown to moderate the intensity, chronicity, or frequency with which either state is *elicited* via the mechanisms classically assumed in this literature (e.g., Ferguson & Eyre, 2006). At the same time, there is a *disturbing* degree of interindividual, interoutcome, and even intraindividual variability in the extent to which (1) prototypical exemplars (e.g., ability, effort) are classified in ways consistent with the traditional attributional dimensions, (2) are inferred reliably from information regarding each dimension's value (e.g., Dresel,

Schober, & Ziegler, 2005), and (3) are strongly or consistently related, as predicted, to the differential elicitation of guilt or shame (cf. Tracy & Robins, 2004).

There are diverse explanations of this variability. One plausible explanation is that some individuals may *not* parse controllability perceptions by calculating two distinct "emotional equations" representing shame's link to a lack of control and guilt's association with control's presence (see Weiner, 1994, 1995). Instead of independently solving these two equations, individuals may more configurally weigh each "cause's" implication for the existence and quality of the person's actual intentions and motives, which also arouses the two emotions, but situates their reasoning regarding them in the richer realm of Heiderian "personal causality" (see Malle, 2004), thereby giving greater *moral* force to both of them. We think the shift in emphasis from a purely causal model to a moral one corrects a *particular* prevailing trend in the self-conscious emotions literature, which has been to equate feelings of shame with uncontrollable self-characteristics and thereby render the person passive and helpless. That people do feel ashamed in these instances is indisputable. Yet, they also feel ashamed for events they could control, a point illustrated by three other studies from Ferguson's lab (including Ferguson, Olthof, & Stegge, 1997; Treadwell, 1999, 2001).

In these three studies, college students acted as transgressors of hypothetical wrongdoings or kept logs of harmful transgressions they actually had perpetrated (e.g., property damage, making the victim late, infidelity), including unintended and uncontrollable harm (accidental), controllable but unintended harm (foreseeable), and avoidable, intended, and ill-motivated harm (angry retaliation). Because several theorists have denied the role of responsibility- or attribution-related perceptions as elicitors of emotional experiences, including guilt (e.g., Parkinson, 1995), as opposed to being mere concomitants or postevent justifications of these experiences, we assessed all judgments both immediately after the event took place (Time 1) and 24 hours later (Time 2). At both time periods, we assessed the felt intensity of guilt and shame, perceptions related to moral and/or causal responsibility, predictions regarding the victims' reactions (e.g., disappointment, anger), and concerns regarding these events' reflection on their character.

Of greatest relevance to this chapter is the correlational evidence linking each emotion to causal-, moral-, and victim-oriented perceptions. Immediate feelings of guilt (residualized for shame) increased as perceived motive justification decreased. Guilt at Time 1 also increased as the agents' ability to avoid the outcome increased, a link that was even stronger at Time 2. In comparison, immediate shame (residualized for guilt) increased as transgressors' motives were rated less justified and with perceived increases in moral responsibility. At Time 2, shame's association with moral responsibility was even stronger, as was shame's link to perceived intentionality, a composite score of the victims' reactions, and worries regarding the event's reflection on their character.

The association of shame with intentionality and its connection with moral, interpersonal, and victim-oriented concerns in these (and our earlier studies) suggested that perceptions of the voluntary nature of one's actions and the harm's production committed greatly affected shame. These are the very types of actions on which people focus in evaluating a person's character. To many, they also are the very criteria involved in labeling an act as "moral" or "immoral," thus supporting the view of shame as a moral emotion (cf. Haidt, 2003; Malle, 2004). Although feelings of guilt were strongly affected by, and associated with, factors concerning the outcome's controllability, readers should note that people felt guilty largely because they did not act to identify and then counteract *any* causal condition necessary to bring about the harmful outcome, including *external* forces in the situations we used (cf. Brickman et al., 1982). This renders guilt a function not only of Heiderian "personal causality," but of the "impersonal causality" that many would consider falling *outside* the realm of moral blame or credit (Ferguson, Stegge, et al., 2000; Malle, 2004). Most of our findings regarding guilt—when disconnected from shame—seemed to implicate guilt as one way to repay a "presumed" debt via emotional self-punishment, and thus avoid the need to blame the self or risk being blamed by others (see Baumeister et al., 1994; Greenspan, 1995). Shame, on the other hand, seems to resonate more with the person's perceived blameworthiness or moral responsibility for the wrongdoing, which is a function of factors related to personal causality (including intentionality).

SHAME AND GUILT REDUX: SUMMARY AND CONCLUSIONS

The sheer hell of shame is apparent when felt regarding uncontrollable self-characteristics, especially when also perceived to be stable and widely influential across domains of one's life (cf. Tangney & Dearing, 2002; Tracy & Robins, 2004). In our view, however, feelings of shame are no more agonizing than feelings of guilt regarding uncontrollable or irreversible unwanted events. To be shamed or humiliated by another, or to bear the brunt of unfounded guilty accusations, especially in service of the victimizer's cruel and selfish needs, cannot possibly be warranted. Instead of focusing on conditions exacerbating either state's unfortunate consequences, previous research has attended primarily to the variety of conditions enhancing guilt's warrant but detracting from shame's (see Tangney & Dearing, 2002), we asked whether particular conditions contributed to similar or different perceptions of the two states' moral warrant and whether this warrant related reliably to judgments of agents' characters.

Findings emanating primarily from our studies with American, Canadian, Dutch, and Russian samples made very clear that a withdrawal/avoidance/self-critical operationalization of "shame," characteristic of widely used protocols, is *not* seen as an intelligible or warranted response to one's minor or isolated wrongdoings. When expressed in response to repeated wrongdoing, however, it may communicate the types of submissive-appeasement displays of shame known to elicit sympathetic understanding (cf. Keltner & Harker, 1998; Weiner, 1994, 1995). Results also suggested that shame as a feeling is extremely warranted when agents are deemed responsible or capable of changing the motives, intentions, or behaviors associated with producing an unwanted state of affairs that could merely taint, or entirely spoil, the self's identity. Agents themselves reported feeling ashamed after engaging in actions that merely *questioned* coveted views of the self, including their moral worthiness, and these feelings seemed to serve as useful reminders of personal aspirations and the role of various states of mind or qualities of the "will" in their attainment or delay.

Very importantly, instead of shame detracting from guilt's value in affirming commitment to relationships, it appeared to actually *strengthen* this perception, which bears out Sabini and Silver's (1997) eloquent defense of shame as well as that of Williams (1993, p. 94):

> By itself, guilt cannot help one to understand one's relations to [those] happenings, or to rebuild the self that has done these things and the world in which that self has to live. Only shame can do that . . . it is only through the experience of shame that we are forced to ask what kinds of failings or inadequacy are the source of the harms, and what those failings mean in the context of our own and other people's lives.

To conclude: Guilt and shame both are affectively infused SOS signals to reconsider one's wrongdoings or failures in light of cherished values and standards. For many years, the literature has depicted guilt and shame as though they were adversaries in an emotional tug of war. Instead of strictly opposing them, we prefer to view them as acting in concert. They both encourage exploration of whether and how the person can take responsibility for upholding or achieving cherished standards. Although they can compete as mutual liabilities, together they serve as useful goads to responsibly promote the self's integrity while also fulfilling one's duties.

ACKNOWLEDGMENTS

We thank the Logan City and Brigham City School Districts, and their children, teachers, and parents for their kind help with the "near moral miss" study. For their generous support, we are indebted to the Van der Gaag Foundation of the Netherlands Royal Academy of Sciences, Professor Willem Koops (Dean, Faculty of Social Sciences, Utrecht University), Professor Joyce Kinkead (Vice Provost for Undergraduate Research, Utah State University [USU]), as well as USU's Honors' and URCO (University Research Creative Opportunity) programs. We express our heartfelt gratitude to this volume's editors (Janet Tracy, Richard Robins, & June Tangney). Tamara Ferguson warmly thanks the many undergraduate and graduate students at USU who contributed their time and energy to the USU-based studies since 1988, including Adam Kynaston, Elina Alexandrova, Stephanie Alberico, Bryant Albrecht, Mike Ashbaker, Margaret ("Annie") Ashcraft, Justin Barker, Jeff Bertuzzi, Shayne Bland, Colleen Cook, Katie Crowell Peterson, Kim Dzatko, Shawn Edmondson, Danielle Grotepas-Sanders, Amanda Hillhouse, Annamarie LaDumas, Angela Smith, Deann Sheppard (Gerity), Russ Vollmer, Shayne Stowell, Teresa Thompson, Chris Treadwell, Irena Turcin, and Starla Weaver. Citations of others' many relevant findings and the instruments we used, which we eliminated due to space limitations, are available upon request.

REFERENCES

Aksan, N., & Kochanska, G. (2005). Conscience in childhood: Old questions, new answers. *Developmental Psychology, 41,* 506–516.

Alberico, S., Anderson, M., Hacker, B., Higley, A., Marsolais, V., Moyes, M., et al. (1998, April). *Guilt and shame elicitors: Unwanted identities, responsibility, and interpersonal consequences.* Poster presented at the joint meeting of the Western Psychological and Rocky Mountain Psychological Associations, Albuquerque, NM.

Alexandrova, E. O., Ferguson, T. J., & Crowley, S. L. (1996, April). *Raising the Iron Curtain: Assessment of guilt and shame in Russia.* Poster presented at the 76th annual convention of the Western Psychological Association, San Jose, CA.

Aronfreed, J. (1968). *Conduct and conscience: The socialization of internalized control over behavior.* New York: Academic Press.

Ausubel, D. P. (1955). Relationships between shame and guilt in the socializing process. *Psychological Review, 62,* 378–390.

Barrett, K. C. (1995). A functionalist approach to shame and guilt. In J. P. Tangney & K. W. Fischer (Eds.), *Self-conscious emotions: The psychology of shame, guilt, embarrassment, and pride* (pp. 25–63). New York: Guilford Press.

Baumeister, R. F., Stillwell, A. M., & Heatherton, T. F. (1994). Guilt: An interpersonal approach. *Psychological Bulletin, 115,* 243–267.

Brickman, P., Rabinowitz, V. C., Karuza, J., Coates, D., Cohn, E., & Kidder, L. (1982). Models of helping and coping. *American Psychologist, 37,* 368–384.

Damasio, A. (2003). *Looking for Spinoza: Joy, sorrow, and the feeling brain.* New York: Harcourt.

Davitz, J. (1969). *Language of emotion.* New York: Academic Press.

Dresel, M., Schober, B., & Ziegler, A. (2005). Nothing more than dimensions?: Evidence for a surplus meaning of specific attributions. *Journal of Educational Research, 99,* 31–43.

Edmondson, R. S. (2002). *Identifying the bases for gender differences in guilt and shame.* Unpublished master's thesis, Utah State University.

Elison, J. (2003). Definitions of, and distinctions between, shame and guilt: A facet theory analysis. *Dissertation Abstracts International: Section B: The Sciences and Engineering, 64,* 1537.

Ferguson, T. J. (1996, August). *Self-report, narrative, and projective indicators of (mal)adaptive features of guilt and shame.* In T. J. Ferguson (Chair), Measure for Measure: Assessing Guilt and Shame across the Life-Span. Symposium conducted at the meeting of the International Society for Research on Emotion, Toronto, Canada.

Ferguson, T. J. (1999). Guilt. In D. Levinson, J. Ponzetti, & P. Jorgensen (Eds.), *Encyclopedia of human emotions* (pp. 301–315). New York: Macmillan Reference/Prentice Hall.

Ferguson, T. J. (2001, April). *Peer and parental contributions to the development of guilt- and shame-proneness.* Paper presented at the annual meeting of the Society for Research in Child Development. Minneapolis.

Ferguson, T. J. (2006). Mapping shame and its functions. *Child Maltreatment, 10,* 377–386.

Ferguson, T. J., Barrett, K. C., Edmondson, R. S., Eyre, H. L., Ashbaker, M., Grotepas-Sanders, D., et al. (2000, February). *Adaptive and maladaptive features of shame.* Paper presented at the annual meeting of the Society for Personality and Social Psychology, Nashville, TN.

Ferguson, T. J., & Barrett, K. C. (2003, October). *Trumping shame with anger: Felt vs. expressed emotions as predictors of youths' problem behaviors.* Paper presented at the Conference on Emotions and Health, Tilburg, The Netherlands.

Ferguson, T. J., & Crowley, S. L. (1997a). Gender differences in the organization of guilt and shame. *Sex Roles, 37,* 19–44.

Ferguson, T. J., & Crowley, S. L. (1997b). Measure for measure: A multitrait–multimethod analysis of guilt and shame. *Journal of Personality Assessment, 69,* 425–441.

Ferguson, T. J., Edmondson, R. S., & Gerity, D. S. (2000, October). *Pain with a purpose: Anticipatory shame and guilt in daily dilemmas.* Paper presented at the annual meeting of the Society of Experimental Social Psychology, Atlanta, GA.

Ferguson, T. J., & Eyre, H. L. (2000). Engendering gender differences in shame and guilt: Stereotypes, socialization, and situational pressures. In A. H. Fischer (Ed.), *Gender and emotion: Social psychological perspectives* (pp. 254–276). Cambridge, UK: Cambridge University Press.

Ferguson, T. J., & Eyre, H. L. (2006). *Reconciling interpersonal versus appraisal views of guilt: Roles of inductive strategies and projected responsibility in prolonging guilty feelings.* Unpublished manuscript submitted for publication.

Ferguson, T. J., & Eyre, H. L., & Ashbaker, M. (2000). Unwanted identities: A key variable in shame–anger links and gender differences in shame. *Sex Roles, 42,* 133–157.

Ferguson, T. J., Eyre, H. L., & Stegge, H. (1996, March). *Multifaceted functions of transient and persistent guilt in adults and children.* Poster presented at the biennial meeting of the Southwestern Society for Research on Human Development, Park City, UT.

Ferguson, T. J., Olthof, T., & Stegge, H. (1997). Temporal dynamics of guilt: Changes in the role of interpersonal and intrapsychic factors. *European Journal of Social Psychology, 27,* 659–673.

Ferguson, T. J., & Stegge, H. (1995). Emotional states and traits in children: The case of guilt and shame. In J. P. Tangney & K. W. Fischer (Eds.), *Self-conscious emotions: Shame, guilt, embarrassment and pride* (pp. 174–197). New York: Guilford Press.

Ferguson, T. J., & Stegge, H. (1998). Measuring guilt in children: A rose by any other name still has thorns. In J. Bybee (Ed.), *Guilt and children* (pp. 19–74). San Diego, CA: AcademicPress.

Ferguson, T. J., Stegge, H., & Damhuis, I. (1990). Guilt and shame experiences in elementary school-age children. In P. J. D. Drenth, J. A. Sergeant, & R. J. Takens (Eds.), *European perspectives in psychology* (Vol. 1, pp. 195–218). New York: Wiley.

Ferguson, T. J., Stegge, H., & Damhuis, I. (1991). Children's understanding of guilt and shame. *Child Development, 62,* 827–839.

Ferguson, T. J., Stegge, H., Eyre, H. L., Vollmer, R., & Ashbaker, M. (2000). Context effects and the (mal)adaptive nature of guilt and shame in children. *Genetic, Social, and General Psychology Monographs, 126,* 319–345.

Ferguson, T. J., Stegge, H., Miller, E. R., & Olsen, M. E. (1999). Guilt, shame, and symptoms in children. *Developmental Psychology, 35,* 347–357.

Frankfurt, H. (1987). Identification and wholeheartedness. In F. Schoeman (Ed.), *Responsibility, character, and the emotions: New essays in moral psychology* (pp. 27–45). New York: Cambridge University Press.

Gibbard, A. (1990). *Wise choices, apt feelings: A theory of normative judgment.* Cambridge, MA: Harvard University Press.

Gilbert, P. (1998). What is shame?: Some core issues and controversies. In P. Gilbert & B. Andrews (Eds.), *Shame: Interpersonal behavior, psychopathology, and culture* (pp. 3–38). New York: Oxford University Press.

Gilbert, P., Pehl, J., & Allan, S. (1994). The phenomenology of shame and guilt: An empirical investigation. *British Journal of Medical Psychology, 67,* 23–36.

Greenspan, P. S. (1995). *Practical guilt.* New York: Oxford University Press.

Haidt, J. (2003). The moral emotions. In R. J. Davidson, K. R. Scherer, & H. H. Goldsmith (Eds.), *Handbook of affective sciences* (pp. 852–870). Oxford, UK: Oxford University Press.

Harder, D. W. (1995). Shame and guilt assessment, and relationships of shame- and guilt-proneness to psychopathology. In J. P. Tangney & K. W. Fisher (Eds.), *Self-conscious emotions: The psychology of shame, guilt, embarrassment and pride* (pp. 368–392). New York: Guilford Press.

Harris, N. (2003). Reassessing the dimensionality of the moral emotions. *British Journal of Psychology, 94,* 457–473.

Heider, F. (1958). *The psychology of interpersonal relations.* New York: Wiley.

Heise, D. R., & O'Brien, J. (1993). Emotion expression in groups. In M.Lewis & J . M. Haviland (Eds.), *Handbook of emotions* (pp. 489–497). New York: Guilford Press.

Keltner, D., & Harker, L. A. (1998). The forms and functions of the nonverbal signal of shame. In P. Gilbert & B. Andrews (Eds.), *Shame: Interpersonal behavior, psychopathology, and culture* (pp. 78–98). Oxford, UK: Oxford University Press.

Kochanska, G. (2002). Committed compliance, moral self, and internalization: A mediational model. *Developmental Psychology, 38,* 339–351.

Kugler, K., & Jones, W. H. (1992). On conceptualizing and assessing guilt. *Journal of Personality and Social Psychology, 62,* 318–327.

Lazowski, L. (1987). Speakers' nonverbal expressions of emotion as moderators of listeners' reactions to disclosures of self-harm and social harm. *Dissertation Abstracts International, 48,* 282–291.

Lewis, H. B. (1971). *Shame and guilt in neurosis.* New York: International Universities Press.

Lindsay-Hartz, J. (1984). Contrasting experiences of shame and guilt. *American Behavioral Scientist, 27,* 689–709.

Luyten, P., Fontaine, J. R., & Corbeleyn, J. (2002). Does the Test of Self-Conscious Affect (TOSCA) measure maladaptive aspects of guilt and adaptive aspects of shame?: An empirical investigation. *Personality and Individual Differences, 33,* 1373–1387.

Malle, B. F. (2004). *How the mind explains behavior: Folk explanations, meaning, and social interaction.* Cambridge, MA: MIT Press.

Mason, M. (2003). Contempt as a moral attitude. *Ethics, 113,* 234–272.

Morris, H. (1971). *On guilt and shame.* Belmont, CA: Wadsworth.

Neslen, J., & Peterson, K. (2005, April). *The pivotal role of shame in perceptions of moral virtue.* Paper presented at the annual meeting of the Rocky Mountain Psychological Association, Phoenix, AZ.

O'Connor, L. E., Berry, J. W., & Weiss, J. (1999). Interpersonal guilt, shame, and psychological problems. *Journal of Social and Clinical Psychology, 18,* 181–203.

Olthof, T., Ferguson, T. J., Bloemers, E., & Deij, M. (2004). Morality- and identity-related antecedents of children's guilt and shame attritions in events involving physical illness. *Cognition and Emotion, 18,* 383–404.

Olthof, T., Schouten, A., Kuiper, H., Stegge, H., & Jennekens-Schinkel, A. (2000). Shame and guilt in children: Differential situational antecedents and experiential correlates. *British Journal of Developmental Psychology, 18,* 51–64.

Ortony, A., Clore, G. L., & Collins, A. (1988). *The cognitive structure of emotions.* Cambridge, UK: Cambridge University Press

Parkinson, B. (1995). *Ideas and realities of emotion.* New York: Routledge.

Sabini, J., & Silver, M. (1997). In defense of shame: Shame in the context of guilt and embarrassment. *Journal for the Theory of Social Behaviour, 27,* 1–15.

Stegge, H., & Ferguson, T. J. (2003, October). *(Mal)adaptive emotional response patterns in children: Guilt, shame, anger and pride.* Paper presented at the Conference on Emotions and Health, Tilburg, The Netherlands.

Strawson, P. (1962). Freedom and resentment. *Proceedings of the British Academy, 48,* 1–25.

Tangney, J. P. (1991). Moral affect: The good, the bad, and the ugly. *Journal of Personality and Social Psychology, 61,* 598–607.

Tangney, J. P. (1995). Recent advances in the empirical study of shame and guilt. *American Behavioral Scientist, 38,* 1132–1145.

Tangney, J. P. (1996). Conceptual and methodological issues in the assessment of shame and guilt. *Behaviour Research and Therapy, 34,* 741–754.

Tangney, J. P., & Dearing, R. L. (2002). *Shame and guilt.* New York: Guilford Press.

Tangney, J. P., Ferguson, T. J., Wagner, P. E., Crowley, S. L., & Gramzow, R. (1996). *The Test of Self-Conscious Affect, Version 2* (TOSCA-2). Unpublished instrument, George Mason University, Fairfax, VA.

Tangney, J. P., Miller, R. S., Flicker, L., & Barlow, D. H. (1996). Are shame, guilt, and embarrassment distinct emotions? *Journal of Personality and Social Psychology, 70,* 1256–1269.

Tangney, J. P., Wagner, P. E., & Gramzow, R. (1989). *The Test of Self-Conscious Affect.* Fairfax, VA: George Mason University.

Tracy, J. L., & Robins, R. W. (2004). Putting the self into self-conscious emotions: A theoretical model. *Psychological Inquiry, 15,* 103–126.

Tracy, J. L., & Robins, R. W. (2006). Appraisal antecedents of shame and guilt: Support for a theoretical model. *Personality and Social Psychology Bulletin, 32,* 1339–1351.

Treadwell, C. L. (1999). *Interpersonal aspects of attribution and emotion.* Unpublished master's thesis, Utah State University, Logan.

Treadwell, C. L. (2001). Changing the role of appraisal and interpersonal factors in guilt induction: Time, perspective, and responsibility. *Dissertation Abstract International, 62,* 4844–4846.

Weaver, S., Miller, M., & Ferguson, T. J. (2005, April). *Victims' perceptions of responsibility and perpetrators' guilty feelings: The eye of the beholders.* Paper presented at the annual meeting of the Rocky Mountain Psychological Association, Phoenix, AZ.

Weiner, B. (1994). Integrating social and personal theories of achievement striving. *Review of Educational Research, 64,* 557–573.

Weiner, B. (1995). *Judgments of responsibility: A foundation for a theory of social conduct.* New York: Guilford Press.

White, J. R., & Ferguson, T. J. (2004, April). *Madness to methods and purpose in pain: studying the beneficial and adverse consequences of shame and guilt.* Paper presented at the annual meeting of the Rocky Mountain Psychological Association, Reno, NV.

Wicker, F. W., Payne, G. C., & Morgan, R. D. (1983). Participant descriptions of guilt and shame. *Motivation and Emotion, 7,* 25–39.

Williams, B. (1993). *Shame and necessity.* Berkeley and Los Angeles: University of California Press.

PART V

SPECIAL TOPICS
AND APPLICATIONS

19

Group-Conscious Emotions

The Implications of Others' Wrongdoings for Identity and Relationships

BRIAN LICKEL
TONI SCHMADER
MARIJA SPANOVIC

Emotions are traditionally viewed as a combination of psychological, physiological, and phenomenological experiences that motivate an individual to behave with respect to certain self-relevant goals. Self-conscious emotions, as described in previous chapters, are a unique class of emotional experiences that require a sense of self-awareness and mark events that have direct relevance to a symbolic sense of self. We feel pride for our accomplishments, shame for our personal flaws, embarrassment for our social foibles, and guilt for our mishandling of situations. Traditionally, emotion theorists have discussed self-conscious emotions in terms of how an *individual* uses these emotions to regulate his or her *own* behavior with respect to certain personal goals or social standards (e.g., Beer, Heerey, Keltner, Scabini, & Knight, 2003). This process of self-regulation is no doubt the key function of self-conscious emotions. We would remind the reader, however, that individuals do not behave or even define themselves within a social vacuum. Rather, being social creatures, our very sense of self is at least in part defined by our associations to other people. Likewise, we carry aspects of our selfhood in our group identities and social relationships. The implication of this assertion is that self-conscious emotions might not only be experienced in response to our own actions and behaviors; the actions of others might also have the potential to elicit self-conscious emotions in us. Our goal in this chapter is to bring together literature on self-conscious emotions with literature on groups and intergroup processes to build a case for our thesis that, at least in some circumstances, the *group* plays a significant role in self-conscious emotions.

For the purposes of our analysis, we are most interested in the emotional reactions people experience when they observe other individuals engage in wrongdoing. Because these are the events of interest, we constrain ourselves to examining negative self-conscious emotions like shame and guilt. In our chapter, we'll discuss a wider array of emotions than just shame and guilt. Nonetheless, the distinctions between these two emotions provide an important starting point for our analysis. Conceptual distinctions between shame and guilt have been discussed in other chapters. In general, however, we subscribe to the theoretical analyses laid out by Tangney and Fischer (1995), stating that shame and guilt can be independently predicted by distinct appraisal processes. We tend to feel ashamed for events that highlight fundamentally flawed aspects of our character and guilty for events that we felt we could have and should have controlled to a greater degree (see also Tracy & Robins, 2004). In addition, the two emotions are also distinguished by the types of behaviors they evoke. People who feel ashamed are motivated to withdraw from an emotion-eliciting event, whereas people who feel guilty are motivated to repair the event in some way (Wicker, Payne, & Morgan, 1983; Tangney, Miller, Flicker, & Barlow, 1996). This distinction between the motivations that these emotions elicit is part of the reason it is critical to predict the distinct type of emotional experience individuals have to a given event.

Given these definitions of shame and guilt, we might first ask whether it is possible to experience these emotions for something another person has done. Reading the literature on self-conscious emotion could easily lead one to conclude that the experience of these emotions *requires* that one has personally committed some wrong. For example, in their classic study of appraisal processes in emotion, Smith and Ellsworth (1985) concluded, "In shame and guilt, unlike the other negative emotions, a sense of self-blame is central. For both emotions subjects always described situations in which they had done something they regretted" (p. 833). More recently, Sabini and Silver (2005) stated that "Shame, embarrassment, and guilt all have to do with recognizing that one has done something infelicitous" (p. 5). These assertions imply that such emotions might only be felt in response to one's own actions.

In contrast, we argue that personal causality is not necessary. Rather, people might readily feel a sense of shame or guilt for the actions of another, assuming that the individual sees that other person as in some way an extension of him- or herself. In fact, at least one set of emotion theorists has allowed for vicarious forms of self-conscious emotions. Ortony, Clore, and Collins (1988) argue that associations with other people can lead to the formation of a cognitive unit between self and other. When the other individual then engages in positive or negative behavior, the strength of the unit formation with the other should predict the intensity of a pride or shame response, respectively. More recently, scholars have begun to empirically investigate when and why people may feel self-conscious emotions for the actions of others. In our chapter, we summarize this recent work and provide a theoretical framework for organizing the findings.

WHY EXPERIENCE SELF-CONSCIOUS EMOTIONS FOR OTHERS' WRONGDOINGS?

Humans are a social species in which important aspects of life are conducted in the context of groups and social relationships. Emotions such as shame and guilt form an important mechanism that regulates people's behavior within social groups (Eisenberg, 2000). However, the pervasive role of groups in human life has another consequence, namely, that members of groups become psychologically bonded together (from the perspective of both outsiders and oneself). Thus, the events and actions that are caused by or affect other ingroup members have the capacity to affect one's self to the extent that one's group affiliation makes these behaviors and events relevant to the goals of one's ingroup (Smith, 1993). Moreover, in our view, people have the capacity to experience self-conscious emotions for the actions of others because it is ultimately functional to do so. Although claims about the evolutionary adaptiveness of emotions are difficult to prove, we take as a basic assumption that the human emotion system is a product of natural selection and has been shaped to aid people in responding to ancestrally recurrent challenges (Cosmides & Tooby, 2000; Tooby & Cosmides, 1990).

Certainly, when discussing self-conscious emotions for events caused by the self, there appears to be a clear adaptive explanation for the behaviors that such emotions motivate. For example, guilt promotes efforts to repair damage to social relationships, and at least under some circumstances is associated with positive relationship functioning (Baumeister, Stillwell, & Heatherton, 1994). Shame, although often considered to be a maladaptive response for the individual who experiences it, might serve as an internal deterrent that prevents individuals from engaging in wrongful behavior in the first place (Heery, Keltner, & Capps, 2005; Tangney et al., 1996). We have recently considered that although shame might motivate avoidance in the short run, it might motivate a desire to change the self over time (Lickel et al., 2007). Finally, the distinct spontaneous nonverbal display associated with embarrassment (Keltner, 1995) indicates to others that one recognizes that one has committed a social transgression. Such displays may have the function of preventing ostracism or aggression from others.

Many emotion scholars accept that self-conscious emotions are probably evolved responses to aid in solving recurring problems associated with group living and managing one's relationships to others. Similarly, the structure of social life provides a ready explanation for why these emotions might also be experienced in response to another's behavior. Human groups are not insular. Instead, our social groups have interactions with other groups. For example, conflict between individual members of two different groups often quickly becomes a conflict between the two groups. Furthermore, our notion of the self gets expanded to include the social groups of which we are members (Tajfel & Turner, 1986). Thus, as social agents, we must worry not only about our own behavior and how it implicates the self, but also about the behavior of fellow group members who may have damaging interactions with members of other groups.

Just as self-conscious emotions for our own actions may promote adaptive interpersonal behaviors, feeling self-conscious emotions for the actions of ingroup members may promote adaptive intergroup behaviors (Lickel, Schmader, & Barquissau, 2004; Lickel, Miller, Stenstrom, Denson, & Schmader, 2006). Thus, for example, when an ingroup member harms a member of an outgroup, apology and restitution for the ingroup member's actions (even if not coming from that person him- or herself) may reduce the extent to which members of the harmed outgroup wish to seek retribution against the ingroup member and the entire ingroup. Likewise, distancing from the ingroup member (a shame-based response), and perhaps even expelling him or her from the group, may signal to the harmed outgroup that this person's actions were those of a single individual and do not reflect the sentiment or goals of the group.

JUDGING THE TYPE OF SIGNIFICANCE FOR THE SELF: TWO GENERAL TYPES OF ASSOCIATION

As we argued above, we think that ultimately humans experience self-conscious emotions for the actions of others because this response is functional. However, this functional explanation does not say much about the details of how and why people experience self-conscious emotions for the actions of others. Elsewhere, we have outlined a process model of the distinct appraisals involved in the experience of vicarious shame and guilt (Lickel et al., 2004; Lickel, Schmader, Curtis, Scarnier, & Ames, 2005). In our view, a differentiated understanding of why people experience self-conscious emotions for the actions of others requires an understanding of the ways in which the actions of others might implicate the self.

Based on the writings of past scholars we highlight two broad types of social association that are important to this process. The first of these, *shared identity*, refers to the extent to which people see themselves as sharing a deep and meaningful similarity to others as defined through a common group membership. In the literature on group processes, these identity-based associations are typically studied in terms of shared membership in a broad social category such as race, religion, nationality, or gender. In some cases, sharing membership in a newly created and somewhat meaningless social group is enough to cue these feelings of shared identity (Tajfel, 1970). Thus, one need not personally know other individuals in one's social group to feel this type of association with them. Moreover, these identities have importance to individuals because they expand their sense of self and most often can provide a source of self-enhancement (Aron & Aron, 1996; Tajfel & Turner, 1986; Tropp & Wright, 2001).

The second type of social association, *interpersonal interdependence*, refers to the extent to which people see themselves as bonded together in an interdependent way with others in a group. Our connections to close friends, family, coworkers, and teammates might provide a sense of shared identity, but they also represent something more. These relationships reflect shared goals, communication, and mutual interdependence. The literatures on close relationships and small-group processes examine the processes represented in these kinds of social associations. Whereas the sense of shared identity is a somewhat abstract concept—part of a symbolic sense of self constructed by reference to others—social relationships are more concrete manifestations of the dynamic processes that exist between people who often know one another well. These ideas of shared identity and interpersonal interdependence have deep and long roots in social psychological theorizing, connecting at least loosely to Tonnies's conceptions of *Gesellschaft* and *Gemeinschaft* (1887/1988; see also Lewin, 1948; more recently, cf. Brewer, 2000; Denson, Lickel, Curtis, Stenstrom, & Ames, 2006; Hamilton, Sherman, & Lickel, 1998; Lickel et al., 2000; Prentice, Miller, & Lightdale, 1994; Wilder & Simon, 1998).

We contend that situations involving an observed wrongdoing can be judged as self-relevant due to one or both of these types of social associations. That is, the event can pose a threat to one's sense of identity and/or to one's social relationships. Furthermore, such self-relevance can stem from one's connection to the wrongdoer or to the individual or individuals victimized by the event. The nature of the perceived self-relevance has implications, we believe, for the distinct type of self-conscious emotional response that will be felt. Below we discuss how identity-based concerns and relational-based concerns can each lead to distinct self-conscious negative emotions that might be felt through this process. Although research on these questions has only begun in the last 5–10 years, we summarize some of what is known on these questions as well as highlight areas for future research.

Existing research on self-conscious emotions has tended to stress the distinction between shame and guilt. Traditional perspectives on these emotions maintain that guilt results from viewing oneself as responsible for some specific, contextually bound negative act, whereas shame includes a broader sense of a flawed personal identity (Tangney &

Fischer, 1995). As we discuss in more detail below, we believe that this distinction between shame and guilt is also important for understanding group-based experiences of these emotions. Furthermore, in translating theory on self-conscious emotion to group-conscious emotion we draw a distinction between identity-based concerns and relational concerns as two distinct types of processes that govern how individuals are associated to their social groups. Given that issues of identity and underlying character are key to feelings of shame, group-based shame, we argue, is linked to concerns about maintaining a positive group identity. In contrast, given guilt's role in maintaining interpersonal relationships, we examine group-based guilt as stemming more from perceptions of how one relates to other members of one's ingroup and to the harmed individual.

Although we focus on shame and guilt in our analysis, we think it is important to consider other emotions that may be evoked because of identity or relational concerns. For example, anger is an emotional reaction that may be evoked in addition to and perhaps even as a result of the shame people feel when they experience identity threats. Considering emotions that might co-occur in situations of intergroup transgression will enable us to better distinguish the unique effects of group-conscious emotion on motivation and behavior while also better understanding the profiles of emotional response in such circumstances. Thus, we discuss a set of emotions (and the behaviors that such emotions evoke) including shame, embarrassment, and anger when we discuss identity-based concerns. Likewise, when we discuss relational concerns, we describe several different forms of guilt, as well as emotional reactions of sympathy. Our goal throughout our discussion is to identify key differences among these emotions, particularly in terms of the behaviors that are evoked by each emotion.

IDENTITY-BASED CONCERNS

Shame

As we mentioned above, shame is most often discussed as an emotion that individuals experience when a flaw in their underlying sense of self is revealed to the individual him- or herself and perhaps to others (Tangney & Fischer, 1995). Although shame can be felt for private events, it typically involves a sense of imagined self-exposure (Smith, Webster, Parrott, & Eyre, 2002). Given that individuals gain a sense of identity from their membership in social groups, individuals might feel vicariously ashamed when they witness others who share their group identity engaging in behaviors that are seen as revealing a flawed social identity. In other words, just as through my own misdeeds I might feel ashamed of *who I am,* when a group member engages in a wrongdoing I might feel ashamed of *who we are.* Indeed, in a recent study, we asked participants to recall several guilt- and shame-evoking events involving the wrongdoing of a family member, friend, or ethnic ingroup member and make ratings of their appraisals and emotional reactions to the wrongdoing (Lickel et al., 2005). The more these individuals rated the person's behavior as being relevant to an identity they shared in common with the person, the more they appraised the event as reflecting poorly on their personal identity and the more ashamed they felt. Interestingly, these measures of perceived identity threat did not predict guilt.

Because a sense of identity threat is central to feeling vicarious shame, members of stigmatized groups might be particularly susceptible to experiencing vicarious shame in response to the negative actions of their ingroup (Schmader & Lickel, 2006a). Because negative stereotypes represent cultural statements about the flaws inherent to certain groups, when a group member engages in behaviors that confirm those stereotypes shame might be a dominant response. In line with this prediction, we have found that Latino college students report feeling greater shame for an ingroup member's negative behavior to the degree that the behavior is seen as highly stereotypical. These judgments of stereotypicality do not predict feelings of guilt, sadness, or anxiety (although they do also predict anger).

In other research, we have further established the causal role of identity-based attributions in predicting vicarious shame by manipulating whether the victimized group blames the character of the ingroup or the behavior of the ingroup (Iyer, Schmader, & Lickel, 2007). In these studies, British and U.S. college students read an article about the poor conditions in the parts of postwar Iraq under their country's command. When this article included embedded quotes from Iraqis that blamed poor conditions on the flawed *character* of the British or the American people, students from that respective country reported more shame than when the quotes were written to simply focus on flawed *behavior*. This manipulation did not lead to increases in guilt.

Taken together, these studies highlight the ideas that a self-conscious emotion like shame can be felt for the actions of others, and that this feeling of shame is particularly intense to the degree that the other person's behavior is construed as a threat to one's sense of identity. It is also important to note that these perceptions of social identity threat do not predict greater feelings of guilt, but instead are unique to the self-conscious emotional experience of shame.

Embarrassment

Embarrassment and shame are similar in that both arise from identity-based concerns, but several scholars have highlighted differences between them (e.g., Babcock & Sabini, 1990; Sabini, Garvey, & Hall, 2001; Smith et al., 2002). While both emotions seem to involve a sense of self-exposure and smallness and motivate avoidance behaviors (Tangney et al., 1996), people feel embarrassed when they think that *others will see them as flawed*, but feel ashamed when they personally fear that they *are flawed* (Sabini et al., 2001). Furthermore, whereas shame more often stems from behavior that oversteps moral proscriptions, prototypical scenarios of embarrassment involve behaviors that go against social convention (Parrott, Sabini, & Silver, 1988). These distinctions between these two emotions suggest they often will co-occur if an individual both fears that the flaw is present and fears what others might think about it. Only embarrassment will result in situations where one does not internalize the sense of a flawed self.

In most of our research on vicarious self-conscious emotions embarrassment is highly correlated with shame and the terms "embarrassed" and "ashamed" load on the same factor (Lickel et al., 2005; Schmader & Lickel, 2006b). However, it is unlikely that shame and embarrassment always co-occur in vicarious situations. In fact, there appears to be an asymmetry to the relationship between these emotions. In one study, participants were asked to recall a time when they felt embarrassed, ashamed, or guilty for another person's behavior and to make ratings of the specific emotions they felt to the event they described (Schmader & Lickel, 2002). Interestingly, people who were asked to recall a time when they felt ashamed for another person's actions reported high levels of both shame and embarrassment. However, people asked to recall a time when they felt embarrassed for another person's actions reported significantly higher levels of embarrassment than shame. Thus, feelings of vicarious shame often involve a component feeling of embarrassment, although vicarious embarrassment can be felt without shame.

Furthermore, when feeling embarrassed for the wrongs carried out by others, we might also imagine that believing in the existence of the flawed identity would be critical for distinguishing embarrassment from shame. For example, when considering emotional responses to the stereotypic actions of ingroup members, we would predict that those individuals who personally endorse the negative stereotype about their group would feel both ashamed and embarrassed. For them, witnessing others who behave stereotypically is a reminder of the flawed social identity they believe they possess. In contrast, those who completely reject the validity of the stereotype might feel embarrassed that their fellow group member would give others the impression that the stereotype is valid, but they might not feel particularly ashamed by the action. This is an intriguing question that merits further study.

Although little research has tried to systematically distinguish vicarious shame from vicarious embarrassment, studies have examined the tendency to experience embarrassment at observing others behaving in awkward situations. This research has found that manipulations that cue an empathic perception of the other person or that establish some prior relationship to the individual increase the tendency to feel a sense of vicarious embarrassment (Miller, 1987). In addition, Shearn, Spellman, and Meirick (1999) show that individuals blush when watching a friend sing and the intensity of this vicarious blushing was not significantly different from that of the actor herself when rewatching the video. Other more recent research shows that a fear of negative evaluation is associated with a propensity to experience vicarious embarrassment among men, although women reported higher levels of vicarious embarrassment regardless of their chronic fear of evaluation (Thorton, 2003). These findings are consistent with our assertion that variables that heighten concern of identity threat or represent greater self–other overlap would intensify feelings of embarrassment.

Anger

Although our focus in this chapter is on self-conscious emotions, it is worth discussing that the types of events that concern us elicit other emotions as well. In fact, our research has revealed that anger is the strongest emotional response that individuals have to the wrongdoings of those with whom they share a group identity. When individuals recall or witness firsthand a member of their ingroup engaging in some wrongful act, their feelings of shame are highly correlated with anger (Schmader & Lickel, 2006a; Johns, Schmader, & Lickel, 2005; Iyer et al., 2007) and both are significantly predicted by appraisals of identity threat (Schmader & Lickel, 2006a; Iyer et al., 2007).

This relationship between vicarious shame and anger is interesting given that personal shame has also been linked to anger and hostility (Tangney, Wagner, Fletcher, & Gramzow, 1992). In the case of personal wrongdoings, it is posited that hostility becomes a defensive response whereby blame is externalized in order to deflect attention from the acknowledgment of one's own failings (Tracy & Robins, 2004). Whereas this external attribution might often be unjustified in cases of personal shame, an external attribution is a more appropriate response to the wrongdoings of ingroup members. Even still, the motive to avoid feeling a reflected sense of shame might fuel a stronger desire to blame and punish a group member who has mismanaged the group identity or broken social norms. For example, in the intergroup literature, it is commonly found that individuals derogate ingroup members particularly harshly when those individuals break the norms of the group (Marques, Yzerbyt, & Leyens, 1988). Ironically, the same behavior enacted by an outgroup member does not receive the same harsh reaction. This derogation no doubt plays a functional role in managing the behavior of group members. Anger is the likely candidate for the emotion that drives this social response, although the self-conscious feeling of shame that accompanies it might also promote efforts to distance oneself and one's social identity from the offending group member.

One interesting question for future research delving into the role of anger in such situations is that the perceived intentionality of the wrongdoing is likely to be a strong predictor of this angry response. Individuals who knowingly engage in negative behaviors that threaten a shared group identity are likely to elicit especially strong feelings of anger from their fellow group members. Furthermore, anger might get expressed as a desire to punish the group member in a public way so as to send the message to the offended outgroup or individual that the action did not go unnoticed and will be dealt with.

GROUP IDENTIFICATION AS A MODERATOR OF IDENTITY-BASED CONCERNS

In discussing how identity concerns affect emotional responses to the wrongdoings of others, one must consider how the individual's identification with the relevant social identity might moderate his or her affective response. Research suggests that identification can enter into the interpretative process at two points. First, one's identification with the group can affect how the act is interpreted during the initial construal of the event. Because individuals who are highly identified with their social group are motivated to see that group in a positive light, identification can inhibit the extent to which they appraise the event as wholly negative or place blame on an ingroup member. For example, Doojse, Branscombe, Spears, and Manstead (1998), in their study of Dutch guilt reactions to their country's history of colonialism, found that identification moderated collective guilt reactions when colonialism was framed as having a mixture of positive and negative consequences. In this condition, people who were highly identified reported less guilt than individuals who were weakly identified. Presumably this effect occurred because identification affected how people construed their country's actions, with highly identified individuals framing their country's history in a positive light. Although shame was not measured in this study, we would predict that this inhibitory effect of identification might be particularly strong on feelings of shame given the sensitivity of shame to identity threat.

In fact, we have found that the biasing effects of identification do occur on people's reports of shame when examining how people react to specific wrongdoings of particular ingroup members. For example, Johns et al. (2005) examined the role of identification with one's national identity in predicting emotional reactions to instances of anti-Arab prejudice after 9-11. For events that were less severe (e.g., racial slurs or jokes that were not directly targeted at an individual as compared to violent hate crimes), highly identified Americans reported less shame than weakly identified Americans. This same relationship was not found for other negative emotions, including guilt, after controlling for the effects on shame. Presumably, the relatively benign nature of these events allowed those with the greatest investment in maintaining a positive social identity the opportunity to rationalize the event and avoid shame.

This research suggests that identification can inhibit the experience of self-conscious emotion for the wrongful behaviors of others. However, there are other circumstances in which group identification can intensify feelings of self-conscious emotion. Specifically, for events that cannot be easily justified or denied and for which blame is clearly placed on an ingroup member, greater identification signals greater inclusion of the group identity in the self-concept (Tropp & Wright, 2001). As Ortony et al. (1988) foresaw, this greater degree of unit association between self and other can then facilitate a greater degree of identity threat, and, as a result, we would argue, a greater degree of shame. Indeed, in Johns et al.'s (2005) study of Americans' emotional reactions to anti-Arab prejudice, highly identified Americans reported more shame for events that were unambiguously severe, prejudicial, and harmful to others. In other words, the relationship between identification and feelings of vicarious shame were significantly moderated by the severity of the event. Thus, high identification is a double-edged sword, minimizing one's emotional reaction when a less severe event can be favorably interpreted or explained away, but increasing the self-relevance (and therefore the emotional reaction) when an unambiguously negative event cannot be framed in a positive light.

The complex role of group identification can also be seen when examining different aspects of what it means to be highly identified with one's group. For example, Tajfel (1978) defines social identity as "that part of an individual's self-concept which derives from . . . knowledge of . . . membership of a social group (or groups) together with the value and emotional significance attached to that membership" (p. 63). This characterization suggests that identification includes both cognitive and affective components. In addition to mere knowledge of category membership, the cognitive component might also include the degree of overlap between one's concept of self and one's concept of group (e.g., Tropp & Wright, 2001). This notion of self–group overlap might be considered conceptually distinct from the affective feeling or valenced attitude one has toward one's group. Recent research suggests that this distinction might have consequences for the emotional response one has to ingroup wrongdoing.

In a recent study, we asked Latino participants to recall a time when a member of their ethnic ingroup behaved stereotypically and to rate their emotional reactions to that episode (Schmader & Lickel, 2006a). Before doing this, they also rated the importance they generally place on their ethnic identity as a component of self-definition (i.e., the cognitive aspect of identification) and the private regard they have for their ethnic identity (i.e., the affective feeling toward the group). These two aspects of identification (which themselves are positively correlated) had different unique relationships with feelings of shame for the ingroup member's actions. The importance placed on ethnic identity predicted more shame for the stereotypical actions of an ethnic ingroup member, but the degree to which Latinos saw their ingroup positively in general predicted less shame for those same acts (Schmader & Lickel, 2006a).

Using a similar framework, Roccas and colleagues (Roccas, Klar, & Liviatan, 2004) use the term *attachment* to refer to the extent to which the group is an important aspect of one's self-concept (the cognitive component) and the term *glorification* to refer to seeing one's group as superior to others (the affective component). Their research indicates that it may be glorification of one's group in particular that leads one to minimize wrongdoings committed by ingroup members (thus minimizing group-based shame or guilt), whereas attachment determines the extent to which an ingroup member's actions are appraised as self-relevant. In their research, high levels of glorification predicted lower levels of shame and guilt for one's group, whereas high levels of attachment predicted greater shame and guilt for the wrongdoings of the ingroup. Together, this research suggests that the feeling of cognitive overlap between self and group might intensify the sting of an ingroup member's negative behavior, while at the same time the affective feeling toward the group might predict a tendency to make group-serving attributions as a way of minimizing the threat to identity.

MOTIVATIONS THAT STEM FROM IDENTITY-BASED EMOTIONS

As discussed earlier, people are concerned about managing their personal and social identities and protecting those identities from being discredited. Because of the nature of typical human social structures, the blameworthy actions of others with whom we share a group membership can potentially discredit us as individuals. Shame, embarrassment, and ingroup-directed anger appear to be prominent affective responses to such situations. In turn, these emotions evoke particular motivational responses that help individuals cope with the event.

As in the literature on self-conscious emotions for personal actions, it appears that group-based shame is particularly linked to a motivation to distance from the shame-provoking event, an association we have now found in numerous studies (Lickel et al., 2005; Johns et al., 2005; Schmader & Lickel, 2006a, 2006b). However, in our work, we have been interested in examining other motivational responses than merely a general desire to distance from the event. For example, in some research we have examined whether there is a distinction between distancing from the event, distancing from the group identity, or distancing from the wrongdoer (Johns et al., 2005). However, we have also examined other strategies that are distinct from distancing. For example, we have found that under some circumstances people are also motivated to personally engage in behaviors that repair the image of the group. In our study of Latinos' reactions to the stereotypical behaviors of an ingroup member, we examined several of these potential responses (Schmader & Lickel, 2006a). Our analyses revealed that shame and anger (but not guilt, sadness, or anxiety) predicted a motivation to distance oneself from the group member who committed the negative act. However, shame was the only emotion that was uniquely predictive of wanting to distance oneself from one's ethnic group or do something to repair the damaged image of the group.

These data suggest, first, that for groups where exit is possible, the negative behaviors of ingroup members can elicit feelings of shame that then motivate individuals to leave the group. This finding contributes to our understanding of the emotional mechanisms that underlie some of the responses that people have to their membership in a group with a devalued identity (Tajfel & Turner, 1986). In addition to providing insight into how people manage their identities, these findings also reveal something interesting and previously unexplored about shame. Shame is typically thought to elicit behaviors that facilitate escape from situations that induce feelings of shame or escape from the shame feeling itself. This assertion has often led to an assumption that shame is always maladaptive because it leads to avoidance behaviors. However, if shame motivates a desire to change the image of the group, this strategy represents a more proactive response to shameful events. In fact, we believe that shame not only motivates this desire to boost the positivity of one's social identity in response to another's wrongdoing, but that it also likely motivates a desire to change one's own identity in response to personal-enacted wrongs. This is an interesting avenue for future research that has implications for what might motivate people to enter into psychotherapy or otherwise seek to change aspects of themselves.

In other applications, understanding the motivations elicited by specific emotions could have implications for the type of collective action individuals are willing to take in response to the wrongs of their ingroup. For example, if we consider the case of war protest, we might expect shame and anger (and guilt) to play a different role in predicting the type of protest message one endorses. In a recent study, we examined British and U.S. college students' reactions of shame, guilt, and ingroup-directed anger for their country's occupation of Iraq (Iyer et al., 2007). As mentioned earlier, a manipulation of identity threat in which Iraqis interviewed in the bogus article criticized the character of one's country (versus the actions of one's country) magnified feelings of shame and ingroup-directed anger (but not guilt). In turn, ingroup-directed anger motivated a variety of political action tendencies, including supporting compensation for Iraqis, confronting ingroup members who support the occupation, and withdrawing from Iraq. Interestingly, although feelings of shame and ingroup-directed anger were correlated, shame predicted only support for withdrawing from Iraq. These two studies indicate that ingroup-directed anger and shame may both a product of identity threat under many circumstances, but have somewhat distinct consequences for behavior. Whereas anger motivates protest in any form against the negative acts of the ingroup, shame primarily motivates a desire to withdraw the group from the shame-eliciting situation.

RELATIONAL-BASED CONCERNS

The preceding discussion summarizes the ways in which feeling a sense of shared identity with a wrongdoer can make one susceptible to feeling self-conscious emotions like shame, embarrassment, and anger when an ingroup member engages in wrongdoing. Situations of observed wrongdoing not only have implications for one's sense of identity but also negatively affect one's social relationships. That is, when we have a sense of relational interdependence with the wrongdoer or the victimized party, these events can have implications for those relationships. We take the perspective that self-conscious emotions like guilt can specifically be understood as responses to these relationship-based concerns.

Guilt

Guilt is an emotion that is thought to be important for signaling that damage has been done to an important social relationship (Baumeister et al., 1994). Whereas shame stems from making a dispositional attribution for a negative event that has occurred, guilt stems from making an internal attribution that is constrained to a specific behavior (Tangney & Fischer, 1995; Tracy & Robins, 2004). Feelings of shame make us want to undo who we are, whereas feelings of guilt make us want to undo only what we have done (Niedenthal, Tangney, & Gavanski, 1994). Prior research on personal feelings of guilt (i.e., guilt for one's own actions), most typically has examined guilt stemming from appraisals of personal responsibility. For example, people feel a sense of guilt when through their actions or inactions harm is done to others. In some cases, neither the behavior nor the consequences were intended, yet the appraisal that one's behavior was the most direct cause of the negative event elicits feelings of guilt. There are, however, other situations in which one feels guilty. For example, people tend to feel a sense of guilt when they become aware that through an unjust practice of distribution they have been unfairly advantaged whereas others have been unfairly disadvantaged (Baumeister et al., 1994). Because these two types of appraisals constitute somewhat different pathways to guilt, we address how each applies to situations of vicarious wrongdoing.

Responsibility-Based Guilt

If we start with the premise that guilt is an emotion that can stem from attributing a negative act to controllable behaviors carried by the self (Tracy & Robins, 2004; Weiner,

1986), we can take two perspectives on how guilty feelings could arise from the observed wrongdoings of others. First, in a process that we have termed *vicarious guilt*, individuals can perceive themselves (rightly or wrongly) as part of a causal chain in which their own behaviors could have had some influence on the behavior of the wrongdoer. For example, a parent might feel guilty when his child pushes another child on the playground, if the parent believes that he should have had a closer eye on what his child was doing. We have argued that it is one's relational independence with a wrongdoer that prompts these appraisals of control. Laypeople have an intuitive theory of social influence in groups and assume that people can and do influence the behavior of others with whom they are interpersonally interdependent. For example, people's folk theories of social influence are known to affect how they judge the collective responsibility of others (Denson et al., 2005; Lickel, Rutchick, Hamilton, & Sherman, 2006; Lickel, Schmader, & Hamilton, 2003). Presumably, these same processes shape how individuals come to feel some indirect responsibility themselves for the actions of others.

We have tested this idea in our study of emotional reactions to wrongful behaviors carried out by individuals associated with respondents' family, friendship, and ethnic identities (Lickel et al., 2005). In this study, the more participants felt a degree of interdependence with the wrongdoer of a given event, the more they thought they should have been able to control the person's actions and the more guilty they felt in response to the event. Ratings of interdependence were weakly (or not) related to appraisals of image threat and feelings of shame. Similarly, in our study of Latino's reactions to the stereotypical behavior of ethnic ingroup members, perceptions of stereotypicality predicted shame and anger, but one's level of interdependence with the group member predicted guilt (Schmader & Lickel, 2006a). These data highlight that we feel ashamed when another person's actions tarnish our social identity, but we are more likely to feel guilty when that person is someone we know well and interact with frequently. It is the interdependence of our relationship to the wrongdoer that cues us to think of how we might have controlled or prevented that person's behavior.

Some might counter that guilt in these situations is not entirely vicarious since it involves seeing oneself as part of a causal chain that led up to the wrongdoing. It is important to note that this emotional response is possible even when it is unrealistic to think that the perceiver could have influenced the other person's actions. The interdependent nature of the relationship makes us believe that we *should have* been able to prevent the behavior, even if we realize that we *could not* actually do so. In addition, many of these situations likely involve a reinterpretation of fairly innocuous behaviors that would not have elicited guilt in the absence of the other person's wrongdoing. For example, a parent might feel guilty for allowing her teenage son to go to a party where the son is later arrested for property damage. If the son had engaged in no wrongdoing, guilt would not be a likely or appropriate response to her behavior (i.e., allowing him to attend the party). In other words, without the other person's wrongdoing, there would be no feeling of guilt. In this sense, the emotional response is vicarious because it is elicited only in response to the other person's actions.

In addition to situations where an interdependent relationship to a wrongdoer cues appraisals of control and feelings of guilt, there are also documented cases of *collective guilt* responses in which an emotional reaction stems from attributing a negative action to one's ingroup as a whole (e.g., Doosje et al., 1998; see also Branscombe & Doosje, 2004). In these cases, even though the individual has no personal responsibility for the wrong and no real ability to influence those directly responsible, the blame placed on an expanded notion of the self as part of a larger group is sufficient to elicit feelings of guilt. For example, in an experiment by Doosje et al. (1998), participants reported greater guilt upon learning that their miminal (i.e., a laboratory-created) group (but not them personally) had a history of discriminating against another minimal group. Simply attributing a negative and relationally harmful act to the ingroup was enough to elevate feelings of guilt. In other work, Iyer, Leach, and Crosby (2003) found that white college students report more guilt for the United States's history of racial discrimination if they are primed to focus on the harm *done by the ingroup* as opposed to focus on the negative consequences for the outgroup. Thus, even though one feels no responsibility for causing the event, the collective self might still feel a sense of responsibility for righting the wrong that has been done.

One thing that is less clear from this work on collective guilt is whether this focus on ingroup responsibility uniquely elevates guilt as opposed to other self-conscious emotions like shame. The studies described earlier generally only measured guilt. Other data suggest that an attribution of ingroup responsibility might increase both guilt and shame reactions. In studies of college students' emotional reactions to their country's involvement in the Iraq war (Iyer et al., 2007), students reported both more shame and more guilt to the degree that they held their country responsible for the negative consequences of the war and occupation. Given that an attribution to the ingroup involves both an assertion of blame and a focus on a now-tarnished social identity, perhaps both relational and identity-based concerns are cued by these situations.

Inequity-Based Guilt

Another form of collective guilt can be elicited by the awareness that one is advantaged in a social system that unfairly disadvantages or even discriminates against other groups. In some of the cases already described, this appraisal process could be playing some role in eliciting guilty feelings. For example, a person who feels guilty for his or her country's occupation or colonization of another country might partly feel guilt because of the blame attribution to the ingroup, but might also feel a degree of guilt for the economic or political advantages that might result from the power exerted against the other nation. Inequity-based guilt might also stem from an assumption that resources are distributed in a zero-sum manner where the advantages that one enjoys are seen as coming at a proportionate cost to others. In more direct evidence for inequity-based collective guilt, Swim and Miller (1999) have shown that white Americans' feelings of guilt for racial discrimination in the United States are largely predicted by beliefs about white privilege. Iyer et al. (2003) have replicated this relationship between white privilege and white guilt and have also shown that there is a link between seeing one's ingroup as perpetrating discrimination and feeling unjustly privileged. Finally, in an experimental test of the role of perceived inequality in predicting guilt, Powell, Branscombe, and Schmitt (2005) manipulated a focus on ingroup privilege or outgroup disadvantage and showed that framing racial inequality in the United States in terms of ingroup advantages increases feelings of collective guilt and also decreases racist attitudes and ingroup identification.

Sympathy

In each of the cases above, the self-conscious feeling of guilt involves a recognition that through the ingroup's actions or unjust distribution others have been harmed. In the first case, one's relation to the perpetrator primes appraisals of personal or group blame. In the second case, one's relation to, and concern for, the victim might be important in cuing a self-conscious feeling of guilt. Related to these guilty feelings are feelings of sympathy for the harmed party. Although sympathy is not itself categorized as a self-conscious emotion, it is an emotional response that likely plays a role in the situations that concern us. For example, insofar as a person has a close relationship to the outgroup or sees him- or herself as similar to the outgroup, his or her reactions of sympathy and perhaps also guilt may be increased.

Several lines of research point in this direction. First, social cognition scholars have documented the effects of perspective taking on judgments of outgroups. Galinsky and Moskowitz (2000) found that when people were instructed to take the perspective of members of an outgroup, their evaluations of the outgroup were improved. Galinsky and Moskowitz argued that this result was likely driven by an increasing overlap between one's self-representation and the cognitive representation of the outgroup. More recently, Ames (2004) has shown that when perceivers make judgments about outgroup members, they switch between projection (using the self as a basis for simulating the thoughts of the target person) and stereotyping, depending on how similar the perceiver is to the target—projection is higher when perceived similarity is high. Thus, when making sense of the thoughts, feelings, and behavior of outgroup individuals, there are at least some instances in which people are likely to use themselves as a basis for judgment, which in turn may increase an individual's feelings of empathy, sympathy, and possibly even guilt.

Based on the same reasoning described above, there have been direct efforts to investigate the extent to which taking the perspective of a harmed outgroup affects sympathy and guilt for their outcomes. For example, Zebel, Doojse, and Spears (2004) discuss a series of studies examining how perspective taking affects collective guilt among the Dutch for the historical actions of their ingroup. One finding from this research is that measures of perspective taking are positively correlated with feelings of guilt. A second finding is that the effect of perspective taking on guilt is moderated by the degree of identification with the ingroup. People who are highly identified with their group exhibit reactance to the perspective-taking manipulation and report lower levels of guilt (than when compared to a no perspective taking condition). These findings suggest potentially interesting questions that might be addressed in the literature on personal guilt, in which it has been argued that perspective taking can increase empathy and guilt for people that one has harmed (e.g., Leith & Baumester, 1998). Ironically, leading those with inflated self-esteem (i.e., narcissism) to take the perspective of others might actually lead to increased threat and therefore less empathy and guilt than when not taking another's perspective. In particular, it may be that such perspective taking might lead to shame and other-directed anger rather than empathy among people high in narcissism.

Another key issue is the extent to which perspective taking differentially affects guilt versus sympathy. The work by Zebel et al. (2004) did not differentiate these responses. However, other work by Iyer et al. (2003) indicates that guilt and sympathy are differentiated with regard to self-focus (see also Miron, Branscombe, & Schmitt, 2006). Sympathy for others is increased when one takes an "other" focus (i.e., tries to take the perspective of the harmed person). In one study (Iyer et al., 2003, Study 2), white participants were either primed to focus attention on how whites had discriminated against blacks (self-focus) or on the consequences of discrimination on blacks (other focus). Feelings of sympathy were higher in the other focus condition, whereas feelings of guilt were higher in the self-focus condition. As we discuss below, these feelings of guilt and sympathy may also have different consequences for intergroup behavior.

MOTIVATIONS THAT STEM FROM RELATIONAL-BASED CONCERNS

Relational concerns, and the emotions that are linked to them, drive at least two types of responses. First, relationship-based concerns may motivate efforts to repair the consequences of the event for people who have been harmed (e.g., Baumeister et al., 1994; Lickel et al., 2005; Tangney et al., 1996). Second, relationship-based concerns may also motivate efforts to change the larger social or intergroup situation that gave rise to the harm in the first place (e.g., Iyer et al., 2003; Swim & Miller, 1999). Although these two motivations may seem closely related, research indicates that there may be somewhat distinct emotional predictors of them.

An early focus of group-based emotion researchers was to examine the extent to which collective guilt motivates apology and/or compensation for outgroups that were harmed historically by one's ingroup. As we discussed earlier, Doojse et al. (1998) studied Dutch reactions to their nation's history of colonialism in Indonesia and found that students felt more guilt when these events were framed in an unambiguously negative way. Interestingly, the same patterns observed for guilt were also observed for participant's ratings of the degree to which Indonesians should be compensated for the historical consequences of Dutch colonialism. Thus, Dutch collective guilt for their nation's historical actions appears to be linked to people's motivation to repair a damaged intergroup relationship. In a different cultural context, McGarty et al. (2005) found that guilt predicted white Australian's support for an official apology to indigenous Australians for their historical mistreatment by the government and white settlers. Studies examining guilt based on perceived inequity have also replicated these patterns (Iyer et al., 2003; Swim & Miller, 1999). For example, Iyer et al. (2003) found that among Americans, white guilt for racial inequalities predicted support for affirmative action programs that are specifically designed to compensate for the advantages of whites over nonwhites.

Finally, in our work focused on vicarious guilt responses to the actions of particular ingroup members, we have also found a link between guilt and efforts to make reparations to others who were harmed by an ingroup member's behavior. In a study examining vicarious shame and guilt reactions in the context of family, friendship, and ethnic group identities (Lickel et al., 2005), we found that guilt predicted reparative behavior (whereas shame promoted distancing behaviors). We have more recently replicated this relationship in a set of studies examining vicarious shame and guilt reactions to the blameworthy actions of romantic partners (Curtis, Lickel, Schmader, & Collins, 2007). In this context as well, vicarious guilt promotes a motivation to repair and/or apologize for the partner's blameworthy actions toward people outside the relationship.

These findings about the role of guilt in promoting intergroup reparations paint a picture of group-based guilt that is consistent with the framing of personal guilt as an adaptive emotion that promotes behaviors that restore damaged social relationships (Baumeister et al., 1994). Although there is evidence for the positive role of guilt in intergroup relations, some scholars have suggested that there might be some limitations to the prosocial consequences of guilt. According to Iyer's viewpoint (e.g., Iyer et al., 2003), situations of intergroup disadvantage can elicit both guilt and sympathy among members of the advantaged group. Both of these emotions relate to efforts to rectify the inequality. Iyer and colleagues argue, however, that if guilt is an emotion that is more focused on the self and sympathy an emotion that is more focused on the other, there might be subtle but important distinctions between the types of reparations these two emotions elicit. If guilt motivates a desire to relieve personal distress (Miron et al., 2006), then reparative attempts might focus on restitution for a specific wrong done in the past. In contrast, if sympathy motivates a desire to relieve distress in the harmed outgroup, then reparative attempts might also include more systemic or long-term changes that will also prevent future harm. In their initial research on this question, Iyer et al. (2003) provide evidence that white Americans' feelings of guilt for race-based inequalities predicted support for compensatory policies to make up for past wrongs, whereas white Americans' sympathy predicted support for policies that would create equal opportunity for blacks in the future. Future work is needed to establish the generalizability of this distinction, but it raises an interesting possibility for the limitations of guilt.

CONCLUSIONS AND FUTURE DIRECTIONS

In this chapter, we have provided an overview of research conducted on self-conscious emotional reactions that people might have to the wrongdoings of others. We have also contrasted these self-conscious emotional experiences to other emotional responses (e.g., anger, sympathy) that are likely to be evoked in these types of situations. Clearly, we have only provided a summary of a young but rapidly expanding body of research. Readers interested in any of the themes we have written about will find more detail and differing perspectives in other recent edited volumes (e.g., Branscombe & Doosje, 2004; Mackie & Smith, 2002). In what follows, we discuss areas that we think should be the focus of future work.

First, we think that scholars studying group-based shame and guilt (and related emotions) should press their work more toward understanding the consequences of these emotions in actually affecting intergroup conflict and prejudice reduction. For example, we have ourselves argued that the behaviors motivated by shame and guilt (e.g., distancing and repair) may play a role in defusing intergroup conflicts before they spiral into retributive aggression (Lickel et al., 2004; Lickel, Miller, et al., 2006). Evidence about these ideas is lacking. However, other scholars are making more direct connections to the role of group-based self-conscious emotions in reducing intergroup prejudice. For example, Powell et al. (2005) found that manipulations that focus attention on how one's ingroup is advantaged over other outgroups led to a marked decrease in prejudice toward the outgroup, and that reduction in prejudice was mediated by guilt.

The preceding point is directed primarily to scholars working within the intergroup relations literatures. However, we also think that work on group-based emotions may raise some interesting questions for researchers studying self-conscious emotions more generally. For example, some intergroup scholars have argued that there may be some limits to the positive benefits of guilt (Iyer et al., 2003). Given the generally positive framing of guilt in much of the traditional scholarship on guilt, we think that this critique provides a stimulus for considering the potential limitations of guilt for one's own actions, particularly in contrast to sympathy for the harmed victim. Although these two emotions might often co-occur, it might be sympathy that is the important predictor of enacting changes that would prevent future wrongs, whereas guilt might simply motivate efforts to repair past wrongs.

In a related vein, we think that scholarship on group-based emotions paints a more positive picture of shame and anger than the intrapersonal approach to shame. For example, in at least two of our studies, anger for an ingroup members' wrongdoing motivates a wide array of potentially beneficial political behaviors, whereas in both studies guilt's connection to positive behaviors was limited (Iyer et al., 2007). Furthermore, in some of our other work, we have found that group-based shame promotes a motivation to disconfirm the negative group image created by an ingroup member's behavior (a motivation distinct from distancing from that person or from the group). We think it is possible that shame for one's own actions may have more positive consequences than traditional emotion research has recognized. In other work, we (Lickel et al., 2007) have found that shame for one's actions is a strong predictor of a motivation to change oneself after a moral transgression (a motivation distinct from apologizing/repairing the event or distancing from it). These are a few of the areas where recent advances in group-based emotion could inform the processes involved in self-conscious emotions more broadly.

The final area where we encourage more research is in understanding the developmental processes and cultural variation associated with group-based emotions. Our work has largely focused on studying adults in Western societies. We believe that the developmental processes underlying group-based self-conscious emotions are likely to be complex, and should emerge relatively late in childhood after individuals have developed not just a sense of self-awareness, but a sense of social identity and perspective taking as well. Understanding developmental processes can also aid in understanding the roots of cultural variation in group-based self-conscious emotions. There is some evidence that group-based shame and guilt are more prevalent in collectivist cultures than elsewhere (Stipek, 1998). However, at present, we do not have a very firm understanding of the nature of cultural variation in collective and group-based self-conscious emotions. This represents a key arena for future work.

Self-conscious emotions are important aspects of our psychology that make humans unique compared to most other species. Just as shame and guilt for one's own actions play an important role in regulating our behavior as individuals, feelings of shame or guilt for the actions of others are likely to play an important role in regulating intergroup and interpersonal relationships. In this chapter, we have identified how identity concerns and relational concerns are critical for predicting when and why a person might feel self-conscious emotions for the negative actions of another person. Not only does research on personal feelings of shame and guilt better inform our understanding of intergroup relations, but research on group-based emotions and intergroup behavior can also yield insights into the basic nature of these emotional experiences. We hope that future research will not only advance our understanding of self-conscious emotions and intergroup relations separately, but that research that integrates these two literatures will flourish as well.

REFERENCES

Ames, D. R. (2004). Inside the mind reader's toolkit: Projection and stereotyping in mental state inference. *Journal of Personality and Social Psychology, 87,* 340–353.

Aron, E. N., & Aron, A. (1996). Love and the expansion of the self: The state of the model. *Personal Relationships, 3,* 45–58.

Babcock, M. K., & Sabini, J. (1990). On differentiating embarrassment from shame. *European Journal of Social Psychology, 20,* 151–160.

Baumeister, R. F., Stillwell, A. M., & Heatherton, T. F. (1994). Guilt: An interpersonal approach. *Psychological Bulletin, 115,* 243–267.

Beer, J. S., Heerey, E. N., Keltner, D., Scabini, D., & Knight, R. T. (2003). The regulatory function of self-conscious emotion: Insights from patients with orbitofrontal damage. *Journal of Personality and Social Psychology, 85,* 594–604.

Branscombe, N. R., & Doojse, B. (Eds.). (2004). *Collective guilt: International perspectives*. New York: Cambridge University Press.

Brewer, M. B. (2000). Superordinate goals versus superordinate identity as bases of intergroup cooperation. In D. Capozza & R. Brown (Eds.), *Social identity processes: Trends in theory and research* (pp. 117–132). London: Sage.

Cosmides, L., & Tooby, J. (2000). Evolutionary psychology and the emotions. In M. Lewis & J. M. Haviland-Jones (Eds.), *Handbook of emotions* (2nd ed., pp. 91–115). New York: Guilford Press.

Curtis, M., Lickel, B., Schmader, T., & Collins, N. (2007). *Reactions to the blameworthy acts of a partner: Vicarious shame and guilt in romantic relationships*. Unpublished manuscript, University of Southern California.

Denson, T., Lickel, B., Curtis, M., Stenstrom, D., & Ames, D. R. (2006). The roles of entitativity and essentiality in judgments of collective responsibility. *Group Processes and Intergroup Relations, 9*, 43–61.

Doojse, B., Branscombe, N. R., Spears, R., & Manstead, A. S. R. (1998). Guilty by association: When one's group has a negative history. *Journal of Personality and Social Psychology, 75*, 872–886.

Eisenberg, N. (2000). Emotion, regulation, and moral development. *Annual Review of Psychology, 51*, 665–697.

Galinsky, A. D., & Moskowitz, G. B. (2000). Perspective-taking: Decreasing stereotype expression, stereotype accessibility, and in-group favoritism. *Journal of Personality and Social Psychology, 78*, 708–724.

Hamilton, D. L., Sherman, S. J., & Lickel, B. (1998). Perceiving social groups: The importance of the entitativity continuum. In C. Sedikides, J. Schopler, & C. A. Insko (Eds.), *Intergroup cognition and intergroup behavior* (pp. 47–74). Mahwah, NJ: Erlbaum.

Heerey, E., Keltner, D., & Capps, L. M. (2005). Making sense of self-conscious emotion: Linking theory of mind and emotion in children with autism. *Emotion, 3*, 394–400.

Iyer, A., Leach, C. W., & Crosby, F. J. (2003). White guilt and racial compensation: The benefits and limits of self-focus. *Personality and Social Psychology Bulletin, 29*, 117–129.

Iyer, A., Schmader, T., & Lickel, B. (2007). Why individuals protest the perceived transgressions of their country: The role of anger, shame, and guilt. *Personality and Social Psychology Bulletin, 4*, 572–587.

Johns, M., Schmader, T., & Lickel, B. (2005). Ashamed to be an American?: The role of identification in predicting vicarious shame for anti-Arab prejudice after 9-11. *Self and Identity, 4*, 331–348.

Keltner, D. (1995). The signs of appeasement: Evidence for the distinct displays of embarrassment, amusement, and shame. *Journal of Personality and Social Psychology, 68*, 441–454.

Leith, K. P., & Baumeister, R. F. (1998). Empathy, shame, guilt, and narratives of interpersonal conflicts: Guilt-prone people are better at perspective taking. *Journal of Personality, 66*, 1–37.

Lewin, K. (1948). *Resolving social conflicts*. New York: Harper.

Lickel, B., Hamilton, D. L., Wieczorkowska, G., Lewis, A., Sherman, S. J., & Uhles, A. N. (2000). Varieties of groups and the perception of group entitativity. *Journal of Personality and Social Psychology, 78*, 223–246.

Lickel, B., Matta, S., Ronquillo, J., Denson, T., Curtis, M., & Schmader, T. (2007). *Motivation to change the self: Another motivation evoked by self-conscious emotions*. Unpublished manuscript, University of Southern California.

Lickel, B., Miller, N., Stenstrom, D., Denson, T. F., & Schmader, T. (2006). Vicarious retribution: The role of collective blame in intergroup aggression. *Personality and Social Psychology Review, 10*, 372–390.

Lickel, B., Rutchick, A., Hamilton, D. L., & Sherman, S. J. (2006). Intuitive theories of group types and relational principles. *Journal of Experimental Social Psychology, 42*, 28–39.

Lickel, B., Schmader, T., & Barquissau, M. (2004). The evocation of moral emotions in intergroup contexts: The distinction between collective guilt and collective shame. In N. R. Branscombe & B. Doosje (Eds.), *Collective guilt: International perspectives* (pp. 35–55). New York: Cambridge University Press.

Lickel, B., Schmader, T., Curtis, M., Scarnier, M., & Ames, D. R. (2005). Vicarious shame and guilt. *Group Processes and Intergroup Relations, 8,* 145–147.

Lickel, B., Schmader, T., & Hamilton, D. L. (2003). A case of collective responsibility: Who else is to blame for the Columbine High School shootings? *Personality and Social Psychology Bulletin, 29,* 194–204.

Mackie, D. M., & Smith, E. R. (Eds.). (2002). *Beyond prejudice: From outgroup hostility to intergroup emotions.* Philadelphia: Psychology Press.

Marques, J. M., Yzerbyt, V. Y., & Leyens, J. P. (1988). The "black sheep effect": Extremity of judgments towards ingroup members as a function of group identification. *European Journal of Social Psychology, 18,* 1–16.

McGarty, C., Pedersen, A., Leach, C. W., Mansell, T., Waller, J., & Bliuc, A. M. (2005). Group-based guilt as a predictor of commitment to apology. *British Journal of Social Psychology, 44,* 659–680.

Miller, R. S. (1987). Empathic embarrassment: Situational and personal determinants of reactions to the embarrassment of another. *Journal of Personality and Social Psychology, 53,* 1061–1069.

Miron, A. M., Branscombe, N. R., & Schmitt, M. T. (2006). Collective guilt as distress over illegitimate intergroup inequality. *Group Processes and Intergroup Relations, 9,* 163–180.

Niedenthal, P. M., Tangney, J. P., & Gavanski, I. (1994). "If only I weren't" versus "If only I hadn't": Distinguishing shame and guilt in counterfactual thinking. *Journal of Personality and Social Psychology, 67,* 585–595.

Ortony, A., Clore, G. L., & Collins, A. (1988). *The cognitive structure of emotions.* New York: Cambridge University Press.

Parrott, W. G., Sabini, J., & Silver, M. (1988). The roles of self-esteem and social interaction in embarrassment. *Personality and Social Psychology Bulletin, 14,* 191–202.

Powell, A. A., Branscombe, N. R., & Schmitt, M. T. (2005). Inequality as ingroup privilege or outgroup disadvantage: The impact of group focus on collective guilt and interracial attitudes. *Personality and Social Psychology Bulletin, 31,* 508–521.

Prentice, D. A., Miller, D. T., & Lightdale, J. R. (1994). Asymmetries in attachments to groups and their members: Distinguishing between common-identity and common-bond groups. *Personality and Social Psychology Bulletin, 20,* 484–493.

Roccas, W., Klar, Y., & Liviatan, I. (2004). Exonerating cognitions, group identification, and personal values as predictors of collective guilt among Jewish-Israelis. In N. R. Branscombe & B. Doosje (Eds.), *Collective guilt: International perspectives* (pp. 130–147). New York: Cambridge University Press.

Sabini, J., Garvey, B., & Hall, A. L. (2001). Shame and embarrassment revisited. *Personality and Social Psychology Bulletin, 27,* 104–117.

Sabini, J., & Silver, M. (2005). Why emotion names and experiences do not neatly pair. *Psychological Inquiry, 16,* 1–10.

Schmader, T., & Lickel, B. (2002). *Distinguishing vicarious shame, guilt, and embarrassment.* Unpublished data, University of Arizona.

Schmader, T., & Lickel, B. (2006a). Stigma and shame: Emotional responses to the stereotypic actions of one's ethnic ingroup. In S. Levin & C. van Laar (Eds.), *Stigma and group inequality: Social psychological approaches* (pp. 261–285). Mahwah, NJ: Erlbaum.

Schmader, T., & Lickel., B. (2006b). The approach and avoidance function of personal and vicarious guilt and shame emotions. *Motivation and Emotion, 30,* 43–56.

Shearn, D., Spellman, L., & Meirick, J. (1999). Empathic blushing in friends and strangers. *Motivation and Emotion, 23,* 307–316.

Smith, C. A., & Ellsworth, P. C. (1985). Patterns of cognitive appraisal in emotion. *Journal of Personality and Social Psychology, 48,* 813–838.

Smith, E. R. (1993). Social identity and social emotions: Toward new conceptualizations of prejudice. In D. M. Mackie & D. L. Hamilton (Eds.), *Affect, cognition, and stereotyping: Interactive processes in group perception* (pp. 297–315).San Diego, CA: Academic Press.

Smith, R. H., Webster, J. M., Parrott, W. G., & Eyre, H. L. (2002). The role of public exposure in moral and nonmoral shame and guilt. *Journal of Personality and Social Psychology, 83,* 138–159.

Stipek, D. (1998). Differences between Americans and Chinese in the circumstances evoking pride, shame, and guilt. *Journal of Cross-Cultural Psychology, 29,* 616–629.

Swim, J. K., & Miller, D. L. (1999). White guilt: Its antecedents and consequences for attitudes toward affirmative action. *Personality and Social Psychology Bulletin, 25,* 500–514.

Tajfel, H. (1970). Experiments in intergroup discrimination. *Scientific American, 223,* 96–102.

Tajfel, H. (1978). *Differentiation between social groups.* London: Academic Press.

Tajfel, H., & Turner, J. C. (1986). Social identity theory of intergroup behavior. In W. Austin & S. Worchel (Eds.), *Psychology of intergroup relations* (2nd ed., pp. 7–24). Chicago: Nelson-Hall.

Tangney, J. P., & Fischer, K. W. (Eds.). (1995). *Self-conscious emotions.* New York: Guilford Press.

Tangney, J. P., Miller, R. S., Flicker, L., & Barlow, D. B. (1996). Are shame, guilt, and embarrassment distinct emotions? *Journal of Personality and Social Psychology, 70,* 1256–1269.

Tangney, J. P., Wagner, P., Fletcher, C., & Gramzow, R. (1992). Shamed into anger?: The relation of shame and guilt to anger and self-reported aggression. *Journal of Personality and Social Psychology, 62,* 669–675.

Thorton, K. C. (2003). When the source of embarrassment is a close other. *Individual Differences Research, 1,* 189–200.

Tönnies, F. (1988). *Community and society.* New Brunswick, NJ: Transaction Books. (Original work published 1887)

Tooby, J., & Cosmides, L. (1990). The past explains the present: Emotional adaptations and the structure of ancestral environments. *Ethology and Sociobiology, 11,* 375–424.

Tracy, J. L., & Robins, R. W. (2004). Putting the self into self-conscious emotions: A theoretical model. *Psychological Inquiry, 15,* 101–125.

Tropp, L. R., & Wright, S. C. (2001). Ingroup identification as the inclusion of ingroup in the self. *Personality and Social Psychology Bulletin, 27,* 585–600.

Weiner, B. (1986). *An attributional theory of motivation and emotion.* New York: Springer-Verlag.

Wicker, F. W., Payne, G. C., & Morgan, R. D. (1983). Participant descriptions of guilt and shame. *Motivation and Emotion, 7,* 25–39.

Wilder, D., & Simon, A. F. (1998). Categorical and dynamic groups: Implications for social perception and intergroup behavior. In C. Sedikides, J. Schopler, & C. A. Insko (Eds.), *Intergroup cognition and intergroup behavior* (pp. 27–44). Mahwah, NJ: Erlbaum.

Zebel, S., Doojse, B., & Spears, R. (2004). It depends on your point of view: Implications of perspective-taking and national identification for Dutch collective guilt. In N. R. Branscombe & B. Doosje (Eds.), *Collective guilt: International perspectives* (pp. 148–168). New York: Cambridge University Press.

20

Shame and Guilt in Antisocial and Risky Behaviors

JEFFREY STUEWIG
JUNE PRICE TANGNEY

The majority of research examining the self-conscious emotions of shame and guilt and subsequent outcomes has focused on psychological adjustment. Less research has focused on if, and how, the moral emotions relate to antisocial and risky behavior. In this chapter we review some of the literature regarding the relationship of shame and guilt to risky behavior, discuss some holes and limitations within the existing literature, and set forth some possible avenues for future research.

Antisocial and risky behavior is a significant problem in our society. Whether it is manifested as substance abuse or criminal behavior in adulthood, risky sexual behavior or delinquency in adolescence, aggression or conduct disorder in childhood, or any type of violence across the spectrum, these behaviors cost society billions of dollars yearly. In addition to the monetary damage these behaviors can cause, there is also an enormous emotional toll—for the victims, the victims' families, and often the perpetrator's families as well. Neighborhoods, workplaces, and school settings can also be significantly disrupted. Understanding the progression of these behaviors and the factors that promote the onset, persistence, desistance, or change in the manifest expression of antisocial tendencies will be useful for designing and implementing interventions across the life course.

DIFFERENCES BETWEEN SHAME AND GUILT

Shame and guilt are both "negative" and uncomfortable emotions and as such are usually correlated. Both also deal with self-evaluative judgments in that we judge ourselves and our actions according to internal standards. There are, however, important conceptual differences between them and important differences in how they associate with other constructs (Tangney, 1990, 1991; Tangney, Stuewig, & Mashek, 2007; Tangney, Wagner, &

Gramzow, 1992; Tracy & Robins, 2006). H. B. Lewis (1971) theorized that the key difference between shame and guilt concerns the distinction between "the self" and "the behavior." Shame focuses less on specific behaviors and more on the evaluation of the entire *self* against internalized standards. Guilt, on the other hand, reflects feelings about *actions* that are inconsistent with internalized standards. The two emotions also lead to different "action tendencies" (Lindsay-Hartz, 1984; Tangney, Miller, Flicker, & Barlow, 1996). When people feel guilt, they are motivated to make reparations for the *behavior*. When people feel shame, they feel awful about *themselves*; they want to hide or disappear. Although both are uncomfortable emotions, shame can be more debilitating and painful. People's phenomenological reports of shame describe feeling powerless and insignificant (Wicker, Payne, & Morgan, 1983).

Researchers have found that shame is substantially related to a variety of poor outcomes including depression, anxiety, eating disorder symptoms, subclinical psychopathy, posttraumatic stress disorder, anger, and low self-esteem (Andrews, Brewin, Rose, & Kirk, 2000; Ashby, Rice, & Martin, 2006; Feiring & Taska, 2005; Ferguson et al., 2000; Stuewig & McCloskey, 2005; Tangney et al., 2007; Tangney, Wagner, & Gramzow, 1992). Conversely, feelings of guilt uncomplicated by shame (Paulhus, Robins, Trzesniewski, & Tracy, 2004; Tangney & Dearing, 2002) are either unrelated or negatively related to psychological symptoms and negatively related to anger and externalization of blame (Paulhus et al., 2004; Quiles & Bybee, 1997; Stuewig & McCloskey, 2005; Stuewig, Tangney, Heigel, & Harty, 2007; Tangney, Wagner, Fletcher, & Gramzow, 1992). (See Tangney, Stuewig, & Mashek, Chapter 2, this volume, and 2007; and Tangney & Dearing, 2002, for a more extensive discussion of both the theoretical and empirical differences between shame and guilt.)

SHAME AND GUILT AS "MORAL" EMOTIONS

Shame and guilt are also often described as "moral" emotions in that they help keep us on the moral path by avoiding temptation, inhibiting aggression, and doing the right thing. It is often suggested that these two "moral" emotions help motivate people to steer clear of risky, aggressive, delinquent, or criminal behavior. This implicit assumption is often revealed by the type of punishment meted out by authority figures (e.g., humiliation of a student in class, shaming sentences used in criminal cases such as making someone walk around with a sign signifying that he or she is a criminal, or any other punishment that sends the message to the individual that he or she is a bad or defective person).

In contrast, others have suggested that overwhelming feelings of shame and guilt will cause people to act out and engage in risky behavior. This may be especially true in the case of shame. In order to escape painful feelings of shame, and to cope with feelings of low self-esteem and hopelessness, the shame-prone individual may misguidedly engage in risky behavior, most likely in an attempt to take back some sense of control over his or her life. Similarly, others have discussed the idea of bypassed or unresolved or unacknowledged shame as leading to anger and hostility (Harris, 2003, 2006; H. B. Lewis, 1971; M. Lewis, 1995; Scheff, 1987), and perhaps other risky behaviors.

However, there have been few empirical studies of how shame and guilt function as "moral" emotions, especially using the self/behavior distinction. So the question arises, Do shame and guilt lead to aggression, delinquency, and other risky behavior or do they keep individuals from engaging in these acts? Or, as we believe, are shame and guilt differentially related to different forms of risky behavior, paralleling their divergent correlates in the domain of psychological adjustment?

EMPIRICAL STUDIES OF THE RELATIONSHIP OF SHAME AND GUILT TO ANTISOCIAL AND RISKY BEHAVIOR

Aggression

H. B. Lewis (1971) was among the first to note a relationship between shame and anger. Specifically, she observed that painful feelings of shame may turn into defensiveness, anger, fury, and sometimes overt aggression. This theme has been further elaborated on by Scheff (1987), Gilligan (1996), M. Lewis (1995), and Tangney (1992; Tangney & Dearing, 2002).

Essentially, an attack on one's core self may give rise to instances of shame-rage or humiliated fury. The pain felt from evaluating oneself as defective or inferior may lead shamed individuals to lash out and blame others in order to regain a sense of control over their lives. This may lead to increasing amounts of shame that subsequently feeds right back into anger and further destructive acts, à la a "shame–rage spiral" as described by Scheff (1987). In contrast to shame-prone people, guilt-prone people tend not to internalize these evaluations about the self; instead, they focus on the behavior and on making amends (Tangney & Dearing, 2002). In this way guilt may serve a protective function against aggression in that it is associated with taking responsibility for one's actions and focusing on reparation. Furthermore, guilt and empathy appear to go hand in hand (Leith & Baumeister, 1998; Stuewig et al., 2007; Tangney, 1991; Tangney & Dearing, 2002), and empathy in turn is negatively correlated with a range of antisocial behaviors including aggression (Jolliffe & Farrington, 2004; Miller & Eisenberg, 1988).

Most empirical work has focused on the differential relationship of shame and guilt to aggression broadly defined and skewed toward the mild/normal range. Tangney's research, for example (Tangney, Wagner, Fletcher, & Gramzow, 1992; Tangney, Wagner, Hill-Barlow, Marschall, & Gramzow, 1996; Tangney & Dearing, 2002), has centered on indices of anger, hostility, and verbal aggression in nonclinical samples of children, adolescents, and adults. The empirical work on shame, guilt, and physical aggression—violence, per se—has been limited and the results are not clear-cut. In one study of undergraduates, Tangney, Wagner, Fletcher, and Gramzow (1992) found no relationship between shame-proneness and the subscales of assault (physical aggression) and verbal hostility as measured by the Buss–Durkee Hostility Inventory (Buss & Durkee, 1957). In a subsequent study, however, Tangney, Wagner et al. (1996), using different versions of the Anger Response Inventory (ARI; Tangney, Wagner, Marschall, & Gramzow, 1991), found a positive correlation between shame-proneness and physical aggression in independent samples of adults, adolescents, and children. Furthermore, there was also a relationship between shame-proneness and verbal aggression for adults, college students, adolescents, and children. Guilt-proneness, on the other hand, was consistently negatively related to verbal and physical aggression across all the participants. In two separate samples of undergraduates, Paulhus et al. (2004) found a positive relationship between shame-proneness and total aggression on the Buss–Durkee Aggression Questionnaire and a negative relationship between guilt-proneness and total aggression. In a study of children between 5 and 12 years of age, externalizing symptoms (e.g., aggression and delinquency) were positively related to shame-proneness for boys and girls; externalizing symptoms were negatively related to guilt-proneness for boys but not for girls (for whom there was a positive relationship) (Ferguson, Stegge, Miller, & Olsen, 1999). In contrast, however, in a sample of 3- to 7-year-olds, Bennett, Sullivan, and Lewis (2005) did not find a direct relationship between shame and externalizing symptoms, although they did find an indirect relationship through anger.

Although the link between shame and overt physical aggression is less consistent than that between shame and anger, this may be due to a restriction of range in the dependent variable. Behaviors such as physical aggression have low base rates in these nonclinical samples. In addition, there are concerns with the operationalization of the dependent variables. Researchers studying nonclinical samples have often not distinguished between related constructs, confounding aggression with anger, hostility, externalization of blame, and/or other problem behavior. For example, the Buss–Durkee Aggression Questionnaire is a combination of verbal aggression, physical aggression, anger, and hostility. Externalizing symptoms are often a mix of not only verbal and physical aggressive items but delinquent items and other more nonspecific items (e.g., loud, jealous, moody, brags, excess talking, stubborn). Use of such measures may be muddying the true relationship of shame versus guilt to aggression. This seems worth examining more closely because withdrawal, a hallmark of shame, is contradictory to approach-oriented behaviors such as physical aggression that would tend to draw more attention to the shame-prone individual. Other related constructs such as anger or externalization of blame, on the other hand, do not necessarily have to be directly expressed to others, and seem to have more consistent relationships with shame (Bennett et al., 2005; Harper, Austin, Cercone, & Arias, 2005; Wicker et al., 1983; Tangney, 1995; Tangney, Wagner, et al., 1996). Furthermore, the relationship between shame, guilt, and aggression is probably more complex than direct effects alone. Further examination of possible mediators of these relationships is needed.

To address some of these issues, we examined the relationship of shame and guilt to two separate forms of aggression (physical and verbal) in multiple samples (Stuewig et al., 2007). We expected that the shame-to-aggression link would be fairly small using these "cleaner" measures of aggression and that any subsequent relationship would be mediated by externalization of blame. In two of the four samples "guilt-free" shame was unrelated to physical aggression ($r = .02$ and $.02$), while in the other two samples it was significantly related ($r = .20$ and $.15$). Similarly, "guilt-free" shame was unrelated to verbal aggression in one of three samples ($r = -.03$), but significantly related in the other two ($r = .13$ and $.31$). To test these relationships in a fuller multivariate environment, we hypothesized that the negative feelings of shame would lead to externalization of blame, which in turn would be related to increased verbal and physical aggression. As such, we expected externalization of blame to fully mediate any relationship between shame-proneness and either type of aggression. Results using path analyses in the separate samples were consistent with a model of no direct relationship between shame-proneness and physical or verbal aggression once externalization of blame was included. There was, however, a significant indirect relationship through externalization of blame in all samples.

In contrast to shame-proneness, guilt-proneness should facilitate empathic feelings and processes, thus reducing outward-directed aggression. As such, we expected guilt-proneness to be negatively related to both types of aggression, both directly and indirectly. Guilt was uniquely related to both verbal and physical aggression in all samples. In the path analyses guilt-proneness showed a significant direct negative relationship to aggression and was also significantly negatively related to aggression indirectly through externalization of blame and empathy.

In summary, although many have theorized about a shame–aggression link, fewer studies have examined this relationship empirically. Although existing studies suggest that the relationship of shame to aggression may not be as strong or as consistent as often assumed in some of the literature, there was little evidence that shame plays any sort of protective or inhibitory role. Guilt-proneness shows a more consistent (and seemingly more robust) inhibitory role vis-à-vis aggression. Nonetheless, aggression can be conceptualized in a number of different ways and it is possible that these relationships depend on the type of aggression that is measured. For example, shame-prone individuals may be less likely to engage in overt physical aggression but more likely to participate in aggressive activities of a covert nature due to their tendency to avoid putting themselves in the spotlight. This differential relationship depending on type of aggression may not be true for guilt because it does not focus as much on the self or the evaluation of the self by others. Additionally, perhaps shame-prone individuals are more likely to engage in reactive aggression due to its immediate and context-dependent nature as opposed to proactive aggression. Moreover, aggregated measures of aggressive behavior over time may not match up with conceptions of the shame–fury episode as described in the clinical literature. If these are sudden, random, and inconsistent actions, they may be missed by survey measures. Inclusion of measures that attempt to isolate and assess sudden and explosive episodes of violence and aggression using both self-reports and other corroborating data such as peer reports or official records may be more informative.

Delinquency/Criminal Behavior

Although aggression is one form of antisocial behavior that has a theoretical relationship to shame and guilt, there are a number of other possible domains of interest. For instance, these self-conscious emotions may also play a role in delinquency and criminal behavior (M. Lewis, 1995). Criminal activity and/or rule breaking in general do not necessarily entail aggression and as such there may be different relationships and pathways linking shame and guilt to these activities. Little psychological research, however, has looked at how shame and guilt relate to criminal or delinquent behavior. There has been some empirical research in the field of criminology that is relevant. Using a rational choice model framework, Grasmick and colleagues (Grasmick, Blackwell, & Bursik, 1993; Grasmick & Bursik, 1990) found shame to be negatively related to the hypothetical intention to commit crimes. Their measures of shame, however, are closer to what psychologists refer to as guilt. As reviewed by Tibbetts (2003), much of the research in criminology (e.g., Elis & Simpson, 1995; Grasmick & Bursik, 1990; Nagin & Paternoster, 1993) not only uses the terms "shame" and "guilt" interchangeably but also does not take into account the important self (shame) versus behavior (guilt) distinction that H. B. Lewis (1971) described.

Tibbetts (1997), in a sample of undergraduates, measured three types of shame: anticipated shame states if offending was exposed, anticipated shame states if offending was not exposed, and shame-proneness. At the bivariate level there was a negative relationship between the two anticipated shame states and the intention to drive drunk or shoplift and no relationship between the Shame-Proneness Scale (SPS; Tibbetts, 1997) and criminal intentions. However, the construct validity of the SPS is not clear, as it contains a substantial number of items that do not capture shame as an emotion but instead seems to measure standards and cognitions (e.g., "living up to the ideals and standards I have committed myself to is important to me" and "I do things because I feel I should, even when I do not want to") and other nonfocal constructs. Finally, as Tibbetts (2003) points out, these relationships may be biased due to the failure to partial out the relationship between shame and guilt (i.e., measuring "guilt-free" shame and "shame-free" guilt) (also see Paulhus et al., 2004). Building on his previous work, Tibbetts used multiple measures of shame and guilt. A new sample of undergraduates completed the SPS, the TOSCA (Tangney, Wagner, & Gramzow, 1989), and the PFQ-2 (Harder & Zalma, 1990). Criminal offending was indexed by number of illegal behaviors (including use of marijuana and other illegal drugs) self-reported by undergraduates over a 6-month period. Criminal offending showed a negative bivariate relationship to TOSCA-shame, SPS-shame, TOSCA-guilt, and PFQ-2-guilt (Tibbetts, 2003). In a multiple regression analysis in which all shame and guilt measures were simultaneously entered as predictors, TOSCA-shame was unrelated to offending whereas TOSCA-guilt remained negatively related.

Although the terminology differs, the work of criminologist John Braithwaite and colleagues is especially relevant to the possible link between the self-conscious emotions and crime (Ahmed, Harris, Braithwaite, & Braithwaite, 2001; Braithwaite, 1989; Makkai & Braithwaite, 1994). Briefly, Braithwaite's reintegrative shaming theory (RST) distinguishes between two types of shaming practices. The first practice, labeled "reintegrative shaming," deals with practices that identify the crime or the behavior, not the individual, as irresponsible, wrong, or bad. While the act is looked down upon, the person is respected, accepted back into society, and given the chance to make atonement for the behavior. This focus on the behavior, not the person, together with Braithwaite's emphasis on apology and remediation, seems much more congruent with the dynamics of guilt, as described in the psychological literature. The second type of shaming practice is labeled "disintegrative shaming" or stigmatization. Here the individual is not forgiven but stigmatized, isolated, and humiliated as a person, in an attempt to instill feelings more akin to our notion of shame. Although there has not been an abundance of empirical research on RST, most studies have been at least partially supportive of the theory (Harris, 2006; Hay, 2001; Makkai & Braithwaite, 1994). Nevertheless, most of this research has focused on the practice of shaming perpetrators, not on whether the perpetrating individual actually experiences shame or guilt and how these emotions are then related to behavior.

Two prospective studies have investigated the long-term effects of shame- and guilt-proneness in the domain of criminal behavior. In the first, shame-proneness in the fifth grade was unrelated to either arrests or convictions reported by the participant at age 18. In contrast, guilt-proneness was negatively related to both (Tangney, Stuewig, Kendall, Reinsmith, & Dearing, 2006). In the second study, Stuewig and McCloskey (2005) examined whether shame or guilt in early adolescence mediated the relationship between maltreatment in childhood and subsequent delinquency and depression measured in late adolescence. "Guilt-free" shame was unrelated to delinquency using either juvenile court records or self-report of delinquency, while adolescents high in "shame-free" guilt were less delinquent. Furthermore, in the full-path models guilt-proneness continued to be negatively related to delinquency even when a number of other variables, including symptoms of conduct disorder in childhood and parenting in adolescence, were integrated in the model.

In short, much of the research in criminology on shame conflicts with the findings of psychology (Tibbetts, 2003). We believe this has more to do with the use of different terminology across fields as opposed to fundamental differences in the underlying constructs themselves. Using the terminology of psychology, guilt seems to have the stronger inhibitory relationship to criminal behavior. Shame's relationship, on the other hand, is still somewhat unclear. Further research is needed to examine if this inconsistent relationship is just due to sampling variability across studies or if there is a true relationship but one moderated by as yet undiscovered variables, such that the inhibiting (or disinhibiting) effects of shame are observed in some contexts but not others.

Other Risky Behaviors

Thus far, we have discussed behaviors that fall solidly into the domain of externalizing behaviors. We believe that shame and guilt may play a role in other maladaptive behaviors, such as substance abuse and risky sexual behavior. While all these behaviors can be classified along an externalizing dimension, it is possible that there are unique relationships to each specific outcome. For instance, although alcohol and drug dependence were part of a higher-order, heritable, externalizing dimension, each lower-order indicator (e.g., drug dependence) shows a substantial amount of residual variance (Krueger, 2002; Krueger et al., 2002). Although the links between shame, guilt, and risky behaviors are often mentioned in the clinical and theoretical literature, we are aware of only a few studies that have attempted to investigate these links.

Substance Use and Abuse

Issues of shame and guilt are often brought up in treatment settings. This is particularly true among clinicians who treat individuals dealing with substance abuse problems (Fossum & Mason, 1986; Potter-Efron, 2002). Furthermore, since people often use substances to improve their mood (Cooper, Frone, Russell, & Mudar, 1995), it would seem probable that individuals high in shame-proneness may be at risk for substance abuse. Again, however, there are relatively few empirical studies evaluating this relationship, especially ones that take into account the self/behavior distinction that we believe to be important in discriminating shame and guilt. The research so far has been fairly consistent. In two studies, adults in recovery programs had lower guilt-prone scores and higher shame-prone scores as compared to individuals in community samples (Meehan et al., 1996; O'Connor, Berry, Inaba, Weiss, & Morrison, 1994). Nonetheless, results focusing on people in recovery programs are tricky to interpret because the elevated levels of shame may be due to other factors such as being in a recovery program as opposed to substance use problems, per se. In another study, using two samples from an undergraduate population and one sample of jail inmates, shame-proneness was consistently positively related to both alcohol and drug problems, while guilt-proneness tended to be negatively related, albeit less consistently (Dearing, Stuewig, & Tangney, 2005). Finally, using prospective data, shame- and guilt-proneness in the fifth grade were related to age of first alcohol use as reported at 18 years of age (Tangney et al., 2006). Whereas those high in shame-proneness tended to start drinking earlier than those low in shame-proneness, and those high in guilt-proneness started drinking at a later age than those low in guilt-proneness. In addition, shame-prone children were more likely to later use heroin, with an analogous trend for uppers and hallucinogens. In contrast, guilt-prone children were less likely to use heroin, with similar trends for marijuana and uppers.

Risky Needle Use and Risky Sexual Behavior

In one study we examined the relationship of shame and guilt to preincarceration HIV risk behavior in a sample of male inmates (Stuewig, Tangney, Mashek, Forkner, & Dearing, in press). Contrary to our hypotheses, shame and guilt were unrelated to risky IV drug use (conceptualized as IV needle use and, among those IV users, frequency of sharing needles with others). There were significant, albeit small, results when focusing on risky sexual behaviors. Guilt was negatively related to both number of sexual partners and an index of risky sexual behavior (unprotected sex: with someone other than a primary partner; with someone who is a needle user; while trading, giving, or getting sex for drugs, money, or gifts). In this domain, shame was not associated with increased risk. In fact, there was a nonsignificant trend suggesting an inverse relationship between shame and number of sexual partners in the year prior to incarceration. Similarly, in a prospective developmental study, children identified as shame-prone in the fifth grade did not differ from their less shame-prone peers on number of sexual partners reported at age 18 (although their was a trend linking higher shame with unprotected sex). The findings for guilt were similar to those observed in the jail sample. Children identified as guilt-prone in the fifth grade were less likely to have unprotected sex and more likely to use birth control as teens, and they had fewer sexual partners (Tangney et al., 2006).

Similar to other domains discussed earlier, we believe that guilt-prone individuals may not only anticipate that their actions may be harmful to the self but with their higher capacity for empathy may recognize the consequences of such activities on others, and as such avoid these risky behaviors. The relationship between shame and risky behavior appears to vary depending on the type of behavior under consideration. Due to the tendency for those high in shame to want to hide, shrink, or disappear, these individuals may not be inclined to place themselves in social situations where frequent sexual encounters are likely to be initiated. In addition, the interpersonal difficulties associated with shame may result in fewer opportunities for multiple sex partners. But when in a sexual relationship shame-prone individuals may not make the safest decisions. This interpretation, however, is highly speculative. Clearly, more research is needed regarding the link between shame and sexual behavior.

Summary of Empirical Studies

We began with the question, Do shame and guilt lead to aggression, delinquency, and other risky behavior, or do they inhibit individuals from engaging in these acts? The literature reviewed suggests that the self-conscious emotions do play a role in antisocial and risky behavior. It may not be, however, a simple one. Broadly speaking, guilt-proneness seems to be consistently negatively related to aggression and criminal behavior. In addition, guilt-prone individuals may have fewer problems with substances and, based on a limited number of studies, appear to engage in less sexual risk taking. In contrast, shame-proneness shows no evidence of protecting individuals from committing aggressive or criminal acts. Furthermore, there is support that shame-prone individuals have issues with anger and externalization of blame that may subsequently lead to verbal and physical aggression. In addition, there is evidence that shame-prone individuals are vulnerable to problems associated with alcohol and drug use. Additional research, both experimental, or laboratory-based, and survey-, or observational-based, focused on identifying mediating and moderating processes, would be useful for further elucidating the complex relationships between these self-conscious emotions and antisocial and risky behavior.

POSSIBLE FUTURE DIRECTIONS

Shame, Guilt, and the Onset of Risky and Antisocial Behavior

Most of the studies conducted thus far have examined simple bivariate, and often contemporaneous, relationships of shame and guilt to risky behavior. It would be useful to systematically investigate not only the concurrent relationship of shame and guilt to antisocial and risky behavior across different ages but also prospective relationships within a strong developmental framework, taking into account concurrent effects and stability over time. It is possible that the relationships between risky behavior and shame and guilt are bidirectional, especially during adolescence and adulthood. But it may be that the roots of this sequence are planted in early childhood.

How might this process work over time? It may be that the propensity to experience shame sets children up for early failure in a number of domains that, in turn, leads to further negative feelings and further failure. These early failures may initiate a pattern of behavior leading to cumulative disadvantages over time. For example, shame-prone individuals may be at increased risk for poor school performance and depression, in part because of the kinds of maladaptive coping strategies that may be adopted by shame-prone individuals (Fee & Tangney, 2000; Kulick, 1998; Stern, 1999) including self-handicapping strategies (Cowman & Ferrari, 2002). In contrast, because guilt involves a focus on behavior, guilt-prone children may be more inclined to recognize when problems arise and feel more capable of taking positive steps. For example, among children and adolescents, proneness to guilt has been associated not only with better study skills but also fewer learning problems and a greater likelihood of applying to college (Bybee & Williams, 1994; Tangney et al., 2006).

Guilt-prone children may learn from their mistakes, focus on the task, and make an effort to improve, while shame-prone children may focus on the failure and what it says about them as a person. Some indirect evidence (Dweck & Leggett, 1988; Dweck, Hong, & Chiu, 1993) suggests that shame may interfere with academic achievement. As time passes the shame-prone individual may just stop trying in school. In turn, failure in school has been linked to a number of poor outcomes including delinquency, substance use, teen pregnancy, contact with the criminal justice system, and so on. As Caspi, Elder, and Bem (1988) noted, "In such cases, behaviors are sustained across time by the progressive accumulation of their own consequences, producing what we have called cumulative continuity" (p. 824). A cycle of low self-esteem, hopelessness, and depression may result, one that in turn is likely to have adverse effects in other important domains: relationships with peers, relationships with parents, prosocial activities, and health-related behaviors, to name a few. Again, evidence suggests that shame-prone children are less popular and less able to manage anger in a constructive fashion (Tangney, Wagner, et al., 1996; Tangney & Dearing, 2002). Likewise they may have inadequate interpersonal problem-solving skills (Covert, Tangney, Maddux, & Heleno, 2003). Understanding the roles shame and guilt play across the life course may add substantially to our knowledge of developmental processes and pathways.

Importantly, research indicates that shame- and guilt-proneness are moderately stable over a 2- to 3-year period (Tangney & Dearing, 2002)—thus, they appear to be at least somewhat malleable. Such malleability makes shame and guilt promising targets for early intervention.

Shame, Guilt, and the Persistence and Desistance of Antisocial Behavior

Thus far, most empirical research has focused on the relationship of shame and guilt to individual differences in antisocial or risky behavior assessed with respect to a single time frame. The moral emotions of shame and guilt, however, may play a role in the persistence or desistance of antisocial and risky behavior, once such behavior is initiated.

Although the stability of antisocial behavior over time is one of the most robust findings in the social sciences (Loeber, 1982; Moffitt, Caspi, Harrington, & Milne, 2002), theorists and researchers have become increasingly interested in the variance left to be explained. Many people who engage in criminal or other risky behavior eventually stop these behaviors—some without any intervention. For others, such behaviors persist over time.

Identifying predictors of such continuity and discontinuity is an important goal (Rutter, Kim-Cohen, & Maughan, 2006). For example, if unique predictors of desistance can be identified in this naturally occurring process, then intervention efforts may be able to focus on strengthening these factors. Each year sizable numbers of adolescents "age out" of delinquency and antisocial behavior as a result of naturally occurring social, psychological, biological, and interpersonal changes (Moffitt, 1993). These changes are not likely to be random. Certain factors and characteristics may identify individuals who will eventually follow this path to desistance. Pinpointing factors that promote change would have direct implications for intervention. As such, a key question is, Are the same factors leading to onset also associated with subsequent desistance? And furthermore, how exactly do these processes of desistance work? And finally, in what ways may external factors and internal characteristics work together in changing a person's antisocial behavior at different developmental stages?

Sampson and Laub's (1993) life-course model proposes that life events influence behavior and modify trajectories. Much of the theory and research thus far has focused on external triggers or characteristics such as employment, marriage, and military service in promoting desistence from criminal behavior. Other common constructs are changes in peer groups (e.g., leaving the gang), education, natural mentors, family stability, living situation, and parenthood (Ackerman, Brown, & Izard, 2003; Sampson & Laub, 1996; Stouthamer-Loeber, Wei, Loeber, & Masten, 2004). Of course, the relevance of many predictors will differ by the age of the individual. Yet only a handful of studies have looked at changes in antisocial behavior as a function of life event "triggers" at different developmental stages. Loeber and Stouthamer-Loeber (1998) explained that "little is known about the stability or the causes of desistance. It cannot be assumed that the causes of desistance from aggression in childhood are the same as the causes of desistance from aggression or violence in adolescence or adulthood" (p. 244). For example, Sampson and Laub (1993) found that a stable work history predicted desistance in adults. For adolescents, this might not be true. In fact, some research has shown that employment in adolescence actually increases delinquent behavior (Hirschi, 1969; Ploeger, 1997; Steinberg & Dornbusch, 1991). It is therefore critical to examine these questions while keeping a developmental framework in mind.

Internal or individual characteristics have received less attention. Researchers have generally not considered explicitly the internal mechanisms through which such environmental triggers effect change. An examination of psychological mediators would add importantly to our understanding of the desistance process. These internal cognitive and emotional mechanisms may represent common pathways across the life course by which developmentally specific life events foster desistence. Here we lay out three broad domains of psychological mechanisms—emotions, individual characteristics, and cognitions—and a few examples of each.

Emotions

We believe the self-conscious emotions of shame and guilt may be important "mechanisms of action" in this desistance process. In addition, the construct of empathy may also play a key role. People at any age who have the ability to experience guilt and empathy may be more likely to desist from antisocial behavior in the future, relative to their less empathic and less guilt-prone peers. Guilt, with its focus on behavior, not the self, may help individuals avoid the downward spiral of repeated delinquency. As they realize that the behavior is incongruent with their standards and values, empathic, guilt-prone individuals may be more likely to desist in the future. Anticipation of painful feelings of shame may also convince people not to engage in antisocial behavior in the future. However, based on the above review of correlates, we believe that to be unlikely. Further, shame-prone people may not anticipate their affective responses to contemplated behaviors as reliably as non-shame-prone people. Once engaged in antisocial, aggressive, or risky behaviors, an individual's proneness to shame may lead to externalization of blame, denial, aggression, and a failure to learn or correct his or her behavior. Such negative outcomes, in turn, engender more feelings of shame, more denial, and more problematic behavior. Or an alternative pathway may be taken. It may be that shame and its relation to negative attributions, depression, and hopelessness may play a role in the persistence of risky behavior. Simply put, it may be easy to get stuck in these destructive cycles when one is shame-prone. Either way, transforming an individual's shame-prone tendencies into the more adaptive guilt-prone style may help individuals break free of these negative cycles.

Temperament/Personality

A number of individual characteristics (e.g., self-control, impulsivity) are related to a variety of later outcomes in life, including delinquency, substance abuse, crime, and antisociality (Krueger et al., 1994; Polakowski, 1994). Here again most of the research has focused on the onset of antisocial behavior or its co-occurrence with factors such as self-control and impulsivity. A notable exception is Moffit's (1993, 2006) work distinguishing between life-course-persistent and adolescent-limited delinquent individuals. Adolescent-limited delinquents (e.g., desisters) tend to be higher in self-control than persisters. Perhaps even within the category of desisters, there are individual differences in self-control that predict who starts this desistence process sooner. Similar to the self-conscious emotions, this process may be common across different ages.

Cognitions

Cognitions represent another avenue of change. How we interpret our lives and actions plays an important role in how we choose to act in the future. Promising directions include Sykes and Matza's (1957) techniques of neutralization (e.g., denial of injury, denial of responsibility); Maruna's (2001) findings that ex-offenders needed to reinterpret their life so as to explain to themselves and others why they are no longer "like that"; and Maruna's (2004) work on attributional style. Similarly, psychologists have proposed models of social information processing (Crick & Dodge, 1994; Dodge, 1980) as well as models of the content of cognitions (Guerra & Slaby, 1990; Slaby & Guerra, 1988). Understanding cognitions across the life course and how they change naturally may prove to be important because they are the basis of cognitive-behavioral therapy and many interventions with criminal offenders (Gendreau, Goggin, French, & Smith, 2006).

The Interplay of Shame and Guilt with Other Internal Characteristics and External Triggers in Antisocial or Risky Behavior

Although research on the relations of external triggers and psychological mechanisms to discontinuity of behavior are promising lines of research in and of themselves, it is the complex interplay among these factors that may lead to the most comprehensive understanding of the desistance or abstinence process. This interplay could manifest in two ways: (1) in connections among psychological mechanisms, and (2) in connections between these mechanisms and external factors.

Regarding the connections among psychological mechanisms, how might emotions, cognitions, and individual characteristics be intertwined? And might these relationships differ depending on the outcome variable of interest? For example, how might shame and guilt (and other self-conscious emotions such as pride) work together with cognitions to predict onset and continuity in antisocial and risky behavior? Some research suggests that the relationship between shame-proneness and aggression is mediated by externalization of blame and/or anger (Bennett et al., 2005; Stuewig et al., 2007) Of course, it is doubtful that this is universal. It seems reasonable that individual differences and situational variables moderate either the entire pathway (moderated mediation) or any of the specific links (e.g., externalization of blame → aggression). For example, the pathway of shame-proneness to externalization of blame to aggression may be more pronounced among individuals who are low in self-control. Those who have higher levels of self-control may be better able to self-regulate, thereby avoiding the transition from shame to externalization of blame or the transition of externalization of blame to overt physical aggression. Similarly, self-control may moderate the direct or indirect pathways leading from guilt-proneness to aggression. Individuals who may be guilt-prone but are not able to self-regulate may continue to have trouble reining in their immediate impulses in aggressive situations.

Furthermore, theoreticians and clinicians often speak of different pathways for shame-prone individuals, as such; cognitions like neutralization techniques may not only be mediators but moderators as well. The link between shame and fury as described by H. B. Lewis (1971) does not necessarily assume an isomorphic relationship. What is it that turns shame into defensiveness, anger, and aggression? It may be that there are different pathways, such that shame-prone individuals who tend to use cognitions that outwardly direct blame are more likely to engage in violent criminal activity while those shame-prone individuals who display other cognitive styles such as helplessness are more likely to engage and continue in substance abuse behavior. Additionally, it is possible that the proposed destructive cycle between shame and risky behavior may depend on situational factors influencing one's evaluation of opportunities or future prospects (Fessler, Chapter 10, this volume; Wiebe, 2004). These types of models along with other complex patterns (e.g., nonlinear, compensatory) need to be further investigated.

Similarly, it is possible that both cognitions and individual characteristics play a role in guilt's relationship to risky and antisocial behavior. Perhaps it is easier for guilt-prone individuals to change their life narrative in order to establish a "noncriminal" identity. Or they may focus on the "recovering" part as opposed to the "addict" part of "recovering addict."

Regarding external events, the impact of life event "triggers" may be mediated or moderated by the propensity to experience shame- or guilt-proneness. For example, individuals who are shame-prone and who have experienced a traumatic event (e.g., child maltreatment) may be especially likely to participate in certain forms of risky behavior (Deblinger & Runyon, 2005). Or it may be that dropping out of school adversely affects those who are already high in shame. In addition, it may be that there are more dynamic processes at play. The internal processes may occur in response to environmental triggers. When thinking about links between external triggers and psychological mechanisms, questions about whether external factors affect *changes* in psychological characteristics arise. In other words, do these internal changes mediate the relationship between external factors and changes in risky behavior, or alternatively do the external factors mediate the relationship between the internal variables and changes in antisocial behavior?

There are a large number of possible external or environmental triggers that may be specific to a developmental level, but all may work through or be associated with developmentally common psychological mechanisms. For adults, a trigger may be loss of employment that may *lead* to increases in shame. For adolescents, dropping out of school may increase one's shame-proneness, which in turn may relate to increases in risky behavior. As Petit (2004) notes, "Emotional and cognitive processes may provide a key connecting link between developmental risk factors and antisocial behavior and violence" (p. 194).

SUMMARY

Researchers in the fields of developmental criminology, developmental psychology, and developmental psychopathology are increasingly emphasizing the importance of studying intraindividual changes in antisocial behavior (LeBlanc & Loeber, 1998; Nagin & Tremblay, 2001; Rutter et al., 2006). The process of desistance from any class of antisocial behaviors—be it conduct disorder, aggression, substance abuse, delinquency, or crime—is likely to be a complex one. Not only may triggers of change depend on the type of antisocial behavior, but also the developmental stage when it is manifested. It is possible that there are similar internal processes working at different developmental stages related to the phenomenon of "aging out" of crime and other risky behavior. From an intervention perspective, it is especially important to understand the processes and mechanisms whereby antisocial behavior is inhibited (Hawkins & Farrington, 1999). Allen, Moor, and Kuperminc (1997) explained that "even slight accelerations in developmental processes that occur naturally at the end of adolescence could lead to sizable reductions in the incidence of antisocial behavior within our society" (p. 550). While there are most likely triggers in the environment (e.g., family stability, living situation, educational opportunities, employment, marriage) that contribute to this desistance process, such events almost certainly work through and with individual factors. We believe that the self-conscious emotions, particularly shame and guilt, are especially promising individual factors that may help to more fully illuminate the life experiences and life changes of individuals. Tracy and Robins (2004) have stated, "We believe the time is ripe to devote greater attention to self-conscious emotions" (p. 104). We echo that statement and believe that there are numerous questions and hypotheses yet to be investigated as to how the self-conscious emotions of shame and guilt can help inform more effective prevention and intervention strategies to reduce antisocial and risky behavior across the lifespan.

ACKNOWLEDGMENTS

This research was supported by Grant No. RO1 DA14694 to June Price Tangney from the National Institute on Drug Abuse.

REFERENCES

Ackerman, B. P., Brown, E., & Izard, C. E. (2003). Continuity and change in levels of externalizing behavior in school of children from economically disadvantaged families. *Child Development, 74,* 694–709.

Ahmed, E., Harris, N., Braithwaite, J., & Braithwaite, V. (2001). *Shame management through reintegration.* Melbourne, Australia: Cambridge University Press.

Allen, J. P., Moore, C. M., & Kuperminc, G. P. (1997). Developmental approaches to understanding adolescent deviance. In S. Luthar, J. Burack, D. Cicchetti, & J. Weisz (Eds.), *Developmental psychopathology: Perspectives on adjustment, risk, and disorder* (pp. 548–567). Cambridge, UK: Cambridge University Press.

Andrews, B., Brewin, C. R., Rose, S., & Kirk, M. (2000). Predicting PTSD symptoms in victims of violent crime: The role of shame, anger, and childhood abuse. *Journal of Abnormal Psychology, 109,* 69–73.

Ashby, J. S., Rice, K. G., & Martin, J. L. (2006). Perfectionism, shame, and depressive symptoms. *Journal of Counseling and Development, 84*(2), 148–156.

Bennett, D. S., Sullivan, M. W., & Lewis, M. (2005). Young children's adjustment as a function of maltreatment, shame, and anger. *Child Maltreatment, 10*(4), 311–323.

Buss, A., & Durkee, A. (1957). An inventory for assessing different kinds of hostility. *Journal of Consulting Psychology, 21,* 343–349.

Braithwaite, J. (1989). *Crime, shame and reintegration.* Melbourne, Australia: Cambridge University Press.

Bybee, J., & Williams, C. (1994). *Does guilt show adaptive relationships with socioemotional competency and academic achievement?* Paper presented at the biennial conference on Human Development, Pittsburgh, PA.

Caspi, A., Elder, G. H., & Bem, D. J. (1988). Moving away from the world: Life-course patterns of shy children. *Developmental Psychology, 24,* 824–831.

Cooper, M. L., Frone, M. R., Russell, M., & Mudar, P. (1995). Drinking to regulate positive and negative emotions: A motivational model of alcohol use. *Journal of Personality and Social Psychology, 69,* 990–1005.

Covert, M. V., Tangney, J. P., Maddux, J. E., & Heleno, N. M. (2003). Shame-proneness, guilt-proneness, and interpersonal problem solving: A social cognitive analysis. *Journal of Social and Clinical Psychology, 22,* 1–12.

Cowman, S. E., & Ferrari, J. R. (2002). "Am I for real?": Predicting imposter tendencies from self-handicapping and affective components. *Social Behavior and Personality, 30,* 119–126.

Crick, N. R., & Dodge, K. A. (1994). A review and reformulation of social information-processing mechanisms in children's social adjustment. *Psychological Bulletin, 115,* 74–101.

Dearing, R. L., Stuewig, J., & Tangney, J. P. (2005). On the importance of distinguishing shame from guilt: Relations to problematic alcohol and drug use. *Addictive Behaviors, 30,* 1392–1404.

Deblinger, E., & Runyon, M. (2005). Understanding and treating feelings of shame in children who have experienced maltreatment. *Child Maltreatment, 10*(4), 364–376.

Dodge, K. A. (1980). Social cognition and children's aggressive behavior. *Child Development, 51*, 162–170.

Dweck, C. S., Hong, Y., & Chiu, C. (1993). Implicit theories: Individual differences in the likelihood and meaning of dispositional inferences. *Personality and Social Psychology Bulletin, 19*, 644–656.

Dweck, C. S., & Leggett, E. L. (1988). A social-cognitive approach to motivation and personality. *Psychological Review, 95*, 256–273.

Elis, L. A., & Simpson, S. S. (1995). Informal sanction threats and corporate crime: Additive versus multiplicative models. *Journal of Research in Crime and Delinquency, 32*, 399–424.

Fee, R., & Tangney, J. P. (2000). Procrastination: A means of avoiding shame and guilt? *Journal of Social Behavior and Personality, 15*, 167–184.

Feiring, C., & Taska, L. (2005). The persistence of shame following sexual abuse: A longitudinal look at risk and recovery. *Child Maltreatment, 10*, 337–349.

Ferguson, T. J., Barrett, K. C., Edmondson, R. S., Eyre, H. L., Ashbaker, M., Grotepas-Sanders, D., et al. (2000, February). *Adaptive and maladaptive features of shame.* Paper presented at the meeting of the Society for Personality and Social Psychology, Nashville, TN.

Ferguson, T. J., Stegge, H., Miller, E. R., & Olsen, M. E. (1999). Guilt, shame and symptoms in children. *Developmental Psychology, 35*, 347–357.

Fossum, M. A., & Mason, M. J. (1986). *Facing shame: Families in recovery.* New York: Norton.

Gendreau, P., Goggin, C., French, S., & Smith, P. (2006). Practicing psychology in correctional settings. In I. Weiner & A. Hess (Eds.), *The handbook of forensic psychology* (3rd ed., pp. 722–750), Hoboken, NJ: Wiley.

Gilligan, J. (1996). Exploring shame in special settings: A psychotherapeutic study. In C. Cordess & M. Cox (Eds.), *Forensic psychotherapy: Crime, psychodynamics and the offender patient, Vol. 2: Mainly practice* (pp. 475–489). London, UK: Jessica Kingsley.

Grasmick, H., Blackwell, B., & Bursik, R. (1993). Changes over time in gender differences in perceived risk of sanctions. *Law and Society Review, 27*, 679–705.

Grasmick, H., & Bursik, R. (1990). Conscience, significant others, and rational choice: Extending the deterrence model. *Law and Society Review, 24*, 837–861.

Guerra, N., & Slaby, R. (1990). Cognitive mediators of aggression in adolescent offenders: Intervention. *Developmental Psychology, 26*, 269–277.

Harder, D. W., & Zalma, A. (1990). Two promising shame and guilt scales: A construct validity comparison. *Journal of Personality Assessment, 55*, 729–745.

Harper, F. W. K., Austin, A. G., Cercone, J. J., & Arias, I. (2005). The role of shame, anger, and affect regulation in men's perpetration of psychological abuse in dating relationships. *Journal of Interpersonal Violence, 20*, 1648–1662.

Harris, N. (2003). Reassessing the dimensionality of the moral emotions. *British Journal of Psychology, 94*(4), 457–473.

Harris, N. (2006). Reintegrative shaming, shame, and criminal justice. *Journal of Social Issues, 62*, 327–346.

Hawkins, J. D., & Farrington, D. P. (1999). Editorial. *Criminal Behaviour and Mental Health, 9*, 3–7.

Hay, C. (2001). An exploratory test of Braithwaite's reintegrative shaming theory. *Journal of Research in Crime and Delinquency, 38*, 132–153.

Hirschi, T. (1969). *Causes of delinquency.* Berkeley and Los Angeles: University of California Press.

Jolliffe, D., & Farrington, D. (2004). Empathy and offending: A systematic review and meta-analysis. *Aggression and Violent Behavior, 9*(5), 441–476.

Krueger, R. F. (2002). Personality from a realist's perspective: Personality traits, criminal behaviors, and the externalizing spectrum. *Journal of Research in Personality, 36*, 564–572.

Krueger, R. F., Hicks, B., Patrick, C., Carlson, S., Iacono, W., & McGue, M. (2002). Etiologic connections among substance dependence, antisocial behavior and personality: Modeling the externalizing spectrum. *Journal of Abnormal Psychology, 111*, 411–424.

Krueger, R. F., Schmutte, P. S., Caspi, A., Moffitt, T. E., Campbell, K., & Silva, P. A. (1994). Personality traits are linked to crime among men and women: Evidence from a birth cohort. *Journal of Abnormal Psychology, 103,* 328–338.

Kulick, M. J. (1998). Shame-proneness and the utilization of coping behaviors and resources. *Dissertation Abstracts International: Section B: The Sciences and Engineering, 58,* 3928.

Le Blanc, M., & Loeber, R. (1998). Developmental criminology updated. In M. Tonry (Ed.), *Crime and justice: A review of research* (Vol. 23, pp. 115–198) Chicago: University of Chicago Press.

Leith, K. P., & Baumeister, R. F. (1998). Empathy, shame, guilt, and narratives of interpersonal conflicts: Guilt-prone people are better at perspective taking. *Journal of Personality, 66,* 1–37.

Lewis, H. B. (1971). *Shame and guilt in neurosis.* New York: International Universities Press.

Lewis, M. (1995). *Shame: The exposed self.* New York: Free Press.

Lindsay-Hartz, J. (1984). Contrasting experiences of shame and guilt. *American Behavioral Scientist, 27,* 689–704.

Loeber, R. (1982). The stability of antisocial and delinquent child behavior: A review. *Child Development, 53,* 1431–1446.

Loeber, R., & Stouthamer-Loeber, M. (1998). Development of juvenile aggression and violence: Some common misconceptions and controversies. *American Psychologist, 53,* 242–259.

Makkai, T., & Braithwaite, J. (1994). Reintegrative shaming and compliance with regulatory standards. *Criminology, 32,* 361–385.

Maruna, S. (2001). *Making good: How ex-convicts reform and reclaim their lives.* Washington, DC: American Psychological Association.

Maruna, S. (2004). Desistance and explanatory style: Ex-prisoners' techniques of shame management. *Journal of Contemporary Criminal Justice, 20,* 184–200.

Meehan, M. A., O'Connor, L. E., Berry, J. W., Weiss, J., Morrison, A., & Acampora, A. (1996). Guilt, shame, and depression in clients in recovery from addiction. *Journal of Psychoactive Drugs, 28,* 125–134.

Miller, P. A., & Eisenberg, N. (1988). The relation of empathy to aggressive and externalizing/antisocial behavior. *Psychological Bulletin, 103,* 324–344.

Moffitt, T. E. (1993). Adolescence-limited and life-course-persistent antisocial behavior: A developmental taxonomy. *Psychological Review, 100,* 674–701.

Moffitt, T. E. (2006). Life-course-persistent versus adolescence-limited antisocial behavior. In D. Cicchetti & D. Cohen (Eds.), *Developmental psychopathology* (2nd ed., Vol. 3, pp. 570–598). New York: Wiley.

Moffitt, T. E., Caspi, A., Harrington, H., & Milne, B. (2002). Males on the life-course persistent and adolescence-limited antisocial pathways: Follow-up at age 26. *Development and Psychopathology, 14,* 179–206.

Nagin, D. S., & Paternoster, R. (1993). Enduring individual differences and rational choice theories of crime. *Law and Society Review, 27,* 467–496.

Nagin, D. S., & Tremblay, R. (2001). Analyzing developmental trajectories of distinct but related behaviors: A group-based method. *Psychological Methods, 6,* 18–34.

O'Connor, L. E., Berry, J. W., Inaba, D., Weiss, J., & Morrison. A. (1994). Shame, guilt, and depression in men and women in recovery from addiction. *Journal of Substance Abuse Treatment, 11,* 503–510.

Paulhus, D. L., Robins, R. W., Trzesniewski, K. H., & Tracy, J. L. (2004). Two replicable suppressor situations in personality research. *Multivariate Behavioral Research, 39,* 301–326.

Petit, G. S. (2004). Violent children in developmental perspective: Risk and protective factors and the mechanisms through which they (may) operate. *Current Directions in Psychological Science, 13,* 194–197.

Ploeger, M. (1997). Youth employment and delinquency: Reconsidering a problematic relationship. *Criminology, 35,* 659–675.

Polakowski, M. (1994). Linking self- and social control with deviance: Illuminating the structure underlying a general theory of crime and its relation to deviant activity. *Journal of Quantitative Criminology, 10,* 41–78.

Potter-Efron, R. (2002). *Shame, guilt, and alcoholism* (2nd ed.). New York: Haworth Press.

Quiles, Z. N., & Bybee, J. (1997). Chronic and predispositional guilt: Relations to mental health, prosocial behavior and religiosity. *Journal of Personality Assessment, 69,* 104–126.

Rutter, M., Kim-Cohen, J., & Maughan, B. (2006). Continuities and discontinuities in psychopathology between childhood and adult life. *Journal of Child Psychology and Psychiatry, 47,* 276–295.

Sampson, R. J., & Laub, J. H. (1993). *Crime in the making: Pathways and turning points through life.* Cambridge, MA: Harvard University Press.

Sampson, R. J., & Laub, J. H. (1996). Socioeconomic achievement in the life course of disadvantaged men: Military service as a turning point, circa 1940–1965. *American Sociological Review, 61,* 347–367.

Scheff, T. J. (1987). The shame–rage spiral: A case study of an interminable quarrel. In H. B. Lewis (Ed.), *The role of shame in symptom formation* (pp. 109–149). Hillsdale, NJ: Erlbaum.

Slaby, R., & Guerra, N. (1988). Cognitive mediators of aggression in adolescent offenders: 1. Assessment. *Developmental Psychology, 24,* 580–588.

Steinberg, L. D., & Dornbusch, S. M. (1991). Negative correlates of part-time employment during adolescence: Replication and elaboration. *Developmental Psychology, 27,* 304–313.

Stern, A. E. (1999). Cognitive and behavioral aspects of shame among preadolescents. *Dissertation Abstracts International: Section B: The Sciences and Engineering, 59,* 4487.

Stouthamer-Loeber, M., Wei, E., Loeber, R., & Masten, A. S. (2004). Desistance from persistent serious delinquency in the transition to adulthood. *Development and Psychopathology, 16,* 897–918.

Stuewig, J., & McCloskey, L. (2005). The impact of maltreatment on adolescent shame and guilt: Psychological routes to depression and delinquency. *Child Maltreatment, 10,* 324–336.

Stuewig, J., Tangney, J. P., Heigel, C., & Harty, L. (2007). *Re-examining the relationship between shame, guilt, and aggression.* Manuscript in preparation.

Stuewig, J., Tangney, J. P., Mashek, D., Forkner, P., & Dearing, R. L. (in press). The moral emotions, alcohol dependence, and HIV risk behavior in an incarcerated sample. *Substance Use and Misuse, 42.*

Sykes, G. M., & Matza, D. (1957). Techniques of neutralization: A theory of delinquency. *American Sociological Review, 22,* 664–670.

Tangney, J. P. (1990). Assessing individual differences in proneness to shame and guilt: Development of the Self-Conscious Affect and Attribution Inventory. *Journal of Personality and Social Psychology, 59,* 102–111.

Tangney, J. P. (1991). Moral affect: The good, the bad, and the ugly. *Journal of Personality and Social Psychology, 61,* 598–607.

Tangney, J. P. (1992). Situational determinants of shame and guilt in young adulthood. *Personality and Social Psychology Bulletin, 18,* 199–206.

Tangney, J. P. (1995). Shame and guilt in interpersonal relationships. In J. P. Tangney & K. W. Fischer (Eds.), *Self-conscious emotions: The psychology of shame, guilt, embarrassment, and pride* (pp. 114–139). New York: Guilford Press.

Tangney, J. P., & Dearing, R. (2002). *Shame and guilt.* New York: Guilford Press.

Tangney, J. P., Miller, R. S., Flicker, L., & Barlow, D. H. (1996). Are shame, guilt and embarrassment distinct emotions? *Journal of Personality and Social Psychology, 70,* 1256–1269.

Tangney, J. P., Stuewig, J., Kendall, S., Reinsmith, C., & Dearing, R. (2006). *Implications of childhood shame and guilt for risky and illegal behaviors in young adulthood.* Unpublished manuscript, Department of Psychology, George Mason University.

Tangney, J. P., Stuewig, J., & Mashek, D. (2007). Moral emotions and moral behavior. *Annual Review of Psychology, 58,* 345–372.

Tangney, J. P., Wagner, P. E., Fletcher, C., and Gramzow, R. (1992). Shamed into anger?: The relation of shame and guilt to anger and self-reported aggression. *Journal of Personality and Social Psychology, 62,* 669–675.

Tangney, J. P., Wagner, P., & Gramzow, R. (1989). *The Test of Self-Conscious Affect (TOSCA).* Fairfax, VA: Department of Psychology, George Mason University.

Tangney, J. P., Wagner, P. E., & Gramzow, R. (1992). Proneness to shame, proneness to guilt, and psychopathology. *Journal of Abnormal Psychology, 103,* 469–478.

Tangney, J. P., Wagner, P. E., Hill-Barlow, D. H., Marschall, D., & Gramzow, R. (1996). The relation of shame and guilt to constructive vs. destructive responses to anger across the lifespan. *Journal of Personality and Social Psychology, 70,* 797–809.

Tangney, J. P., Wagner, P. E., Marschall, D., & Gramzow, R. (1991). *The Anger Response Inventory.* Fairfax, VA: Dept. of Psychology of George Mason University.

Tibbetts, S. G. (1997). Shame and rational choice in offending decisions. *Criminal Justice and Behavior, 24,* 234–255.

Tibbetts, S. G. (2003). Self-conscious emotions and criminal offending. *Psychological Reports, 93,* 101–126.

Tracy, J. L., & Robins, R. W. (2004). Show your pride: Evidence for a discrete emotion expression. *Psychological Science, 15*(3), 194–197.

Tracy J. L., & Robins, R. W. (2006). Appraisal antecedents of shame, guilt, and pride: Support for a theoretical model. *Personality and Social Psychology Bulletin, 32*(10), 1339–1351.

Wicker, F. W., Payne, G. C., & Morgan, R. D. (1983). Participant descriptions of guilt and shame. *Motivation and Emotion, 7,* 25–39.

Wiebe, R. P. (2004). Expanding the model of human nature underlying self-control theory: Implications for the constructs of self-control and opportunity. *Australian and New Zealand Journal of Criminology, 37,* 65–84.

21

Wrestling with Nature

An Existential Perspective on the Body and Gender in Self-Conscious Emotions

TOMI-ANN ROBERTS
JAMIE L. GOLDENBERG

All human beings must wrestle with nature. But nature's burden falls more heavily on one sex.

—Paglia (1990, p. 9)

The "self-consciousness" of self-conscious emotions has important existential and psychological significance. Based on terror management theory, we posit that the human ability to reflect on the self as an object of attention makes evident the vulnerability of the physical and, consequently, mortal body. In addition, objectification theory specifies that women in particular are especially prone to reflect on and evaluate their own bodies with respect to cultural standards. In this chapter, we integrate these two theoretical perspectives, and in doing so we highlight an existential underpinning of some of the self-conscious emotions and specifically emphasize the relevance of the awareness and evaluation of one's physical body in emotional manifestations, such as embarrassment, shame, self-disgust, and also pride. For each of these emotions, we find that, as Camille Paglia (1990) said, "Nature's burden falls more heavily on one sex" (p. 9). Our combined view, then, helps explain gender differences in these self-conscious emotions, and also predicts that, in situations in which the physical body is made salient, women will experience self-conscious emotional consequences more than men.

TERROR MANAGEMENT THEORY AND THE PROBLEM OF THE BODY

Terror management theory (TMT; e.g., Greenberg, Pyszczynski, & Solomon, 1986), derived from the ideas of Ernest Becker (e.g., 1971, 1973), posits that self-awareness plays a critical role in the human condition. The capacity to be self-aware is a tremendously adaptive mechanism, enabling a great degree of flexibility in responding to our environment; however, the ability to reflect on one's self also renders one conscious of the irrefutable fact that one's existence is doomed to come to an end. Such awareness creates a heavy burden for human beings. As the main character in John Cassavette's film *Shadows* recognized, "It is perfectly obvious—man, in contrast to other animals, is conscious of his own existence and therefore conscious of the possibility of nonexistence; ergo, he has anxiety."

However, following Becker, TMT posits that human beings use these same sophisticated cognitive capabilities that render us aware of our existential condition to develop means of "managing" this potential "terror" by conceiving of oneself as an integral part of a symbolic reality that is more meaningful and lasting than one's own individual physical existence. From the perspective of Becker (1973) and TMT, children originally identify with their parents and other close relationship figures to protect them from the anxiety associated with their sense of vulnerability (see also Bowlby, 1969, and Mikulincer, Florian, & Hirschberger, 2003, for a recent expansion of TMT). Thus, living up to parental standards of value leads to feelings of security and protection from anxiety. However, Becker argued that as children's cognitive sophistication develops and they recognize the inevitability of their own death, as well as their parents' inability to provide protection from the certainty of this outcome, the security blanket broadens and the standards of value shift to the larger cultural definitions of what it means to be a worthwhile person. In particular, fears about death are posited to be assuaged via a culturally specified system of meaning and by living up to the standards of one's particular anxiety-buffering worldview (i.e., self-esteem).

In support of this hypothesis, a large body of research demonstrates that people respond to reminders of their mortality (mortality salience) by clinging more rigidly to their cultural worldview and striving to maintain self-esteem. For example, mortality salience causes individuals to like others who support their views (e.g., Greenberg et al., 1990), recommend harsher penalties against others who transgress against cultural standards (Florian & Mikulincer, 1997), and express greater discomfort when they themselves violate a cultural norm (Greenberg, Simon, Porteus, Pyszczynski, & Solomon, 1995). Further, people try more fervently to measure up to personally relevant cultural standards when primed with mortality salience (e.g., Taubman Ben-Ari, Florian, & Mikulincer, 1999). Thus, self-esteem offers a shield of protection from psychological threats posed by the awareness of death.

The body, however, represents a special problem for humankind (for reviews, see Goldenberg, 2005; Goldenberg, Pyszczynski, Greenberg, & Solomon, 2000). For if death is such a central concern, it follows that people should also be threatened by that which reminds them of their mortal nature. The body, which aches, bleeds, and grows old, may make evident a trajectory toward which death can be the only end. Moreover, bodies exude all sorts of scents and substances that reinforce the reality of one's physical, and thus mortal, nature. The body therefore poses a psychological burden: for if, as TMT suggests, human beings cope with the existential threat associated with the awareness of impending death through symbolic constructions of meaning and value, then reminders of the physicality of the body should threaten the efficacy of these defenses. As Becker (1973) surmised, "[Humans] have a symbolic identity that brings [them] sharply out of nature" (p. 26), but the body reminds us that we are "hopelessly in it"; it is this paradox that makes the body such a problem.

It makes sense from this context that people's relationship with their bodies would be marked by a great deal of ambivalence, that people do not unequivocally embrace their physical body and its potential for pleasure, and, moreover, that existential concerns would underlie such threats. Experimental evidence supports this. For example, Goldenberg et al. (2001) showed that after a mortality salience induction, participants responded more negatively to an essay that described the biological similarities between humans and animals (i.e., our "creatureliness") relative to an essay emphasizing human uniqueness. In other research (Goldenberg, Cox, Pyszczynski, Greenberg, & Solomon, 2002), after reading this same essay emphasizing human creatureliness, and thus influenced by mortality salience, people reported decreased interest in the physical aspects of sex and thinking about physical sex increased the accessibility of death-related thoughts. For although one might expect that thinking about death could promote more positive reactions to sex for a number of reasons (e.g., to pass on one's genes, to experience life-affirming pleasure), our perspective implies that threats associated with the physical aspects of sex can pose a barrier to sex's more obvious redeeming qualities. Furthermore, in other research (Goldenberg et al., 2006; Goldenberg, Pyszczynski, McCoy, Greenberg, & Solomon, 1999), it has been found that individuals who are high in neuroticism and thus less successful at constructing defenses against mortality concerns (because they tend to be emotionally reactive and prone to a negative interpretation of events) exhibited the associative link between the physicality of the body and death in the absence of any explicit reminder of humans' "creaturely" or animal nature.

Becker (1973) argued that the "denial of death" is supported by the emotion of disgust. Although disgust probably evolved out of an evolutionary advantage associated with aversive reactions to dangerous food products (e.g., bitter berries), Rozin, Haidt, and McCauley (e.g., 2000) have theorized that, in humans, disgust is an ideological response to that which is offensive to the self because of its nature or origin, rather than a sensory response such as distaste. And, consistent with our position, Rozin et al. (2000) found that stimuli that blur the human–animal boundary (i.e., those that involve the fundamentals of animal life: eating, excreting, grooming, reproduction, injury, death and decay) are most likely to elicit disgust. We deem certain foods, sex, and bodily functions as disgusting because these things violate the "temple" of the body, which must be guarded against degradation, and by expressing disgust we can psychically distance ourselves from animals that we consider inferior. Such theorizing roots the emotion of disgust in an existential framework in which the ability to reflect on one's self, and to be threatened by one's physical nature, is critical in the experience of disgust. Consistent with this position, Goldenberg et al. (2001) found that people are more disgusted by bodily products and by animals after thinking about their own death. Cox, Goldenberg, Pyszczynski, and Wiese (in press) showed that the accessibility of death-related thoughts increases when people are exposed to pictorial representations of disgusting stimuli (e.g., an unflushed toilet).

It follows from TMT, however, that people can defend against the existential threat associated with the body by subjecting it to cultural regulations, prescriptions, and standards. In this way, the body is transformed into a symbolic entity and thus becomes, rather than a reminder of death, a vehicle for defense against it. In support of this analysis, a number of experiments have shown that although mortality salience increases distancing from and disgust in response to the physical aspects of the body, it does not increase distancing from its more symbolic reflections (e.g., the romantic aspects of sex; Goldenberg et al., 2002; Goldenberg et al., 1999). Goldenberg et al. (2002) also found that when people were primed with the idea that humans are unique (in contrast to a creatureliness prime), they did not at all distance from the body in response to mortality salience; and, moreover, people who derive a great deal of self-worth from their body tended to cling to it when primed with thoughts of death (Goldenberg, McCoy, Pyszczynski, Greenberg, & Solomon, 2000). These findings support the proposition that people defend against the threat of the physicality of the body by transforming it into a symbolic entity, and thus making the body a viable source of self-esteem. From the perspective of TMT, this means that an individual's basis of self-esteem is contingent on meeting the culture's prescriptions for an appropriate body. Such efforts require constant vigilance and a great deal of emotional resources. To date research has focused on showing the effects of mortality salience on efforts to attain the culture's standards (e.g., thinness for women; Goldenberg, Arndt, Hart, & Brown, 2005). However, we lay out a position in which such efforts may contribute to the experience of self-conscious emotions in women. For when it comes to the body, especially women's bodies, the standards are often narrowly defined, extreme, and unattainable for most (Fredrickson & Roberts, 1997; see also Goldenberg & Roberts, 2004).

OBJECTIFICATION THEORY AND SELF-OBJECTIFICATION

We turn now to our second theoretical perspective that we believe can inform an understanding of self-conscious emotions. Objectification theory (Fredrickson & Roberts, 1997), like TMT, is a perspective that also emphasizes the role of self-awareness, but focuses on the cultural emphasis placed on women's bodies in particular, and the development of a gendered form of self-consciousness that ensues when cultural standards for the body's appearance are internalized.

Objectification theory builds on feminist frameworks (e.g., Bordo, 1993) that argue that women's bodies are targeted for sexualized evaluation and scrutiny. This evaluation occurs both in interpersonal encounters and also in our interactions with the media, which seamlessly align viewers of female bodies with a sexualizing gaze. Sexual "objectification" occurs when women's bodies or body parts are separated from their humanity, or regarded as if they are capable of representing them (Bartky, 1990). Objectification can occur along a continuum, from pornographic treatment or even rape at one end, to the seemingly benign use of women's bodies as decorative features in popular media at the other. Sexual objectification occurs with "endless variety and monotonous similarity" (Rubin, 1975, p. 159); the images are everywhere, and constitute the cultural milieu in which we live.

But not all women's bodies or features of women's bodies are presented in these ubiquitous images. Women's bodies are acceptable and deemed "beautiful" only under certain conditions. For example, Wolf (1991) has shown that the images of the idealized female bodies to which we are exposed by the U.S. media are invariably of youth, slimness, and whiteness, and that these images are increasingly broadcast worldwide. Other cultures have alternate standards for feminine beauty, such as necks elongated with stacks of golden necklaces among the Karen of Upper Burma. However, regardless of the particular features deemed essential by a culture for feminine beauty, we have argued elsewhere that it is precisely when the more creaturely functions of women's bodies are actually or symbolically removed from the presentation, that the body is deemed publicly acceptable and attractive (Goldenberg & Roberts, 2004). So women's bodily functions are kept exceedingly discreet; for example, while breast-feeding in public is considered unseemly or even disgusting, push-up bras, which symbolically transform breasts into sexual objects, are sold via nationally televised commercials.

Simone deBeauvoir (1952) was the first to argue that the cultural milieu of sexual objectification functions to socialize girls and women to treat themselves as objects to be evaluated on the basis of appearance, and that this constitutes a risk factor for their self-esteem. Indeed, research shows that other people's evaluations of their bodily appearance have a far greater impact on how women are treated than how men are, at home, at school, and at work (cf. Unger, 1979). Given this, it behooves women to be vigilant in regard to their physical appearance as a way of anticipating others' treatment of them. Objectification theory posits that women come to internalize an observer's perspective on their own bodies, an effect termed "self-objectification." Self-objectification, then, involves thinking about and valuing one's own body more from a third-person perspective, focusing on observable body attributes, than from a first-person perspective, focusing on privileged or nonobservable body attributes.

This perspective on the body constitutes a particular form of self-consciousness, and, indeed, ample research has demonstrated that inducing self-objectification leads to self-conscious emotional consequences. Studies show that women engage in the practices of self-objectification more than do men overall, and that situationally inducing self-objectification leads women to experience greater self-conscious emotional and behavioral consequences than men (e.g., Fredrickson, Roberts, Noll, Quinn, & Twenge, 1998). For example, both men and women asked to try on and evaluate swimwear experienced body-focused self-consciousness, describing themselves with more appearance terms than those asked to try on a sweater. That is, they both reported a sense of being "on display" while in swimwear, despite the fact that no actual observers were present. This finding ties objectification theory with some theories of self-conscious emotions, which argue that an externalized observer, or a sense of exposure, is a prerequisite of such emotions as shame and embarrassment (e.g., Leary, 2004; M. Lewis, 2000). However, and germane to our argument in this chapter, men appear to experience the self-consciousness of self-objectification in a more lighthearted manner than women. In this study, men in swimsuits reported feeling more silly and foolish, whereas women reported feeling more ashamed, disgusted, and repulsed.

We have recently argued that the sexual objectification of women may serve the existential function of divorcing women from their animal nature (Goldenberg & Roberts, 2004). That is, following the TMT framework in which living up to cultural standards associated with the body provides symbolic protection from existential concerns, objectification can provide a kind of symbolic drapery that transforms "natural" women (who menstruate, give birth, and lactate) into "objects" of beauty and desire. Given that reminders of one's own animal nature are existentially threatening because they are also reminders of our mortality, it makes sense that women themselves would also willingly participate in the flight from the creaturely body through self-objectification—that is, monitoring of one's own appearance in an effort to attain cultural standards for the body. Indeed, experimental research has demonstrated that priming existential concerns with a standard mortality salience paradigm increases both men's and women's tendencies to objectify women's bodies in general, as well as women's tendencies to objectify their own bodies (Grabe, Routledge, Cook, Andersen, & Arndt, 2005). And, in other research, reminders of mortality have repeatedly been shown to increase women's concern with the appearance of their own body (e.g., Goldenberg et al., 2005; Routledge, Arndt, & Goldenberg, 2004). So the effort women expend to slim, refashion, conceal, sanitize, deodorize, depilitate, and even surgically alter their bodies may provide a kind of existential protection from reminders of their creaturely, mortal nature. Such efforts not only cost time and money, but also come with a heavy psychological price for girls' and women's self-esteem (see Fredrickson & Roberts, 1997).

GENDERED EMOTIONAL EXPRESSION IN THE SELF-CONSCIOUS ANIMAL

We have thus far delineated a framework in which we suggest that our self-conscious nature renders us aware of the facts of our existence: that we are physical creatures destined to die. We have also specified that this creates a situation in which the body is a central problem with which human beings must deal. And, moreover, women appear to bear the brunt of the burden of the body. We hope to have made the case that a great deal of energy goes into managing the "terror" associated with the body and death. But yet we do not do so without emotional repercussions.

We now turn our attention to the expression of emotion in the self-conscious animal, with hope that a theoretical perspective informed by TMT and objectification theory can extend previous insights into self-conscious emotions. We believe our combined perspective provides an explanatory scheme for gender differences in a number of self-conscious emotions, and, further, that when the physical body is placed at the forefront of social interaction, why it is that women are more likely to experience self-conscious emotions as a result. Much of our argument here is likely relevant particularly to Western culture, where standards for the body have been influenced so heavily by a Judeo-Christian dualist framework. We would predict fewer negative self-conscious emotional outcomes in cultures where creaturely aspects of the body are more publicly acceptable.

In his original discourse on emotional expression, Darwin (1872/1965) noted that although there is continuity between the emotional experience of our species and that of others, there are some emotions that are unique to humans: the emotions of self-consciousness. Following Darwin, a number of theorists have delineated conditions necessary for the experience of a handful of such emotions. In discussing embarrassment, Arnold Buss (1980, p. 132) asked, "What do older children and adults possess—lacking in animals, infants, and the severely mentally retarded—that is required for blushing to occur?" In response, he stated, "Animals, infants and the severely mentally retarded are not aware of themselves as social objects." The supposition that ability to reflect on one's own existence is necessary to experience the so-called self-conscious emotions is generally agreed upon (e.g., M. Lewis, 1997; Tracy & Robins, 2004a) and sets the stage for an existential perspective on self-conscious emotions.

Theorists such as M. Lewis (see also Fischer & Tangney, 1995; Stipek, 1995) suggest that in addition to involving reflecting on one's self, the experience of self-conscious emotions depends also on the evaluation of one's self against some standard. Thus, to experience such emotions, individuals must internalize some view of the world that is meaningful and provides a context for which their own selves and behaviors can be perceived as significant. Falling short of such standards leads to negative self-conscious emotions, such as embarrassment, shame, and, we suggest, self-disgust. Positive evaluations can lead to feelings of pride. This framework is consistent with our perspective in which children first strive to attain parental standards and later strive to achieve cultural standards as a means of existential protection and suffer emotional ramifications as a result of failure.

Of course, the existential framework that we have proposed points to the central importance of the awareness of one's body in terms of the potential for terror and, consequently, as a domain in which it is particularly important to attain relevant standards. Following Becker (1971), we note that the first standards a child must obtain are those rooted in the body: children receive praise (and anxiety reduction) when they master developmental bodily milestones (e.g., rolling over, potty training). As the child grows, praise-worthy events become less rooted in biology, and in fact, regulation of the body (Freud's repression of impulses) becomes a requirement for appropriate behavior. Based on objectification theory, we further point out that the standards for girls' and women's bodies are often particularly stringent and that gender differences in the experience of self-conscious emotions may result as a consequence of women's striving (and often failing) to conform. With these suppositions in mind, we turn now to four self-conscious emotions: embarrassment, shame, self-disgust, and pride.

Embarrassment

Embarrassment occurs when unwanted events threaten the social image we wish to maintain (R. S. Miller, 1996). We feel embarrassed when our public presentation is inept or unbecoming. It is not surprising from the perspective of TMT and objectification theory that the experience of embarrassment often involves an inappropriate presentation of the body. Most of us can think of terribly embarrassing moments when our bodies betrayed us: we burped or farted in public, we stumbled and fell, an item of clothing slipped and revealed too much skin. Keltner and Buswell (1996) found that four out of five of the most frequently cited antecedents of embarrassment recalled by participants involved the physical body. These situations were physical pratfalls, such as slipping in the mud; loss of control over the body, such as vomiting after drinking too much; shortcomings in physical appearance, such as walking around with toilet paper stuck to one's shoe; and failure at privacy regulation, such as accidentally walking in on others engaged in sexual relations. It is as if, in embarrassment, the physical body asserts itself, tripping us up as it were. Public attention is drawn not to our ideas or to our soul, but to our physical self, and this incites the embarrassed display: gaze aversion, smile control, and sometimes a blush. Given the prominence of the body in situations where embarrassment occurs, we would go so far as to argue that this self-conscious emotion seems to be about regulating the physical body in public. Indeed, we note that in most of the embarrassing situations that Keltner and Buswell (1996) cite the connection between the body and its animal nature (e.g., bathroom needs, sex) is salient.

The embarrassed response apparently provides an appeasement function. That is, we like others when they show a blush or embarrassed reaction to their own faux-pas, much more than those who do not (Keltner & Buswell, 1997). So the display of the embarrassed expression seems to have evolved to lead others to help remedy social transgressions (Keltner & Anderson, 2000). If I burp in public, and show the embarrassed expression by blushing and saying "Oops!," I draw others toward me in recognition that I have violated social norms of bodily propriety, but I understand those norms and adhere to them typically. If, on the other hand, I burp in public and show no sign of remorse, I am likely to be responded to with disgust and disapproval.

It is consistent with our perspective that women show stronger and more frequent embarrassment than men (R. S. Miller, 1992). This is perhaps because women's bodies provide more opportunities for embarrassment. In addition to the body functions both sexes share, women bleed monthly, get pregnant, give birth, and lactate. There are simply more occasions for embarrassing body-function betrayals. In addition, however, social norms of femininity require greater control over the body. Feminine propriety dictates that a woman who burps in public ought to be more embarrassed than a man. In a study in which a male or a female experimenter excused him- or herself to either use the restroom or to get some paperwork, results showed that participants rated the female experimenter more negatively in the bathroom condition than the control, but no differences were found for the male experimenter (Roberts & MacLane, 2002).

Objectification theory would predict, too, that the caprices of the fashion industry, combined with the stigma that women who reveal "too much skin" suffer, undoubtedly means that women experience more embarrassing moments with respect to states of undress. In one study, mortality salience led women to report that touching their breasts in the context of a breast self-examination is embarrassing (Goldenberg, 2001), and in other research reminders of one's physical nature actually led women to inhibit actual breast exam behavior (Goldenberg, Arndt, Hart, & Turrisi, 2004). Further, studies show that women suffer more "appearance anxiety" than do men; underlying this chronic vigilance concerning the body's appearance is the fear of embarrassment (Dion, Dion, & Keelan, 1990).

Shame

Freud argued that shame involves "symbolic nakedness" (Yorke, 1990). We like this conception because we would also argue that the moments that involve the most burning shame for us inevitably involve the creaturely body in some way. The Renaissance fresco by Masaccio known as *The Expulsion from the Garden of Eden* is perhaps one of the most dramatic depictions of shame, and its links to the physical body. In it, Adam and Eve are shown naked, and mortified with shame, as an angel above them exiles them forever from their happiness.

Several conceptions of the self-conscious emotions argue that shame and embarrassment are very close relatives, with shame being the more morally weighty of the two (e.g., Keltner & Buswell, 1996; Tangney, Miller, Flicker, & Barlow, 1996). Whereas embarrassment follows relatively trivial violations of norms and is always experienced in the presence of others, shame follows from the failure of the self to achieve standards and can often be experienced alone. Not surprisingly, then, some researchers have found that the experience occurs developmentally later than embarrassment (e.g., M. Lewis, 1997)—once children have internalized parental and later societal standards, in line with Becker's (1971) conceptualization. Having attention drawn to one's body alone can incite the blush of embarrassment; having a body that fails to conform to sociomoral standards of conduct or appearance can lead to shame. In embarrassment, the public presentation of self is inept, whereas in shame the entire self is deemed deficient (Shott, 1979).

The relationship between shame and the body is evident in the derivation of the word itself. *Shame* derives from the Germanic word for "cover" (*Oxford English Dictionary*). Darwin (1872/1965) argued that the emotion of shame reflects a strong urge for concealment, and that the expression of shame involves body gestures that are designed to make the person as small as possible. People who are ashamed describe wanting to hide or even disappear (Tangney, 1993). When shamed, it seems our bodies feel not just foolish or awkward, but rather enormous, ugly, or offensive under the painful (real or imagined) gaze of others.

Shame stemming specifically from concerns about the body is related to the fear of eliciting disgust and social rejection from others, and can have powerful consequences. Research shows that many people with "shameful" diseases or conditions (e.g., obesity, hemorrhoids, venereal diseases, acne) may actually avoid medical help (Lazare, 1997). Acne is an interesting example, for it is a skin condition that is considered relatively innocuous by the medical community, and yet sufferers can experience profound shame because of it (Kellett & Gilbert, 2001). As with so many conditions in which the physical body is found lacking, observers make moral judgments about the cleanliness of the acne sufferer (despite the fact that acne is not caused by "dirt" on the skin). So acne sufferers not only feel ashamed because their facial skin does not conform to standards of attractiveness, but also because they are considered dirty and unhygienic. Interestingly, most commercials for acne medication show a person (usually a teenager) hiding in the house, as if to say, "If you have such a condition, you should be hiding."

As with embarrassment, in shame again we find an important gender difference linked to body concerns. Women have been shown, in general, to experience more shame than men (H. B. Lewis, 1971). And women's greater shame-proneness appears to be rooted in existential concerns. For example, Arndt and Goldenberg (2004) demonstrated that self-focus led to increased shame for women but not for men. Following from objectification theory, it makes sense that focus on the self is likely to lead women more so than men to focus on the body and its shortcomings. Further, Goldenberg et al. (2005) found that mortality salience led women, but not men, to restrict their consumption of a fattening snack food and, further, mortality salience led women to perceive their bodies as more discrepant from ideal and this perceived discrepancy mediated their restricted eating. In the future, research on TMT would benefit from measuring shame directly; these finding, however, are consistent with our hypothesized impact of existential concerns on women's shame experiences.

Indeed, gender differences in body shame are particularly pronounced. One study of children found that many more girls than boys feel ashamed of their bodies (Offer, Ostrov, & Howard, 1984). Studies of undergraduates also show more body shame reported by women than by men (e.g., McKinley, 1998). Women's comparison of their own bodies to the mythical, idealized, slim bodies portrayed by the media is a recipe for shame (Wolf, 1991). Indeed, weight dissatisfaction is practically universal among women. Because weight is considered an attribute over which people have personal control, women feel ashamed of their moral "failure" to be thinner (Quinn & Crocker, 1999; Silberstein, Striegel-Moore, & Rodin, 1987). Women also experience more shame about sex than do men (Oliver & Hyde, 1993). But, interestingly, the Kinsey survey of sexual practices showed that U.S. women were more ashamed when asked about their weight than when asked how often they masturbated (Kinsey, Pomeroy, Martin, & Gebhard, 1953). So it appears that physical attractiveness, and particularly body weight, trumps all other concerns when it comes to women's shame. Empirical studies bear this out. For example, Goldenberg and Au (2004) found that women who felt negatively about their body weight (but not other aspects of their body) responded to negative weight-related feedback (as operationalized by viewing one's body in a distorted mirror that made one's appearance shorter and heavier) with increased feelings of shame. In addition, women, but not men, experienced increases in body shame when trying on swimwear but not a sweater (Fredrickson et al., 1998). And in a study in which participants were primed with body appearance words such as "attractiveness" and "physique," women responded with greater feelings of shame than did men (Roberts & Gettman, 2004).

Menstruation is another area where women suffer the stigma of body-based shame.

It is, after all, known popularly as "the curse." The rhetoric around menstrual product advertising is often designed to appeal to women's feelings of shame regarding this bodily event (Simes & Berg, 2001). For example, a current print advertisement for Tampax tampons depicts a sad-looking puppy dog sitting on a woman's lap. The copy reads, "Certain leaks can be forgiven." By implying that menstrual leaks are *un*forgivable, the ad illustrates the cultural mandate that menstruation be covered up lest women suffer terrible shame. Indeed, when girls are asked about menarche, a primary emotional response that emerges is shame (e.g., Moore, 1995). Being exposed as a menstruating person is not just embarrassing, it is shameful. Again, the link to hygiene supports our contention that self-conscious emotions about body functions such as menstruation have their roots in existential concerns. The taboos surrounding contact with menstrual blood that exist across cultures stem from deep-seated fears of contamination (Delaney, Lupton, & Toth, 1988). Thus, the shame many women feel about menstruation is a reflection, in part, of a view of the self as a source of contamination or pollution. It is not surprising, then, that just about the time of menarche (and also at the onset of sexual objectification by others) is when girls' self-image and body esteem in particular tends to decrease compared to those of boys (e.g., Rosenblum & Lewis, 1999). Furthermore, Roberts (2004) showed that the extent to which women self-objectify is related to feelings of shame about their menstruation. That is, the more women subscribe to self-objectifying standards for their bodily appearance, the more shame they feel toward the natural body function of menstruation.

Returning to Masaccio's fresco, we are struck by the differing portrayals of Adam and Eve's shame. In a poignant illustration of our contention that the creaturely body burdens women more than men with self-conscious emotions, Adam is shown covering his eyes whereas Eve is shown covering her breasts and her genital area. Indeed "nature's burden falls more heavily on one sex," and thus the depiction of shame in this painting focuses differentially on the sight, or intelligence, of men, and on the body functions of women. It may be, further, that Adam is shielding his eyes from having to look at Eve's naked body.

Self-Disgust

"We can become the other to ourselves" (W. I. Miller, 1997, p. 51) and experience disgust directed toward the self. Some have argued that self-disgust, or self-loathing, is part of the subjective experience of shame (e.g., H. B. Lewis, 1971). Whether self-disgust is its own self-conscious emotion, or a specialized, perhaps harsher, version of shame, is yet to be determined. However, it is clear that individuals can experience self-disgust, and that this is a particularly negative self-conscious feeling state in which, again, we find the body and gender to be particularly relevant.

We propose that disgust is especially likely to be directed at one's self when one fails to maintain certain societal standards of conduct, primarily with respect to the cultural prescriptions requiring the concealment of our physical, animal nature. The emotional reaction of disgust toward oneself, thus, meets commonly endorsed criteria for a self-conscious emotion in that it involves self-evaluation against internalized cultural standards (e.g., Tracy & Robins, 2004a). If "cleanliness is next to Godliness," and if, as Freud (1961) argued, soap is the yardstick of civilization, then our efforts to maintain appropriate hygiene are motivated in large part to earn and sustain others' social acceptance of us, to "civilize" ourselves as it were. Furthermore, the lengths to which we go to conceal indecent bodily functions, and generally maintain and enhance our physical appearance, may also be viewed as efforts to control our own feelings of self-disgust. Consistently, research shows that those whose bodies violate social norms, or those who perceive their bodies to be socially unacceptable, feel self-disgust. For example, disgust is linked to the self-image in those who suffer from body image disorders such as body dismorphic disorder (Phillips & Heining, 2002). Obesity is associated with feelings of disgust toward one's own "grotesque" body (Stunkard & Mendelson, 1967). Homosexuals seeking counseling sometimes display profound self-disgust and self-contempt regarding their bodies and sexuality (Cornett, 1993; Taywaditep, 2001).

Consistent with a perspective informed by objectification theory, in which women's bodies are held to more rigorous standards and women are particularly apt to reflect on their own failures, research shows that women are more likely to experience disgust directed toward the bodily self than are men. For example, in the experiment in which women and men were asked to try on and evaluate themselves in swimwear in front of a mirror, both showed predictable levels of self-consciousness (Fredrickson et al., 1998). Viewing their bodies in swimsuits brought the body front and center for all participants; however, women's reactions were far less lighthearted than men's. Women in swimsuits were more likely to respond to their bodies with "disgust, distaste and revulsion" than were men. In another study, in which participants were primed with words that typically appear on fashion and body magazine covers (e.g., weight, attractiveness, physique), women showed increased feelings of self-disgust (e.g., "I feel disgusted with myself") but men did not (Roberts & Gettman, 2004).

Menstruation is a bodily function heavily associated with pollution and hygiene, and here women again have more opportunities for self-disgust. The marketing of menstrual products emphasizes cleanliness, secrecy, and decorum (Coutts & Berg, 1993), promising women a sanitized, deodorized, and fresh bodily presentation. The message delivered by the media is fraught with disgust-related rhetoric; the way to handle the hygienic crisis of one's period is through frequent bathing and "sanitary napkin" changing (Crawford & Unger, 2004). Indeed, it's no wonder women heed the advertiser's warnings. When menstrual status is made known, women are treated with disgust-like responses. For example, Roberts, Goldenberg, Power, and Pyszczynski (2002) showed that the mere presence of a wrapped tampon led both men and women to physically distance themselves from a female confederate. Although self-disgust has not been measured in the context of TMT research, disgust toward the body and its by-products was shown to increase in response to mortality salience. Thus it makes sense that one's own body, especially when it fails to conform to appropriate standards for hygiene or appearance, can be perceived as more disgusting after mortality salience.

One study showed that the extent to which women self-objectify predicted self-disgust and contempt toward their menstrual cycles (Roberts, 2004). In other words, internalizing the cultural standards of feminine attractiveness exacts a cost for women in terms of self-conscious emotions regarding the physical body and its functions. The great lengths to which women go to conceal, sanitize, and deodorize their bodies' functions illustrate their flight from the creaturely, existentially threatening body. When such efforts fail, women anticipate others' social rejection and thus feel disgusted with themselves.

W. I. Miller (1997) has written, "Disgust works to support shame in public settings, but it has a more private and secret life" (p. 162). We believe this private, or self-directed, disgust deserves attention as a particularly noxious self-conscious emotion, one likely to be experienced especially by women in a culture in which sex and reproduction are at the very core of what is existentially threatening to our efforts at "civilized" social interaction. Whether self-disgust deserves its own place as a self-conscious emotion is a matter of debate. However, we would argue that our perspective, informed by both TMT and objectification theory, raises the status of this feeling state, and we encourage more work in this area.

Pride

Thus far, we have discussed only the dark side of self-conscious emotions. It is not surprising, from our existential framework, that reflecting on one's self as an object can result in a number of negative emotional states, and that women are more likely than men to suffer self-conscious emotions when the physical body is made salient. Recently, one more positive emotion, pride (see Tracy & Robins, Chapter 15, this volume), has begun to receive some attention. Pride, in a sense, is the flip side of shame (e.g., Brown & Marshall, 2001; Scheff, 1988). It can be understood as the emotional response to reflecting on one's self favorably. Consistent with this definition, it is not surprising that self-esteem is closely associated with pride (and conversely with shame; Brown & Marshall, 2001). Only humans can feel self-conscious about their bodies, and they also are the only creatures who can feel proud about their bodies.

From a Beckerian perspective, it makes sense that feelings of pride originate in relation to the mastery of bodily functions. The first standards to which an infant is exposed are those surrounding basic bodily functions (e.g., eating, sleeping, and defecating). Much like Freud's conceptualization, the basis for parental approval results in increased control (and repression) of one's bodily functions (e.g., potty training), but unlike Freud, Becker (1971; see also Brown, 1959) suggested that regulation of the body functions to boost self-esteem and thereby ward off existentially rooted anxiety. Thus, the body, which begins as a natural source of pleasure, becomes transformed into a symbol through which one can obtain self-esteem by living up to parental and later cultural standards.

Findings that people who derive a great deal of self-worth from their physical body cling to this aspect of their self when primed with thoughts of death (Goldenberg, McCoy, et al., 2000) is consistent with this position. In this research, participants with high levels of body esteem more highly identified with their bodily self after a mortality salience induction. Goldenberg, McCoy, et al. (2000) also showed that under such conditions sex can even be desired as a means of demonstrating one's pride about one's body. In this sense, the body can become a source of pride, a positive reflection on one's self, an achievement.

The domains, however, in which women can experience pride have traditionally been more limited than those for men. For decades feminists (e.g., de Beauvoir, 1952; Woolf, 1929) have been pointing out inequities in opportunities to exert competence in nonbodily domains, such as academics and careers. Furthermore, when women do obtain the same level of success as men, it is less likely that they will experience pride, as they are often criticized for failing to conform to appropriate gender roles, or even appropriately "feminine" bodily self-presentation (Fiske, Bersoff, Borgida, Deaux, & Heilman, 1991). So while males have more opportunity for feeling proud of nonbodily accomplishments, for girls and women, beginning in adolescence, the body remains the central domain about which society judges. Certainly males can (if they choose) make their body central to self-evaluation through sportsmanship. The difference here, however, is that for women the body is no longer treated as a realm of competency, but rather as an object to be evaluated by others (e.g., sex object). Not surprisingly, girls who do involve themselves in sports reap psychological benefits (Pedersen & Seidman, 2004). However, on the whole, beginning in adolescence, males demonstrate significantly more pride in their bodies than do their female counterparts, and this difference has been associated with gender differences in depression, starting at about the same age (e.g., Allgood-Merten, Lewinsohn, & Hops, 1990; Grant et al., 1999). Consistently, Robins, Trzesniewski, Tracy, Gosling, and Potter (2002) found that self-esteem for males and females starts to diverge in adolescence, with girls' self-esteem dipping more than that of boys, and that males' self-esteem was consistently higher throughout adulthood with this difference narrowing in old age.

It is worth noting, however, that although some nonbodily domain of pride (e.g., success in the male workplace) have been less accessible for women, women do have a bodily domain, independent of bodily appearance, in which they can take pride. Women typically perform the critical role of bearing and nurturing children. Although we have suggested that women's reproductive responsibilities have been used to derogate them and that they can be a source of embarrassment, shame, and even self-disgust, it makes sense that the creaturely female body *can* be a source of pride: "I have the body that bore these children, and I have used this body to raise healthy offspring who do me proud." However, even here Glick and Fiske (2001) have shown that it is often women's nurturing capacities that are highlighted in "benevolent sexist" attitudes toward women. Such attitudes portray women as *either* competent and autonomous (the aggressive career woman) *or* likable and worthy (the nurturing, selfless mother). In other words, to the extent that women can take pride in their reproductive and nurturing capacities, it seems to come at the expense of being taken seriously in other, nonbodily domains.

It is easy to see that the physical body is involved in the expression of pride. Darwin (1872/1965) observed that a proud person holds the head and spine erect, making himor herself appear as large as possible and displaying dominance. Tracy and Robins (2004b) have shown that indeed this bodily expression of pride is widely recognized and identified as such. Furthermore, Darwin proposed that the upright position of the body not only reflects and conveys felt pride, but may influence it. Indeed, some research has shown that individuals feel more pride when given positive feedback in the context of an upright posture as opposed to a stooped one (e.g., Stepper & Strack, 1993). However, in keeping with our position that the physical body damns women more than men, Roberts and Arefi-Afshar (in press) recently showed that men rated their performance on a cognitive task more highly and felt more satisfaction when upright as opposed to stooped, whereas the inverse effect was found for women, who rated themselves more highly when stooped as opposed to upright. We interpret this counterintuitive effect through the lens of objectification theory. Upright posture, with breasts prominent, may feel not especially prideful but instead may induce self-consciousness for women, since it can be viewed not so much as a signal of dominance but rather as sexually open or inviting. Thus, the positive proprioceptive aftereffects of erect posture may not be as readily available for women as for men in an objectifying culture.

So we can see that there is a dark side to even the most optimistic of the self-conscious emotions. Pride is not always considered a positive emotion. Tracy and Robins (2003) suggest that when pride is not based on actual achievement, it can become hubristic and more accurately relates to narcissism than to self-esteem. This may be particularly true when it comes to women's bodies, since when they are positively evaluated it is usually based on appearance rather than health, functioning, or competence. So women are not only provided with fewer opportunities to feel proud of their bodies, but when they do, it is likely that the pride experienced is more in line with Tracy and Robin's narcissistic, hubristic pride. Indeed, Freud (1933) called such pride in women *vanity*.

CONCLUSION

We have painted a portrait of a self-conscious animal that is driven to compare itself with standards. This picture is consistent with that of other researchers who have studied self-conscious emotions (e.g., M. Lewis, 1997; Tracy & Robins, 2004a). However, from our perspective, comparison of one's self to standards serves an existential function; attainment of first parental and then cultural standards provides security in the face of the awareness of death. In short, by maintaining faith in one's cultural worldview and living up to its standards of value (acquiring self-esteem), people can feel as if they are part of something larger, more meaningful, and more enduring than their own physical, corporeal life.

In our framework, the body takes center stage. As Becker (1971) suggested, "We spend our lives searching in mirrors to find out who we 'really are' " (p. 36). The physical body that reflects back to us in those mirrors poses an existential threat because it makes evident to us our human creatureliness and our vulnerability to death. Following Becker and TMT, we argue that therefore we "drape" the body with symbolic meanings, such that culture becomes our mirror, telling us precisely how the body should appear. We suggest that successes and failures in attaining cultural standards for the body play a significant role in the experience of self-conscious emotions. Further, and in line with objectification theory, it seems that for women the cultural mirror is a far harsher critic. And thus bodily self-consciousness in women magnifies the experience of such emotions as embarrassment, shame, and self-disgust, and even takes the air out of the experience of pride.

REFERENCES

Allgood-Merten, B., Lewinsohn, P. M., & Hops, H. (1990). Sex differences and adolescent depression. *Journal of Abnormal Psychology, 99*, 53–63.

Arndt, J., & Goldenberg, J. L. (2004). From self-awareness to shame-proneness: Evidence of causal sequence among women. *Self and Identity, 3*, 27–37.

Bartky, S. L. (1990). *Femininity and domination: Studies in the phenomenology of oppression.* New York: Routledge.

Becker, E. (1971). *The birth and death of meaning* (2nd ed.). New York: Free Press.

Becker, E. (1973). *The denial of death.* New York: Free Press.

Bordo, S. (1993). *Unbearable weight: Feminism, Western culture, and the body.* Berkeley and Los Angeles: University of California Press.

Bowlby, J. (1969). *Attachment and loss: Attachment.* New York: Basic Books.

Brown, J. D., & Marshall, M. A. (2001). Self-esteem and emotions: Some thoughts about feelings. *Personality and Social Psychology Bulletin, 27*, 575–584.

Brown, N. O. (1959). *Life against death: The psychoanalytical meaning of history.* Middletown, CT: Wesleyan Press.

Buss, A. H. (1980). *Self-consciousness and social anxiety.* San Francisco: Freeman.

Cornett, C. (1993). Dynamic psychotherapy of gay men: A view from self psychology. In C. Cornett (Ed.), *Affirmative dynamic psychotherapy with gay men* (pp. 45–76). Northvale, NJ: Aronson.

Coutts, L. B., & Berg, D. H. (1993). The portrayal of the menstruating woman in menstrual product advertisements. *Health Care for Women International, 14,* 179–191.

Cox, C. R., Goldenberg, J. L., Pyszczynski, T., & Weise, D. (in press). Disgust, creatureliness, and the accessibility of death-related thoughts. *European Journal of Social Psychology.*

Crawford, M., & Unger, R. K. (2004). *Women and gender: A feminist psychology* (4th ed.). Boston: McGraw-Hill.

Darwin, C. (1965). *The expression of the emotions in man and animals.* Chicago: University of Chicago Press. (Original work published 1872)

de Beauvoir, S. (1952). *The second sex.* New York: Knopf.

Delaney, J., Lupton, M. J., & Toth, E. (1988). *The curse: A cultural history of menstruation.* Urbana: University of Illinois Press.

Dion, K. L., Dion, K. K., & Keelan, J. P. (1990). Appearance anxiety as a dimension of social-evaluative anxiety: Exploring the ugly duckling syndrome. *Contemporary Social Psychology, 14,* 220–224.

Fischer, K. W., & Tangney, J. P. (1995). Self-conscious emotions and the affect revolution: Framework and overview. In J. P. Tangney & K. W. Fischer (Eds.), *Self-conscious emotions: The psychology of shame, guilt, embarrassment, and pride* (pp. 3–24). New York: Guilford Press.

Fiske, S. T., Bersoff, D. N., Borgida, E., Deaux, K., & Heilman, M. E. (1991). Social science research on trial: Use of sex stereotyping research in *Price Waterhouse v. Hopkins. American Psychologist, 46,* 1049–1060.

Florian, V., & Mikulincer, M. (1997). Fear of death and the judgment of social transgressions: A multidimensional test of terror management theory. *Journal of Personality and Social Psychology, 73,* 369–380.

Fredrickson, B. L., & Roberts, T. (1997). Objectification theory: Toward understanding women's lived experiences and mental health risks. *Psychology of Women Quarterly, 21,* 173–206.

Fredrickson, B. L., Roberts, T., Noll, S. M., Quinn, D. M., & Twenge, J. M. (1998). That swimsuit becomes you: Sex differences in self-objectification, restrained eating and math performance. *Journal of Personality and Social Psychology, 75,* 269–284.

Freud, S. (1933). Femininity. In J. Strachey (Ed. and Trans.), *New introductory lectures on psychoanalysis* (pp. 139–167). New York: Norton.

Freud, S. (1961). *Civilization and its discontents.* (J. Strachey, Ed. and Trans.). New York: Norton.

Glick, P., & Fiske, S. T. (2001). An ambivalent alliance: Hostile and benevolent sexism as complementary justifications for gender inequality. *American Psychologist, 56,* 109–118.

Goldenberg, J. L. (2001, August). *Human corporeality: What's the matter?* Paper presented at the annual meeting of the International Conference on Experimental Existential Psychology, Amsterdam, The Netherlands.

Goldenberg, J. L. (2005). The body stripped down: An existential account of ambivalence toward the physical body. *Current Directions in Psychological Science, 14,* 224–228.

Goldenberg, J. L., Arndt, J., Hart, J., & Brown, M. (2005). Dying to be thin: The effects of mortality salience and body-mass index on restricted eating among women. *Personality of Social Psychology Bulletin, 31,* 1400–1412.

Goldenberg, J. L., Arndt, J., Hart, J., & Turrisi, R. (2004). *Existential discomfort with the creaturely body and women's reluctance to perform breast self-examinations.* Manuscript submitted for publication.

Goldenberg, J. L., & Au, M. (2004). The effects of weight self-esteem and negative feedback on women's experience of shame. Unpublished data, University of California, Davis.

Goldenberg, J. L., Cox, C. R., Pyszczynski, T., Greenberg, J., & Solomon, S. (2002). Understanding human ambivalence about sex: The effects of stripping sex of meaning. *Journal of Sex Research, 39,* 310–320.

Goldenberg, J. L., Hart, J., Pyszczynski, T., Warnica, G. M., Landau, M., & Thomas, L. (2006). Terror of the body: Death, neuroticism, and the flight from physical sensation. *Personality and Social Psychology Bulletin, 32,* 1264–1277.

Goldenberg, J., McCoy, S., Pyszczynski, T., Greenberg, J., & Solomon, S. (2000). The body as a source of self-esteem: The effect of mortality salience on identification with one's body, interest in sex, and appearance monitoring. *Journal of Personality and Social Psychology, 79,* 118–130.

Goldenberg, J. L., Pyszczynski, T., Greenberg, J., & Solomon, S. (2000). Fleeing the body: A terror management perspective on the problem of human corporeality. *Personality and Social Psychology Review, 4,* 200–218.

Goldenberg, J. L., Pyszczynski, T., Greenberg, J., Solomon, S., Kluck, B., & Cornwell, R. (2001). I am not an animal: Mortality salience, disgust, and the denial of human creatureliness. *Journal of Experimental Psychology, 130,* 427–435.

Goldenberg, J. L., Pyszczynski, T., McCoy, S. K., Greenberg, J., & Solomon, S. (1999). Death, sex, love, and neuroticism: Why is sex such a problem? *Journal of Personality and Social Psychology, 77,* 1173–1187.

Goldenberg, J. L., & Roberts, T.-A. (2004). The beast within the beauty: An existential perspective on the objectification and condemnation of women. In J. Greenberg, S. L. Koole, & T. Pyszczynski (Eds.), *Handbook of experimental existential psychology* (pp. 71–85). New York: Guilford Press.

Grabe, S., Cook, A., Routledge, C., Arndt, J., & Anderson, C. (2005). In defense of the body: The effect of mortality salience on female body objectification. *Psychology of Women Quarterly, 29,* 33–37.

Grant, K., Lyons, A., Landis, D., Cho, M. H., Scudiero, M., Reynolds, L., et al. (1999). Gender, body image, and depressive symptoms among low-income African American adolescents. *Journal of Social Issues, 55,* 299–316.

Greenberg, J., Pyszczynski, T., & Solomon, S. (1986). The causes and consequences of a need for self-esteem: A terror management theory. In R. F. Baumeister (Ed.), *Public self and private self* (pp. 189–212). New York: Springer-Verlag.

Greenberg, J., Pyszczynski, T., Solomon, S., Rosenblatt, A., Veeder, M., Kirkland, S., et al. (1990). Evidence for terror management: II. The effects of mortality salience on reactions to those who threaten or bolster the cultural worldview. *Journal of Personality and Social Psychology, 58,* 308–318.

Greenberg, J., Simon, L., Porteus, J., Pyszczynski, T., & Solomon, S. (1995). Evidence of a terror management function of cultural icons: The effects of mortality salience on the inappropriate use of cherished cultural symbols. *Personality and Social Psychology Bulletin, 21,* 1221–1228.

Kellett, S., & Gilbert, P. (2001). Acne: A biopsychosocial and evolutionary perspective with a focus on shame. *British Journal of Health Psychology, 6,* 1–24.

Keltner, D., & Anderson, C. (2000). Saving face for Darwin: The functions and uses of embarrassment. *Current Directions in Psychological Science, 9,* 187–192.

Keltner, D., & Buswell, B. N. (1996). Evidence for the distinctness of embarrassment, shame and guilt: A study of recalled antecedents and facial expressions of emotion. *Cognition and Emotion, 10,* 155–171.

Keltner, D., & Buswell, B. N. (1997). Embarrassment: Its distinct form and appeasement functions. *Psychological Bulletin, 122,* 250–270.

Kinsey, A. C., Pomeroy, W. B., Martin, C. E., & Gebhard, P. H. (1953). *Sexual behavior in the human female.* Oxford, UK: Saunders.

Lazare, A. (1997). Shame, humiliation and stigma in the medical interview. In M. R. Lansky & A. P. Morrison (Eds.), *Widening the scope of shame* (pp. 383–396). Hillsdale, NJ: Analytic Press.

Leary, M. R. (2004). Digging deeper: The fundamental nature of "self-conscious" emotions. *Psychological Inquiry, 15,* 129–131.

Lewis, H. B. (1971). *Shame and guilt in neurosis.* New York: International Universities Press.

Lewis, M. (1997). The self in self-conscious emotions. In J. G. Snodgrass & R. L. Thompson (Eds.), *Self across psychology: Self-recognition, self-awareness and the self-concept* (pp. 119–142). New York: New York Academy of Sciences.

Lewis, M. (2000). Self-conscious emotions: Embarrassment, pride, shame and guilt. In M. Lewis & J.

M. Haviland-Jones (Eds.), *Handbook of emotions* (2nd ed, pp. 623–636). New York: Guilford Press.

McKinley, N. M. (1998). Gender differences in undergraduates' body esteem: The mediating effect of objectified body consciousness and actual/ideal weight discrepancy. *Sex Roles, 39,* 113–123.

Mikulincer, M., Florian, V., & Hirschberger, G. (2003). The existential function of close relationships: Introducing death into the science of love. *Personality and Social Psychology Review, 7,* 20–40.

Miller, R. S. (1992). The nature and severity of self-reported embarrassing circumstances. *Personality and Social Psychology Bulletin, 18,* 190–198.

Miller, R. S. (1996). *Embarrassment: Poise and peril in everyday life.* New York: Guilford Press.

Miller, W. I. (1997). *The anatomy of disgust.* Cambridge, MA: Harvard University Press.

Moore, S. M. (1995). Girls' understanding and social construction of menarche. *Journal of Adolescence, 18,* 87–104.

Offer, D., Ostrov, E., & Howard, K. I. (1986). The self-image of normal adolescents. *New Directions for Mental Health Services, 22,* 5–17.

Oliver, M. B., & Hyde, J. S. (1993). Gender differences in sexuality: A meta analysis. *Psychological Bulletin, 114,* 29–51.

Paglia, C. (1990). *Sexual personae: Art and decadence from Nefertiti to Emily Dickinson.* New York: Random House.

Pedersen, S., & Seidman, E. (2004). Team sports achievement and self-esteem development among urban adolescent girls. *Psychology of Women Quarterly, 28,* 412–422.

Phillips, M. L., & Heining, M. (2002). Disgust and the self. In D. J. Castle & K. A. Phillips (Eds.), *Disorders of body image* (pp. 13–23). Petersfield, UK: Wrightson Biomedical.

Quinn, D. M., & Crocker, J. (1999). When ideology hurts: Effects of belief in the Protestant ethic and feeling overweight on the psychological well being of women. *Journal of Personality and Social Psychology, 77,* 402–414.

Roberts, T.-A. (2004). "Female trouble:" The Menstrual Self-Evaluation Scale and women's self-objectification. *Psychology of Women Quarterly, 28,* 22–26.

Roberts, T.-A., & Arefi-Afshar, Y. (in press). Not all who stand tall are proud: Gender differences in the proprioceptive effects of upright posture. *Cognition and Emotion.*

Roberts, T.-A., & Gettman, J. (2004). "Mere exposure": Gender differences in the negative effects of priming a state of self-objectification. *Sex Roles, 51,* 17–27.

Roberts, T.-A., Goldenberg, J. L., Power, C., & Pyszczynski, T. (2002). "Feminine protection": The effects of menstruation on attitudes toward women. *Psychology of Women Quarterly, 26,* 131–139.

Roberts, T.-A., & MacLane, C. (2002, February). *The body disgusting: How knowledge of body functions affects attitudes toward women.* Paper presented at the annual meeting of the Society for Personality and Social Psychology, Savannah, GA.

Robins, R. W., Trzesniewski, K. H., Tracy, J. L., Gosling, S. D., & Potter, J. (2002). Global self-esteem across the lifespan. *Psychology and Aging, 17,* 423–434.

Rosenblum, G. D., & Lewis, M. (1999). The relations among body image, physical attractiveness, and body mass in adolescence. *Child Development, 70,* 50–64.

Routledge, C., Arndt, J., & Goldenberg, J. L. (2004). A time to tan: Proximal and distal effects of mortality salience on sun exposure intentions. *Personality and Social Psychology Bulletin, 30,* 1347–1358.

Rozin, P., Haidt, J., & McCauley, C. R. (2000). Disgust. In M. Lewis & J. Haviland (Eds.), *Handbook of emotions* (2nd ed., pp. 637–653). New York: Guilford Press.

Rubin, G. (1975). The traffic in women: Notes on the political economy of sex. In R. Reiter (Ed.), *Toward an anthropology of women* (pp. 157–210). New York: Monthly Review Press.

Scheff, T. J. (1988). Shame and conformity: The deference-emotion system. *American Sociological Review, 53,* 395–406.

Shott, S. (1979). Emotion and social life: A symbolic interactionist analysis. *American Journal of Sociology, 84,* 1317–1334.

Silberstein, L. R., Streigel-Moore, R., & Rodin, J. (1987). Feeling fat: A woman's shame. In H. B. Lewis (Ed.), *The role of shame in symptom formation* (pp. 89–108). Hillsdale, NJ: Erlbaum.

Simes, M. R., & Berg, D. H. (2001). Surreptitious learning: Menarche and menstrual product advertisements. *Health Care for Women International, 22,* 455–469.

Stepper, S., & Strack, F. (1993). Proprioceptive determinants of emotional and nonemotional feelings. *Journal of Personality and Social Psychology, 64,* 211–230.

Stipek, D. (1995). The development of pride and shame in toddlers. In J. P. Tangney & K. W. Fischer (Eds.), *Self-conscious emotions: The psychology of shame, guilt, embarrassment, and pride* (pp. 237–254). New York: Guilford Press.

Stunkard, A., & Mendelson, M. (1967). Obesity and body image: Characteristic disturbances in the body image of some obese persons. *American Journal of Psychiatry, 123,* 1296–1300.

Tangney, J. P. (1993). Shame and guilt. In C. G. Costello (Ed.), *Symptoms of depression* (pp. 161–180). New York: Wiley.

Tangney, J. P., Miller, R. S., Flicker, L., & Barlow, D. H. (1996). Are shame, guilt and embarrassment distinct emotions? *Journal of Personality and Social Psychology, 79,* 1256–1269.

Taubman Ben-Ari, O., Florian, V., & Mikulincer, M. (1999). The impact of mortality salience on reckless driving—A test of terror management mechanisms. *Journal of Personality and Social Psychology, 76,* 35–45.

Taywaditep, K. J. (2001). Marginalization among the marginalized: Gay men's antieffeminacy attitudes. *Journal of Homosexuality, 42,* 1–28.

Tracy, J. L., & Robins, R. W. (2003). "Death of a (narcissistic) salesman": An integrative model of fragile self-esteem. *Psychological Inquiry, 14,* 57–62.

Tracy, J. L., & Robins, R. W. (2004a). Putting the self into self-conscious emotions: A theoretical model. *Psychological Inquiry, 15,* 103–125.

Tracy, J. L., & Robins, R. W. (2004b). Show your pride: Evidence for a discrete emotion expression. *Psychological Science, 15,* 194–197.

Unger, R. K. (1979). Toward a redefinition of sex and gender. *American Psychologist, 34,* 1085–1094.

Wolf, N. (1991). *The beauty myth: How images of beauty are used against women.* New York: Anchor Books.

Woolf, V. (1929). *A room of one's own.* New York: Harcourt, Brace.

Yorke, C. B. (1990). A psychoanalytic approach to the understanding of shame. *Sigmund Freud House Bulletin, 14,* 14–28.

22

Overvalued and Ashamed

Considering the Roles of Self-Esteem and Self-Conscious Emotions in Covert Narcissism

JENNIFER K. BOSSON
JENNIFER L. PREWITT-FREILINO

Over the past 30 years, empirical investigations into narcissism have yielded a rich body of knowledge about the personal and interpersonal tendencies associated with this construct. Despite these advances, research into some aspects of narcissism lags behind theory due to limitations in our measurement capabilities. For example, the feelings of shame and underlying self-doubt that theoretically fuel narcissistic self-regulation have proven difficult to capture empirically, given narcissists' tendencies toward grandiose posturing and categorical denial of negativity or weakness. Recently, however, the emergence of new, unobtrusive tools for assessing shame-proneness (Tangney, Wagner, & Gramzow, 1992) and self-esteem (Bosson, Swann, & Pennebaker, 2000) has allowed researchers fresh access into the well-guarded inner worlds of narcissists. Here, we capitalize on these recent methodologies to test a model that links implicit and explicit self-esteem, cognitive attributional style, self-conscious emotions, and narcissistic personality.

To summarize the key features of our model, we begin by assuming that discrepancies between people's implicit (automatic, uncontrolled) and explicit (conscious, controlled) self-esteem lie at the heart of narcissistic self-regulation. Implicit/explicit self-esteem discrepancies emerge when people receive relatively extreme messages about their self-worth early in life from caregivers, but encounter repeated doses of environmental feedback that challenge the credibility of these messages. In such cases, people's outcomes conflict routinely with their implicit self-representations and, if they make certain attributions for these outcomes, they will consequently experience certain self-conscious emotions on a regular basis. Chronic experiences with certain self-conscious emotions can, in turn, shape people's explicit self-esteem such that it differs in valence from their implicit self-esteem. In the context of the resulting fragile self system, narcissistic—that is, defensively self-aggrandizing—personality tendencies take root.

When first conceptualizing the specifics of our model, we assumed that narcissistic personality tendencies reflect *low implicit* self-esteem combined with *high explicit* self-esteem. Several theorists have proposed that narcissistic self-regulation reflects the individual's continual efforts to maintain positive explicit self-views in the face of negative implicit beliefs that derive from unreliable, cold, and/or abusive caregiving (Kernberg, 1975; Kohut, 1977; Morf & Rhodewalt, 2001). Indeed, Tracy and Robins (2003) recently proposed a developmental model of self-conscious emotions and narcissism similar to the one we outline here, in which they asserted that low implicit/high explicit self-esteem discrepancies fuel narcissism. Some empirical work also supports this account of narcissism, in that people high in explicit self-esteem, but low in implicit self-esteem, scored particularly high on several measures of narcissism and self-aggrandizement (Bosson, Brown, Zeigler-Hill, & Swann, 2003; Jordan, Spencer, Zanna, Hoshino-Browne, & Correll, 2003). Thus, both theory and research provided sound justification for our assumption that a combination of low implicit and high explicit self-esteem drives the narcissistic personality.

Very soon, however, we realized that this conceptualization of the link between discrepant implicit/explicit self-esteem and narcissism might be incomplete. For instance, research suggests that narcissism is a multifaceted construct, some components of which correlate positively with explicit self-esteem, and others of which correlate negatively with explicit self-esteem (e.g., Dickinson & Pincus, 2003; Emmons, 1984, 1987; Millon, 1981; Rathvon & Holmstrom, 1996; Rose, 2002; Wink, 1991). Some aspects (or types) of narcissism are thus characterized by low, rather than high, explicit self-esteem. Second, pilot data collected in the first author's lab suggested that, whereas high scores on some indices of narcissism were characterized by a pattern of low implicit self-esteem combined with high explicit self-esteem, high scores on other narcissism indices were characterized by *high implicit* and *low explicit* self-esteem. Finally, shame—a self-conscious emotion that theoretically plays a central role in narcissism (H. B. Lewis, 1971; Morrison, 1989)—correlates positively with some components of narcissism, but negatively or not at all with others (Gramzow & Tangney, 1992; Tangney, Burggraf, & Wagner, 1995; Watson, Hickman, & Morris, 1996).

Given the possibility of different forms of narcissism that stem from different patterns of discrepant implicit and explicit self-esteem, we focus here on developing a model of shame-driven (or *covert*) narcissism. Although our approach admittedly shares several key components and assumptions with other social-personality models of narcissism (Jordan et al., 2003; Otway & Vignoles, 2006; Tracy & Robins, 2003), it is novel in its (1) consideration of different patterns of discrepant self-esteem stemming from different developmental histories, and (2) emphasis on the distinction between two types of narcissism. While fleshing out the details of our model, we looked frequently to Millon's (1981) social learning theory of narcissism, which deviates from many classical accounts by positing that some forms of narcissism emerge in response to parental overvaluation rather than parental neglect or abuse.

As shown in Figure 22.1, our model begins with individuals who have unusually high implicit self-esteem, presumably due to parental overvaluation (e.g., overindulgence, pampering). When these individuals' personal outcomes fall short of their overblown expectancies, and they attribute their failures to some inadequacy of the self, they will experience shame on a regular basis (path *a*). To defend against painful shame feelings, these

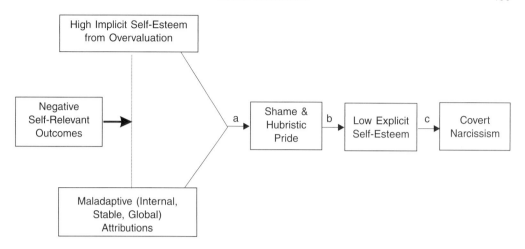

FIGURE 22.1. Covert narcissism as a function of self-esteem, cognitive attributional style, and self-conscious emotions.

individuals suppress shame and convert it into hubristic pride, an all-encompassing feeling of superiority that is distinct from more adaptive and circumscribed feelings of achievement-oriented, or "authentic," pride (M. Lewis, 2000; Tracy & Robins, 2004, 2007). Although hubristic pride is a positively valenced feeling state, it does not protect the individual from the harmful effects of chronic shame. Shame feelings therefore chip away at explicit self-esteem, ultimately creating a discrepancy between high implicit and low explicit self-esteem (path *b*). The vulnerability engendered by this self-esteem discrepancy, in turn, promotes covert narcissistic tendencies toward entitlement and exploitativeness (path *c*).

In what follows we define the primary constructs in our model, clarify the links among them, and summarize the literatures on which our logic is based. Next, we present the results of a preliminary test of our ideas, and discuss their implications for our model. Throughout this chapter, we link our ideas and findings to current social-personality research on implicit and explicit self-esteem, self-conscious emotions, and narcissism (e.g., Bosson et al., 2003; Jordan et al., 2003; Robins, Tracy, & Shaver, 2002; Tracy & Robins, 2003).

THE MODEL

As noted, we assume that a pattern of high implicit and low explicit self-esteem underlies covert narcissism. We therefore begin by defining implicit and explicit self-esteem and discussing their developmental origins.

Implicit and Explicit Self-Esteem

Consistent with several influential conceptualizations, we define "self-esteem" as an attitude that individuals hold about the self (Coopersmith, 1967; Rosenberg, 1965) or, more specifically, an evaluation of one's lovability and competence (Harter, 1990; Tafarodi & Swann, 2001). As do other types of attitudes, the self-attitude presumably operates—that is, influences behavior—via both implicit (automatic, uncontrolled) and explicit (conscious, controlled) processes (Epstein, 1990; Fazio, 1990). Whereas the implicit effects of the self-attitude on people's psychological and behavioral responses occur spontaneously, in the absence of conscious self-reflection or other higher-order cognitive processes, the explicit effects of the self-attitude result from deliberate self-reflection (Greenwald & Banaji, 1995; Koole, Dijksterhuis, & van Knippenberg, 2001). In their efforts to understand how these different processes influence the self, social-personality psychologists are increasingly emphasizing the importance of measuring and understanding both implicit and explicit self-esteem (e.g., Bosson et al., 2003; Greenwald & Farnham, 2000; Hetts, Sakuma, & Pelham, 1999; Jones, Pelham, Mirenberg, & Hetts, 2002; Jordan et al., 2003).

We define *explicit self-esteem* as people's consciously controlled, verbalized evaluations of the self—or, the self-attitude that is captured via self-reports and other explicit measurement techniques. In contrast, we define *implicit self-esteem* as the affect that is elicited automatically by stimuli that prime the self—or, the self-attitude that is captured via cognitive priming tasks and other implicit measures (Fazio & Olson, 2003). Unlike self-report scales, implicit measures of self-esteem do not require respondents to answer direct questions about their attitudes toward the self. Instead, implicit measures seek to circumvent respondents' conscious control by, for example, priming the self and assessing the speed with which respondents can subsequently identify positive versus negative stimuli (e.g., Hetts et al., 1999) or measuring the positivity of respondents' reactions to self-associated stimuli (e.g., Koole et al., 2001; Nuttin, 1985).

Whereas implicit and explicit self-esteem measures presumably assess the same underlying construct, they tend to be uncorrelated or, at best, weakly associated (Bosson et al., 2000). Although this fact raises legitimate concerns about the validity of both types of measures (see Bosson, 2006; Farnham, Greenwald, & Banaji, 1999), a discussion of these measurement issues is beyond the scope of this chapter. Instead, we begin here by assuming that low correlations between implicit and explicit self-esteem scores emerge because some people's implicit and explicit reactions to the self truly differ in valence. To explain how such discrepancies might emerge, we look to Epstein's (1990) cognitive–experiential self-theory (CEST).

According to CEST, human information processing is characterized by two separate systems. The evolutionarily older *experiential* system operates automatically, holistically, and intuitively, and is thus adapted for immediate action. In contrast, the relatively young *cognitive* system operates deliberatively, and is thus adapted for rational decision making and delayed action. These systems work in tandem to provide people with two different ways of "knowing" the self and the world. For example, people develop implicit beliefs about the self via implicit learning processes such as classical and operant conditioning and other emotion-based experiences, and they develop explicit beliefs about the self via logical, rational analyses of self-relevant experiences. Whereas self-relevant information that gets processed automatically and heuristically should form the basis of people's implicit self-esteem, information that is processed in an effortful, piecemeal fashion should form the basis of explicit self-esteem. Note that the type of processing that occurs, experiential versus cognitive, may depend on features of the information being processed (e.g., whether it is affect-laden or affect-free, nonverbal or verbal), as well as features of the individual doing the processing (e.g., whether motivation and ability to engage in effortful processing are high versus low; see Fazio, 1990).

Although beliefs about the self acquired via the experiential and cognitive systems often coincide, they need not (Epstein & Morling, 1995). From the perspective of CEST, discrepancies between individuals' implicit and explicit self-esteem might arise if they receive different messages, or arrive at different conclusions, about their worth via these different routes. For example, subtle, nonverbal rejection from a primary caregiver may lead an individual to develop negative implicit beliefs about her worth (Bowlby, 1969; Mikulincer, 1995) that, through repeated activation, become "consolidated into [her] cognitive-affective architecture" (Koole et al., 2001, p. 669). If subsequent interactions provide this individual with feedback indicating that she is lovable and competent (e.g., verbal acceptance from peers, success at reaching goals), she may develop positive explicit beliefs about her worth that coexist with her negative implicit ones. Conversely, as suggested by our model, overvaluation by caregivers may lead an individual to develop excessively favorable implicit self-views. Subsequent negative outcomes (e.g., rejection from peers, failure to reach goals) might then lead this individual to construct negative explicit self-esteem alongside her positive implicit self-esteem.

Note our assumption that implicit self-esteem develops earlier in life than explicit self-esteem. Because explicit self-esteem is language-based, requires self-awareness, and derives from conscious analysis of self-relevant outcomes, it cannot take hold until individuals pass certain developmental milestones (Lewis & Brooks-Gunn, 1979). In contrast, implicit belief systems emerge developmentally prior to explicit ones (e.g., Seger, 1994), and reflect the quality of early interactions with caregivers and other relationship partners (Bartholomew & Horowitz, 1991; Bowlby, 1969). Empirical research linking implicit self-esteem to early social relationships is sparse, but promising. For example, Hetts and Pelham (2003) found that individuals who are born near the Christmas holiday tend to exhibit lower implicit self-esteem than individuals born at other times of the year, presumably because the former often got overlooked by family and friends on their birthday. Furthermore, DeHart, Pelham, and Tennen (2006) found that respondents higher in implicit self-esteem recalled having mothers who were more nurturing and less overprotective during their childhood, and mothers' reports of their parenting style similarly predicted respondents' implicit self-esteem. Despite these encouraging findings, we note that no existing empirical work links parental overvaluation to high implicit self-esteem in the manner suggested by our model.

In contrast to implicit self-esteem, explicit self-esteem should reflect the individual's judgments of his or her worth based on conscious assessments of self-relevant feedback and outcomes. According to our model, covert narcissism grows from a discrepancy between extremely high implicit self-esteem—rooted in parental overvaluation, coddling, and favoritism—and relatively low explicit self-esteem, which develops when the individual repeatedly assesses his or her outcomes as falling below expectations. More specifically, we suggest that repeated failure experiences lead to shame-proneness in some high implicit self-esteem individuals, and that shame ultimately forms the basis of their low explicit self-esteem. To clarify the proposed link between shame-proneness and explicit self-esteem, we turn to M. Lewis's (1992, 2000) cognitive-attributional theory of self-conscious emotions.

Cognitive Attributions and Self-Conscious Emotions

According to M. Lewis's (1992, 2000) cognitive-attributional theory, self-conscious emotions arise from attribution processes in which the individual makes an internal attribution (i.e., takes personal responsibility) for a self-relevant outcome. A *self-relevant out-*

come is an assessment of one's behavior or performance with regard to an internalized, personally valued standard or goal (Lewis, Sullivan, Stanger, & Weiss, 1989; Tangney, 2002; Tracy & Robins, 2004). To illustrate, a woman who considers social skills to be a central component of her self-concept may assess her interpersonal conduct during a business meeting as either exceeding, matching, or falling short of her desired social self-representation (Higgins, 1987). If the woman makes such an assessment and then takes personal responsibility for it (e.g., "That was *my* doing"), she should experience a self-conscious emotion.

The specific self-conscious emotion felt is determined by two additional cognitive processes: (1) an evaluation of the self-relevant outcome as either a success or a failure, and (2) an attribution to either global and stable or specific and unstable causes (M. Lewis, 1992, 2000). The first of these decisions has implications for the valence of the resulting self-conscious emotion. To the extent that a self-relevant outcome exceeds or meets one's standard, positively valenced feelings of either hubristic pride or authentic pride should occur. Conversely, if an outcome falls short of one's standard, negative emotion should occur in the form of either shame or guilt. The second decision—the attribution of the outcome to global and stable versus specific and unstable causes—determines how "fully" the self is implicated in the resulting emotion. Attributions to a global, stable cause will result in self-conscious emotions that subsume the whole self, that is, shame and hubristic pride. Alternatively, attributions to a specific, unstable cause will produce self-conscious emotions—specifically, guilt and authentic pride—that implicate one's actions in a given context rather than one's self in totality.

As illustrated in Figure 22.1, we propose that self-conscious emotions that engulf the self, that is, shame and hubristic pride, play central roles in covert narcissism (see also Tracy & Robins, 2003). These emotions should arise when individuals high in implicit self-esteem experience repeated failure outcomes and attribute these outcomes to internal, global, and stable causes (path *a*).

Before proceeding, it is worth considering why some individuals with high implicit self-esteem might develop a shame-promoting attributional style. Logically, it seems that high implicit self-esteem should bias people to process self-relevant information in a positive, self-enhancing manner, thus mitigating the tendency toward shame-promoting attributions for negative outcomes. In the case of individuals whose high implicit self-esteem stems from parental overvaluation, however, self-enhancing attributions for repeated failures may, over time, become unsustainable as the reality of one's personal limitations belies one's idealistic expectations. After all, repeated failures to attain "perfection" must surely reflect something internal, stable, and global about the individual—namely, that she or he is not, and will never be, perfect. From our perspective, then, the grandiose standards instilled by overvaluing parents can foster a pattern of disappointing outcomes that becomes difficult to blame on external, specific, and unstable causes. As such, even individuals high in implicit self-esteem are vulnerable to developing a shame-promoting attributional style.

Returning to path *a*, research documents a link between the tendency to make internal, global, and stable attributions for negative self-relevant outcomes and a chronic proneness to shame (Feiring, Taska, & Lewis, 2002; Nolen-Hoeksema, Girgus, & Seligman, 1992; Tangney et al., 1992; Tracy & Robins, 2005; Weiner, 1985). That is, to the extent that people blame their negative outcomes on their own pervasive and persistent inadequacies, they react to such outcomes with all-encompassing feelings of humiliation and worthlessness. Also consistent with M. Lewis's (1992, 2000) model, Tracy and

Robins (2007) found that internal, stable attributions for positive self-relevant outcomes predicted a proneness to hubristic pride, but they did not measure the globality dimension of attributions (and instead focused on the controllability dimension). One question we therefore address in the upcoming test of our model is whether hubristic pride indeed arises from internal, global, and stable attributions for positive self-relevant outcomes.

Unlike M. Lewis's (1992, 2000) attributional account of hubristic pride, our model proposes that this self-conscious emotion often emerges defensively, to protect the self against the painful feelings of shame that arise following failures. Because shame is such a debilitating emotion (Tangney, 2002), some shame-prone individuals suppress their shame reactions and replace them with hubristic pride, a grandiose feeling of superiority (Horney, 1950; H. B. Lewis, 1971; Nathanson, 1987). For example, when shame arises, people may defend against it by externalizing blame for the shame-eliciting event, while at the same time recalling or seeking opportunities for self-enhancement at the expense of others (Robins et al., 2001). Over time, the tendency toward shame elicits a concurrent tendency to respond to personal successes with hubristic pride. Ultimately, however, attempts to protect the self from shame by evoking hubristic pride fail, and shame chips away at explicit self-esteem (path *b*).

Because the self is implicated so fully in the emotion of shame, episodes of shame should provide much of the raw data from which people abstract generalized, explicit assessments of self-worth (Malatesta & Wilson, 1988; Moretti & Higgins, 1990; Scheff, 1988). Consistent with this assumption, research shows that temporary feelings of shame covary with immediate decrements in self-esteem (Gruenewald, Kemeny, Aziz, & Fahey, 2004), and shame-proneness correlates negatively with baseline self-esteem (Harder, Cutler, & Rockart, 1992; Leith & Baumeister, 1998; Sorotzkin, 1985; Tangney & Dearing, 2002). Thus, to the extent that people chronically react to negative outcomes with shame, they will gradually (at least explicitly) deem themselves less lovable, competent, and worthy. Implicit self-esteem, on the other hand, because it is overlearned and difficult to control, should be relatively less affected by repeated failure experiences (Hetts et al., 1999). As a result, individuals with high implicit self-esteem who make internal, global, and stable attributions for negative self-relevant outcomes should develop low explicit self-esteem, but retain their high implicit self-esteem (at least for some time). According to our model, then, these high implicit/low explicit self-esteem people will be vulnerable to developing covert narcissism.

The Narcissistic Personality: Types, Origins, and Measurement

The narcissistic personality is characterized by heightened levels of self-importance, entitlement, exhibitionism, vanity, power striving, and exploitativeness (Raskin & Hall, 1979). Within this broad constellation of traits, researchers find evidence for two distinct forms of narcissistic personality (Dickinson & Pincus, 2003; Wink, 1991). One form, often called *overt* or grandiose narcissism, is characterized by high explicit self-esteem, subjective happiness (Rose, 2002), and low levels of shame (Gramzow & Tangney, 1992; Watson et al., 1996); a second form, often called *covert* or vulnerable narcissism, is characterized by low explicit self-esteem, unhappiness, and shame-proneness. Thus, although both types of narcissists are "extraordinarily self-absorbed and arrogant" (Rose, 2002, p. 380), overt narcissists enjoy several psychological benefits that covert narcissists do not share.

Historically, theorists have disagreed about the developmental origins of narcissism, with some linking it to parental undervaluation and others linking it to parental over-valuation. According to parental undervaluation models, narcissistic personality tenden-cies reflect the individual's continual efforts to shore up support for grandiose, but frag-ile, explicit self-views that mask underlying feelings of inferiority and self-doubt (Brown & Bosson, 2001; Kernberg, 1975; Morf & Rhodewalt, 2001). More specifically, inade-quate and insensitive parenting leads some individuals to associate the self with negative affect (low implicit self-esteem). To protect against this negative self-relevant affect, nar-cissists defensively construct highly positive explicit self-views that they maintain through various intra- and interpersonal self-enhancement strategies. From this perspective, then, the narcissist's grandiose posturing reflects his or her efforts to defend the self against deep-seated feelings of inferiority instilled by uncaring or insufficiently attentive parents.

Parental overvaluation models, in contrast, tie narcissistic personality traits to exces-sive pampering at the hands of parents (Adler, 1938/1964; Capron, 2004; Millon, 1981). According to these models, some parents "pamper and indulge their youngsters in ways that teach them that their every wish is a command, that they can receive without giving in return, and that they deserve prominence without even minimal effort" (Millon, 1981, p. 175). Consequently, these youngsters learn to associate the self with positive affect and develop extremely favorable implicit self-representations. Millon acknowledges that parental praise is not problematic when it is well earned, but notes also that the "idyllic existence" fostered by parents who spoil their children "cannot long endure; the world beyond home will not be so benign and accepting" (p. 167). Thus, in many cases of parental overindulgence, reality eventually intervenes—in the form of personal failures, humiliations, weaknesses, and the like—and undermines the individual's explicit self-esteem. From this perspective, narcissists' tendencies toward entitlement and exploita-tiveness reflect the overblown implicit expectations their parents instilled in them, while their shame-proneness reflects their chronic perception of themselves as falling short of these expectations.

Here, we link these different developmental accounts of narcissism to the different types of narcissism identified above (see also Capron, 2004; Emmons, 1984; Freud, 1914/1957; Otway & Vignoles, 2006). Specifically, we suggest that parental undervaluation drives overt narcissism, whereas parental overvaluation drives covert narcissism. Individuals who receive insensitive or uncaring parenting should develop low implicit self-esteem, but subsequent successes may convince them—at least explicitly—that they are lovable and competent. As a result, these individuals will possess low implicit self-esteem combined with high explicit self-esteem, and will self-regulate by rigorously pursuing self-enhancement strategies (overt narcissism). Conversely, individuals whose parents overindulge and spoil them should develop high implicit self-esteem, but subsequent failures should teach them that they are not as "special" as their parents led them to feel. Consequently, these indi-viduals will possess high implicit self-esteem combined with low explicit self-esteem, and will self-regulate by exploiting and manipulating others (covert narcissism; see Figure 22.1, path *c*).

If our logic is correct, implicit and explicit self-esteem should interact differently to predict measures of overt and covert narcissism. Some research does suggest that implicit and explicit self-esteem interact to predict narcissistic tendencies, but this work generally operationalizes narcissism as total scores on Raskin and Hall's (1979; Raskin & Terry, 1988) Narcissistic Personality Inventory (NPI). When NPI scores are computed by sum-ming (or averaging) across all of the NPI items, the resulting index appears to capture overt—as opposed to covert—narcissism: total NPI scores correlate negatively with shame-proneness, depression, anxiety, and neuroticism, and positively with self-esteem, actual–ideal self-congruency, and self-handicapping (Emmons, 1984; Harder & Lewis, 1987; Raskin & Novacek, 1989; Rhodewalt & Tragakis, 2003; Watson, Taylor, & Morris, 1987). As noted earlier, and consistent with our logic regarding the implicit and explicit self-esteem bases of overt narcissism, Jordan et al. (2003) found that high scores on the total NPI were characterized by low implicit self-esteem and high explicit self-esteem. Similarly, Bosson et al. (2003) found that low implicit/high explicit self-esteem discrepancies predicted stronger tendencies toward overt narcissism.

To differentiate overt from covert narcissism, Emmons (1984, 1987) factor-analyzed the NPI and found evidence of four distinct factors. Of these, one factor (titled Exploitativeness/Entitlement, or EE) appears to tap into covert narcissism. The remaining three factors—titled Leadership/Authority (LA), Superiority/Arrogance (SA), and Self-Absorption/Self-Admiration (SS)—tap overt features of the narcissistic personality. For example, whereas LA and SS narcissism correlate positively with self-esteem and negatively with shame-proneness and depression, EE narcissism correlates negatively with self-esteem and positively with tendencies toward shame and depression (Gramzow & Tangney, 1992; Watson et al., 1987). We therefore wondered whether high implicit/low explicit self-esteem predicts EE narcissism, and low implicit/high explicit self-esteem predicts LA, SA, and/or SS narcissism. In what follows, we present the results of an investigation whose purpose was to test these proposed links, as well as the previously described paths, in our model.

TESTING THE MODEL

We conducted a correlational study to test the basic assumptions of the model depicted in Figure 22.1. To this end, we recruited 133 native English speakers (93 women and 40 men) to complete measures of implicit and explicit self-esteem, cognitive attributions for successes and failures, proneness to self-conscious emotions, and overt and covert narcissism. Given the preliminary nature of this investigation, we used a cross-sectional design and relied on people's self-reports. Because our model is a work-in-progress, we allowed ourselves considerable flexibility to pursue statistical analyses that tested not only our primary paths, but also additional links of interest among our theoretical constructs.

To assess implicit self-esteem, we measured people's preferences for their first- and last-name initials. Compared to other implicit measures of self-esteem, name letter preferences demonstrate acceptable test–retest reliability and predictive validity (Bosson et al., 2000; Koole et al., 2001). Liking for first and last initials was correlated, $r = .35$, $p .001$, so we averaged them to yield an index of implicit self-esteem. To measure explicit self-esteem, we combined Rosenberg's (1965) 10 global self-esteem items with Tafarodi and Swann's (2001) 16 self-liking and self-competence items ($\alpha = .96$). As in other research, explicit and implicit self-esteem scores did not correlate, $r = .07$, $p > .44$.

Our measure of cognitive attributional style was an abbreviated version of Anderson, Jennings, and Arnoult's (1988) Attributional Style Assessment Test-III (ASAT-III). This scale requires respondents to imagine 10 failure scenarios (e.g., "You just attended a party for new students and did not make any new friends") and 10 success scenarios (e.g., "You just received a high score on the midterm in a class"), and to generate one major cause of each outcome. Respondents then rate each cause in terms of its locus (*caused by other people or circumstances* vs. *caused by me*), its globality (*specific to a few situations* vs. *relevant to many situations*), and its stability (*not at all stable* vs. *very stable*). We created measures of attributional style by combining across the locus, globality, and stability items of the ASAT-III separately for the failure (α = .79) and success (α = .83) scenarios.

To assess shame-, hubristic pride-, guilt-, and authentic pride-proneness, we used the Test of Self-Conscious Affect (TOSCA; see Tangney et al., 1992). This measure presents respondents with 15 self-relevant scenarios, 10 of which describe negative outcomes (e.g., "You make a mistake on an important project at work . . . and your boss criticizes you") and five of which describe positive outcomes (e.g., "You put off making a difficult phone call. At the last minute you make the call and . . . all goes well"). After imagining themselves in each scenario, respondents rate the likelihood of experiencing a variety of self-conscious emotions including shame (e.g., "You would feel incompetent") and guilt (e.g., "You would feel that you deserve to be reprimanded"). In response to the positive scenarios only, respondents rate the likelihood of experiencing *alpha pride* and *beta pride*, which correspond, respectively, to hubristic pride (e.g., "You would feel competent and proud of yourself") and authentic pride (e.g., "You would feel your hard work had paid off"). Following Gramzow and Tangney (1992), we computed separate shame (α = .77), guilt (α = .72), hubristic pride (α = .47), and authentic pride (α = .51) scores by averaging these items across the scenarios. We then created "pure" measures of shame and hubristic pride by regressing shame onto guilt and hubristic pride onto authentic pride, and saving the standardized residuals; we also created pure measures of guilt and authentic pride this way.

To assess narcissism, we used Raskin and Terry's (1988) 40-item version of the NPI. Following Emmons (1984), we computed separate EE, LA, SA, and SS subscales. The EE subscale (α = .55) assesses tendencies toward interpersonal entitlement and manipulation; the LA subscale (α = .75) captures assertiveness and a strong leadership striving; the SA subscale (α = .53) captures an arrogant sense of superiority over others; and the SS subscale (α = .63) captures a tendency toward vain self-absorption. To obtain statistically pure indices of these four narcissism components, we regressed EE onto LA, SA, and SS, and saved the standardized residuals as our index of EE narcissism. We then repeated this procedure on the other three narcissism subscales.

Do High Implicit/Low Explicit Self-Esteem Discrepancies Fuel Covert Narcissism?

Path a

The first path in our model links implicit self-esteem and cognitive attributional style with self-conscious emotions. Specifically, we propose that people with high implicit self-esteem who make maladaptive (i.e., internal, stable, global) attributions for negative self-relevant outcomes should be prone to shame and hubristic pride.

Before testing this path, we investigated the links between specific attributional styles and self-conscious emotions. To do this, we regressed shame- and guilt-proneness separately onto the index of failure attributions, and hubristic and authentic pride-proneness onto the index of success attributions. In support of M. Lewis's (1992, 2000) theory, a tendency to make internal, global, and stable attributions for failures predicted shame, β = .25, p < .01. However, failure attributions were unrelated to guilt, t < 1, and success attributions predicted neither hubristic nor authentic pride, ts < 1. Instead, and consistent with our model, hubristic pride following positive outcomes was associated with a tendency to make internal, global, and stable attributions for failures, $\beta = .22$, $p = .01$. Although by no means definitive, this finding suggests that hubristic pride may arise defensively to ward off painful feelings associated with failure-based shame. Additional support for this assumption is provided by the fact that our respondents who were high in shame-proneness tended also to score high in hubristic pride, $r = .35$, $p < .01$. We therefore averaged shame and hubristic pride to create an index of narcissistic self-conscious emotions.

To test path *a* in our model, we regressed this measure of narcissistic emotions onto implicit self-esteem, attributional style, and their interaction (implicit self-esteem and attributional style were uncorrelated, $r = -.001$). A significant interaction emerged, $\beta = .19$, $p = .02$, and predicted values of narcissistic emotions appear in Figure 22.2. Consistent with our logic, people who have positive, affective reactions to the self, but who attribute failure experiences to internal, global, and stable causes, experience more shame and hubristic pride than do high implicit self-esteem people with a more adaptive attributional style.

Path b

The next path in our model links narcissistic self-conscious emotions to explicit self-esteem. Specifically, a tendency to experience shame and hubristic pride should be associated with lower explicit self-esteem. The results of a regression analysis provided strong support for this path, $\beta = -.44$, $p < .001$.

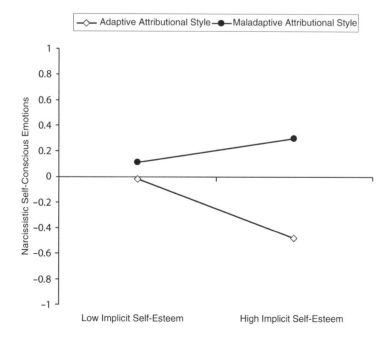

FIGURE 22.2. Narcissistic self-conscious emotions (shame- and hubristic pride-proneness) as a function of implicit self-esteem and cognitive attributional style. Predicted values are calculated at 1 *SD* above and below the mean on implicit self-esteem and attributional style.

We also tested the indirect path, implied by our model, linking high implicit self-esteem and a maladaptive attributional style to low explicit self-esteem. That is, we tested whether implicit self-esteem and attributional style interacted to predict explicit self-esteem. A regression analysis revealed that they did, $\beta = -.18$, $p = .04$; predicted values of explicit self-esteem as a function of implicit self-esteem and attributional style are shown in Figure 22.3. Consistent with our logic, people with high implicit self-esteem who make internal, global, and stable attributions for failures exhibit relatively low explicit self-esteem.

We also explored whether shame and hubristic pride mediated the path from implicit self-esteem and attributional style to explicit self-esteem. When we entered these narcissistic emotions into the regression model described above, the emotion index was negatively related to explicit self-esteem, $\beta = -.40$, $p < .001$, and the interaction of implicit self-esteem and attributional style was no longer significant, $\beta = -.10$, $p = .21$. This suggests that shame and hubristic pride at least partially mediate the link between attributional style and explicit self-esteem among people high in implicit self-esteem.

Path c

The final direct path in our model links low explicit self-esteem to covert narcissism. A regression analysis revealed the expected association in that people lower in explicit self-esteem scored higher in EE narcissism, $\beta = -.32$, $p < .001$.

We followed this analysis up by testing the indirect path from discrepant (high implicit/low explicit) self-esteem to covert narcissism. Specifically, we regressed the index of EE narcissism onto implicit and explicit self-esteem and their interaction. The interaction

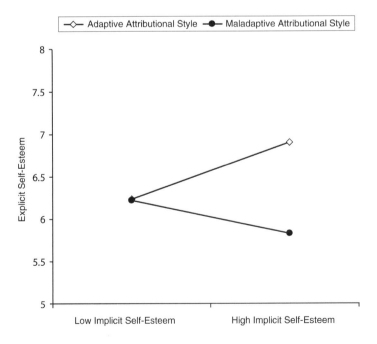

FIGURE 22.3. Explicit self-esteem as a function of implicit self-esteem and cognitive attributional style. Predicted values are calculated at 1 *SD* above and below the mean on implicit self-esteem and attributional style.

approached significance, $\beta = -.14$, $p < .10$, and the predicted values presented in Figure 22.4 reveal a pattern that is consistent with our model: people high in implicit self-esteem, but low in explicit self-esteem, scored the highest in covert narcissism.

Finally, to establish further the role of self-conscious emotions in covert narcissism, we conducted four simple regression analyses in which we predicted EE narcissism from the four self-conscious emotion indices. Consistent with our model and past work (Gramzow & Tangney, 1992; Tracy & Robins, 2003), people higher in both shame and hubristic pride scored higher in EE narcissism, $\beta s > .18$, $ps < .04$. EE narcissism was also negatively related to guilt, $\beta = -.20$, $p = .02$, and it was unrelated to authentic pride, $t < 1$.

To summarize, we found evidence consistent with our model of shame-prone narcissistic self-regulation. People with high implicit self-esteem who attributed negative outcomes to internal, global, stable causes tended toward greater shame and hubristic pride, as well as lower explicit self-esteem. Discrepant (high implicit/low explicit) self-esteem, in turn, marginally significantly predicted a tendency toward covert narcissism.

Do Low Implicit/High Explicit Self-Esteem Discrepancies Fuel Overt Narcissism?

Based on our current theorizing, as well as past theory and research (Bosson et al., 2003; Brown & Bosson, 2001; Jordan et al., 2003; Tracy & Robins, 2003), we also expected implicit and explicit self-esteem to interact in predicting measures of overt narcissism. However, the anticipated low implicit/high explicit self-esteem pattern did not emerge. When we regressed LA, SA, and SS narcissism (as well as total NPI scores) separately onto explicit self-esteem, implicit self-esteem, and their interaction, the interaction did not approach significance in any model, $ps > .14$. Moreover, the highest overall scores on

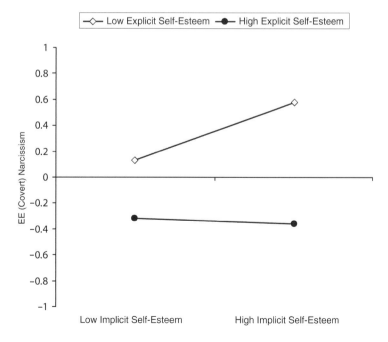

FIGURE 22.4. Covert narcissism as a function of implicit and explicit self-esteem. Predicted values are calculated at 1 *SD* above and below the mean on implicit and explicit self-esteem.

most of the indices of overt narcissism (LA, SS, and total NPI) were obtained by people with congruent, not discrepant, high self-esteem (i.e., high implicit *and* high explicit self-esteem). Although the highest scores on SA narcissism were obtained by people with high explicit and low implicit self-esteem, the implicit/explicit interaction did not even approach significance in this model, $t < 1$. Thus, we found no support for the idea that low implicit and high explicit self-esteem combine to fuel overt narcissism. Unfortunately, space constraints prevent additional empirical investigations into the links between low implicit/high explicit self-esteem and other constructs in our model.

DISCUSSION

The goals of this chapter were to lay the theoretical groundwork and present some preliminary empirical support for a model linking self-esteem, attributional style, self-conscious emotions, and narcissistic personality. More specifically, we sought to link different patterns of discrepant implicit/explicit self-esteem with different types of narcissism, in the context of a broad developmental model. In the final analysis, our efforts met with mixed success.

In the "pluses" column, we found fairly straightforward evidence of a form of shame-prone narcissism characterized by high implicit/low explicit self-esteem discrepancies. In this sense, our findings are consistent with theoretical models that propose a central role of shame in driving narcissism (Broucek, 1991; H. B. Lewis, 1971; Morrison, 1989; Tracy & Robins, 2003; Watson et al., 1996). Moreover, the findings presented here both replicate and extend Gramzow and Tangney's (1992) work on the link between shame-proneness and narcissism. First, in replicating Gramzow and Tangney's computational approach, our findings confirm that researchers interested in capturing shame-prone narcissism should compute statistically pure indices of both shame-proneness and covert (EE) narcissism. Researchers who do not separate shame from guilt and overt from covert narcissism may fail to find the straightforward shame–narcissism link we obtained here. Second, in demonstrating an association between hubristic pride and narcissism, our findings extend Gramzow and Tangney's analysis of the role of self-conscious emotions in narcissism. Specifically, our findings suggest that covert narcissists may defend against painful feelings of shame by conjuring overinflated feelings of hubristic pride (Nathanson, 1987). Indeed, many of the covert narcissist's entitled and exploitative behaviors may occur in the service of regulating the all-encompassing, but oppositely valenced, self-conscious emotions of shame and hubristic pride.

Another plus of the current work is that we attempt to make sense of inconsistencies in the narcissism literature by proposing that different types of parental treatment produce different types of narcissism (see also Emmons, 1984; Otway & Vignoles, 2006). To do this, we begin with the basic assumption that narcissistic tendencies emerge within vulnerable self systems characterized by underlying discrepancies between implicit and explicit reactions to the self. Such discrepancies, however, may take (at least) two different forms: whereas some people exhibit strongly favorable implicit reactions to the self combined with relatively negative explicit ones, others exhibit unfavorable implicit reactions to the self combined with extremely positive explicit ones. Because implicit self-esteem is theoretically rooted in early interpersonal dynamics with caregivers, we suggest that different types of parental treatment might predispose individuals toward these different types of self-esteem discrepancies—and, consequently, toward the different types of narcissism—by instilling in them rather extreme implicit attitudes toward the self. Parental undervaluation may create unrealistically low implicit self-esteem, which ultimately fuels overt (i.e., grandiose, non-shame-prone) narcissism, and parental overvaluation should create unrealistically high implicit self-esteem, which fuels covert (i.e., vulnerable, shame-prone) narcissism.

In the "minuses" column, the empirical investigation presented here allowed only a partial test of our theoretical model. After all, our model posits developmental processes that unfold across time, and the cross-sectional design used here was inadequate to the task of capturing cause-and-effect relations among our constructs of interest. Moreover, some features of our model—including parental treatment and early failure experiences—were assumed rather than assessed in our investigation. That is, we did not measure directly the quality or type of caregiving that respondents received in childhood, nor did we query them about early experiences with self-relevant outcomes that challenged their implicit self-representations. Until these variables are measured directly, all of our assumptions about the role of early life experiences in shaping narcissism remain speculative.

Furthermore, several crucial factors in our model have yet to be elucidated. For instance, we suggest that people with high implicit self-esteem who make maladaptive attributions for negative outcomes will suffer decrements in explicit self-esteem via repeated feelings of shame. However, our claims as to why some high implicit self-esteem individuals develop a maladaptive attributional style remain purely speculative at this point. Similarly, our model assumes that some people react to shame by evoking hubristic pride, but we have yet to clarify the variables that predict this tendency. Finally, as noted earlier, although our model shares several basic features with other recent approaches to narcissism, some of our key assumptions diverge. For instance, whereas we propose that parental overvaluation should lead to excessively high implicit self-esteem, Tracy and Robins (2003) propose that such overvaluation should produce *low* implicit self-esteem as children defensively dissociate their explicit and implicit selves so as to keep painful feelings of inferiority out of awareness. Moreover, whereas we propose that different parenting styles should predict different types of narcissistic personality, Otway and Vignoles (2006) recently found that both overt *and* covert narcissism were predicted by high levels of both indiscriminate parental praise (overvaluation) *and* parental coldness (undervaluation). Clearly, additional work should focus on refining the constructs and paths in our model, accounting for discrepancies between our findings and those of other researchers, and comparing the predictive utility of our model with that of similar approaches.

Perhaps the most disappointing shortcoming of the current investigation was our failure to find evidence that low implicit/high explicit self-esteem discrepancies drive overt narcissism. The null effects we obtained in analyses on overt narcissism are troubling not only because they fail to support our model, but also because they are inconsistent with both empirical (Bosson et al., 2003; Jordan et al., 2003) and theoretical (Brown & Bosson, 2001; Tracy & Robins, 2003) accounts of narcissism. One possible reason for the puzzling findings presented here is that researchers have used different methods to tap implicit self-esteem. Whereas Jordan et al. (2003) measured implicit self-esteem with the Implicit Association Test (IAT; Greenwald & Farnham, 2000)—and found that people low in IAT self-esteem but high in explicit self-esteem earned particularly high total NPI scores—we relied here on people's preferences for their name initials as our measure of implicit self-esteem. Given that these different indices of implicit self-esteem do not correlate with each other (Bosson et al., 2000), it is perhaps not surprising that patterns obtained with one index do not replicate with a different implicit self-esteem index.

Another possibility is that subtle features of the measurement context may influence the performance of implicit self-esteem indices in ways that are difficult for researchers to discern. Although implicit self-esteem appears relatively stable across long periods of time (Hetts et al., 1999), it may actually fluctuate more than explicit self-esteem in response to momentary, self-relevant experiences (Jones et al., 2002). If this is the case, then perhaps we failed to replicate past narcissism findings because we did not control for contextual variables that affect people's immediate feelings of implicit self-esteem (Bosson, 2006). This explanation, however, seems insufficient given that we did find evidence for the role of implicit self-esteem in driving covert narcissism.

Of course, we cannot say for sure why we found no evidence that low implicit and high explicit self-esteem combine to predict overt narcissism. For now, this issue remains unresolved, and we count ourselves among a small but dedicated group of researchers who strive to understand the role of implicit self-esteem in narcissism. The ideas and findings presented here reflect this goal, and we hope that they serve the important purpose of inspiring additional efforts.

REFERENCES

Adler, A. (1964). *Social interest: A challenge to mankind.* New York: Capricorn Books. (Original work published 1938).

Anderson, C. A., Jennings, D. L., & Arnoult, L. H. (1988). Validity and utility of the attributional style construct at a moderate level of specificity. *Journal of Personality and Social Psychology, 55,* 979–990.

Bartholomew, K., & Horowitz, L. M. (1991). Attachment styles among young adults: A test of a four-category model. *Journal of Personality and Social Psychology, 61,* 226–244.

Bosson, J. K. (2006). Assessing self-esteem via self-reports and nonreactive instruments: Issues and recommendations. In M. Kernis (Ed.), *Self-esteem issues and answers: A sourcebook of current perspectives* (pp. 88–95). London: Psychology Press.

Bosson, J. K., Brown, R. P., Zeigler-Hill, V., & Swann, W. B. Jr. (2003). Self-enhancement tendencies among people with high explicit self-esteem: The moderating role of implicit self-esteem. *Self and Identity, 2,* 169–187.

Bosson, J. K., Swann, W. B. Jr., & Pennebaker, J. W. (2000). Stalking the perfect measure of self-esteem: The blind men and the elephant revisited? *Journal of Personality and Social Psychology 79,* 631–643.

Bowlby, J. (1969). *Attachment and loss: Vol. 1. Attachment.* New York: Basic Books.

Broucek, F. J. (1991). *Shame and the self.* New York: Guilford Press.

Brown, R. P., & Bosson, J. K. (2001). Narcissus meets Sisyphus: Self-love, self-loathing, and the never-ending pursuit of self-worth. *Psychological Inquiry, 12,* 210–213.

Capron, E. W. (2004). Types of pampering and the narcissistic personality trait. *Journal of Individual Psychology, 60,* 77–93.

Coopersmith, S. (1967). *The antecedents of self-esteem.* San Francisco: Freeman.

DeHart, T., Pelham, B. W., & Tennen, H. (2006). What lies beneath: Parenting style and implicit self-esteem. *Journal of Experimental Social Psychology 42,* 1–17.

Dickinson, K. A., & Pincus, A. L. (2003). Interpersonal analysis of grandiose and vulnerable narcissism. *Journal of Personality Disorders 17,* 188–207.

Emmons, R. A. (1984). Factor analysis and construct validation of the Narcissistic Personality Inventory. *Journal of Personality Assessment, 48,* 291–300.

Emmons, R. A. (1987). Narcissism: Theory and measurement. *Journal of Personality and Social Psychology, 5,* 11–17.

Epstein, S. (1990). Cognitive-experiential self-theory. In L. A. Pervin (Ed.), *Handbook of personality: Theory and research* (pp. 165–192). New York: Guilford Press.

Epstein, S., & Morling, B. (1995). Is the self motivated to do more than enhance and/or verify itself? In M. H. Kernis (Ed.), *Efficacy, agency, and self-esteem* (pp. 9–29). New York: Plenum Press.

Farnham, S. D., Greenwald, A. G., & Banaji, M. R. (1999). Implicit self-esteem. In D. Abrams & M. A. Hogg (Eds.), *Social identity and social cognition* (pp. 230–248). Malden, MA: Blackwell.

Fazio, R. H. (1990). A practical guide to the use of response latency in social psychological research. In C. Hendrick & M. S. Clark (Eds.), *Research methods in personality and social psychology* (pp. 74–97). Thousand Oaks, CA: Sage.

Fazio, R. H., & Olson, M. A. (2003). Implicit measures in social cognition research: Their meaning and use. *Annual Review of Psychology 54*, 297–327.

Feiring, C., Taska, L., & Lewis, M. (2002). Adjustment following sexual abuse discovery: The role of shame and attributional style. *Developmental Psychology, 38,* 79–92.

Freud, S. (1957). On narcissim: An introduction. In J. Strachey (Ed. and Trans.), *The standard edition of the complete psychological works of Sigmund Freud* (Vol. 14, pp. 67–104). London: Hogarth Press. (Original work published 1914)

Gramzow, R., & Tangney, J. P. (1992). Proneness to shame and the narcissistic personality. *Personality and Social Psychology Bulletin, 18,* 369–376.

Greenwald, A. G., & Banaji, M. R. (1995). Implicit social cognition: Attitudes, self-esteem, and stereotypes. *Psychological Review 102*, 4–27.

Greenwald, A. G., & Farnham, S. D. (2000). Using the Implicit Association Test to measure self-esteem and self-concept. *Journal of Personality and Social Psychology, 79,* 1022–1038.

Gruenewald, T. L., Kemeny, M. E., Aziz, N., & Fahey, J. L. (2004). Acute threat to the social self: Shame, social self-esteem, and cortisol activity. *Psychosomatic Medicine, 66,* 915–924.

Harder, D. W., Cutler, L., & Rockart, L. (1992). Assessment of shame and guilt and their relationships to psychopathology. *Journal of Personality Assessment, 59,* 584–604.

Harder, D. W., & Lewis, S. J. (1987). The assessment of shame and guilt. In J. N. Butcher & C. D. Spielberger (Eds.), *Advances in personality assessment* (Vol. 6, pp. 89–114). Hillsdale, NJ: Erlbaum.

Harter, S. (1990). Causes, correlates, and the functional role of global self-worth: A life-span perspective. In J. Kolligian & R. Sternberg (Eds.), *Perceptions of competence and incompetence across the life-span* (pp. 67–98). New Haven, CT: Yale University Press.

Hetts, J. J., & Pelham, B. W. (2003). *The ghosts of Christmas past: Reflected appraisals and the perils of near Christmas birthdays.* Unpublished data.

Hetts, J. J., Sakuma, M., & Pelham, B. (1999). Two roads to positive self-regard: Implicit and explicit self-evaluation and culture. *Journal of Experimental Social Psychology, 35,* 512–559.

Higgins, E. T. (1987). Self-discrepancy: A theory relating self and affect. *Psychological Review, 94,* 319–340.

Horney, K. (1950). *Neurosis and human growth: The struggle toward self-realization.* Oxford, UK: Norton.

Jones, J. T., Pelham, B. W., Mirenberg, M. C., & Hetts, J. J. (2002). Name letter preferences are not merely mere exposure: Implicit egotism as self-regulation. *Journal of Experimental Social Psychology, 38,* 170–177.

Jordan, C. H., Spencer, S. J., Zanna, M. P., Hoshino-Browne, E., & Correll, J. (2003). Secure and defensive high self-esteem. *Journal of Personality and Social Psychology, 85,* 969–978.

Kernberg, O. F. (1975). *Borderline conditions and pathological narcissism.* New York: Aronson.

Kohut, H. (1977). *The restoration of the self.* New York: International Universities Press.

Koole, S. L., Dijksterhuis, A., & van Knippenberg, A. (2001). What's in a name: Implicit self-esteem and the automatic self. *Journal of Personality and Social Psychology, 80,* 669–685.

Leith, K. P., & Baumeister, R. F. (1998). Empathy, shame, guilt, and narratives of interpersonal conflicts: Guilt-prone people are better at perspective taking. *Journal of Personality, 66,* 1–37.

Lewis, H. B. (1971). Shame and guilt in neurosis. *Psychoanalytic Review, 58,* 419–438.

Lewis, M. (1992). *Shame: The exposed self*. New York: Free Press.

Lewis, M. (2000). Self-conscious emotions: Embarrassment, pride, shame, and guilt. In M. Lewis & J. M. Haviland-Jones (Eds.), *Handbook of emotions* (2nd ed., pp. 623–636). New York: Guilford Press.

Lewis, M., & Brooks-Gunn, J. (1979). *Social cognition and the acquisition of self*. New York: Plenum Press.

Lewis, M., Sullivan, M. W., Stanger, C., & Weiss, M. (1989). Self development and self-conscious emotions. *Child Development, 60,* 146–156.

Malatesta, C. Z., & Wilson, A. (1988). Emotion cognition interaction in personality development: A discrete emotions, functionalist analysis. *British Journal of Social Psychology, 27,* 91–112.

Mikulincer, M. (1995). Attachment style and the mental representation of the self. *Journal of Personality and Social Psychology, 69,* 1203–1215.

Millon, T. (1981). *Disorders of personality: DSM-III, Axis II*. New York: Wiley.

Moretti, M. M., & Higgins, E. T. (1990). The development of self-esteem vulnerabilities: Social and cognitive factors in developmental psychopathology. In R. J. Sternberg & J. Kolligian Jr. (Eds.), *Competence considered* (pp. 286–314). New Haven, CT: Yale University Press.

Morf, C. C., & Rhodewalt, F. (2001). Unraveling the paradoxes of narcissism: A dynamic self-regulatory processing model. *Psychological Inquiry, 12,* 177–196.

Morrison, A. (1989). *Shame: The underside of narcissism*. Hillsdale, NJ: Analytic Press.

Nathanson, D. L. (1987). The shame/pride axis. In H. B. Lewis (Ed.), *The role of shame in symptom formation* (pp. 183–205). Hillsdale, NJ: Erlbaum.

Nolen-Hoeksema, S., Girgus, J. S., & Seligman, M. E. (1992). Predictors and consequences of childhood depressive symptoms: A 5-year longitudinal study. *Journal of Abnormal Psychology, 101,* 405–422.

Nuttin, M. J. Jr. (1985). Narcissism beyond gestalt and awareness: The name letter effect. *European Journal of Social Psychology, 15,* 353–361.

Otway, L. J., & Vignoles, V. L. (2006). Narcissism and childhood recollections: A quantitative test of psychoanalytic predictions. *Personality and Social Psychology Bulletin, 32,* 104–116.

Raskin, R. N., & Hall, C. S. (1979). A narcissistic personality inventory. *Psychological Reports, 45,* 590.

Raskin, R., & Novacek, J. (1989). An MMPI description of the narcissistic personality. *Journal of Personality Assessment, 53,* 66–80.

Raskin, R., & Terry, H. (1988). A principal-components analysis of the Narcissistic Personality Inventory and further evidence of its construct validity. *Journal of Personality and Social Psychology, 54,* 890–902.

Rathvon, N., & Holmstrom, R. W. (1996). An MMPI-2 portrait of narcissism. *Journal of Personality Assessment, 66,* 1–19.

Rhodewalt, F., & Tragakis, M. W. (2003). Self-esteem and self-regulation: Toward optimal studies of self-esteem. *Psychological Inquiry, 14,* 66–70.

Robins, R. W., Tracy, J. L., & Shaver, P. R. (2001). Shamed into self-love: Dynamics, roots, and functions of narcissism. *Psychological Inquiry, 12,* 230–236.

Rose, P. (2002). The happy and unhappy faces of narcissism. *Personality and Individual Differences, 33,* 379–392.

Rosenberg, M. (1965). *Society and the adolescent self-image*. Princeton, NJ: Princeton University Press.

Scheff, T. J. (1988). Shame and conformity: The deference-emotion system. *American Sociological Review, 53,* 395–406.

Seger, C. A. (1994). Implicit learning. *Psychological Bulletin, 115,* 163–196.

Sorotzkin, B. (1985). The quest for perfection: Avoiding guilt or avoiding shame? *Psychotherapy: Theory, Research, Practice, Training, 22,* 564–571.

Tafarodi, R. W., & Swann, W. B. Jr. (2001). Two-dimensional self-esteem: Theory and measurement. *Personality and Individual Differences, 31,* 653–673.

Tangney, J. P. (2002). Self-conscious emotions: The self as a moral guide. In A. Tesser & D. Stapel (Eds.), *Self and motivation: Emerging psychological perspectives* (pp. 97–117). Washington, DC: American Psychological Association.

Tangney, J. P., Burggraf, S. A., & Wagner, P. E. (1995). Shame-proneness, guilt-proneness, and psychological symptoms. In J. P. Tangney & K. W Fischer (Eds.), *Self-conscious emotions: The psychology of shame, guilt, embarrassment, and pride* (pp. 343–367). New York: Guilford Press.

Tangney, J. P., & Dearing, R. L. (2002). *Shame and guilt.* New York: Guilford Press.

Tangney, J. P., Wagner, P., & Gramzow, R. (1992). Proneness to shame, proneness to guilt, and psychopathology. *Journal of Abnormal Psychology, 101,* 469–478.

Tracy, J. L., & Robins, R. W. (2003). "Death of a (narcissistic) salesman": An integrative model of fragile self-esteem. *Psychological Inquiry, 14,* 57–62.

Tracy, J. L., & Robins, R. W. (2004). Putting the self into self-conscious emotions: A theoretical model. *Psychological Inquiry, 15,* 103–125.

Tracy, J. L., & Robins, R. W. (2007). The psychological structure of pride: A tale of two facets. *Journal of Personality and Social Psychology, 92,* 506–525.

Watson, P. J., Hickman, S. E., & Morris, R. J. (1996). Self-reported narcissism and shame: Testing the defensive self-esteem and continuum hypotheses. *Personality and Individual Differences, 21,* 253–259.

Watson, P. J., Taylor, D., & Morris, R. J. (1987). Narcissism, sex roles, and self-functioning. *Sex Roles, 16,* 335–350.

Weiner, B. (1985). An attributional theory of achievement motivation and emotion. *Psychological Review, 92,* 548–573.

Wink, P. (1991). Two faces of narcissism. *Journal of Personality and Social Psychology, 61,* 590–597.

23

Runaway Nationalism

Alienation, Shame, and Anger

THOMAS J. SCHEFF

Most contemporary discussions of blind nationalism and violence are entirely descriptive (see, e.g., Kressel, 2002). Psychological explorations of collective "evil" are also largely descriptive, even though they refer to the most basic component of ethnocentrism, the "us–them" attitude. Both Baumeister (1997) and Staub (2003) have written about collective violence, but both lack an explicit theory of individual and collective dynamics.

Haidt and Algoe (2004) have taken the idea of ethnocentrism several steps further. First, they use the vivid terminology of "saints" (us) and "devils" (them) which is helpful because it suggests vast intensity of feeling. Second, they propose that emotions drive sanctifying and devil making. Finally, they introduce the idea of moral amplification, how us–them attributions are magnified by moral feelings.

This chapter proposes a similar dynamic of ethnocentrism, involving the division of the world into two contending groups, with the possibility of limitless amplification. Unlike Haidt and Algoe (2004), who use a correlational argument, this chapter describes a model of causal process, one that proposes a second-by-second feedback system with biosocial components (unacknowledged emotions and alienation) that produces collective violence.

A first step into a dynamic theory of nationalism is suggested by Durkheim's (1915) idea that any enduring religion requires the interplay between belief, on the one hand, and ritual, on the other. He proposed that the elemental basis for religion is the reciprocal relation of belief to ritual, and vice versa. Belief leads to ritual, and ritual to belief, in a feedback loop. Organized religions can be viewed as social systems arising out of the interaction between belief and ritual, ideas and actions.

Viewing religion as a social system can further understanding of blind allegiance to nations or ethnic groups. But more detail will be needed. In particular, we need to understand how blind nationalism is generated not only in the world of ideology and action, but also in the emotional/relational world (E/RW). How is nationalism forged out of belief, ritual, emotion, and relationships?

Benedict Anderson (1991) has suggested that a nation is an "imagined community." Although he does not develop the idea, this phrase suggests what might be seen as an anomaly. We all know many people personally, our neighbors and work associates and members of our own families. Yet we may identify with, and will lay down our lives to protect, the millions of fellow citizens who we not only do not know, but have never, and will never, meet. For reasons considered below, it may be much easier to identify with imagined people you do not know then real ones that you do.

The social theory of G. H. Mead (1936) and recent discussions of infatuation may be next steps toward further understanding. Mead argued that the self is social, a response to a community that is, in great part, imagined. The core of this theory is what he called "taking the role of the other," by which he meant viewing a situation not only from our own point of view, but also from the point of view of the other(s). His concept of "the generalized other" makes it clear that role taking refers not only to people that we know, but also to those that we only imagine. Although Mead did not explicitly discuss the possibility of identifying with the imagined other, his theory implies it.

One example of an imagined point of view that one might identify with is posterity: one imagines what future generations might think of one's self, and judges one's self from that point of view. A more common generalization of the other would be for an American person to imagine the point of view of all other Americans, and identify with that imagined point of view. The only step remaining for forming an "us and them" mentality would be to idealize the one at the expense of the other.

Imagining the point of view of the other(s) occurs not only in nationalism, but is a commonplace requirement of everyday life for everyone. Since ordinary language is extremely ambiguous, one must take the point of view of the other in order to understand even fairly simple statements. A crucial part of the context of any message is the point of view of the person(s) from whom one received the message. As Cooley (1922) said, "We live in the minds of others' without knowing it" (p. 208). But the "us and them" mentality requires not only imagining the points of view of two communities, but also identifying with one and rejecting the other.

One problem with Mead's scheme is that he did not worry about variability in the accuracy with which we imagine the point of view of the other(s). His theory seems to imply accuracy, which cannot possibly be always, or even, typically, true. I return to this issue below, in the discussion of infatuation and voter education. The other issue pursued here, more extensively than the issue of accuracy, is the emotional aspects of role taking. Neither Mead nor Anderson has anything to say about emotions. This chapter suggests that emotions play a dominant part in the kind of identification and rejection that leads to aggression.

Most discussions of nationalism give little or no attention to the role of emotions. For example, it has been argued that military service simply involves the meeting of one's obligations, as in any other institution (Hinde & Watson, 1994). The willingness of soldiers to die for others is viewed as simply normative. It is probably true that much of what goes on in the human world can be explained in this way: we merely follow the rules. Perhaps this kind of explanation is best for understanding the everyday world. But it is also true that everyday some rules are broken or ignored. Moreover, in times of change or crisis, all rules may be ignored. Without invoking the E/RW, it is difficult to understand the fervor of nationalism. Untold millions of people have gratuitously laid down their lives, and taken the lives of others, in the name of their nation or other imagined communities.

Such willingness is understandable when it is quite clear that one's group is in danger because of a threat by another group. But current and past history suggests that most citizens support killing and being killed purely "on spec," even without plausible evidence of threat. Many would argue that the war on Iraq is one instance, and that World War I, which commenced without any real attempt at peacemaking, and with little immediate threat (Scheff, 1994), is another.

Few people would be willing to die for their neighborhood, county, state, trade, or professional association. My own professional association is the American Sociological Association (ASA). Although I have been laying down dollars every year for many years in order to belong, I would not kill to avoid a hostile takeover by another discipline. The ASA may have a few such members, disciplinary patriots. For the rest of us, we may wage war with words, yes, but not with bombs and bullets.

There is another, much smaller group that may demand blind loyalty: the immediate family. An earlier study (Scheff, 1995) illustrated this dynamic. In conflict-ridden families, the child will often identify with, and idealize, one parent and vilify the other. This pattern is particularly prevalent in, but not limited to, families of divorced parents.

This chapter proposes that infatuation and shame/rage are the key elements of the social and psychological dynamics shared by families, gangs, aggressive nations, and ethnic groups in conflict.

INFATUATION AND HATRED

To begin to understand the social/psychological dynamics of fervent nationalism, it will be necessary to understand what is meant by "love of country," on the one hand, and "hatred" of its supposed enemies, on the other. These terms, in vernacular usage, may not be as simple and straightforward as they seem. They can be used as mystifications that both distort and hide the nature of the E/RW.

The use of ordinary words, rather than well-defined concepts, is a pressing problem in all of social science. For example, there have been a vast number of studies of alienation and of self-esteem that assume these words need not be defined. Although there are many, many standardized scales for measuring alienation and self-esteem, there have been few attempts to decide, conceptually, what it is that these scales are supposed to be measuring.

To this day, most key concepts in social science are quite ambiguous. Some of them, such as alienation and self-esteem, may involve too many potentially orthogonal meanings (such as individual, relational, cognitive, and emotional dimensions) to be measured by a single instrument. Others, such as irrationality or context, for example, may be mere residual categories, conceptually empty boxes, because they encompass the enormously wide variety of different kinds of things that remain after their polar opposite has been explored in detail. Rationality is a fairly specific idea since it involves rules of logic and evidence; irrationality is all other approaches. Similarly, the immediate situation is what we see before us in the present; the context is everything else: past, present, future, here and elsewhere. Rationality and situation are bounded domains, irrationality and context are boundless.

Ambiguity in the Meaning of Love

The word *love* provides a vivid example of the first kind of ambiguity, a kind of umbrella word that encompasses many different facets. According to Harold Bloom, Aldous Huxley suggested that "we use the word love for the most amazing variety of relationships, ranging from what we feel for our mothers to what we feel for someone we beat up in a bordello, or its many equivalents" (Bloom, 1998, p. 549).

The comment about beating someone up out of love is probably not an exaggeration. A recent set of experiments suggests that people's condemnation of murder is softened if they are told that it was caused by jealousy (Peunte & Cohen, 2003). People seem to entertain the idea that one can love someone so much that one kills them, loving them to death.

Solomon (1981, pp. 3–4) elaborates on the broad sweep of the word *love:*

> Consider . . . the wealth of meticulous and fine distinctions we make in describing our feelings of hostility: hatred, loathing, scorn, anger, revulsion, resentment, envy, abhorrence, malice, aversion, vexation, irritation, annoyance, disgust, spite and contempt, or worse, "beneath" contempt. And yet we sort out our positive affections for the most part between the two limp categories, "liking" and "loving." We distinguish our friends from mere acquaintances and make a ready distinction between lovers and friends whom we love "but not that way." Still, one and the same word serves to describe our enthusiasm for apple strudel, respect for a distant father, the anguish of an uncertain romantic affair and nostalgic affection for an old pair of slippers.

In modern societies the broad use of the word *love* may defend us against the painful absence of true intimacy and community. The idea seems to be that *any* kind of relationship that has positive elements in it, even if mixed with extremely negative ones, can be named love.

What Does Love Mean?

One place to seek definitions is the dictionary. In the English language unabridged dictionaries provide some *two dozen* meanings for love, most of them applicable to romantic or other human relationships. These are the first two meanings in the *American Heritage Dictionary* (1992):

1. A deep, tender, ineffable feeling of affection and solicitude toward a person, such as that arising from kinship, recognition of attractive qualities, or a sense of underlying oneness.
2. A feeling of intense desire and attraction toward a person with whom one is disposed to make a pair; the emotion of sex and romance.

These two definitions are of great interest because they touch upon several complexities. Particularly daunting is the idea that love is ineffable (indescribable). I can sympathize with this idea because genuine love seems to be quite complex. Both popular and scholarly accounts flirt with the idea that one of the crowning qualities of love is that it is mysterious and therefore indescribable.

Contradicting this idea, I have developed definitions of love, both in its romantic and nonromantic forms, that might be used instead of the vernacular word (Scheff, 2006).

My definition of romantic love contains three components. Two are physical: sexual attraction and attachment. One is cognitive/emotional; I call it "attunement" (balanced mutual awareness between self and other). My definition of nonromantic love omits sexual attraction, but involves the other two "A's," attachment and attunement.

This definition of the attunement component is based on an earlier approach to defining love by Solomon (1994) as *shared identity*: "love [is] shared identity, a redefinition of self which no amount of sex or fun or time together will add up to. . . . Two people in a society with an extraordinary sense of individual identity mutually fantasize, verbalize and act their way into a relationship that can no longer be understood as a mere conjunction of the two but only as a complex ONE. (p. 235)

Although Solomon does not use terms like "mutual awareness" or "intersubjectivity," such concepts are clearly implied. In passing, he also implies another aspect of what I would call "genuine love," that one's individual identity is held in balance with identifying with the other(s). One's own autonomous self is valued no more than the other(s), but also no less. It is this feature that differentiates between true solidarity and engulfment. The implication is that moments of unity with the other(s) are, in the long run, balanced against moments of individual autonomy. See also Aron, Mashek, and Aron (2004, pp. 27–41), on including the other in one's self. Their idea is a step toward the idea of attunement, but still couched in individualistic terms.

Many attempts to define love propose that it has three components. However, none of them make attunement (mutual knowledge) one of the three. This idea is sometimes referred to, however, albeit indirectly and indistinctly. For example, Sternberg (1988) defines love as involving commitment, passion, and intimacy. He breaks intimacy down into 10 parts, one of which is mutual understanding. His definition therefore hints at the attunement component in my definition. However, his treatment of mutual understanding as one of nine other aspects of intimacy diminishes its importance, as does his failure to make clear what he means by "mutual understanding."

The idea of attunement can be used to distinguish love from look-alikes such as infatuation and engulfment. What most patriots profess to be "love" of their country lacks the perquisite of balanced shared identity. Love of country is closer to being what might be called "infatuation." Similarly, what is called "hatred of national enemies" could be a gloss on a complex process of hiding feelings of inadequacy and alienation under the cover of "pride" in one's country, as is discussed below. The meaning of love and pride are so ambiguous in ordinary language that they can easily be used in the service of defensive maneuvers like denial and projection.

Genuine love requires detailed knowledge of the other(s). Having only an image of the other's appearance, say, or infatuation is self-generated fantasy. Collective infatuation is not only self-generated, but also socially amplified. Nations, like fan clubs, can whip their participants into an ecstasy of adoration. Unlike fan clubs, nations also do the opposite, amplifying individual negative feelings into orgies of hatred and rage.

Both individual and collective infatuation can be an enormously arresting, intense experience. The idealization of a mere image of the other(s), unlike genuine love, has no reality check, and therefore can spiral into infinity. The great never-ending stream of poetry of romantic infatuation bears witness to the infinitely intense experience of the "lover."

Tennov (1979) interviewed "lovers" about their state of mind. She describes it as "limerance," an unusual word that means trance. Most of the informants were lost in what Sappho called "the love-trance." The idea that those who are infatuated are in a trance has ominous political implications, if, as I suggested above, those who profess love of country are actually infatuated. Unable to perceive and think clearly, such persons would be at the mercy of the "love" object.

Intense infatuation forms the dominant emotion in the propaganda of any nation preparing for war. One clear example occurred in the patriotic novels, lyrics, and poetry of France during the period between wars with Germany (1871–1914: Scheff, 1994). Most exiguous was the "military poetry" of the right-wing extremist Paul de Roulede. His *Songs of a Soldier* (1872) gushed passionate "love" for the glory of France, and demanded revenge on Germany as necessary for the honor of France. It went through an unprecedented 83 editions by 1890, making it one of the most popular books ever published in France.

The infatuation-trance of extreme nationalism is like the naked trust that small children have for their parents. For the first 6 years of life, at least, most children form an idealized image of their parents as authorities who can do no wrong, like gods on earth. It appears that for many adults, whether or not they retain this nursery image of the actual parent, they transfer it to their government. It is very difficult to overcome such an image, no matter the mounting evidence that it is untrue.

Collective Hatred and Rage

Collective hatred, like collective "love," can achieve much higher levels of intensity than that of individuals, but the spiral is much more hidden and complex. To understand this process, it may be necessary to forego everyday, vernacular explanations. I propose that "hatred" is the commonly used word for hidden vulnerable emotions, particularly grief, fear, and shame. Dictionary definitions of hatred focus on hostility as the key component.

> Hatred: 1. To feel hostility or animosity toward. To detest. 2. To feel dislike or distaste for: I hate washing dishes
> Animosity: Bitter hostility or open enmity; active hatred. (*American Heritage Dictionary*, 2000)

The inclusion of animosity in the definition is important because it emphasizes the intensity that is usually involved in hatred, counteracting the scaling down of the word in everyday, nonconflict situations, as in encounters with dirty dishes. The definition of animosity includes both bitter hostility, an attitude that may or may not be expressed, and open enmity.

The key to the intensity or bitterness of hatred seems to be an emotion that is a hidden component of rage and aggression: unacknowledged shame or humiliation. (For the purpose of this discussion, I treat shame and humiliation as the same emotion, since both signal disconnect). One way to deal with the feeling that one has been rejected as unworthy is to "reject the rejector," rather than to blame one's self as unworthy. This is the process that is discussed below as a technique of neutralization, but in the relatively new language of emotions, instead of being framed entirely in cognitive and behavioral terms.

Hidden, covert shame, in combination with either hidden or overt rage, may be the primary components of hatred. The first step is to discuss intense rage. An immediate problem in making this argument persuasive is the difficulty of describing in words the experience of rage and other compelling emotions. When readers are sitting in the comfort of their study, feeling more or less safe and secure, it will take some effort to help them visualize the intensity of "war fever," or of the feelings that lead to massacre on a vast scale. The intensity and primitiveness of humiliated fury beggars verbal description.

Most social science writing on violent conflict assumes a "realist" or materialist perspective, that the real causes of human conduct always involve physical, rather than social and psychological, reality. But eliminating emotional and relational elements as causes of violence may be a gross error. It is easy to do because of the difficulty of conveying emotional states in words. Those who map mountains without also viewing them can easily loose touch with their vast immensity.

I am not arguing that material conditions are unimportant, only that violence is caused by a combination of physical and social/psychological elements. I will consider hatred first at the level of individuals, then at the collective level, showing how both hatred and violence are products of unacknowledged emotions, which are in turn generated by alienation and by cultural scripts for demonizing purported enemies.

Shame and Hate

As already indicated, rage seems to be a composite affect, a sequence of two elemental emotions, shame and anger. This idea has been advanced by other authors, notably Kohut (1971), Lewis (1971), Gilligan (1997), and Tangney and Dearing (2002). Kohut proposed that violent anger of the kind he called "narcissistic rage" was a shame/anger compound. Lewis suggested that shame and anger have a deep affinity, and that one can find indications of unacknowledged shame occurring just prior to any episode of intense hostility. (For further elaboration on the implications of shame/anger sequences, see Tangney & Dearing, 2002.)

This sequence has been shown in many transactions during psychotherapy sessions by Lewis (1971), in four marital quarrels by Retzinger (1991), and in Hitler's writings and speeches (Scheff, 1994). Retzinger demonstrated that prior to each of the 16 episodes of angry escalation in her cases, there had been first an insult by one party, indications of unacknowledged shame in the other party, and finally intense hostility in that party. This sequence can be seen as the motor of violence, since it connects the intense emotions of shame and anger to overt aggression.

Although there has been little research focused explicitly on pure, unalloyed anger, indications from the studies of discourse by Lewis (1971) and Retzinger (1991), and my own work (such as Scheff, 1990), suggest that pure anger is rare and unlikely to lead to violence or even social disruption. On the contrary, anger by itself is usually brief and instructive. A person who is frustrated and unashamed of his or her anger is mobilized to tell what is going on, and to do what is needed, without making a huge scene.

In my own case, I can testify that most of my experiences of anger have involved shame/anger, either in the form of humiliated fury, or in a more passive form, what Labov and Fanshel (1977) call "helpless anger." Both of these variants are long-lasting and extremely unpleasant. Shame-induced anger is unpleasant while happening, and even more unpleasant when over, since it is typically accompanied by a sense of being foolish and out of control.

Episodes of pure anger are rare, and the experience is entirely different. Looking back on my own such experiences, I notice that I did not raise my voice, nor did I put anyone down nor engage in any other kind of excess. I simply told my view of what was going on directly, rapidly, and with no calculation or planning. I was overcome with what might be called "machine-gun mouth." Everyone who was present for one of these communications suddenly became quite respectful. I didn't feel out of control, even though my speech was completely spontaneous; on the contrary, I was wondering why I had not had my say before. It would seem that anger without shame has only a signal function, to alert self and others to one's frustration.

When anger has its source in feelings of rejection or inadequacy, and when the latter feelings are not acknowledged, a continuous spiral of shame/anger may result, which may be experienced as hatred and rage. Rather than expressing and discharging one's shame through laughter ("Silly me" or "Silly us"), it is masked by rage and aggression. One can be angry one is ashamed, and ashamed that one is angry, and so on, working up to a loop of unlimited duration and intensity. This loop may be the emotional basis of lengthy (even lifelong) episodes of hatred that seem intense beyond endurance.

Shame/Rage and Hypermasculinity

Spanish has a word for it, *machismo*, which means the extreme exaggeration of masculine traits. Since there is no comparable word in English, I will make up one: *hypermasculinity*. An earlier essay (Scheff, 2003) proposed that physical aggression or complete withdrawal is a common component of hypermasculinity, which in turn has social/emotional bases: (1) no affectional attachments, (2) a single overarching obsession, and (3) complete repression of shame. Only to the extent that all three of these conditions are fully met is silence or destructive violence likely. The earlier essay used Hitler's biographies to show how completely episodes from his life illustrate all three of these conditions. Although women with this pattern would be as likely as men to commit or condone violent acts, men appear to qualify much more frequently and fully than do women.

Most men are trained from early childhood to suppress all vulnerable emotions, especially fear, grief, and shame. Parents and male children usually confound fear with cowardice and grief and shame with weakness. After thousands of episodes of intentional suppression, men learn to numb out these feelings automatically. In terms of the theory proposed here, the repression of shame is the core process in hypermasculinity, because it numbs out both fear and conscience. Killing or maiming other humans would be intensely painful if the automatic shame response was still in play.

In her essay "Let Them Eat War," Hochschild (2005) suggests a similar mechanism of defense to explain why working-class men, against their own economic interests, support our "cowboy president." She argues that Bush covers his own fears and other vulnerable emotions by aggressive action, a pattern that these males also follow or would like to follow. This analysis suggests how reactionary leaders generate support among their followers (as was the case with Hitler's appeal to the Germans). Their appeal is largely social and emotional, rather that economic or ideological.

Collective hatred and violence seem to depend on the suppression of other vulnerable emotions, not just shame. Volkan (2004) has made a convincing case that the most lethal violence is caused by the humiliation of groups that have suppressed collective grief. Many groups, he notes, have what he calls "chosen traumas," a historical episode of massive loss. For example, he shows that the chosen trauma of the Serbs, their loss of the Battle of Kosovo in 1389, has taken on such a great symbolic/emotional value that reference to it is needed to understand the tragedies in Bosnia in 1992 and Kosovo in 1999 (p. 50).

Particularly relevant to the understanding of mass violence is Volkan's (2004) idea that chosen traumas may give rise to collective feelings of entitlement to revenge. He also makes the connection between collective and individual emotions:

> Serious threats to large-group identity, such as shared helplessness and humiliation, are perceived by members of that large group as *individually* wounding and *personally* endangering: they induce a collective response of anxiety or terror. (p. 33)

This linking of personal and collective responses makes sense in terms of responses to 9/11 that I have seen in persons close to me. Out of my large extended family, only two persons (both in-laws) reacted in this way. But their response exactly illustrates Volkan's point; they went into an aggressive posture, continually declaring their hatred of "the enemy" and their love for their country. They exhibit blind trust for the present Bush regime, in exactly the way that Volkan proposes.

My own initial reaction to 9/11 was also extreme, but in a different way. Rather than becoming aggressive, I sank into depression. After watching the assault on the towers on TV many times, I fell into a trance-like state of disorientation and horror. This state persisted even after I finally turned off the TV. The next day, however, a different kind of episode occurred that lifted me out of depression.

As I was driving in my car, I heard radio interviews of survivors from the World Trade Center. I noticed that several of them mentioned that when they were running down the stairs to escape, they were quite surprised to see policemen and firemen running up the stairs. Many of these men sacrificed their own lives trying to help others escape. After turning off the radio, as I was thinking of the courage of these men, I burst into tears. I cried for a long time, convulsively, like a baby. After the crying episode, I felt like I was myself again.

What happened? My interpretation is that seeing the towers fall had left me in a state of helpless humiliation, grief, and fear. Like most men, I was unable to manage these particular emotions, since at some level I am still ashamed of them. So I suppressed them, leading to my depression. But I felt pride when I identified with the brave men who sacrificed their lives helping others. The pride countered my shame, leading to an episode of effective mourning. A comparison of my episode, and the failure to mourn by my two in-laws, illustrates Volkan's idea about the importance of unresolved grief and shame in collective responses to trauma

Conditions for Intergroup Hatred

One elemental source of hatred may be the shame of not belonging, forming groups that reject the group(s) supposedly rejecting them. The culture of such groups generates *techniques of neutralization* that encourage hatred and mayhem. Just as there is rage generated by threatened or damaged bonds at the level of the individual, there are also social and cultural spirals that give rise to collective hatred and rage.

Elsewhere (Scheff, 1997, Chap. 3), I have described how *bimodal alienation* generates violence at the collective level. Bimodal alienation between groups occurs when there is "isolation" *between* them, but "engulfment" *within* them. On the one hand, members of group A are distant from members of group B, and vice versa. But, on the other hand, members of each group are infatuated with each other, to the point that they give up important parts of themselves in order to be completely loyal to the group. A very wealthy and influential person in my local community said to me, "I am a patriot. When my country wants something, I give it, no questions asked." I replied, "Suppose you have doubts?" He answered, "Not possible. My country comes first." Idealizing the nation means suppressing one's thoughts and feelings.

The initial motor in this theory is the need to belong. It makes sense that the German language has the most beautiful word for home, in the sense of the place that you belong: *das Heimat*. As both Elias (1995) and I (Scheff, 1994) have argued, historically the Germans have long had an unsatisfied yearning for a place in which they belong, and have had great difficulty in managing the feeling of rejection, of not belonging and being accepted. Members of a group who feel not accepted both by foreigners and in their own group are in a position to surrender their individual identity in order to be accepted, giving rise in the German case to the principle of *obrigkeit* (blind loyalty and obedience). Bimodal alienation (isolation between groups and engulfment within them) may be the fundamental condition for intergroup conflict.

Under the condition of bimodal alienation, a special culture develops within each group that encourages the acting out of unacknowledged resentment and hatred. There are various ways of characterizing this culture, but for my purposes I will describe it in terms of "techniques of neutralization." This idea was originally formulated in criminology (Sykes & Matza, 1957) to explain how and why teenagers engage in delinquent behavior, how a special culture develops among them that neutralizes the norms in their larger culture that oppose crime. But the idea has also been carefully applied by Alverez (1997) to the behavior of the German people in tolerating or actually engaging in genocide during the Holocaust.

Alverez shows how each of Sykes and Matza's five techniques of neutralization can be used to explain the special culture that developed during the Nazi regime, a culture that neutralized the norms in the larger culture that forbid murder. The first technique is denial of responsibility. Alverez shows that this technique in the German case usually took the form that the perpetrator was only carrying out orders from above. The second neutralization technique, denial of injury, took the form under the Nazi regime of special language that hid or disguised what was actually being done, euphemisms in which killing became "special treatment," "cleansing" (also applied to the massacres in Bosnia), and many other similar examples. The third technique, denial of the victim, asserts that the victim actually brought on his or her own downfall. In the German case, Hitler and his followers believed that the Jews were involved in a conspiracy to enslave the whole world, so that killing them was self-defense. Although a fiction, many Germans appeared to have believed it to be literally true.

The fourth neutralization technique, condemning the condemners, in the German case, involved claims made by the German government and the media that other countries that were condemning Germany were historically guilty of worse crimes, such as the treatment of blacks and Native Americans in the United States and the treatment of native peoples in the French, British, and Spanish colonies. The fifth neutralization technique described by Sykes and Matza, appealing to higher loyalties, was used by German perpetrators of genocide in thinking of themselves as patriots, nobly carrying out their duty. Alverez himself added a sixth category, denial of humanity, to those formulated by Sykes and Matza because of its special relevance to the Holocaust. Typical Nazi propaganda portrayed Jews and other non-Aryans as subhuman, filled with bestial impulses, such as the urge for destruction, primitive desires, and unparalleled evil. Although dehumanization often accompanies intergroup conflict, it seems in the German case that it was explicitly orchestrated by the government.

Any one of these six techniques can serve to encourage violence by neutralizing society's norms against aggression and murder. To the extent that they are all implemented together, as they apparently were under the Nazi regime, a whole society can forgo moral values in order to engage in wholesale slaughter.

The dynamics described here can be found in our nation's current policies as well. The manipulation of fear, shame, and rage in the public seems to be the key element in the Bush regime strategy. Finding plausible outside enemies serves to protect its political and economic maneuvers from criticism. The framing of aggression against Iraq for the past decade by the U.S. government has made ample use of techniques of neutralization. Denial of victim has been especially important, in that our government makes the claim, with no evidence, that Iraq poses a threat to the United States and to the world. The war against Iraq has made frequent use of the denial of injury. One example is the use of the phrase "collateral damage" to disguise the killing of civilian men, women, and children. Another example is the idea that the purpose of the war is to "liberate," rather than to control, Iraq. The idea that the United States is liberating Iraq is also an appeal to higher loyalties.

The idea of techniques of neutralization suggests the cultural foundation for collective violence. In the remainder of this chapter, I focus on the potential for reducing the emotional bases of violence by dealing with shame and alienation that has gone unacknowledged.

PRACTICAL APPLICATIONS OF THEORY

How can spirals of unresolved grief, unacknowledged shame, and anger be avoided or slowed when they are occurring? One answer may lie in the direction of effective mass mourning and acknowledgment of shame. Acknowledgment, however, does not refer to merely verbal acknowledgment, as in the routine confessions in Alcoholics Anonymous and its spin-offs. Acknowledgment is one of those terms, like "working through" in psychoanalysis, that play a central role in professional discourse, but are seldom defined or even illustrated through concrete examples.

This discussion points toward several paths for conciliation between belligerent groups. My theory of protracted conflict suggests that the foremost cause is mass alienation within and between the groups. Any steps that would decrease mass alienation would lessen the potential for conflict. Some examples follow.

An earlier essay on alienation (Scheff, 1997, Chap. 4) proposed that teachers need to be retrained to be aware of the way in which they reject working-class and minority students. I also suggest classes on family relations that would help young people form stable families. Also in that essay I recommend reform for welfare programs to lessen rejection and shame. Young men form the bulk of combatants for intergroup and international conflict. If they could be better integrated into work or welfare, school, and family, they would be less vulnerable to pressure to fight an external and, often what amounts to, an imagined enemy.

At the level of culture, to undermine the sources of intergroup conflict, we may need to counter the techniques of neutralization (Sykes & Matza, 1957; Alverez, 1997) that are used to foment hatred and violence toward purported enemies. Although there are attempts to control hatred in the mass media, they still have not been comprehensive enough to help reduce the pressure toward violence. An obvious example is the continuing sexism and violence toward women in commercial films, not to mention fringe films. Although racism and xenophobia has been toned down somewhat, it still forms an undercurrent in many current films. It seems particularly flagrant in "action" films. Needless to say, both sexism and racism are rife in most of the old films that are constantly being rerun on TV.

Learning to identify and acknowledge shame and rage in self and others is also a fundamental direction toward decreasing conflict. I have proposed in this chapter that alienation and unacknowledged shame are basic causes of destructive conflict, as important as material causes. Obviously material interests matter in human affairs. They are topics of quarrels. But these interests can always be negotiated, if there is no unacknowledged emotion, in a way that allows parties maximum benefit or perhaps least destructive outcomes. Unacknowledged shame figures large because it makes rational negotiation of interest difficult or even impossible, given the elements of insult and rejection when shame is not acknowledged by both parties.

How does one awaken persons from a trance? Changing individuals would require long-term projects. One approach would be to introduce courses on emotional/relational issues in early schooling. A course on mediation and conflict resolution could be introduced in middle schools and a course on dating and family communications at the high school level.

I have been teaching a course on communication for many years to university students in their freshman year. Most of the students have been very receptive. A large majority in every class seem to understand that their own communication practices can be improved, and so can those of the people in their life. The majority act as if they have been awakened from a trance. Their faces show shock the first time they realize their own part in causing a difficulty that they had been attributing to the other person. They find it easiest to see their own role in difficulties with roommates. Next, they acknowledge their own roles in problems with their parents. Last, they admit to their own roles in difficulties with their lovers, which is a struggle because that relationship is so conflicted and immediate. Only a bare majority make it that far in 10 weeks. If the class lasted 20 weeks, probably everyone would.

Even if all schools introduced such courses—itself unlikely—major changes in the management of the E/RW would still be a long time coming. In the meanwhile, it might be worth the effort to try to make changes at the collective level. One thing that might work is institutions based on the Truth and Reconciliation Committee that proved to be effective in the transformation of relationships in South Africa. A by-product of the acknowledgment of aggression by the perpetrators, and of suffering by the victims and their kin, is the acknowledgment of shame and rage.

Perhaps in the future it will be necessary to institute a project to clarify the origins and emotional, political, and economic origins and consequences of the war on Iraq. A first step might be to form committees on the Gulf War, since there are many questions that need to be raised. One would be the origins of that war. Ramsey Clark (1994), the U.S. attorney general during Carter's presidency, has claimed that the United States instigated this war through Kuwait, and by deceiving Iraq. Another issue would be the treatment of the U.S. veterans of that war, especially the claims that many were sickened by the war, but have been unable to get treatment.

At a more general level, it may be necessary to pursue reforms that could make the sentiments that the majority hold for their country less like infatuation and more like love, warts and all, and the sentiments that they hold toward the enemy less like blind hatred and more like understanding or at least objectivity. Most supporters of the Iraq war do not even know where Iraq is, much less the history of U.S. interference in that country. Perhaps they do not want to know. But in any case, one reform that might help would be the requirement that citizens pass an examination before being allowed to vote.

Getting knowledge relevant to the major issues of the day is not easy, even for a scholar. One problem is the complexity and depth of many of the issues. Another is the poor job the mass media do. Can relevant knowledge be made available to everyone? The World Wide Web may provide new opportunities for publicly consumed knowledge that can be presented in an easily accessible format.

CONCLUSION

This chapter concerns the emotional/relational components of blind infatuation and hatred, how they are generated, and how they might be overcome. I have proposed that there is always an irrational component in mass infatuation and hatred that is the product of unacknowledged shame and alienation. Can anything be done? A number of strategies are offered whereby teachers, policymakers, and the media can facilitate mass mourning and acknowledgment of shame, decrease mass alienation, counter techniques of neutralization, and enhance communication without engendering destructive experiences of shame.

ACKNOWLEDGMENTS

This chapter is based in part on Chapter 11 in my book on Erving Goffman (Scheff, 2006). I am indebted to Bernard Phillips for his advice on both versions, and to June Tangney for her advice on this one.

REFERENCES

Alverez, A. (1997). Adjusting to genocide: Techniques of neutralization and the Holocaust. *Social Science History, 21,* 139–178.

American Heritage dictionary of the English language, the (3rd ed.). (1992). Boston: Houghton Mifflin.

Anderson, B. (1991). *Imagined communities.* London: Verso.

Aron, A., Mashek, D., & Aron, E. (2004). Closeness as including other in the self. In A. Aaron and D. Mashek (Eds.), *Handbook of closeness and intimacy* (pp. 4–43). Mahwah, NJ: Erlbaum.

Baumeister, R. (1997). *Evil: Inside human violence and cruelty.* New York: Freeman.

Bloom, H. (1998). *Shakespeare: The invention of the human.* New York: Riverhead Books.

Clark, R. (1994). *The fire this time: U.S. war crimes in the Gulf.* Emeryville, CA: Thunder's Mouth Press.

Cooley, C. H. (1922). *Human nature and the social order.* New York: Scribner's.

Durkheim, E. (1915). *Elementary forms of the religious life.* Glencoe, IL: Free Press.

Elias, N. (1995). *The Germans: Power struggles and the development of habitus in the nineteenth and twentieth centuries.* Cambridge, UK: Polity Press.

Gilligan, J. (1997). *Violence.* New York: Vintage Books.

Haidt, J., & Algoe, S. (2004). Moral amplification and the emotions that attach us to saints and demons. In J. Greenberg, S. L. Koole, & T. Pyszczynski (Eds.), *Handbook of experimental existential psychology.* New York: Guilford Press.

Hinde, R., & Watson, H. (Eds.). (1994). *War, a cruel necessity?: The bases of institutionalized violence.* London: Tauris.

Hochschild, A. (2004). Let them eat war. *European Journal of Psychotherapy, Counseling and Health,* 6(3), 1–10.

Kohut, H. (1971). Thoughts on narcissism and narcissistic rage. In *The search for the self* (pp. 77–108). New York: International Universities Press.

Kressel, N. (2002). *Mass hate.* Boulder, CO: Westview Press.

Labov, W., & Fanshel, D. (1977). *Therapeutic discourse.* New York: Academic Press.

Lewis, H. (1971). *Shame and guilt in neurosis.* New York: International Universities Press.

Mead, G. H. (1936). *Mind, self, and society.* Chicago: University of Chicago Press.

Phillips, B., & Kinkaid, H. (Eds.). (2002). *Beyond Babel: Reconstructing sociology.* Hawthorne, NY: Aldine de Gruyter.

Puente, S., & Cohen, D. (2003). Jealousy and the meaning of love. *Personality and Social Psychology Bulletin,* 29, 449–460.

Retzinger, S. M. (1991). *Violent emotions: Shame and rage in marital quarrels.* Newbury Park, CA: Sage.

Scheff, T. (1979). *Catharsis in healing, ritual, and drama.* Berkeley and Los Angeles: University of California Press.

Scheff, T. (1990). *Microsociology: Discourse, emotion and social structure.* Chicago: University of Chicago Press.

Scheff, T. (1994). *Bloody revenge: Emotions, nationalism, war.* Boulder, CO: Westview Press.

Scheff, T. (1995). Conflict in family systems: The role of shame. In J. P. Tangney & K. W. Fischer (Eds.), *Self-conscious emotions.* New York: Guilford Press.

Scheff, T. (2003). Male emotions and violence. *Human Relations,* 56, 727–749.

Scheff, T. (2006). *Goffman unbound!: A new paradigm for social science.* Boulder, CO: Paradigm.

Scheff, T., & Retzinger, S. (1991). *Emotion and violence: Shame/rage spirals in interminable conflicts.* Lexington, MA: Lexington Books.

Solomon, R. (1981). *Love: Emotion, myth, and metaphor.* Garden City, NY: Anchor Press/Doubleday.

Solomon, R. (1994). *About love: Re-inventing romance for our times.* Lanham, MD: Littlefield Adams.

Sternberg, R. (1988). Triangulating love. In R. Sternberg & M. L. Barnes (Eds.), *The psychology of love.* New Haven, CT: Yale University Press.

Staub, E. (2003). *The psychology of good and evil.* Cambridge, UK: Cambridge University Press.

Sykes, G., & Matza, D. (1957). Techniques of neutralization: A theory of delinquency. *American Sociological Review,* 22, 664–670.

Tangney, J. P., & Dearing, R. L. (2002). *Shame and guilt.* New York: Guilford Press.

Tennov, D. (1979). *Love and limerance.* Chelsea, MI: Scarborough House.

Volkan, V. (2004). *Blind trust: Large groups and their leaders in times of crisis and terror.* Charlottesville, VA: Pitchstone.

PART VI

ASSESSMENT

24

Assessing Self-Conscious Emotions

A Review of Self-Report and Nonverbal Measures

RICHARD W. ROBINS
ERIK E. NOFTLE
JESSICA L. TRACY

In this chapter, we provide an overview of measures of self-conscious emotions (embarrassment, guilt, pride, and shame). The goal of the chapter is to help researchers identify and select measures of self-conscious emotions that meet their diverse needs. Self-conscious emotions are typically assessed through either self-report scales or coding of nonverbal behavior. We first summarize the extant self-report measures and then describe nonverbal coding schemes for each self-conscious emotion previously found to have a recognizable nonverbal expression (i.e., embarrassment, pride, and shame).

SELF-REPORT MEASURES OF SHAME, GUILT, EMBARRASSMENT, AND PRIDE

In this section, we summarize the self-report measures available for shame (and humiliation), guilt, embarrassment, and pride. For each emotion, we organize the available measures into three sections: (1) trait or dispositional scales, (2) state or online feeling scales, and (3) state and trait scales of related constructs. Within each of the three sections, the scales are ordered chronologically, by date of publication. Reflecting the field's tendency to focus on clinically relevant emotions, considerably more effort has been devoted to developing self-report measures of shame and guilt than pride or embarrassment. As a result, the vast majority of scales included here assess shame and guilt.

For each specific scale, we provide (1) relevant references; (2) a brief description of the scale and the way it was developed; (3) an indication of whether the scale is "frequently used," "occasionally used," or "rarely used," based on a citation analysis of the scale name and relevant publications ("frequently used" = cited at least 50 times; "rarely used" = cited fewer than 10 times); and (4) psychometric information about the length, reliability, and format of the scale. The scale format is classified into one of the following four categories (adapted from Tangney & Dearing, 2002):

   1. *Situation-based* scales: Participants read a set of situations, preselected because they presumably elicit specific emotions, and then rate the extent to which they would feel a particular emotion (or set of emotions) in each situation. For example, participants might be asked to rate their level of embarrassment during the following situation: "Suppose you tripped and fell while entering a bus full of people" (Modigliani, 1968).
   2. *Scenario-based* scales: Participants read hypothetical scenarios and then choose which of a set of responses they would be most likely to perform, or rate the likelihood that they would choose each response. These scales differ from situation-based measures in that they usually include multiple response options, and the response options typically refer to behaviors and thoughts in addition to feelings. For example, a participant might read: "You make a mistake at work and find out a coworker is blamed for the error," and be asked to choose whether he or she would be more likely to respond with: "(a) You would think the company did not like the coworker; (b) You would think 'Life is not fair'; (c) You would keep quiet and avoid the coworker; (d) You would feel unhappy and eager to correct the situation" (Tangney, Dearing, Wagner, & Gramzow, 2000).
   3. *Statement-based* scales: Participants rate the degree to which they experience different feelings, cognitions, and/or related behaviors specified in sentences or phrases. For example, a participant might be asked to rate the extent to which he or she agrees or disagrees with the statement, "I want to sink into the floor and disappear" (Marschall, Sanftner, & Tangney, 1994).
   4. *Adjective-based* scales: Participants rate the extent to which they experience different feelings, such as happy, sad, ashamed, etc. Many adjective-based scales were designed to assess either traits or states, depending on the instructions (e.g., "Indicate to what extent you feel this way in general, that is, on the average" or "Indicate to what extent you feel this way right now, that is, at the present moment)"; Watson & Clark, 1994).

Shame

A. Trait Measures of Shame

A1. SHAME AND EMBARRASSMENT SCALES OF THE DIFFERENTIAL EMOTIONS SCALE (DES-II)

   Mosher, D. L., & White, B. B. (1981). On differentiating shame and shyness. *Motivation and Emotion, 5,* 61–74. [includes full scales]
   A revision of Izard, Dougherty, Bloxom, and Kotsch's (1974) DES-II scale (which has been revised a number of times subsequently and now includes statements; see A6, below). This revision includes sets of emotion adjectives to measure distinct emotions. Using the rational method (i.e., devising items rationally, based on face validity, to represent hypothesized constructs), the previous shame/shyness scale was separated into two scales representing shame and shyness and additional adjectives were added. In addition, a new scale for embarrassment was added. Mosher and White's shame, shyness, and embarrassment scales have not been used frequently by researchers, although the DES itself is frequently used. Izard's most recent version of the DES (the DES-IV; see A6, below)

now includes separate scales to assess shame and shyness, but not embarrassment. In general, the DES can be used as either a trait or a state measure, although most researchers have tended to use it to measure emotional dispositions. [RARELY USED]

Scale characteristics: shame-humiliation (three items: ashamed, humiliated, disgraced); embarrassment (three items: embarrassed, self-conscious, blushing).

Response format: Adjective measure with a 5-point rating scale (1 = "very slightly or not at all"; 5 = "very strongly").

A2. MEASURE OF SUSCEPTIBILITY TO GUILT AND SHAME

Cheek, J. M., & Hogan, R. (1983). Self-concepts, self-presentations, and moral judgments. In J. Suls & A. G. Greenwald (Eds.), *Psychological perspectives on the self* (Vol. 2, pp. 249–273). Hillsdale, NJ: Erlbaum. [includes full scale]

A set of items were derived from past scales and from participants' responses to an open-ended questionnaire. The items were selected to reflect a differentiation between inner moral affects (guilt) and outer moral affects (shame). [RARELY USED]

Scale characteristics: guilt (five items; α = .63); shame (five items; α = .73).

Sample item: "Breaking or losing something I have borrowed from a friend."

Response format: Statement-based measure with a 5-point scale (1 = "not at all"; 2 = "a little"; 3 = "a fair amount"; 4 = "much"; 5 = "very much").

A3. ADAPTED SHAME/GUILT SCALE (ASGS)

Hoblitzelle, W. (1987). Differentiating and measuring shame and guilt: The relation between shame and depression. In H. B. Lewis (Ed.), *The role of shame in symptom formation* (pp. 207–235). Hillsdale, NJ: Erlbaum. [includes full scale]

A set of items were added to Gioiella's (1979) Shame/Guilt Survey (and some items tapping into anxiety were removed), using the rational method. This scale was designed as a trait measure of shame and guilt, but it could be easily used as a state measure. [RARELY USED]

Scale characteristics: total scale (30 items; α = .90), shame (10 items: bashful, mortified, shy, humiliated, abashed, embarrassed, depressed, chided, reproached, ashamed; α = .86), guilt (12 items: condemned, unethical, immoral, delinquent, unconscionable, inappropriate, wicked, criminal, liable, indecent, unscrupulous, imprudent; α = .88).

Response format: Adjective-based measure with a 7-point scale.

A4. DIMENSIONS OF CONSCIENCE QUESTIONNAIRE (DCQ)

Johnson, R. C., Danko, J. P., Huang, Y. H., Park, J. Y., Johnson, S. B., & Nagoshi, C. T. (1987). Guilt, shame and adjustment in three cultures. *Personality and Individual Differences, 8,* 357–364. [includes full scale]

Johnson, R. C., Kim, R. J., & Danko, G. P. (1989). Guilt, shame and adjustment. A family study. *Personality and Individual Differences, 10,* 71–74. [adds five additional items, which are included]

Gore, E. J., & Harvey, O. J. (1995). A factor analysis of a scale of shame and guilt: Dimensions of Conscience Questionnaire. *Personality and Individual Differences, 19,* 769–771.

Items were written to distinguish guilt-inducing situations from those that induced shame; additional items come from related measures and from guilt stories collected from undergraduates. The current version of the scale uses a psychometrically sound subset of the original 121 items. [OCCASIONALLY USED]

Scale characteristics (Johnson et al., 1987): shame (13 items; α = 84), guilt (15 items; α = .81).

Scale characteristics (Gore & Harvey, 1995): Shame 1: Social impropriety (10 items; α = .77), Shame 2: Exposed inadequacy (five items; α= .70), Guilt 1: Impersonal transgression (six items; α = .88), Guilt 2: Harm to another person (six items; α = .88), Guilt 3: Trust/oath violation (three items; α = .73).

Sample item: "Strongly defending an idea or point of view in a discussion only to learn later that it was incorrect."

Response format: Situation-based measure with a 7-point scale (1 = "not at all bad"; 7 = "as bad as I possibly could feel").

A5. HARDER PERSONAL FEELINGS QUESTIONNAIRE–2 (PFQ2)

Harder, D. W., & Zalma, A. (1990). Two promising shame and guilt scales: A construct validity comparison. *Journal of Personality Assessment, 55,* 729–745. [includes full scale]

Harder, D. W., & Lewis, S. J. (1987). The assessment of shame and guilt. In J. N. Butcher & C. D. Spielberger (Eds.), *Advances in personality assessment* (Vol. 6, pp. 89–114). Hillsdale, NJ: Erlbaum.

Harder, D. W. (1995). Shame and guilt assessment and relationships of shame and guilt proneness to psychopathology. In J. P. Tangney & K. W. Fischer (Eds.), *Self-conscious emotions: The psychology of shame, guilt, embarrassment, and pride* (pp. 368–392). New York: Guilford Press.

A set of items were added to the earlier PFQ (Harder & Lewis, 1987), using the rational method, and several original items were expanded. The original PFQ was devised using the rational method to assess affective tendencies in clinical settings, and was later found to differentiate between clinical shame and guilt. [OCCASIONALLY USED]

Scale characteristics: shame (10 items: embarrassed; feeling ridiculous; self-consciousness; feeling humiliated; feeling "stupid"; feeling "childish"; feeling helpless, paralyzed; feelings of blushing; feeling laughable; feeling disgusting to others; α = .78); guilt (six items: mild guilt; worry about hurting or injuring someone; intense guilt; regret; feeling you deserve criticism for what you did; remorse; α = .72).

Response format: Adjective/statement measure with a 5-point scale (0 = "never experience the feeling"; 4 = "experience the feeling continuously or almost continuously").

A6. SHAME, GUILT, AND HOSTILITY INWARD SUBSCALES OF THE DIFFERENTIAL EMOTIONS SCALE–IV (DES-IV)

Izard, C. E., Libero, D. Z., Putnam, P., & Haynes, O. M. (1993). Stability of emotion experiences and their relations to traits of personality. *Journal of Personality and Social Psychology, 64,* 847–860. [includes full scale]

A set of items were generated from cross-cultural labels for emotion expressions, which were later expanded into short statements for ease of use with varied groups. This scale is based on Izard's differential emotions theory (Izard, 1991). The guilt scale measures self-blame, regret, and wrongdoing. The shame scale seems conceptually closer to current conceptions of embarrassment than shame, whereas the hostility-inward scale seems closer to clinical conceptions of shame. [FREQUENTLY USED]

Scale characteristics: shame (three items: feel embarrassed when anybody sees you make a mistake; feel like people laugh at you; feel like people always look at you when anything goes wrong; α = .60); guilt (three items: feel regret, sorry about something you did; feel like you did something wrong; feel like you ought to be blamed for something; α = .72); hostility–inward (three items: feel you can't stand yourself; feel mad at yourself; feel sick about yourself; α = .75).

Response format: Statement-based measure with a 5-point scale (1 = "rarely or never"; 2 = "hardly ever"; 3 = "sometimes"; 4 = "often"; 5 = "very often")

A7. INTERNALIZED SHAME SCALE (ISS)

Cook, D. R. (1994). *Internalized Shame Scale: Professional manual.* Menomonie, WI: Channel Press. [includes full scale]

Cook, D. R. (1996). Empirical studies of shame and guilt: The Internalized Shame Scale. In D. L. Nathanson (Ed.), *Knowing feeling: Affect, script, and psychotherapy* (pp. 132–165). New York: Norton. [includes full scale]

[*German version*] Wolfradt, U., & Scharrer, F. (1996). The Internalized Shame Scale (ISS): Conceptual aspects and psychometric properties of a German adaptation/Die "Internalisierte Scham-Skala"(ISS): Konzeptuelle Aspekte und psychometrische Eigenschaften einer deutschsprachigen Adaptation. *Zeitschrift für Differentielle und Diagnostische Psychologie, 17,* 201–207.

A set of statements were written to describe the phenomenology of the shame experience. One subscale taps into internalized shame, whereas the other measures negative global evaluations of the self (this subscale consists primarily of items from the Rosenberg Self-Esteem Scale). This scale is used primarily in the clinical literature. [FREQUENTLY USED]

Scale characteristics: internalized shame (24 items; α = .96); (negative) self-esteem (six items; α = .95).

Sample item: "I would like to shrink away when I make a mistake."

Response format: Statement-based measure with a 5-point scale (0 = "never"; 1 = "seldom"; 2 = "sometimes"; 3 = "often"; 4 = "almost always").

A8. OTHER AS SHAMER SCALE (OAS)

Goss, K., Gilbert, P., & Allan, S. (1994). An exploration of shame measures. I. The Other as Shamer scale. *Personality and Individual Differences, 17,* 713–717. [includes full scale]

This statement-based scale is a modification of a subset of the items from the Internalized Shame Scale (Cook, 1994). The original statements were rewritten to reflect a person's perception of what others feel about him or her rather than what he or she feels about him- or herself. This scale has been used in both the clinical and personality literatures. Gilbert and Allan (1994) have also constructed a measure to assess the submissive behavior that often accompanies experiences of shame (see below in part C of the Shame measures). [RARELY USED]

Scale characteristics: total scale (18 items), inferiority (seven items), emptiness (four items), how others behave when they see me make mistakes (six items) [one item included in total scale is not an item on any of the subscales].

Sample item: "I think that other people look down on me."

Response format: Statement-based measure with a 5-point scale (0 = "never"; 1 = "seldom"; 2 = "sometimes"; 3 = "often"; 4 = "almost always").

A9. BRIEF SHAME RATING SCALE (BSRS)

Hibbard, S. (1994). An empirical study of the differential roles of libidinous and aggressive shame components in normality and pathology. *Psychoanalytic Psychology, 11,* 449–474. [includes full scale]

A set of items were taken from Hoblitzelle's (1987) Adapted Shame/Guilt Scale (ASGS; see A3, above) and Harder and Lewis's (1987) Personal Feelings Questionnaire (PFQ; see A5, above) to examine libidinous and aggressive aspects of shame. The two facets of shame were validated with relevant existing scales. [RARELY USED]

Scale characteristics: total scale (11 items; .96), disgraced/humiliated (BSRS1; seven items: disgraced, mortified, helpless/paralyzed, abashed, humiliated, ashamed, depressed; α = .96), bashful/shy (BSRS2; four items: bashful, shy, embarrassed, blushing/near blushing; α = .97).

Response format: Adjective-based measure with a 5-point scale (1 = "rarely, not much like this"; 5 = "often, very much like this")

A10. SHAME–GUILT SCALE [NO SPECIFIC TITLE GIVEN]

Diener, E., Smith, H., & Fujita, F. (1995). The personality structure of affect. *Journal of Personality and Social Psychology, 69,* 130–141. [includes full scale]

A set of items were generated to measure "shame-guilt" using the rational method, including adjectives that varied in intensity. This is a measure of negative self-conscious emotions, which has been used as a brief measure in the personality literature. [OCCASIONALLY USED]

Scale characteristics: shame (four items: shame, guilt, regret, embarrassment; α = .78).

Response format: Adjective-based measure with a 7-point rating scale (1 = "never"; 4 = "about half the time"; 7 = "always").

A11. TEST OF SELF-CONSCIOUS AFFECT–3 (TOSCA-3)

Tangney, J. P., Dearing, R. L., Wagner, P. E., & Gramzow, R. (2000). *The Test of Self-Conscious Affect–3 (TOSCA-3).* Fairfax, VA: George Mason University. [includes full scale; current version]

Tangney, J. P., & Dearing, R. L. (2002). *Shame and guilt.* New York: Guilford Press. [includes TOSCA-3 and also TOSCA-A and TOSCA-C for assessing the same dimensions in adolescents and children, respectively]

Hanson, R. K., & Tangney, J. P. (1995). *The Test of Self-Conscious Affect—Socially Deviant Populations (TOSCA-SD).* Ottawa, Canada: Corrections Research, Department of the Solicitor General of Canada. [includes full scale]

The original scale was generated from participants' (college students and other adults) descriptions of personal experiences of pride, guilt, and shame. These descriptions formed the basis for the fifteen scenarios (five positive and 10 negative) that comprise the scale. A separate set of descriptions written by adults not attending college formed the basis for the multiple-choice-styled response set. The current version (TOSCA-3) drops one of the original scenarios and adds two new scenarios. These scales are dispositional measures, and are very frequently used in the social-personality literature to assess shame- and guilt-proneness. [FREQUENTLY USED]

Scale characteristics: alpha pride (five items, α = .48), beta pride (five items, α = .51), guilt (16 items, α = .78), shame (16 items, α = .77); also externalization (16 items, α = .75) and detachment (11 items, α = .72). [alphas from Tangney & Dearing, 2002]

Sample item: "You are driving down the road and you hit a small animal. (A) You would think the animal shouldn't have been on the road. (B) You would think: 'I'm terrible.' (C) You would feel: 'Well, it's an accident.' (D) You'd feel bad you hadn't been more alert driving down the road."

Response format: Scenario-based measure that includes sets of responses, each representing a different affective tendency (guilt-proneness, shame-proneness, externalization, pride in one's self (alpha pride), pride in one's behavior (beta pride), and detachment. All responses are rated on a 5-point scale (1 = "not likely"; 5 = "very likely").

A12. SHAME AND EMBARRASSMENT SCENARIOS [NO SPECIFIC TITLE GIVEN]

Sabini, J., Garvey, B., & Hall, A. L. (2001). Shame and embarrassment revisited. *Personality and Social Psychology Bulletin, 27,* 104–117. [includes full scales]

Two sets of items were generated by the rational method to describe scenarios that were likely to elicit shame and embarrassment. In the first set, 10 scenarios were written for shame and 10 were written for embarrassment. In the second set, six items were written for shame, which were turned into embarrassment scenarios by adding one additional sentence to each scenario. For all scenarios, participants rate their expected levels of shame and embarrassment (as well as other affects listed below). Although the measure was designed to contrast the eliciting conditions of shame and embarrassment, it can also be used as a trait measure of shame and embarrassment. [OCCASIONALLY USED]

Scale 1 characteristics: Shame Scenarios (10 items), Embarrassment Scenarios (10 items). [For shame and embarrassment experienced in both types of scenarios, αs = .85–.91.]

Scale 2 characteristics: Shame Scenarios [six items; shame (α = .73), embarrassment (α = .74)], Embarrassment Scenarios [six items; shame (α = .61), embarrassment (α = .78)].

Sample item: "You are at a public beach and you feel like going for a swim. The waves are rough but there are other people swimming near you. As you dive in, you realize that your bathing suit has fallen down and that people are staring at you."

Response format: Situation-based measures with 7-point rating scales for six emotions (anger, shame, fear, guilt, embarrassment, and regret; 1 = "not at all"; 7 = "extremely").

A13. SHAME–GUILT PROPENSITY SCALE [ITALIAN LANGUAGE ONLY]

Battacchi, M. W., Codispoti, O., Marano, G. F., & Codispoti, M. (2001). Toward the evaluation of susceptibility to shame and sense of guilt: The Shame–Guilt Propensity Scale/Per la valutazione delle suscettibilità alla vergogna e al senso di colpa: La scala SSCV. *Bollettino di Psicologia Applicata, 233,* 19–31. [RARELY USED]

A14. EXPERIENCE OF SHAME SCALE (ESS)

Andrews, B., Qian, M., & Valentine, J. D. (2002). Predicting depressive symptoms with a new measure of shame: The Experience of Shame Scale. *British Journal of Clinical Psychology, 41,* 29–42. [includes full scale]

[*Chinese version*] Qian, M., Andrews, B., Zhu, R., & Wang, A. (2000). The development of the Shame Scale for Chinese college students. *Chinese Mental Health Journal, 14,* 217–221.

A set of items were devised, based on interviews with depressed populations and the rational method, to measure characterological shame (four aspects), behavioral shame (three aspects), and bodily aspects of shame. For each type of shame, items reflecting experiential, cognitive, and behavioral aspects were written. This scale has been used in the personality and clinical literatures. [RARELY USED]

Scale characteristics: total scale (25 items; α = .92); characterological (12 items; α = .90); behavioral (nine items; α = .87); bodily (four items; α = .86).

Sample item: "Have you tried to conceal from others the sort of person you are?"

Response format: Statement-based measure with a 4-point scale (1 = "not at all"; 2 = "a little"; 3 = "moderately"; 4 = "very much")

A15. COMPASS OF SHAME SCALE (COSS)

Elison, J., Lennon, R., & Pulos, S. (2006). Investigating the Compass of Shame: The development of the Compass of Shame Scale. *Social Behavior and Personality, 34,* 221–238. [includes full scale]

Elison, J., Pulos, S., & Lennon, R. (2006). Shame-focused coping: An empirical study of the compass of shame. *Social Behavior and Personality, 34,* 161–168.

A set of items were developed to assess use of the four shame-coping styles described by Nathanson (1992). For each scenario, participants indicate the frequency with which they tend to make each of four responses, representing each of the four subscales (see below). [RARELY USED, BUT NEW SCALE]

Scale characteristics: Withdrawal (12 items; α = .89); Attack Other (12 items; α = .85); Attack Self (12 items; α = .91); Avoidance (12 items; α = .74).

Sample item: "When I feel others think poorly of me . . . I want to escape their view."

Response format: Scenario-based measure with a 5-point scale (1 = "Never"; 2 = "Seldom"; 3 = "Sometimes"; 4 = "Often"; 5 = "Almost Always").

B. State Measures of Shame

B1. STATE SHAME AND GUILT SCALE (SSGS)

Marschall, D., Sanftner, J., & Tangney, J. P. (1994). *The State Shame and Guilt Scale.* Fairfax, VA: George Mason University. [includes full scale]

Tangney, J. P., & Dearing, R. L. (2002). *Shame and guilt.* New York: Guilford Press. [includes full scale]

A set of items were written using the rational method, based on Lewis's (1971) theory, to assess phenomenological aspects of shame and guilt. [RARELY USED]

Scale characteristics: shame (five items; α = .89), guilt (five items; α = .82), pride (five items; α = .87).

Sample item: "I want to sink into the floor and disappear."

Response format: Statement-based measure with a 5-point scale (1 = "not feeling this way at all"; 3 = "feeling this way somewhat"; 5 = "feeling this way very strongly").

C. Measures of Constructs Related to Shame

Note: For space reasons, we do not include the many measures of shyness, even though some conceptions of shame include shyness as a low-intensity variant of shame (for an elaboration on this distinction, see Mosher & White, 1981).

C1. SOCIAL AVOIDANCE AND DISTRESS SCALE

Watson, D., & Friend, R. (1969). Measurement of social-evaluative anxiety. *Journal of Consulting and Clinical Psychology, 33,* 448–457.

Leary, M. R. (1991). Watson and Friend's Social Avoidance and Distress Scale. In J. P. Robinson, P. R. Shaver, & L. S. Wrightsman (Eds.), *Measures of personality and social psychological attitudes* (pp. 177–179). San Diego, CA: Academic Press. [includes full scale]

A set of items were devised to measure (behavioral) social avoidance using the rational method. Thus, the scale does not measure shame directly, but measures social avoidance, which is a behavioral aspect of shame. The scale is primarily used in the anxiety literature. [FREQUENTLY USED]

Scale characteristics: total scale (28 items; α = .90), social avoidance (14 items; α = .87).

Sample item: "I often want to get away from people."

Response format: True–false statement measure, but many researchers have used it with a 5-point rating scale (Leary, 1991).

C2. FEAR OF NEGATIVE EVALUATION SCALE (FNE)

Watson, D., & Friend, R. (1969). Measurement of social-evaluative anxiety. *Journal of Consulting and Clinical Psychology, 33,* 448–457.

Leary, M. R. (1983). A brief version of the Fear of Negative Evaluation Scale. *Personality and Social Psychology Bulletin, 9,* 371–375. [includes abbreviated scale]

Corcoran, K., & Fischer, J. (1987). *Measures for clinical practice: A sourcebook.* New York: Free Press.

Leary, M. R. (1991). Watson and Friend's Fear of Negative Evaluation Scale. In J. P. Robinson, P. R. Shaver, & L. S. Wrightsman (Eds.), *Measures of personality and social psychological attitudes* (pp. 165–167). San Diego, CA: Academic Press. [includes full scale]

The Fear of Negative Evaluation Scale (FNE; Watson & Friend, 1969) is a 30-item instrument that measures a specific aspect of social anxiety: the fear of loss of social approval. Each item is answered true or false. The FNE is highly reliable and correlates with social approval, desirability, and measures of anxiety (Corcoran & Fischer, 1987). Leary (1983) created an abbreviated (12-item) version of the FNE. [FREQUENTLY USED]

Scale characteristics (Watson & Friend, 1969): total scale (30 items; KR-20 = .92).

Scale characteristics (Leary, 1983): total scale (12 items; α = .90).

Sample item: "I become tense or jittery if I know someone is sizing me up."

Response format: The original scale (Watson & Friend, 1969) uses a true–false statement format; the abbreviated scale (Leary, 1983) uses a 5-point scale (1 = "not at all characteristic of me"; 5 = "extremely characteristic of me").

C3. FEAR OF APPEARING INCOMPETENT SCALE

Good, L., & Good, K. (1973). An objective measure to avoid appearing incompetent. *Psychological Reports, 32,* 1075–1078.

A set of items were written to assess trait aspects of the fear of appearing incompetent. This scale does not directly assess shame, but has been used as a proxy measure of shame (Hoblitzelle, 1987). [RARELY USED]

Scale characteristics: total scale (36; .89).

Sample item: "I would very much like to be less apprehensive about my capabilities."

Response format: True–false statement measure.

C4. PUBLIC AND PRIVATE SELF-CONSCIOUSNESS SCALES

Fenigstein, A., Scheier, M. F., & Buss, A. H. (1975). Public and private self-consciousness: Assessment and theory. *Journal of Consulting and Clinical Psychology, 43,* 522–527. [includes full scale]

Scheier, M. F., & Carver, C. S. (1985). The Self-Consciousness Scale: A revised version for use with general populations. *Journal of Applied Social Psychology, 15,* 687–699. [includes full scale]

[*Swedish version*] Nystedt, L., & Smari, J. (1989). Assessment of the Fenigstein, Scheier, and Buss Self-Consciousness Scale: A Swedish translation. *Journal of Personality Assessment, 53,* 342–352.

[*Turkish version*] Ruganci, R. N. (1995). Private and public self-consciousness subscales of the Fenigstein, Scheier and Buss Self-Consciousness Scale: A Turkish translation. *Personality and Individual Differences, 18,* 279–282.

A set of items was devised using the rational method to describe behaviors indicative of a self-conscious person. Scheier and Carver (1985) revised the items for use with the general population. This scale is a frequently used measure of both public and private aspects of self-consciousness. Public self-consciousness has been found to be positively related to shame-proneness (Tangney & Dearing, 2002), and both aspects are negatively related to self-esteem (Turner, Scheier, Carver, & Ickes, 1978). [FREQUENTLY USED]

Scale characteristics: total scale (23), Private Self-Consciousness (10), Public Self-Consciousness (7).

Sample item: "I'm always trying to figure myself out."

Response format: Statement-based measure with a 5-point scale (0 = "extremely uncharacteristic"; 4 = "extremely characteristic").

Response format for Scheier and Carver's revision. 4-point scale (0 = "not at all like me"; 3 = "a lot like me")

C5. DEVALUATION–DISCRIMINATION, SECRECY, AND WITHDRAWAL

Link, B. G., Cullen, F. T., Struening, E., Shrout, P. E., & Dohrenwend, B. P. (1989). A modified labeling theory approach to mental disorders: An empirical assessment. *American Sociological Review, 54,* 400–423. [includes full scale]

These three statement-based measures are stigma-related measures for current and former mental patients, and are highly relevant to shame measurement. [OCCASIONALLY USED]

Scale characteristics: devaluation–discrimination (12 items; α = .76), secrecy (five items; α = .71), withdrawal (seven items; α = .67).

Sample item: "Most people would willingly accept a former mental patient as a close friend."

Response format: Statement-based measure with a 6-point scale (1 = "strongly agree"; 6 = "strongly disagree").

C6. SUBMISSIVE BEHAVIOUR SCALE (SBS)

Allan, S., & Gilbert, P. (1997). Submissive behaviour and psychotherapy. *British Journal of Clinical Psychology, 36,* 467–488. [includes full scale]

Gilbert, P., & Allan, S. (1994). Assertiveness, submissive behaviour and social comparison. *British Journal of Clinical Psychology, 33,* 295–306.

[*Adolescent version*] Irons, C., & Gilbert, P. (2005). Evolved mechanisms in adolescent anxiety and depression symptoms: The role of the attachment and social rank systems. *Journal of Adolescence, 28,* 325–341. [includes full scale]

This scale was developed from open-ended descriptions of behavioral acts originally collected by Buss and Craik (1986), which were then rated for "submissiveness." Gilbert and Allan (1994) retained the 16 items rated as most prototypical of this dimension for the scale. This scale has been used in both the clinical and personality literatures. [RARELY USED]

Scale characteristics: total scale (18 items), inferiority (seven items), emptiness (four items), how others behave when they see me make mistakes (six items). [one item included in total scale is not an item on any of the subscales]

Sample item: "I think that other people look down on me."

Response format: Statement-based measure with a 5-point scale (0 = "never"; 1 = "seldom"; 2 = "sometimes"; 3 = "often"; 4 = "almost always").

C7. EDUCATIONAL SOCIALIZATION SCALE (ESS)

Bempechat, J., Graham, S. E., & Jimenez, N. V. (1999). The socialization of achievement in poor and minority students: A comparative study. *Journal of Cross-Cultural Psychology, 30,* 139–158. [includes full scale]

This statement-based measure assesses shame and guilt in the context of academic achievement. [RARELY USED]

Scale characteristics: total scale (17 items), shame (four items: "My parents make me feel ashamed if I do badly in school," "I feel ashamed if I do badly in school," "My parents feel ashamed if I do badly in school," "My parents punish me when I don't do well in school"; α = .73) guilt (two items: "I feel badly because my parents work so hard to give me a good education," "I feel badly that my parents have to work so hard"; α = .65)

Response format: Statement-based measure with a 5-point scale (1 = "never"; 5 = "almost every day").

C8. HUMILIATION INVENTORY (HI)

Hartling, L. M., & Luchetta, T. (1999). Humiliation: Assessing the impact of derision, degradation, and debasement. *Journal of Primary Prevention, 19,* 259–278. [includes full scale]

A set of items were generated through interviews, expert consultations, and literature reviews pertaining to relevant constructs. This scale assesses the shame-related emotion of humiliation, but not shame directly. [RARELY USED]

Scale characteristics: total scale (32 items; α = .96), fear of humiliation (FHS; 20 items; α = .94), cumulative humiliation (CHS; 12 items; α = .95).

Sample item: "At this point in your life, how much do you fear being laughed at?"

Response format: Statement-based measure with a 5-point scale (1 = "not at all"; 5 = "extremely").

C9. BODY IMAGE GUILT AND SHAME

(See description in item C4 of the Guilt measures section.)

Guilt

A number of self-report scales have been developed to measure guilt. Some of them tap into specific subdomains, such as Mosher's Sex Guilt Scale, but many are aimed at domain-general measurement of trait and state guilt. Shame scales A2–A6, A11, and A13 also have subscales for trait guilt and thus are not listed below; Shame scale B1 also has a subscale for state guilt and thus is not listed below.

A. Trait Measures of Guilt

A1. GUILT SUBSCALE OF THE BUSS–DURKEE HOSTILITY–GUILT INVENTORY

Buss, A. H., & Durkee, A. (1957). An inventory for assessing different kinds of hostility. *Journal of Consulting Psychology, 21,* 343–349. [includes full scale]

A set of items were developed using the rational method, with guilt defined as "feelings of being bad, having done wrong, or suffering pangs of conscience" (Buss & Durkee, 1957, p. 344). This scale is a supplementary measure of guilt developed as part of a widely used hostility measure because of clinical links between the two constructs. It is rarely used as an independent measure of guilt, in part because it seems to assess a blend of guilt and shame (e.g., Tangney, Wagner, Fletcher, & Gramzow, 1992, p. 675). [RARELY USED]

Scale characteristics: guilt (nine items).

Sample item: "When I do wrong, my conscience punishes me severely."

Response format: True–false statement-based measure.

A2. MOSHER TRUE–FALSE AND FORCED-CHOICE GUILT INVENTORIES

Mosher, D. L. (1966). The development and multitrait-multimethod matrix analysis of three measures of three aspects of guilt. *Journal of Consulting Psychology, 30,* 25–29.

Mosher, D. L. (1968). Measurement of guilt in females by self-report inventories. *Journal of Consulting and Clinical Psychology, 32,* 690–695.

Mosher, D. (1987). Revised Mosher Guilt Inventory. In C. M. Davis, W. L. Yarber, & S. L. Davis (Eds.), *Sexuality-related measures: A compendium* (pp. 152–155). Lake Mills, IA: Graphic. [includes full scale]

True–false version. A set of items were taken from the Mosher Incomplete Sentences Test (MIST) and administered to students in a true–false format: items representing the top and bottom 27% were chosen.

Forced-choice version. Guilt-prone and non-guilt-prone completions of the incomplete sentences that were matched on social desirability were selected. Subscales were developed from the original MIST categorizations for both the true–false and forced-choice inventories. [FREQUENTLY USED]

Scale characteristics (true–false version): sex guilt (35 items; α = .91), hostile guilt (37 items; α = .84), morality-conscience guilt (31 items; α = .84).

Scale characteristics (forced choice): sex guilt (28 items; α = .97), hostile guilt (29 items; α = .96), morality-conscience guilt (22 items; α = .92).

Sample items: "I punish myself when I make mistakes." *(true–false version).* "A guilty conscience . . . a) does not bother me too much; b) is worse than a sickness to me." *(forced choice).*

Response format: Statement-based measure with a true–false or forced-choice response option.

A3. PERCEIVED GUILT INDEX

Otterbacher, J. R., & Munz, D. C. (1973). State-trait measure of experiential guilt. *Journal of Consulting and Clinical Psychology, 40,* 115–121. [includes full scale]

A set of adjectives and phrases describing subjective experiences of guilt were generated by students, and were then rated for the extremity with which they described a guilty reaction. Items representing a spectrum from "not guilty" to "extremely guilty" were then derived based on factor analyses. This scale has been used in the applied and clinical realms. [OCCASIONALLY USED]

Scale characteristics: Participants select one item out of the following 11 items to either describe how they feel "at the moment" (state version) or how they "normally feel" (trait version): 1 = innocent, 2 = undisturbed, 3 = restrained, 4 = pent-up, 5 = fretful, 6 = chagrined, 7 = reproachable, 8 = marred, 9 = degraded, 10 = disgraceful, 11 = unforgivable.

Response format: Adjective-based measure.

A4. REACTION INVENTORY—GUILT

Evans, D. R., Jessup, B. A., & Hearn, M. T. (1974, April). *Development of a reaction inventory to measure guilt* (Research Bulletin No. 287). London, Canada: Department of Psychology, University of Western Ontario. [includes full scale]

Evans, D. R., Jessup, B. A., & Hearn, M. T. (1975). Development of a reaction inventory to measure guilt. *Journal of Personality Assessment, 39,* 421–423. [includes subscale items but not full measure]

A set of items were developed from interviews with students about situations that had made them feel guilty. Situations named by at least two students were retained for the inventory. [RARELY USED]

Scale characteristics: total scale (50 items; α = .52), intentional behavior disrupting interpersonal relations (seven items), self-destructive behavior (four items), behavior contrary to moral or ethical principles (seven items), unintentional behavior disrupting interpersonal relationships (six items).

Sample item: "Finding out you have hurt someone's feelings."

Response format: Situation-based measure with a 5-point scale of how much guilt each situation made the person feel (1= "not at all"; 2 = "a little"; 3 = "a fair amount"; 4 = "much"; 5 = "very much").

A5. GUILT MEASURE [PORTUGUESE LANGUAGE ONLY]

Sigelmann, E., & Fernandes, L. M. (1986). Development of a guilt measure/ Desenvolvimento de uma medida de culpa. *Arquivos Brasileiros de Psicologia, 38,* 76–83. [includes full scale (in Portuguese)] [RARELY USED]

A6. SITUATIONAL GUILT SCALE (SGS)

Klass, E. T. (1987). Situational approach to assessment of guilt: Development and validation of a self-report measure. *Journal of Psychopathology and Behavioral Assessment, 9,* 35–48. [for the complete scale, contact Ellen Tobey Klass at *eklass@hunter. cuny.edu*]

A set of items were generated from students' descriptions of situations in which they experienced guilt. These were then rated by a separate sample of students for the degree to which they would likely produce guilt. The best items were retained and factor-analyzed to create subscales. In this scale, participants rate how guilty they anticipate they would feel in response to guilt-inducing situations. It is used primarily in the clinical literature. [RARELY USED]

Scale characteristics: total guilt (22 items; α = .92), interpersonal harm guilt (nine items; α = .88), norm violation guilt (five items; α = .74), self-control failure guilt (six items; α = .76).

Sample item: "You have always given a present at holidays to one of your relatives, who always gives one to you. However, this year you did not get around to buying a present and didn't give anything though he/she gave you a present. It is now the middle of February, and you still haven't done anything about getting a present for him/her."

Response format: Situation-based measure with a 5-point scale (1 = "not at all"; 2 = "slightly"; 3 = "moderately"; 4 = "considerably"; 5 = "very") for each of four terms (regretful, disappointed in myself, guilty, and ashamed), rated for each situation.

A7. FEAR OF PUNISHMENT/NEED FOR REPARATION SCALES

Caprara, G. V., Manzi, J., & Perugini, M. (1992). Investigating guilt in relation to emotionality and aggression. *Personality and Individual Differences, 13,* 519–532. [includes full scale]

[*Italian version*] Caprara, G. V., Perugini, M., Pastorelli, C., & Barbaranelli, C. (1990). Esplorazione delle dimensioni comuni della colpa e dell'aggressivita: Contributo empirico [Exploration of the common dimensions of guilt and aggression: Empirical contribution]. *Giornale Italiano di Psicologia, 17,* 665–681.

A set of items were generated from students' descriptions of characteristics they thought were most typical of guilt, which were then rated for guilt-prototypicality by a second sample of students. The highly prototypical guilt items were then given to a third sample and factor-analyzed, resulting in two factors, which served as the basis for two subscales. It has primarily been used in personality research. [OCCASIONALLY USED]

Scale characteristics: Fear of Punishment (23 items; α = .91), Need for Reparation (15 items; α = .80). The two scales include additional filler items.

Sample item: "It sometimes happens that I feel my conscience is not completely clear."

Response format: Statement-based measure with a 6-point scale (0 = "completely false for me"; 5 = "completely true for me").

A8. GUILT (AND SELF-ASSURANCE) SUBSCALES OF THE POSITIVE AND NEGATIVE AFFECT SCHEDULE—EXPANDED FORM

Watson, D., & Clark, L. A. (1994). *The PANAS-X: Manual for the Positive and Negative Affect Schedule—Expanded form.* University of Iowa. [includes full scale; also available at *www.psychology.uiowa.edu/faculty/Clark/PANAS-X.pdf*]

Watson, D. (2000). *Mood and temperament.* New York: Guilford Press.

Developed through factor analyses of a set of 60 mood adjectives from Zevon and Tellegen (1982) and 16 additional positive mood terms. The PANAS-X can be used as both a state and a trait measure, and is frequently used in personality and social psychology to measure specific affects, as well as general positive and negative affect. The self-assurance subscale identifies someone who is feeling (or tends to feel) not only confident but also daring. The guilt subscale, despite its label, appears to be a general measure of negative self-conscious emotions; for example, it includes both "ashamed" and "guilty." [FREQUENTLY USED]

Scale characteristics: guilt (six items: guilty, ashamed, blameworthy, angry at self, disgusted with self, dissatisfied with self; α = .87), self-assurance (six items: proud, strong, confident, bold, daring, fearless; α = .83).

Response format: Adjective-based measure with a 5-point scale (1= "very slightly or not at all"; 2 = "a little"; 3 = "moderately"; 4 = "quite a bit"; 5 = "extremely").

A9. INTERPERSONAL GUILT QUESTIONNAIRE (IGQ-45 AND IGQ-67)

O'Connor, L. E., Berry, J. W., Weiss, J., Bush, M., & Sampson, H. (1997). Interpersonal guilt: The development of a new measure. *Journal of Clinical Psychology, 53,* 73–89. [for the complete scale, contact Lynn O'Connor at *LynnOC@aol.com*]

[*German version*] Albani, C., Blaser, G., Körner, A., Geyer, M., Volkart, R., O'Connor, L., et al. (2002). The German Short Version of the Interpersonal Guilt Questionnaire: Validation in a population-based sample and clinical application/Der "Fragebogen zu interpersonellen schuldgefühlen." *Psychotherapie Psychosomatik Medizinische Psychologie, 52,* 189–197.

A set of items were generated by clinicians, based on clinical observation and theory, to measure irrational and damaging aspects of guilt. This measure has been used in the clinical literature. [OCCASIONALLY USED]

Scale characteristics (IGQ-45): survivor guilt (26 items; α = .79), separation/disloyalty guilt (five items; α = .64), omnipotent responsibility guilt (eight items; α = .74), and self-hate guilt (six items; α = .85).

Scale characteristics (IGQ-67): survivor guilt (22 items; α = .85), separation/disloyalty guilt (15 items; α = .82), omnipotent responsibility guilt (14 items; α = .83), and self-hate guilt (16 items; α = .87).

Sample item: "If something bad happens to me I feel I must have deserved it."

Response format: Statement-based measure with a 5-point scale.

B. State Measures of Guilt

B1. GUILT INVENTORY (GI)

Jones, W. H., & Kugler, K. (1990). *Preliminary manual for the Guilt Inventory (GI).* Unpublished manuscript, University of Tennessee, Knoxville. [includes full scale]

Jones, W. H. (2000). The Guilt Inventory. In J. Maltby, C. A. Lewis, & A. Hill (Eds.), *A handbook of psychological tests* (pp. 723–724). Lampeter, Wales, UK: Edwin Mellen Press. [includes full scale]

Kugler, K., & Jones, W. H. (1992). On conceptualizing and assessing guilt. *Journal of Personality and Social Psychology, 62,* 318–327.

A set of items were developed using the rational method to assess trait and state guilt and general moral standards. This scale assesses both recent experiences of, and general tendencies to experience, maladaptive forms of guilt and regret. It is used primarily in clinical and personality research. [FREQUENTLY USED]

Scale characteristics: trait guilt (20 items; α = .89), state guilt (10 items; α = .84), moral standards (15 items; α = .88).

Sample item: "I have recently done something that I deeply regret."

Response format: Statement-based measure with a 5-point scale (1 = "strongly disagree"; 2 = "disagree"; 3 = "undecided"; 4 = "agree"; 5 = "strongly agree").

B2. GUILT SCALE [NO TITLE GIVEN]

Berrios, G. E., Bulbena, A., Bakshi, N., Dening, T. R., Jenaway, A., Markar, H., et al. (1992). Feelings of guilt in major depression: Conceptual and psychometric aspects. *British Journal of Psychiatry, 160,* 781–787. [includes full scale]

A set of items were developed through the rational method (with reference to clinical observations) to assess the guilt that sometimes accompanies clinical depression. This scale seems to measure aspects of both guilt and shame. [RARELY USED]

Scale characteristics: cognitive/attitudinal guilt (four items: been ashamed of something done; feeling as if you have committed a sin; feeling you must die to pay for your sins; feeling like praying to God for forgiveness), mood/feeling guilt (three items: feeling wicked for no reason; feeling guilty for no reason; feeling people know that you're a bad person).

Response format: Statement-based measure with a 4-point scale.

B3. GUILT SUBSCALE OF THE POSITIVE AND NEGATIVE AFFECT SCHEDULE— EXPANDED FORM

(See description in A8, above.)

C. Measures of Constructs Related to Guilt

C1. CHILDREN'S INTERPRETATIONS OF INTERPERSONAL DISTRESS AND CONFLICT (CIIDC)

Zahn-Waxler, C., Kochanska, G., Krupnick, J., & Mayfield, A. (1988). *Coding manual for Children's Interpretations of Interpersonal Distress and Conflict.* Bethesda, MD: Laboratory of Developmental Psychology, National Institute of Mental Health.

Zahn-Waxler, C., Kochanska, G., Krupnick, J., & McKnew, D. (1990). Patterns of guilt in children of depressed and well mothers. *Developmental Psychology, 26,* 51–59. [includes sample items]

This measure is an interview designed for use with children. Guilt can be assessed through a complex and rigorous system for coding children's verbal responses to stories. [RARELY USED]

C2. TRAUMA-RELATED GUILT INVENTORY (TRGI)

Kubany, E. S., Haynes, S. N., Abueg, F. R., Manke, F. P., Brennan, J. M., & Stahura, C. (1996). Development and validation of the Trauma-Related Guilt Inventory (TRGI). *Psychological Assessment, 8,* 428–444. [includes full scale]

Structured interviews were performed in order to assess trauma-related guilt in Vietnam veterans. Based on these interviews, a team of psychologists generated an item pool, which was then refined through factor analyses and reliability analyses. This scale assesses three broad aspects of a trauma-related guilt experience, as well as more specific subfacets. It is used primarily in the clinical and counseling literatures. [RARELY USED]

Scale characteristics: global guilt (four items; α = .90), distress (six items; α = .86), guilt cognitions (22 items; α = .86). Subscales of guilt cognitions scale: Hindsight-Bias/Responsibility (seven items; α = .82), Wrongdoing (five items; α = .75), Lack of Justification (four items; α = .67).

Sample item: "I blame myself for what happened."

Response format: Statement-based measure with a 5-point scale.

C3. BODY IMAGE GUILT AND SHAME

Thompson, T., Dinnel, D. L., & Dill, N. J. (2003). Development and validation of a Body Image Guilt and Shame Scale. *Personality and Individual Differences, 34,* 59–75. [for the complete scale, contact Ted Thompson at *t.thompson@utas.edu.au*]

A set of items focused on guilt- and shame-proneness about one's body and body-related behaviors were devised using the rational method and formed into a scale using the TOSCA (Tangney & Dearing, 2002) as a model. [RARELY USED]

Scale characteristics: guilt (14 items; α = .88), shame (14 items; α = .91).

Sample item: "You find that your clothes from last summer are very tight around your waist (A) You would feel undisciplined and overweight. (B) You would go out and buy a six-month membership to a gym. (C) You would think: 'Well, it's time to buy some new clothes anyway!' (D) You would think: 'I've been very busy over the last year, with no time to exercise.'"

Response format: Scenario-based measure that includes sets of responses, each representing a different affective tendency (guilt-proneness and shame-proneness; also included, similar to Tangney & Dearing, 2002, externalization and detachment). All responses are rated on a 5-point scale (1 = "not likely"; 5 = "very likely").

C4. EDUCATIONAL SOCIALIZATION SCALE (ESS)

(See C7 in the Shame measures section.)

Embarrassment

In contrast to guilt and shame, there are relatively few scales designed to measure embarrassment, as either a state or a trait. This is, in part, because researchers have tended to view embarrassment as a mild form of shame.

A. Trait Measures of Embarrassment

A1. EMBARRASSABILITY SCALE

Modigliani, A. (1968). Embarrassment and embarrassability. *Sociometry, 31,* 313–326.

Leary, M. R. (1991). Modigliani's Embarrassability Scale. In J. P. Robinson, P. R. Shaver, & L. S. Wrightsman (Eds.), *Measures of personality and social psychological attitudes* (pp. 173–176). San Diego, CA: Academic Press. [includes full scale]

Modigliani, A. (1971). Embarrassment, facework, and eye contact: Testing a theory of embarrassment. *Journal of Personality and Social Psychology, 17,* 15–24.

A set of items were devised to represent embarrassing situations using the rational method. This scale measures trait embarrassment, as well as embarrassment in response to different social situations. It is used in both the social and the personality literatures. [OCCASIONALLY USED]

Scale characteristics: total scale (26 items; α = .88).

Sample item: "Suppose you tripped and fell while entering a bus full of people."

Response format: Situation-based measure with a 5-point scale (1 = "I would not feel the least embarrassed: not awkward or uncomfortable at all"; 5 = "I would feel strongly embarrassed: extremely self-conscious, awkward, and uncomfortable").

A2. SUSCEPTIBILITY TO EMBARRASSMENT SCALE

Kelly, K. M., & Jones, W. H. (1997). Assessment of dispositional embarrassability. *Anxiety, Stress, and Coping, 10,* 307–333. [includes full scale]

Maltby, J., & Day, L. (2000). The reliability and validity of a susceptibility to embarrassment scale among adults. *Personality and Individual Differences, 29,* 749–756.

A set of items were developed using the rational method to assess "the tendency to feel emotionally exposed, vulnerable, and concerned about making mistakes in front of other people" (Kelly & Jones, 1997, p. 321). The scale thus measures the personality attributes of easily embarrassed people, and has been used primarily in the social-personality literature. [RARELY USED]

Scale characteristics: total scale (25 items; α = .90).

Sample item: "I often worry about looking stupid."

Response format: Statement-based measure with a 7-point scale (1 = "Not at all like me"; 7 = "Very much like me").

A3. EMBARRASSMENT SCALE OF THE DIFFERENTIAL EMOTIONS SCALE (DES-II)

(See description in A1 of the Shame measures section.)

A4. EMBARRASSMENT SCENARIOS [NO SPECIFIC TITLE GIVEN]

(See description in A12 of the Shame measures section.)

B. State Measures of Embarrassment

B1. SITUATIONAL EMBARRASSMENT SCALE [ARABIC LANGUAGE ONLY]

Alansari, B. M. (1996). *Situational Embarrassment Scale manual.* Kuwait: University Book Home.

Alansari, B. M. (2002). Situational Embarrassment Scale. In B. M. Alansari (Ed.), *Sourcebook of objective personality scales: Standardization for Kuwaiti society* (pp. 70–89). Kuwait: New Book Home. [RARELY USED]

B2. EMBARRASSMENT SCALE OF THE DIFFERENTIAL EMOTIONS SCALE (DES-II)

(See description in A1 of the Shame measures section.)

C. Measures of Constructs Related to Embarrassment

Note: For space reasons, we do not include the many measures of shyness and social anxiety, even though these constructs are conceptually related to embarrassment (e.g., Cheek & Briggs, 1990; Leary, 1991; Miller, 1986).

Pride

A. Trait Measures of Pride

A1. ALPHA AND BETA PRIDE SUBSCALES OF THE TEST OF SELF-CONSCIOUS AFFECT

(See description in A11 of the Shame measures section.)

A2. SELF-ASSURANCE SUBSCALE OF THE POSITIVE AND NEGATIVE AFFECT SCHEDULE—EXPANDED FORM

(See description in A8 of the Guilt measures section.)

A3. AUTHENTIC AND HUBRISTIC PRIDE SCALES

Tracy, J. L., & Robins, R. W. (2007). The psychological structure of pride: A tale of two facets. *Journal of Personality and Social Psychology, 92,* 506–525.

The scales were empirically derived from a series of studies assessing participants' subjective feelings during a pride experience and their chronic dispositional tendencies to experience pride. The initial item set came from three sources: (1) labels applied to the pride nonverbal expression (Tracy & Robins, 2004a); (2) words listed in response to a request to list all pride-related words (Tracy & Robins, 2007); and (3) thesaurus synonyms for words that emerged from (1) and (2) and that were rated as highly prototypical of pride. The scales measure two empirically derived facets of pride, which the authors have labeled "authentic" and "hubristic," but which are based on earlier theoretical accounts (Lewis, 2000; Tangney, Wagner, & Gramzow, 1989; Tracy & Robins, 2004b). Each scale can be used to assess state or trait pride. In the trait version, participants are asked to rate the extent to which they "generally feel" each of the items. In the state version, participants are asked to rate the extent to which each item describes their current feelings. The two scales are fairly independent (for trait pride, $r = .09$, n.s.; for state pride, $r = 14$, $p < .05$). [NEWLY DEVELOPED]

Scale characteristics: Authentic pride scale (seven items, including "accomplished," "like I am achieving," "confident," "fulfilled," "productive," "like I have self-worth," and "successful"; $\alpha = .88$); Hubristic pride scale (seven items, including "arrogant," "conceited," "egotistical," "pompous," "smug," "snobbish," and "stuck-up"; $\alpha = .90$)

Response format: 5-point scale (1 = "not at all"; 2 = "somewhat"; 3 = "moderately"; 4 = "very much"; 5 = "extremely").

B. State Measures of Pride

B1. SELF-ASSURANCE SUBSCALE OF THE POSITIVE AND NEGATIVE AFFECT SCHEDULE—EXPANDED FORM

(See description in A8 of the Guilt measures section.)

B2. PRIDE SUBSCALE OF THE STATE SHAME AND GUILT SCALE (SSGS)

(See description in B1 of the Shame measures section.)

B3. AUTHENTIC AND HUBRISTIC PRIDE SCALES

(See description in A3 of the Pride trait measures section.)

C. Measures of Constructs Related to Pride

C1. NARCISSISTIC PERSONALITY INVENTORY (NPI)

[*Note:* There are numerous measures of narcissism. We include only the NPI because it is the most widely used scale and assesses individual differences in the normal range of narcissistic tendencies, rather than clinical levels of narcissism.]

Raskin, R., & Terry, H. (1988). A principal-components analysis of the Narcissistic Personality Inventory and further evidence of its construct validity. *Journal of Personality and Social Psychology, 54,* 890–902. [for the complete scale, contact Richard W. Robins at *rwrobins@ucdavis.edu*]

Emmons, R. A. (1987). Narcissism: Theory and measurement. *Journal of Personality and Social Psychology, 52,* 11–17.

Raskin, R. N., & Hall, C. S. (1981). The Narcissistic Personality Inventory: Alternate form reliability and further evidence of construct validity. *Journal of Personality Assessment, 45,* 159–162.

Items were developed based on the DSM-III behavioral criteria for the narcissistic personality disorder, however the scale is assumed to assess subclinical levels of narcissistic tendencies. Most researchers use Raskin and Terry's (1988) 40-item version of the original 54-item scale. Raskin and Terry (1988) and Emmons (1987) both developed subscales of the NPI, a subset of which are relevant to pride and are described below. [FREQUENTLY USED]

Scale characteristics (Raskin & Terry, 1988): total scale (40 items; α = .83), superiority (five items; α = .54), self-sufficiency (six items; α = .50), vanity (three items; α = .64).

Scale characteristics (Emmons, 1987): total scale (54 items; α = .87), Self-Absorption/Self-Admiration (nine items; α = .81), Superiority/Arrogance (11 items; α = .70).

Sample item: "(A) The thought of ruling the world frightens the hell out of me. (B) If I ruled the world it would be a much better place."

Response format: Statement-based measure with a forced-choice response option (for each pair of statements, participants are required to select the statement they agree with more strongly).

C2. REGULATORY FOCUS QUESTIONNAIRE (RFQ)

Harlow, R. E., Friedman, R. S., & Higgins, E. T. (1997). *The Regulatory Focus Questionnaire*. New York: Department of Psychology, Columbia University.

Higgins, E. T., Friedman, R. S., Harlow, R. E., Idson, L. C., Ayduk, O. N., & Taylor, A. (2001). Achievement orientations from subjective histories of success: Promotion pride versus prevention pride. *European Journal of Social Psychology, 31,* 3–23. [includes full scale]

A set of items was generated using the rational method, and was validated on several large samples of undergraduates using a variety of criteria. This measure is used in both basic and applied social psychology to measure regulatory styles and strategies to achieve success, but is not typically used as a trait measure of pride. [RARELY USED]

Scale characteristics: promotion pride (six items; α = .73), prevention pride (five items; α = .80).

Sample item: "How often have you accomplished things that got you 'psyched' to work even harder?"

Response format: Statement-based measure with a 5-point scale.

C3. STATE SELF-ESTEEM SCALE (SSES)

Heatherton, T. F., & Polivy, J. (1991). Development and validation of a scale for measuring state self-esteem. *Journal of Personality and Social Psychology, 60,* 895–910. [includes full scale]

Linton, K. E., & Marriott, R. G. (1996). Self-esteem in adolescents: Validation of the State Self-Esteem Scale. *Personality and Individual Differences, 21,* 85–90.

Developed from factor analyses of the Janis and Field (1959) Feelings of Inadequacy Scale and its revisions. This scale does not measure pride directly, but assesses the related construct of momentary feelings of self-worth. This scale is used primarily in the social-personality literature. [FREQUENTLY USED]

Scale characteristics: total scale (20 items; α = .92), performance (seven items; α = .80), social (seven items; α = .80), appearance (six items; α = .83). [alphas from Lakey & Scoboria, 2005]

Sample item: "I feel that others respect and admire me."

Response format: Statement-based measure with a 5-point scale (1= "not at all"; 2 = "a little bit"; 3 = "somewhat"; 4 = "very much"; 5 = "extremely").

NONVERBAL INDICATORS OF SELF-CONSCIOUS EMOTIONS

Building on the large body of research demonstrating that each so-called basic emotion (i.e., anger, fear, disgust, happiness, sadness, surprise) is associated with a distinct, universally recognized facial expression (Ekman, 2003), several researchers have attempted to find reliably identified nonverbal expressions for the self-conscious emotions. As with the basic emotions, a key criterion for determining whether a particular self-conscious emotion has a distinct nonverbal expression is whether such an expression is recognizable; thus, researchers have conducted judgment studies showing that embarrassment, pride, and shame are associated with expressions that observers reliably agree signify each emotion (Izard, 1971; Keltner, 1995; Tracy & Robins, 2004a). In these studies, participants are typically shown photographs of posed expressions and asked to choose which, if any, emotion is conveyed by each expression. If agreement levels are higher than what would be expected by chance (usually defined by the number of options presented), it is then assumed that the expression does, in fact, signify a particular emotion (but see Russell, 1994). Embarrassment, pride, and shame have nonverbal expressions that are recognized across cultures (Haidt & Keltner, 1999; Izard, 1971; Tracy & Robins, 2004a), and, in the case of pride and shame, by members of a preliterate culture that is highly isolated from the Western world (Tracy & Robins, 2006). These findings suggest the expressions are not simply culture-specific socialized gestures (like the "thumb's up" sign) and may in fact be a universal part of human nature.

Posed, recognizable expressions for each self-conscious emotion were derived from anecdotal observations and observational studies in which participants' nonverbal behaviors were recorded or coded during an embarrassing, prideful, or shaming experience (Keltner, 1995; Belsky & Domitrovich, 1997; Lewis, Alessandri, & Sullivan, 1992; Stipek, Recchia, & McClintic, 1992; Weisfeld & Beresford, 1982).

The finding of universal basic emotion recognition led to the development of an elaborate coding scheme for each basic emotion, based on the specific facial muscle movements involved in each expression (i.e., the Facial Action Coding Scheme, or FACS; Ekman & Friesen, 1978). In this scheme, each critical facial muscle movement is assigned an "action unit" (AU). Notably, the self-conscious emotion expressions seem to involve more than the face; they cannot be accurately identified without the perception of head movements, postural positions, or arm positions. FACS includes codes for head movements, but not for body and postural movements, so elements of certain self-conscious emotion expressions (e.g., pride) are not captured by the extant scheme.

In Table 24.1, we describe the facial and nonfacial actions that have been found to be associated with the recognizable expression of each self-conscious emotion; where possible, we also report the relevant AUs.

In general, the availability of a nonverbal coding scheme for an emotion greatly enhances a researcher's ability to study that particular emotion by circumventing the limitations of self-report. Self-report measures of emotions require that participants (1) be aware of their emotions, (2) be willing to disclose their emotions, and (3) can distinguish among different yet similar emotional experiences. Research suggests that all three of these assumptions are frequently not met: emotions are often experienced at an implicit level (Kihlstrom, Mulvaney, Tobias, & Tobis, 2000; Shaver & Mikulincer, 2005); research participants are often unwilling to openly discuss their feelings, particularly feelings of shame (H. B. Lewis, 1971; Scheff, Retzinger, & Ryan, 1989), and in many situations it is not socially acceptable for them to do so (Zammuner, 1996; Zammuner & Frijda, 1994); and similar emotions, such as shame and guilt, are frequently confused by laypeople (Tangney & Dearing, 2002). For these reasons, nonverbal expressions, which are less under voluntary control than are verbal self-reports, may be crucial to an accurate assessment of an individual's emotional response to a particular event (Ekman, 2003). However, given that expressions occur very quickly, are more difficult to assess (videotaping is typically required), are time-consuming to code (several distinct expressions can occur within a matter of seconds), and can only be used to assess states, not traits, researchers may want to use both approaches and seek convergences (or psychologically meaningful divergences) across methods.

TABLE 24.1. Facial and Nonfacial Actions Associated with Self-Conscious Emotions

Emotion	Nonverbal expression	Mean recognition rates (Western samples)	Cross-cultural recognition	Relevant citations
Embarrassment (dynamic display)	Gaze down, followed by lip press, then smile, then head turn away, then gaze shift	53–61%		Keltner, D. (1995). Signs of appeasement: Evidence for the distinct displays of embarrassment, amusement, and shame. *Journal of Personality and Social Psychology, 68,* 441–454.
Embarrassment (static "snapshot image" display)	Non-Duchenne smile, lip press, gaze down, head movement to the left and down, face touch (AUs 12, 24, 51, 54, 64)	40–56%	United States, India	Haidt, J., & Keltner, D. (1999). Culture and facial expression: Open-ended methods find more expressions and a gradient of recognition. *Cognition and Emotion, 13,* 225–266. Keltner, D. (1995). Signs of appeasement: Evidence for the distinct displays of embarrassment, amusement, and shame. *Journal of Personality and Social Psychology, 68,* 441–454. Keltner, D., & Buswell, B. (1997). Embarrassment: Its distinct forms and appeasement functions. *Psychological Bulletin, 122,* 250–270.
Pride	Head tilted back approximately 15 degrees (AU 53b or 53c), small non-Duchenne smile (AU 12a or 12b), expanded posture (shoulders back, chest out), and arms either (a) akimbo with hands on hips; (b) raised above the head with hands in fists; or (c) crossed on chest	74–84%; recognition is highest for arm position (a), then (b), then (c)	United States, Italy, Burkina Faso (preliterate)	Tracy, J. L., & Robins, R. W. (2004). Show your pride: Evidence for a discrete emotion expression. *Psychological Science, 15,* 194–197. Tracy, J. L., & Robins, R. W. (2006). *The nonverbal expression of pride: Evidence for cross-cultural recognition.* Manuscript under review.
Shame	Head and gaze down (AUs 54, 64)	47–73%	United States, England, Germany, Sweden, France, Switzerland, Greece, Japan, Burkina Faso (preliterate)	Izard, C. E. (1971). *The face of emotion.* East Norwalk, CT: Appleton-Century-Crofts. Keltner, D. (1995). Signs of appeasement: Evidence for the distinct displays of embarrassment, amusement, and shame. *Journal of Personality and Social Psychology, 68,* 441–454. Tracy, J. L., & Robins, R. W. (2006). *The nonverbal expression of pride: Evidence for cross-cultural recognition.* Manuscript under review.

Note. Two recognizable embarrassment expressions have been documented, so both are included here. The dynamic version, which takes place over a 5-second time course, is typically better recognized, but the static version shares a central feature with all other recognizable emotion expressions—it can be recognized from a single snapshot image. To date, no research has found a reliably recognizable nonverbal expression of guilt.

REFERENCES

Belsky, J., & Domitrovich, C. (1997). Temperament and parenting antecedents of individual difference in three-year-old boys' pride and shame reactions. *Child Development, 68*, 456–466.

Buss, D. M., & Craik, K. H. (1986). Acts, dispositions, and clinical assessment: The psychopathology of everyday conduct. *Clinical Psychology Review, 6*, 387–406.

Cheek, J. M., & Briggs, S. R. (1990). Shyness as a personality trait. In W. R. Crozier (Ed.), *Shyness and embarrassment: Perspectives from social psychology* (pp. 315–337). New York: Cambridge University Press.

Ekman, P. (2003). *Emotions revealed: Recognizing faces and feelings to improve communication and emotional life.* New York: Times Books.

Ekman, P., & Friesen, W. V. (1978). *Facial action coding system: Investigator's guide.* Palo Alto, CA: Consulting Psychologists Press.

Gioiella, P. P. (1979). The relationship of relative shame/guilt proneness to the attribution of responsibility under no shame and shame arousal (Doctoral dissertation, New York University, 1979). *Dissertation Abstracts International, 40*, 24–32.

Izard, C. E. (1971). *The face of emotion.* East Norwalk, CT: Appleton-Century-Crofts.

Izard, C. E. (1991). *The psychology of emotions.* New York: Plenum Press.

Izard, C. E., Dougherty, F. E., Bloxom, B. M., & Kotsch, W. E. (1974). *The Differential Emotions Scale: A method of surveying the subjective experience of discrete emotions.* Unpublished manuscript, Vanderbilt University.

Janis, I. L., & Field, P. B. (1959). A behavioral assessment of persuasibility: Consistency of individual differences. In C. Hovland & I. Janis (Eds.), *Personality and persuasibility* (pp. 29–54). Oxford, UK: Yale University Press.

Keltner, D. (1995). Signs of appeasement: Evidence for the distinct displays of embarrassment, amusement, and shame. *Journal of Personality and Social Psychology, 68*, 441–454.

Kihlstrom, J. F., Mulvaney, S., Tobias, B. A., & Tobis, I. P. (2000). The emotional unconscious. In E. Eich, J. F. Kihlstrom, G. H. Bower, J. P. Forgas, & P. M. Niedenthal (Eds.), *Cognition and emotion* (pp. 30–86). New York: Oxford University Press.

Lakey, B., & Scoboria, A. (2005). The relative contribution of trait and social influences to the links among perceived social support, affect, and self-esteem. *Journal of Personality, 73*, 361–388.

Leary, M. R. (1991). Social anxiety, shyness, and related constructs. In J. Robinson, P. Shaver, & L. Wrightsman (Eds.), *Measures of personality and social psychological attitudes* (pp. 161–194). San Diego, CA: Academic Press.

Lewis, H. B. (1971). *Shame and guilt in neurosis.* New York: International Universities Press.

Lewis, M. (2000). Self-conscious emotions: Embarrassment, pride, shame, and guilt. In M. Lewis & J. M. Haviland-Jones (Eds.), *Handbook of emotions* (2nd ed., pp. 623–636). New York: Guilford Press.

Lewis, M., Alessandri, S. M., & Sullivan, M. W. (1992). Differences in shame and pride as a function of children's gender and task difficulty. *Child Development, 63*, 630–638.

Miller, R. S. (1986). Embarrassment: Causes and consequences. In W. H. Jones, J. M. Cheek, & S. R. Briggs (Eds.), *Shyness: Perspectives on research and treatment* (pp. 295–311). New York: Plenum Press.

Nathanson, D. L. (1992). *Shame and pride.* New York: Norton.

Russell, J. A. (1994). Is there universal recognition of emotion from facial expressions?: A review of the cross-cultural studies. *Psychological Bulletin, 115*, 102–141.

Scheff, T. J., Retzinger, S. M., & Ryan, M. T. (1989). Crime, violence, and self-esteem: Review and proposals. In A. M. Mecca, N. J. Smelser, & J. Vasconcellos (Eds.), *The social importance of self-esteem* (pp. 165–199). Berkeley and Los Angeles: University of California Press.

Shaver, P. R., & Mikulincer, M. (2005). Attachment theory and research: Resurrection of the psychodynamic approach to personality. *Journal of Research in Personality, 39*, 22–45.

Stipek, D., Recchia, S., & McClintic, S. (1992). Self-evaluation in young children. *Monographs of the Society for Research in Child Development, 57* (Serial No. 226).

Tangney, J. P., Wagner, P., Fletcher, C., & Gramzow, R. (1992). Shamed into anger?: The relation of shame and guilt to anger and self-reported aggression. *Journal of Personality and Social Psychology, 62,* 669–675.

Tangney, J. P., Wagner, P., & Gramzow, R. (1989). *The Test of Self-Conscious Affect.* Fairfax, VA: George Mason University.

Tracy, J. L., & Robins, R. W. (2004a). Show your pride: Evidence for a discrete emotion expression. *Psychological Science, 15,* 194–197.

Tracy, J. L., & Robins, R. W. (2004b). Putting the self into self-conscious emotions: A theoretical model. *Psychological Inquiry, 15,* 103–125.

Tracy, J. L., & Robins, R. W. (2006). *The nonverbal expression of pride: Evidence for cross-cultural recognition.* Manuscript under review.

Turner, R. G., Scheier, M. F., Carver, C. S., & Ickes, W. (1978). Correlates of self-consciousness. *Journal of Personality Assessment, 42,* 285–289.

Weisfeld, G. E., & Beresford, J. M. (1982). Erectness of posture as an indicator of dominance or success in humans. *Motivation and Emotion, 6,* 113–131.

Zammuner, V. L. (1996). Felt emotions, and verbally communicated emotions: The case of pride. *European Journal of Social Psychology, 26,* 233–245.

Zammuner, V. L., & Frijda, N. H. (1994). Felt and communicated emotions: Sadness and jealousy. *Cognition and Emotion, 8,* 37–53.

Zevon, M., & Tellegen, A. (1982). The structure of mood change: An idiographic/nomothetic analysis. *Journal of Personality and Social Psychology, 43,* 111–122.

Author Index

Subject Index

485